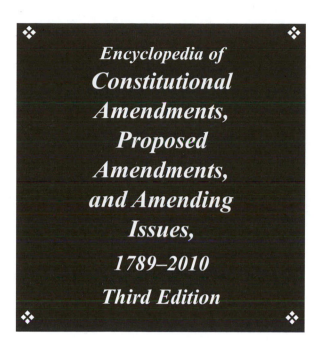

Encyclopedia of
Constitutional
Amendments,
Proposed
Amendments,
and Amending
Issues,
1789–2010
Third Edition

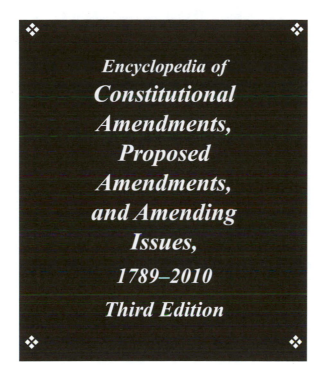

Encyclopedia of
***Constitutional
Amendments,
Proposed
Amendments,
and Amending
Issues,
1789–2010***
Third Edition

VOLUME ONE
A–M

John R. Vile

ABC-CLIO

Santa Barbara, California • Denver, Colorado • Oxford, England

Library of Congress Cataloging-in-Publication Data

Vile, John R.
  Encyclopedia of constitutional amendments, proposed amendments, and amending issues, 1789-2010 / John R. Vile. — 3rd ed.
      p. cm.
  Includes bibliographical references and index.
  ISBN 978-1-59884-316-3 (alk. paper) — ISBN 978-1-59884-317-0 (ebook)
  1. Constitutional amendments—United States. I. Title.
  KF4557.V555 2010
  342.7303--dc22   2010002113

ISBN: 978-1-59884-316-3
EISBN: 978-1-59884-317-0

14 13 12 11 10   1 2 3 4 5

This book is also available on the World Wide Web as an eBook.
Visit www.abc-clio.com for details.

ABC-CLIO, LLC
130 Cremona Drive, P.O. Box 1911
Santa Barbara, California 93116-1911

This book is printed on acid-free paper ∞
Manufactured in the United States of America

This book is dedicated to three great teachers, scholars, and gentlemen: Henry J. Abraham, Alpheus T. Mason, and Walter F. Murphy

❖ CONTENTS ❖

❖ A TO Z LIST OF ENTRIES ❖

❖ FOREWORD ❖

I am one who believes that the single most important provision of any constitution is its amending clause. This is not, obviously, to deny the importance of how a given constitution allocates decision-making authority or protects individual rights. But unless one is deluded into believing that a given constitutional text, whether with regard to allocating power or recognizing rights, is doubly perfect—that is, perfect with regard to the issues and contexts within which it was originally written and then perfect throughout time, when both issues and contexts might well be quite different—one must agree that changes even in foundational documents will be necessary. Indeed, I drew the title for a book that I edited, *Responding to Imperfection: The Theory and Practice of Constitutional Amendment*, from a letter written by George Washington to his nephew, Bushrod Washington: "The warmest friends and best supporters the Constitution has do not contend that it is free from imperfections; but they found them unavoidable and are sensible if evil is likely to arise there from, the remedy must come hereafter." Although many have insisted on portraying the founders as "demigods" whose views on constitutional wisdom we are obligated to follow, Washington himself—who was, of course, president of the Constitutional Convention in Philadelphia before becoming the first president of the United States—was becomingly more modest. "I do not think," he wrote, "we are more inspired, have more wisdom, or possess more virtue, than those who will come after us." Fortunately, "there is a Constitutional door open" to provide any necessary remedies, as future generations, themselves inspired by their own mixtures of wisdom and experience, will take advantage of Article V. From this perspective, one pays most fealty to the father of our country by contemplating the potential presence of imperfections and then working politically to amend the Constitution as a means of truly achieving the "more perfect Union" that is the ultimate aspiration of anyone who joins in our constitutional covenant.

Anyone who shares my (and Washington's!) view of the importance of amendment knows that John Vile is nothing less than a treasure. He is by far our most persistent student of amendment, with unending fascination for everything thought by anyone—whether truly wise or really quite daffy—to be an imperfection and what, therefore, has been proposed as a responsive amendment. But, of course, proposal is quite literally only the beginning of a complex process, and Professor Vile is well aware of every last facet of the process and its implications for the success or failure of proposals for reform.

Professor Vile is also aware of every theoretical debate surrounding amendment. He mentions one of them in his preface: Does Article V set out an exclusive process of amendment per se, or an exclusive procedure only for something we might call "textual" amendments? The very use of this adjective is designed to suggest the possibility that textual amendments are only a subset of a wider set of amendments that include, in their complete description, what can only be described as nontextual amendments that have entered our notion of what the Constitution means even in the absence of a formal Article V process. Another theoretical question, which he addressed in his own contribution to Responding to Imperfection, is whether the Constitution is open to limitless change, so long as the formalities of Article V are followed. This allows the possibility that anything might be added to the Constitution should the requisite number of votes be cast in support. That is, the only protection against the reinstitution of slavery, the establishment of the United States as a religious theocracy, or whatever else may be one's worst nightmare is [Page xviii] the procedural difficulty established by Article V. But some constitutions, including the German constitution, rule out certain categories of amendments—in Germany's case, any amendment that would undercut the constitution's commitment to protecting "human dignity"—and at least some persons have suggested the same is true of our own Constitution, whether or not it is spelled out clearly.

And, of course, there is the Constitution's wild card, the Article V procedure by which a brand-new convention can be called by Congress on petition of two-thirds of the states. (Presumably, Congress has no discretion in the matter once the states unite in their call.) Although there is little doubt that the generation of the framers anticipated that this would actually become part of the American system of government (after all, most states have experienced constitutional conventions and, indeed, the replacement of an outmoded constitution by one thought more suitable to the times) this part of Article V has, of course, basically become a dead letter. One of the reasons is that the Constitution gives no clue at all as to the procedures that would structure a new convention. For starters, would a second convention be required to adopt the same voting rule—one state, one vote—as that followed by the framers in Philadelphia? With regard to these issues as well, Professor Vile's encyclopedia provides essential guidance for any scholar or layperson trying to wrestle with the truly knotty problems posed by this aspect of our Constitution.

There is little point in going on. It is enough to scan the "List of Entries" to appreciate the comprehensiveness of Professor Vile's grasp of his subject. Most encyclopedias are the handiwork of an editor who commissions others to write the entries. There was no need to follow that route in this case, for anyone who thinks about constitutional amendment knows that the expert—the possessor of literally encyclopedic knowledge—is John Vile. We are all fortunate to have this absolutely up-to-date third edition in hand even as we can be confident that, if developments warrant, Professor Vile will be busy preparing a fourth edition for scholars (and others) who depend on him!

Professor Sanford Levinson, W. St. John Garwood, and W. St. John Garwood Jr. Regents Chair in Law, University of Texas Law School

How This Edition Differs from Earlier Editions and from Works by Other Scholars

When I wrote the first edition of this encyclopedia, I was determined to write the most comprehensive and up-to-date volume of its kind. Although I think it accomplished this objective, a book, like a constitution, can profit from amendments, and this will be the third edition of this work (previous editions were dated 1996 and 2003). Each time, the publishers and I have sought not only to add new entries but also to update, and at times to pare down, earlier entries.

Like earlier editions, this volume includes not only proposals that members of Congress have introduced in that body but also proposals that ordinary citizens have made, especially for comprehensive changes. Since the last edition Professors Sanford Levinson and Larry Sabato have both written books advocating a series of constitutional changes, and it is a pleasure not only to include these but also to continue to find similar sets of proposals from earlier in American history that I have previously missed.

The first edition of my *Encyclopedia* was published at a time when others were also turning renewed attention to the amending process. Professor David Kyvig published his *Explicit and Authentic Acts* (1996a), another important contribution to our understanding of existing amendments, in the same year as the Encyclopedia's first edition. In 2000 Kris Palmer in turn edited another major review of existing amendments in his *Constitutional Amendments, 1789 to the Present*, with Pendergast, Pendergast, and Sousanis subsequently publishing a three-volume survey of amendments under the editorship of Elizabeth Shaw Grunow the following year (2001) entitled *Constitutional Amendments: From Freedom of Speech to Flag Burning*.

Valuable though these other resources are, the third edition of the *Encyclopedia of Constitutional Amendments*, like the earlier ones, is unique on today's market in its central focus on short explanatory essays that group and describe not only existing amendments but also proposed amendments that were not successful and proposed new or revised constitutions. Such proposals continue to multiply, and the ability to find them is increasing with technological advances. Once limited to books and pamphlets, proposals for new constitutions and amendments are increasingly finding their way onto the Internet, and they too have been included in this volume.

In the second edition, the publishers and I tried our best to keep everything within a single volume. This publication finally bows to the almost inevitable necessity of going to two volumes. Avoiding length for length's sake, we have cut back redundancies in existing entries and have continued to strive for leaner entries throughout the book. We aim to see that this third edition remains an indispensable tool for those who are interested in constitutional amendments, proposed amendments, and amending issues. I have continued to update sources and have added additional cross-references to help those who are conducting research.

Previous Works on the Subject

Members of state ratifying conventions and of Congress began proposing amendments to the Constitution even before all the states had joined the Union, and such proposals have continued at a steady pace ever since. Individual proposals, especially those in the Bill of Rights and later in the post–Civil War period, were often subject to intense dispute and occasional scholarly analysis, but no major compilation of amendments proposed in Congress was prepared until 1896. At this time, Professor Herman Ames, soon to be a historian at the University of Pennsylvania, published a book, which had begun as his Ph.D. dissertation, covering the constitutional amendments that members of Congress had proposed during the nation's first 100 years. The American Historical Association awarded this book its first prestigious Justin

Winsor Prize, and the volume's continuing relevance was recognized with its replication in 1970 and again in 2002. In addition to describing the subjects of proposed amendments in his text, Ames included a list of the topics of the 1,736 amendments proposed in the nation's first century. He also included a comprehensive index and bibliography. One hundred years later, his book is still readable and useful.

In 1929, M. A. Musmanno, then a Pennsylvania lawyer and later a judge, analyzed the 1,370 amendments that members of Congress had proposed since Ames wrote his book. In part because Musmanno's volume was published as a government document and in part because it covered a shorter time period and was therefore less comprehensive than Ames's, it is less well known but is still a valuable resource.

Although literally hundreds of articles, essays, and books have subsequently addressed the subject of amendments and proposed amendments, no author sought to survey the field in the same comprehensive manner as did Ames and Musmanno until I published the first edition of this *Encyclopedia* in 1996. Once between the time that Ames and Musmanno wrote (Tansill 1926) and several times afterward, lists of amendments proposed in Congress during designated periods have been published (*Proposed Amendments* 1957, 1963, 1969; Davis 1985; Harris 1992). In 2003, I was privileged to edit a set of three volumes that has republished and updated existing listings of these proposed amendments along with Ames's and Musmanno's analyses. I also included a compilation of state petitions to Congress for constitutional conventions that relied largely on a compilation by Michael Stokes Paulsen (1993) (also see Van Sickle and Boughey 1990). These lists and analyses, as well as more recent entries that are now available on the Internet, form the starting point and vital foundation of my study.

From the time that Musmanno wrote to the time that ABC-CLIO published the first edition of this book, the number of proposed amendments grew from just over 3,000 to about 10,000; this number has now grown to more than 11,700 (see Number of Proposed Amendments). It has been both a pleasure and a challenge to compile a book to cover all these proposals. I recognize the impossibility of being an expert on every subject discussed in this volume, as well as the difficulty of covering everything of importance in essays short enough to be of value for a general reader or high school or college student. My knowledge of the limitations of both editions of this work has been balanced by the realization of how useful it is to have a book that provides a starting point for an analysis of individual proposals and issues.

Current Interest in the Amending Process

Interest in various scholarly topics waxes and wanes over time, but interest in the amending process had clearly increased in the decade prior to my first edition of this *Encyclopedia*, and it continues to wax today. Recent years have witnessed numerous scholarly treatments of amendments and constitutional change.

Bruce Ackerman's sophisticated theory of constitutional moments, which has now been explicated in two of three anticipated volumes of *We the People* (1991, 1996), had salted discussion of amending issues with terms like "constitutional moments" and "dualist democracy," and has received the most attention (given the number of citations in law reviews, one might indeed refer, with little exaggeration, to "Ackermania"), but many other authors have also addressed the topic. Another Yale professor, Akhil Reed Amar (1988), has advanced the challenging thesis, which he continues to reiterate, that it is possible to amend the Constitution outside of Article V channels, and Walter Murphy (1980) revived interest in the idea that there may be certain implicit limits on the subject of constitutional amendments. Donald Lutz (1994) examined a number of challenging hypotheses about constitutional change in an influential article in the *American Political Science Review* that also compares the U.S. system with that in other nations and points out how much more difficult the American process is in comparison to those of most other nations. In addition to writing several scholarly articles and leading a number of panels at meetings of the American Political Science Association on the subject of constitutional change, Professor Sanford Levinson of the University of Texas (1995) has compiled a book of essays presenting theoretical views of leading scholars on the subject. More recently, Melissa Schwartzberg (2004, 2007) has examined the theoretical origins of constitutional change, and her scholarship promises continuing insights in the years ahead.

At the time of my first edition of this *Encyclopedia*, the putative ratification of the Twenty-seventh Amendment in 1992, as well as the attempt to extend the ratification deadline of the proposed Equal Rights Amendment, had spawned a great deal of commentary on the amending procedure. Much of it had taken its point of departure from an earlier essay by Walter Dellinger (1983) that asked whether such issues should be considered political questions and a response by Laurence Tribe (1983). Both before and after the first edition of this *Encyclopedia*, there has been renewed interest in the still-unused Article V constitutional convention mechanism. Russell Caplan's book on the subject (1988) complemented legislation that Orrin Hatch sponsored to deal with such unresolved convention issues (See Vile 1993c, 466–483).

Just prior to the first edition of this Encyclopedia, the Republican electoral victories of 1994 and the Contract with America focused considerable attention on specific amending proposals, such as the balanced budget amendment, term limits, flag desecration, prayer in schools, and the item veto. What is therefore so interesting about most current academic works is that so many focus primarily on the theory of constitutional amendments and constitutional change.

At the time of my first edition, Bernstein and Agel's (1993) survey of amendments was a notable exception that has since been joined by the Kyvig, Palmer, and Pendergast, Pendergast, and Sousanis volumes identified above. Although adhering to generally high scholarly standards, Bernstein's book, like Kyvig's, succeeded in reaching a popular audience in a fashion that earlier works—most notably the judicious treatment of amendments by Alan P. Grimes (1978)—never quite managed. (The Palmer book and the Pendergast, Pendergast, and Sousanis volumes seem more appropriate to reference libraries, with the latter especially appropriate for high schools.) In any case, Bernstein and Agel's work and Kyvig's, as well as other

new books—Michael Vorenberg's account of the Thirteenth Amendment in *Final Freedom* (2001) is an especially noteworthy contribution to the literature—have necessarily focused chiefly on amendments that have been adopted rather than those that have been proposed. This third edition of the *Encyclopedia of Constitutional Amendments*, like the first two, thus has a unique niche in the literature and on the reference shelf.

Although their short discussion of proposed amendments was lively (Bernstein with Agel 1993, 169–198), it may unintentionally have left many readers with the impression that most proposed amendments have been trivial or ridiculous. If this impression were true, one might well question the value of this book, but the study of proposed amendments is far from a trivial pursuit. Undoubtedly, there are proposed amendments (just as there are proposed laws) that are naive, unnecessary, or ridiculous—proposals, for example, to outlaw war, to give the president authority over the air force, or to take citizenship away from all nonwhites. Sometimes proposals are wiser than they seem. Many point to real problems or identify areas for future legislation, if not amendment.

It is a rare issue indeed that has not been introduced as an amendment at some point in historyThe study of such proposals thus provides a unique window into American history and politics. The fact that the goals of proposed amendments are often achieved by other means testifies not so much to the inadequacy of the amending process as to the dynamics of the U.S. federal system.

I am fascinated with the theoretical arguments about constitutional amendments, but I think that it is important to keep such scholarship anchored in actual practice. I have written all three editions of this book to address topics of interest to those with theoretical inclinations, while keeping the primary focus on amendments and proposed amendments.

Subjects Covered in This Book
Amendments and Proposed Amendments

Altogether, there are more than 525 entries in this book. The majority deal with the 27 amendments that have been ratified and with the approximately 11,700 others that have been proposed. Why, then, are there not 11,700 entries? Clearly, the number 11,700 records the approximate number of amendments that have been individually introduced and not the number of subjects that have been addressed. For example, there have been almost 1,000 proposals for the Equal Rights Amendment, and, while this amendment raised related issues, most such proposals can be discussed in a single essay. Similarly, there are hundreds of proposals dealing with reform of the electoral college, abortion, prayer in schools, balanced budgets, term limits, and so on. In most cases, I have grouped the discussion of proposals relating to a single topic in one essay rather than composing separate entries for each proposal. I have also included entries on new proposals, like the one to permit flag salutes (a reaction to a U.S. Circuit Court of Appeals opinion stating that the words "under God" made the salute an impermissible establishment of religion when recited in public schools).

A quick perusal of the Ames and Musmanno volumes, as well as indexes to subsequent lists of amendments, demonstrates that no two authors divide the thousands of proposals in the same manner. Moreover, I cannot guarantee that I have covered all topics. I typically had to work from the titles of amendments rather than from the actual texts, and in some cases where I was able to perform checks, the titles of amendments turned out to be inaccurate or deceptive. Sometimes, I found it impossible to ascertain the content of a proposal, or I had to make educated guesses about what motivated a particular amendment or which proposals to group in the same essay.

From the second session of the Seventy-fourth Congress to the present, the Legislative Reference Service of the Library of Congress has compiled an annual listing of all proposed laws and amendments and their sponsors. For recent Congresses this information may be further supplemented by my own published reprints and update issued by the Law Book Exchange (Vile 2003) and by materials available on the Web site for the Library of Congress, generally by combing through lists of joint resolutions (which is the way that amending proposals are most generally introduced). Such compilations are extremely helpful, but they are surely far from foolproof. Sometimes the *Congressional Record* was an aid, but this record was often silent about the motivation or meaning of a proposed amendment. In some cases, I have called the staffs of members of Congress who have proposed obscure amendments, but often such members had long since retired, and an educated guess was the best that I could do.

Major Constitutional Reforms Introduced outside Congress

Given the breadth of current musings about the amending process, a book limited describing amendments and proposed amendments did not seem adequate to meet the needs of a modern researcher. I therefore included a number of related types of entries.

One class of entry moves outside Congress to consider major reform proposals to rewrite the Constitution or substantially to alter it. This was the subject of my own first book (Vile 1991c). Historian Stephen Boyd (1992) also addressed this topic in a book compiling the texts of 10 proposed alternative constitutions. At the time of the first edition of this *Encyclopedia*, my own continuing research revealed that even when these results were combined, our books did not identify all such proposals, and so I included summaries of added proposals I have found from the period that Boyd and I originally covered. In addition, well over a dozen new proposals have been published or posted on the Internet since the first edition of this book (including a proposed constitution by Jim Davidson for a new nation in the Caribbean to be named "Oceana," but which is clearly designed to influence American thinking on the subject in a more libertarian direction), at which time I knew of no such proposals. I have continued to locate proposals that were published before the first edition of this work, and I am almost certain that there must be even more that continue to rest in obscurity. Still, the approximately 85 such proposals that are known make a fascinating supplement to discussions of more piecemeal reforms and should prove useful for further scholarly comparison and analysis. They also highlight the fact that a new constitution or set of amendments is a potentially viable option to more piecemeal change. Although I do not have comparative data from other nations where formal constitutional change, and even regime changes, are often much more frequent, I like to think that there may be something uniquely American about the idea of private citizens sitting down and deciding to put pen to paper to draft a new constitution or set of amendments; if such proposals continue to multiply at the present rate, they may eventually merit another separate volume, but for now, I have included all that I could find here, including some that are fairly bizarre. It is particularly interesting to see a recent proliferation of proposals by individuals influenced by Ayn Rand, by futurists, and by students of public choice, the latter of which now merit a separate entry.

When I have been able to identify the authors of proposed constitutions or multiple amendments, I have described them under their authors' names. Where I had no names, as, for example, a proposal under the pseudonym Virginia Vanguard, I used the description of the plan or, in this case, the pseudonym, that the author provided. I have also provided at least a brief biographical sketch of each such individual for whom biographical information was available.

Influential Individuals

I have listed two other types of entries under individual names. One type discusses individuals who have had an important impact on how we think about the amending process. Although I have argued elsewhere that American thinkers have been influenced on the subject by previous writers (Vile 1992, 1–21), I limited my focus to Americans, including such individuals as William Penn, George Washington, Thomas Jefferson, John C. Calhoun, Sidney George Fisher, Francis Lieber (a new entry in this edition), and Woodrow Wilson.

In a similar vein, I included entries, several of which are new, on individuals such as Susan B. Anthony, John Bingham, Everett McKinley Dirksen, Frederick Douglass, Alexander Hamilton, James Madison, George Mason, Elizabeth Cady Stanton, Gregory Watson, and Frances Willard who were especially influential in for-

mulating or pressing for the adoption of various amendments. Where it was appropriate, I mentioned the names and parties of individuals who supported amendments within the entries on proposed amendments. I found a Congressional Quarterly (2000) volume, fortunately updated and expanded since the first edition of this *Encyclopedia*, to be particularly useful in identifying the political parties of such individuals.

I reserved separate entries for a select number of individuals, including those listed above, whose roles in providing for an individual amendment or set of amendments were extraordinary. I included more entries on the Nineteenth Amendment, which provided for women's suffrage, than on others. I did so because this movement was clearly a grassroots effort and because the amendment was advocated so long before it was finally adopted. Support for this amendment thus spanned more than a generation of active supporters.

In this book, I omitted American reformers who were not specifically concerned with constitutional amendments. Researchers interested in such individuals will find Alden Whitman's volume on the subject (1985) to be especially helpful.

Influential Organizations

I included some entries on organizations that influence the adoption of amendments—especially the drive for national alcoholic prohibition, which culminated in the Eighteenth Amendment, and the drive for women's suffrage that culminated in the Nineteenth Amendment. I quickly realized, however, that literally hundreds of organizations have labored for or against one or another amendment and that there was no feasible way to discuss all of them here. Readers who are interested in such modern groups should find Clement Vose's magisterial discussion in *Constitutional Change* (1972) useful. Books focusing on the Eighteenth, Nineteenth, and Twenty-first Amendments often describe such groups and their influences in much greater detail than I do here.

Supreme Court Decisions

Another group of entries in this book consists of Supreme Court decisions. These particularly interest me, because I teach American constitutional law. Moreover, as I completed entries on proposed amendments for all three editions of this book, I have been frequently struck by the continual interplay between Supreme Court decisions and constitutional amendments, a number of which have overturned such decisions. Even more often, Court decisions have served as catalysts for amending proposals. When I was aware of such connections, I included them in individual entries on proposed amendments. When warranted, I wrote separate essays on such decisions. I have added entries on new decisions in subsequent editions of the book while recognizing that most amendments have been the subject of numerous subsequent decisions and that it was necessary to choose judiciously among them.

In addition to the Supreme Court decisions that have prompted amending proposals, there is another set of important decisions—namely, those dealing with specific amending issues. Although the Supreme Court declared in *Coleman v. Miller* (1939) that issues surrounding the amending process were political questions for Congress to resolve, it had settled a number of important amending issues in prior cases. Moreover, several subsequent court decisions have called into question the legitimacy of the Coleman precedent. I included summaries of such relevant cases.

Unresolved Issues

I have continued to include essays on key amending issues. These include discussions of the constitutional convention mechanism; whether there are implicit limits on the amending process; whether states can rescind ratification of pending amendments; whether governors and presidents have a role in the process; whether there are time limits on such ratifications; whether constituents should be able to instruct their representatives on introducing amendments; and so on.

Miscellaneous

From time to time, I included related entries in this book that seemed useful but did not really fit into any of the above categories. It seemed appropriate, for example, to include an entry on constitutional commissions, even though this is primarily a mechanism for state constitutional change. Similarly, I included notes on the officers that have been designated to certify amendments, and essays on such miscellaneous topics as the Articles of Confederation, the Confederate constitution, the Virginia and Kentucky Resolutions, the Louisiana Purchase, the Hartford Convention, the Peace Convention, the Contract with America, and critical elections. I have also included essays on the Magna Carta, the English Bill of Rights, and the Virginia Declaration of Rights.

This edition continues to include essays that are designed to illumine the overall impact of the amending process. These include the following entries: Consensus and the Amending Process, Deliberation and the Amending Process, Democracy and Constitutional Amendments, Enforcement Clauses in Amendments, Entrenchment Clauses, Federalism and the Amending Process, Implementation Dates of Amendments, the Living Constitution (which helps explore the links between constitutional amendment and constitutional interpretation), the Placement of Constitutional Amendments, Progress and the Amending Process, the Relevance of Constitutional Amendments, Separation of Powers and the Amending Process, Social and Economic Rights, Supermajorities, Supreme Court Decisions Reversed by Constitutional Amendments, and Unintended Consequences of Constitutional Amendments, Voting Rights.

The Form of This Book

Ames (1896) and Musmanno (1929) discussed proposed amendments in narrative form. Others simply listed the subjects of amendments with their respective resolution numbers, who proposed them, and the dates in which they did so. The publication by the Law Book Exchange of a previously mentioned work reprinting and updating these earlier lists (Vile 2003) should be a boon to scholars of the subject. This *Encyclopedia* will remain a worthy and, for most people, a more accessible accompaniment in that I have organized this book as an encyclopedia of separate entries, each consisting of an essay on an amendment, a proposed amendment, or one of the related themes mentioned above. I chose this format so that the information would be accessible to high school students, college students, and general readers, as well as to advanced researchers in law, political science, and history.

Although such an approach arguably sacrifices some continuity, I have attempted to preserve continuity in four ways. First, I have added a list of entries to the front of this edition of the book to provide readers with an initial overview of all the topics covered. Second, I have grouped multiple entries together under such headings as Congress, the Judiciary, the Presidency, Slavery, States, and Taxation. Third, individual entries are extensively cross-referenced—even more in this edition than in the previous two. Fourth, I have included fairly generous references that students and scholars can consult for further information. Individuals interested more generally in the amending process should find the bibliography and index, both of which have been extensively altered for this edition, to be especially useful. Because I make so many references to the Constitution and its amendments, they are also included in an appendix.

As one who has now been studying and teaching the subject for more than 35 years, I have long been convinced that the United States Constitution is an important document and that the constitutional amending process is a particularly critical part of it. Many governments in the early American colonies were based on charters, and colonial Americans often associated such charters not only with written scriptures but also with the idea of a covenant, which was a particularly pervasive scriptural theme. When, after exhausting all legal routes to reform, the colonies collectively declared their independence of Britain, most states began to write their own constitutions and declarations of rights. So, too, the Continental Congress began work on the Articles of Confederation. Ratified in 1781, it proved to be an important, if largely ineffective, prologue to the Constitution that followed.

There were many problems with the articles, which was a far less democratic document than today's Constitution. There was, for example, no independent executive, and each state had a single vote in Congress. The major problem with the government under the articles, however, was that it did not secure adequate powers for the national government. States were, for example, responsible for coining their own money and raising the taxes that they paid to the national government, and they began enacting trade barriers against one another that hurt economic development.

These problems were compounded by the fact that when Congress recommended changes, all 13 state legislatures had to approve. This obstacle was so formidable that, despite palpable problems, the states were unable to adopt any amendments during the time that the articles were in operation. Moreover, when the founders eventually wrote a new Constitution, they bypassed the mechanism for unanimous state ratification, specifying in Article VII that the new document would go into effect when approved by special constitutional conventions in nine or more states (see Ratification of the U.S. and/or Future U.S. Constitutions), a mechanism subsequently used to ratify the Twenty-first Amendment.

Establishing the Amending Process

Fifty-five delegates from twelve states met in Philadelphia from May through September 1787 to formulate the existing constitution. Delegates represented the diversity of state interests, most notably those associated with population size, the issue of slavery, and distinct regional interests. The government formulated by the delegates to the Constitutional Convention differed in significant respects from that under the Articles of Confederation. Although states were retained in a newly devised federal system, congressional powers were significantly expanded. The new government contained three branches of government rather than one. These included a bicameral Congress in which the people were represented according to population in the larger house; a single executive, chosen by an independent electoral college, with powers to enforce congressional legislation; and an independent judiciary, whose members would serve "during good behavior."

Especially after vigorous debates persuaded defenders of the Constitution to form a Bill of Rights, the results of the Convention deliberations were generally accepted as an improvement over the Articles of Confederation. Observers also recognized that they embodied imperfect compromises. Moreover, even had the delegates been capable of creating a perfect document, it would have required alteration during the course of time. The delegates knew from their experience under British rule that a constitution that could not be altered would likely break, or end up being broken through revolution.

The framers allowed considerable play within the joints of the instrument that they had created—for example, the judicial system soon began exercising the power known as judicial review, by which it interpreted the Constitution and laws made under its authority and declared acts that it considered to be unconstitutional to be void. In addition to providing or allowing for such mechanisms, the framers of the Constitution prudently constructed a process of formal constitutional amendment. This process, which Article V of the Constitution outlines, is difficult, but it was considerably easier than the process that was in place under the Articles of Confederation. The new process would proceed in two steps. Two-thirds majorities of both Houses of Congress would propose amendments (an alternative mechanism for two-thirds of the states to petition Congress to call a constitutional convention has never been utilized), and three-fourths of the states would have to ratify them. At congressional specification, states could ratify amendments either through their existing legislatures, or, as in the case of the Constitution itself, through special constitutional conventions called for this purpose. The only permanent stated restriction on the amending process, known as an entrenchment clause, protected the Connecticut Compromise by providing that the government could not deprive any state of its equal suffrage in the U.S. Senate without its consent.

The History of Amendments in America

The constitutional amending process has not been utilized as frequently as might have been anticipated, but this process has been important in updating the document and in keeping it current with popular sentiments. It is possible that the Constitution would not have even been ratified had it not contained an amending mechanism. One of the key arguments of those who opposed ratification of the new Constitution, the Anti-Federalists, was that the document was inadequate without a bill of rights specifying the liberties that individuals would have against the newly created national government. Initially rebuffed by Federalist supporters of the Constitution, such proponents later recognized that the easiest way to head off a second convention that might attempt to undo the work of the first was to agree to accede to the adoption of such a bill of rights. Significantly, James Madison, who is often identified as the "father" of the U.S. Constitution, went on to shepherd the Bill of Rights through the first Congress.

The 10 amendments that the states subsequently ratified were appended to the end of the document (see Placement of Constitutional Amendments) and continue to be generally revered by the American people (see Reverence for the Constitution). More importantly, citizens may invoke them in court when they believe that their rights specified there have been violated. These rights are described in much greater detail in this book. It is sufficient to note here that these guarantees include protections of religious and political liberty that the First Amendment established. They provide for a right to bear arms (Second Amendment); prohibit the government from quartering troops in citizens' homes without their consent (Third Amendment); prohibit "unreasonable searches and seizures" (Fourth Amendment); and provide for a variety of rights for individuals who are accused of crimes, those who are on trial, and even for those who are being punished after being convicted of crimes (Fifth through Eighth Amendments). The Ninth Amendment indicates that the people retain other rights that have not been delegated to the new government, while the tenth and final provision of the Bill of Rights was designed to ease the fear that the new government would destroy the existing states.

The states ratified two amendments from 1791 to 1865, and rejected a third proposal relating to titles of nobility. The Eleventh Amendment reversed an early Supreme Court decision, thus demonstrating that the amending process fit within the newly created system of checks and balances, and protected state sovereignty by clarifying the circumstances in which states could be sued. The Twelfth Amendment remedied defects in the electoral college, which in the wake of the development of political parties was no longer operating in the manner that the framers had anticipated. In the meantime, many citizens came increasingly to revere the new Constitution, even though it proved incapable of averting the Civil War. Congress did propose the Corwin Amendment, which might have headed off war, but it would have done so at the high cost of permanently guaranteeing the existence of slavery in those states that wanted to keep it.

At war's end there was considerable sentiment for attempting to correct the problems that had led to the conflict. Three amendments were eventually ratified with this purpose in mind. The historic Thirteenth Amendment (1865) abolished involuntary servitude except as a punishment for crime. The Fourteenth Amendment (1868) contained a number of provisions. The most important overturned the polarizing *Dred Scott* decision of 1857 by defining citizenship so that it applied to "all persons [including blacks] born or naturalized within the United States," and by guaranteeing "privileges and immunities," "due process," and "equal protection" to all such persons. This amendment later became the vehicle through which the U.S. Supreme Court eventually applied most of the provisions in the Bill of Rights to the states. Initially, the Bill of Rights had applied only to actions by the federal government. Although it proved far from effective during most of the first century of its existence, the Fifteenth Amendment (1870) prohibited discrimination in voting on the basis of race.

Another hiatus in amendments occurred between 1865 and 1913, after which four amendments were ratified in the next seven years. Usually associated with the Progressive Era in American politics with its increased emphasis on direct democracy, these amendments, respectively, overturned another Supreme Court decision to allow for a national income tax (the Sixteenth Amendment); provided that U.S. Senators would thereafter be selected directly by the voters, rather than by state legislatures (the Seventeenth Amendment); established national alcoholic prohibition (the Eighteenth Amendment); and prohibited discrimination in voting on the basis of sex (the Nineteenth Amendment). The latter amendment was ratified more than 70 years after the Seneca Falls Convention had first brought the issue into the public limelight.

States ratified eight amendments from 1933 through 1992. These included a number of proposals to deal with what might be considered constitutional housekeeping matters. Thus, the Twentieth Amendment altered the terms under which new presidents and legislators took office with a view of decreasing the power of political "lame ducks." The Twenty-second Amendment (1951) limited the terms that a president could serve. The Twenty-fifth Amendment (1967) provided for cases of presidential disability and for the replacement of vice presidents. The Twenty-seventh Amendment, originally proposed as part of the Bill of Rights and belatedly ratified in 1992, provided for an intervening election between the time that congressional pay raises were adopted and when they went into effect. In a more substantive development, the Twenty-first Amendment (1933) had in turn provided for the repeal of the Eighteenth Amendment.

Other amendments adopted since the Progressive Era, like the earlier Fifteenth and Nineteenth Amendments, have widened voting rights. The Twenty-third Amendment (1961) provided for representation in the electoral college for residents of the District of Columbia. The Twenty-fourth Amendment (1964) eliminated poll taxes in federal elections, and the Twenty-sixth Amendment (1971) lowered voting ages to 18.

An amendment that Congress proposed to eliminate child labor eventually proved to be unnecessary in light of changing judicial interpretations of the Constitution. States also rejected amendments to give the District of Columbia voting representation in Congress or mandate equal rights for women. However, many of the goals of the second proposal, like the early child labor amendment, were brought about through altered judicial interpretations of the Constitution.

The Importance of Existing Amendments
Many developments have occurred without being incorporated into constitutional amendments, and at least one contemporary scholar has accordingly questioned the importance of the amending process—a bet that he somewhat hedges by excluding the Bill of Rights from his account (Strauss 2001). I would concede that one clearly could not write a complete account of American constitutional history simply on the basis of the text of the U.S. Constitution and its subsequent amendments. Just as clearly, one could not write such a history without also taking such amendments into account (see Relevance of Constitutional Amendments).

The Preamble of the Constitution begins with the words, "We the People." Through their representatives, the amending process continues to give the people their most direct mechanism for altering or adding provisions that they think are needed. In addition to solving a number of structural problems in the Constitution that have emerged throughout the nation's history, amendments have edged the nation much closer to democracy than when it began (see Democracy and Constitutional Amendments). Amendments have guaranteed important rights that continue to be expanded and enforced in courts; brought an end to legal chattel slavery, expanded citizenship, and extended equal rights to all; and have significantly expanded voting rights by eliminating barriers based on race, sex, age, and wealth (by eliminating the poll tax).

Although one might quibble with one or another amendment that has been ratified in the nation's history, it is difficult to imagine that many Americans would trade the original unamended Constitution for the one that is in effect today. With or without amendments, we might hope that governments would not abuse freedoms of speech or religion, deny rights to individuals indicted or on trial for crimes, reimpose slavery, or take away voting rights for African Americans, women, or 18-year-olds. Still, almost all of us probably feel more secure knowing that there is now specific constitutional language governing such matters.

Significantly, some nations, such as Great Britain, that have long relied on an unwritten constitution have been increasingly giving consideration to the adoption of a written document.

The Importance of Amending Proposals

Altogether, Congress has proposed 33 amendments (for those not ratified, see Failed Amendments) by the necessary two-thirds majorities. Of these, 27 have been adopted. (Each is described in this book under its number, e.g., First Amendment). For every amending proposal that has been adopted, there have been hundreds that have been introduced in Congress but either never seriously considered or rejected—a number that is somewhat misleading because many proposals that have been introduced in Congress are duplicative. Despite their lack of success, such proposals not only serve to illumine possible alternatives to existing constitutional provisions but also important constitutional concerns of earlier generations as well as our own.

Between publication of the first edition of this Encyclopedia in 1996 and the present, scholars have added numerous other books and articles to the subject of constitutional amendments and proposed amendments. The First, Second, Fourth, Tenth, Eleventh, and Fourteenth Amendments are among those that appear currently "hot." Debates continue about the merits of a balanced budget amendment, an amendment providing for congressional term limits, amendments limiting taxes, a religious equality amendment, an anti-flag-desecration amendment, and a victims' rights amendment. Debates have resurfaced about the possibility that Congress might still ratify the Equal Rights Amendment. Individuals like Representative Jesse Jackson Jr. (D-IL) have proposed new amendments to provide constitutional protections for social and economic rights such as a right to work, to education, to health care, and to a clean environment. Scholars have devoted renewed attention to the issue of whether there should be mandatory retirement ages for members of the judiciary and to the issue of gay marriages.

The presidential election of 2000, which produced the first electoral college winner who did not garner a majority of the popular votes in more than 100 years, renewed questions about the desirability of continuing, reforming, or eliminating the current electoral college system by an amendment or through other means. The September 11, 2001, terrorist attack on the World Trade Center in New York and the Pentagon just outside Washington DC has, in turn, led to renewed questions as to whether an amendment needs to be adopted to provide for a situation in which numerous members of the House of Representatives might be simultaneously killed or incapacitated—the Constitution currently permits state governors to make temporary replacements of U.S. Senators but does not have a similar provision for members of the House.

The Author's View of Constitutional Change

In previous books, I have taken positions on most contemporary issues relative to the amending process. At some point in my life, I will probably write an article indicating those proposals that I think are most meritorious. I continue to believe that a constitutional amendment for replacing massive losses of members of the U.S. House of Representatives, and possibly members of the U.S. Supreme Court (along the lines of what the Twenty-fifth Amendment did for presidents and vice-presidents) warrants expedited consideration (see Congress, Emergency Functioning). I am also fascinated by a "Truth-in-Legislation" Amendment that my friends Brannon Denning and Brooks Smith have suggested, essentially requiring that each legislative bill would address one subject and that it would be specified within the bill (see Truth-in-Legislation Amendment). For the most part, however, I often find myself on constitutional matters agreeing with the listener to a congressional speech who noted, "It contained some good things that were not new, and some new things that were not good" (Moore 1925, 15). Although I continue to believe that it is important not to clutter the constitution with proposals that could be effected through legislation, I am increasingly wary of arguments that would preclude consideration of the amending option simply because of unanticipated consequences. The founders included an amending process for a reason, and the supermajorities required in Article V appear more than adequate to weed out those that are unwise or improvident

Despite my fascination with proposals for major constitutional overhauls, I do not currently think that such an overhaul is necessary. I do believe, however, that we have sometimes unthinkingly privileged constitutional changes effected through judicial decision making over those effected through amendments.

During his debate with Stephen Douglas for the Illinois Senate seat that both were seeking, Abraham Lincoln, who was strongly committed to the rule of law, opposed the Supreme Court's decision in *Scott v. Sandford* (1857). In so doing, he recognized that if the Supreme Court could decide each issue with finality the first time it came up, then "the people will have ceased to be their own rulers, having, to that extent, practically resigned their government into the hands of that eminent tribunal" (Murphy, Fleming, and Barber 1995, 317).

In a similar fashion, I believe that it is a mistake to argue that the judiciary and other branches of government have the right to bring about drastic changes in our understanding of the Constitution but that the written document that serves as the fundament for such interpretations must somehow remain untouched. Moreover, I believe that there are occasions when the precision of an amendment is preferable to a more ambiguous ruling that is so frequently tied to the specific facts of an individual case.

Those who worry that any diminution of the Bill of Rights (or other sections of the Constitution) will lead to an avalanche of proposals are, I believe, too fearful. Moreover, if changes in constitutional understandings were actually incorporated into the text, they could serve both as tools of public instruction and as firm bases for judicial decisions. Such arguments, it should be recalled, were among the primary reasons that Thomas Jefferson argued for, and James Madison agreed to, incorporating a bill of rights into the Constitution in the first place.

❖ ACKNOWLEDGMENTS ❖

It is impossible to write a book of this length and breadth without accumulating a number of scholarly debts, and I have mustered my share. In writing the first edition, I acknowledged owing special thanks to Henry Rasof of ABC-CLIO for initially contacting me about this project and subsequently providing useful suggestions and editorial help and to Susan McRory, Susan Ficca, Jennifer Job, and Linda Lotz for their work in turning the manuscript into a book. For this edition, I owe primary thanks to Holly Heinzer, acquisition editor, Alex Mikaberidze, submission editor, and editors Alysia Cooley, Dave Mason, Ray Stoia, and project manager Lisa Connery.

At the outset of the first edition of this project, four individuals read the suggested entries and made helpful suggestions: Professor Barbara Perry of Sweet Briar College, Donna Clilders of Denison University, and Mark Byrnes and Thomas Van Dervort of Middle Tennessee State University (MTSU). At some point in my writing of the three editions of this book, I have called upon most members of the Political Science and History Departments at MTSU for help, including Mark Byrnes, Robb McDaniel, Tyson King-Meadows, Francine Sanders, Jack Turner, Anne Sloan, David Carlton, Everett Cunningham, Lisa Langenbach, and Clyde Willis in the Political Science Department and Jan Leone (who was especially helpful in alerting me to individuals who were influential in the adoption of the Nineteenth Amendment), Bob Hunt, David Rowe, Thad Smith, Fred Rolater, Nancy Rupprecht, Andrew Guilliford, and Lewright Sikes in the History Department. Sarah Peveler, a graduate student at MTSU, and Professor Richard V. Pierard from the History Department at Indiana State University also provided useful information on the Christian Amendment, and Charles Nored gave me access to his files on Christian Reconstructionism. John C. Fortier of the American Enterprise Institute provided information on current plans for an amendment to ensure the continuity of Congress in cases of massive loss of life or incapac-itation of members. Gary Freedom at McNeese State University directed me to sources on cultural and linguistic rights, and Steve Dillard provided information on the proposed Victims' Rights Amendment and recent court decisions. I also received great encouragement from Henry J. Abraham at the University of Virginia and several helpful bibliographical references from Brannon P. Denning, who since the first edition of this book has completed an additional law degree at Yale and is now a prolific professor of law at the Cumberland School of Law at Samford University, and with whom I continue to enjoy corresponding and writing about the amending process.

I have been blessed to teach on a campus that has an especially helpful and friendly library staff. In my first edition I expressed special thanks to Betty McFall and Amy Carr in the MTSU interlibrary loan department, who cheerfully and efficiently handled numerous requests for materials from other libraries. Also, Peggy Colflesh in the Periodicals Department kept me informed as each new issue of *Index to Legal Periodicals* arrived, and Rhonda Armstrong proved helpful in tracking down citations. Library staff members have changed since my first edition, but their willingness to help has not. I have been especially grateful not only for a beautiful new library facility on our campus, but also for an increasing number of indexes on the Internet that have enabled me to access far more journals from my desk than I was once able to do.

On a related note, I am especially grateful to David Huckabee of the Legislative Reference Service at the Library of Congress. Convinced of the value of my project and apparently sympathetic to my own lack of computer savvy, he twice provided written copies of the proposed amendments for my first edition and subsequently taught me how to find such proposals on the Internet on my own for the second and third editions. I also received help from Mike Gillette in the National Archives and Records Administration and from Michael White in the Federal Register's Office.

Student aides at MTSU did much of the "grunt work" for the first edition of this project. Initially they helped compile 12 long boxes of note cards on which we recorded and labeled the nearly 11,000 proposed amendments that were listed in existing books and reports—a task with which my wife and daughters helped. MTSU student aides subsequently helped by running library errands and by writing and compiling the cards that served as the basis for the entries and bibliography for this book. Aides who helped on the first edition of this project included Kathy Aslinger, Felicia Emery Rasori, Pamela Russell-Short, Clint Petty, Megan Kingree, Jaime Sparks, Robert Fletcher, Jason Reid, and Stephanie Corbin. I am especially indebted to my aide Jenny Picklesimer. In addition to doing more than her share of work transferring amending proposals to note cards, she proved to be an adept and competent proofreader. My former secretary, Clare Christian, also helped coordinate the work of student aides on these and related projects.

Because I have just recently worked with the Law Book Exchange on updating the list of proposed amendments, I did not do additional note cards for this project. I did, however, enlist the help of my secretary, Pam Davis, as well as a temporary secretary, Brooke Hamilton, for typing and Web searches. David Dedman, a student aide, helped locate library sources for this second edition, as did my daughter Virginia Vile, who is now a lawyer. Her twin sister Rebekah did her own part by finishing two degrees in record time and getting a full-time job, of which my wife and I are also proud. I also owe thanks to Dawn Johnson, who helped me track down source citations for the second edition.

Middle Tennessee State University has proved to be a very supportive community in which to work. I appreciate my cooperative colleagues and students, and especially the encouragement I received from students in my constitutional law classes and on the mock trial teams I help coach. I owe special thanks to Dr. John McDaniel, dean of the College of Liberal Arts, and to the Faculty Research Committee at MTSU. Both provided release time for me to work on the first edition of this project. In a similar fashion, I am now grateful to the staff of the University Honors College where I am now employed.

I also owe special thanks to my wife, Linda, and to my twin daughters for allowing me to forgo income from one summer of teaching and to devote extensive time from a spring semester and a second summer to speed this project along. More generally, my family made daily sacrifices for a husband and father who sometimes appeared to be more concerned with his scholarship than with their needs. I appreciate their sacrifices and sincerely hope that they can take pride in this volume.

Finally, I relied extensively on the work of previous scholars, especially those who compiled lists and analyses of prior amendments. Despite all my debts, the responsibility for this book is ultimately mine. Any errors in fact or judgment that have crept in must be laid at my own door.

A

ABINGTON V. SCHEMPP (1963)

This 8-to-1 Supreme Court decision stimulated a number of proposed amendments to restore prayer and Bible reading in public schools. The decision covered both *Abington v. Schempp,* involving a Unitarian family in Pennsylvania, and another case in Baltimore involving an atheistic mother and son (*Murray v. Curlett*). *Abington* extended the Supreme Court's controversial opinion of the previous year in *Engel v. Vitale,* which had invalidated the recitation of a state-composed prayer in public schools. *Abington* held that, even in the absence of comments, student-led Bible reading and recitation of the Lord's Prayer during school time and under the supervision of public school teachers violated the establishment clause of the First Amendment, as applied to the states through the due process clause of the Fourteenth Amendment.

Justice Tom C. Clark's majority opinion focused on the "wholesome 'neutrality'" that the state was obligated to follow in regard to religion (*Abington* 1963, 222). Denying that his decision was antireligious or secularistic, Clark said that religion must depend for its support on the home, church, and individual conscience (*Abington* 1963, 226). Clark found that the practices in question were devotional rather than being simply discussions of historical or literary material or nonsectarian attempts to foster morality. He therefore ruled that they lacked an overriding "secular legislative purpose" and that they had as their "primary effect" the promotion of religion (*Abington* 1963, 222).

Justice William Brennan's extensive concurring opinion insisted that establishment clause concerns need to be related to modern historical and educational developments rather than to any narrow view of the framers' original intent. He also denied that the failure to adopt the Blaine Amendment in the 19th century—itself stimulated in part by judicial decisions (see *The Bible in the Public Schools* 1967)—precluded application of the establishment clause to the states. In addition, Brennan discussed previous unsuccessful attempts to adopt the Christian Amendment, which would recognize God in the Constitution (*Abington* 1963, 256–258).

Justice Potter Stewart's dissenting opinion extended his earlier dissent in *Engel* by focusing on his paramount concern with religious freedom. Stewart argued that, because students were permitted to absent themselves from the devotional practices and because there was no direct showing of coercion, such practices represented acceptable accommodations of the exercise of the majority's religious beliefs.

Abington indicated that, despite intense criticism and pressure for an amendment to overturn *Engel,* the Court was not going to back away from its earlier opinion. Still, early studies indicated that many public schools ignored the decision. One school superintendent responded to a survey by saying, "I am of the opinion that 99 percent of the people in the United States feel as I do about the Supreme Court's decision—that it was an outrage, and that Congress should have it amended. The remaining 1 percent do not belong in this free world" (Birkby 1973, 117).

Abington arguably increased pressure for an amendment to permit prayer in schools and for other state and congressional legislation to accommodate majority religious practices. Although a 6-to-3 majority of the Court in *Wallace v. Jaffree* (1985) struck down a state law providing for a moment of silence, it did so primarily because the law favored prayer over alternative meditative activities; the Court thus left open the possibility that it would uphold laws that did not express such a preference. In *Lee v. Weisman* (1992), however, the Supreme Court extended its ruling in *Abington* to outlaw prayers led by members of the clergy at high school graduations, a decision subsequently extended in *Santa Fe Independent School District v. Doe* (2000) to student-led prayers at football games. Issues like prayer in schools and the posting of the Ten Commandments continue to divide those who believe that schools should be imparting moral values from those who fear any state intervention in matters of religion or conscience. Such issues have reemerged in recent Supreme Court decisions involving the application of criminal laws to individuals who are acting on the basis of religious conviction and in the controversy over the need for a Religious Equality Amendment.

See also Blaine Amendment; Christian Amendment; *Engel v. Vitale;* First Amendment; Prayer in Public Schools; Religious Equality Amendment.

For Further Reading:

Abington School District v. Schempp, 374 U.S. 203 (1963).

The Bible in the Public Schools. 1870. Cincinnati, OH: Robert Clarke & Co. Reprint, New York: Da Capo Press, 1967. Introduction by Robert G. McCloskey.

Birkby, Robert H. 1973. "The Supreme Court and the Bible Belt: Tennessee Reaction to the "Schempp' Decision," In *The Impact of Supreme Court Decisions: Empirical Studies*, 2d ed., ed. Theodore L. Becker and Malcolm M. Feeley. New York: Oxford University Press.

Murray, William J. 1982. *My Life without God.* Nashville, TN: Thomas Nelson.

Santa Fe Independent School District v. Doe, 530 U.S. 290 (2000).

Smith, Rodney K. 1987. *Public Prayer and the Constitution: A Case Study in Constitutional Interpretation.* Wilmington, DE: Scholarly Resources.

Solomon, Stephen D. 2007. *Ellery's Protest: How One Young Man Defied Tradition and Sparked a Battle Over School Prayer.* Ann Arbor: University of Michigan Press.

ABOLITIONISTS

The ratification of the Thirteenth Amendment in 1865 followed not only the Civil War but also more than 30 years of agitation by abolitionists. The transition from widely held antislavery sentiments to pressure for immediate abolition occurred in the 1820s. It coincided both with the elimination of slavery in the British Empire and with American religious revivals led by Charles G. Finney and others (Pease and Pease 1965, xxx–xxxii).

William Lloyd Garrison, editor of the *Liberator,* was the best-known abolitionist and advocate of "immediatism" (Pease and Pease 1965, xxix). Garrison founded the New England Anti-Slavery Society. Like the individuals who supported such groups (among them Harriet Beecher Stowe, author of *Uncle Tom's Cabin*), these organizations usually proved better able to denounce slavery than to propose practical plans for its elimination. Like other reform groups, the abolitionists were torn by debates. Controversial issues included how to eliminate slavery, whether violence like that carried out by John Brown was appropriate, whether established religions were friends or foes, how to tie together the rights of blacks and women (many of whom were active in the abolitionist and temperance movements and who, after being disappointed by the Fourteenth and Fifteenth Amendments, lobbied for the Nineteenth Amendment), what role blacks should play in the movement, and what attitude to take toward the U.S. Constitution (Pease and Pease 1965, xlvii–lv).

Some abolitionists, such as Boston's Robert Rantoul, thought that the Constitution was an antislavery document. Others, such as ex-slave

Frederick Douglass, argued that the document should be narrowly construed so as not to sanction slavery. Others, such as congressman (and ex-president) John Quincy Adams, wanted a constitutional amendment. William Lloyd Garrison saw the Constitution as a slave document (Pease and Pease 1965, lvii–lxii). Ultimately, the doctrine of natural rights, grounded in the language of the Declaration of Independence, provided the strongest argument against slavery (see Douglass's Fourth of July Oration in Storing 1970, 28–38).

Abolitionists helped form the National Liberty Party in 1840, the Free-Soil Party later in the decade, and the Republican Party in 1854. The Republicans nominated Abraham Lincoln in 1860, and his election led to the Civil War. Even those abolitionists who had previously resisted political action supported Lincoln during the war and became strong advocates of the Emancipation Proclamation, of the Thirteenth and Fourteenth Amendments, and of the Union and the Constitution, whose utility many of them had previously doubted (Pease and Pease 1965, lxxxi).

See also Brown, John; Declaration of Independence; Fifteenth Amendment; Fourteenth Amendment; Nineteenth Amendment; Thirteenth Amendment.

For Further Reading:

Basker, James G. ed. 2005. *Early American Abolitionists: A Collection of Anti-Slavery Writings, 1760-1820.* New York: Gilder Hehrman Institute of American History.

Dillon, Merton L. 1974. *The Abolitionists: The Growth of a Dissenting Minority.* De Kalb: Northern Illinois University Press.

Pease, William H., and June H. Pease, eds. 1965. *The Antislavery Argument.* Indianapolis, IN: Bobbs-Merrill.

Storing, Herbert, ed. 1970. *What Country Have I? Political Writings by Black Americans.* New York: St. Martin's Press.

tenBroek, Jacobus. 1951. *The Antislavery Origins of the Fourteenth Amendment.* Berkeley: University of California Press.

Wiecek, William M. 1977. *The Sources of Antislavery Constitutionalism in America, 1760–1848.* Ithaca, NY: Cornell University Press.

ABORTION

Long regarded as a matter for state legislative regulation, access to abortion became a major federal issue during the 1970s. Prior to this time, abortion regulations had varied significantly from state to state, allowing the procedure to women in some states (whether residents or those wealthy enough to travel there for that purpose), but effectively denying access to it in other states, where women's choice to resort to illegal abortion procedures posed a threat to their health.

In *Roe v. Wade* (1973), the U.S. Supreme Court upheld a challenge to a restrictive Texas law in an opinion that Justice Harry Blackmun authored. Tracing the origin of abortion laws to the 19th century, Blackmun identified three primary objects of such laws—deterring immoral sexual conduct (not raised as an issue in *Roe*), protecting the health of women, and protecting the life of the fetus. Arguing that the justices could no more agree on when human life began than could philosophers and religious authorities, Blackmun concentrated chiefly on the role of antiabortion laws in protecting women's health. Relying on the right to privacy that the Court had articulated in *Griswold v. Connecticut* (1965), Blackmun decided that during the first trimester, or first three months, of pregnancy, the decision as to whether to have an abortion was between a woman and her doctor. During the second trimester, as abortion became riskier, the state could specify appropriate medical precautions to safeguard a woman's health. In the third trimester, when fetuses are generally considered to be "viable" outside their mothers' wombs, the Court allowed states to prohibit abortion, except in cases where the life or health of the mother was at stake. Advocates of abortion strongly supported the opinion in *Roe,* but critics, including some who favored a woman's right to procure an abortion, argued that the Court had usurped the states' lawmaking authority or the right of the people to settle the matter by adopting a constitutional amendment on the subject.

Since *Roe,* the Supreme Court has rendered many other decisions relative to abortion. In recent years, the Court has accepted a number of state laws requiring parental notification for minors seeking abortion (with a judicial bypass for minors shown to be capable of making the decision on their own), waiting periods, and other restrictions—while rejecting attempts to give fathers a veto over the procedure and still keeping the procedure legal. In *Maher v. Roe* (1977), the Court decided that states were not obligated to provide Medicaid funding for abortion and could prefer funding births over abortion procedures. In *Gonzales v. Carhart,* 550 U.S. 124 (2007), the Court upheld a federal law that limited late-term "partial-birth" abortions, although it had earlier struck down a state law on the subject in *Stenberg v. Carhart,* 530 U.S. 914 (2000).

Numerous proposals have been tried to restrict abortion through constitutional amendments. Some proposed amendments would restrict the procedure altogether, while others would leave the matter for decision at the state level, where it was prior to 1973. Urged to reconsider its central holding in *Roe,* the Supreme Court ruled in *Planned Parenthood of Southeastern Pennsylvania v. Casey* (1992) that abandoning the decision in *Roe* would destabilize the law and send the wrong signal to those who had lobbied against it. Should the Court ever reverse *Roe,* its supporters may well be the ones advancing an amendment to reinstitute the right it protected.

Debates between self-designated prochoice and prolife advocates (the first favoring and the second disfavoring, or desiring to limit, legal access to abortion) continue to be very emotional, with human life amendments proposed in every session of Congress.

See also *Griswold v. Connecticut;* Right to Life.

For Further Reading:

Balkin, Jack, ed. 2007 *What Roe v. Wade Should Have Said: The Nation's Top Legal Experts Rewrite America's Most Controversial Decision.* New York: NYU Press.

Burgess, Susan R. 1992. *Contest for Constitutional Authority: The Abortion and War Powers Debates.* Lawrence: University Press of Kansas.

Maher v. Roe, 432 U.S. 464 (1977).

Planned Parenthood of Southeastern Pennsylvania v. Casey, 500 U.S. 833 (1992).

Roe v. Wade, 410 U.S. 113 (1973).

Tribe, Laurence H. 1990. *Abortion: The Clash of Absolutes.* New York: W. W. Norton & Company.

ACKERMAN, BRUCE (1943–)

Ackerman, who is Sterling Professor of Law and Political Science at Yale University, has written a number of articles and the first two volumes of a projected three-volume set of books (*We the People*) designed to explicate processes of change in the United States. Ackerman argues that the United States is a "dualist democracy," in which periods of ordinary democratic politics are interrupted by periods of intense constitutional lawmaking, often designed to remove certain matters of fundamental rights from the reach of ordinary politics. Ackerman is particularly interested in those major regime changes that have occurred outside of the normal politics of ordinary Article V amending processes.

Ackerman argues that there have been three major changes in American history—that inaugurated by the Constitutional Convention of 1787, that brought about by the Civil War, and that which resulted from the New Deal in the 1930s and 1940s. None of these "constitutional moments" have strictly followed the Article V scenario. Moreover, constitutional interpretation often involves the creative synthesis of insights from different constitutional moments.

Typically, successful periods of "higher lawmaking" involve four phases: a signaling phase, a proposal, a time of mobilized popular deliberation, and a period of legal codification by the Supreme Court (Ackerman 1991, 266–267). If any of these phases is short circuited—as, for example, in Reagan's unsuccessful nomination of Robert Bork to the U.S. Supreme Court—there may be a failed constitutional moment.

Widely critiqued and reviewed, Ackerman's work directs attention to the importance of extra-constitutional changes and to the fact that some such changes are more important than others.

In addition, Ackerman has proposed adding a referendum provision to the Constitution. Under Ackerman's proposal, presidents would be able to propose amendments in their second term. Such proposals would become law if approved by two-thirds of both houses of Congress and subsequently approved by three-fifths of the voters in each of the two succeeding presidential elections (Ackerman 1991, 54–55).

Ackerman has suggested that nations seeking to write new constitutions or revise existing ones might want to look to modified parliamentary systems rather than either to the U.S. model or to the more pure parliamentary model used in Great Britain (Ackerman 2000). Ackerman has also joined another law professor in arguing for a system whereby individuals can anonymously donate "patriot dollars" to candidates and political organizations that they favor, thereby circumventing some of the perceived problems with current campaign contribution limits (Ayers and Ackerman 2002).

See also Article V; Initiative and Referendum; Parliamentary System.

For Further Reading:

Ackerman, Bruce. 2000. "The New Separation of Powers." *Harvard Law Review* 113 (January): 633–729.

———. 1998. *We the People: Transformations.* Cambridge, MA: Harvard University Press.

———. 1989. "Constitutional Politics/Constitutional Law." *Yale Law Journal* 99 (December): 453–547.

———. 1988. "Transformative Appointments." *Harvard Law Review* 101: 1164–1184.

———. 1984. "The Storrs Lectures: Discovering the Constitution." *Yale Law Journal* 93: 1013–1072.

———. 1979. "Unconstitutional Convention." *New Republic* 180 (3 March): 8–9.

Ayers, Ian, and Bruce A. Ackerman. 2002. *Voting with Dollars: A New Paradigm for Campaign Finance.* New Haven, CT: Yale University Press.

Vile, John R. 1993. *Contemporary Questions Surrounding the Constitutional Amending Process.* Westport, CT: Praeger.

Weiser, Philip J. 1993. "Ackerman's Proposal for Popular Constitutional Lawmaking: Can It Realize His Aspirations for Dualist Democracy?" *New York University Law Review* 68 (October): 907–959.

ADAMS, A. R.

A. R. Adams, who is otherwise unidentified, wrote a book in 1996 entitled *The Fourth Constitution* that outlines a very detailed proposal for replacing the U.S. Constitution. Adams calls his constitution the fourth on the basis that the Declaration of Independence, the Articles of Confederation, and the current Constitution were the first three. On the back cover of his book, Adams says his aim is to author "an egalitarian, merit-based democracy that adds economic and social rights to the political rights of all citizens."

Adams's proposal calls for establishing a unicameral congress of 600 representatives who would be limited to three three-year terms, and who would be limited to $3,000 of campaign expenses. The people would select the chief executive from among seven candidates nominated by Congress. Twenty-one justices, serving 10-year terms, would head the Supreme Court. Adams further sought to guarantee full employment, "egalitarian, managed health care" for all, "universal higher education," and national military training and public service duty for all (ix). The Fourth Constitution would further provide for balancing the federal budget, eliminating the national debt, and punishing environmental polluters. Adams proposed to eliminate states and replace them with 600 congressional districts, each containing 100 wards and being subdivided into 10 precincts.

Adam's constitution begins with a set of self-evident "verities," which include a classification of the Constitution of 1789 as "a plutocracy" (2)—a term denoting a regime governed by the wealthy. He devotes 83 pages of his book to the new legislative branch. Here, as elsewhere in his proposal, he outlines an order of chapel services for Congress that includes singing "My Country 'Tis of Thee" and reciting the Gettysburg Address, the Three Parts of the Tenets of American Citizenship, and the Desiderada (9).

Adams would make lobbying a felony (13) and would forbid omnibus bills (14). He would institute a progressive income tax that would take up to 70% of upper incomes; he would further supplement this with a 99% inheritance tax and with sumptuary taxes (15–16), which would not apply to "vegetarian diet controlled caféterias" (17). Property owners would pay a tax on all space above 970 square feet. Individual incomes would be limited to 25 times that of the lowest.

Article I outlines a variety of compulsory measures to improve the environment, including ex post facto punishments and mandated organic farming. It would also provide for balancing trade with foreign nations. Each ward would be a planned community. Individuals convicted of sexual crimes would be neutered, and tobacco and alcohol would be heavily regulated.

Health care would include the right to assisted suicide and would be limited for individuals who were obese or who practiced other unhealthy lifestyles. The government would provide a "Department of Rehabilitation" for unwed mothers, who would be closely supervised and regulated. Couples would be limited to two children and would be forbidden from divorce if they had children under the age of 18. Adams would mandate abortions and birth control for unwed mothers and sterilize individuals who might pass on hereditary diseases.

Adams would provide youth rehabilitation centers, and would replace all existing private pensions with one issued by the government. He would mandate English as the official language and make numerous regulations regarding the content of public education, including provision for school uniforms and a daily chapel call. Although affirming freedom of speech, Adams's proposal calls for numerous governmental controls over the electronic media, including restrictions on advertising.

Article II outlines the responsibilities of the president. The top vote getter would serve as president, with the individual coming in second becoming vice president.

Article III specifies that members of the Supreme Court would select their chief justice. Local counts would take cases against "Scolds (those troublesome and angry persons who, by brawling and wrangling among his or her neighbors increases discords) and against Common Nuisances (those disturbers of the peace who interrupt the peace, quiet, and good order of the neighborhood by unnecessary and distracting noices, such as keeping dogs that bark by day and night, playing radios and sound systems at a volume that can be heard outside the house or vehicle, and any conduct which tends to annoy all good citizens)." (93–94) Article III also contains provisions currently found in the Fourth, Fifth, Sixth, Seventh, and Eighth Amendments, sometimes modified by accompanying case law.

Article IV specifically abolishes existing state lines, which are to be replaced by the new congressional districts. It also provides for national referendums. The latter provision also includes modified forms of a number of current constitutional amendments. It would specifically modify the First Amendment to provide for limiting freedoms that "in any manner or degree infringe upon the rights of others to their privacy, to their tranquility, to their peace and quiet of mind and body or to the public peace and quiet" (106).

Article V provides for "The Tenets of American Citizenship." These include "Duties or Legal Obligations," "Moral Obligations," and "Values or Personal Obligations."

Article VI provides for congressional districts to play the role that states currently play in ratifying amendments. Article VII deals with miscellaneous matters, and Article VII provides for ratification of the document "In a concurrent referendum with the first election of Representatives to the first congress" (111).

See also Bill of Responsibilities; Social and Economic Rights.

For Further Reading:

Adams, A. R. 1996. *The Fourth Constitution of the United States of America.* Salt Lake City, UT: A. R. Adams Publishing.

ADAMS, FREDERICK UPHAM (1859–1921)

An inventor and engineer before becoming labor editor of the *Chicago Tribune,* Adams published a utopian novel, *President John Smith* (1896), that sold more than 750,000 copies.

After copious initial chapters analyzing American politics and business cycles, the novel told the story of a onetime federal judge who ran for president as a Populist. After being cheated out of the presidency when he fell one vote short of a majority in the Electoral College, the judge called a convention that met in Omaha and wrote a new constitution, under which he served as the first president. This constitution was based on majority rule and socialism and reflected populist themes that would continue into the Progressive Era.

Adams's proposed constitution, submitted by the Smith character in his novel to popular approval by the people, contained eight articles. The first provided for a president selected by direct popular vote and subject to recall. The plan made no provisions for a vice president; if the president died, he was to be temporarily succeeded by the secretary of state until a special election could be called. (Although Adams constantly referred to a "direct" or "popular" vote throughout his proposed constitution, he continued to use the pronoun "he," and does not appear to have contemplated nationwide voting by women, which came in 1920 with the adoption of the Nineteenth Amendment.)

Article II provided for a cabinet of 12 officers—including a superintendent of education—popularly elected and also subject to recall. The Senate was eliminated, with the cabinet taking over some of its functions—ratifying treaties, for example, by a two-thirds vote.

Article III provided for a unicameral Congress of 200 members. Fifty members could submit legislation directly to the people for approval by referendum. All major legislation was to be so approved.

The Supreme Court, outlined in Article IV, would have five members appointed by the president, approved by the people, and subject to retirement by the people's majority vote. Although it would exercise judicial review of state and local laws, the Court would have no power to declare laws adopted by the people to be unconstitutional. Instead, it would be required to give advisory opinions to Congress on ways to make its legislation acceptable.

Article V dealt with currency matters (valuing the dollar on "the average productivity of one hour's work"), and Articles VI and VII provided for the use of the government's power of eminent domain to take over unoccupied land and to socialize basic industries.

Article VIII provided for constitutional repeal, revision, and amendment by majority vote. The constitution contained no bill of rights or definition of citizenship such as that in the Fourteenth Amendment.

At the conclusion of his novel, Adams asked readers to consider forming a "Majority Rule Club" in their vicinity. Adams also advocated his ideas in a socialist magazine that he renamed the *New Times*. Boyd (1992, 96) reports that Adams appears to have abandoned his plans for a new constitution by the turn of the century, and his project has been largely ignored ever since.

See also Progressive Era.

For Further Reading:

Adams, Frederick U. 1896. *President John Smith: The Story of a Peaceful Revolution*. Chicago: Charles H. Kerr & Company. Reprint New York: Arno Press, 1970.

Boyd, Steven R., ed. 1992. *Alternative Constitutions for the United States: A Documentary History*. Westport, CT: Greenwood Press.

ADAMSON V. CALIFORNIA (1947)

Justice Stanley Reed delivered a 5-to-4 ruling for the U.S. Supreme Court in *Adamson v. California* that had broad implications for the interpretation of the Bill of Rights and the Fourteenth Amendment. In *Adamson,* the Court reaffirmed an earlier decision in *Twining v. New Jersey* (1908) by deciding that the Fifth Amendment guarantee against self-incrimination did not apply to the states through the due process clause of the Fourteenth Amendment. States were thus free, as California had authorized, to permit comment on defendants' failure to testify in their own defense.

Reed thus reaffirmed the doctrine of selective incorporation, which Justice Benjamin Cardozo had articulated in *Palko v. Connecticut* (1937). By this doctrine, the Court did not apply the entire Bill of Rights to the states via the due process clause but only those guarantees that were most fundamental. Similarly, in his concurring opinion in *Adamson,* Justice Felix Frankfurter defended the view that the due process clause was not intended to serve as shorthand for the Bill of Rights and "neither comprehends the specific provisions by which the founders deemed it appropriate to restrict the federal government nor is confined to them" (*Adamson* 1947, 66).

In a dissenting opinion joined by Justice William O. Douglas, Justice Hugo Black, a former U.S. senator from Alabama who believed that his service as a senator had given him special understanding of how to read congressional debates, argued that John Bingham and other sponsors (whose views Black analyzed in a 32-page appendix) had designed the first section of the Fourteenth Amendment to overturn the Supreme Court's decision in *Barron v. Baltimore* (1833) and apply the Bill of Rights to the states. Although advocating such total incorporation, which the Court had rejected in the *Slaughterhouse Cases* (1873) and subsequent decisions, Black favored limiting the due process clause to specific guarantees in the Bill of Rights, thus avoiding the "natural-law–due-process formula" (*Adamson* 1947, 90) that Black identified with prior judicial abuses.

Although substantively agreeing with Black, Justices Frank Murphy and Wiley Rutledge argued for "total incorporation plus" (Abraham and Perry 2003, 99), or the view that although the due process clause had been intended to apply the protections of the Bill of Rights to the states, it might also include additional rights. The Court has followed this philosophy, or the related doctrine that has been called "selective incorporation plus," in cases like *Griswold v. Connecticut* (1965), *Roe v. Wade* (1973), and similar cases when articulating a constitutional right to privacy.

Since *Adamson,* the Court has, by a process of selective incorporation, approached Black's goal of total incorporation by applying all but five guarantees in the Bill of Rights to the states. (The five yet to be incorporated are the Second

Amendment's right to bear arms, the Third Amendment's limitation on quartering troops, the Fifth Amendment's right to a grand jury indictment, the Seventh Amendment's right to a petit jury in civil cases, and the Eighth Amendment's right to be free of excessive bails and fines.) In *Griffin v. California* (1965), the Court specifically applied the self-incrimination provision it had rejected in *Adamson.*

See also *Barron v. Baltimore;* Bingham, John; Fifth Amendment; Fourteenth Amendment**;** Incorporation; *Palko v. Connecticut.*

For Further Reading:

Abraham, Henry J., and Barbara Perry. 2003. *Freedom and the Court: Civil Rights and Liberties in the United States,* 8th ed. New York: Oxford University Press.

Adamson v. California, 332 U.S. 46 (1947).

AFFIRMATIVE ACTION

Although not specifically mentioning race, the Constitution of 1787 permitted slavery and even counted slaves as three-fifths of a person for purposes of representation in the House of Representatives and direct taxation. In [*Dred*] *Scott v. Sandford* (1857), Chief Justice Roger Taney declared that blacks were not, and could not be, American citizens. The Fourteenth Amendment overturned this decision by assuring citizenship in Section 1 to "all persons born or naturalized in the United States and subject to the jurisdiction thereof" and guaranteed basic "privileges and immunities," "due process," and "equal protection" to all such citizens. Section 5 further gave Congress power to enforce these provisions.

Initially giving the amendment a narrow reading in such decisions as the *Slaughterhouse Cases* (1873), the *Civil Rights Cases* (1883), and *Plessy v. Ferguson* (1896), the Supreme Court reversed course in *Brown v. Board of Education* (1954) and outlawed discriminatory Jim Crow laws that had provided for racial segregation. Congress followed with legislation such as the Civil Rights Act of 1964, which used federal commerce powers to outlaw discrimination in places of public accommodation and in hiring.

Questions soon arose as to whether the government could now use racial classifications that had once discriminated against minorities to improve minority representation and compensate for the effects of past discrimination. Generally, liberals approved of such affirmative action plans as effective means of enforcing the Fourteenth Amendment, whereas conservatives opposed them as impositions of "reverse discrimination." The Supreme Court has faced this issue in a large number of cases. In *Regents of the University of California v. Bakke* (1978), Justice Lewis Powell voted with four other members of the Court to strike the use of strict racial quotas at the medical school at the University of California at Davis but joined four other justices in deciding that some consideration of race was appropriate to assure diversity in university admissions. Representative James Collins (R) of Texas introduced an amendment in 1978 to prohibit "denial of equal opportunity because of quotas or ratios based on race, color, national origin, religion, or sex" (H.J. Res. 1035). Senator Orrin Hatch (R) of Utah subsequently introduced amendments against affirmative action in 1980 and 1981. The Senate held hearings on the subject in 1981.

Since its decision in *Richmond v. Croson Company* (1989), in which it overturned a 30-percent set-aside program for minority contractors that was established by the Richmond City Council, the U.S. Supreme Court has subjected affirmative action programs to greater scrutiny. In *Adarand Constructors, Inc. v. Pena* (1995), the U.S. Supreme Court announced that it would apply three principles to affirmative action cases. First, it would be "skeptical" of racial classifications, subjecting them to strict scrutiny; second, it would require "consistency" in the treatment of classifications based on race, whether such classifications applied to racial majorities or minorities; and third, it would require "congruence" between what it would permit states and the national government to do (in previous cases, the Court had sometimes given the national government greater leeway under the enforcement clauses of the Thirteenth through Fifteenth Amendments).

The U.S. Supreme Court issued two important affirmative action decisions in 2003. In *Gratz v. Bollinger,* it ruled that the assignment of a designated number of entrance "points" to minority applicants violated the equal protection clause of the Fourteenth Amendment. In *Grutter v. Bollinger,* however, it upheld the Michigan Law School's more diffuse considerations of diversity for its admission system. In *Ricci v. DeStefano*, 129 s. ct. 2659 (2009), a case involving New Haven, Connecticut firefighters, the Supreme Court limited affirmative action remedies in the workplace.

See also Fourteenth Amendment; *Scott v. Sandford.*

For Further Reading:

Affirmative Action and Equal Protection. 1981. Hearings before the Senate Subcommittee on the Constitution of the Committee on the Judiciary, 97th Cong., 1st sess., on S.J. 41, 4 May, 11, 18 June, and 16 July. Washington DC: U.S. Government Printing Office.

Eastland, Terry. 1996. *Ending Affirmative Action: The Case for Colorblind Justice.* New York: Basic Books.

Fiscus, Ron. 1992. *The Constitutional Logic of Affirmative Action.* Durham, NC: Duke University Press.

Gratz v. Bollinger, 539 U.S. 244 (2003).

Grutter v. Bollinger, 539 U.S. 306 (2003).

Perry, Barbara A. 2007. *The Michigan Affirmative Action Cases.* Lawrence: University Press of Kansas.

Regents of the University of California v. Bakke, 438 U.S. 265 (1978).

Schmidt, Peter. 2002. "Next Stop, Supreme Court? Appeals Court Upholds Affirmative Action at University of Michigan Law School." *The Chronicle of Higher Education* 48 (24 May): A24–26.

AGAR, HERBERT (1897–1980)

Herbert Agar was an author, historian, and editor for the *Louisville Courier-Journal.* During World War II, he also wrote a book, *A Time for Greatness,* in which he called for national spiritual and political renewal in order to save civilization. He presented his ideas for governmental reform in a chapter entitled "Can We Make Government Accountable and Understandable?" (Vile 1991c, 87–89).

There, as elsewhere in his book, Agar drew a distinction between two types of government. One was a "multipleagency system" of government like that of the United States, "which seeks to partition and separate the powers of government and to distribute them among various agencies, so that authority will always be subject to checks." The other was a system like that in Great Britain, which "concentrates power in the executive, and sets up a representative body whose sole task is to watch and criticize the executive" (Agar 1942, 83–84). Although Agar's initial critique of the U.S. government seemed to favor a parliamentary system of concentrated responsibility, he noted that he was not suggesting "that the Parliamentary form of government is necessarily to be preferred," but rather that it "has much to teach us about the solution of the problem" (Agar 1942, 257).

As one who spent much of his life in England, Agar drew several lessons from the British system. He believed that the executive should be responsible for formulating the budget, with the legislature serving as critic rather than having the authority to add to it. More generally, Agar believed that it was the responsibility of the executive to prepare all needed measures and the function of Congress to act on them, "rejecting them, refining them, proposing alternatives, or accepting them as they are" (Agar 1942, 261).

Agar argued that the American founders intended for the federal system to be closer to this accountability model than it turned out to be in practice. Agar tied the system's failure to achieve this accountability to the Washington administration. He cited the first Senate's unwillingness to serve as a type of privy council in formulating treaties and Congress's refusal to allow Alexander Hamilton to appear on the House floor and "establish direct relations between the heads of Cabinet departments and Congress" (Agar 1942, 265). Agar noted, "if the administration were allowed to bring its bills upon the floor of Congress and there to defend them, the executive could create policy and the Congress, unable to retreat into the darkness itself, would see to it that there was nothing hidden or obscure or unexplained about the measures proposed" (Agar 1942, 277).

Because Agar believed that the American founders had actually intended to have a more accountable system than the one that developed, he held out the possibility that reform might be achieved by "constitutional reinterpretation" rather than by amendment. He indicated, however, that "if the task cannot be done by reinterpretation, it will have to be done by revision, even if that involves a constitutional convention" (Agar 1942, 278).

See also Parliamentary System.

For Further Reading:

Agar, Herbert. 1942. *A Time for Greatness.* Boston: Little, Brown.

Vile, John R. 1991. *Rewriting the United States Constitution: An Examination of Proposals from Reconstruction to the Present.* New York: Praeger.

AGRICULTURE

Although the U.S. Constitution was written when the nation was chiefly agricultural, and leading statesmen—including Thomas Jefferson—favored the development of an agrarian republic, the document makes no specific mention of the subject. Undoubtedly, many of the founders anticipated that any agricultural regulations that were needed would be enacted by the states. Although the Supreme Court sometimes struck down such regulations under its interpretation of the due process clause of the Fourteenth Amendment, most 19th-century agricultural regulation was exercised at the state level; prices charged by grain elevator operators and railroads were frequent subjects of state concern in the latter half of the century.

Democratic Texas senator Morris Sheppard, however, proposed an amendment in 1916 and 1917, giving Congress power to purchase, improve, and sell land and to make loans for the purpose of promoting farm ownership (S.J. Res. 127; S.J. Res. 76). Similarly, New York's Republican representative Fiorello La Guardia proposed an amendment in 1917 (probably related to the U.S. war effort), allowing Congress to regulate "production, conservation, and distribution of foodstuffs and fuel" (H.J. Res. 107). World War I resulted in the War Time Prohibition Act, which went into effect in 1919, more than six months prior to the Eighteenth Amendment (C. May 1989, 66), which constitutionalized the ban on alcohol (but was later overturned by the Twenty-First Amendment).

The Great Depression accented the interdependency between agriculture and other aspects of the economy, and a number of Franklin Roosevelt's New Deal programs were directed toward or included agricultural regulation. Most notable were the National Industrial Recovery Act and the Agricultural Adjustment Act. Initially, the Supreme Court struck down both laws. In *Schechter Poultry Corporation v. United States* (1935), often called the "Sick Chicken" case, the Court declared that the first law, which permitted industries to set codes of fair competition to be approved by the president, was unconstitutional. The Court believed that the law permitted excessive delegation of congressional powers. In *United States v. Butler* (1936), the Court decided that the processing tax on agricultural commodities sanctioned by the Agricultural Adjustment Act invaded state police powers protected by the Tenth Amendment (Kershen 1992, 22). The latter decision especially appears to have sparked a number of proposed amendments giving Congress the power to legislate for agriculture. Democrat Samuel Dickstein of New York proposed one such amendment the day after the decision, and another dozen or so proposals were introduced within the next two years. Some proposals referred only to agriculture, whereas others included regulation of commerce, industry, and labor.

Subsequent Supreme Court decisions in *Mulford v. Smith* (1939) and *Wickard v. Filburn* (1942) upheld a revised Agricultural Adjustment Act under a broad reading of the commerce clause. In the latter case, the Court even recognized congressional authority over crops that were grown for home consumption. With the Supreme Court's broad reading of the commerce clause, less restrictive interpretations of state police powers, and greater judicial deference to governmental regulations in the area of economic policies, congressional proposals for amendments to increase federal powers over agriculture have ceased. Debates continue over desirable farm policies and especially over the wisdom and/or necessity of federal crop supports and subsidies.

See also Jefferson, Thomas; Tenth Amendment.

For Further Reading:

Kershen, Drew L. 2005. "Agriculture." In *The Oxford Companion to the Supreme Court of the United States,* ed. Kermit L. Hall. 2d ed. New York: Oxford University Press, 26–27.

May, Christopher N. 1989. *In the Name of War.* Cambridge, MA: Harvard University Press.

AIR FORCE

Article II, Section 2 of the U.S. Constitution designates the president as "Commander in Chief of the Army and Navy of the United States," as well as of state militias when called to national service. The air force, for which there was no specific warrant in 1787, was subsequently developed and separated from the other two services in 1947. The following January, Republican representative Claude Bakewill of Missouri introduced an amendment (H.J. Res. 298) designating the president commander in chief of this branch as well. Failure to adopt the amendment does not appear to have lessened presidential powers in this area, but at least one advocate of a new constitution believes the current document's failure to mention the air force is a significant omission (Scott 1999, 214).

See also Scott, Rodney.

For Further Reading:

Scott, Rodney. 1999. *The Great Debate: The Need for Constitutional Reform.* Chicago: Rampant Lion Press.

ALBANY PLAN OF UNION

In early America, the colonies were created and governed by royal, corporate, or proprietary charters, which eventually served as models for state and national constitutions. Even during the Articles of Confederation and the early years of the U.S. Constitution, the former colonies continued jealously to guard their rights. Unsurprisingly, the first real plan proposed for a North American union, the Albany Plan of Union, was ultimately neither adopted by the colonies nor pushed by the English themselves. This plan, authored chiefly by Benjamin Franklin just before the French and Indian War in 1754 and proposed by delegates from the northern colonies and from the Iroquois Nations, remains significant in pointing the direction to a possible future union.

The plan had a brief preamble and 25 sections. The preamble proposed making "humble application" to the British Parliament for "one general government" in America. The new government was to be "administered by a President-General" appointed by the king and a "Grand Council" chosen by individual colonial assemblies (Section 1). This unicameral council was to have 48 representatives from 11 colonies (Section 2); the representatives would meet in Philadelphia when convened by the president-general. Members would serve for three-year terms, with reapportionment to be provided for based on the proportion of taxes paid by each colony, but with the stipulation (somewhat akin to the later Connecticut Compromise) that no state would have more than seven or fewer than two delegates (Section 5).

The Grand Council, like the current House of Representatives, would have had the right to choose its own speaker and could not be arbitrarily dismissed by the president-general. The latter's assent would, however, be required for all acts. The Grand Council was to have power to make war or peace with Indian tribes, regulate Indian trade, make purchases from the Indians, and found and govern new settlements (Sections 10–15). The Grand Council could also "make laws, and levy such general duties, imposts, or taxes, as to them shall appear most equal and just" (Section 16). The Grand Council would transmit laws to the king in council in Great Britain; in a provision resembling a modern-day legislative veto, such laws were to become effective "if not disapproved within three years after presentation" (Section 21).

The speaker of the Grand Council was designated to succeed the president-general in the case of his death, until the Crown could make a new appointment (Section 22). The president-general was responsible for commissioning all military officers with the consent of the Grand Council, thus establishing civilian control over the military. A final section (Section 25) granted that "the particular military as well as civil establishments in each Colony [will] remain in their present state . . . ." The plan does not appear to have provided for a specific amending mechanism.

Although the plan was never adopted, many of the delegates who attended the Congress that established the Articles of Confederation or the subsequent Constitutional Convention (where Benjamin Franklin was the oldest member present) were undoubtedly aware of this proposal. The specific features of both documents diverge in many respects from the Albany Plan of Union, but principles like the division of power between the executive and legislative branches (without, however, specification for an independent judiciary) and civilian control of the military are similar to those in the current Constitution.

See also Articles of Confederation.

For Further Reading:

"Albany Plan of Union," http://www.constitution.org/bcp/albany.htm. Accessed April 27, 2002.

Newbold, Robert C. 1955. *The Albany Congress and Plan of Union of 1754.* New York: Vantage Press.

Olson, Alison Gilbert. 1960. "The British Government and Colonial Union, 1754." *William and Mary Quarterly,* 3rd Ser. 17 (January): 22–34.

ALCOHOLIC PROHIBITION

See Eighteenth Amendment.

ALIENS

Article I, Section 8 of the U.S. Constitution entrusts Congress with the power to provide a "uniform Rule of Naturalization." Section 1 of the Fourteenth Amendment further extends citizenship to all persons born in the United States or naturalized. Although the United States is a nation of immigrants, disputes about the status of noncitizens, or aliens, date at least as far back as the Alien Acts of 1798. Federalists adopted the Alien Acts, along with the Sedition Acts, partly because they believed that immigrants (especially those from France and Ireland) were more supportive of the Republican stance against the British than of Federalist Anglophile policies (Urofsky 1988, 171). Since that time, amendments have been introduced both to restrict and to expand the rights of such individuals.

Laws Restricting Aliens

Most proposals would affect states where aliens reside rather than the aliens themselves. Such proposals, especially prominent in the 1930s and 1940s, but continuing into the 21st century, would exclude aliens from the population count used to apportion representatives in the House (for example, H.J. Res. 263, 1930). Section 2 of the Fourteenth Amendment currently provides that such apportionment be based on "the whole number of persons in each State, excluding Indians not taxed." Excluding aliens from the count would thus reduce representation for states with large immigrant populations, such as California, Florida, and Texas.

Subject to restrictions against discrimination such as those found in the Fifteenth, Nineteenth, Twenty-Fourth, and Twenty-Sixth Amendments (each of which protects citizens only), states set their own qualifications for voting and office-holding. Thus, there have also been a number of proposals, most prominent from the 1890s to about 1921, which would prevent states from extending either or both privileges to aliens. Many advocates of such restrictions were connected to the Progressive movement and hoped that such restrictions would remove a source of support for corrupt political machines (Welch et al. 1993, 171). This was clearly an objective that could be reached by state law; today, all states include citizenship as a requirement for voting and holding office.

Additional proposals relating to the rights of aliens have sought to allow states to regulate their employment or, as in a proposal introduced by Democratic representative Thomas Wilson of Mississippi in 1927, to prohibit citizens born overseas from serving as representatives (H.J. Res. 103). Such a proposal would effectively extend the ban on office-holding (itself controversial) that now applies, under Article II, Section 1 of the Constitution, only to the presidency.

A number of individuals who competed for the presidential nomination in 2008, most Republicans, proposed measures to cut governmental benefits for illegal aliens and to make it more difficult for them to enter the United States.

Laws Protecting Aliens

A New York representative introduced three proposals from 1917 to 1919 to prevent states from passing discriminatory laws against aliens. An earlier proposal in 1913 would have granted Congress the "exclusive power to legislate on questions affecting rights and privileges of aliens resident in [the] United States" (H.J. Res. 88). All these proposals appear to have been directed primarily at laws passed by California that discriminated against immigrant Japanese. Laws such as those restricting landholding by Japanese or separating Asian children from those of Anglo-Saxon stock in schools sometimes conflicted with U.S. treaties and embarrassed U.S. foreign policy at a time when Japan was becoming a major world power (Daniels 1968, 31–45). During World War II, the United States sequestered more than 100,000 Japanese Americans in detention camps.

Related to the question of the treatment of aliens is the question of citizenship. Concerned with providing disincentives for those coming to the United States illegally, advocates of the Birthright Citizenship Amendment have sought to limit the extension of citizenship to individuals born on U.S. soil to those whose mothers are either U.S. citizens or who are, in the least, legally in the United States.

See also Birthright Citizenship Amendment; Citizenship, Definition of; Congress, Representation in; Fourteenth Amendment; Immigration, Illegal; Voting Rights, Constitutional Amendment Related to.

For Further Reading:

Daniels, Roger. 1968. *The Politics of Prejudice.* New York: Antheneum.

Davis, Jeffrey. 2008. *Justice across Borders: the Struggle for Human Rights in U.S. Courts.* Cambridge: Cambridge University Press.

Urofsky, Melvin I. 1988. *A March of Liberty: A Constitutional History of the United States.* New York: Alfred A. Knopf.

Welch, Susan, et al. 1993. *Understanding American Government,* 2nd ed. Minneapolis–St. Paul, MN: West.

ALTERNATIVE U.S. CONSTITUTIONS, PROPOSED

The United States is based on fundamental law in a written constitution, which in turn succeeded a previous written document, the Articles of Confederation. Many reformers have subsequently attempted not simply to author individual amendments to the Constitution but also to rewrite the entire document, or to append major revisions to it that often have exceeded the length of the original Constitution itself.

Proposals have varied so much that it is difficult to generalize about them. They appear to span most of American history. After the presidential election of 1801, Virginia's Edmund Pendleton offered a number of proposals that he thought were necessary to secure Democratic-Republican principles. Then–West Point cadet Simon Willard Jr.'s prolix proposal for reforming and renaming the nation Columbia in 1815 (see Willard, Simon, Jr.) is another early one. In addition to leading to secession and the writing and implementing of the Confederate Constitution in the South, the period around the U.S. Civil War precipitated at least two proposals for

new constitutions, one by the notorious abolitionist John Brown and the other by a lesser-known New York writer named William B. Wedgwood. Since then, proposals appear to have been chiefly prompted by "crises (or perceived crises) and constitutional anniversaries" (Vile 1991c, 156). Proposals have been identified from the period of Reconstruction, the Progressive Era, both World Wars, the Great Depression, the 1960s and 1970s, and anniversary celebrations of the Declaration of Independence and the U.S. Constitution. Several proposals over the last decade or so have centered on the fact that the nation has entered a new century and, indeed, a new millennium. Increasingly, such proposals are beginning to appear on the Internet, where their effect is even less easy to measure.

Some proposals can be grouped together. Many call for the following: establishing a parliamentary system of government in place of the existing system based on separation of powers; strengthening or weakening one or another of the existing branches of government; strengthening the national government against centrifugal state tendencies; "downsizing" or decentralizing existing powers or even allowing portions of the nation to secede; recognizing more individual political rights; moving the United States in a more socialistic or libertarian direction; guaranteeing a set of social and economic rights; and stringing together lists of proposed alterations, often overlapping with popular measures that members of Congress are introducing into that body at the time, and so forth. There are undoubtedly others who are hoping for more violent revolutionary changes that would fall outside the parameters of this book.

Because of this diversity of perspectives, it is difficult, if not impossible, to identify a "reform" tradition. Not only do proposed alternative U.S. constitutions vary significantly, but most were written in response to specific crises or with little or no knowledge of the proposals that preceded them.

Although many proposed major sets of changes or alternative constitutions have been written by academic scholars or practitioners like Woodrow Wilson, William Y. Elliott, Leland Baldwin, Rexford Tugwell, Chester J. Antieau,

Richard Labunski, Sanford Levinson, and Larry Sabato, others have been authored by fairly ordinary citizens, some of whom have preferred to remain anonymous. Some have attempted to rewrite the entire Constitution, whereas others have preferred to incorporate changes into the existing text. There may indeed be something peculiarly American about the idea of sitting down to rewrite the Constitution.

Many authors of alternate constitutions have paid little attention to how they might be implemented. Others have proposed liberalizing existing constitutional amending mechanisms; convening, or persuading Congress or the states to convene, constitutional preconventions, conventions, or commissions; convincing states to serve as laboratories for proposed changes; or introducing and/or ratifying proposals by initiative or referendum. Such initiatives and referendums appear to be increasing in popularity among proponents of new major constitutional alterations; some such advocates believe that the Internet and other forms of modern technology have increased the chances for citizen participation in constitution-making and approval.

There continues to be not only fairly strong support for the existing constitutional document but also fairly widespread fear of, and resistance to, the idea of wholesale constitutional alterations that might threaten existing rights or result in unintended consequences. To date, the Article V convention mechanism has never been utilized, and only one of 27 amendments adopted (the Twenty-First, repealing national alcoholic prohibition) has been ratified through the convention mechanism rather than being ratified by existing state legislatures. Alternate constitutions provide fascinating reading, cast interesting light on their authors, help illumine the nature of earlier historical time periods, point to strengths and weaknesses of existing constitutional structures, explain existing delineations of governmental powers and individual rights and possible alternatives, and serve as storehouses of possible future reforms.

See also Confederate States of America, Constitution of; Constitutional Conventions; Parlimanctary Systems; Reverence for the Constitution; Unintended Consequences of Constitutional Amendments; individual names of authors for constitutions that they have proposed.

For Further Reading:

Boyd, Stephen R., ed. 1992. *Alternative Constitutions for the United Sates: A Documentary History.* Westport, CT: Greenwood Press.

Mount, Steve. "Constitutional Topic: Rewriting the Constitution." http://www.usconstitution.net.consttop_newc.html. Accessed June 23, 2008.

Vile, John R. 1991. *Rewriting the United States Constitution: An Examination of Proposals from Reconstruction to the Present.* New York: Praeger.

Vile, John R. 1993. "The Long Legacy of Proposals to Rewrite the U.S. Constitution." *PS: Political Science and Politic*s 26 (June): 208.

AMAR, AKHIL REED (1958–)

Amar is a professor of law at Yale University and has written articles analyzing a number of constitutional amendments as well as books on the Bill of Rights (Amar 1997, 1998). Like Bruce Ackerman, Amar argues that the procedures in Article V of the U.S. Constitution are not the exclusive legal mechanisms for amending the Constitution. Unlike Ackerman, who focuses on "constitutional moments," Amar believes either that a majority of voters could petition Congress to call a constitutional convention or that Congress could submit amendments to a popular vote or referendum (Amar 1988, 1994).

Amar bases his argument on the extralegal fashion in which the current Constitution was adopted, on ideas of popular sovereignty current at the nation's founding, and on such constitutional provisions as the Preamble and the First, Ninth, and Tenth Amendments. Amar's argument may also receive some support from experience with amending mechanisms at the state level, although there is one prominent example of such an experiment going awry (*Luther v. Borden* [1849]). If accepted, Amar's view would negate the need for a number of proposed procedural changes in the amending process. Dow (1990), Vile (1990–1991), and Monaghan (1996) have questioned the constitutional support for Amar's views.

Amar's views have served as one of the supports for the National Initiative for Democracy, which met in Williamsburg, Virginia, in February 2002 with hopes of amending the U.S. Constitution through a national referendum.

See also Ackerman, Bruce; National Initiative for Democracy.

For Further Reading:

Amar, Akhil R. 2005. *America's Constitution: A Biography.* New York: Random House.

———. 1997. *The Constitution and Criminal Procedure: First Principles.* New Haven, CT: Yale University Press.

———. 1994. "The Consent of the Governed: Constitutional Amendment outside Article V." *Columbia Law Review* 94 (March): 457–508.

———. 1992. "The Bill of Rights as a Constitution." *Yale Law Journal* 100 (Winter): 1131–1210.

———. 1988. "Philadelphia Revisited: Amending the Constitution outside Article V." *University of Chicago Law Review* 55 (Fall): 1043–1104.

Dow, David R. 1990. "When Words Mean What We Believe They Say: The Case of Article V." *Iowa Law Review* 76 (October): 1–66.

Monaghan, Henry P. 1996. "We the People[s], Original Understanding, and Constitutional Amendment." *Columbia Law Review* 96 (January): 121–177.

Vile, John R. 1990–1991. "Legally Amending the United States Constitution: The Exclusivity of Article V's Mechanisms." *Cumberland Law Review* 21: 271–307.

AMENDING PROCESS

See Article V of the U.S. Constitution.

AMENDING PROCESS, PROPOSALS FOR CHANGING

Article V of the U.S. Constitution delineates an amending process. It requires two-thirds majorities of both houses of Congress or a special convention called by two-thirds of the states to propose amendments, and three-fourths of the state legislatures, or special state conventions, to ratify an amendment. Members of Congress have introduced about 150 proposals, many redundant, to alter this procedure.

Proposals for Popular Initiative or Referendum

A common proposal appears to have first surfaced around the time of the outbreak of the Civil War as a means of averting conflict by incorporating various slavery compromises into the Constitution. It would provide for some kind of popular initiative or referendum on amendments. Such proposals, which embody a form of direct democracy, were especially common during the Progressive Era, which spanned the first two decades of the 20th century, at which time there was a great deal of scholarly criticism of the amending process for being too "rigid" (Vile 1992, 135–156). Common variants (for example, S.J. Res. 22, 1919) provided that amendments would be initiated by 500,000 or more voters and ratified by a majority of voters in either a majority of the states or in three-fourths thereof. Similarly, Wisconsin's Republican senator Robert La Follette proposed in 1912 and 1913 that amendments become effective after being proposed by 10 states or a majority of Congress and being ratified by a majority vote of citizens in a majority of the states (Musmanno 1929, 194). In 1923, Senator James W. Wadsworth of New York and Representative Finis J. Garrett of Tennessee proposed a "back to the people" amendment that would allow states to require a popular vote to affirm or overturn a state legislature's ratification of an amendment (Vose 1972, 246). Three years earlier, in *Hawke v. Smith* (*I* and *II*), the Court had invalidated such a provision in the Ohio state constitution.

Akhil Reed Amar, a contemporary Yale law professor, has argued that the mechanisms in Article V are not exclusive and that citizens already have the right to propose or ratify amendments by popular majorities (Amar 1988). Similarly, Bruce Ackerman has proposed an alteration to Article V, whereby a president could propose an amendment in his second term that could be ratified by a three-fifths vote in the next two elections (Ackerman 1991, 54–55). There have been a number of recent plans, most notably one by the National Initiative for Democracy in 2002, which have called for amending the constitution through referendums.

Proposed Changes in
Ratification Procedures

Three sets of changes have been proposed that would alter current ratification procedures. One would limit the power of lame duck legislatures by requiring that one or both houses of a state legislature ratifying an amendment must have been elected after the amendment was proposed. The House of Representatives actually added such a requirement to the Twentieth Amendment, which shortened the lame duck terms for the president and members of Congress, but it was dropped in conference committee (Grimes 1978, 108). In a related vein, some proposals (for example, H.J. Res. 242, 1919) specify that a certain majority must be present when such state ratification votes are taken.

A second set of proposals has attempted to set a time limit, usually five to eight years, during which states must ratify amendments. Currently, the Constitution sets no such limits, and although the Supreme Court decided in *Dillon v. Gloss* (1921) that amendments should be ratified relatively contemporaneously, in *Coleman v. Miller* (1939) the Court suggested that such decisions might be "political questions." In 1992, the archivist of the Library of Congress and a vote in Congress certified the validity of the Twenty-Seventh Amendment, even though it was not ratified until more than 200 years after being proposed.

A third set of proposals would tackle another unresolved issue by explicitly providing for state rescission of amendments prior to ratification by the necessary three-fourths majority (Musmanno 1929, 206).

Proposals Offered by the
Council of State Governments

A meeting of the Council of State Governments in December 1962 resulted in a number of state petitions to Congress for amendments to liberal-ize the amending process. The council was clearly shaken by the Supreme Court decision in *Baker v. Carr* (1962) and its implications for judicial review of state legislative apportionment. The Council proposed eliminating the convention mechanism (and the myriad of questions surrounding it) and allowing three-fourths of the states to ratify identical texts of amendments proposed by two-thirds of the states. A similar amendment was proposed again in 1990 (Tolchin 1990, A12); more recently, some state advocates have proposed allowing three-fourths of the states to propose an amendment that would become valid in two years unless two-thirds majorities of both houses rejected it ("Conference of the States" 1995); Representative Thomas J. Bliley (R-VA) proposed allowing two-thirds of the states to petition for an amendment, which, unless disapproved by two-thirds majorities in Congress, would then be resubmitted to the states for three-fourths approval (Thierer 1999). In two additional proposals offered by the Council of State Governments and severely criticized at the time by scholars (for example, Swindler 1963 and C. Black 1963), the council proposed amendments allowing states to apportion themselves without judicial oversight and setting up a Court of the Union with the power to overturn Supreme Court decisions (Vile 1991c, 98–99).

Although the proposals by the Council of State Governments prompted scholarly attention, a number of similar proposals had been introduced in Congress during the previous decade. They would have enabled states to ratify amendments that had been proposed by two-thirds majorities in both houses of the legislatures of 12 states and transmitted to the U.S. secretary of state and the secretary of state within each state.

Other Proposals

One of the earliest proposed changes affecting the amending process was introduced in 1826 and would have limited the introduction of such proposals to every 10 years (H.J. Res. 232, 325); by way of comparison, a proposal introduced by New York's Progressive (and later Republican) representative Walter Chandler in 1916 (H.J.

Res. 315) would have provided for constitutional conventions to meet every 30 years to propose amendments. This embodied an idea advocated by Thomas Jefferson, who thought that a new constitution should be considered each generation. Other proposals have called for making ratification by state conventions (an alternative ratification method specified in Article V and used to ratify the Twenty-First Amendment) the exclusive method of state ratification. Still other members of Congress have proposed making the amending process easier by reducing the required two-thirds majorities in Congress to one-half or three-fifths, by permitting less than two-thirds of the states to call a convention to propose amendments, or by reducing the necessary ratification majority of the states from three-fourths to two-thirds (Musmanno 1929, 192–193). By contrast, an amendment offered by Rhode Island when it ratified the Constitution in 1790 would have required the consent of 11 or more of the original 13 states for any amendments proposed after 1793 (Ames 1896, 292). Consistent with concerns about the antidemocratic impact of judicial review that were expressed in the Progressive Era, Democrat James Doolittle of Kansas introduced a proposal in February 1914 that would have automatically submitted amendments dealing with U.S. laws invalidated by judicial review to states for their acceptance (H.J. Res. 221).

See also Ackerman, Bruce; Amar, Akhil Reed; Corwin Amendment; *Coleman v. Miller;* Council of State Governments; Crittenden Compromise; *Dillon v. Gloss;* Initiative and Referendum; National Initiative for Democracy; Ratification of Amendments; Rescission of Ratification of Pending Amendments.

For Further Reading:

Ackerman, Bruce. 1991. *We the People: Foundations.* Cambridge, MA: Belknap.

Amar, Akhil R. 1988. "Philadelphia Revisited: Amending the Constitution outside Article V." *University of Chicago Law Review* 55 (Fall): 1043–1104.

Ames, Herman. 1896. *The Proposed Amendments to the Constitution of the United States during the First Century of Its History.* New York: Burt Franklin. 1970 reprint.

Black, Charles L., Jr. 1963. "The Proposed Amendment of Article V: A Threatened Disaster." *Yale Law Journal* 72 (April): 957–966.

"Conference of the States: An Action Plan to Restore Balance in the Federal System." 1995. Concept paper adopted by the Council of State Governments, the National Governors' Association, and the National Conference of State Legislatures. 1 February.

Grimes, Alan P. 1978. *Democracy and the Amendments to the Constitution.* Lexington, MA: Lexington Books.

Levinson, Sanford. 1996b. "The Political Implications of Amending Clauses." *Constitutional Commentary* 13 (Spring): 107–123.

Musmanno, M. A. 1929. *Proposed Amendments to the Constitution.* Washington DC: U.S. Government Printing Office.

Swindler, William. 1963. "The Current Challenge to Federalism: The Confederating Proposals." *Georgetown Law Review* 52 (Fall): 1–41.

Thierer, Adam D. March 2, 1999. "The Bliley 'States' Initiative': Empowering States and Protecting Federalism." No. 576. The Heritage Foundation Executive Memorandum.

Tolchin, Mark. 1990. "Fifteen States Rally behind Calls for Amendment to Gain More Powers." *New York Times,* 26 June, A12, col. 3–6.

Vile, John R. 1992. *The Constitutional Amending Process in American Political Thought.* New York: Praeger.

———. 1991c. *Rewriting the United States Constitution: An Examination of Proposals from Reconstruction to the Present.* New York: Praeger.

Vose, Clement E. 1972. *Constitutional Change: Amendment Politics and Supreme Court Litigation since 1900.* Lexington, MA: D. C. Heath.

AMENDMENT, DEFINITION

The *American Heritage Dictionary of English Language,* 4th edition (New York: Houghton Mifflin 2006) defines "amendment" as "1. The act of changing for the better; improvement. 2. A correction or alteration, as in a manuscript. 3. a. The process of formally altering or adding to a document or record. b. A statement of such an alteration or addition." Sanford Levinson has described "amendment" as "an extraordinarily rich word" (1990a, 25). This richness derives in part from the tension between the first two definitions cited above. An amendment may refer to an improvement suggested by progress in human understanding or the accumulation of greater experience and wisdom. The better understandings of the evils of slavery reflected in the post–Civil War Amendments or in the capacities of women as reflected in the Nineteenth Amendment could serve as examples. The idea of amendment can also refer to a correction of errors that have arisen either because of flaws in the original language or structure or from changes brought about through the course of time. The adoption of the Twelfth Amendment correcting flaws in the original Electoral College mechanism would be a good example. In the Bible, the term "amend" is sometimes used to exhort individuals or nations to correct moral faults, as when the prophet Jeremiah tells his countrymen to "amend your ways" (KJV, Jer. 7:3, 5). This usage may be related to the idea of "mending" torn clothes.

Scholars have made periodic attempts to distinguish "constitutional amendment" from "constitutional interpretation" or "revision" and to delineate what kinds of changes require amendments and which can be effected through other means. Historical practice appears to demonstrate that such lines, if they exist at all, are relatively fluid (Vile 1994a, 73–76). The only specific remaining qualification to the existing amending procedures that are delineated within the U.S. Constitution provides that states shall not be deprived of their equal suffrage in the U.S. Senate without their consent. Some advocates of additional substantive limits on amendments base their arguments in part on the idea that the term "amendment" implicitly mandates the adoption of changes consistent with the principles and character of the document being amended.

The Constitutional Convention was originally called essentially to amend the Articles of Confederation and ended up replacing them instead. This example always opens the possibility that another constitutional convention, perhaps one even bypassing the specific mechanisms now outlined in Article V, could use convention or popular ratification of its proposals to bypass existing ratification mechanisms.

The fear may well be relatively groundless (see Weber and Perry 1989), but concern that a second convention might become a "runaway" body that could "throw out the baby with the bathwater" appears to be a key reason that this mechanism has yet to be utilized.

See also Constitutional Amendments, Limits on; Entrenchment Clauses; Progress and the Amending Process.

For Further Reading:

Levinson, Sanford. 1990a. "On the Notion of Amendment: Reflections on David Daube's 'Jehovah the Good.'" *S'vara: A Journal of Philosophy and Judaism* 1 (Winter): 25–31.

Vile, John R. 1994a. *Constitutional Change in the United States: A Comparative Study of the Role of Constitutional Amendments, Judicial Interpretations, and Legislative and Executive Actions.* Westport, CT: Praeger.

Weber, Paul J., and Barbara A. Perry. 1989. *Unfounded Fears: Myths and Realities of a Constitutional Convention.* New York: Praeger.

AMES, HERMAN (1865–1935)

Ames was a historian at the University of Pennsylvania who compiled the first comprehensive list and analysis of proposed amendments to the Constitution. Altogether, Ames compiled 1,736 proposals—many with multiple parts—that had been offered in the first 100 years under the Constitution. The central part of Ames's book, which was honored in 1897 by the American Historical Association, was a narrative analysis of proposed amendments according to subject. An appendix listed the date, subject, and other relevant information about proposed amendments (Ames 1896, 306–422).

In discussing the history of U.S. constitutional amendments, Ames divided the amendments proposed in the first 100 years into four periods: 1789–1803, 1804–1860, 1860–1870, and 1870–1889. He associated the first period with "the perfection of details," the second with "general alterations," the third with "slavery and reconstruction," and the fourth with "general emendations" (Ames 1896, 19). Significantly, Ames's volume was published during the second longest period in U.S. history, from 1871 through 1912 (the first was from 1804 to 1865), during which no amendments were successfully proposed and ratified. Acknowledging that many proposals had failed because they "were suggested as cures for temporary evils, . . . were trivial or impracticable, [or] . . . found a place in that unwritten constitution which has grown up side by side with the written document," Ames identified "insurmountable constitutional obstacles" as the central barriers to amendments (Ames 1896, 301). Although suggesting—like other critics from the Progressive Era (Vile 1992, 140–141)—that "the majorities required are too large," Ames did not specify what majorities he would regard as ideal (Ames 1896, 304).

Ames's work has been reprinted, along with all nonoverlapping subsequent collections of amending topics proposed in Congress (Vile 2003).

For Further Reading:

Ames, Herman. 1896. *The Proposed Amendments to the Constitution of the United States during the First Century of Its History.* New York: Burt Franklin. 1970 reprint.

Vile, John R., ed. 2002. *Proposed Amendments to the U.S. Constitution, 1787–2001.* 3 Vols. Union, NJ: The Law Book Exchange.

ANNAPOLIS CONVENTION

In 2000 Richard Labunski, a journalism professor at the University of Kentucky, advocated creating a preconvention as a way of inducing states to call an Article V convention. Although the circumstances were much different, the convention that proposed the U.S. Constitution was itself preceded by a preconvention, albeit a fairly truncated one. In 1785, representatives of Virginia and Maryland met at George Washington's home at Mt. Vernon, Virginia, to discuss conflicts they were having with navigation on the Potomac River at a time when Congress had no power over such interstate commerce. James

Madison and others used this meeting as a chance to call a broader meeting of the states on the topic of navigation.

When this new meeting convened in Annapolis, Maryland, on September 11, 1786, there was outward cause for pessimism. Only New York, New Jersey, Pennsylvania, Delaware, and Virginia had sent delegates, and they had no authority to act on behalf of all 13 states. Nonetheless, the 12 delegates, who included New York's Alexander Hamilton and Virginia's Edmund Randolph and James Madison, unanimously chose Delaware's John Dickinson as chair and proceeded to deliberate. They unanimously reported their findings to Congress in a report dated September 14, 1786, apparently in the deft hand of Alexander Hamilton (Solberg 1958, 54).

The genius of Hamilton's prose lay in his effort to use the Annapolis Convention as a springboard for a still broader discussion of problems under the Articles of Confederation. He did so by drawing from the commission of the three delegates from New Jersey, whose legislature had authorized them "to consider how far a uniform system in their commercial regulations and *other important matters,* might be necessary to the common interest and permanent harmony of the several States" (Solberg 1958, 56). Hamilton used this commission to suggest that other states, too, might recognize that "regulating trade is of such comprehensive extent, and will enter so far into the general System of the federal government, that to give it efficacy, and to obviate questions and doubts concerning its precise nature and limits, may require a correspondent adjustment of other parts of the Foederal System" (Solberg 1958, 57–58).

Accordingly, the delegates to Annapolis proposed a meeting of commissioners

to meet at Philadelphia on the second Monday in May next, to take into consideration the situation of the United States, to devise such further provisions as shall appear to them necessary to render the constitution of the Foederal Government adequate to the exigencies of the Union; and to report such an Act for that purpose to the United States in Congress assembled, as when agreed to, by them, and afterwards confirmed by the Legislatures of every State, will effectually provide for the same. (Solberg 1958, 58–59)

Fortunately for this resolution, the winter of 1786–1787 witnessed, among other disturbances, Shay's Rebellion in Massachusetts. The apparent inability of the government under the Articles of Confederation to meet this contingency, as well as the cogency of Hamilton's argument for considering questions of trade within a larger context, persuaded additional states to appoint delegates to the Constitutional Convention. Eventually, delegates from all the states except Rhode Island met in Philadelphia to propose what became the Constitution of the United States. Although passed on to the states for approval by Congress, Article VII of the new Constitution bypassed existing state legislatures by providing that the new Constitution would instead be approved by special conventions called within each state.

See also Constitutional Convention of 1787; Hamilton, Alexander; Labunski, Richard; Madison, James.

For Further Reading:

Calvert, Jane E. 2009. *Quaker Constitutionalism and the Political Thought of John Dickinson.* New York: Cambridge University Press.

Labunski, Richard. 2000. *The Second Constitutional Convention: How the American People Can Take Back Their Government.* Versailles, KY: Marley and Beck Press.

Meyerson, Michael I. 2008. *Liberty's Blueprint: How Madison and Hamilton Wrote the Federalist Papers, Defined the Constitution, and Made Democracy Safe for the World.* New York: Basic Books.

Solberg, Winton, ed. 1958. *The Federal Convention and the Formation of the Union.* Indianapolis: The Bobbs-Merrill Company, Inc.

ANTHONY, SUSAN BROWNELL (1820–1906)

Susan B. Anthony was a schoolteacher who was initially interested in the temperance and anti-slavery movements. She subsequently devoted her efforts to women's suffrage and has been called "the greatest individual in the American suffrage movement" (Kraditor 1981, 12).

Although she was a friend of Frederick Douglass, like her close friend Elizabeth Cady Stanton, Anthony opposed ratification of the Fourteenth and Fifteenth Amendments, which Douglass supported, when the proposed amendments failed to extend to women the rights accorded to African American men; indeed, Anthony declared that she "would sooner cut off my right hand than ask for the ballot for the black man and not for woman" (quoted in McFeely 1991, 266). Anthony and Stanton subsequently established women's suffrage as an "independent feminist movement" (Dubois 1978, 202) and founded the National Woman Suffrage Association in 1869. The same year, women who had supported the Fourteenth and Fifteenth Amendments founded the rival American Woman Suffrage Association. From 1868 to 1870, Anthony edited *The Revolution,* and in 1872 she was tried and convicted in New York State for voting (*United States v. Anthony*). The amendment that eventually became the Nineteenth Amendment was first introduced in Congress in 1878 (Kraditor 1981, 206) and is often called the Susan B. Anthony Amendment. However, it was not proposed by the necessary majorities in Congress until 1919, and the states ratified it in 1920. In the interim, the two leading suffrage organizations had merged into the National American Woman Suffrage Association (NAWSA), with Stanton serving as its first president from 1890 to 1892 and Anthony serving from 1892 to 1900, after which time Carrie Catt became president.

See also Fifteenth Amendment; Fourteenth Amendment; Nineteenth Amendment; Stanton, Elizabeth Cady.

For Further Reading:

Dubois, Ellen C. 1978. *Feminism and Suffrage: The Emergence of an Independent Women's Movement in America, 1848–1869.* Ithaca, NY: Cornell University Press.

Hammond, Rayne L. 2000. "Trial and Tribulation: The Story of *United States v. Anthony.*" *Buffalo Law Review* 48 (2000): 981–1045.

Kraditor, Aileen S. 1981. *The Idea of the Woman's Suffrage Movement, 1890–1920.* New York: W. W. Norton.

McFeely, William S. 1991. *Frederick Douglass.* New York: W. W. Norton.

ANTIEAU, CHESTER (1913–)

In 1995 Chester Antieau, a professor emeritus of constitutional law at Georgetown University, published a book designed to offer changes in the Constitution as the nation approached the year 2000. The book is divided into three parts. The first identifies rights the Supreme Court already implicitly recognizes that should be recognized explicitly. The second discusses existing constitutional provisions that need amendment. The third highlights additional rights that should be included in the Constitution. In defending his proposals, Antieau makes constant reference to earlier legal theorists and philosophers; to previous historical documents and events; to treaties, international human rights declarations, and conventions; and to provisions in the constitutions of a variety of foreign nations and the 50 states.

The four rights that courts implicitly recognize which Antieau believes should be added to the Constitution are freedom of association, freedom of enterprise, freedom of movement, and the right of privacy. Antieau does not address the difficulties to which judicial enforcement of economic rights led during the New Deal. He does note, however, that the right of privacy could be in conflict with the right to life, but he does not indicate how he would resolve this issue.

Antieau proposes a number of changes to existing constitutional provisions. He wants to expand the guarantees in the Eighth Amendment specifically to protect "the inherent dignity of the human person," to outlaw torture, and to stipulate a right to bail (Antieau 1995, 37). He advocates changing the grounds for impeachment to "serious misconduct to the harm of the nation" (Antieau 1995, 56) and proposes establishing special nonlegislative tribunals to try such impeachments. Antieau wants to modify the Seventh Amendment to eliminate jury trials in civil cases. He further advocates allowing the president to exercise a line item veto, eliminating the pocket veto, and allowing Congress to override presidential vetoes by less than a two-thirds majority. Antieau supports allowing the Supreme Court to issue advisory opinions and wants to withdraw federal diversity jurisdiction from the federal courts. He favors state-appointed counsel for indigents in civil as well as criminal cases, giving particular attention to cases of child custody. Antieau would allow naturalized citizens to be eligible for the presidency and favors the introduction of constitutional amendments by popular initiative. He also wants the First Amendment to recognize the right of both the public and the press to have access to information.

Many of the rights that Antieau would add to the Constitution are social and economic rights like those contained in other 20th-century constitutions, including the right to an education; the right to a healthy environment; and the right to adequate social services, such as housing, health care, employment, food, clothing, and social security. He emphasizes the importance of a number of interrelated rights of movement, including the rights of asylum, departure, emigration, voluntary expatriation, and entry and return and the freedom from exile and deportation. Miscellaneous proposals would establish the people's right to recall members of Congress, the right to conscientious objection to military service, and the right not to be executed.

Although Antieau presents an interesting array of proposals, his overall scheme is fairly piecemeal. He does not discuss in any depth the degree to which the listing of social and economic rights would provide cures for such ills. He also does not discuss at any length the impact that new constitutional guarantees might have on the power of the judiciary and on the current scheme of separation of powers.

See also Social and Economic Rights.

For Further Reading:

Antieau, Chester J. 1995. *A U.S. Constitution for the Year 2000.* Chicago: Loyola University Press.

ANTI-FEDERALISTS

Even before the Constitution was written, there were individuals such as Virginia's Patrick Henry and Richard Henry Lee who feared the creation of a new national government. They were concerned that it would result in undue consolidation of the states, accent aristocratic tendencies, and jeopardize individual liberties. After the Constitution was proposed for ratification by the states, these forces opposed to a new government became known as Anti-Federalists. They led a vigorous opposition both in public debates and in the state ratifying conventions for the new Constitution, noting that it was not being adopted according to the forms specified under the Articles of Confederation. The Anti-Federalists were hindered in their debate by the superior organization of the Federalists, who were pushing for the Constitution; by the support of George Washington and Benjamin Franklin for the new Constitution; and by the general consensus that the existing Articles were inadequate.

The two most important outcomes of the debate between the Federalists and Anti-Federalists were arguably the writing of a series of 85 essays in defense of the new Constitution, known as *The Federalist Papers,* and the adoption of the first 10 amendments to the Constitution, known as the Bill of Rights. Although the Constitutional Convention had barely touched on this issue, the lack of a bill of rights quickly became an important Anti-Federalist rallying point. Federalists initially responded, in *The Federalist Papers* and elsewhere, by arguing in somewhat contradictory fashion that the Constitution already protected important rights (prohibitions against bills of attainder and ex post facto laws, for example) and that additional rights were unnecessary or inappropriate. Anti-Federalists indicated that they would press the states either to propose a second convention or to ratify the new Constitution conditionally. Key Federalists, among them James Madison, indicated that they would support a bill of rights once the new Constitution was adopted. This promise—kept by James Madison, who, as a member of the U.S. House of Representatives, proposed and shepherded the Bill of Rights during the First Congress—undoubtedly aided, and may have been essential to, ratification of the document. Initially applying only to the national government and not to the states, the Bill of Rights had little direct impact on governmental operations until the judicial incorporation of the Bill of Rights into the due process clause of the Fourteenth Amendment, which largely occurred in the 20th century.

At the state ratifying convention, a number of Anti-Federalists argued that the amending process in Article V of the U.S. Constitution was too difficult (Vile 1992, 32–33). The weakness of this argument was that the new process requiring proposal by two-thirds of both houses of Congress (or by a convention called by two-thirds of the states) and ratification by three-fourths of the states was considerably easier than the process under the Articles of Confederation. This process had required unanimous state consent to amendments proposed in Congress.

See also Bill of Rights; Federalists; Fourteenth Amendment; Incorporation; Madison, James; Mason, George.

For Further Reading:

Gillespie, Michael L., and Michael Lienesch, eds. 1989. *Ratifying the Constitution.* Lawrence: University Press of Kansas.

Hamilton, Alexander, James Madison, and John Jay. 1787–1788. *The Federalist Papers.* Reprint, New York: New American Library, 1961.

Kenyon, Cecelia, ed. 1985. *The Antifederalists.* Boston: Northeastern University Press.

Lash, Kurt T. 1994. "Rejecting Conventional Wisdom: Federalist Ambivalence in the Framing and Implementation of Article V." *American Journal of Legal History* 38 (April): 197–231.

Main, Jackson T. 1961. *The Antifederalists: Critics of the Constitution, 1781–1788.* Chicago: Quadrangle Books.

Storing, Herbert, ed. 1981. *The Complete AntiFederalist.* 7 vols. Chicago: University of Chicago Press.

Vile, John R. 1992. *The Constitutional Amending Process in American Political Thought.* New York: Praeger.

ANTIMISCEGENATION LAWS

See Intermarriage.

ANTIPOLYGAMY LAWS

See Marriage, Divorce, and Parenting.

ANTI-SALOON LEAGUE

Founded in the 1890s, the Anti-Saloon League was one of the organizations that led the push for adoption of the Eighteenth Amendment and national alcoholic prohibition. The league existed in tension with the Prohibition Party, which had been established in 1869 and, in many ways, had been modeled on the antislavery campaign that had resulted in the Civil War and the eventual adoption of the Thirteenth Amendment. Whereas the Prohibition Party ran its own candidates, the Anti-Saloon League adopted a "balance-of-power policy" (Blocker 1976, 162) that enabled it to ally itself with whatever party was willing to adopt its stance as part of its platform. The Prohibition Party was, for a time at least, tempted by an alliance with the Populist Party and its broad agenda of social reform. By contrast, the Anti-Saloon League "posited the existence of a unified constituency closely associated with the churches, the major political parties, and the free enterprise system" (Blocker 1976, 207). The saloon was often viewed as a center of foreign—and Catholic—influence and machine politics (Grimes 1978, 84). By focusing on this institution, the league was especially successful in appealing to middle- and upper-class white Protestant progressives.

The failure of Prohibition and the adoption of the Twenty-First Amendment led to problems for the league. By 1948, it had split into the National Temperance League and the Temperance Education Foundation (Blocker 1976, 235). The Prohibition Party continues to field candidates but is a minor force in current American politics.

See also Eighteenth Amendment; Twenty-First Amendment.

For Further Reading:

Blocker, Jack S., Jr. 1976. *Retreat from Reform: The Prohibition Movement in the United States, 1890–1916.* Westport, CT: Greenwood Press.

Grimes, Alan P. 1978. *Democracy and the Amendments to the Constitution.* Lexington, MA: Lexington Books.

Kerr, K. Austin. 1985. *Organized for Prohibition: A New History of the Anti-Saloon League.* New Haven, CT: Yale University Press.

APPROPRIATENESS OF AMENDMENTS

See Citizens for the Constitution, the Constitutional Amendment Initiative.

ARCHIVIST OF THE UNITED STATES

The Archivist of the United States, who heads the National Archives and Records Administration (NARA), is currently responsible for certifying constitutional amendments. The secretary of state performed this function by custom through 1818 and by statute until 1951. Congress then transferred the duty to the administrator of general services, who published the *Federal Register.* Congress transferred both functions to the archivist in 1984. The provision of the code specifying the archivist's authority is relatively brief. It provides that:

Whenever official notice is received at the National Archives and Records Administration that any amendment proposed to the Constitution of the United States has been adopted, according to the provisions of the Constitution, the Archivist of the United States shall forthwith cause the amendment to be published, with his certificate, specifying the

States by which the same may have been adopted, and that the same has become valid, to all intents and purposes, as a part of the Constitution of the United States (1 U.S.C. § 106(b) (1984)).

Under this provision, the archivist submits amendments that Congress has proposed to state governors, who then submit them to the state legislatures. Sometimes states ratify amendments, however, even before they receive official notice. Whenever they act, they send their proposals to the archivist, who in turn gives them to the Office of the Federal Register (OFR) to check for "facial legal sufficiency and an authenticating signature" ("Constitutional Amendment Process," archives Web site). If the necessary three-fourths of the states respond, the archivist then certifies the validity of the amendment, and it is published in the *Federal Register* and in U.S. Statutes at Large ("Constitutional Amendment Process," archives Web site).

On May 18, 1992, after 40 states had ratified it, archivist Don Wilson certified ratification of the Twenty-Seventh Amendment and had it published the next day in the *Federal Register.* This was controversial because of the long time that had elapsed between the amendment's proposal in 1789 (as the second of 12 amendments submitted to the states) and its putative ratification in 1992. Senators Robert Byrd and Charles Grassley criticized Wilson for not submitting the issue to Congress, as the secretary of state had done with the controversial Fourteenth Amendment. It is not clear, however, that an amendment must be certified or published before it becomes part of the Constitution. Moreover, although Congress subsequently voted to confirm Wilson's judgment (Bernstein with Agel 1993, 246–247), this too was probably legally unnecessary (Dellinger 1983, 402).

Brendon Ishikawa has questioned whether it is appropriate for members of the executive branch, like either the secretary of state or the archivist, to certify amendments. Pointing to the Supreme Court's declaration in *Hollingsworth v. Virginia* (1798) that a president's signature was not necessary to the validity of constitutional amendments, Ishikawa notes that "the very nature of the powers of the executive branch is to faithfully execute the laws, rather than to pass

judgment upon the validity of the constitutional amendment" (1997, 591). Acknowledging that his solution would not be without problems of its own, most notably the precedent in *Coleman v. Miller* (1939) essentially renouncing such review, Ishikawa believes that courts could more fairly and effectively determine matters involving procedural questions surrounding the ratification of amendments (1997, 592–593).

See also *Coleman v. Miller;* Fourteenth Amendment*; Hollingsworth v. Virginia;* Office of the Federal Register; Ratification of Amendments; Secretary of State; Twenty-Seventh Amendment.

For Further Reading:

Bernstein, Richard B., with Jerome Agel. 1993. *Amending America: If We Love the Constitution So Much, Why Do We Keep Trying To Change It?* New York: Random House.

"Constitutional Amendment Process," http://www.archives.gov/federal_register/constitution/amendment_process.html.

Dellinger, Walter. 1983. "The Legitimacy of Constitutional Change: Rethinking the Amending Process." *Harvard Law Review* 97 (December): 380–432.

Ishikawa, Brendon T. 1997. "Everything You Always Wanted to Know about How Amendments Are Made, but Were Afraid to Ask." *Hastings Constitutional Law Quarterly* 24 (Winter): 545–597.

ARTICLE V OF THE U.S. CONSTITUTION

This article delineates the constitutional amending process. Consistent with the view that constitutional law is designed to be paramount to ordinary law, the process in Article V is considerably more difficult than the process for adopting legislation that is spelled out in Article I, Section 7. Article V provides two ways for amendments to be proposed and two ways for them to be ratified. To date, all amendments have been proposed by a two-thirds vote of both houses of Congress, but two-thirds of the states may also petition Congress to call a convention to propose such amendments. Moreover, calls that fall short of a mandate may still exert pressure on Congress to act—as they did, for example, in pressuring Congress to propose the Seventeenth Amendment, which provided for direct election of senators. Legislatures in three-fourths of the states have ratified all but one of the existing 27 amendments, but Congress may stipulate that ratification be effected by special conventions called in each of the states. This latter procedure was specified by the delegates to the Constitutional Convention of 1787, with respect to the Constitution itself, and by Congress in the case of the Twenty-First Amendment, which repealed national alcoholic prohibition.

Limits

Article V delineates two substantive limits on the amending process. One, dealing with slave importation, is no longer relevant. The second prohibits states from being denied their equal vote in the U.S. Senate without their consent. Although a number of Supreme Court decisions have rejected the notion that there are additional limits on the amending process, some contemporary scholars (W. Murphy 1980, for example) believe that the issue is still viable. The argument was raised by those who questioned the legitimacy of amendments proposed in the wake of *Texas v. Johnson* (1989) and *United States v. Eichman* (1990) to prohibit flag desecration.

Origins

Article V is important because it offers a peaceful alternative to the kind of revolution that the colonists were forced to proclaim in the Declaration of Independence. Although philosophers had been discussing the need for constitutional change for centuries, formal amending mechanisms were necessitated by the development of written constitutions and thus originated in colonial charters first granted by William Penn. Such mechanisms also appeared in most of the state constitutions written during the American Revolutionary War period. Early state constitutions provided for amendment by legislative action, by state conventions, or through a council of censors (Vile 1992, 25). The Articles of

Confederation provided for amendments to be approved by Congress and ratified by unanimous consent of the state legislatures. The unanimity requirement made this provision ineffective and served to caution the framers of the U.S. Constitution about devising an amending process that was too difficult.

The Constitutional Convention

Delegates to the Constitutional Convention of 1787 generally agreed that a formal amending process was needed. The Virginia Plan proposed that congressional consent to such amendments should not be required, and the first formal proposal that emerged at the convention specified that Congress should call a convention to propose amendments at the request of two-thirds of the states (Farrand 1966, 2:159). George Mason expressed concern that this mechanism might be used to subvert the states, Alexander Hamilton thought that Congress should be able to propose amendments on its own, and James Madison argued that the convention mechanism was too vague. Therefore, a new proposal was offered: two-thirds majorities in Congress would propose amendments when Congress so chose or when it was petitioned by two-thirds of the state legislatures. The clause entrenching the slave importation agreement was added at this time (Farrand 1966, 2:559). Two days before the Constitution was signed, the proposed amending provision was altered so that Congress could propose amendments or states could petition Congress to call a convention to propose amendments. The convention mechanism was designed to circumvent Congress. If Congress refused to propose amendments, then a convention could do so. The convention adopted this alteration after George Mason expressed fears that amendments would be impossible if Congress proved to be unresponsive (Farrand 1966, 2:559–560). The clause protecting state representation in the Senate was also added then.

Principles of Article V

Article V embodies a number of distinct concerns and principles. Consistent with the desire that the Constitution be paramount to ordinary legislation, the process is intended to be difficult, but not impossible (Ginsburg 1989–1990; Vile 1993a, 101–105). There is no constitutional provision, such as that which Thomas Jefferson advocated, for automatic constitutional revision or review at periodic intervals. Consistent with federalism, the article allows states to initiate, and requires that they ratify, amendments. Consistent with the desire for deliberation, the process involves at least two stages and requires supermajorities for each one. Consistent with suspicions of entrenched power and an emphasis on popular sovereignty, Article V offers a pathway around a recalcitrant Congress.

The History of Article V
Although scholars have praised the amending process throughout most of U.S. history (with scholars writing around the Civil War and the Progressive Era sometimes being exceptions), the process has arguably proved more difficult in practice than was anticipated (Berry 1987). This difficulty is particularly evident when the federal process is compared with counterparts at the state level or with processes in most foreign countries (Lutz 1994) or when the history of the amending process is examined (Grimes 1978; Bernstein with Agel 1993). The primary obstacle has been the difficulty of proposing amendments by the requisite majority of both houses of Congress, especially the Senate. Although more than 11,000 such proposals have been introduced in Congress—many redundant and centering around a few major issues—only 33 have been reported to the states for ratification by the necessary majorities. Of these proposals, 27 have been ratified.

Many of these amendments fall into distinct clusters. The first 10 amendments, the Bill of Rights, were ratified in 1791 and were the result of Anti-Federalist criticisms of the new Constitution. The Thirteenth, Fourteenth, and Fifteenth Amendments were ratified from 1865 to 1870 after the Civil War. Four amendments were ratified from 1913 to 1920, at the end of the Progressive Era. Many amendments have helped make the U.S. system of government considerably more democratic than it was when it was established. Expansions of the franchise—for example, in the Fifteenth (African Americans), Nineteenth (women), and Twenty-Sixth Amendments (18- to 21-year-olds)—have been especially important. Proposals for new or substantially altered constitutions have rarely stirred more than passing interest (see Boyd 1992; Vile 1991c).

Alternative Means of Change
The difficulty of the amending process has encouraged other means of change (Lutz 1994). Judicial interpretations of the Constitution have contributed to its flexibility, but congressional practices and presidential initiatives have also proved important (Vile 1994a). An unwritten constitution has grown up around and supplemented the words of the written document. Although written constitutional provisions have the capacity to trump conflicting customs and usages, changes can often be effected to fill in constitutional gaps and silences. On at least four occasions (the Eleventh, the Thirteenth and Fourteenth, the Sixteenth, and the Twenty-Sixth Amendments), amendments have overturned Supreme Court decisions. The Supreme Court, in turn, interprets such amendments. At times, it may construe such provisions more restrictively or more expansively than their authors intended.

Unresolved Issues
In early American history, the Supreme Court resolved some important issues. In *Hollingsworth v. Virginia* (1798), for example, it decided that the president did not need to sign constitutional amendments. In *Dillon v. Gloss* (1921), it ruled that ratification of amendments should reflect a contemporary consensus. In *Coleman v. Miller* (1939), however, the Court decided that such issues were political questions for the elected branches of government to solve. Many such issues remain unresolved. A number of them center on the still unused convention mechanism (Caplan 1988). Other such questions involve whether states have the power to rescind ratification of amendments prior to the time a three-fourths majority is mustered, whether states should be permitted to ratify amendments they have previously rejected, and how long states have to ratify amendments. This last issue was prominent in the case of the Twenty-Seventh

Amendment, which was putatively ratified more than 200 years after it was originally proposed by Congress. Additional issues involve what conditions Congress can place on proposed amendments and whether Congress can extend a previously specified ratification date, as it did in the case of the failed Equal Rights Amendment (Vile 1992, 45–54).

A number of procedural changes in the constitutional amending process have been proposed to clarify these questions or to make the amending process easier. Akhil Reed Amar (1988) suggests that Article V mechanisms may not be the exclusive means by which formal constitutional changes can be effected. He believes that such changes might also be effected by popular initiative or ratified by referendum. Professor Bruce Ackerman (1991), who believes that major changes have been instituted without following the letter of the Article V process, favors adopting an amendment to allow for ratification of amendment by referendum. Professor William J. Quirk, who believes members of Congress have conspired to hold power while granting excessive powers both to the president and the courts, favors changing the Constitution so that three-fourths of the states can bypass Congress in proposing and ratifying amendments (2008, 202–293).

See also Ackerman, Bruce; Amar, Akhil Reed; *Coleman v. Miller; Dillon v. Gloss;* Entrenchment Clauses; *Hollingsworth v. Virginia;* Ratification of Amendments.

For Further Reading:

Ackerman, Bruce. 1991. *We the People: Foundations.* Cambridge, MA: Belknap.

Amar, Akhil R. 1988. "Philadelphia Revisited: Amending the Constitution outside Article V." *University of Chicago Law Review* 55 (Fall): 1043–1104.

Bernstein, Richard B., with Jerome Agel. 1993. *Amending America: If We Love the Constitution So Much, Why Do We Keep Trying to Change It?* New York: Random House.

Berry, Mary F. 1987. "How Hard It Is to Change." *New York Times Magazine,* 13 September, 93–98.

Boyd, Steven R., ed. 1992. *Alternative Constitutions for the United States: A Documentary History.* Westport, CT: Greenwood Press.

Caplan, Russell L. 1988. *Constitutional Brinkmanship: Amending the Constitution by National Convention.* New York: Oxford University Press.

Farrand, Max, ed. 1966. *The Records of the Federal Convention.* 4 vols. New Haven, CT: Yale University Press.

Ginsburg, Ruth B. 1989–1990. "On Amending the Constitution: A Plea for Patience." *University of Arkansas at Little Rock Law Journal* 12: 677–694.

Grimes, Alan P. 1978. *Democracy and the Amendments to the Constitution.* Lexington, MA: Lexington Books.

Lutz, Donald S. 1994. "Toward a Theory of Constitutional Amendment." *American Political Science Review* 88 (June): 355–370.

Murphy, Walter F. 1980. "An Ordering of Constitutional Values." *Southern California Law Review* 53: 703–760.

Quirk, William J. 2008. *Courts & Congress: America's Unwritten Constitution.* New Brunswick, NJ: Transaction Publishers.

Vile, John R. 1994. *Constitutional Change in the United States: A Comparative Study of the Role of Constitutional Amendments, Judicial Interpretations, and Legislative and Executive Actions.* Westport, CT: Praeger.

———. 1993a. *Contemporary Questions Surrounding the Constitutional Amending Process.* Westport, CT: Praeger.

———. 1993b. *The Theory and Practice of Constitutional Change in America: A Collection of Original Source Materials.* New York: Peter Lang.

———. 1992. *The Constitutional Amending Process in American Political Thought.* New York: Praeger.

———. 1991c. *Rewriting the United States Constitution: An Examination of Proposals from Reconstruction to the Present.* New York: Praeger.

ARTICLES OF CONFEDERATION

After the Revolutionary War and before the Constitution of 1787, the newly liberated states established a league of friendship among themselves, which was governed by a document known as the Articles of Confederation. Pennsylvania's John Dickinson was largely responsible for writing the document, but the Continental Congress, which approved it in 1777, modified his handiwork so as to keep major powers at the state level. Requiring unanimous state approval, the Articles did not officially go into effect until Maryland, which had been holding out until the larger states renounced their claims to western lands, ratified it in 1781.

Formed when states were extremely jealous of their powers and suspicious of strong executive power, such as that which George III had exercised during the colonial period, the Articles embodied the principle of state sovereignty. Article II provided that "each state retains its sovereignty, freedom, and independence, and every Power, Jurisdiction and right, which is not by this confederation expressly delegated to the United States, in Congress assembled" (Solberg 1958, 42). Whereas the current U.S. Constitution is based on the division of power among three branches, the unicameral legislative branch—in which each state had an equal vote—dominated the Articles. This branch, however, was not entrusted with power over interstate commerce, and on key matters, the consent of nine or more states was required. State legislatures elected, and could recall, members of the Confederation Congress, who further depended on the states for raising revenue and mustering armies.

Article XIII provided for an amending process. Congress would vote on amendments, which were then to be approved by all 13 state legislatures. This process ultimately proved too wooden, and despite several attempts, including two that fell but a single state shy of adoption (Bernstein with Agel 1993, 12), no amendments survived the gauntlet of unanimous state ratification.

Although the government under the Articles helped defeat the British, provided a useful transition from British to American rule, and was responsible for such achievements as the Northwest Ordinance of 1787, contemporaries came to agree that it did not provide for an adequate central authority. Accordingly, when the Constitutional Convention of 1787 met, the delegates decided to start with a new plan rather than attempt to revise the existing document. Ignoring the provision of Article XIII, the delegates specified that the new document would go into effect when ratified by nine of the states. The convention delegates further provided that the new document would be ratified not by the existing state legislatures, which would lose power to the new Congress, but by special conventions called within the states. Thus, technically, at least, the new system was adopted illegally (Kay 1987; Ackerman and Katyal 1991). Article V of the U.S. Constitution continued the two-step process for amendment, providing that two-thirds of both houses would propose amendments that three-fourths of the states would have to ratify.

Particularly in early American history, debates arose between individuals who believed that the new Constitution simply added some congressional powers while continuing to reserve key powers to the states that were part of a continuing "compact," and those who thought that the new government was intended to be significantly different and that it had effectively created a new nation of "We the People." Although the outcome of the Civil War put to rest extreme views of state sovereignty, debate continues over the appropriate role for states based on the new Constitution.

See also Constitutional Convention of 1787.

For Further Reading:

Ackerman, Bruce, and Ned Katyal. 1991. "Our Unconventional Founding." *University of Chicago Law Review* 62 (Spring): 475–573.

Bernstein, Richard B., with Jerome Agel. 1993. *Amending America: If We Love the Constitution So Much, Why Do We Keep Trying to Change It?* New York: Random House.

Dougherty, Ketih L. 2001. *Collective Action under the Articles of Confederation.* Cambridge: Cambridge University Press.

Jensen, Merrill. 1966. *The Articles of Confederation.* Madison: University of Wisconsin Press.

Johnson, Calvin H. 2003–2004. "Homage to Clio: The Historical Continuity from the Articles of Confederation into the Constitution." *Constitutional Commentary* 20 (Winter): 463–513.

Kay, Richard S. 1987. "The Illegality of the Constitution." *Constitutional Commentary* 4 (Winter): 57–80.

Solberg, Winton, ed. 1958. The Federal Convention and the Formation of the Union. Indianapolis, IN: Bobbs-Merrill.

ASSOCIATION, FREEDOM OF

The Supreme Court has recognized a right of association under the First Amendment. For example, it declared in a unanimous decision written by John Marshall Harlan II in *National Association for the Advancement of Colored People v. Alabama ex rel. Patterson* (1958, 460) that freedom of association was essential to "effective advocacy" and "an inseparable aspect of the 'liberty' assured by the Due Process Clause of the Fourteenth Amendment, which embraces freedom of speech." The Court accordingly voided an Alabama law requiring that the state chapter of the NAACP disclose the list of its members, who might then be subject to reprisals.

Ironically, when two Florida congressmen (Republican Charles Bennett and Democrat Donald Matthews) introduced amendments designed to preserve freedom of association in 1963 (H.J. Res. 728 and 775), their objective was to insulate the areas of private business, housing, and education from the effects of the Supreme Court's decision in *Brown v. Board of Education* (1954), which had mandated racial desegregation. Such an amendment would have permitted states to segregate students by race and sex in public schools, subject to the "separate but equal" standard originally established in *Plessy v. Ferguson* (1896) but repudiated in *Brown* (*Congressional Record,* 16909–10, 19449 (1963)).

The freedom of association under the First Amendment was one of the bases cited in *Griswold v. Connecticut* (1965) as a foundation for the right of privacy. This right was expanded in *Roe v. Wade* (1973) to include the right of a woman to obtain an abortion, at least in the first two trimesters of pregnancy.

See also First Amendment; *Griswold v. Connecticut.*

For Further Reading:

Guy-Urid, E. Charles, 2003. "Racial Identity, Electoral Structure, and the First Amendment Right of Association." *California Law Review* 91 (October): 1209–1280.

National Association for the Advancement of Colored People v. Alabama ex rel. Patterson, 356 U.S. 449 (1958).

Vile, John R., David Hudson Jr., and David Schultz. 2009. *Encyclopedia of the First Amendment.* Washington DC: CQ Press.

ATTORNEY GENERAL

Although she remained in office throughout both of Bill Clinton's terms, Attorney General Janet Reno, like her successor, John Ashcroft, was surrounded by controversy. Most prominent were the disputes surrounding her response to the Branch Davidian religious movement led by David Koresh (he died along with most of his followers when the building burned after being attacked by the FBI in Waco, Texas), and, later, for the handling of the immigration of Elian Gonzales (whose mother had died at sea while bringing him from Cuba to the United States, but who was eventually returned, at the insistence of the U.S. and Cuban governments, to his father in Cuba).

Perhaps motivated by the former issue (the latter did not occur until 1999), Democrat Ralph Hall of Texas proposed an amendment in August 1998 vesting the responsibility of the current attorney general in an elected official (see Vile 2003, 3:1692). Currently, the attorney general is a cabinet officer, indeed one of the first so established, appointed by the president with the advice and consent of the U.S. Senate. If the attorney general were elected, that individual would presumably be more accountable to the American people, but, similarly, it might be difficult to hold the president personally accountable for performing the duty vested in the presidency to enforce the laws of the United States.

See also Cabinet.

For Further Reading:

Vile, John R., ed. 2003. *Proposed Amendments to the U.S. Constitution, 1787–2001.* 3 Vols. Union, NJ: Law Book Exchange.

B

BACON, SELDEN (1861–1946)

Bacon was the spokesman for a group of New York lawyers in the late 1920s and early 1930s. He argued in a pamphlet and a follow-up article that the Tenth Amendment implied limits on the amending process in addition to those explicitly stated in Article V (see Vile 1992, 169–170). Bacon contended that Roger Sherman had inserted the words "to the United States" in the Tenth Amendment specifically to limit Article V—the amending process being such a power "not delegated to the United States" but given to the states or their people. By this addition, Sherman hoped to close the potential loophole that the delegates to the Constitutional Convention of 1787 had created whereby Article V might strip people of their liberties (S. Bacon 1930, 780).

According to Bacon's interpretation, matters that the Tenth Amendment reserved to the people could be effected only through the use of the convention method of ratification. Bacon cited the Eighteenth Amendment, which provided for national alcoholic prohibition, as an amendment requiring such popular ratification (S. Bacon 1930, 793). He argued that its effects on personal liberty were significantly different from previous amendments that the Supreme Court had recently upheld against similar challenges. Although Henry Taft (1930) attempted to refute his arguments, Bacon reiterated them before the Supreme Court in arguing the case of *United States v. Sprague* (1931). Even though the Court rejected Bacon's arguments, similar arguments continue to interest both modern proponents of substantive limits on the amending process and those who favor ratification of amendments by referendum.

See also Constitutional Amendments, Limits On; Eighteenth Amendment; Tenth Amendment; *United States v. Sprague.*

For Further Reading:

Bacon, Selden. 1930. "How the Tenth Amendment Affected the Fifth Article of the Constitution." *Virginia Law Review* 16 (June): 771–791.

Taft, Henry. 1930. "Amendment of the Federal Constitution: Is the Power Conferred by Article V Limited by the Tenth Amendment?" *Virginia Law Review* 16 (May): 647–658.

Vile, John R. 1992. *The Constitutional Amending Process in American Political Thought.* New York: Praeger.

BAILEY, MARTIN J. (1927–2000)

One of the most unusual texts of a new constitution was published posthumously in a book by Martin J. Bailey, a longtime economist (PhD Johns Hopkins University) at Emory University and other institutions who also held a variety of governmental positions. Entitled *Constitution for a Future Country* (2001), the proposed constitution and accompanying text justifying it are among the most detailed and complex ever to be offered.

Bailey, whose views were chiefly influenced by the public choice school of economics, whose proponents concentrate on the ties between economic choices and political institutions, believed that existing governments are riddled by inefficiencies. These largely occur because special interests organize and lobby for legislation to give themselves great benefits at only minimal costs to the public at large, who therefore have less incentive to organize against them. Bailey estimated that close to 50 percent of governmental spending is wasteful and could be sharply reduced if governments were given fewer monopolies and if individuals could express their true preferences when it came to what programs they were willing to support through taxation.

Although Bailey's model serves as a clear alternative to that of the United States, he thought that a proposal like his own has the best chance in a new nation. Speaking of existing countries and the possibility of initiating change by constitutional convention, he notes that:

> Every such country already has too many entrenched interests for such a convention to have an appreciable chance of success. The only hope for its adoption is in a new country of unusually prudent voters with unusually perspicacious leaders. (Bailey 2001, 168)

Bailey might have added that it would also help if the nation were composed chiefly of economists familiar with, and supportive of, such mechanisms as "a Lindahl tax [designed so that citizens favor taxes that benefit them and oppose those that are overly costly], the "Thomson Insurance Mechanism," and the "Vickrey-Clarke-Groves, or VCG mechanism," all of which his book features prominently.

Bailey identified what he considered to be the seven prime characteristics of his proposal. They were:

1. stratified random selection of official legislators [selected by chance rather than through elections];
2. a demand-revealing process [designed to ascertain public will] in each official legislature;
3. estimated Lindahl taxes;
4. potentially generous compensation for legislators based on all relevant outcomes, combined with competition among legislatures;
5. protection from bribery and extortion;
6. referenda with combined demand–revealing mechanisms; [and]
7. monitoring and enforcement of the performance of approved programs. (Bailey 2001, 51)

Bailey's model would provide for legislators to not only be randomly selected but, once chosen, to be sealed off from their constituents and forbidden to correspond with them. (This author knows of only one other such proposal, drafted by Jim Davidson for a hypothetical country called "Oceana.") Competition would be encouraged in Bailey's system among both courts (which would have to support themselves through user fees) and legislatures, but ultimately the people would settle almost every question through use of referenda. Governments would be strictly limited in their powers. Significantly, Bailey would put strict limits on judicial constructions of his document. He specified in a provision on the judiciary that:

> The courts shall interpret the law as it [was] meant when enacted, and shall not amend or modify the law. The only law, in addition to this constitution, shall be statute law. The courts shall interpret the constitution in terms of the meaning it had at the time it was ratified and similarly for the interpretation of each constitutional amendment and of each law. (Bailey 2001, 110)

Although Bailey's constitution puts great emphasis on freedom of contract and other property-related rights, he devotes significantly less attention to traditional civil liberties. Perhaps because he was so confident that the mechanisms he had devised would be effective, his section on civil liberties is one of the sketchiest of his constitution:

> Bill of rights. Standard stuff, including strict prohibition of retroactive laws. Strict

prohibition of involuntary servitude in any form, except that in the case of foreign invasion or an imminent threat of same, the government may use emergency powers to compel military service for up to a maximum of sixty days by citizens represented in official legislatures and qualified to vote, whose compensation shall be provided by law. Freedom of association and of political expression shall not include freedom to form coalitions or conspiracies by voters having the purpose of misrepresenting the harms to them of legislative proposals on the ballot. (Bailey 2001, 99)

As theories of public choice become increasingly prominent in the academic community, some of Bailey's proposals are likely to reemerge elsewhere.

See also Davidson, Jim; Public Choice and Constitutional Amendments.

For Further Reading:
Bailey, Martin J. 2001. *Constitution for a Future Country.* New York: Palgrave.

BAKER V. CARR (1962)

Baker v. Carr was the 6-to-2 decision in which Justice William Brennan declared for the Supreme Court that matters of state legislative apportionment were not political questions unfit for judicial resolution, but were justiciable under the equal protection clause of the Fourteenth Amendment. The decision remanded for consideration a Tennessee scheme of state legislative apportionment that favored rural counties and had not been altered since 1901, and it overturned an earlier plurality opinion in an Illinois case, *Colegrove v. Green* (1946). It also prepared the way for the Court to apply a one-person, one-vote standard for apportionment in both houses of a state legislature in *Reynolds v. Sims* (1964).

Focusing on a state matter rather than on a dispute among the three branches of the nation-al government, *Baker v. Carr* did not overturn the Court's decision in *Luther v. Borden* (1849), which identified the question of whether a state government is republican as a political question. *Baker* also seems to have left standing the decision in *Coleman v. Miller* (1939), entrusting decisions about the ratification of amendments to the elected branches (discussed in *Baker* 1962, 214–215).

In *Baker,* Brennan identified six factors involved in political questions:

[1.] a textually demonstrable constitutional commitment of the issue to a coordinate political department; [2.] or a lack of judicially discoverable and manageable standards for resolving it; [3.] or the impossibility of deciding without an initial policy determination of a kind clearly for nonjudicial discretion; [4.] or the impossibility of a court's undertaking independent resolution without expressing lack of the respect due coordinate branches of government; [5.] or an unusual need for unquestioning adherence to a political decision already made; [6.] or the potentiality of embarrassment from multifarious pronouncements by various departments on one question. (*Baker* 1962, 217)

Brennan noted that the citizens of Tennessee had no initiative and that the state amending process made it difficult for the people to initiate changes in the apportionment process (*Baker* 1962, 193–194). Justices Douglas and Clark wrote concurring opinions, and Justices Frankfurter and Harlan authored vigorous dissents questioning the wisdom of judicial intervention in this complex area and suggesting that the framers of the equal protection clause had not intended for it to apply to such controversies.

Baker and follow-up opinions stimulated calls for amendments in Congress and increased public opposition to the Warren Court. In a move led by Illinois senator Everett Dirksen, the states fell but a single vote short of mustering the necessary two-thirds majority needed to force Congress to call a special constitutional convention on the subject. The decision also generated controversial proposals for amendments by the Council of State Governments. Scholars have both praised (Ely 1980) and criticized the Court for its apportionment decisions (Elliott 1974). In recent years, the primary controversies involving apportionment have centered less on the justiciability of the issue (or on subsequent controversies over "one person, one vote") than on the degree to which such districts can be gerrymandered so as to create districts that are composed predominately of minority-race members. Although in decisions such as *Shaw v. Reno* (1993), *Bush v. Vera* (1996), and *Shaw v. Hunt* (1996), the Court has indicated that it looks unfavorably on districts drawn strictly on the basis of race, it has arguably yet to set clear standards in this area, in part vindicating Frankfurter and Harlan's concern about the complexity of judicial decision making in regard to this issue.

See also Council of State Governments; Dirksen, Everett McKinley; Political Questions; *Reynolds v. Sims;* States, Legislative Apportionment.

For Further Reading:
Baker v. Carr, 369 U.S. 186 (1962).
Elliott, Ward. 1974. *The Rise of Guardian Democracy.* Cambridge, MA: Harvard University Press.
Ely, John Hart. 1980. *Democracy and Distrust.* Cambridge, MA: Harvard University Press.
Irons, Peter, and Stephanie Guitton, eds. 1993. *May It Please the Court.* New York: New Press.
Lee, Calvin B. T. 1967. *One Man One Vote: WMCA and the Struggle for Equal Representation.* New York: Charles Scribner's Sons.

BALANCED BUDGET AMENDMENT

Among the powers the Constitution grants to Congress in Article I, Section 8 is the power "to borrow Money on the credit of the United States."

Although governmental debt was not uncommon in the 18th and 19th centuries, amendments were offered in the 1820s and 1830s for spending federal surpluses. Later in the 19th century, Section 4 of the Fourteenth Amendment indicated that the United States would honor its own, but not Confederate, debt.

In the 1870s and 1880s, amendments were introduced to limit the national debt, but the last several decades have been the most active period for such proposed amendments. Hundreds of proposals have been introduced during this time. One commentator noted that, in this respect, "the balanced budget amendment has shown itself to be the constitutional equivalent of the Energizer bunny" (Kyvig 1995, 99). In 1969, the National Taxpayers Union was formed to support the balanced budget amendment. Although generally associated with conservatives, this group has also mustered some support among liberals, including then Illinois Democratic senator Paul Simon.

At one time or another, as many as 32 of the needed 34 states have petitioned Congress to call a convention to address the balanced budget amendment, although some have since withdrawn their petitions. Moreover, on several occasions, Congress has voted on a balanced budget amendment. In August 1982 the Senate voted 69 to 31 for a balanced budget amendment, but it stalled in the House of Representatives. In 1986, a balanced budget amendment fell a single vote short of the needed majority in the Senate. In 1990, it was seven votes shy of the needed majority in the House, and in 1992, it fell only nine votes short (Kyvig 1995, 114, 118–119). After the Republican gains in the 1994 congressional elections, a balanced budget amendment passed the House of Representatives, but it subsequently came up a single vote shy of adoption in the Senate. One of the amendment's supporters, Republican Senate Majority Leader Robert Dole of Kansas, ultimately cast his vote against the amendment. This parliamentary maneuver allowed him to reintroduce the measure in 1996, just before he retired to run for president. On June 6, 1996, the amendment fell two votes short of the needed majority. The vote in the Senate was even closer on March 4, 1997, when the Senate vote of 66 to 34 fell a single vote shy of the required two-thirds vote, despite the fact that all 55 Senate

Republicans voted in favor of the measure. The vote was attributed in part to a last-minute defection by Democrat Robert G. Torricelli of New Jersey, who had advocated such an amendment in his Senate campaign and previously voted three of three occasions for a similar measure (Taylor 1997, 577).

Although the idea of a balanced budget appears relatively simple on the surface, its supporters are motivated by different objectives, and these are sometimes in tension. Like earlier supporters of an amendment to limit the percentage of income that could be collected through the income tax that was sanctioned in the Sixteenth Amendment, many supporters see the balanced budget mechanism primarily as a means of curtailing the increased activities and expenditures of the federal government since the New Deal was introduced in the 1930s and 1940s. Others anticipate that such an amendment would require the government to increase taxes to pay for current programs.

Differences in objectives and approaches are reflected in the variety of amendments that have been introduced in Congress on the subject. These have included proposals to limit governmental expenditures to a fixed percentage of the gross national product; to require Congress to stay in session until it proposes a balanced budget; to prevent expenditures from exceeding revenues except in cases of war or emergency; to require every appropriation measure to be accompanied by a revenue-raising measure; to require the approval of an extraordinary majority of Congress to raise taxes; to require the approval of an extraordinary majority of Congress to raise the ceiling on the debt; to mandate increased taxes in certain deficit situations; to begin paying back the national debt; and to provide for a taxpayer's bill of rights. Some such proposals have been tied to prohibitions against unfunded federal mandates or to proposals for a presidential line-item veto.

Two questions that dog the balanced budget amendment are those of appropriateness and enforceability. To the extent that the amendment appears to sanction one, possibly transient, economic theory over another, some argue that it has no place in a constitution intended to endure over time ("Balanced Budget Amendment" 1983). Other questions center on who would have standing to sue under such an amendment, how the amendment would be enforced, and, particularly, what role the courts would play in its enforcement (see J. Bowen 1994). At least since 1937, U.S. courts have generally taken a hands-off approach to economic affairs, and such an amendment might, wisely or unwisely, inject courts back into such controversies. Moreover, legislation designed to achieve balanced budgets—most notably the Balanced Budget and Emergency Deficit Control Act of 1985, better known as the Gramm-Rudman-Hollings law—initially proved relatively unsuccessful in ending deficits. To some, this suggests that stronger medicine is needed; others fear that an amendment might prove similarly unenforceable and that it would ultimately bring disrespect on the Constitution.

At the end of George W. Bush's administration, Congress adopted a bank bailout plan that costs hundreds of billions of dollars. The Obama administration proposed further stimulus money, which Congress allocated, to create jobs, save the automobile industry, and help with home mortgages. These proposals both show that members of both parties consider deficit spending to be an appropriate tool to be used in circumstances and that deficit spending is likely to continue for the near future.

See also Hamilton, Alexander; Jefferson, Thomas; Public Choice and Constitutional Amendments.

For Further Reading:
"The Balanced Budget Amendment: An Inquiry into Appropriateness." 1983. *Harvard Law Review* 96 (May): 1600–1620.

Bowen, James W. 1994. "Enforcing the Balanced Budget Amendment." *Constitutional Law Journal* 4 (Spring): 565–620.

Davidson, James D. 1992. "Yes, to Save Congress from Itself." *The World & I* 7 (August): 110, 112–115.

Fink, Richard H., and Jack C. High, eds. 1987. *A Nation in Debt: Economists Debate the Federal Budget Deficit.* Frederick, MD: University Publications of America.

Ishikawa, Brendon T. 2000. "The Stealth Amendment: The Impending Ratification and Repeal of a

Federal Budget Amendment." *Tulsa Law Journal* 33 (Winter): 353–381.

Kyvig, David E. 1995. "Reforming or Resisting Modern Government? The Balanced Budget Amendment to the U.S. Constitution." *Akron Law Review* 28 (Fall/Winter): 97–124.

McIntyre, Robert S. 1992. "No, It Would Wreck the Economy." *The World & I* 7 (August): 111, 116–117, 119.

Moore, W. S., and Rudolph G. Penner, eds. 1980. *The Constitution and the Budget: Are Constitutional Limits on Tax, Spending and Budget Powers Desirable at the Federal Level?* Washington DC: American Enterprise Institute for Public Policy Research.

Savage, James D. 1988. *Balanced Budgets and American Politics.* Ithaca, NY: Cornell University Press.

Taylor, Andrew. 1997. "Senate Again One Vote Short; GOP Says House Will Act," *Congressional Quarterly,* 55 (8 March): 577–578.

BALDWIN, LELAND
(1897–1981)

Baldwin was a retired professor of history from the University of Pittsburgh when he proposed a new constitution in a 1972 book entitled *Reframing the Constitution: An Imperative for Modern America.* Identifying the existing system of federalism, separation of powers, and a weak party system as some of the problems in the current government, Baldwin described his plan as "a modified version of the Cabinet or Parliamentary form" (Baldwin 1972, 96).

Baldwin's plan called for the creation of a unicameral Congress consisting of 200 elected members. It would also have up to 15 congressmen-pro-forma to serve as a type of shadow cabinet and enough appointed congressmen-at-large to give the majority party a 55 percent voting majority of the membership. This constitution would entrust Congress with more explicit powers (the administration of some of which could, however, be delegated to the states), and members would be elected to five-year terms, subject to prior dissolution.

The president, similar to a prime minister, would preside over Congress and be its executive arm. Like members of Congress, the president would serve for a five-year term, subject to a vote of no confidence. The vice presidency would be eliminated. Instead, Congress would elect a successor in case of presidential death or disability.

The courts would be headed by a new body designated as the Senate and consisting of 50 law senators (two from each of the 15 new states described below and others elected on the basis of population apportionment) and 50 senators-at-large. Senators would be appointed for life but would retire at age 70. The chief justice, who would be selected by the Senate, would preside over that body and would live in the White House and serve as head of state. The entire Senate would vote on matters of constitutional interpretation. The Senate could suspend the writ of habeas corpus and exercise similar power in times of emergency. It could also dissolve Congress, conduct investigations, and impose reforms on state governments. In cases of conflict between the president and Congress, the chief justice and two-thirds of the Senate could dissolve Congress.

Baldwin provided mechanisms to recognize political parties and to nominate and select the elected branches. He also proposed dividing existing states into 15 new ones. Alaska would be given the option of becoming a commonwealth or joining a group of northwestern states. Each state would draw up a new constitution consolidating existing governments and providing for a unicameral legislature and an appointive senate.

The Bill of Rights would be modified, in accord with the 20th-century incorporation process, to apply to both the states and the national government. Baldwin would broaden protections against discrimination to cover "sex, race, color, religion, or birth out of wedlock." He would explicitly vest Congress with power over gun ownership, thus modifying the current Second Amendment.

Baldwin also wanted to liberalize the constitutional amending process. He would empower two-thirds majorities of the Senate or the Congress to propose amendments, subject to ratification by either three-fourths of the state legislatures or a majority of the electorate.

Alternatively, one-half of the states could propose amendments. Baldwin also specified mechanisms for calling a new constitutional convention.

See also Parliamentary System.

For Further Reading:

Baldwin, Leland. 1972. *Reframing the Constitution: An Imperative for Modern America.* Santa Barbara, CA: ABC-CLIO.

Boyd, Steven R., ed. 1992. *Alternative Constitutions for the United States: A Documentary History.* Westport, CT: Greenwood Press.

Vile, John R. 1991c. *Rewriting the United States Constitution: An Examination of Proposals from Reconstruction to the Present.* New York: Praeger.

BANKING

The U.S. Constitution neither specifically mentions banking nor authorizes Congress to establish corporations. Congressional authority to establish a national bank was a major issue in the administration of George Washington and contributed to the emerging split between the Federalist and Republican Parties. Secretary of the Treasury Alexander Hamilton, who would soon be a leading Federalist, favored broad federal powers and emphasized the development of commerce and industry; he accordingly argued that the bank was constitutional. Secretary of State Thomas Jefferson, who would soon lead the Republican Party, was wary of broad federal powers and emphasized agricultural development; he, and Attorney General Edmund Randolph, accordingly argued that the bank was unconstitutional. Washington sided with Hamilton, and Congress created a bank with a 20-year charter. Although this charter lapsed, Congress reestablished the bank in 1816.

Maryland challenged the constitutionality of this bank and attempted to tax its branch in Baltimore. In *McCulloch v. Maryland* (1819), Chief Justice John Marshall decided that the national government could establish the bank under the doctrine of implied powers. He also voided Maryland's tax on the bank. This decision did not, however, prevent Andrew Jackson (who associated banks with eastern monied interests) from vetoing a bank bill that was introduced during his administration. He also had his secretary of the treasury, Roger Taney (later a chief justice of the U.S. Supreme Court), move monies from the national bank to various state institutions.

Three amendments proposed in Congress in 1793 and 1794 would have made bankers ineligible to serve in Congress. Amendments proposed in 1813 and 1814 would have specifically authorized a bank. A spate of proposals made immediately after *McCulloch* and reflecting resolutions voted on in a number of state legislatures would have prohibited branches of the national bank outside the District of Columbia.

At least three proposals from 1837 to 1840, apparently stimulated by the panic of 1837, would have prohibited the issuance of state bank notes. Oklahoma Democratic senator Thomas Gore introduced a proposal in 1933, probably in response to the Great Depression, that would have required states to get congressional consent before chartering banks (S.J. Res. 18).

See also Congress, Powers of; *McCulloch v. Maryland.*

For Further Reading:

Legislative and Documentary History of the Bank of the United States Including the Original Bank of North America, compiled by M. St. Clarke and D.A. Hall. 1967 reprint of 1832. 1832 ed. in Washington by Gales & Seaton; 1967 ed. in New York by Augustus M. Kelley.

Jefferson, Thomas. 1791. "Opinion of the Constitutionality of a National Bank." In *Documents of American Constitutional and Legal History,* ed. Melvin I. Urofsky. New York: Alfred A. Knopf, 1989, 132–146.

BANKRUPTCY

Although the Constitution grants Congress power in Article I, Section 8 to make "uniform

Laws on the subject of Bankruptcies throughout the United States," Congress did not create a lasting system of national legislation until 1898 (Coleman 1992, 73). A proposal introduced in 1822 would have allowed states to adopt legislation in the interim (Ames 1896, 265). With some reservations, this was basically what the Supreme Court agreed to in a 4-to-3 decision in *Ogden v. Saunders* (1827), in which Chief Justice John Marshall, author of an earlier case on state insolvency laws in *Sturges v. Crowinshield* (1819), dissented.

Congress modified the 1898 system with the adoption of the Bankruptcy Reform Act of 1978, which established a new Bankruptcy Court. Although the new system has not been without problems, it has not stimulated further proposals for constitutional amendments.

See also Congress, Powers of.

For Further Reading:

Ames, Herman. 1896. *The Proposed Amendments to the Constitution of the United States during the First Century of Its History.* Reprint, New York: Burt Franklin, 1970.

Coleman, Peter J. 2005. "Bankruptcy and Insolvency Legislation." In *The Oxford Companion to the Supreme Court of the United States,* ed. Kermit L. Hall. 2nd ed., New York: Oxford University Press, 72–74.

———. 1974. *Debtors and Creditors in America: Insolvency, Imprisonment for Debt, and Bankruptcy, 1607–1900.* Madison: State Historical Society of Wisconsin.

BARRON V. BALTIMORE (1833)

In this 7-to-0 decision (there were only seven justices at this time) authored by Chief Justice John Marshall, the Supreme Court decided that the first 10 amendments to the Constitution, known as the Bill of Rights, applied only to the national government and not to the states. In this case, the city of Baltimore had diverted streams that subsequently filled a wharf owned by Barron and rendered it useless. Citing the takings clause of the Fifth Amendment, Barron argued that the government had illegally deprived him of his property without just compensation. In response, Marshall argued that the Constitution had been designed to limit the national government rather than the state governments. He pointed out that provisions of the Constitution that did limit the states (those found in Article I, Section 10, for example) concerned matters relevant to the national government and had been explicitly applied to the states. Marshall further noted that if individuals had desired alterations in their own state constitutions, they would have called conventions rather than use "the unwieldy and cumbrous machinery of procuring a recommendation from two-thirds of Congress and the assent of three-fourths of their sister states" (*Barron* 1833, 250).

When James Madison introduced his initial version of the Bill of Rights, Madison proposed an amendment limiting the states, but his proposal had failed for lack of congressional support. The Fourteenth Amendment, which was ratified in 1868, provided protections against state deprivations of privileges and immunities, due process rights, and equal protection for U.S. citizens. Some supporters of the amendment, including Congressman John Bingham, knew about *Barron v. Baltimore* and apparently hoped that the Fourteenth Amendment would overturn it. Although Justice John Marshall Harlan I agreed, the rest of the Supreme Court initially rejected this interpretation. In the 20th century, although never officially embracing the doctrine of total incorporation that Harlan and later Justice Hugo Black advocated, the Court has gradually used the due process clause of that amendment (in a development generally referred to as selective incorporation) to apply almost all the guarantees found in the Bill of Rights to the states as well as to the national government.

See also *Adamson v. California;* Bingham, John; Fifth Amendment; Incorporation; *Palko v. Connecticut.*

For Further Reading:

Barron v. Baltimore, 32 U.S. 243 (1833).

Courtner, Richard. 1981. *The Supreme Court and the Second Bill of Rights: The Fourteenth Amendment and the Nationalization of Civil Rights*. Madison: University of Wisconsin Press.

Schwartz, Bernard. 1992. *The Great Rights of Mankind: A History of the American Bill of Rights*. Madison, WI: Madison House.

BEASLEY, ROBERT E. (DATES UNKNOWN)

Robert Beasley, a Californian who seems otherwise to have faded into obscurity, proposed a new constitution for the United States in a pamphlet published in 1864 in both English and Spanish and titled *A Plan to Stop the Present and Prevent Future Wars*. His plan, which actually preceded his proposed constitution, called for all persons to vote on whether to continue the Civil War, with nonvoters to be penalized by a $1,000 fine. If the vote was affirmative, all would then be placed in the army and "compelled to assist in prosecuting the war" (Beasley 1864, 3). The constitution, constantly referred to as being for "the sovereign States of North and South America," followed.

Under this plan, the House of Representatives would consist of two representatives from each state and the Senate of one from each. The Senate would have to vote on charges of impeachment by three-fifths rather than two-thirds, and members of Congress would receive $5 for each day of service plus expenses. Perhaps in response to Lincoln's forceful actions in prosecuting the war, only Congress would have the power to suspend the writ of habeas corpus.

The president and vice president would not be permitted to serve for consecutive terms. Each voter would write the name of his preferred candidate for president on a ballot, with the Senate deciding tie votes. The president would receive a yearly salary of $40,000. His power to pardon would be restricted in cases of "lying, larceny, and impeachment" (Beasley 1864, 13). He could also be removed from office for "conviction of lying, larceny or other high crimes and misdemeanors" (Beasley 1864, 14).

Most of the provisions of the Bill of Rights would be incorporated. Government officers convicted of stealing were to be fined, with proceeds to go toward the construction of a national cemetery. Those stealing over $10,000 were to be "hung with a rope by the neck until dead" and denied burial in this cemetery (Beasley 1864, 16).

States were to be prohibited from interfering in the domestic affairs of other states and would be expelled from the Union for 50 years for so doing. States could secede and keep government property within their boundaries. Beasley would further provide for the purchase of "white servants" from Europe to become citizens after 15 years (Beasley 1864, 18). Slaveholders would be able to take their slaves into the territories, thus affirming the 1857 decision in *Scott v. Sandford*, with states subsequently deciding whether to have slavery according to the principle of popular sovereignty. The national government could call on each state for a quota of troops; if the quota were not met, "all the males and half the females in his State" would be drafted (Beasley 1864, 20). Neither slavery nor polygamy would exclude a state from the Union. In language similar to that later used in the Fourteenth Amendment, voting in federal elections and office-holding were to be limited to "white male citizens of the age of twenty-one years and upwards" (Beasley 1864, 20).

Beasley would have officially adopted the Monroe Doctrine and authorized Congress to carry it out. Adjacent islands could be admitted into the Union after 1900, but states in Europe, Asia, and Africa would have to wait until after 2000. States would have the power to prohibit their citizens from interfering in the "domestic concerns" of their neighbors or "lying to their own or their neighbor's dumb brutes [presumably slaves], or unnecessarily abusing them in any way" (Beasley 1864, 21).

Beasley identified himself as one of the "sovereign people" of Rio Vista, California, who doubted that he was "a servant of God" (Beasley 1864, 3), but he proposed four scriptures "as admonitions to all people" (Beasley 1864, 21). These dealt with the subjection of wives to husbands, instructions for familial relations, master-slave relations, and the proper allocation of responsibilities between Caesar and God.

Secret political parties were to be outlawed, and political parties could not nominate individuals for office. Amendments were to be ratified by five-sixths (rather than three-fourths) of the states, and ratification by conventions in five states would be sufficient to inaugurate the new government.

In an addendum, Beasley asserted, in apparent reference to slaves, that "whatsoever God has made inferior, man cannot make equal or superior" (Beasley 1864, 23). He further proposed a census for after the war and laws "that will give every one a chance to have a husband or a wife," and he suggested that the seat of government should be "within one or two hundred miles of the 'Isthmus of Panama'" (Beasley 1864, 24).

From 1914 to 1940, Democratic representative Louis Ludlow of Indiana introduced an amendment designed to require a popular referendum before the nation could enter into war, an idea that was revived briefly during the Vietnam Era. Beasley's proslavery constitution was otherwise overtaken by events, and it appears to have quickly faded from public view.

See also Initiative and Referendum; Slavery, Protection for.

For Further Reading:

Beasley, Robert. 1864. *A Plan to Stop the Present and Prevent Future Wars: Containing a Proposed Constitution for the General Government of the Sovereign States of North and South America.* Rio Vista, CA: Robert Beasley.

Bolt, Ernest C., Jr. *The War Referendum Approach to Peace in America, 1914–1941.* Charlottesville, VA: University Press of Virginia, 1977.

BECKER, THEODORE L. (1932–)

In 1976, when he was a professor of law and political science at the University of Hawaii, Becker offered a series of proposed constitutional reforms in a textbook entitled *American Government: Past—Present—Future.* He referred to his plan as a type of *eutopia*—that is, a "good" or "desirable" place—as opposed to a *utopia,* which literally means "no place" (Becker 1976, 432).

In an attempt to increase governmental responsiveness and accountability, Becker favors a national presidential primary (NPP). However, his ultimate aim is to institute a presidential election tournament (PET), whereby candidates would emerge (as in organized athletic contests) first from the states, then from one of four regions, then from either the East or the West, and finally from the contest between those two champions, with campaign costs funded by the government. Becker would also institute a vote of "no confidence" as a means of executive recall and suggests that voting should be a compulsory, perhaps even a paid, activity. Citizens would, however, be given a "no preference" option (Becker 1976, 459).

Becker favors a unicameral rather than bicameral Congress. He would also establish an "executive Committee, Council, or Cabinet" to run its affairs (Becker 1976, 467). He anticipates a legislature of from 500 to 1,000 people in which at least half of the representatives are selected at random. He also favors a national initiative and referendum process that might be effected by home cable television or computer hookups.

Becker would like to see presidents run for office on a ticket that includes members of their cabinet. Contrary to precedents in *Myers v. United States* (1926) and elsewhere that vests such power exclusively in the executive, the president would, in turn, have to get 60 percent approval of Congress to fire a cabinet member (Becker 1976, 474). Congress and ombudsmen, who would form a "countergovernment" (Becker 1976, 509), would provide greater administrative oversight.

Becker also anticipates numerous reforms of the judicial and criminal justice systems. He favors either setting up a national appeals court to ease the Supreme Court's workload or appointing 18 Supreme Court justices who would work on nine-judge panels. Judges would serve for 12 to 15 years rather than for life and would retire at age 70. As in Congress, a good portion of the judges would be chosen by lottery, albeit from members of the bar, with all judges undergoing at least six months' training at a judicial academy. Members of the lay public would preside in many trials, the state's peremptory challenges for jurors would be eliminated, jury pools would be widened, and jury pay would be increased.

Becker favors the repeal of all so-called victimless crime laws, such as those prohibiting consensual sex, gambling, drug use, and the like.

In 1992, Becker—then at Auburn University—
was working with Barry Krusch, author of *The
21st Century Constitution* (1992), to develop a
national network of individuals interested in a second constitutional convention. As a class project,
Becker had previously organized a simulated constitutional convention in Hawaii. Becker is one of
the supporters of the National Initiative for
Democracy, or Philadelphia II, which is designed
to amend the U.S. Constitution by referendum.
Becker continues to be an advocate of using modern technology to strengthen direct democracy
within the United States.

See also Krusch, Barry; National Initiative
for Democracy.

For Further Reading:

Becker, Theodore L. 1976. *American Government: Past—Present—Future.* Boston: Allyn and
Bacon.

Becker, Theodore Lewis, and Christa Daryl Sla-
ton. 2000. *The Future of Teledemocracy.* Westport,
CT: Praeger.

Krusch, Barry. 1992. *The 21st Century Constitution: A New America for a New Millennium.* New
York: Stanhope Press.

BIBLE READING IN SCHOOLS

See *Abington v. Schempp; Engel v. Vitale;*
Prayer in Public Schools.

BILL OF RESPONSIBILITIES

The first person known to have used the word
"responsibility" was James Madison (Adair,
1965, 137). Although individual rights and
responsibilities are arguably correlative, the
Constitution currently provides protection for
the former largely without specifying the latter.
Rexford Tugwell and Jeremy Miller have been
among the proponents of a new constitution that
lists such responsibilities in the proposed document. More generally, some commentators have
argued that American laws should devote more
attention to citizen duties than they currently do
(Glendon 1991, 76–108).

As part of its contribution to the bicentennial
of the U.S. Constitution, the Freedoms Foundation in Valley Forge, in consultation with a number of scholars, developed a one-page bill of
responsibilities. It is based on the presumption,
stated in a one-paragraph preamble, that
"[f]reedom and responsibility are mutual and
inseparable" and that "we can ensure enjoyment
of the one only by exercising the other."

Perhaps as a parallel to the Bill of Rights, the
Foundation's Bill of Responsibilities was divided into 10 parts. These included the responsibilities "to be fully responsible for our own actions
and for the consequences of those actions; to
respect the rights and beliefs of others; to give
sympathy, understanding and help to others; to
do our best to meet our own and our families'
needs; to respect and obey the laws; to respect
the property of others, both private and public;
to share with others our appreciation of the benefits and obligations of freedom; to participate
constructively in the nation's political life; to
help freedom survive by assuming personal
responsibility for its defense; and to respect the
rights and to meet the responsibilities on which
our liberty rests and our democracy depends"
(Freedoms Foundation 1985, italics omitted).
Each of these responsibilities is followed by a
brief explanation.

Another bill of responsibilities that is circu-
lating on the Internet is attributed to Judith H.
Ross, who is otherwise unidentified. She
believes her list of 10 responsibilities is similar
to what "the Founding Fathers might suggest." It
says that each citizen should be "loyal," "honor
the flag," and "pledge allegiance to your country." Ross believes a citizen should not be a
"hyphenated American or an expatriate of another country who is here solely for economic
advantage." Citizens should "obey the law and
work through peaceful means to achieve
change." A citizen should "speak up when the

criminal or legislative actions of any persons threaten the welfare of your family or your nation." Citizens should further "consider the welfare of ALL the citizens" even at the cost of "personal sacrifice." They should support themselves, their immediate families, and their neighbors. They should seek "to make a difference" in the lives of their families, their communities, and their nation. They should be "educated and informed" and "should use wisdom in selecting those who will lead." Citizens should also "value and defend human life." Finally, citizens should honor their "freedom of worship and . . . defend that right for every citizen in this country."

Both these bills of responsibilities appear to have been offered for citizen reflection rather than in the hopes that they would be adopted, like the Bill of Rights, as a set of constitutional amendments.

See Also Madison, James; Miller, Jeremy; Tugwell, Rexford.

For Further Reading:

Adair, Douglas, 1965. "The Federalist Papers," *The William and Mary Quarterly,* 3rd ser. 22 (1965): 131–139.

Blitz, Mark. 2005. *Duty Bound: Responsibility and American Public Life.* Lanham, MD: Rowman and Littlefield.

Freedoms Foundation. 1985. "Bill of Responsibilities." Valley Forge, PA: Freedom Foundation.

Glendon, Mary A. 1991. *Rights Talk: The Impoverishment of Political Discourse.* New York: Free Press.

Rose, Judith H. "An American Bill of Responsibilities." http://charltonrose.com/misc/billresp. Accessed May 17, 2008.

BILL OF RIGHTS

Collectively, the first 10 amendments to the U.S. Constitution are designated the Bill of Rights. These amendments are almost as venerated as the original document. Curiously, the subject of such a bill received little attention at the Constitutional Convention of 1787, although some debate was stirred near the end of the convention when George Mason of Virginia, who had

authored his state's path-breaking declaration of rights in 1776, proposed a motion for such a bill. Similarly, Virginia's Richard Henry Lee tried unsuccessfully to get the Congress under the Articles of Confederation to add a bill of rights before sending the Constitution to the states for approval (Schwartz 1992, 105).

The Federalist–Anti-Federalist Controversy

The absence of such a bill quickly became one of the rallying points for Anti-Federalists opposed to the new Constitution. Federalist proponents of the document initially argued that such a bill was unnecessary and could even prove dangerous in the event that key rights were omitted. Leading proponents of the Constitution subsequently realized that adding a bill of rights would be far less likely to jeopardize the new document than the prospect of a second convention, which many Anti-Federalists were advocating (Labunski, 2007).

Actions by Congress

In the process of ratifying the U.S. Constitution, eight states submitted more than 100 substantive amendment proposals (Schwartz 1992, 157). Although President George Washington had expressed approval for such a bill in his inaugural address, many Congressmen wanted to postpone consideration of a bill of rights until the new Constitution had been more thoroughly tested, but Madison especially believed that such a bill was essential to gaining the confidence of those who had opposed ratification of the document (Vile 1993c, 137–160).

Madison formulated a list of nine amendments with 42 separate rights for congressional consideration (Lutz 1992, 55); most of Madison's proposals dealt with individual political rights rather than guarantees for state sovereignty, which some Anti-Federalists had sought. In the course of debate and deliberation, Congress deleted four of Madison's proposed amendments. They would have provided a declaration of the people's right to alter the government, applied guarantees of freedom of conscience and the press to the states (thus anticipating the later incorporation controversy), limited certain appeals to the Supreme Court, and explicitly mentioned the doctrine of separation of powers (Schwartz 1992, 169). All 12 amendments that subsequently emerged from House and Senate action (including action by a Committee of Eleven, which included Madison, in the House, and conference reports in both houses) were based on Madison's original draft, with changes related "to form rather than substance" (Schwartz 1992, 169). Madison did not succeed in incorporating proposals into the constitutional text; instead, the Congress followed Roger Sherman's suggestion to append the Bill of Rights to the end of the document. The House voted to accept the Bill of Rights on September 24, 1789, with the Senate concurring the following day (Schwartz 1992, 186).

Twenty-six of the rights on Madison's original list were found in the state constitutions, nine were found in five of seven contemporary constitutions, four were found in six, and thirteen were found in all seven existing state documents (Lutz 1992, 67; also see Conley and Kaminski 1992); many of these rights, in turn, originated in colonial charters (Lutz 1992, 68–69). Whereas the first eight amendments contain provisions protecting individual rights (with special attention to the rights of political participation and rights for those accused of criminal behavior), the Ninth and Tenth Amendments are directed toward different concerns and are thus sometimes excluded from discussions of the first eight amendments. Unlike many 20th-century bills of rights, the U.S. version does not attempt to guarantee social and economic rights.

State Ratification

The first 10 amendments became part of the Constitution with their ratification by Virginia in late 1791. Secretary of State Thomas Jefferson notified the state governors of this ratification on March 1, 1792 (Schwartz 1992, 186). In 1939, the sesquicentennial of the adoption of the U.S. Constitution, Connecticut and Georgia added their ratifications in a symbolic display that illustrates the Bill of Rights' grip on the popular mind (Schwartz 1992, 191).

The Incorporation Controversy

For all the attention that this part of the Constitution receives, the Bill of Rights was not the source of frequent judicial decision making in the nation's first 100 years when the courts interpreted the Bill of Rights as a limitation only on the actions of the national government and not on the states, where most early legislating took place. The wording of the First Amendment—beginning with "Congress shall make no law"—appeared to confirm that the Bill of Rights applied only to actions of the national government. Chief Justice John Marshall confirmed this view in *Barron v. Baltimore* (1833), where he cited the debates over the Bill of Rights as proof.

Among the supporters of the Fourteenth Amendment, which was ratified in 1868, at least some advocates—among them Congressman John Bingham, who was largely responsible for authoring the first section—were motivated by a desire to overturn *Barron v. Baltimore*. Initially, the Court rejected this incorporation doctrine in the *Slaughterhouse Cases* (1873) and other contemporary decisions. In the early 20th century, however, the Supreme Court adopted the view of selective incorporation, under which courts applied individual guarantees to the states via the due process clause of the Fourteenth Amendment on a piecemeal basis. Over time, all but five provisions were so applied to the states, with the Warren Court proving particularly active in this area (Hall 1991, 8). The result is that the Bill of Rights has had considerably more influence in the 20th century than in the 19th.

The Bill of Rights Today

Whereas the Warren Court generally interpreted the Bill of Rights expansively, subsequent Courts have been more cautious about expanding such rights and have, in many cases, narrowed but not abandoned earlier rulings. As a consequence, some advocates of expanded rights now argue that those seeking expanded protections for individual rights should look increasingly to their own state constitutions and their state bills of rights for protection, with the federal Bill of Rights serving more as a floor than a ceiling. A number of individuals who have written and proposed new constitutions in recent years, especially libertarians, have significantly expanded the attention they devote in such documents to rights, often articulating rights like privacy and travel that courts have recognized but that have not been formally added to the existing constitutional text. Consistent with practice in a number of states prior to the adoption of the U.S. Bill of Rights, a number of recent proposals list rights at the beginning of their documents rather than appending them to the end. The current Bill of Rights focuses on political rights, or rights against the government. A number of proponents of new rights, among them Congressman Jesse Jackson Jr., have focused on social and economic rights, which governments would be obligated to provide.

See also Anti-Federalists; *Barron v. Baltimore;* Federalists; Fourteenth Amendment; Incorporation; Jackson, Jesse L., Jr.; Madison, James; Magna Carta; Placement of Constitutional Amendments; Social and Economic Rights; Virginia Declaration of Rights.

For Further Reading:

Alderman, Ellen, and Caroline Kennedy. 1991. *In Our Defense: The Bill of Rights in Action.* New York: William Morrow.

Amar, Akhil R. 1992. "The Bill of Rights as a Constitution." *Yale Law Journal* 100 (Winter): 1131–1210.

Bill of Rights Institute, 2006. *The Bill of Rights and You: Rights and Responsibilities.* Arlington, VA.

"The Bill of Rights." 1991. Bicentennial issue of *Life* (Fall).

Bodenhamer, David J., and James W. Ely Jr., eds. 1993. *The Bill of Rights in Modern America after 200 Years.* Bloomington, IN: Indiana University Press.

Bryant, Irving. 1965. *The Bill of Rights: Its Origin and Meaning.* Indianapolis, IN: Bobbs-Merrill.

Cogan, Neil H., ed. 1997. *The Complete Bill of Rights: The Drafts, Debates, Sources, and Origins.* New York: Oxford University Press.

Conley, Patrick T., and John P. Kaminski, eds. 1992. *The Bill of Rights and the States: The Colonial and Revolutionary Origins of American Liberties.* Madison, WI: Madison House.

Finkelman, Paul. 1991. "James Madison and the Bill of Rights: A Reluctant Paternity." 1990. *Supreme Court Review,* eds. Gerhard Casper, Dennis J. Hutchinson, and David Strauss. Chicago: University of Chicago Press.

Grimes, Alan P. 1978. *Democracy and the Amendments to the Constitution.* Lexington, MA: Lexington Books.

Hall, Kermit L., ed. 1991. *By and for the People: Constitutional Rights in American History.* Arlington Heights, IL: Harlan Davidson.

Kurland, Philip B., and Ralph Lerner, eds. 1987. *The Founders' Constitution.* Vol. 5. Chicago: University of Chicago Press.

Labunski, Richard. 2006. *James Madison and the Struggle for the Bill of Rights.* New York: Oxford University Press.

———. 2007. "The Second Convention Movement, 1787–1789." *Constitutional Commentary* 24 (Fall): 567–600.

Lutz, Donald S. 1992. *A Preface to American Political Theory.* Lawrence: University Press of Kansas.

Mason, Alpheus T., and Gordon E. Baker. 1985. *Free Government in the Making: Readings in American Political Thought.* 4th ed. New York: Oxford University Press.

Peck, Robert S. 1992. *The Bill of Rights and the Politics of Interpretation.* St. Paul, MN: West.

Schwartz, Bernard. 1992. *The Great Rights of Mankind: A History of the American Bill of Rights.* Madison, WI: Madison House.

Schwartz, Bernard, ed. 1980. *The Roots of the Bill of Rights.* 5 vols. New York: Chelsea House.

Stone, Geoffrey R., Richard A. Epstein, and Cass R. Sunstein, eds. 1992. *The Bill of Rights in the Modern State.* Chicago: University of Chicago Press.

Vile, John R. 1993c. "Three Kinds of Constitutional Founding and Change: The Convention Model and Its Alternatives." *Political Research Quarterly* 46: 881–895.

———. 1991b. "Proposals to Amend the Bill of Rights: Are Fundamental Rights in Jeopardy?" *Judicature* 75 (August–September): 62–67.

BINGHAM, JOHN A. (1815–1900)

John Bingham was a lawyer and Republican congressman from Ohio from 1854 to 1873. Supreme Court Justice Hugo Black once described Bingham as "the [James] Madison of the first section of the Fourteenth Amendment" (*Adamson v. California* 1947, 74). Bingham, who served on the congressional Joint Committee of Fifteen on Reconstruction, drafted all of Section 1 of the Fourteenth Amendment except for the first sentence, which defines citizenship (Thaddeus Stevens appears to have been most responsible for the other sections of the amendment).

Dispute continues about Justice Hugo L. Black's argument that Bingham specifically intended for the privileges and immunities clause and the due process clause of the Fourteenth Amendment to overturn the Court's decision in *Barron v. Baltimore* (1833) and apply all of the Bill of Rights to the states (a process usually referred to as incorporation). There is no doubt that Bingham, who had been a strong foe of slavery and a defender of the principle of equality announced in the Declaration of Independence, was a strong advocate for the rights of African Americans, whom he hoped to protect through this amendment.

Sometimes called "the Cicero of the House" (Beauregard 1989, 97), Bingham was a special judge advocate who led the successful prosecution of the Lincoln assassins, a leader in the unsuccessful impeachment trial of President Andrew Johnson, chairman of the House Judiciary Committee from 1869 to 1873, and a minister plenipotentiary to Japan from 1873 to 1885.

See also *Barron v. Baltimore;* Black, Hugo Lafayette; Incorporation.

For Further Reading:

Adamson v. California, 332 U.S. 46 (1947).

Aynes, Richard L. 2003. "The Continuing Importance of Congressman John A. Bingham and the Fourteenth Amendment." *Akron Law Review* 36: 589–615.

Beauregard, Erving E. 1989. *Bingham of the Hills: Politician and Diplomat Extraordinary.* New York: Peter Lang.

Curtis, Michael Kent. 2003. "John A. Bingham and the Story of American Liberty: The Lost Cause Meets the 'Lost Clause.'" *Akron Law Review* 36: 617–669.

Nabers, Deak. 2006. *Victory of Law: The Fourteenth Amendment, the Civil War, and American Literature, 1852–1867.* Baltimore: The Johns Hopkins University Press.

BIRTHRIGHT CITIZENSHIP AMENDMENT

More than a dozen members of the U.S. House of Representatives have supported an amendment, which California representative Elton Gallegly first introduced in October 1991, to deny citizenship to persons born in the United States whose mothers are not legal residents. If adopted, this amendment, which former California Republican Governor Pete Wilson has supported, would modify the first clause of the Fourteenth Amendment, which specifies that "all persons born or naturalized in the United States, and subject to the jurisdiction thereof, are citizens of the United States and of the State wherein they reside." The Fourteenth Amendment originally was adopted to overturn the unpopular decision in *Scott v. Sandford* (1857), wherein Chief Justice Roger Taney and a majority of the Supreme Court had declared that blacks were not and could not be citizens of the United States whether they were born here or not. At least one attorney, who focuses chiefly on the intent of its authors rather than on actual language of the provision, has argued that the Fourteenth Amendment is already subject to an interpretation that excludes children of illegal aliens from citizenship (Wood 1999).

On the surface, Gallegly's amendment resembles proposals that were introduced earlier in the century by members of Congress from the West Coast and designed to limit citizenship to persons born in the United States of parents who were eligible for citizenship. The primary purpose of these earlier proposals was to restrict property ownership by children born to legal Japanese immigrants living in the United States. At the time, the parents of such children were ineligible for citizenship and were prevented from owning property in the state of California (Musmanno 1929, 180–181).

By contrast, Gallegly's proposal is aimed at the problem of providing government services to illegal immigrants at a time when the nation is facing a rising tide of immigrants. Like earlier Japanese immigrants, most modern immigrants are from non-European nations. Although it appears that legal immigrants generally pay their own way, some argue that illegal immigrants often cost governments more in spending on social programs than the immigrants contribute in taxes (Welch et al. 1993, 9). The costs of such illegal immigration tend to fall disproportionately on states such as Florida, Texas, and California, which have large immigrant populations.

To the extent that illegal immigrants come to the United States in the expectation that their children born here will become citizens, the birthright citizenship amendment might deter immigration by such aliens and any problems they might bring with them. Those who oppose this amendment fear any erosion of the Fourteenth Amendment. They also note that the proposed amendment would treat illegal alien fathers and mothers differently and would penalize children for the status of their parents, over which they have no control (see "Birthright Citizenship Amendment" 1994). In *Plyler v. Doe* (1982), the Supreme Court used such arguments to strike down a Texas law that allowed the public schools to exclude children of illegal aliens. Although the principle may be valid, the Supreme Court might be reluctant to apply such analysis to void an amendment.

One proposed variant of the birthright citizenship amendment, which would have only prospective effect, would deny citizenship to individuals born in the United States who do not have at least one natural parent who is a U.S. citizen or lawful permanent resident. This proposal would classify children of illegal aliens as "permanent lawful residents" who would not be permitted to naturalize until they were 18 years old, and then only contingent upon have no felony conviction on their records. Congress could further require that they have resided in the United States for at least five years (Hsieh 1998).

In a much different vein, Congress adopted a law, entitled the Child Citizenship Act, that went into effect in February 2001. It provided that most children under 18 who have been adopted from abroad by an American parent are now automatic citizens ("Children Adopted Abroad" 2001, 12).

See also Citizenship, Definition of; Fourteenth Amendment.

For Further Reading:

Barnhart, Sara Catherine. 2008. "Second Class Delivery: The Elimination of Birthright Citizenship as a Repeal of 'The Pursuit of Happiness,'" *Georgia Law Review* 42 (Winter): 525–567.

"Children Adopted Abroad Win Automatic Citizenship," 2001. *Migration World Magazine* 19 (March): 12.

Hsieh, Christine J. 1998. "Note: American Born Legal Permanent Residents? A Constitutional Amendment Proposal." *Georgetown Immigration Law Journal* 12 (Spring): 511–529.

Musmanno, M. A. 1929. *Proposed Amendments to the Constitution.* Washington DC: U.S. Government Printing Office.

Schuck, Peter H., and Rogers M. Smith. 1985. *Citizenship without Consent: Illegal Aliens in the American Polity.* New Haven, CT: Yale University Press.

Welch, Susan, et al. 1993. *Understanding American Government.* 2d ed. Minneapolis–St. Paul, MN: West.

Wood, Charles. 1999. "Losing Control of America's Future: The Census, Birthright Citizenship, and Illegal Aliens." *Harvard Journal of Law and Public Policy* 22 (Spring): 465–522.

BLACK, HUGO LAFAYETTE (1886–1971)

President Franklin D. Roosevelt appointed Hugo Black, then a second-term senator from Alabama who had supported both the New Deal and FDR's court-packing plan (but whose one-time membership in the Ku Klux Klan was not revealed until after his confirmation), to the Supreme Court in 1937. Black served there for 34 years, including the entire tenure of the Warren Court. Many of his decisions significantly influenced thinking about the meaning of key constitutional amendments and the role of the Court in interpreting the Constitution.

In *Coleman v. Miller* (1947), Black wrote a concurring opinion stating that procedural questions surrounding the amending process were "political questions" for Congress to resolve.

In *Adamson v. California* (1947), Black articulated the view, repeated in numerous subsequent cases, that John Bingham and other authors of the first section of the Fourteenth Amendment intended for it to incorporate all the provisions of the Bill of Rights and make them applicable to the states. Black saw these and other guarantees as both a floor and a ceiling for the federal judiciary (Yarbrough 1988, 264); although judges were obliged to apply all the provisions of the Bill of Rights to the states, they should wait for the people to amend the Constitution via Article V before going any further. Despite his otherwise broad interpretation of the Fourteenth Amendment, Black argued in a dissenting opinion in *Connecticut General Life Insurance Co. v Johnson* (1938) that the word "person" in that amendment did not, as his colleagues believed, include corporations.

In a number of cases, Black accused his brethren of short-circuiting this democratic process by reading their own views into the document. In *Griswold v. Connecticut* (1965), saying that Article V was "good for our Fathers" and "good enough for me" (*Griswold* 1965, 522), Black rejected the Court's expansive reading of privacy rights in striking down a state birth-control law. In *Harper v. Virginia State Board of Elections* (1966), Black also dissented from a Supreme Court decision invalidating a state poll tax on the basis of a judicial reading of the equal protection clause of the Fourteenth Amendment that was unsupported by an act of Congress: "when a 'political theory' embodied in the Constitution becomes outdated . . . a majority of the Supreme Court are not only without constitutional power but are far less qualified to choose a new constitutional political theory than the people of this country proceeding in the manner provided by Article V" (*Harper* 1966, 678).

Similarly, in *Katz v. United States* (1967), Black dissented from the Court's decision using the Fourth Amendment to forbid warrantless electronic searches. Black doubted that it was the Court's function to "'keep the Constitution up to date' or 'to bring it into harmony with the times'"; the Court was not intended to be "a continuously functioning constitutional convention" (*Katz* 1967, 373).

Black was also known for his view, articulated in *New York Times Co. v. United States* (1971) and elsewhere, that the freedom of speech guaranteed in the First Amendment is absolute. In his view, however, this amendment did not extend full protection to symbolic speech (see Black's dissent in *Tinker v. Des Moines Independent Community School District* [1969]). On another First Amendment issue, Black was a strong advocate of separation of church and state, and he authored the Court's decision in *Engel v. Vitale* (1962) outlawing prayer in public schools and prompting numerous calls for a constitutional amendment.

In *Oregon v. Mitchell* (1970), Black helped precipitate the Twenty-sixth Amendment by ruling that a provision in the 1970 Voting Rights Act Amendments of 1970 lowering the minimum voting age to 18 would apply to federal but not to state elections.

See also *Adamson v. California;* Bingham, John; *Coleman v. Miller; Engel v. Vitale;* First Amendment; Fourteenth Amendment; *Griswold v. Connecticut; Harper v. Virginia State Board of Elections;* Incorporation; *Oregon v. Mitchell;* Twenty-sixth Amendment.

For Further Reading:

Black, Hugo L. 1969. *A Constitutional Faith.* New York: Alfred A. Knopf.

Dunne, Gerald T. 1977. *Hugo Black and the Judicial Revolution.* New York: Simon and Schuster.

Freyer, Tony. 1990. *Hugo L. Black and the Dilemma of American Liberalism.* Glenville, IL: Scott, Foresman.

Griswold v. Connecticut, 381 U.S. 479 (1965).

Newman, Roger K. 1994. *Hugo Black: A Biography.* New York: Pantheon Books.

Yarbrough, Tinsley E. 1988. *Mr. Justice Black and His Critics.* Durham, NC: Duke University Press.

BLACK PANTHERS

While the mainline civil rights groups organized during the 1960s followed Dr. Martin Luther King Jr. in pursuing desegregation through nonviolent means, others responded to continuing discrimination and oppression by heeding Malcolm X's exhortation to defend their rights "by any means necessary" (quoted in Bloom 2000, 84).

African American college students Bobby Seale and Huey Newton founded the Black Panther Party in Oakland, California, in October of 1966. Admirers of revolutionary thinkers and leaders (including Karl Marx, Mao Tsetung, and Che Guevara) from throughout the world, party members, later joined by Eldridge Cleaver, pursued a strategy of "armed self-defense" that led them into frequent and often bloody conflicts with the police. As the party's reputation for militancy spread, new chapters were established in cities throughout the nation.

The Black Panther Party engaged in one of the more bizarre attempts to rewrite the Constitution from September 5 to 7, 1970, when about 6,000 members met at Temple University in Philadelphia in a "Revolutionary People's Convention" (Vile 1991c, 102–104). David Hilliard, the party chief of staff, stated the convention's hope of composing a "constitution that will guarantee and deliver to every American citizen the inviolable human rights to life, liberty and the pursuit of happiness" ("Panthers Plan New Convention" 1971, 503). Clearly, however, the Panthers intended to move beyond these fairly conventional-sounding aims.

The party's founder and minister of defense, Huey Newton, had recently been released from prison, where he had been serving time for the murder of a police officer. His presence at the convention was a drawing card for Easterners to catch a glimpse of him and assess his leadership and speaking abilities (Pearson 1994, 226). However, no new constitution emerged from the Panthers' deliberations, and a subsequent gathering at Howard University in November 1970 was a failure.

Convention discussions centered on a number of subjects, ranging from socialism to women's liberation to human rights (Moore 1970, 1298). The *U.S. News and World Report* identified the primary proposals as:

- Abolishment of present political boundaries; creation of independent, self-governing communities from which political power would flow upward.
- A rotating police force of volunteers, under community control, with community councils, instead of courts, to deal with criminals.
- A national defense force of volunteers, trained in guerilla warfare.
- Free housing, health care, education, and daycare centers for children.
- U.S. support of the Communist Vietcong in South Vietnam and the Communist Pathet Lao in Cambodia; return of Taiwan to Red China; "liberation" of Palestine from "Zionist colonialism." ("Rising Clamor for Black Separatism" 1970, 82)

The Panthers' convention had little success, and by the late 1970s the party dissolved (Jeffries 1998, 118). The convention gives some insight, however, into the political turmoil of the era and shows an attempt to use a fairly traditional tool, the constitutional convention, in the hope of achieving fairly radical changes.

See also Social and Economic Rights.

For Further Reading:

Bloom, Joshua. 2000. "Black Panther Party." In *Civil Rights in the United States*. 2 vols. Edited by Waldo E. Martin Jr. and Patricia Sullivan. New York: Macmillan Reference USA. I: 84–85.

Jeffries, Judson L. 1998. "Black Panther Party." In *The Encyclopedia of Civil Rights in America*. Edited by David Bradley and Shelley Fisher Fishkin. Armond, NY: M. E. Sharpe, Inc.

Moore, Trevor W. 1970. "A Rumbling in Babylon: Panthers Host a Parley." *Christian Century* 87 (28 October): 1296–1300.

"Panthers Plan New Convention." 1971. In *Facts on File Yearbook, 1970*. Vol. 30. New York: Facts on File.

Pearson, Hugh. 1994. *The Shadow of the Panther: Huey Newton and the Price of Black Power in America*. Reading, MA: Addison-Wesley.

"Rising Clamor for Black Separatism." 1970. *U.S. News and World Report* 69 (21 September): 82.

Vile, John R. 1991c. *Rewriting the United States Constitution: An Examination of Proposals from Reconstruction to the Present*. New York: Praeger.

BLAINE AMENDMENT

Modern controversies over prayer and Bible reading in schools date back more than a century, to the time when Catholics, Jews, and others increasingly challenged an unofficial Protestant establishment. These religious minorities objected both to Protestant religious exercises in public schools (readings, for example, from the King James Bible) and to the unavailability of government funding for nonpublic schools.

In 1875, President Ulysses S. Grant delivered a speech advocating an amendment requiring states to fund a system of free public schools and preventing any public funds from being allocated to parochial schools. Representative and former House Speaker James G. Blaine of Maine (the noted orator and unsuccessful Republican presidential nominee in the election of 1884) subsequently introduced an amendment applying the establishment and free exercise clauses of the First Amendment directly to the states and prohibiting public support of parochial schools (H.R. 1, 1875). Blaine, then seeking the Republican nomination for president, appears to have been motivated largely by political concerns (Green 1992, 40–51).

Some modern scholars cite debates over this amendment as evidence that contemporaries did not believe that the Fourteenth Amendment had intended to incorporate the provisions of the Bill of Rights and apply them to the states (A. Meyer 1951; F. O'Brien 1965). Steven Green (1992) has argued, however, that these debates are inconclusive on this point and that participants were more concerned about contemporary religious controversies.

Blaine's proposal stimulated considerable debate, including a proposed amendment by Democratic congressman William O'Brien of Maryland in 1876 forbidding all religious tests and prohibiting ministers from holding public office. Democrats in the House Judiciary Committee accepted Blaine's proposal but weakened it by including a provision that "this article shall not vest, enlarge, or diminish legislative power in the Congress," thus making it declaratory only (Green 1992, 58). This amended version passed the House by a vote of 180 to 7. The Senate deleted the Democratic addition to the amendment. This body, however, added a clause providing that the proposed amendment "shall not be construed to prohibit the reading of the Bible in any school or institution" (cited by Green 1992, 60). This was an apparent reaction to a series of decisions by school boards prohibiting religious instruction and Bible reading in public schools. One such decision had been upheld by the Ohio State Supreme Court in 1872 (Green 1992, 46–47). The Senate vote of 28 to 16 fell four votes shy of the majority needed to send it on to the states (Green 1992, 67), but a number of states adopted versions of the Blaine amendment (E. Larson 1993).

Variations of the Blaine amendment continued to be introduced in Congress throughout the 19th and early 20th centuries; one scholar cited 19 proposals in addition to Blaine's (F. O'Brien 1965, 210). Such proposals were supported by a group called the National League for the Protection of American Institutions (A. Meyer 1951, 944–945). An amendment introduced by Senator Henry Blair of New Hampshire in 1888, although intended to exclude public school teachings of doctrines "peculiar to any sect," would nonetheless have required states to educate children "in virtue, morality, and the principles of the Christian religion" (F. O'Brien 1965, 196). Proposals intended to permit religious exercises in school were stimulated anew by Supreme Court decisions in *Engel v. Vitale* (1962) and *Abington v. Schempp* (1963) relating to prayer and Bible reading in public schools. Proposals for a religious equality amendment have been stimulated by the opinion that religious believers have suffered discrimination and that their free exercise rights have not been fully protected.

See also *Abington v. Schempp; Engel v. Vitale;* First Amendment; Fourteenth Amendment; Prayer in Public Schools; Religious Equality Amendment.

For Further Reading:

Green, Steven K. 1992. "The Blaine Amendment Reconsidered." *American Journal of Legal History* 36 (January): 38–69.

Hamburger, Philip. 2002. *Separation of Church and State.* Cambridge, MA: Harvard University Press.

Klinkhammer, Marie C. 1965. "The Blaine Amendment of 1875." *Catholic Historical Review* 21: 15–49.

Larson, Edward J. 1993. "The 'Blaine Amendment' in State Constitutions." In *The School-Choice Controversy: What Is Constitutional?* ed. James W. Skillen. Grand Rapids, MI: Baker Books.

Meyer, Alfred W. 1951. "The Blaine Amendment and the Bill of Rights." *Harvard Law Review* 64: 939–945.

O'Brien, F. William. 1963. "The Blaine Amendment, 1875–1876." *University of Detroit Law Journal* 41 (December): 137–205.

Symposium: "Separation of Church and States: An Examination of State Constitutional Limits on Government Funding for Religious Institutions." *The First Amendment Law Review,* vol. 2. (Winter) 2003. [This issue has several articles related to the Blaine Amendment.]

BOEHNER V. ANDERSON

John Boehner (R-OH) and other members of Congress cited the belatedly ratified "Madison," or Twenty-seventh Amendment, when challenging two provisions of the Ethics Reform Act of 1989. The first provision provided for a congressional cost of living increase (COLA) to go into effect at the first of each year. The second modified an earlier provision by establishing a citizen board to recommend quadrennial adjustments to congressional salaries to see that they were consistent with those in the private sector.

The Twenty-seventh Amendment provides that "No law, varying the compensation for services of the Senators and Representatives shall take effect until an election of Representatives shall have intervened." In examining the Ethics Reform Act of 1989, U.S. District Judge Stanley Sporkin lauded the law for limiting outside honoraria that members of Congress could receive and essentially depoliticizing the issue of congressional pay. Judge Sporkin found the contention that Congress would have to enact "a separate law for each and every raise, including a COLA" to be "an extremely strained reading of the 27th amendment—a reading for which the plain language of the amendment

provides no support" (*Boehner v. Anderson,* 142). Similarly, he denied that each COLA "constitutes a separate law, which varies Congress' compensation before an election has intervened and which therefore violates the 27th Amendment" (*Boehner v. Anderson,* 143). He noted that "each year the COLA becomes effective by the terms of the 1989 Act; no additional law is necessary. In short, each COLA is not a law and, therefore, is not subject to the requirements of the 27th Amendment" (*Boehner v. Anderson,* 143).

Judge Ruth Bader Ginsburg (subsequently a U.S. Supreme Court justice) wrote the decision for the U.S. Circuit Court for the District of Columbia affirming the lower court opinion. Since the Ethics Reform Law was adopted in 1989 and did not mandate the first COLA increase until 1991, she found that it met the Twenty-seventh Amendment's criterion for an intervening election. She further rejected Boehner's subsequent challenge to the cancellation of the 1994 COLA on the basis that it represented a new argument not considered in the lower court and arguably in conflict with Boehner's stated premise that his pay raise had constituted an "injury" that gave him judicial standing. Because no pay increase had been effected under the quadrennial provision, and none was scheduled prior to 1999, Ginsburg ruled that this provision was not yet ripe for review.

These decisions could arguably call the effectiveness of the Twenty-seventh Amendment into question. They do not directly address the question of the legitimacy of the amendment's belated ratification. First proposed as part of the Bill of Rights in the late 18th century, it was not ratified until 1992.

See also Twenty-seventh Amendment.

For Further Reading:
Boehner v. Anderson, 809 F. Supp. 138 (D.D.C. 1992).

Boehner v. Anderson, 30 F.3d 156 (D.C. Cir. 1994).

Vermeule, Adrian. 2002. "The Constitutional Law of Official Compensation." *Columbia Law Review* 102 (March): 501–538.

BOERNE, CITY OF V. FLORES (1997)

Momentum has grown in recent years for adoption of a Religious Equality Amendment. Proponents believe that such an amendment has been necessitated by a number of decisions by the U.S. Supreme Court, including *City of Boerne v. Flores* (1997).

In 1990 the U.S. Supreme Court issued a decision in *Employment Division v. Smith* in which it decided that a state could deny unemployment benefits to individuals who had broken a state law criminalizing the use of drugs, including peyote, that Smith and a colleague had ingested as part of their religious exercises as members of a Native American church. In previous cases, the Supreme Court had usually required a state to demonstrate a "compelling governmental interest" when a law of general applicability fell with particular force on a religious exercise, but in *Smith,* the Court distinguished such cases by arguing that they had all involved the exercise not simply of freedom of religion but also of related rights. In *Smith,* the Court ruled that states did not need to show a compelling governmental interest in cases where laws of general applicability incidentally burdened religious practices.

Concerned that this new approach did not adequately protect the freedom of religious exercise guaranteed in the First Amendment of the U.S. Constitution, Congress adopted the Religious Freedom Restoration Act (RFRA) of 1993. Justified as an exercise of congressional enforcement authority under Section 5 of the Fourteenth Amendment, RFRA sought to reverse *Smith* by reinstituting the "compelling governmental interest" test in such cases.

When St. Peter Catholic Church in Boerne, Texas, subsequently attempted to expand its facilities, it came into conflict with a zoning ordinance designed to preserve the architectural heritage of the city. Archbishop Flores sought an exemption under the provisions of RFRA. In a ruling that illumines the contemporary Supreme Court's understanding of Section 5 of the Fourteenth Amendment and that has led to renewed calls for a constitutional amendment to do what

RFRA was unable to do, the Supreme Court, in a decision written by Justice Anthony Kennedy, declared RFRA to be unconstitutional.

Reaffirming the *Smith* decision, Justice Kennedy interpreted Section 5 of the Fourteenth Amendment as a "remedial" rather than as a "substantive" power. Citing John Marshall's opinion in *Marbury v. Madison* (1803), which had established judicial review of congressional legislation, Kennedy noted that, if Congress could use Section 5 of the Fourteenth Amendment to redefine the Constitution, "no longer would the Constitution be 'superior paramount law, unchangeable by ordinary means.' It would be on a level with ordinary legislative acts, and, like other acts, . . . alterable when the legislature shall please to alter it" (*Boerne,* 529). Kennedy further argued that remedial legislation must establish both proportionality in addressing problems to which it is directed as well as "congruence between the means adopted and the legitimate end to be achieved" (*Boerne,* 533). By contrast, Kennedy pointed out that the compelling governmental interest test was "the most demanding test known to constitutional law" (*Boerne,* 534). He further noted that:

> The substantial costs RFRA exacts, both in practical terms of imposing a heavy litigation burden on the States and in terms of curtailing their general regulatory power, far exceed any pattern or practice of unconstitutional conduct under the Free Exercise Clause as interpreted in Smith. (*Boerne,* 534)

Kennedy's opinion was joined by Chief Justice Rehnquist and by Justices John Paul Stephens, Clarence Thomas, and Ruth Bader Ginsburg. Antonin Scalia wrote a concurring opinion. Justices Sandra Day O'Connor, Stephen Breyer, and David Souter continued to question the Supreme Court's earlier decision in *Smith,* and Congress subsequently adopted the Religious Land Use and Institutionalized Persons Act of 2000 (RLUIPA) that more specifically focused on federal land use regulations and persons who were institutionalized. The Court upheld a portion of this law in *Cutter v. Wilkinson,* arguably undermining some pressure for a constitutional amendment.

See also First Amendment; Fourteenth Amendment; Religious Equality Amendment.

For Further Reading:

Boerne, City of v. Flores, 521 U.S. 507 (1997).

Cutter v. Wilkinson, 544 U.S. 709 (2005).

Employment Division v. Smith, 494 U.S. 872 (1990).

Greenawalt, Kent. 1998. "Reflections on City of *Boerne v. Flores*: Why Now Is Not the Time for Constitutional Amendment: The Limited Reach of *Boerne v. Flores.*" *William and Mary Law Review* 29 (February): 689–698.

―――. 1998. "Should the Religion Clauses of the Constitution be Amended?" *Loyola of Los Angeles Law Review* 32 (November): 9–25.

BOUNDARY, U.S. AND CANADA

See Minnesota Boundary.

BRICKER AMENDMENT

Although the idea appears to have been the original brainchild of Seattle attorney and one-time head of the American Bar Association, Frank Holmann Richards, Senator John Bricker, a conservative Republican senator from Ohio, spearheaded a drive in the 1950s for a constitutional amendment related to treaties and executive agreements. A substitute for this amendment came only one vote shy of being proposed by the necessary two-thirds majority in the Senate in 1954 (the vote was 60 in favor to 31 against). Following its first introduction in 1951, more than 65 proposals like Bricker's were offered over the next 10 years. By 1954 the issue was described as "a major question of national policy" (Schubert 1954, 258), and proponents of the amendment continued offering amending resolutions into the 1980s.

Support for such amendments can be traced to a number of developments. A Supreme Court decision in *Missouri v. Holland* (1920) had suggested that Congress could exercise powers under the authority of treaties that it did not have under the Constitution. *United States v. Pink* (1942) appeared to magnify further executive powers under executive agreements. Some individuals expressed concern that the United Nations and a series of conventions it had drawn up might be used to undermine state sovereignty, afford fewer protections than Americans were accustomed to under the Bill of Rights, or interfere with purely domestic concerns. Such fears were, in turn, heightened by a California District Court opinion in *Fujii v. California* (1950) that overruled a portion of the state's Alien Land Law on the basis of a provision in the U.N. Charter (Tananbaum 1988, 5).

Supporters of an amendment emphasized different concerns. With a view toward *Missouri v. Holland,* Bricker's original proposal called for repeal of the supremacy clause in Article VI of the Constitution and substitution of a phrase more clearly indicating that treaties had to be made "in pursuance" of the Constitution and not simply under its authority. Bricker's original proposal would also have limited the reach of treaties and executive agreements with regard to individual rights, the form of government, and matters lacking in "mutuality of interest" or those within the U.S. "domestic jurisdiction." In addition, it called for publication of executive agreements and for their termination within six months of the end of a president's term (Tananbaum 1988, 221).

The American Bar Association supported an alternative proposal directed more toward the protection of states' rights. It provided that "a treaty shall become effective as internal law of the United States only through legislation by Congress which it could enact under its delegated powers in the absence of such treaty" (Tananbaum 1988, 222). The proposal by Georgia senator Walter George that the Senate came close to proposing provided both that "a provision of a treaty or other international agreement which conflicts with this Constitution shall not be of any force or effect" and that agreements other than treaties "shall become effective as internal law in the United States only by an act of Congress" (Tananbaum 1988, 225).

President Eisenhower worked belatedly and largely behind the scenes against such proposals—although he publicly supported something known as the Knowland-Ferguson Proposal that would have prohibited treaties from violating the Constitution and would have required a roll-call vote on treaties (Garrett 1972, 195)—which he considered unnecessary and thought might tie his hands in foreign negotiations. Supreme Court decisions in *Rice v. Sioux City Memorial Park* (1955) and *Reid v. Covert* (1957) also allayed some of the concerns that had been raised in earlier cases. In the *Reid* case, Justice Hugo Black stated that "no agreement with a foreign nation can confer power . . . which is free from the restraints of the Constitution" (*Reid v. Covert* 1957, 16).

One scholar on the subject believes that the Bricker controversy alerted Eisenhower to the need to consult Congress on foreign policy matters. This scholar also believes that the controversy was a factor in delaying U.S. ratification of the U.N. Genocide Convention until 1986 (Tananbaum 1988, 218–219). Another scholar has noted that the Bricker controversy presaged some of the controversies during the Vietnam War over the respective powers of the legislative and executive branches in the area of foreign policy (Garrett 1972).

Recent years have witnessed increased American participation in such international organizations as the World Trade Organization (WTO) and in agreements with foreign nations such as those involved in the North American Free Trade Agreement (NAFTA). The latter created a free-trade zone within the United States, Canada, and Mexico, which might later be expanded throughout the hemisphere. Under the Trade Act of 1974, such agreements, which sometimes vest considerable discretion in international boards not directly accountable to the American people, have been given expedited review through the so-called fast track mechanism. This mechanism, which some scholars have compared to an informal constitutional amendment (Ackerman and Golove 1995), substitutes approval by a majority vote of both houses of Congress for a treaty requiring a two-thirds vote in the Senate. Under this arrangement, however, congressional floor debate is truncated, and Congress is limited to an up or down vote (Thomas 2000).

See also *Missouri v. Holland;* Treaties, Ratification of.

For Further Reading:

Ackerman, Bruce, and David Golove. 1995. "Is NAFTA Constitutional?" *Harvard Law Review* 108 (February): 801–929.

Garrett, Stephen A. 1972. "Foreign Policy and the American Constitution: The Bricker Amendment in Contemporary Perspective." *International Studies Quarterly* 16 (June): 187–220.

Nelson, Richards. 2006. "The Bricker Amendment and Congresses Failure to Check the Inflation of the Executive's Foreign Affairs Powers, 1951–1954." *California Law Review* 94 (January): 175–213.

Schubert, Glendon. 1954. "Politics and the Constitution: The Bricker Amendment during 1953." *Journal of Politics* 16 (May): 257–298.

Tananbaum, Duane. 1988. *The Bricker Amendment Controversy: A Test of Eisenhower's Political Leadership.* Ithaca, NY: Cornell University Press.

Thomas, Chantal. 2000. "Constitutional Change and International Government." *Hastings Law Journal* 52 (November): 1–46.

BROWN, JOHN (1800–1859)

John Brown was the fervent abolitionist who led a bloody attack on proslavery settlers in Pottawatomie, Kansas, in May 1856 and on the arsenal at Harpers Ferry, Virginia (now West Virginia), in October 1859. Although he had hoped to encourage a slave revolt by the latter action, he did not succeed in this endeavor, a number of his sons were killed in the raid, and he was subsequently hanged.

Brown and 45 followers held a constitutional convention on May 8, 1858, in Chatham, Ontario. There they voted on a provisional constitution Brown had composed consisting of a preamble and 48 articles. It was designed to create an initial government for the free state that Brown hoped his attack on Harpers Ferry would create (Oates 1970, 243).

The unicameral Congress was to consist of five to ten members serving three-year terms and elected by the persons "connected with the organization" (Fogleson and Rubenstein 1969, 48). The president, vice president, and five members of the Supreme Court were to be selected in similar fashion, with the executive also serving a three-year term, and all subject to impeachment and removal. Members of the three branches were to choose the commander in chief for a three-year term, with a treasurer, secretary of state, secretary of war, and secretary of the treasury chosen in a similar manner. The Constitution addressed recruiting for government posts and for the army and dealt with court-martials, the treatment of prisoners and neutrals, deserters, and captured property.

All persons in the organization were responsible for laboring "for the common good," with prohibitions on "profane swearing, filthy conversation, indecent behavior, or indecent exposure of the person, or intoxication or quarreling" and "unlawful intercourse of the sexes" (Fogleson and Rubenstein 1969, 57). The constitution also called for respecting "the marriage relation" (Brown's own two marriages had resulted in 20 children) and for setting aside Sunday for rest and for "moral and religious instruction and improvement, relief of the suffering, instruction of the young and ignorant, and the encouragement of personal cleanliness" (Fogleson and Rubenstein 1969, 57–58).

Article 46 of Brown's constitution proclaimed its intention to "amend and repeal" rather than dissolve the Union. It further specified that "our flag shall be the same that our fathers fought under in the Revolution" (Fogleson and Rubenstein 1969, 59).

Those who signed the document elected Brown as commander in chief, but the office of president was left vacant after two black nominees both declined to serve (Oates 1970, 246).

See also Abolitionists; Slavery Insurrections.

For Further Reading:

Fogleson, Robert M., and Richard E. Rubenstein. 1969. *Mass Violence in America: Invasion at Harper's Ferry.* New York: Arno Press.

Oates, Stephen B. 1970. *To Purge This Land with Blood: A Biography of John Brown.* New York: Harper and Row.

Renehan, Edward J., Jr. 1995. *The Secret Six: The True Tale of the Men Who Conspired with John Brown.* New York: Crown.

BROWN V. BOARD OF EDUCATION (1954)

Few, if any, 20th-century cases better demonstrate the ability of the Supreme Court to alter current understandings of the Constitution—and thus provide a substitute for constitutional amendment—than this case. Here the Court overturned the doctrine of "separate but equal" that it had sanctioned in *Plessy v. Ferguson* (1896) and declared that segregation would have no place in U.S. public education. This opinion, in turn, sparked both support and opposition, including numerous attempts to trim the power of the Court in succeeding decades.

In delivering the unanimous opinion for the Court, Chief Justice Earl Warren recognized that the intention of those who wrote the Fourteenth Amendment could not be fully ascertained. Instead, he chose to focus on the importance of education in the modern context. Relying in part on contemporary psychological studies, Warren argued that racial segregation generated feelings of inferiority that adversely affected the motivation of minority students to learn (*Brown* 1954, 494).

A companion case, *Bolling v. Sharpe* (1954), extended the prohibition on segregation to the District of Columbia under authority of the due process clause of the Fifth Amendment, which, unlike the Fourteenth Amendment, applied to the national rather than the state governments. In the following year, the Court issued *Brown v. Board of Education II,* in which it declared that local school authorities, subject to the supervision of U.S. district courts, were responsible for seeing that desegregation was implemented "with all deliberate speed" (*Brown II* 1955, 301). Other decisions later applied the desegregation decision in *Brown* to areas outside the field of education.

Initially *Brown* stirred both passionate support and passionate opposition, including numerous amending proposals. Subsequent decisions involving race have led to proposed amendments dealing with affirmative action policies, state control of schools, and school busing.

Few contemporary constitutional scholars disagree with what the Court did in the *Brown* decision, and many believe that the case rectified a fundamental error in constitutional interpretation in the *Plessy* decision. Scholars continue to debate whether the decision can be, or needs to be, squared with the "original intent" of those who wrote and ratified the Fourteenth Amendment (McConnell 1995). The decision also raises the issue of the level of generality by which the Constitution, and its amendments, should be interpreted. Should constitutional interpreters be bound by the original intent of the framers regarding segregation generally, or segregation in schools specifically, or by the framers' and ratifiers' wider intent, or perhaps, in plainer language, as regards "equal protection of the laws"?

Brown proclaimed that education had assumed increased importance in American life. Later decisions, most notably *San Antonio Independent School District v. Rodriguez* (1973), however, refused to declare that education was a "fundamental right" that states had to fund equally for all. A number of state courts have subsequently concluded that their own constitutions require stricter funding standards than the U.S. Supreme Court has attributed to the U.S. Constitution, and some proponents of national constitutional amendments have favored adding one specifically guaranteeing the right to an education.

See also Affirmative Action; Education, Right to; Fourteenth Amendment; *Plessy v. Ferguson;* School Busing; Social and Economic Rights.

For Further Reading:

Kluger, Richard. 1975. *Simple Justice: The History of* Brown v. Board of Education *and Black America's Struggle for Equality.* 2 vols. New York: Alfred A. Knopf.

McConnell, Michael W. 1995. "Originalism and the Desegregation Decisions." *Virginia Law Review* 81 (May): 947–1140.

San Antonio Independent School District v. Rodriguez, 411 U.S. 1 (1973).

Wilkinson, J. Harvie, III. 1979. *From* Brown *to* Bakke: *The Supreme Court and School Integration: 1954–1978.* New York: Oxford University Press.

BUSING

See School Busing.

C

CABINET

The U.S. Constitution does not specifically mention the president's cabinet, but the institution began in the administration of George Washington and consists of the heads of major executive departments. These individuals may also give the president advice, although most modern presidents (and some early presidents like Andrew Jackson, who was known for relying upon his "kitchen cabinet") rely more on their personal staffs for this function. The cabinet has grown from its original three officers—the secretary of state, secretary of treasury, and attorney general—to 15. George W. Bush proposed in June 2002 that the 15th cabinet-level department be created for the Secretary of Homeland Security, headed by former Pennsylvania governor Tom Ridge, whose position was created in the aftermath of the terrorist attacks against the United States of September 11, 2001. Ridge was confirmed in January 2003.

In April 1818, Democratic Representative William Lewis of Virginia introduced an amendment containing provisions, whereby Congress would appoint members of the cabinet and the judiciary, with members of Congress apparently to be excluded from consideration as executive officers. Similarly, Whig representative Joseph Underwood of Kentucky introduced a proposal in 1842 to deprive the president of the power to select certain cabinet officers.

Article I, Section 6 of the U.S. Constitution prevents members of Congress from simultaneously serving as executive officers, and practice dictates that cabinet officers do not appear on the floor of Congress to answer questions. In the 1890s, Gamaliel Bradford argued for a bill introduced by Democratic representative George H. Pendleton of Ohio to allow the former—because the practice is not forbidden by the Constitution, it would not require an amendment (G. Bradford 1891, 1893; Cobb 1924). At about the same time, Republican representatives William Barrett and Ernest Roberts of Massachusetts introduced amendments to enable members of Congress to serve as cabinet officers, an idea that Supreme Court Justice and Harvard law professor Joseph Story had previously advocated (Story 1833, 2:333–337). Curiously, Woodrow Wilson, who had been an early advocate of parliamentary-oriented reforms, nixed an idea proposed by outgoing President William Howard Taft that would have granted cabinet officers nonvoting seats in Congress (Sundquist 1986, 51).

Allowing cabinet officers to hold dual memberships in the cabinet and in Congress would weaken the separation of powers and move the United States closer to a parliamentary system of government, in which cabinet members are regularly selected from the legislature (Lowell 1886). The parliamentary model has been a favorite of those seeking wholesale reform of the U.S. Constitution (Vile 1991c, 157–158) but has also been subject to intense criticism (see Sargentich 1993). Although enabling members of Congress to serve on the cabinet might improve executive liaison with Congress, the pressures on an individual responsible for heading an executive agency and representing constituents from a district or state would be immense.

In the 19th century, at least three members of Congress proposed to give Congress power either to appoint or remove the Secretary of the

Treasury, whose work is closely tied to the congressional power of the purse. In 1998, Texas Representative Ralph Hall introduced an amendment calling for the election of the attorney general, who is a cabinet officer. Other proposals for a new U.S. Constitution, including a number that want to "downsize" existing government or provide for educational reform, have called for the elimination of one or more cabinet posts.

See also Attorney General; Congress, Members' Eligibility for Other Offices; Parliamentary System; Treasury, Department of; Wilson, Woodrow.

For Further Reading:
Bradford, Gamaliel. 1893. "Congress and the Cabinet—II." *Annals of the American Academy of Political and Social Sciences* 4 (November): 289–299.

———. 1891. "Congress and the Cabinet." *Annals of the American Academy of Political and Social Sciences* 4 (November): 404–424.

Cobb, Frank. 1924. "A Twentieth Amendment." In *Cobb of "The World": A Leader in Liberalism,* ed. John L. Heaton. New York: E. P. Dutton.

Lowell, A. Lawrence. 1886. "Ministerial Responsibility and the Constitution." *Atlantic Monthly* 57: 180–193.

Sargentich, Thomas O. 1993. "The Limits of the Parliamentary Critique of the Separation of Powers." *William and Mary Law Review* 34 (Spring): 679–739.

Story, Joseph. 1833. *Commentaries on the Constitution of the United States.* 3 vols. Boston: Hilliard, Gray and Company. Reprint, New York: Da Capo Press 1970.

Sundquist, James L. 1986. *Constitutional Reform and Effective Government.* Washington DC: Brookings Institution.

Vile, John R. 1991. *Rewriting the United States Constitution: An Examination of Proposals from Reconstruction to the Present.* New York: Praeger.

CALHOUN, JOHN C.
(1782–1850)

Along with Henry Clay and Daniel Webster, John C. Calhoun was one of the congressional giants of the early 19th century. Calhoun served as a member of the South Carolina leg-islature (1808–1809), member of the House of Representatives (1811–1817), secretary of war (1817–1825), vice president (1825–1832), secretary of state (1844–1845), and senator from South Carolina (1832–1844, 1845–1850). Despite his ability, his greatness has been somewhat diminished by his strong defense of slavery and of an extreme form of states' rights.

In addition to defending slavery as a positive good, Calhoun was among the South's strongest advocates of the doctrines of nullification and secession, which eventually led to disunion and civil war. In Calhoun's *Disquisition on Government,* he outlined his theory of concurrent majorities, which was intended to provide each major interest or portion of the community with "a concurrent voice in making and executing the laws or a veto on their execution," thus preserving the status quo absent a consensus to change it (Calhoun 1953, 20). Calhoun's central concern was protection of regional interests, particularly slavery. But others have noted that the principle could be extended to others, indeed, even to racial minorities (Kuic 1983).

In his *Discourse on the Constitution and Government of the United States,* Calhoun lavishly praised the constitutional amending process, calling it the "*vis medicatrix* of the system" (Calhoun 1851–1856, 295) and describing it (somewhat counter to James Madison's description in *The Federalist Papers*) as a purely federal mechanism that embodied Calhoun's own view of concurrent majorities. Calhoun also gave the amending process a critical role in his theory of nullification, which would have entrusted states with the power to challenge federal legislation. On occasions when a state questioned the legitimacy of federal power, Calhoun called upon the majority exercising such disputed power to validate its view by adopting a constitutional amendment. Even here, however, Calhoun preserved the states' right to challenge amendments that exceeded implicit limits on the constitutional amending process (Vile 1992, 86).

During the nullification crisis of the 1820s and early 1830s, in which Calhoun opposed higher federal tariffs and challenged President Andrew Jackson's assertion of federal authority, Calhoun advocated calling a constitutional convention to resolve the controversy. He appeared to anticipate a body whose power "was much broader than that actually set forth in the exact language of the amending article" (Pullen 1948, 45).

Late in life, Calhoun came to fear that the amending process might be used, as it later would be in the Thirteenth Amendment, to abolish the institution of slavery, which he had defended. Accordingly, in his *Discourse,* Calhoun advocated creating a dual executive representing the North and the South, with each executive required to approve acts of congressional legislation before they became law (Calhoun 1851–1856, 392). Ironically, the very amending supermajorities that Calhoun praised were an obstacle to such a proposal.

A series of proposals introduced by Ohio's Democratic representative Clement Vallandigham in February 1861 and designed to forestall war appear to share features of Calhoun's thinking. One part of this proposal would have divided the nation into four sections, and another would have required a majority from all sections if a vote were so demanded by one-third or more of the senators.

Specifically distinguishing his own federalism-preserving proposal from that of Calhoun, a graduating law school student introduced what he described as a States' Repeal Amendment in 1996. It sought to protect the values of the Tenth Amendment and of federalism by granting states the power, if exercised within two years after the adoption of federal legislation, to repeal such laws by either two-thirds of the state legislatures or by conventions held within two-thirds of the states (O'Brien 1996).

For Further Reading:

Calhoun, John C. 1953. *A Disquisition on Government and Selections from the Discourse.* Edited by C. Gordon Post. Indianapolis, IN: Bobbs-Merrill. [Originally published as part of *The Works of John C. Calhoun.* Edited by Richard K. Crallé. New York: D. Appleton and Company, 1851–1856.]

———. 1851–1856. *The Works of John C. Calhoun.* Edited by Richard K. Crallé. New York: D. Appleton and Company. Reprint, New York: Russell and Russell, 1968.

Coit, Margaret L. 1961. *John C. Calhoun: American Portrait.* Boston: Houghton Mifflin.

Kuic, Vukan. 1983. "John C. Calhoun's Theory of the 'Concurrent Majority.'" *American Bar Association* 69: 482–486.

Niven, John. 1988. *John C. Calhoun and the Price of Union: A Biography.* Baton Rouge: Louisiana State University Press.

O'Brien, Aaron J. 1996. "States' Repeal: A Proposed Constitutional Amendment to Reinvigorate Federalism." *Cleveland State Law Review* 44: 547–576.

Pullen, William R. 1948. *Applications of State Legislatures to Congress for the Call of a National Constitutional Convention, 1788–1867.* Master's thesis, University of North Carolina at Chapel Hill.

Read, James H. 2009. *Majority Rule versus Consensus: The Political Thought of John C. Calhoun.* Lawrence: University Press of Kansas.

Vile, John R. 1992. *The Constitutional Amending Process in American Political Thought.* New York: Praeger.

Wood, W. Kirk. 2008. *Nullification, A Constitutional History, 1776–1833,* Vol. 1: *James Madison, Not the Father of the Constitution.* Lanham, MD: University Press of America.

CAMPAIGN CONTRIBUTIONS AND EXPENDITURES

Members of Congress introduced a number of amendments calling for congressional regulation of campaign contributions and expenditures in the 1920s. A proposal introduced by Democrat Thomas Rubey of Missouri in 1926 demonstrates the difficulty of overly specific regulation in this ever-changing area. It would have excluded from office senators who had knowingly authorized the expenditure of more than $10,000 or representatives who had authorized more than $5,000 for their nomination and election (H.J. Res. 279).

Members of Congress introduced numerous laws regulating campaign contributions and expenditures in the 1970s, 1980s, and 1990s. Such laws typically call for limits on contributions or campaign expenditures or disclosures of contributions made by individuals or political action committees. The Supreme Court examined provisions of the Federal Election Campaign Act of 1971 (subsequently amended in 1974) in *Buckley v. Valeo* (1976) for conformity with the First Amendment. In this case, the Court upheld congressionally imposed requirements for disclosure of campaign contributions as well as limits on the amount of money that an individual could contribute to another's campaign as reasonable efforts to combat corruption or its appearance. The Court, however, struck down limits on the monies that wealthy individuals such as Ross Perot and Steve Forbes could contribute to their own campaigns as well as congressionally imposed limits on overall spending. The Court did accept limits on the spending of presidential candidates who had voluntarily accepted such campaign limits in exchange for public funding. The Court ruled that other limits on personal expenditures or campaign spending interfered with free speech rights guaranteed under the First Amendment. The Supreme Court effectively reaffirmed the Buckley precedent in *Nixon v. Shrink Missouri Government PAC* (2000), when it ruled that states had similar rights to regulate the size of campaign contributions to candidates. The majority opinion was written by Justice David Souter and joined by five other justices. Justice Anthony Kennedy favored overruling *Buckley*'s distinction between campaign expenditures and contributions to permit the states or Congress to attempt to regulate both (thereby lessening the perceived need for any constitutional amendment permitting this), whereas Justices Clarence Thomas and Antonin Scalia thought that Buckley had provided inadequate reasoning for limiting the contributions of individuals to candidates running for office.

The 1980s and 1990s brought a number of new proposals for constitutional amendments permitting either state or congressional regulation in this area. Some such proposals were aimed directly at *Buckley v. Valeo*. Thus, a House Joint Resolution (No. 11), introduced in 1991, specified that campaign expenditures are not to be considered a form of protected speech under the First Amendment. A proposal introduced by Iowa Republican representative James A. Leach in February 2001 would specifically restrict monies that an individual could spend on his or her own campaign.

There is frequent criticism of the rising costs of political campaigns, the need for officeholders to engage in constant fundraising, and the possibility that officeholders are improperly influenced by campaign contributions. Still, previous legislation in this area has often spawned loopholes and proved ineffective. Moreover, expenditure limits might further advantage incumbents, who already have significant advantages when running for reelection. President George W. Bush reluctantly signed a campaign spending law, the McCain-Feingold Campaign Reform Act, or Bipartisan Campaign Reform Act (BCRA) of 2002. This law is designed to limit so-called soft money expenditures that are spent on behalf of a candidate but not under the candidate's direction. The Supreme Court narrowly upheld the act in *McConnell v. Federal Election Commission,* 540 U.S. 93 (2003). In *Randall v. Soprrell,* 548 U.S. 230 (2006), by contrast, it overturned stringent spending and contributions limits that Vermont had imposed on candidates for state office.

John Francis Lee of Corpus Christi, Texas, who has identified himself in e-mail correspondence as "an ordinary private citizen of the USA, in despair over the present corrupt state of the American political class" (private e-mail correspondence with author dated June 25, 2002) has posted a proposal for "Amendment 28" on the Internet. His proposal has nine sections and is aimed, in part, at the decision in *Buckley v. Valeo.* The first, and most important, would prohibit candidates for elected office from accepting or soliciting "campaign funds except individually, from those citizens of the United States eligible to vote for the office in question" (Lee, http://www.28amen. org). A second section would limit the value of any single contribution to the equivalent of 40 hours of work at minimum wage or $100. Section 3 would impose similar limits on individuals' contributions to their own campaigns. Section 4 would limit solicitations to the "calendar year of the contested election." Section 5 would require recording and reporting requirements for all contributions, and Section 6 would apply to primary and related elections. Section 7 would distribute all unspent campaign funds to the U.S. Treasury, Section 8 would exempt a candidate's expenditures for "personal expenses such as for food, clothing, transportation, or shelter," and Section 9 would provide congressional enforcement power including imprisonment and fines.

The complexity of the subject appears to breed complex remedies. Thus, Neal Rechtman has appended a proposed amendment, with five sections, one of which he divides into 10 subsections, to his novel *The 28th Amendment,* which he published in 2007, and which he hoped to implement. The first section would provide that "all direct costs and expenses" of U.S. senatorial and presidential campaigns "shall be paid out of public funds," and Section 2 would prohibit private use of nonpublic funds. Section 3 would entrust the states and Congress with acquiring and allocating such funds. Section 4, with its 10 subsections, would further establish "minimum requirements" for state and congressional regulations. Subdivision 7 would limit such elections to "no more than 100 days." Section 5 would impose a 25-year ratification deadline on the amendment (2007, 258–260).

For Further Reading:

Alexander, Herbert E. 1992. *Financing Politics: Money, Elections and Political Reform,* 4th ed. Washington DC: Congressional Quarterly Press.

Bingham, Jonathan. 1986. "Democracy or Plutocracy? The Case for a Constitutional Amendment to Overturn *Buckley v. Valeo.*" *Annals of American Political and Social Sciences* 486 (July): 103–114.

Lee, John Francis. 2002. "Amendment 28," http://www.28thamen.org/. Accessed June 21, 2002.

Limitations of Expenditures in Elections. 18 February 1990. Printed Hearings. Senate.

Nixon v. Shrink Missouri Government PAC, 528 U.S. 377 (2000).

Rechtman, Neal. *The 28th Amendment.* Minneapolis, MN: Bascom Hill Publishing Group.

Sorauf, Frank J. 1988. *Money in American Elections.* Glenview, IL: Scott, Foresman. http://www.Amendment-28.com.

CAPITAL PUNISHMENT

The issue of governmentally imposed death penalties is highly emotional. Fundamental moral values, assessments of the deterrent value of such punishments, and judgments as to whether the death penalty impacts certain groups in a discriminatory fashion are all likely to shape individual attitudes.

The Fifth and Fourteenth Amendments specify that no person shall be "deprived of life, liberty, or property, without due process of law." Taken together with the Fifth Amendment requirement of a grand jury in cases of "capital" crimes, such evidence is fairly conclusive that the American founders did not intend to outlaw the death penalty. Still, the death penalty is subject to the provision in the Eighth Amendment against "cruel and unusual punishments." Moreover, some scholars believe that the Eighth Amendment ought to be interpreted in light of evolving moral standards that, throughout most of the world, have led to the abolition of the death penalty (see the dissent of Justice Arthur Goldberg to a denial of certiorari in *Rudolph v. Alabama,* 375 U.S. 889 [1963]). Still, despite massive efforts to overturn the death penalty (Epstein and Kobylka 1992), prior to 1968, the Supreme Court had never invalidated a death penalty on such grounds (White 1991, 4).

The first proposed constitutional change in the death penalty appears to have been in 1901, when Pennsylvania republican Congressman Henry Cassel proposed the penalty for destruction of U.S. property; he also proposed deportation or lifetime imprisonment for members of anarchical societies. In the 1940s, Democratic representative Walter Huber proposed abolishing the death penalty for all crimes other than treason. New York representative Adam Clayton Powell proposed abolition of the death penalty in 1961, and his proposal was followed later in the decade by a number of others.

By far the largest number of amendments proposed in relation to capital punishment have called for permitting states to impose this penalty. Some proposals have also called for a federal death penalty in cases of treason or air piracy. Most proposals to uphold state impositions of the death penalty were prompted by the Supreme Court's decision in *Furman v. Georgia* (1972), where it had decided that the death penalty, as states then administered it, was too arbitrary, and hence unconstitutional. States rushed to adopt new laws.

By the time the Court rendered its next significant decision on the death penalty in *Gregg v. Georgia* (1976), 34 states had passed death penalty laws, and Congress had adopted such a penalty for cases of air piracy. In *Gregg*, the Court upheld the validity of the death penalty in cases in which there was a bifurcated trial that separated the decision on guilt or innocence from the decision on a penalty and when aggravating and mitigating circumstances were considered. In a companion case, *Woodson v. North Carolina,* the Court reversed a mandatory death penalty for first-degree murder cases.

The death penalty remains the subject of intense political debate, heightened by fears that, in some states, the penalty, which is irrevocable, may have been applied to individuals who were innocent. The Court continues to hear cases involving the degree of discretion to be awarded to juries in death penalty cases and the number of appeals that defendants may file in such cases. Few justices appear inclined to accept the views advocated by former Justices Thurgood Marshall, William Brennan, and Harry Blackmun that such a penalty violates the cruel and unusual punishment clause per se, but recent Supreme Court decisions in *Adkins v. Virginia* (2002) and *Roper v. Simmons* (2005) have prohibited application of the penalty to individuals who were retarded or to individuals who committed crimes prior to the age of 18.

In 2008, the Supreme Court issued a decision in the case of *Kennedy v. Louisiana,* deciding that a state could not execute an individual for the rape of a minor (in this case, an 8-year-old stepdaughter) that did not result in her death. The previous month, Representative Paul C. Broun of Georgia introduced amendments to provide either for the death penalty or for castration of individuals who were convicted of the rape of a child under the age of 16. Representative Steve Chabot proposed an amendment providing for capital punishment for such offenses the day after the Court issued its decision in Kennedy.

By contrast, Representative Henry Gonzalez, a Mexican American Democrat from Texas, proposed in 1994 eliminating the death penalty completely.

See also Eighth Amendment; Fifth Amendment; Fourteenth Amendment.

For Further Reading:

Barone, Michael, and Grant Ujifusa. 1994. *The Almanac of American Politics 1994.* Washington DC: National Journal.

Epstein, Lee, and Joseph F. Kobylka. 1992. *The Supreme Court and Legal Change: Abortion and the Death Penalty.* Chapel Hill: University of North Carolina Press.

Meltsner, Michael. 1974. *Cruel and Unusual: The Supreme Court and Capital Punishment.* New York: William Morrow.

White, Welsh S. 1991. *The Death Penalty in the Nineties: An Examination of the Modern System of Capital Punishment.* Ann Arbor: University of Michigan Press.

CASCOT SYSTEM FOR SOCIAL CONTROL OF TECHNOLOGY

See Marduke, P. G.

CATT, CARRIE LANE CHAPMAN (1859–1947)

Carrie Lane Chapman Catt was a former teacher and school superintendent who survived the deaths of two husbands to be a major force in the second generation of leadership in the movement for women's suffrage. This movement culminated in the ratification of the Nineteenth Amendment.

In 1889, Catt was elected secretary of the Iowa Woman Suffrage Association. In 1895, she chaired the National Organization Committee of the National American Woman Suffrage Association (NAWSA); in 1900, she succeeded Susan B. Anthony as president of that organization, serving until 1904. She also served as president from 1915 to 1920, when the Nineteenth Amendment (also called the Susan B. Anthony Amendment) was ratified. Catt was a strong organizer with a determined "faith in God's eternal law for the evolution of the race" (quoted in

Fowler 1986, 57). Before her reelection as NAWSA president, Catt was active in the International Woman Suffrage Alliance as well as in the New York State Woman Suffrage Party. Catt's decision as NAWSA president "to concentrate on a constitutional amendment rather than proceeding state by state" (Fowler 1986, 30)—as many southern suffragette advocates who favored states' rights wanted (see Wheeler 1993)—is often credited with resulting in the ratification of the Anthony Amendment.

After states ratified the Nineteenth Amendment, Catt continued to be active in a number of concerns, including the League of Women Voters, which she founded in 1920, and several organizations devoted to world peace. Catt also helped organize the Woman's Centennial Congress of 1940.

See also Anthony, Susan Brownell; Nineteenth Amendment.

For Further Reading:

Fowler, Robert B. 1986. *Carrie Catt: Feminist Politician.* Boston: Northeastern University Press.

Wheeler, Margorie S. 1993. *New Women of the New South: The Leaders of the Woman Suffrage Movement in the Southern States.* New York: Oxford University Press.

Congress currently interprets these provisions so as to include both legal and illegal aliens, giving some extra representation to states with large populations of illegal aliens and also making them eligible for federal funds based on population formulas. At least one attorney, who points out that illegal aliens can be legally deported at any time and thus lack the stability of other state residents, has argued that Congress already has the power, which he thinks it should exercise, to authorize the Census Bureau to exclude illegal aliens from census counts. He has further argued that, if the courts do not accept such an interpretation, which is based more on what he considers to be the original intent of the framers of the constitutional provisions than on the word "persons," he favors a constitutional amendment to exclude such illegal aliens from the count (Wood 1999). Several members of Congress have also proposed such an amendment.

See also Birthright Citizenship Amendment; Congress, Representation in; Immigration, Illegal; Three-Fifths Clause.

For Further Reading:

Wood, Charles. 1999. "Losing Control of America's Future: The Census, Birthright Citizenship, and Illegal Aliens," *Harvard Journal of Law and Public Policy* 22 (Spring): 465–522.

CENSUS

Although each state is represented equally in the Senate, representation in the U.S. House of Representatives is based on population. Article I, Section 2 of the Constitution provides that representation in the House shall be based on an "enumeration," or census, conducted every 10 years. Section 2 of the Fourteenth Amendment eliminated the notorious three-fifths clause (by which "such other persons," namely slaves, had been counted as three-fifths of a person for purposes of representation and taxation), and further specified that "Representatives shall be apportioned among the several States according to their respective numbers, counting the whole number of persons in each State, excluding Indians not taxed."

CHANDLER V. WISE (1939)

Chandler v. Wise was a companion case to *Coleman v. Miller* (1939). Taxpayers, citizens, and voters had challenged Kentucky's ratification of the child labor amendment. They argued that it should be voided because of its prior rejection by the legislature and a majority of other states and because it had not been ratified within a reasonable time, a requirement seemingly mandated in *Dillon v. Gloss* (1921). They sought a court order requiring that the state governor, who had certified and forwarded the amendment before becoming aware of the suit, notify the secretary of state that Kentucky's ratification was invalid.

The Supreme Court rejected this request by a 7-to-2 decision written by Chief Justice Hughes, with Justices Black and Douglas concurring and Justices McReynolds and Butler dissenting. Consistent with the decision in *Coleman v. Miller,* the majority decided that "after the Governor of Kentucky had forwarded the certification of the ratification of the amendment to the Secretary of State of the United States there was no longer a controversy susceptible of judicial determination" (*Chandler v. Wise* 1939, 477–478).

See also Child Labor Amendment; *Coleman v. Miller;* Ratification of Amendments; Time Limits on Amendments.

For Further Reading:
Chandler v. Wise, 307 U.S. 474 (1939).

CHILD LABOR AMENDMENT

Throughout history, children have worked alongside their parents. Industrialization and the accompanying rise of manufacturing and mining, however, created situations in which children often worked long hours in hazardous and unhealthy circumstances without parental supervision and protection and in circumstances that precluded adequate time for them to receive an education. By 1900, "one child in six between the age of ten and fifteen was gainfully employed, and there were more than 1,750,000 child laborers in America" (S. Wood 1968, 3). Many of the reform organizations associated with the Progressive movement coalesced around opposition to child labor; the most effective organization, the National Child Labor Committee (NCLC), was established in April 1904.

Initially, this committee and other organizations focused on reform at the state level, but despite successes in many states, the resulting legislation was not uniform and was especially weak in the South. There, children were frequently employed in the textile industry, and weak regulations depressed adult wages and gave southern manufacturers a labor advantage.

By 1912, the NCLC had concluded that national legislation was needed. A number of Supreme Court decisions, among them *Champion v. Ames* (a 1903 case upholding congressional powers to regulate interstate transportation of lottery tickets), suggested that such powers were within congressional authority. In 1914, at least one member of Congress wanted to proceed instead by constitutional amendment.

In 1916, Congress passed the Keating-Owen bill, attempting to discourage child labor by prohibiting for 30 days the interstate transportation of goods made by companies employing children under the age of 14 or violating standards set for the employment of children between ages 14 and 16. President Woodrow Wilson reconsidered his earlier constitutional reservations and encouraged the passage of and signed this bill, which has been described as "the crowning achievement of progressivism" (S. Wood 1968, 78).

Progressive hopes were dashed in *Hammer v. Dagenhart* (1918), when the Supreme Court declared in a 5-to-4 decision written by Justice William Rufus Day that the Keating Owen bill violated the liberty of contract, which the Court associated with the Fifth and Fourteenth Amendments. With his reasoning called into serious question by Justice Oliver Wendell Holmes's vigorous dissenting opinion, Day attempted to distinguish between the congressional regulation of items that were in themselves harmful and the regulation of those that were not. The Court also viewed the law as an unconstitutional regulation of manufacturing rather than as a legitimate exercise of commerce power. The decision has been called "a breach—not a temporary breach—in constitutional interpretation that signaled return, for almost a generation, to conservative jurisprudence" (S. Wood 1968, 182).

Although several congressmen proposed a constitutional amendment to reverse this decision, a majority settled instead on an amendment to the Revenue Act of 1919 that leveled a 10-percent tax on goods produced by child labor. In an 8-to-1 decision written by Chief Justice William Howard Taft (*Bailey v. Drexel Furniture Company* [1922]), the Court subsequently struck down that law too, arguing that the provisions were designed as a penalty rather than a tax and that they unfairly impinged on state police powers in violation of federal principles, especially the Tenth Amendment.

Samuel Gompers, who headed the American Federation of Labor, subsequently called a meeting that organized the Permanent Conference for the Abolition of Child Labor. Congress in turn proposed the child labor amendment in 1924 by a vote of 197 to 69 in the House and 61 to 23 in the Senate. Omitting references to women, which some proposals had included, it read as follows:

> Section 1. The Congress shall have power to limit, regulate, and prohibit the labor of persons under 18 years of age. Section 2. The power of the several States is unimpaired by this article except that the operation of state laws shall be suspended to the extent necessary to give effect to legislation enacted by this Congress (Grimes 1978, 102).

By 1924, however, the American labor movement was weak, Progressive sentiment was waning, and there was widespread disappointment with the Eighteenth Amendment's attempt to enact national alcoholic prohibition. The proposed child labor amendment also faced strong opposition. In what one scholar identified as "an instructive, almost eerie, parallel with the ERA [Equal Rights Amendment]" (Mansbridge 1986, 31), this waning commitment to reform was combined with concerns as diverse as states' rights, parental control over children, the rights of private religious schools, and communist influence. Such fears were fanned by opposition groups such as the American Bar Association; the Sentinels of the Republic; a publication known as *Woman Patriot,* which had previously opposed women's suffrage; the *Southern Textile Bulletin,* edited by David Clark; and southern industrial leaders (Trattner 1970, 170–174). Some believe that the amendment might have had a better chance of adoption had it set the age for child labor at 16 rather than at 18 and that the word "employment" might have seemed less threatening than "labor" to those who were concerned that the amendment might give the federal government undue influence over life on the farm or life within individual households (Aldous 1997).

As 1925 ended, only four states had ratified and 19 had rejected the proposed amendment (Grimes 1978, 103). The tide seemed to turn with the coming of the New Deal. Some states that had previously rejected the amendment now reversed themselves, an action that was challenged in the courts. In *Coleman v. Miller* (1939) the Supreme Court ruled that the validity of such appeals, as well as the issue of whether they had come within a reasonable time, were "political questions" for Congress to resolve. Eventually, 28 states ratified the amendment.

In the meantime, child labor provisions were incorporated in regulations adopted through the National Industrial Recovery Act, a law subsequently invalidated in the 1935 decision in *Schechter Poultry Corp. v. United States* (Trattner 1970, 190–200). Child labor provisions were subsequently added to the Fair Labor Standards Act of 1938 and were upheld in *United States v. Darby Lumber Co.* (1941), when the Supreme Court explicitly overturned *Hammer v. Dagenhart* and declared that it would no longer be bound by earlier restrictive interpretations of the Fifth and Tenth Amendments. As an amendment issue, child labor has subsequently been moot.

See also *Coleman v. Miller;* Eighteenth Amendment; Equal Rights Amendment; Fifth Amendment; Fourteenth Amendment; Tenth Amendment.

For Further Reading:

Aldous, Joan. 1997. "The Political Process and the Failure of the Child Labor Amendment." *Journal of Family Issues* 18 (January): 71–92.

Davidson, Elizabeth H. 1939. *Child Labor Legislation in the Southern Textile States.* Chapel Hill: University of North Carolina Press.

Freedman, Russell. 1994. *Lewis Hine and the Crusade against Child Labor.* New York: Clarion Books.

Grimes, Alan P. 1978. *Democracy and the Amendments to the Constitution.* Lexington, MA: Lexington Books.

Mansbridge, Jane J. 1986. *Why We Lost the ERA.* Chicago: University of Chicago Press.

Report on the Condition of Women and Children as Wage Earners. 1910–1913. U.S. Department of Labor. 19 vols. Washington DC: U.S. Government Printing Office.

Trattner, Walter I. 1970. *Crusade for the Children: A History of the National Child Labor Committee and Child Labor Reform in America.* Chicago: Quadrangle Books.

Wood, Stephen B. 1968. *Constitutional Politics in the Progressive Era: Child Labor and the Law.* Chicago: University of Chicago Press.

CHISHOLM V. GEORGIA (1793)

This important case from the pre-Marshall Supreme Court was the first such decision overturned by an amendment, in this case the Eleventh. At issue was whether a citizen of another state—here, the executor of the estate of a Charleston, South Carolina, merchant from whom Georgia had purchased supplies in 1777 but whom it had not paid—could sue a state without its consent. Asserting state sovereignty, Georgia refused even to argue its case.

The decision was a seriatim decision, with each justice writing a separate opinion, in which all the justices (Blair, Wilson, Cushing, and Jay) except Iredell agreed. The majority decided that, under the general principles and structures of the Constitution and the specific language of Article III (which extended judicial power to controversies "between a State and Citizens of another State"), a state was subject, both as a defendant and as a plaintiff, to federal judicial jurisdiction. Justice Wilson's opinion was an especially far-reaching discussion of how the U.S. Constitution recognized the people, rather than rulers or governments, as sovereign. However, the Court's ruling contradicted explicit assurances that the Federalists had given the Anti-Federalists during debates over the ratification of the Constitution (Mason and Stephenson 2002, 157).

Although not dealing directly with the constitutionality of a federal law, this case clearly anticipated the exercise of judicial review prior to John Marshall's decision in *Marbury v. Madi-*

son (1803). Justice Iredell thus noted that an act of Congress exceeding constitutional authority would be void "because it would be inconsistent with the Constitution, which is a fundamental law paramount to all others, which we are not only bound to consult but sworn to observe" (*Chisholm v. Georgia* 1793, 433).

Justice Cushing seemed to anticipate, if not invite, an amendment when he noted that "if the Constitution is found inconvenient in practice in this or any other particular, it is well that a regular mode is pointed out for amendment" (*Chisholm v. Georgia* 1793, 468). Subsequent decisions interpreting the Eleventh Amendment, most notably *Hans v. Louisiana* (1890), confirmed the understanding of state sovereign immunity advocated by the dissenters in *Chisholm* rather than that advocated by the majority. In recent years, the Eleventh Amendment has begun to figure more prominently in U.S. Supreme Court decision-making. Thus, in *Seminole Tribe of Florida v. Florida* (1996), the Court used the Amendment to reject a suit brought by Native American Seminoles, who charged that the state of Florida had refused to negotiate with them in good faith to authorize casino gambling on their reservations.

See also Eleventh Amendment; Federalists; Supreme Court Decisions Reversed by Constitutional Amendments.

For Further Reading:

Chisholm v. Georgia, 2 U.S. (2 Dall.) 419 (1793).

Mason, Alpheus T., and Donald G. Stephenson Jr. 2007. *American Constitutional Law: Introductory Essays and Selected Cases.* 15th ed. Upper Saddle River: Pearson/PrenticeHall.

Mathis, Doyle. 1967. "*Chisholm v. Georgia:* Background and Settlement." *Journal of American History* 54: 19–29.

Seminole Tribe of Florida v. Florida, 517 U.S. 44 (1996).

CHRISTIAN AMENDMENT

Unless one counts the reference to "the Year of our Lord one thousand seven hundred and eighty-seven" that is sometimes appended to Article VII of the U.S. Constitution, the document contains no direct reference to God. Instead, a provision in Article VI of the Constitution prohibits any "religious Test" as a condition of office, and the First Amendment both prohibits the "establishment" of religion and of guarantees of its "free exercise."

The Reformed Presbyterian Church, whose roots were in the Scottish Covenant tradition, considered the absence of a specific reference to, and acknowledgment of, God to be a fatal flaw. Members of this denomination accordingly refused to participate in voting or holding office. Some members participated in the War of 1812, however, and a group of "New Side" Reformers (who believed that they should support the government under the Constitution) eventually split from the "Old Side" Reformers in 1833. The Reformed Presbyterian Church remained a small denomination, and it does not appear to have significantly influenced public opinion in the nation's early years.

As the controversy over slavery developed and intensified, however, many abolitionists also began to denounce the Constitution as a flawed document. Although abolitionists typically regarded the Constitution's acquiescence in slavery rather than its failure to acknowledge God as its fatal weakness, the two critiques often merged. Reformed Presbyterians viewed the Constitution's acquiescence in slavery as a logical consequence of its failure to acknowledge the Almighty.

Ironically, when the Confederate states drafted their constitution, they rewrote their preamble specifically to invoke "the favor and guidance of Almighty God" (DeRosa 1991, 135). For their part, in 1859, the Reformed Presbyterians had passed their first resolution specifically calling on the Union to acknowledge God. Typical of many subsequent proposals, their amendment called for

1. An express acknowledgment of the being and authority of God. 2. An acknowledgment of submission to the authority of Christ. 3. That it should recognize the paramount obligation of God's law, contained in the Scriptures of the Old and New Testaments. 4. That it may be rendered, in all its

principles and provisions, clearly and unmistakably adverse to the existence of any form of slavery within the national limits. (Jacoby 1984, 55–56).

In February 1863, a convention composed of members of a number of religious denominations met in Xenia, Ohio. It supported a proposal by Presbyterian layman John Alexander for a constitutional amendment to acknowledge "the rulership of Jesus Christ and the supremacy of the divine law" (Borden 1979, 159). The National Association to Secure the Religious Amendment of the Constitution subsequently chose Alexander as its first president. The *Christian Statesman* was the official journal of this organization, which was later renamed the National Reform Association. One of the association's most prominent members was Judge William Strong, who later served on the Supreme Court from 1870 to 1880, although it was Justice David Josiah Brewer who, in *Church of the Holy Trinity v. United States,* 143 U.S. 457, 471 (1982), specifically identified the United States as "a Christian nation" (see Green 1999).

The National Reform Association held conventions, presented petitions, published and distributed literature, and otherwise pressed for an amendment. The association received a diplomatic but noncommittal reply when it met with President Lincoln in February 1864. The association's mission was aided both by the soul-searching that the Civil War occasioned and by Lincoln's use of religious concepts in explaining and justifying the war.

The movement for a Christian amendment had its greatest prominence in the period from 1872 to 1875. One historian noted that during this time there were "a striking number of conflicts which raised fears that the historic Protestant basis of American society and government was being lost" (Jacoby 1984, 290). The period was also notable for support for the Blaine Amendment, which would have prohibited state aid to parochial schools, often administered by and associated with Roman Catholics.

In 1876, proponents of the Christian Amendment presented petitions with over 35,000 signatures to the House of Representatives. In that same year, the National Reform Association succeeded in keeping the Centennial Exposition from opening on Sunday. By then, however, the association faced increasing opposition from individuals who feared that an amendment recognizing God or Jesus might undermine the liberty of non-Christians and nonbelievers that was guaranteed by the establishment clause of the First Amendment. The association also appears to have somewhat diluted its own effectiveness by endorsing other causes with Christian backing, including the rising temperance movement that eventually resulted in the adoption of the Eighteenth Amendment.

Since 1947, more than 55 proposals in Congress have called for variations of the Christian Amendment. Sponsors have included Republican congressman, and later independent candidate for president in 1980, John Anderson. Modern proposals may have been stimulated in part by contemporary Supreme Court decisions relative to prayer and Bible reading in the public schools, but there have been far more calls for amendments specifically designed to reverse these decisions than to recognize God in the Constitution.

The National Reform Association dissolved in 1945, but the National Association of Evangelicals (NAE) subsequently took up its cause. The NAE supported an amendment under which "this nation devoutly recognizes the authority and law of Jesus Christ, Savior and Ruler of all nations, through whom are bestowed the blessings of Almighty God" (Borden 1979, 167). The NAE later supported a version of the Religious Equality Amendment that mentions God but is chiefly concerned with guaranteeing religious liberty.

Some individuals, including the Christian Reconstructionists, believe that the current U.S. Constitution is already predicated upon Christian principles, a view that seems to be widely shared by Americans who have found it difficult to accept Supreme Court decisions relative to prayer and other religious exercises in public schools. Thus, the 2000 Platform of a group known as the Constitution Party begins its preamble by acknowledging God and solemnly declaring "that the foundation of our political position and moving principle of our political activity is our full submission and unshakable faith in our Savior and Redeemer, our Lord Jesus Christ." Before getting into

such particulars as opposition to another constitutional convention, advocacy of gun control, opposition to the New World Order and the like, the platform proceeds to announce that

> The U.S. Constitution established a Republic under God, rather than democracy; our Republic is a nation governed by a Constitution that is rooted in Biblical law, administered by representatives who are Constitutionally elected by the citizens; [and] in a Republic governed by Constitutional law rooted in Biblical law, all Life, Liberty and Property are protected because law rules ("Constitution Party 2000 National Platform").

After the Ninth U.S. Circuit Court of Appeals ruled in *Newdow v. United States Congress* (2002) that it was unconstitutional under the establishment clause for school students to recite the pledge of allegiance with the words "under God" (a decision that the U.S. Supreme Court subsequently declared to be moot since it decided that the petitioner who brought the case did not have standing), a number of members of Congress introduced amendments to overturn this ruling. Some specifically contained the words "under God." If adopted, such an amendment would, by directly mentioning God, accomplish one of the aims of those who originally favored the Christian Amendment.

See also Abolitionists; Blaine Amendment; Confederate States of America, Constitution of; Flag Salute; Religious Equality Amendment.

For Further Reading:

Borden, Morton. 1979. "The Christian Amendment." *Civil War History* 25 (June): 156–167.

DeRosa, Marshall L. 1991. *The Confederate Constitution of 1861: An Inquiry into American Constitutionalism.* Columbia: University of Missouri Press.

Green, Steven K. 1999. "Justice David Josiah Brewer and the 'Christian Nation' Maxim." *Albany Law Review* 63:427–476.

Handy, Robert T. 1971. *A Christian America: Protestant Hopes and Historical Realities.* New York: Oxford University Press.

Jacoby, Steward O. 1984. *The Religious Amendment Movement: God, People and Nation in the Gilded Age.* 2 vols. PhD dissertation, University of Michigan.

Kramnick, Isaac, and R. Laurence Moore. 1996. *The Godless Constitution: The Case against Religious Correctness.* New York: W. W. Norton.

Morton, Robert K. 1933. *God in the Constitution.* Nashville, TN: Cokesbury Press.

Proceedings of the National Convention to Secure the Religious Amendment of the Constitution of the United States held in Pittsburgh, February 4, 5, 1874, with an Account of the Origin and Progress of the Movement. 1874. Philadelphia: Christian Statesman Association.

Randall, Jaynie. "Sundays Excepted." *Alabama Law Review* 59 (2008): 507–537.

CHURCH, JOSEPH (1918–)

Psychologist Joseph Church has advanced what the cover of his 1982 book, *America the Possible: Why and How the Constitution Should Be Rewritten,* described as "An Iconoclastic View of the Social, Political, and Economic Order in the U.S.—with Some Startling Suggestions for Change" (Church 1982). Born in Gardner, Massachusetts, in 1918, Church was educated at the New School for Social Research, Cornell University, and Clark University. He subsequently taught at Vassar College and, beginning in 1965, at Brooklyn College of the City University of New York. Church's other books deal largely with topics of childhood and adolescence, but this hardly deterred him from advancing wide-ranging views of contemporary American problems and what he believes to be their solutions. He is particularly disturbed by the continuing influence of what he considers to be myths—especially those generated by religion and Victorian sexual morality—and he expresses his ideas about family organization, the economy, and law and order as well as describes the outlines of what he would include in a new constitution. Acknowledging that he has "no faith in human perfectibility," Church states that he does "have a strong faith in human

improvability, and this is enough" (Church 1982, 29).

In outlining "the dimensions of a humane society," Church stresses the goals of greater human fulfillment; the need for greater egalitarianism; and the need for the nation to withdraw from foreign military alliances and commitments, to provide for human physical needs, and to advance democracy. In contrast to those who argue for constitutional brevity, Church notes that such an approach is "dangerously misguided." He explains:

> We have learned a great deal about how societies work in the nearly 200 years that our present Constitution has been in effect. It would be foolish or insane not to incorporate that learning into a new document. We do not want to accord the people in power great flexibility in decision making. They have all too consistently made the wrong decisions, sometimes out of avarice and self interest, but often out of sheer stupidity. (Church 1982, 81)

Church's ideas on the family are among his most provocative and are based on "the libertarian premise that the state should interfere as little as possible in the private lives of individuals" (Church 1982, 87). He is willing to allow any consensual living arrangements that individuals care to choose, including homosexual marriages and "living together" arrangements. He is not opposed to prostitution or even bestiality "as long as the animals are not made to suffer" (Church 1982, 94). (He did not explain how the presence of such suffering would be ascertained.) Apart from laws against rape, he is willing to lower the age of consent and to permit "noncoercive sex with children" (Church 1982, 94), as well as abortion on demand—at least early during a pregnancy. He hopes to abolish the stage of adolescence by allowing children to declare themselves to be independent, a decision that would, however, be irrevocable—children so emancipated would be permitted to drive, have access to pornography, consume alcohol or other drugs, decide whether to attend school, and, of course, engage in sexual relations. They would also qualify for his proposed "universal living-allowance program" (Church 1982, 119). High schools and colleges would be replaced by "research institutes staffed by scholars and scientists" (Church 1982, 123). Church's ideas on economic organization, although not quite so shocking to ordinary sensibilities, are equally provocative.

In the chapter of his book entitled "The New Constitution," Church indicates that he respects those who framed the Constitution and what they wrote, but that there are "reasons to start again" (Church 1982, 234). He wants the new constitution to stress "the democratic, humanitarian, and idealistic foundations of both the Declaration of Independence and the Constitution" as well as "to reassert the supremacy of the people" (Church 1982, 234–235). Aware of proposals advanced by both Rexford Guy Tugwell and Dwight Macdonald, Church wants to go even further.

Church's first proposal calls for abolishing the presidency. He associates the presidency with war and with aggrandizement of power, and he hopes to replace the office with a chief administrator (CA) selected by Congress. With the CA now becoming a mere administrative arm of the legislative branch, the new "balance of powers" within government would consist of "the legislature, the judiciary, and the electorate" (Church 1982, 244). Church also advocates replacing existing states with new arrangements, perhaps allowing for divisions into an urban and a rural America. Most, if not all, funding of programs like education and health care would be provided from national progressive income taxes on personal (albeit not corporate) income, but local groups would apparently maintain authority over the daily operations of such programs. The people would in turn have broad authority that they would exercise through the referendum, initiative, and recall processes (Church 1982, 248).

The most distinctive aspect of Church's proposal (which does not present actual new constitutional language) is how many principles he squeezes into the preamble of his proposed document. The preamble should, he says, "make explicit that ours is a pluralistic society and that the rule of the majority must not work hardships on any minority or group of minorities" (Church 1982, 249). It should affirm electoral supremacy through referendums, initiatives, and recall, mechanisms that would go so far as to allow voters to accept or reject budgets on a line-by-line basis (Church 1982, 250). The preamble would apparently include provisions for "something approaching fulltime voting" and the establishment of "fulltime polling sites" (Church 1982, 253). The preamble would "include the basics of our foreign policy," including the guiding principle of "peaceful coexistence," a dissolution of all foreign alliances, a commitment to work through the United Nations, and a commitment to free trade (Church 1982, 254–255). The preamble would also limit arm sales by governments and by private individuals and set a figure for "the maximum desirable population size of the nation," which Church estimates would be "200 million souls" (Church 1982, 257). The preamble should also "establish that the foundation of our society is the rights set forth in the various amendments to the original Constitution" (Church 1982, 258).

After setting forth the principles to be covered in his prolix preamble, Church discusses other matters. He expresses a near conspiratorial view of existing political parties in the United States but is not altogether clear about what would replace them. Congress would continue to be bicameral, and it would provide health care and a universal living allowance for all. The current Senate would be replaced by a House of Delegates based on the representation of special interest groups—delegates being selected through a system of "preferential balloting of the kind used in many nongovernmental organizations" (Church 1982, 263). Members of both houses would serve five-year terms, subject to voter recall.

Although Church would eliminate the states, he provides for "the right of secession to any part of the country, big or small, that wants to go it alone." This provision is coupled with two provisos. The first, intended to avoid idle threats, provides that secession "would be irrevocable for a period of fifty years." The second provides for "free migration into and out of the seceding territory for a period of five years" (Church 1982, 267).

The judiciary would be significantly altered. All courts would operate "with a uniform system of laws" (Church 1982, 268). Church would establish "a second system of courts of legislative review, culminating in a second Supreme Court" (Church 1982, 268). Much like the Council of Revision that the Constitutional Convention of 1787 rejected, the new courts would review all acts of legislation at the times of their passage, without waiting for cases to arise. Judges would not only be elected, but they would be permitted, if not expected, to campaign for their offices (Church 1982, 269).

Church hopes to draw a clear line between legality and morality. In reviewing current constitutional provisions, he favors spelling out many current guarantees more concretely. Thus, he favors a constitution that specifies the exclusionary rule, limits the use of grants of immunity, and the like. Church favors the nationalization of many industries and of "our national resources" (Church 1982, 275). Although opposed to capital punishment, he favors a constitutional right to die and specifies that "the means of suicide should always be made available upon request" to prisoners (Church 1982, 279).

Church is particularly concerned about what he considers to be the "antiquated" provisions of the First Amendment. In addition to desiring to eliminate tax exemptions for churches and the government provision of chaplains, Church proposes changing the national motto to "In Humankind We Trust" (Church 1982, 282). He thinks that the Government Printing Office should "grant to every citizen the right to publish, at public expense, a pamphlet of up to ten pages a year, to be distributed through the same channels as other government publications" (Church 1982, 284). He thinks that the Constitution should specify "the right of American citizens to travel abroad" (Church 1982, 285).

Church is relatively vague as to how his own proposals might be put into effect. Noting that he is a "man of thought, not of action," he suggests that his main efforts were devoted to "consciousness raising" (Church 1982, 287). As he observes,

My primary hope lies not in economic, legal, and political revolution, but in a psychocultural revolution, whereby we come to realize that we have built our social institutions in a quicksand of false assumptions and that these illfounded institutions needlessly deform our humanity. From this sort of awareness, institutional changes could flow quite readily—not necessarily painlessly, but in a manageable way (Church 1982, 294).

See also Initiative and Referendums; Macdonald, Dwight; Tugwell, Rexford.

For Further Reading:

Church, Joseph. 1982. *America the Possible: Why and How the Constitution Should Be Rewritten*. New York: Macmillan and Company.

"Joseph Church," Contemporary Authors Online, Gale, 2002, http://www.galenet.com. Updated February 27, 2002.

CITIZENS FOR THE CONSTITUTION, THE CONSTITUTIONAL AMENDMENT INITIATIVE

In 1999, the Century Foundation published a document entitled *Great and Extraordinary Occasions: Developing Guidelines for Constitutional Change*. As part of the constitutional amendments initiative co-chaired by former Republican congressman Mickey Edwards (OK) and former Democratic congressman Abner Mikva (IL) and endorsed by a large number of scholars and political figures, the document was designed to lead to reconsideration of what appeared to be excessive resort to the constitutional amendment process in the 104th and 105th Congresses. Kathleen Sullivan, a law professor at Stanford University, wrote an article decrying what she regards as "constitutional amendment fever" that was included as an appendix to the Century Foundation report.

The Century Foundation document proposes eight guidelines intended to introduce self-restraint into the constitutional amending process. The first five guidelines relate primarily to the content of amendments, while the last three relate chiefly to procedural issues. The guidelines are applied especially negatively to the proposed amendments relating to a federal balanced budget, to victims' rights, to the Flag Desecration Amendment, and to the failed Equal Rights Amendment. The report relies in part on the perception that the Eighteenth Amendment, which had (before being repealed by the Twenty-First) provided for national alcoholic prohibition, was an example of what could happen when the amending process enacted temporarily popular, but ultimately unwise, social policies. The report also drew negative lessons from prolix state constitutions that often draw little distinction between legal and political matters.

The Foundation's first consideration is that proposed amendments should "address matters that are of more than immediate concern and that are likely to be recognized as of abiding importance by subsequent generations" (Citizens for the Constitution 1999, 9). The second consideration suggests that amendments should be assessed for whether they "make our system more politically responsive or protect individual rights" (11). The third consideration suggests that amendments should not be adopted when the results could be achieved by ordinary political means. A fourth consideration asks whether a proposed amendment is "consistent with related constitutional doctrine that the amendment leaves intact" (17). The fifth consideration asks whether proposed amendments "embody enforceable, and not purely aspirational, standards" (19).

The last three considerations deal primarily with the degree of scrutiny that proponents of amendments give to their proposals. Thus, guideline six suggests that the proponents of amendments need to consider the manner in which their proposals will "interact with other constitutional provisions and principles" (21). Guideline seven centers on the need for "full and fair debate" (22) over the merits of proposed amendments, considering both questions of policy and operation. Guideline eight suggests that amendments should be proposed with "nonextendable deadline[s]" for ratification (24).

Although apparently written independently, an article by law professor J. B. Ruhl, examining proposals for an Environmental Quality Amendment, also seeks to establish two sets of filters through which amendments should pass. The first would "define whether an amendment to dictate a particular social policy generally is socially acceptable and institutionally necessary given conditions in the social and political realms" (254), whereas the second would "test the implementability of specific proposals to embody the social policy decision" (254). Under the first category, Ruhl argues that amendments should be "1. [s]upported by broad social approval [and] 2. [n]ot capable of being fully implemented through other political and legal institutions" (254). Under the second category, Ruhl argues that amendments should be "1. [r]educible to legal principles that are binding in effect"; 2. sufficiently clear to minimize unanticipated interpretations; [and] 3. [e]nduring even in the face of shifting political climates" (Ruhl 1999, 254).

In contrast to Ruhl, Adrian Vermeule, a professor of law at the University of Chicago, has critiqued what he describes as "the generic case against constitutional amendment" that he believes is embodied in Professor Sullivan's analysis of the Constitutional Amendment Initiative. Vermeule believes that Sullivan has engaged in what he calls a "nirvana illusion," by emphasizing the dangers of using the constitutional amending process without recognizing that changes brought through judicial interpretation have their own drawbacks. Vermeule argues that the supermajority requirements spelled out in Article V already make the process difficult and that establishing further norms against amendments will result in "pernicious double-counting, producing an excessively low rate of amendment" (2006, 256). Vermeule argues that if the process is too easy, which he doubts, then it should be amended to make it more difficult. He analyzes comparative costs and benefits of amendment and judicial interpretations (269–271) much in the manner of John Vile (1994).

See also Equal Rights Amendment.

For Further Reading:

Chemerinsky, Erwin. 2000. "Citizens for the Constitution," *Insights on Law & Society* 1 (Fall): 14–15.

Citizens for the Constitution. 1999. *Great and Extraordinary Occasions.* New York: Century Foundation, Inc.

The Constitution Project. "Constitutional Amendments Initiative." http://www.constitutionproject.org/constitutional.Indexcfm?categoryId=4. Accessed June 21, 2008.

Presser, Stephen B. 2000. "Constitutional Amendments: Dangerous Threat or Democracy in Action?" *Texas Review of Law and Politics* 5 (Fall): 209–225.

Ruhl, J. B. 1999. "The Metrics of Constitutional Amendments: Why Proposed Environmental Quality Amendments Don't Measure Up," *Notre Dame Law Review* 74 (January): 245–281.

Vergeule, Adrian. 2006. "Constitutional Amendments and the Constitutional Common Law," in eds. Richard W. Bauman and Tsvi Kahana. *The Least Examined Branch: The Role of Legislatures in the Constitutional State.* New York: Cambridge University Press, 229–272.

Vile, John R. 1994. *Constitutional Change in the United States: A Comparative Study of the Role of Constitutional Amendments, Judicial Interpretations, and Legislative and Executive Actions.* Westport, CT: Praeger.

CITIZENSHIP, DEFINITION OF

Although the Constitution of 1787 refers to "citizens" in a number of places (in specifying qualifications for officeholders, for example), nowhere does it specifically define such citizenship. This omission enabled Chief Justice Roger Taney to argue in *Scott v. Sandford* (1857) that blacks were not and could not be citizens and thus had no right to appear in U.S. courts.

Democratic representative Thomas Florence of Pennsylvania (1861) and Whig senator Garrett Davis of Kentucky (1864) unsuccessfully tried to write Taney's understanding explicitly into the Constitution. Instead, the first sentence of the Fourteenth Amendment overturned *Scott* and extended citizenship to "all persons born or naturalized in the United States and subject to the jurisdiction thereof."

In *United States v. Wong Kim Ark* (1898), the Supreme Court decided that citizenship extended to children born in the United States to parents who were Chinese citizens. Only children born to diplomatic personnel in the United States, children born to foreigners during hostile occupations, or Indians subject to tribal governance were considered exempt from U.S. jurisdiction and citizenship. Citizenship has subsequently been referred to as a qualification for voting in the Fifteenth, Nineteenth, Twenty-Fourth, and Twenty-Sixth Amendments, although state laws rather than provisions of the U.S. Constitution currently bar aliens from the franchise.

Justice Harry Blackmun's decision in *Roe v. Wade* (1973) voiding most state abortion regulations rested in part on the view that *citizenship* as used in the Fourteenth Amendment and elsewhere in the Constitution refers only to postnatal life. This decision has prompted numerous calls for a right to life amendment.

A number of proposed amendments related to qualifications for the presidency have sought to repeal the provision in Article II, Section 1 of the U.S. Constitution that limits the presidency to "natural born" citizens. The term "natural born" is not itself completely luminous, as indicated by a resolution adopted by the U.S. Senate on April 30, 2008, recognizing that the Republican presidential nominee, John McCain, who had been born to U.S. citizens on a military base in the Panama Canal Zone in 1936, was natural born. Barack Obama and Hillary Clinton, both of whom were vying for the Democratic nomination, were among those who supported the resolution.

Concerned that some individuals are illegally entering the United States with the purpose of obtaining citizenship for their children or that, in the least, this is an additional incentive for illegal immigration, proponents of a birthright citizenship amendment have also proposed limiting citizenship to those born in the United States of at least one parent who is either a citizen or is, in the least, legally within the boundaries of the nation.

See also Birthright Citizenship Amendment; Fourteenth Amendment.

Further Reading:

Heater, Derek. 2004. *A Brief History of Citizenship.* New York: New York University Press.

Hisch, Christine J. 1998. "American Born Legal Permanent Residents? A Constitutional

Amendment Proposal." *Georgetown Immigration Law Journal* 12 (Spring): 511–529.

Smith, Page. 1995. *Democracy on Trial: The Japanese American Evacuation and Relocation in World War II.* New York: Simon and Schuster.

CITIZENSHIP, DUAL

In September 1942, in conjunction with a bill to limit anticipated immigration from Europe following the end of World War II, Republican senator Rufus Holman of Oregon, chair of an ad hoc committee on defense (Irons 1983, 51), introduced a resolution to grant Congress the power to prohibit dual citizenship (S.J. Res. 163). In his speech before the Senate (Holman 1942), Holman referred specifically to Japanese Americans, some of whom held joint citizenship in the United States and Japan. Such dual citizenship arose from the fact that, in addition to the principle of jus soli (law of the soil), Japan applied the doctrine of jus sanguinis (law of the blood). This latter principle allowed people born abroad of Japanese nationals to maintain joint citizenship—citizenship that could, however, be renounced and did not apply to Japanese born in the United States after 1925 (see Justice Murphy's dissenting opinion, *Korematsu v. United States* [1944], 237 n.4).

Such dual citizenship contributed to suspicions that Japanese Americans constituted a disloyal "fifth column." Such fears were used in *Hirabayashi v. United States* (1943) and *Korematsu v. United States* (1944) to justify curfews for Japanese Americans and their exclusion from certain areas of the West Coast. This exclusion was accompanied by an executive order detaining some 112,000 Japanese American citizens in camps during World War II. During the Reagan administration, Congress passed a law providing monetary compensation for living victims of this detention.

For Further Reading:

Holman, Rufus. 1942. "Restriction of Immigration." *Congressional Record,* 77th Cong., 2d sess., Vol. 88, pt. 6: 7193–7194.

Irons, Peter, ed. 1989. *Justice Delayed: The Record of the Japanese Internment Cases.* Middletown, CT: Wesleyan University Press.

CITIZENSHIP, LOSS OF

The Constitution provided no definition of national citizenship prior to the Fourteenth Amendment. This did not stop Congress from proposing an amendment in 1810 providing that a person would "cease to be a citizen" upon accepting, without congressional approval, "any title of nobility or honour . . . from any emperor, king, prince, or foreign power" (Anastaplo 1989, 298–299). The origins of this amendment relative to titles of nobility are obscure. If it had been adopted, it would have provided a sanction for a similar provision already in Article I, Section 9 of the Constitution.

In *Trop v. Dulles* (1958), the Supreme Court struck down the application of a law providing for forfeiture of citizenship to a native-born American who had deserted during a time of war as "cruel and unusual punishment" prohibited by the Eighth Amendment. On the same day, however, in *Perez v. Brownell* (1958), the Supreme Court, in a 5-to-4 vote, upheld a provision of the Nationality Act of 1940, whereby Congress provided that individuals voting in foreign elections would forfeit their citizenship. The Court saw this as a reasonable exercise of power under congressional authority to regulate foreign affairs.

In *Afroyim v. Rusk* (1967), the Court reversed itself in another 5-to-4 decision and ruled that the Fourteenth Amendment protects against loss of citizenship except by voluntary renunciation. Several members of Congress subsequently proposed amendments from 1967 through 1969 to give Congress authority to provide by law for loss of nationality and citizenship.

See also Titles of Nobility.

For Further Reading:

Anastaplo, George. 1989. *The Constitution of 1787: A Commentary.* Baltimore: Johns Hopkins University Press.

Gordon, Charles. 1982. "The Power of Congress to Terminate United States Citizenship." *Connecticut Law Review* 4 (Spring): 611–632.

CITIZENSHIP, OFFICEHOLDING RIGHTS

New York's state ratifying convention proposed a resolution, never introduced in Congress, that would have excluded non-native-born citizens not only from the presidency and vice presidency but also from Congress (Ames 1896, 74). Northeastern Federalists reintroduced this idea during debates over the Alien and Sedition Acts (Kuroda 1994, 109), when many immigrants were more sympathetic to the Democratic-Republican Party. Federalists introduced similar proposals during the War of 1812. Since that time, there has been far more concern (as yet unsuccessful) with lifting the ban on non-native-born citizens to run for president than on excluding such citizens from Congress.

See also Presidency, Qualifications for.

For Further Reading:

Ames, Herman. 1896. *The Proposed Amendments to the Constitution of the United States during the First Century of Its History.* Washington DC: U.S. Government Printing Office. Reprint, New York: Burt Franklin, 1970.

Kuroda, Tadahisa. 1994. *The Origins of the Twelfth Amendment: The Electoral College in the Early Republic, 1878–1804.* Westport, CT: Greenwood Press.

CIVIL RIGHTS CASES (1883)

The Supreme Court's 8-to-1 decision in the *Civil Rights Cases* (1883) was one of the most important 19th-century decisions with respect to the interpretation of the Thirteenth and Fourteenth Amendments. At issue was the constitutionality of the Civil Rights Act of 1875, a law that attempted to guarantee equal access to public accommodations without respect to race.

In his opinion for the Court, Justice Joseph P. Bradley struck down this law on the basis that Section 1 of the Fourteenth Amendment, providing that "no state shall deny" specified individual rights, did not give Congress the power to interfere with actions of private individuals that had the same effect. As he summarized the purposes of the amendment.

> It does not authorize Congress to create a code of municipal law for the regulation of private rights; but to provide modes of redress against the operation of state laws, and the action of state officers executive or judicial, when these are subversive of the fundamental rights specified in the Amendment (*Civil Rights Cases* 1883, 11).

Bradley further denied that discrimination by private individuals constituted a "badge of servitude" prohibited by the Thirteenth Amendment.

In his dissenting opinion, Justice John Marshall Harlan accused the Court of giving "too narrow and artificial" a reading to the Thirteenth and Fourteenth Amendments. He pointed out that Congress had, in the Civil Rights Act of 1866, exercised similar power under authority of the Thirteenth Amendment. He argued that places of public accommodation ceased to be merely private but were clothed with a public interest. Moreover, rather than reading the Thirteenth and Fourteenth Amendments simply as negative prohibitions, Harlan argued (with particular emphasis on the definition of citizenship in Section 1 of the Fourteenth Amendment and the enforcement provisions of both amendments) that they were intended to be positive grants of power to government to protect individual rights. Not only did Harlan's arguments lose in this case, but in *Plessy v. Ferguson* (1896), the Supreme Court subsequently upheld state-sanctioned racial discrimination.

The Court's distinction between state action and private action has never been repudiated. Largely as a consequence, when Congress adopted the Civil Rights Act of 1964 outlawing discrimination in places of public accommodation, it relied primarily on its power to regulate commerce between the states. The Supreme Court upheld its authority under this provision in *Heart of Atlanta Motel v. United States* (1964) and *Katzenbach v. McClung* (1964). Only in recent years has the U.S. Supreme Court begun to indicate that Congress may have reached the outer limits of its power under the commerce clause and that, especially in exercising power dealing with areas like criminal law that have traditionally been handled by the states, the Court may require Congress to do more than simply indicate that it is evoking its power under the commerce clause.

See also Fourteenth Amendment; Thirteenth Amendment.

For Further Reading:

Civil Rights Cases, 109 U.S. 3 (1883).

Madry, Alan R. 1994. "Private Accountability and the Fourteenth Amendment: State Action, Federalism and Congress." *Missouri Law Review* 59 (Summer): 499–568.

CIVIL SERVICE REFORM

Although the Constitution mentions a number of appointed offices (members of the cabinet and the courts, for example), nowhere does it detail requirements for lesser officeholders. The so-called patronage, or spoils system ("to the victor belong the spoils"), allowed an incoming administration to dismiss such appointed officials and replace them with its own supporters, a fact that Senator James Hillhouse cited when he proposed changing the method of presidential selection in 1808. Such a system, later associated with the administration of President Andrew Jackson, can lead to cronyism, but it also helps both to keep government fairly responsive to public opinion and to undercut earlier notions that an office was a form of property.

The growth of government during the Civil War led to increasing concern about the corruption and incompetence that sometimes accompanied a system of personal appointment. Members of Congress proposed several amendments calling for civil service reform in the

1870s, but legislative action eventually proved effective with the passage of the Pendleton Act in 1883. This act created a system whereby candidates for government jobs qualified by fulfilling objective criteria of employment and taking competitive examinations. Reaction to the assassination of President James Garfield by a disappointed office seeker helped generate support for this act (Rosenbloom 1971, 80).

Initially covering about 10 percent of the federal civilian workforce, today the civil service system applies to about 90 percent. In 1935, an amendment was proposed to establish the civil service merit principle more firmly in the federal government (H.J. Res. 378), but the prior history of civil service reform suggests that if this reform is desirable, it can be accomplished through regular legislative action.

See also: Hillhouse, James.

For Further Reading:

Rosenbloom, David H. 1971. *Federal Service and the Constitution: The Development of the Public Employment Relationship.* Ithaca, NY: Cornell University Press.

Van Riper, Paul P. 1958. *History of the United States Civil Service.* Evanston, IL: Row, Peterson.

CLAIMS AGAINST THE UNITED STATES

Despite the doctrine of sovereign immunity, limiting suits against the states, Congress designates certain classes of cases that can be brought against the government. Since 1855, most of these cases have been heard by the U.S. Court of Claims, which was redesignated in 1982 as the U.S. Claims Court. This court relieves Congress of passing special bills to deal with such matters (Abraham 1998, 166).

After the Civil War, 16 proposed amendments sought to limit claims resulting from the war, most by denying claims by those who had been disloyal to the Union. One such proposal received a favorable vote of 145 to 61 in the House of Representatives in 1878 but was not voted on in the Senate. Several proposals would have provided a time limit within which war claims could be filed (Ames 1896, 248). On three occasions between 1905 and 1907, Republican representative Joseph Keifer of Ohio introduced amending resolutions to enlarge the power of the Court of Claims and limit Congress to appropriating money for claims settled by this or other authorized commissions (Musmanno 1929, 151–152).

As of 1982, appeals from the U.S. Court of Claims are heard by the U.S. Court of Appeals for the Federal Circuit. It is considered a legislative court created under Article I of the Constitution rather than an Article III constitutional tribunal; judgments of this court are still subject to review by the Supreme Court.

For Further Reading:

Abraham, Henry J. 1998. *The Judicial Process: An Introductory Analysis of the Courts of the United States, England, and France.* 7th ed. New York: Oxford University Press.

Ames, Herman. 1896. *The Proposed Amendments to the Constitution of the United States during the First Century of Its History.* Reprint, New York: Burt Franklin, 1970.

Musmanno, M. A. 1929. *Proposed Amendments to the Constitution.* Washington DC: U.S. Government Printing Office.

CLARK, WALTER (1846–1924)

Walter Clark, then chief justice of the North Carolina Supreme Court, presented a speech later published as part of his papers (1906), in which he advocated a number of constitutional changes. These proposals reflected his perspective as a progressive Democrat who believed that the Constitution had been a conservative reaction to a more democratic beginning symbolized by the Declaration of Independence (for critique, see Smith 1906). Clark aimed almost all of his proposals, at least one of which he thought would require a constitutional convention, at increasing the power of the people and reducing the power of plutocrats, who he believed exerted control through their selection of federal judges and senators.

Two of Clark's proposals were eventually achieved by constitutional amendments. One, effected by the Seventeenth Amendment, called for direct election of the Senate. Another, later effected by the Twentieth Amendment, was to change the inauguration dates to reduce the lame duck sessions of Congress.

None of Clark's other proposals have yet been adopted. One such proposal—made without reference to the Article V entrenchment clause that appears to make such a change impossible absent state consent—called for eliminating the equality of state representation in the Senate and granting each state one senator for each million inhabitants or fraction thereof over three-quarters of a million. Another proposal called for replacing the current Electoral College system with a proportional plan dividing state votes among candidates according to the proportion of the popular votes each one received. Clark's primary objective in making such a change was to take away the advantage of pivotal states and candidates who come from them. Clark also favored changing the term of the president to six years and making him ineligible for reelection. In addition, Clark advocated removing postmasters from presidential patronage and providing that they would be elected from their districts.

As a judge, however, Clark devoted his greatest attention to the federal judiciary. In his speech, he advocated the election of judges to fixed terms—elsewhere he also suggested popular recall, congressional overrides of judicial decisions, abolition of judicial review, or alterations of judicial jurisdiction (Vile 1991c, 60 n.9). Clark did not believe that the framers of the Constitution had intended to vest judges with the power to declare laws to be unconstitutional (judicial review). He believed such power had been abused in a number of ways. He cited the Supreme Court decision invalidating the income tax (later overturned by the Sixteenth Amendment), the Court's opinion in *Lochner v. New York* (1905) striking down a New York wage regulation of bakers, and other judicial interferences with state autonomy. In what might otherwise appear to be a surprising recommendation coming from a progressive spokesman, Clark suggested, "Nothing can save us from the centripetal force but the speedy repeal of the fourteenth amendment, or a recasting of its language in terms that no future court can misinterpret it" (Clark 1906, 565). As a way of eliminating those judges who were then serving life terms, Clark suggested that Congress could abolish all judge-ships below the Supreme Court and then have new ones elected. He also suggested that Congress could curb the jurisdiction of the Supreme Court (Clark 1906, 568).

However radical such proposals might appear, they were consistent with Clark's continuing belief that "the remedy for the halting, halfway popular government which we have is more democracy" (Clark 1906, 572).

Clark was a strong advocate of women's rights and of women's suffrage (see Clark 1913), which was, of course, embodied in the Nineteenth Amendment.

See also Nineteenth Amendment; Progressive Era; Seventeenth Amendment, Twentieth Amendment.

For Further Reading:

Clark, Walter. 1913. Address by Chief Justice Walter Clark Before the Federation of Women's Clubs, New Bern, NC. 8 May 1913. Electronic Edition. http://doesouth.unc.edu/nc/clark13/clark13.html. Accessed July 9, 2008.

———. 1906. "Some Defects of the Constitution of the United States." In *The Papers of Walter Clark*. Vol. 2, 1902–1924, ed. Aubrey L. Brooks and Hugh T. Lefler. Reprint, Chapel Hill, NC: University of North Carolina Press, 1950.

Smith, Goldwin. 1906. "Chief Justice Clark on the Defects of the American Constitution." *North American Review* 183 (1 November): 845–851.

Vile, John R. 1991. *Rewriting the United States Constitution: An Examination of Proposals from Reconstruction to the Present.* New York: Praeger.

CLINTON V. CITY OF NEW YORK (1998)

In this case, the U.S. Supreme Court voted by a 6-to-3 majority to invalidate a provision of the Line Item Veto Act that went into effect on January 1, 1997. This act effectively entrusted the president with a line item veto of matters relating to taxing and spending. The Court had rejected a challenge to this act in *Byrd v. Raines* (1997) on the basis that the members of Congress who brought the case did not have proper standing to sue. In *Clinton,* the Court majority agreed that the litigants, New York State and hospitals located there, as well as a farmers' cooperative, did have such status, after President Clinton canceled tax exemptions from which each stood to benefit.

The Line Item Veto Act had allowed the president to cancel items that involved "(1) any dollar amount of discretionary budget authority; (2) any item of new direct spending; or (3) any limited tax benefit" (cited in *Clinton* 1998, 436). In making such a decision, the president was responsible for determining that such cancellations would "(i) reduce the Federal budget deficit; (ii) not impair any essential Government functions; and (iii) not harm the national interest" (cited in *Clinton* 1998, 436). If the president exercised such authority, designed to reduce budget deficits, then Congress could adopt a "disapproval bill" rejecting the president's actions, although he in turn would have had authority to veto this bill.

The Supreme Court decided that the authority vested in the president under the Line Item Veto Act was significantly different from that vested in this office under the U.S. Constitution. The Court observed that

> The constitutional return takes place *before* the bill becomes law; the statutory cancellation occurs *after* the bill becomes law. The constitutional return is of the entire bill; the statutory cancellation is of only a part. Although the Constitution expressly authorizes the President to play a role in the process of enacting statutes, it is silent on the subject of unilateral Presidential action that either repeals or amends part of duly enacted statutes (*Clinton* 1998, 439).

The majority concluded that this law was an illegal attempt to bypass the "'finely wrought' procedures that the Framers designed" (*Clinton* 1998, 440) and, more specifically, the presentment clause permitting the president to veto laws that have been passed by both houses of Congress.

As long as the majority view of the Court prevails, the only way that the President could be given a line item veto is through constitutional amendment. Such proposals, which have been advocated for well over a century, continue to be introduced in Congress.

See also Presidency, Veto Power of.

For Further Reading:

Byrd v. Raines, 521 U.S. 811 (1997).

Clinton v. City of New York, 524 U.S. 417 (1998).

Garry, Patrick M. 2006. "The Unannounced Revolution: How the Court Has Indirectly Effected a Shift in the Separation of Powers." *Alabama Law Review* 57 (Spring): 689–723.

U.S. Term Limits, Inc. v. Thornton, 514 U.S. 779 (1995).

COERCIVE USE OF FEDERAL FUNDS

When the national government provides billions of dollars a year in aid to the states, the ability to condition this aid on certain state behaviors can result in a significant measure of federal control. From 1943 to 1993, six states (Pennsylvania, Nevada, Oklahoma, Tennessee, Arizona, and South Dakota) petitioned Congress to call for a convention limiting federal coercion through this funding mechanism.

Although some studies suggest that federal conditions on the use of funds more frequently lead to intergovernmental bargaining than to the direct cutoff of funds (O'Toole 1985, 202–203), states sometimes comply with federal policies rather than risk the loss of aid. Thus, just over half of the states accepted small bonuses that the national government offered to them regulating billboards on interstate highways, but the threat to withhold 10 percent of state constructive funds brought the rest into line (O'Toole 1985, 213). The national government enacted similar laws to get states to reduce speed limits to 55 miles per hour at the time of the Arab oil embargo in the early 1970s

(laws that were subsequently repealed), to get states to raise the legal drinking age from 18 to 21, and, more recently, to encourage states to lower the level of alcohol in the blood for determining legal intoxication from 0.10 to 0.08.

In *United States v. Butler* (1936), while striking down the Agricultural Adjustment Act on Tenth Amendment grounds (a decision that was later overturned), the Supreme Court ruled that congressional power to tax and spend under Article I, Section 8 was, as Alexander Hamilton had previously argued, an independent power that could be used to advance the general welfare.

In *South Dakota v. Dole* (1987), the Court, in a 7-to-2 decision, upheld a law withholding 5 percent of a state's federal funds for road construction when the state sold alcohol to individuals under 21. In so ruling, the Court established four conditions: (1) the exercise of taxing and spending power must be in pursuit of the general welfare, with the Court indicating a general willingness to defer to congressional judgments; (2) Congress must clearly state its intentions; (3) conditions must be related to a federal interest (identified in this case as safe interstate travel); and (4) the behavior rewarded must not violate another constitutional provision (*Dole* 1987, 207–208). In this same case, the Court rejected arguments that the federal conditions were in possible violation of state control of alcohol guaranteed in the Twenty-First Amendment.

See also Tenth Amendment.

For Further Reading:

O'Toole, Lawrence J., Jr., ed. 1985. *American Intergovernmental Relations: Foundations, Perspectives, and Issues.* Washington DC: Congressional Quarterly.

South Dakota v. Dole, 483 U.S. 203 (1987).

COLEMAN, CHARLES H. (1900–1971)

One of the most modest attempts to rewrite the Constitution was offered by Dr. Charles Coleman of Eastern Illinois University in a 1938 publication of the National Council for the Social Studies. Divided into nine articles, Coleman's proposal was actually somewhat shorter than the existing U.S. Constitution. Coleman suggested that such a change would not require a convention but could be adopted by Congress as an amendment after a joint committee held hearings on the subject.

Article One of the new constitution dealt with citizenship, basically drawing from the Fourteenth, Fifteenth, and Nineteenth Amendments. Article Two dealt with the legislative branch. Innovations would have included giving the president power to determine the conditions under which appropriate monies were spent, four-year terms for the House and eight-year terms for the Senate, and a prohibition (similar to that later ratified in the Twenty-Seventh Amendment) on salary increases during a term of office. Congress would have been given a number of new enumerated powers, including the power "to regulate corporations," "to regulate the conditions of labor," "to promote the conservation of natural resources," and "to encourage agriculture" (Coleman 1938, 24–25). Treaties would be approved by a majority of both houses rather than by a two-thirds vote of the Senate.

Article Three described the executive department. The Electoral College would be retained, but individual electors would be eliminated. Also, the vice presidency would be eliminated. Article Four, the judicial article, contained few innovations other than prohibiting individuals convicted of treason from serving in public office. Similarly, Article Five basically repeated provisions relative to relations among the states that are currently found in Article IV of the Constitution.

Article Six dealt with prohibitions on the national government, on the states, and on both. Secession was specifically forbidden to the states. The due process clause and equal protection clause, albeit not the entire Bill of Rights, applied to both sets of government.

Article Seven specified that amendments could be ratified by two-thirds of the states, as long as such states contained at least three-fourths of the population. Article Eight contained the supremacy clause, and Article Nine

provided that the new constitution would go into effect when ratified by conventions in 36 states. A building on the campus of Eastern Illinois University is named in Coleman's honor.

See also: Twenty-seventh Amendment.

For Further Reading:

Coleman, Charles. 1938. *The Constitution up to Date.* Bulletin no. 10. Cambridge, MA: National Council for Social Studies.

Vile, John R. 1991. *Rewriting the United States Constitution: An Examination of Proposals from Reconstruction to the Present.* New York: Praeger.

COLEMAN V. MILLER (1939)

This decision involved a suit brought by Kansas legislators questioning the constitutionality of the state's putative ratification of the Child Labor Amendment. At issue was whether the lieutenant governor had the right to cast the deciding vote in the state senate. Litigants also argued that the proposed amendment had lost its validity because state legislatures in Kansas and other states had previously rejected it and because the 13-year gap between the amendment's proposal and ratification was unreasonable.

Chief Justice Charles Evans Hughes's opinion for the Court accepted the right of state senators to bring their suit on the basis that the issues they raised were federal rather than state matters. As to the lieutenant governor's role, the Court pronounced itself "equally divided" (*Coleman* 1939, 447), thus leaving in place the ruling by the Kansas Supreme Court validating his role. Although he did not repudiate language in *Dillon v. Gloss* (1921) providing for the ratification of amendments within a reasonable time, Hughes decided that the effect of prior rejection and the lapse of time between proposal and ratification were "political questions" for Congress to resolve. Law professor Walter Dellinger has criticized Hughes's decision for relying on the anomalous precedent set by congressional promulgation of the disputed Fourteenth Amendment (Dellinger 1983, 389–405).

Four justices, led by Hugo Black, would have stated the political questions doctrine even more broadly. Justice Butler's dissent relied on *Dillon v. Gloss* (1921) to declare that Kansas's ratification was invalid because it was not contemporary with the amendment's proposal.

Coleman has never been overturned and may have been partly confirmed when Congress voted to accept the long-delayed ratification of the Twenty-Seventh Amendment (first proposed in 1789) in 1992. Continuing scholarly criticisms of *Coleman,* as well as judicial modifications of the "political questions" doctrine and a district court decision in *Idaho v. Freeman* (1981), however, cast some doubt on *Coleman's* continuing validity. Although there would be a danger in allowing courts to declare amendments, especially amendments that might be aimed at judicial decisions themselves, invalid on the basis of their content, some scholars argue that courts are generally adept at handling the kinds of procedural issues that amending controversies often pose. (See, for example, Ishikawa 1997, 594.)

See also Child Labor Amendment; *Dillon v. Gloss; Idaho v. Freeman;* Political Questions; Ratification of Amendments; Twenty-seventh Amendment.

For Further Reading:

Coleman v. Miller, 307 U.S. 433 (1939).

Dellinger, Walter. 1983. "The Legitimacy of Constitutional Change: Rethinking the Amending Process." *Harvard Law Review* 97 (December): 380–432.

Ishikawa, Brendon T. 1997. "Everything You Always Wanted to Know about How Amendments Are Made, but Were Afraid to Ask." *Hastings Constitutional Law Quarterly* 24 (Winter): 545–597.

"Sawing a Justice in Half." 1939. *Yale Law Journal* 48: 1455–1458.

COLONIAL CHARTERS

Although many American states wrote their first constitutions during the Revolutionary War period, most had previously attempted to defend their liberties on the basis of colonial charters that had been issued to them, usually by the king. A scholar who has examined such charters identified eight elements that most had in common:

the identification of a grantor; the creation or identification of a grantee; a statement of the reason for the grant; a statement of what was being granted; the license or exclusive use given by the grant; a statement of how the grant was to be administered; specific restrictions or limits on the grant; and the reciprocal duties owed the grantor by the grantee (Lutz 1988, 35).

In the period preceding the outbreak of the Revolutionary War, U.S. patriots argued that their rights as English citizens derived from their loyalty to the king, who had issued the charters, rather than from any acceptance of parliamentary authority (Reid 1993). Both state and federal constitutions later incorporated provisions of these colonial charters.

Charters that William Penn granted in 1682 to 1683 to Pennsylvania appear to have been the first to provide explicitly for an amending process. Such changes required extraordinary majorities—namely, a six-sevenths majority of the Assembly. This and a number of subsequent charters also presaged future entrenchment clauses, such as that in Article V, which guarantees that no state shall be deprived of its equal representation in the Senate without its consent. Early charters also reflected concerns for rights, such as those later protected in the U.S. Bill of Rights. In the charter granted to Delaware in 1701, William Penn thus provided "That the First Article of this Charter relating to Liberty of Conscience, and every Part and Clause therein, according to the true Intent and Meaning thereof, shall be kept and remain, without any Alteration, inviolably for ever" (Thorpe 1909, 560–561).

Whereas early charters were viewed primarily as grants from the king to his people, later constitutions more clearly resembled compacts, or covenants (with especially deep roots in the Calvinist religious tradition), made collectively by the people by virtue of their own authority (Lutz

1988, 37–38). This foundation in popular sovereignty, in turn, provides the theoretical foundation for the people's right to alter their constitution.

See also Bill of Rights; Entrenchment Clauses; Penn, William.

For Further Reading:

Covenant, Polity, and Constitutionalism. 1980. Special issue of *Publius: The Journal of Federalism* (Fall).

Lutz, Donald S. 1988. *The Origins of American Constitutionalism.* Baton Rouge: Louisiana State University Press.

Reid, John P. 1993. *Constitutional History of the American Revolution: The Authority of Law.* Madison: University of Wisconsin Press.

Thorpe, Francis N. 1909. *The Federal and State Constitutions Colonial Charters and Other Organic Laws of the States, Territories, and Colonies Now or Heretofore Forming the United States of America.* 7 vols. Washington DC: U.S. Government Printing Office.

COMMITTEE ON THE CONSTITUTIONAL SYSTEM

The bicentennial of the U.S. Constitution provided a time for reflection about American constitutionalism and the prospect of constitutional change (Vile 1991c, 125). The nonpartisan Committee on the Constitutional System, which had already served as a sounding board for changes (Robinson 1985), issued a report in January 1987 that received considerable attention. The committee, consisting of a number of prominent politicians and scholars, was co-chaired by Senator Nancy Landon Kassebaum of Kansas; C. Douglas Dillon, a former secretary of the treasury; and Lloyd N. Cutler, former counsel to President Carter and later to President Clinton.

Noting signs of strain in the system the framers had created, the committee traced such phenomena as divided government, lack of cohesion, lack of accountability, and the inability to replace failed or deadlocked governments to the separation of powers and to a number of developments that had undercut the power of political parties. The committee majority agreed on three proposals to strengthen such parties: to allow party officeholders to serve as uncommitted delegates to national nominating conventions, to require all states to provide an optional straight-ticket voting mechanism, and to permit public funding of political campaigns. It also recommended three proposals to improve legislative-executive collaboration: to change congressional terms so that members of the House of Representatives would serve for four years and members of the Senate for eight, to allow members of Congress to serve in the cabinet, and to allow majorities of both houses of Congress to approve treaties. The committee also favored a constitutional amendment allowing Congress to set limits on campaign spending.

The committee offered a number of other proposals, which did not have the majority support of its members, for consideration. These included encouraging the president to appear before Congress, allowing the minority party to form a "shadow cabinet," requiring straight-ticket voting, scheduling elections for Congress after the president and vice president were selected, calling for new elections when the government was deadlocked, and convening conventions every 10 years to make recommendations on how better to divide state and federal responsibilities.

Although committee reforms fell far short of the wide-ranging changes that some favored, they stirred considerable debate and diverse criticism. Thus, political scientist Jeanne Hahn (1987) argued that committee reforms would further entrench the status quo and put more power in the hands of elites. Political scientist James Ceaser critiqued those elements of the plan that imitated the parliamentary model. Defending separation of powers, he blamed most modern political problems on "reformism, collectivism, whiggism [congressional dominance of government], and judicial activism" (Ceaser 1986, 187). The widespread veneration for the Constitution that the bicentennial celebrations evoked probably worked against changes at that time (Vile 1991c, 162).

See also Cutler, Lloyd; Divided Government; Parliamentary System.

For Further Reading:

Ceaser, James W. 1986. "In Defense of Separation of Powers." In *Separation of Powers—Does It Still*

Work? ed. Robert A. Goldwin and Art Kaufman. Washington DC: American Enterprise Institute.

Hahn, Jeanne. 1987. "Neo-Hamiltonianism: A Democratic Critique." In *The Case against the Constitution from AntiFederalists to the Present,* ed. John F. Manley and Kenneth M. Dolbeare. New York: M. E. Sharpe.

Robinson, Donald. 1985. *Reforming American Government: The Bicentennial Papers of the Committee on the Constitutional System.* Boulder, CO: Westview Press.

Vile, John R. 1991. *Rewriting the United States Constitution: An Examination of Proposals from Reconstruction to the Present.* New York: Praeger.

COMMUNISM

On July 7, 1965, Mississippi sent petitions to Congress to call conventions to propose three amendments. One was directed at overturning Supreme Court decisions—most notably *Reynolds v. Sims* (1964) (applying the "one person one vote" standard)—dealing with apportionment of state legislatures. A second petition—most likely a continuing reaction to the Supreme Court's desegregation decision in *Brown v. Board of Education* (1954) and subsequent cases—called for giving states exclusive control over public education. The third proposed an amendment designed to control communism.

Mississippi pointed to "the existence of the world Communist conspiracy and the fact that the Communist Party, U.S.A., operates as an arm of such conspiracy in seeking to bring about the overthrow of the Government of the United States by force and violence." The state further observed that "the Supreme Court of the United States through its various decisions has circumscribed, limited, or invalidated such congressional enactments" ("House Resolution 14" 1965, 15770). Mississippi accordingly asked for an amendment designed to invest Congress with the power to control communism. It would prevent the dissemination of communist propaganda in the United States and allow for the expulsion of noncitizens engaged in disseminating such propaganda. At the time, many individuals in the deep South associated communists with the civil rights movement.

The concern with Supreme Court decisions relating to communism appears to have been more prevalent in the late 1950s than in the period that Mississippi offered its amendment. In a number of decisions from 1955 to 1957, the Supreme Court overturned convictions of American communists. Thus, in *Pennsylvania v. Nelson* (1956), the Court invalidated a state antisedition law on the basis that federal legislation, most notably the Smith Act, already occupied this field. Similarly, in *Watkins v. United States* (1957) it overturned a citation for contempt against a labor leader who had refused to answer certain questions before the House Un-American Activities Committee (HUAC) about possible communist associates. These decisions prompted the unsuccessful Jenner bill, in which Congress attempted to restrict judicial jurisdiction over such cases (W. Murphy 1962). In a number of subsequent decisions, *Barenblatt v. United States* (1959) being the most prominent, the Court appeared to retreat from its earlier rulings (Belknap 1992, 172). In *Barenblatt,* the Court refused to use the First Amendment to extend exemptions for witnesses testifying before congressional committees.

See also *Brown v. Board of Education;* First Amendment.

For Further Reading:

Belknap, Michael R. 1992. "Communism and the Cold War." In *The Oxford Companion to the Supreme Court of the United States,* ed. Kermit L. Hall. New York: Oxford University Press.

"House Resolution 14." *Congressional Record* 89th Cong., 1st sess., 1965, Vol. 111, pt. 12: 15770.

Murphy, Walter F. 1962. *Congress and the Court.* Chicago: University of Chicago Press.

CONCURRENT POWERS

Because the United States has a federal system, some powers are exercised exclusively, or predominantly, by the state or national governments. A larger number of powers—for example, taxation—are shared; these are called concurrent powers. Section 2 of the Eighteenth Amendment, which imposed national alcoholic prohibition, entrusted Congress and the states with "concurrent power to enforce this article." The national government interpreted this clause expansively in the *National Prohibition Cases* (1920), even upholding provisions of the Volstead Act that outlawed beer and wine.

Perhaps with such contemporary construction of the Eighteenth Amendment in mind, New York Democratic representative Frank Oliver (H.J. Res. 42, 5 December 1927) proposed construing "concurrent power" so as to prevent an act of Congress from invalidating an act adopted by a state. Although the Twenty-First Amendment repealed the Eighteenth, the national government and the states share an increasing number of powers. An expert on federalism has argued that contemporary federalism thus more closely resembles a "marble cake" arrangement than a "layer cake" scheme (Grodzins 1966).

One of the proposals for a constitutional amendment to prevent flag desecration, while not specifically using the term concurrent powers, would have provided for them. It would have specified that "The Congress and the States shall have power to prohibit the physical desecration of the flag of the United States" (cited in Dorsen 2000, 425).

See also Eighteenth Amendment; Enforcement Clauses; Flag Desecration; National Prohibition Cases; Twenty-first Amendment.

For Further Reading:

Dorsen, Norman. 2000. "Flag Desecration in Courts, Congress, and Country." *Thomas M. Cooley Law Review* 17 (Michaelmas Term): 417–442.

Grodzins, Morton. 1966. *The American System: A New View of the Government in the United States.* Chicago: Rand McNally.

CONFEDERATE DEBT

Article VI of the U.S. Constitution provided that the new government would accept the validity of debts contracted under the Articles of Confederation. During discussions of the Fourteenth Amendment after the Civil War, members of Congress expressed fears that the former rebels might one day gain office with the intention of either repudiating federal debts that had been used to wage the war or assuming the debts that the Southern states had made to prosecute the conflict. Several proposals were introduced to prevent either contingency (Flack 1908, 133–136). Section 4 of the Fourteenth Amendment subsequently both guaranteed "the validity of the public debt of the United States . . . including debts incurred for payment of pensions and bounties for services in suppressing insurrection or rebellion" and repudiated either federal or state payment of "any debt or obligation incurred in aid of insurrection or rebellion against the United States, or any claim for the loss or emancipation of any slave."

See also Articles of Confederation; Fourteenth Amendment.

For Further Reading:

Flack, Horace E. 1908. *The Adoption of the Fourteenth Amendment.* Baltimore: Johns Hopkins. Reprint, Gloucester, MA: Peter Smith, 1965.

CONFEDERATE STATES OF AMERICA, CONSTITUTION OF

The constitution that bears the greatest similarity to that of the United States was the one the 11 Confederate States of America adopted after deciding to secede from the Union in 1861. Written by the Committee of Twelve and debated by a convention held in Montgomery, Alabama, in March 1861 (C. R. Lee 1963), the document replaced a similar provisional constitution adopted the previous month. The new constitution was subsequently approved by the Confederate Congress and by the Southern states; approval by five states was necessary for the document to go into effect. Reflecting the philosophy of John C. Calhoun and other Southern constitutionalists (DeRosa 1991, 18–37), the Confederate constitution was built on the doctrine of state sovereignty. It also included a number of provisions designed to control federal spending on special interests.

Although the Confederate constitution followed the outline of the U.S. Constitution, several provisions were different. The preamble included an acknowledgment of God. The constitution explicitly referred to slaves rather than using euphemisms. It permitted two-thirds majorities of state legislatures to impeach judicial or other federal officials acting within a state. In imitation of parliamentary systems, it permitted Congress to grant a seat on the floor of Congress for members of the cabinet to discuss measures but did not, like the provisional constitution, allow members of Congress to hold other offices. The permanent constitution gave the president an item veto of appropriations bills and prohibited congressional appropriations for internal improvements other than aids to navigation and harbor improvements. Although prohibiting slave importation, the document explicitly affirmed the right to property in the form of slaves. Appropriations required a two-thirds vote of both houses of Congress, with a provision that all appropriations bills "shall specify in federal currency the exact amount of each appropriation, and the purposes for which it is made." Bills were limited to a single subject.

The president and vice president were to serve single six-year terms and were chosen by an electoral college rather than, as under the provisional constitution, by Congress. The constitution granted the chief executive explicit power to remove department heads at his pleasure and others for specified grievances. Although the constitutional arrangement of the courts was not significantly altered, the Confederate states, perhaps remembering the consolidating effect of U.S. Supreme Court decisions, never got around to establishing their own equivalent.

The constitution did not explicitly prohibit membership by free states, but it did require a vote of two-thirds of both houses to admit new states. The constitution also explicitly granted the government the right to acquire new territory where the right to own slaves was protected.

The provisional Confederate constitution had permitted amendments by a two-thirds vote in Congress (Urofsky 1988, 400). The permanent constitution provided no method for Congress to propose amendments but allowed three states to request Congress to summon a convention to propose amendments. These required ratification by two-thirds of the states. No such amendments were adopted during the Confederate States' brief life.

Article VII of the Confederate Constitution provided that the document would go into effect when ratified by "conventions of five States." The U.S. Constitution had required ratification by nine of 13, but it was predicated on a Union of all, whereas the Confederate Constitution was premised on the notion that there were now two separate peoples.

The Confederate constitution provided a number of innovations for the consideration of future reformers (see, for example, Schouler 1908). The circumstances surrounding the constitution's adoption also contributed to fears of a runaway revolutionary convention (Jameson 1887, 257). Although their motivations are quite different and are often associated with the idea that the existing American government has become too large and impersonal and needs "downsizing," a number of recent proponents of new constitutions have advocated recognizing a right of states or localities to secede.

See also Calhoun, John C.; Constitutional Conventions.

For Further Reading:

Davis, William C. 1994. *"A Government of Our Own": The Making of the Confederacy.* New York: Free Press.

DeRosa, Marshall L. 1991. *The Confederate Constitution of 1861: An Inquiry into American Constitutionalism.* Columbia, MO: University of Missouri Press.

Jameson, John A. 1887. *A Treatise on Constitutional Conventions: Their History, Powers, and Modes of Proceeding.* 4th ed. Chicago: Callaghan and Company.

Lee, Charles Robert, Jr. 1963. *The Confederate Constitutions.* Chapel Hill: University of North Carolina Press.

Schouler, James. 1908. "A New Federal Constitution." In *Ideals of the Republic,* ed. James Schouler. Boston: Little, Brown.

Urofsky, Melvin I. 1988. *A March of Liberty: A Constitutional History of the United States.* New York: Alfred A. Knopf.

CONFESSIONS

One of the most prominent symbols of the activist Warren Court was its decision in *Miranda v. Arizona* (1966). In this case, the Court decided by a 5-to-4 vote that it would no longer accept confessions in cases of custodial police interrogation unless police had informed suspects of their rights. These included notification that they had the right to remain silent, that any statements they made could be used against them, that they had the right to an attorney, and that the state would provide an attorney if they were too poor to afford one.

The Court based this decision on its reading of the self-incrimination clause of the Fifth Amendment as applied to the states via the due process clause of the Fourteenth Amendment. *Miranda* prompted "a firestorm of criticism" by those concerned that it would hamstring law enforcement (Bodenhamer 1992, 121). Within a month, North Carolina Democratic senator Sam Ervin (a constitutional expert who would later chair the Senate Watergate Committee) introduced an amendment to permit the use of "voluntary" confessions and withdraw the jurisdiction of federal courts to "reverse, modify, or set aside" determinations by trial courts that such confessions were voluntary (Ervin 1966, 112). Several other such amendments were introduced from 1966 to 1968, including at least one that would have permitted police to question individuals outside the presence of counsel (H.J. Res. 1260, 1966).

"Although Ervin's amendment was not adopted, disputes continue over both the use of confessions and the appropriate extent of federal habeas corpus review. The Court under Warren Burger and William Rehnquist has allowed a limited number of exceptions to the *Miranda* rules (*New York v. Quarles* [1984], for example, accepted a "public safety" exception, and other cases have permitted slight divergences in wording), but most observers have concluded that the *Miranda* warnings did not have the significant negative impact on confessions that many had anticipated (Bodenhamer 1992, 123). Indeed, some scholars think that the kind of "bright-line" rule established in *Miranda* has actually made it easier for police officers to do their jobs effectively by clearly letting them know what is required of them. Lower courts have also tightened up the number of habeas corpus reviews they will accept. Thus, in *Stone v. Powell* (1976), the Supreme Court decided not to accept federal habeas corpus review of Fourth Amendment claims that had already been given a full hearing in state courts. Federal habeas corpus review continues to be controversial, especially in cases involving the death penalty. Habeas corpus review is now granted in about half of such cases, often significantly delaying executions (Hoffman and Stuntz 1994, 119).

See also Ervin, Sam J., Jr.; Fifth Amendment; Fourteenth Amendment.

For Further Reading:

Bodenhamer, David J. 1992. *Fair Trial: Rights of the Accused in American History.* New York: Oxford University Press.

Ervin, Sam. "Implications of Supreme Court Decision in *Miranda v. Arizona.*" *Congressional Record,* 89th Cong., 2d sess., 1966, Vol. 112, pt. 13: 16721–2e.

Hoffman, Joseph L., and William J. Stuntz. 1994. "Habeas after the Revolution." In *Supreme Court Review.* Chicago: University of Chicago Press.

CONGRESS, AGE OF MEMBERS

As a means of securing a minimal level of maturity, the framers of Article I, Sections 2 and 3 of the U.S. Constitution set age minimums of 25 and 30 for members of the House of Representatives and the Senate, respectively. These sections did not establish any maximum or mandatory retirement age.

The states ratified the Twenty-Sixth Amendment in 1971. It lowered the national voting age to 18—most states had previously set the age at

21. Perhaps stimulated by this change, the rest of the decade witnessed numerous amending proposals to lower the minimum age for members of Congress. Democratic representative Robert Drinan of Massachusetts called for lowering the minimum age of members of the House to 22 years and senators to 27 years.

The 1970s also saw the introduction of a number of proposals to set a mandatory retirement age for members of Congress. Proposed retirement ages ranged from 65 to 75. Some of these proposals would also have altered the length of congressional terms, set a maximum age for judges, or set limits on the total number of terms or consecutive terms that members of Congress could serve—a proposal that continues to generate a great deal of contemporary interest and discussion. With no such limits in place, South Carolina's Republican senator Strom Thurmond (a Dixiecrat candidate for president in 1948) assumed chairmanship of the Senate Judiciary Committee after the congressional elections in 1994 at the age of 92, although, after complaints, he subsequently gave in to committee members' desire for greater autonomy (Hook and Cassata 1995, 466). In 1996, Thurmond was elected to another six-year term in the Senate, but he retired in 2003, at the age of 100, and died later that year. If adopted, congressional term limits would probably reduce the average age of members of Congress.

See also Congress, Term Limits; Twenty-Sixth Amendment.

For Further Reading:

Hook, Janet, and Donna Cassata. 1995. "Low-Key Revolt May Spur Thurmond to Give Colleagues Freer Hand." *Congressional Quarterly Weekly Report* 53 (11 February): 466.

CONGRESS, ATTENDANCE OF MEMBERS

The Constitution makes no provision for the attendance of members of Congress, and some have been frequently absent. For example, Adam Clayton Powell, the flamboyant Harlem representative whose expulsion from the House was voided by the Supreme Court in *Powell v. McCormack* (1969), was present for only 30 percent of all roll call votes in the 82nd Congress and only 54 percent when he became chair of the House Education and Labor Committee (Weeks 1971, 4–5).

Amendments were introduced throughout the 1970s to declare the seats of House and Senate members vacant for excessive absences. One of the earliest, introduced by Maine's Republican senator Margaret Chase Smith, would have declared a vacancy whenever members failed to be present for a total of 200 or at least 60 percent of roll call votes (S.J. Res. 192, 1972). Some later proposals would have raised this minimum to 70 percent. By the end of the 1970s, some proposals included exemptions for absences due to hospitalization necessitated by illness or accidents. The September 11, 2001 terrorist attacks on the World Trade Center and the Pentagon have centered attention more recently not on members of Congress who are physically able to attend and do not, but on replacing large numbers of members who might be killed or incapacitated in similar incidents.

See also Congress, Emergency Functioning.

For Further Reading:

Weeks, Kent M. 1971. *Adam Clayton Powell and the Supreme Court.* New York: Dunellen.

CONGRESS, COMMERCE POWERS

Congress has frequently and effectively used the commerce clause of the Constitution to justify its exercise of powers. Indeed, between 1789 and 1950, it was the most frequently litigated provision in the Constitution (Steamer 1992, 167). Located in Article I, Section 8 among the powers of Congress, this provision—which was lacking in the Articles of Confederation—grants Congress power "to regulate Commerce with foreign Nations, and among the several States, and with the Indian Tribes." Without this, or an equivalent, provision, the expansion of federal powers in the 20th century might have required adoption of a number of amendments.

Early in U.S. history, Chief Justice John Marshall gave an expansive reading to the commerce clause, using congressional powers to strike down conflicting state regulations—most notably in *Gibbons v. Ogden* (1824), invalidating a grant of a steamboat monopoly by the state of New York. The question of whether federal power prohibited all state commercial regulations was more difficult. In *Cooley v. Board of Wardens* (1852), the Court adopted the doctrine of "selective exclusiveness," under which it decided whether a particular area of commerce was one that required a single uniform national rule or whether it was one, like the Philadelphia pilotage regulation upheld in *Cooley,* in which some state variation was permissible.

As the United States industrialized, the national government turned increasingly to the commerce clause for authority to regulate activities not otherwise delineated in the Constitution. The Court found itself picking and choosing among those activities it was willing to allow Congress to regulate. The Court's belief in laissez-faire economics, and its development of the doctrine of substantive due process, often led it to hedge congressional commerce powers through various limiting doctrines. Thus, in *United States v. E.C. Knight Company* (1895), the Court held that Congress could not prevent the acquisition of a near monopoly in the sugar-refining industry. It reasoned that manufacturing and production were distinct from subsequent commerce and that monopoly was a local rather than a national matter. From the 1890s through 1937, the Court also distinguished between the regulation of goods that were harmful and those that were not (see, for example, the decision in *Hammer v. Dagenhart* [1918] invalidating a national child labor law); the control of goods that had a "direct" effect and those that had only an "indirect" effect on commerce; and the regulation of goods that were within the "stream of commerce" and those that were not.

From the 1920s through the 1930s, members introduced a number of amendments to give Congress more explicit authority over areas such as the regulation of coal, oil, and gas; agriculture; minimum wages; child labor; hours of labor; and other such matters that Congress might otherwise have regulated under its commerce powers. President Franklin Roosevelt effectively resurrected the commerce clause with his New Deal programs, but many went down to defeat, prompting his Court-packing plan to add one justice (up to 15) for every justice over the age of 70.

Although Congress rejected Roosevelt's plan, the Court subsequently reversed course in 1937 and began reading the commerce clause quite expansively. By 1964, the Court, in *Heart of Atlanta Motel v. United States* and *Katzenbach v. McClung,* upheld the public accommodations section of the Civil Rights Act of 1964 under authority of the commerce clause. Although the Court read one implicit restriction into federal commerce powers in *National League of Cities v. Usery* (1976), when it limited the scope of federal wage regulations as applied to state employees, it subsequently reversed course in *Garcia v. San Antonio Metropolitan Transit Authority* (1985), essentially leaving states to the protections provided by the structure of existing governmental institutions and renewing some calls for strengthening the Tenth Amendment or otherwise strengthening states' rights.

In 1995, in *United States v. Lopez,* Chief Justice William Rehnquist wrote the Supreme Court's 5-to-4 decision striking down the federal Gun-Free School Zones Act, which prohibited possession of a gun within 1,000 feet of a school, as exceeding federal powers under the commerce clause. Citing *National Labor Relations Board v. Jones & Laughlin Steel Corp.* (1937), Rehnquist wrote that "the scope of the interstate commerce power 'must be considered in light of our dual system of government and may not be extended so as to embrace effects upon interstate commerce so indirect and remote that to embrace them, in view of our complex society, would effectively obliterate the distinction between what is national and what is local and to create a completely centralized government'" (*Lopez* 1995, 556). He further ruled that the exercise of congressional power under the commerce clause was limited to the use of the "channels" of interstate commerce; the "instrumentalities" of such commerce; or "those activities having a substantial relation to interstate commerce, those activities that substantially affect interstate commerce" (*Lopez* 1995, 558–559).

Applying similar limitations in *United States v. Morrison* (2000), the Court decided that a section of the Violence Against Women Act of 1994 interfered with state police powers and had not, despite congressional attempts to do so, been adequately tied to commercial regulation and that it therefore exceeded congressional powers under the commerce clause.

See also Congress, Powers of; Marshall, John; Tenth Amendment.

For Further Reading:

Benson, Paul R., Jr. 1970. *The Supreme Court and the Commerce Clause, 1937–1970.* New York: Denellen.

Bittker, Boris I. 1999. *Bittker on the Regulation of Interstate and Foreign Commerce.* Gaithersburg, MD: Aspen Law & Business.

Denning, Brannon P. 2008. "Reconstructing the Dormant Commerce Clause Doctrine." *William and Mary Law Review* 50 (November): 417–516.

Frankfurter, Felix. 1964. *The Commerce Clause under Marshall, Taney and Waite.* Chicago: Quadrangle Books.

Maltz, Earl. 1995. "The Impact of the Constitutional Revolution of 1937 on the Dormant Commerce Clause—A Case Study in the Decline of State Autonomy." *Harvard Journal of Law and Public Policy* 19 (Fall): 121–145.

Steamer, Robert J. 2005. "Commerce Power." In *The Oxford Companion to the Supreme Court of the United States,* ed. Kermit L. Hall. 2d ed. New York: Oxford University Press, 193–196.

United States v. Lopez, 514 U.S. 549 (1995).

CONGRESS, COMMITTEE COMPOSITION

Although the U.S. Constitution does not delineate the role of congressional committees, Congress would have difficulty operating without them. Committees allow for smaller groups to expedite business and allow members to develop their expertise by specializing in areas of particular interest to them.

Party leaders make committee assignments, with the majority party appointing committee chairs. Seniority is an important but not exclusive factor in such determinations. The majority party may attempt to enhance its control by assigning a greater proportion of its members to key committees. House Republicans complained about such policies in the 1980s and early 1990s, when Democrats held a majority, but Republicans were unsuccessful when they challenged such rules in court (Davidson and Oleszek 1994, 211). A number of amendments were also introduced. One introduced on July 1, 1992, proposed that membership on congressional committees be apportioned either equally or according to the proportion of members each party held in the House (H.J. Res. 522). Each party has some incentive to treat the other fairly in the area because each knows that the party in power today may be out of power after the next election, and that the rules applied by the majority party to the minority party when it is in power will likely be applied to it when it becomes the minority party.

For Further Reading:

Davidson, Roger H., and Walter J. Oleszek. 1994. *Congress and Its Members.* 4th ed. Washington DC: Congressional Quarterly.

CONGRESS, DISTRICT REPRESENTATION

Article I, Section 2 of the U.S. Constitution requires that members of the House of Representatives be inhabitants of the states that elect them, but it does not require that they live in their districts. Indeed, although the Constitution apportions representatives according to a state's population, nowhere does it require that such representatives be selected by districts.

In the nation's early history, a number of states selected representatives through the use of a general ticket (Ames 1896, 56). This situation led to 34 resolutions from 1820 through 1826 proposing to amend the Constitution to require election of representatives by districts. In 1819, 1820, and 1822, these resolutions passed in the Senate but were not voted on in the House. In 1842, Congress passed a law accomplishing the same objective, and petitions for such an amendment subsequently ceased (Ames 1896, 56–57).

Most scholars believe that the single-member district system of representation contributes to the maintenance of a two-party system. To win any seats in the House of Representatives, a political party's candidate must get a plurality of the votes in one or more districts. By contrast, in systems that use a scheme of proportional representation, minor parties may be rewarded with some seats even if they do not capture a plurality of any single district (for a general analysis of electoral systems, see Sartori 1994, 27–79). Although early Americans often looked suspiciously at political parties, many modern reformers have aimed to strengthen them (American Political Science Association 1950; Shogan 1982; however, see also Krusch 1992, 98, who would prohibit members of Congress from being party members).

One reason that the Court in *Colegrove v. Green* (1946) rejected the opportunity to reapportion Illinois congressional districts was its fear that a judicial remedy might require statewide elections. Subsequent decisions accepting justiciability over such questions and mandating approximate equality of districts, most notably *Baker v. Carr* (1962) and *Wesberry v. Sanders* (1964), have worked within the existing single-member district scheme. Michael Lind has proposed replacing the single-member districts in the House of Representatives with a system of proportional representation, in part as a way of eliminating partisan and racial gerrymandering (1995, 315).

See also Gerrymandering; States, Legislative Apportionment.

For Further Reading:

American Political Science Association, Committee on Political Parties. 1950. *Toward a More Responsible Two-Party System.* New York: Rinehart.

Ames, Herman. 1896. *The Proposed Amendments to the Constitution of the United States during the First Century of Its History.* Reprint, New York: Burt Franklin, 1970.

Krusch, Barry. 1992. *The 21st Century Constitution: A New America for a New Millennium.* New York: Stanhope Press.

Lind, Michael. 1995. *The Next American Nation: The New Nationalism and the Fourth American Revolution.* New York: The Free Press.

Sartori, Giovanni. 1994. *Comparative Constitutional Engineering: An Inquiry into Structures, Incentives and Outcomes.* New York: New York University Press.

Shogan, Robert. 1982. *None of the Above.* New York: New American Library.

CONGRESS, EMERGENCY FUNCTIONING

World War II ended in 1945 after the United States dropped atomic bombs that wiped out the Japanese cities of Hiroshima and Nagasaki. Shortly thereafter, a protracted cold war developed between the United States and the Soviet Union. In 1949, Russia exploded its first atomic bomb, and hydrogen bombs followed in the next decade. By the 1960s, both powers had enough weapons to destroy each other, and although this precarious balance of terror served to deter world war, it also raised popular fears of a war-induced apocalypse.

In such an atmosphere, concerns arose about the possibility that a war might cripple the government. From 1945 through 1962, there were more than 30 proposals to provide for emergencies (Davidson 2002, 4). The problem was most acute in dealing with the House of Representatives. Under the terms of Article I, Section 2, Clause 4 of the Constitution, state executives fill vacancies in the House by issuing "Writs of Election," which would require a substantial lapse of time and could leave some states unrepresented in that body in the interim. By contrast, under the terms of Article I, Section 3, Clause 2, governors can temporarily fill vacancies in the U.S. Senate until the next meeting of the legislature. The Seventeenth Amendment, in turn, provides that "the legislature of any State may empower the executive thereof to make temporary appointments until the people fill the vacancies by election as the legislature may direct." Thus, there is a constitutionally designated mechanism for filling temporary vacancies in the Senate until an election can be held, but not in the House (Davidson 2002, 1–3).

The most common proposal allowed for state governors, acting under authority of a presidential proclamation, to make temporary appointments whenever the number of vacancies in the House of Representatives exceeded 145 (this proposal reflects the fact that the nation's federal system of government—with 50 separate centers of power spread throughout the nation—might make it somewhat less vulnerable to catastrophe than unitary systems without such sovereign subunits). Congress has held a number of hearings on the subject, and proposals for providing temporary replacements for House members in the case of massive casualties or incapacities passed the Senate in 1954 by a vote of 70 to 1, and in 1955 by a vote of 76 to 3. Although a proposal introduced by Tennessee Democratic senator Estes Kefauver on the subject and adopted by the Senate in 1960 was not ultimately successful, it became the catalyst for an amendment to repeal the poll tax (Bernstein with Agel 1993, 137).

After the horrific terrorist attack by two airplanes on the World Trade Center and another on the Pentagon on September 11, 2001, renewed attention was given to operations in case of an attack on the government. In December 2001, Representative Brian Baird, a Washington Democrat, proposed an amendment to vest state governors with the power to appoint members of the House to 90-day terms when a quarter or more were killed, disabled, or missing ("Thinking the Unthinkable" 2001, 11). Some question has arisen as to whether governors should have to appoint individuals from the same party as the members that they would be replacing, but the requirement for providing for temporary Senate vacancies contains no such provision.

See also Twenty-fifth Amendment.

For Further Reading:

Bernstein, Richard B., with Jerome Agel. 1993. *Amending America: If We Love the Constitution So Much, Why Do We Keep Trying to Change It?* New York: Random House.

"Continuity of Congress," http://www.aeipolitical corner.org/continuity.htm and http://www.continuity ofgovernment.org. Accessed November 21, 2002.

Davidson, Michael. 2002. "Notes on Proposed Constitutional Amendments on Temporary Appointments of Members of the House." www.aeipolitical corner.org/continuity.htm. Accessed May 16, 2002.

Ornstein, Norman. 2002. "Preparing for the Unthinkable: Bush's 'Shadow Government' Plan Is a Start—But Only a Start." *The Wall Street Journal,* 11 March, A18.

"Thinking the Unthinkable." 2001. *State Legislatures* 27 (December): 11.

Zuckerman, Edward. 1984. *The Day after World War III.* New York: Viking Press.

CONGRESS, FILIBUSTERS IN SENATE

One of the Senate's most hallowed folkways is the filibuster, which has been in use since 1841. This procedure permits members to delay or stop action on a pending bill by monopolizing floor debates in the hope that its sponsors will eventually concede. The first limits were imposed on this mechanism in 1917, after Woodrow Wilson called a group of antiwar progressives opposed to his plans to arm merchant ships "a little group of willful men [who] have rendered the government of the United States helpless and contemptible" (Gettlinger 1994, 3198). In 1975, the Senate modified an earlier rule and permitted a cloture vote by three-fifths of the entire membership rather than the previously required two-thirds of those present and voting (S. Smith 1989, 342). Such cloture votes are still quite difficult to achieve, however, and with some other changes in the way filibusters are conducted, their number has actually increased, with one-half of the total occurring since 1975 (Gettlinger 1994, 3198).

At least four proposed amendments would have altered filibuster procedures. Two proposals introduced in 1916 by West Virginia Democratic senator William Chilton were designed to cut off debate, one after 10 days and the other after 20 hours. In 1969, Democratic senator Mike Mansfield of Montana offered a proposal preventing the Senate from limiting or closing debate by less than three-fifths of those present and voting (S.J. Res. 36). Similarly, in the 90th congress (2005–2006), a member introduced an amendment to require unanimous consent to close debate on "any measure, motion, or other matter pending before the Senate."

Although filibusters are often associated in the popular mind with racist senators opposed to progressive civil rights legislation (the longest filibuster was one by South Carolina Senator Strom Thurmond that lasted over 24 hours opposing the Civil Rights Bill of 1957), the mechanism allows for delay by any senator with strong views.

Debate was renewed over the filibuster when Democrats sought to use it to block confirmation of George W. Bush's nominees to lower federal courts during his first term. Seven Democrats and seven Republicans—the so-called "Gang of 14," eventually agreed to help secure up or down votes on the nominees and to reserve the filibuster for more extraordinary matters (Nelson 2008, II, 1405).

For Further Reading:

Gettlinger, Stephen. 1994. "New Filibuster Tactics Imperil Next Senate." *Congressional Quarterly* 52 (5 November): 3198.

Musmanno, M. A. 1929. *Proposed Amendments to the Constitution.* Washington DC: U.S. Government Printing Office.

Nelson, Michael, ed. 2008. *Guide to the Presidency,* 2 vols., 4th ed. Washington DC: CQ Press.

Smith, Steven. 1989. "Taking It to the Floor." In *Congress Reconsidered,* eds. Lawrence C. Dodd and Bruce I. Oppenheimer. Washington DC: Congressional Quarterly.

CONGRESS, IMMUNITY OF MEMBERS

To insulate members of Congress from political reprisals and to ensure free and open debate,

Article I, Section 6 of the U.S. Constitution specifies that they "shall in all Cases, except Treason, Felony and Breach of the Peace, be privileged from Arrest during their Attendance at the Session of their respective Houses." It further provides that "for any Speech or Debate in either House, they shall not be questioned in any other Place." At least seven proposals have been introduced from 1917 to 1983 to alter one or both of these provisions.

The congressional privilege against arrest is not as broad as it may appear, since the Supreme Court has held that it applies only to civil arrests, which are no longer carried out (R. Baker 1992, 175). The Court's interpretation appears to call into question the need for an amendment introduced in 1983 allowing members going to or returning from Congress to be arrested for traffic violations (H.J. Res. 318).

The most common proposals for alterations have focused on the speech and debate clause and have been directed toward preventing members of Congress from using the congressional platform for libeling individuals—although making it difficult to prove, American courts still recognize libel as an exception to the freedoms of speech and press protected by the First Amendment. Generally, the Court has interpreted the speech and debate clause liberally. It has thus extended protection beyond the floor of Congress to remarks members make before committees. Moreover, in *Gravel v. United States* (1972), the Court extended some collateral protection to congressional aides, who were described as congressional alter egos.

In *Hutchinson v. Proxmire* (1979), however, a case involving Wisconsin Democratic senator William Proxmire's much-publicized "Golden Fleece" Awards, the Court ruled that members of Congress could be sued if statements in their press releases were libelous. Similarly, in *United States v. Brewster* (1972), the Court held that the speech and debate clause did not provide a defense for a member of Congress convicted of taking a bribe. Also, in *Gravel v. United States* (1972), the Court said that congressional immunity did not extend to contracts that members of Congress made with book companies. It further decided that a grand jury could inquire into how members of Congress got classified information. In that case, Alaska Democratic senator

Mike Gravel had obtained a copy of the Pentagon Papers and read them into the record of a subcommittee he chaired. Two days after he had done so, California Republican representative Charles Gubser introduced an amendment (H.J. Res. 754) providing that members of Congress could be prosecuted for disclosing classified information.

See also First Amendment.

For Further Reading:

Baker, Richard A. 1992. "Congress, Arrest and Immunity of Members of." In *The Oxford Companion to the Supreme Court of the United States,* ed. Kermit L. Hall. New York: Oxford University Press.

Betts, James T. 1967. "The Scope of Immunity for Legislators and Their Employees." *Yale Law Journal* 77 (December): 366–389.

Johnson, Carrie. 2008. "Congressmen use clause to dodge prosecution." *The Tennessean,* November 1, 2008, p. 1A, 12A.

CONGRESS, LEGISLATIVE VETO

The doctrine of separation of powers suggests that Congress makes the laws, the president enforces them, and the courts interpret them. The reality is considerably more complex. Sometimes because of inadequate drafting, sometimes because of the complexity of the subject, and sometimes because Congress has made a conscious attempt to avoid or defer controversial decisions, administrative agencies issue numerous rules to implement congressional laws. Congress is understandably concerned that such rules do not usurp its own legislative functions. After numerous reports of agency abuse and incompetence, "criticism of agency rulemaking . . . reached a shrill pitch in the 1970s" (L. Fisher 1991, 142). Although several laws and amendments were introduced in Congress to grant itself a veto over all agency regulations, such attempts failed.

Congress increasingly turned to the so-called legislative veto mechanism, whereby one or both houses granted wide rulemaking power to a particular agency while reserving the power to veto administrative decisions that Congress did not approve. Although the mechanism had been used for about 50 years and made Congress somewhat more willing to delegate power to administrative agencies than it otherwise would have been, most presidents were on record as challenging the constitutionality of this mechanism. In *Immigration and Naturalization Service v. Chadha* (1983), a case involving congressional revocation of a decision by the INS to grant permanent resident status to an East Indian from Kenya who held a British passport, the Supreme Court outlawed such vetoes. It declared that they were contrary to the presentment clause, which allows the president the chance to veto all legislation, and, in the immediate case, to the bicameralism requirement specifying that all legislation pass both houses of Congress (Craig 1988). Within days, an amendment was introduced (H.J. Res. 313) to reinstate the legislative veto mechanism. Although such an amendment was not adopted, Congress has developed a number of informal mechanisms, often at the congressional committee level, by which it still maintains oversight of legislative rule making (L. Fisher 1993, 286–288).

For Further Reading:

Craig, Barbara H. 1988. *Chadha: The Story of an Epic Constitutional Struggle.* New York: Oxford University Press.

Fisher, Louis. 1991. *Constitutional Conflicts between Congress and the President,* 3d ed. Lawrence: University Press of Kansas.

CONGRESS, MEMBERS' ELIGIBILITY FOR OTHER OFFICES

Article I, Section 6 of the U.S. Constitution provides that "no Person holding any Office under the United States, shall be a member of either House during his Continuance In Office." The latter part of this clause is one obstacle to the establishment of a parliamentary system, under which cabinet officers would be selected from among members of congress.

Article I, Section 6 also prohibits a member of Congress from being appointed "to any civil Office under the Authority of the United States, which shall have been created, or the Emoluments whereof shall have been encreased [sic] during such time." Throughout the 19th century, there were over 30 attempts to extend this ban to exclude appointment to any civil office, sometimes making exceptions for appointments to the judiciary and sometimes extending the ban for two years after a member of Congress left office (Ames 1896, 30–33). Andrew Jackson offered one such proposal. He may have been influenced by the "corrupt bargain" he alleged had been struck when, after the four-way presidential election of 1824 involving Jackson, Henry Clay, William Crawford, and John Quincy Adams, Clay shifted his support to Adams, who subsequently rewarded him with an appointment as secretary of state (Van Deusen 1937, 179–195). At least four amending proposals introduced from 1929 to 1945 have sought a ban similar to that advocated in the 19th century.

Controversies sometimes arise when members of Congress have been suggested for, or appointed to, judicial posts or cabinet offices for which salaries have been increased during their tenure. As a remedy, Congress generally adopts legislation reducing the pay for the appointee to that in effect at the beginning of the appointee's term. Thus, when President Clinton appointed Texas Senator Lloyd Bentsen as secretary of treasury, Congress passed a law reducing "'the compensation and other emoluments attached to the office of Secretary of the Treasury' to those in effect on January 1, 1989" (Paulsen 1994, 909). Although acknowledging that such legislation meets "the rationale" behind the emoluments clause, a law professor has argued that it actually violates the constitutional "rule" itself (Paulsen 1994, 911). This suggests either that current practices should be altered or that an amendment should be adopted to bring the Constitution in line with current practice.

See also Parliamentary System.

For Further Reading:

Ames, Herman. 1896. *The Proposed Amendments to the Constitution of the United States during the First Century of Its History.* Reprint, New York: Burt Franklin, 1970.

Paulsen, Michael S. 1994. "Is Lloyd Bentsen Unconstitutional?" *Stanford Law Review* 46 (April): 907–918.

Van Deusen, Glyndon. 1937. *The Life of Henry Clay.* Boston: Little, Brown.

CONGRESS, OVERRIDING JUDICIAL DECISIONS

No power that courts exercise is any more important or more controversial than the power of judicial review. This allows courts to strike down state and federal laws or executive orders that they find to be unconstitutional. Not explicitly stated in the Constitution, the power is arguably an important ancillary to the doctrines of separation of powers, federalism (in the case of unconstitutional state laws), and the supremacy of a written constitution. Chief Justice John Marshall first exercised and justified this power to strike down a federal law in *Marbury v. Madison* (1803), a decision that continues to be at the center of scholarly debate (Alfange 1994).

The power of judicial review is controversial, partly because it is not stated in the Constitution. It also stirs controversy because judges are neither elected by nor directly accountable to the people, and they can accordingly thwart democratic wishes. Its exercise thus presents what Alexander Bickel has called "the countermajoritarian difficulty" (Bickel 1986, 16).

Many proposals have been made to rein in judicial review. From just before the Court's turnaround in 1937 through the 1980s, at least 25 proposals were advanced that would have allowed Congress to overturn such decisions. Although other majorities have been suggested, the most common proposal would allow Congress to override court decisions by a two-thirds vote. If adopted, this would give Congress power over judicial decisions equivalent to that which it now exercises over presidential vetoes.

Congress already has the power to override decisions of the Court that are based simply on statutory interpretation. In such cases, which are relatively frequent, Congress can simply adopt new laws to clarify its intentions (Eskridge 1991; Paschal 1991). Currently, if Congress wishes to override a constitutional interpretation of the courts, it must proceed by constitutional amendment. Congress so acted in the case of the Eleventh, Fourteenth, Sixteenth, and Twenty-sixth Amendments. An amendment granting Congress power to make such reversals by a two-thirds vote, without subsequent consent of three-fourths of the states, could significantly impact the operation of the current amending process. The impact of a more recent proposal encouraging Congress to draft amendments to overturn specific decisions from seven months to a year after the Supreme Court's yearly term is more difficult to measure (T. Baker 1995).

See also Marshall, John; Supreme Court Decisions Reversed by Constitutional Amendments.

For Further Reading:

Alfange, Dean, Jr. 1994. "*Marbury v. Madison* and Original Understandings of Judicial Review: In Defense of Traditional Wisdom." In *Supreme Court Review, 1993*. Chicago: University of Chicago Press.

Baker, Thomas E. 1995. "Exercising the Amendment Power to Disapprove of Supreme Court Decisions: A Proposal for a 'Republican Veto.'" *Hastings Constitutional Law Quarterly* 22 (Winter): 325–357.

Bickel, Alexander. 1986. *The Least Dangerous Branch: The Supreme Court at the Bar of Politics*. 2d ed. New Haven, CT: Yale University Press.

Eskridge, William N., Jr. 1991. "Overriding Supreme Court Statutory Interpretations Decisions." *Yale Law Journal* 101 (November): 331–455.

Hamburger, Philip. 2008. *Law and Judicial Duty*. Cambridge, MA: Harvard University Press.

Paschal, Richard A. 1991. "The Continuing Colloquy: Congress and the Finality of the Supreme Court." *Journal of Law and Politics* 8 (Fall): 143–226.

West Coast Hotel v. Parrish, 300 U.S. 379 (1937).

CONGRESS, POWERS OF

The U.S. Constitution serves both to grant and limit powers. The document lists, or enumerates,

most congressional powers in Article I, Section 8. These include powers like the power to coin money, to raise taxes, and to regulation interstate commerce that the Articles of Confederation did not vest in its congress as well as powers over war and peace that Congress shares with the president.

Not long after the Constitution was ratified, a dispute arose over whether Congress could create a national bank, as Secretary of the Treasury, Alexander Hamilton, desired or whether it was unconstitutional, as Secretary of State, Thomas Jefferson thought. President Washington and Congress eventually sided with Hamilton, who argued that the power to create a bank was a "necessary and proper" measure for carrying into effect other powers, but Democratic-Republicans believed this decision, along with an eventual Supreme Court decision legitimizing the bank in *McCulloch v. Maryland* (1819) stretched the idea of enumerated powers to the breaking point.

Significantly, a number of early Democratic-Republican presidents vetoed internal improvements laws that they thought exceeded congressional authority. Proposed amendments have sought to give Congress power to control the air force (the Constitution mentions only land and sea forces), to establish a bank, to regulate trade marks, to regulate child labor, to provide for a national university, to restrict polygamy, to pass laws involving environmental protection, to provide public housing, medical care, minimum wages, pensions, workers' compensation laws, and enact price controls, or provide for numerous other social and economic rights.

Congress is often able to regulate such matters through its taxing, commerce, general welfare, or war-related powers, and presidents who have sought a larger congressional role may be reluctant to propose specific amendments to do so for fear of making it appear that they are asking for powers that the Constitution does not currently grant. Since the New Deal, courts have generally, albeit not always, deferred to congressional claims that matters were related to such powers, although on occasion, the Court will rule that such powers trench on state police powers under the Tenth Amendment. The Court's decision in *United States v. Morrison* (2000), invalidating the provision of the Violence

Against Women Act that allowed individuals to bring civil suits in federal courts to redress such violence led Casey Westover, then a clerk for a federal judge, to propose an amendment providing that "Congress shall have the power to legislate in furtherance of the general welfare" (327).

The Thirteenth, Fourteenth, and Fifteenth Amendments all granted Congress power to enforce protections for all citizens, while other amendments prohibiting discriminatory voting have also included such congressional enforcement clauses. The Sixteenth Amendment, legitimizing the federal income tax, remains the primary example of an amendment that has increased congressional powers. The Eighteenth Amendment, providing for national alcoholic prohibition, was another, but was repealed by the Twenty-first Amendment.

See also agriculture, Air Force, Articles of Confederation, child labor, Eighteenth Amendment, environmental protection, Fifteenth Amendment, Fourteenth Amendment, internal improvements, McCulloch v. Maryland, minimum wages, national bank, polygamy, Sixteenth Amendment, social and economic rights, Tenth Amendment, Thirteenth Amendment.

Further Reading:

Beck, J. Randy. 2002. "The New Jurisprudence of the Necessary and Proper Clause," *University of Illinois Law Review* 2002: 581–649.

Johnson, Calvin H. 2005. "The Dubious Enumerated Power Doctrine." *Constitutional Commentary* 22 (Spring): 25–95.

Kip, Frederic E. n.d. *Equal Opportunity for All as Against Special Benefits to a Privileged Few.* "Kypsburg," Montclair, New Jersey.

Westover, Casey L. 2003. "The Twenty-eighth Amendment: Why the Constitution Should Be Amended to Grant Congress the Power to Legislative in Furtherance of the General Welfare." *John Marshall Law Review* 36 (Winter): 327–369.

CONGRESS, PRIVATE BILLS

Most congressional laws are public laws that are phrased in general terms and refer to broad classes of individuals. Indeed, the 18th-century French philosopher Jean-Jacques Rousseau argued that just laws were necessarily general, always considering "the subjects as a body and actions by their genera or species, never one man in particular or one unique individual action" (Rousseau 1978, 190). Despite such admonitions, Congress sometimes adopts private laws to provide relief for a single individual. From 1989 to 1991, such laws accounted for only 2.4 percent of the total, but the number was as high as 90 percent from 1905 to 1907 (Congressional Quarterly 1991, 359–360), during which time such bills were often the target of the presidential veto power.

Approximately 20 proposals were introduced from 1876 to 1909 to prohibit or limit private bills, but the number of private bills has been reduced both by the adoption of legislation and by the establishment of courts to hear claims that used to occupy congressional attention. Moreover, members of Congress who have introduced private bills or promised to introduce private bills for personal gain—as in the Abscam investigation—have been successfully prosecuted (*Congressional Quarterly* 1991, 166–167). No amendments related to private bills have been introduced in recent years. However, as concerns have been raised about the way members of Congress often add special provisions to laws to benefit individual constituents or groups of constituents, there has been some renewed discussion of a "Truth-in-Legislation" Amendment that would limit legislation to a single topic and/or require that the content of legislation match that of its heading. Proponents of an item veto have made similar arguments on its behalf, as have opponents of federal "earmarks," who believe that such programs add to federal deficits.

See also Truth-in-Legislation Amendment.

For Further Reading:

Congressional Quarterly. 1991. *Guide to Congress.* 4th ed. Washington DC: Congressional Quarterly.

Morehead, Joe. 1985. "Private Bills and Private Laws: A Guide to the Legislative Process." *Serials Librarian* 9 (Spring): 115–125.

Rousseau, Jean-Jacques. c.1762. *On the Social Contract with Geneva Manuscript and Political*

Economy, ed. Roger D. Masters. Reprint, New York: St. Martin's Press, 1978.

Kravitz, Walter, 1993. *American Congressional Dictionary.* Washington DC: Congressional Quarterly.

CONGRESS, QUORUM

Article I, Section 5 of the Constitution specifies that a majority of each house of Congress constitutes a quorum, or the number of members required to do business. The House can evade this provision by working as a Committee of the Whole, in which case only 100 members must be present (Kravitz 1993, 215). Either house may also operate with less than a quorum as long as no member objects.

Under current law, a quorum is measured on the basis of living members of the House. This means that a House of Representatives decimated by a terrorist attack could continue to operate until elections were held for replacements (state governors can already make temporary appointments in the case of senators), but it could prove highly undesirable to have a large number of states effectively disenfranchised during such a time of crisis when important legislation might be considered (M. Davidson 2002, 6).

In 1883, Democratic Representative Joseph Wheeler of Alabama introduced an amending resolution to reduce the quorum to one-third of the members of each house (Ames 1896, 39). In 1947 and 1949, Republican representative Charles Plumley of Vermont introduced resolutions that would accept an individual's quorum call only when one-fifth of the members present called for one.

See also Congress, Emergency Functioning.

For Further Reading:

Ames, Herman. 1896. *The Proposed Amendments to the Constitution of the United States during the First Century of Its History.* Reprint, New York: Burt Franklin.

Davidson, Michael. January 20, 2002. "Notes on Proposed Constitutional Amendments on Temporary Appointments of Members of the House," www.aeipoliticalcorner.org/continuity.htm. Accessed May 16, 2002.

CONGRESS, RECALL OF MEMBERS

Although the Constitution provides for the impeachment and conviction of officials guilty of criminal misconduct, it does not permit the recall of individuals on grounds of incompetence or unrepresentativeness, and the U.S. Supreme Court's decision in *Cook v. Gralike* (2001) has limited the ability of states to attempt to "instruct" members of Congress or penalize them when they fail to heed such directives. There have been a number of proposed amendments to recall members of Congress, a practice that was permitted under Article V of the Articles of Confederation (Solberg 1958, 43).

The first such proposals focused on senators and came from Virginia representatives from 1803 to 1810. Such proposals, which seem to have reflected concerns over states' rights rather than popular democracy, would have allowed the state legislatures to recall and replace senators. Such proposals may have reflected a view—prominent at the time of the American Revolution—that such legislators were subject to instruction by their constituents, in this case, the state legislatures (G. Wood 1969, 188–196). Interestingly, at least three senators, including future president John Tyler, resigned in the 19th century when they were unable to follow the wishes of the state legislatures that had selected them (Ames 1896, 65). Similarly, John Quincy Adams resigned his seat after the Massachusetts legislature elected his successor nine months early (Leish 1968, 1:178).

The recall, like the initiative and referendum, was popular with reformers in the Progressive Era. Most 20th-century proposals would permit voters to recall both senators and members of the House. A 1987 Gallup poll indicated that 67 percent of the people favored such a mechanism (Cronin 1989, 132). Advocates believe that such a mechanism would promote democracy and accountability. Opponents fear that it might undermine representative government.

See also Constituent Instructions for Amending Constitutions; *Cook v. Gralike;* Initiative and Referendum; Progressive Era.

For Further Reading:

Ames, Herman. 1896. *The Proposed Amendments to the Constitution of the United States during the First Century of Its History.* Reprint, New York: Burt Franklin, 1970.

Cronin, Thomas E. 1989. *Direct Democracy: The Politics of Initiative, Referendum, and Recall.* Cambridge, MA: Harvard University Press.

Leish, Kenneth W., ed. 1968. *The American Heritage Pictorial History of the Presidents of the United States.* 2 vols. n.p.: American Heritage.

Solberg, Winton, ed. 1958. *The Federal Convention and the Formation of the Union.* Indianapolis, IN: Bobbs-Merrill.

Wood, Gordon S. 1969. *The Creation of the American Republic, 1776–1787.* New York: W. W. Norton.

CONGRESS, REPRESENTATION IN

One of the most difficult issues the delegates to the Constitutional Convention faced was the issue of representation. Advocates of the Virginia Plan wanted states to be represented in both houses of Congress according to population. Advocates of the New Jersey Plan wanted to preserve the system under the Articles of Confederation, whereby states were represented equally. In the Connecticut, or Great, Compromise, delegates agreed to allocate representation in the House by population and to give states equal representation in the Senate. The only remaining stated substantive limit on the amending process provides that no state shall be deprived of such representation without its consent. This provision did not deter two members of Congress from introducing resolutions in 1882 and 1892 to increase the number of senators for more populous states.

The Constitutional Convention was also torn by debates between the slave and free states. The former wanted slaves to count for purposes of congressional representation but not for taxation, whereas the free states had opposite interests. In one of the least defensible parts of the Constitution, the delegates settled on a three-fifths formula, which they incorporated into Article I, Section 2. Under this formula, "three-fifths of such other persons [slaves]" were to count for purposes of taxation and representation (Vile 1993a, 27–28). When the Thirteenth Amendment prohibited slavery, the Southern states—dominated by Democrats who had fought against the Union—actually stood to gain representation. When Section 2 of the Fourteenth Amendment subsequently obliterated the three-fifths clause by providing that representation would now be based on "the whole number of persons in each State, excluding Indians not taxed," it also provided a mechanism to reduce representation for those states that restricted the vote other than to males under the age of 21 or those who were guilty of crimes or of participation in rebellion. These provisions followed numerous resolutions for amendments that had been introduced in Congress. In part because it was difficult to ascertain how many people were actually being deprived of the franchise, this provision was never actually put into effect (*Congressional Quarterly* 1991, 742).

A number of reforms relating to representation have been proposed in the 20th century. The 1920s witnessed several proposals to require reapportionment after each decennial census. The topic was then of particular concern, because this was the only time in U.S. history that Congress, faced for the first time with an apparent majority of urban residents, failed to reapportion after such a census (*Congressional Quarterly* 1991, 742–743). Several subsequent proposals would have limited the number of senators from new states. Some would have based representation on the number of U.S. citizens and legal resident aliens within each state rather than on a state's total population, which the Census Bureau now tries to record. The current method of apportionment arguably rewards states with large numbers of illegal aliens with extra representation. At least one scholar, who focuses chiefly on the intention he believes lies behind the census provisions in Article I and the Fourteenth Amendment rather than their explicit reference to "persons," already believes Congress has the authority to exclude illegal aliens from existing counts (C. Wood 1999). A proposal has been made for reapportioning representation in the House after each presidential election, based on the number of voters in such elections. Another proposal (perhaps goaded by the large number of lawyers who are elected to Congress) called for apportioning representatives according to vocation. Others proposed increasing the number of members of the Senate.

The Constitution guarantees that each state will have at least one member in the House of Representatives, and law now caps House membership at 435. This has inevitably meant that, however influential Supreme Court decisions such as *Wesberry v. Sanders* (1964) have been in mandating numerical equality among districts in the same state, interstate numerical equality of districts has been impossible to attain. Thus, in 1980, Nevada and Maine both had two seats, although the former had a population of 787,000 and the latter a population of 1,125,000. By contrast, South Dakota, with a population of 690,000, got only one seat (Butler and Cain 1992, 18). Throughout American history, a number of different mechanisms have been used to ascertain representatives for states with a fraction over or under what they would receive simply on the basis of population (Butler and Cain 1992, 19). The method now used is known as the method of equal proportions and was developed in 1921 by Edward V. Huntington of Harvard and adopted by Congress in 1941. After assigning each state a seat,

"priority numbers" for states to receive second seats, third seats, and so on are calculated by dividing the state's population by the square root of $n(n-1)$ where "n" is the number of seats for that state. The priority numbers are then lined up in order and the seats given to the states with priority numbers until 435 are awarded" (*Congressional Quarterly* 1991, 745).

The Court upheld this method of apportionment in *U.S. Department of Commerce v. Montana* (1992), in which Montana protested its loss of a House seat that reduced its representation to one member. Such situations have led to a number of calls to give each state at least two representatives.

See also Congress, Size of; Constitutional Convention of 1787; Fourteenth Amendment; Thirteenth Amendment.

For Further Reading:

Butler, David, and Bruce Cain. 1992. *Congressional Redistricting: Comparative and Theoretical Perspectives.* New York: Macmillan.

Congressional Quarterly. 1991. *Guide to Congress.* 4th ed. Washington DC: Congressional Quarterly.

Vile, John R. 1993. *Contemporary Questions Surrounding the Constitutional Amending Process.* Westport, CT: Praeger.

Wood, Charles. 1999. "Losing Control of America's Future: The Census, Birthright Citizenship, and Illegal Aliens." *Harvard Journal of Law and Public Policy* 22 (Spring): 465–522.

CONGRESS, SENATE REPRESENTATION

The U.S. Senate is one of the institutions of government most frequently subject to criticism, especially for granting states equal representation regardless of their population. This was such a fundamental compromise at the Constitutional Convention of 1787 that it was entrenched within Article V, the amending article, by the provision that no state could be denied its equal suffrage within the Senate without its consent.

Today's Senate is more democratic than that of the first Congress. The Seventeenth Amendment, ratified in 1913, provided for senators to be chosen by direct popular election rather than by the state legislatures, as previously was the case. Critics, however, continue to see the equal state representation in the U.S. Senate as undemocratic and undesirable (Dahl 2001, 17–18). Such criticisms relate directly to the amending process, because the only used mechanism specified in this process requires two-thirds majorities of both houses of Congress to propose amendments. Although not focusing on this aspect of this representation, two public choice advocates have identified what they consider to be three negative consequences of this arrangement. They include unjustifiable redistribution of wealth "from the large population states to the small ones," away from racial minorities, and away from large states that might otherwise be able "to block federal homogenizing legislation that they consider disadvantageous" (Baker and Dinkin 1997, 23).

Having come to these conclusions, the scholars note that the current constitution, and especially the current entrenchment clause within Article V, makes reform very unlikely. They do offer a number of novel suggestions for possible changes. These include the possibility of repealing the entrenchment clause before reconfiguring representation in the Senate (Baker and Dinkin 1997, 68–72) or allowing larger states to divide. In what would be every high school geography student's nightmare, the authors suggest that California might divide into 65 new states (Baker and Dinkin 1997, 72). The authors also argue that the Supreme Court might interpret the Fifth or Fifteenth Amendments to inaugurate changes (Baker and Dinkin 1997, 74–81). Finally, they suggest that the large states might simply engage in a "work stoppage" (Baker and Dinkin 1997, 81) or even that the issue could become salient enough to prompt a popular revolt (Baker and Dinkin, 83–84).

Drawing from practice in the early republic, Terry Smith, a Fordham law professor, has argued that states could, under existing provisions, including the Seventeenth Amendment, choose to elect senators in two separate districts, a plan that he believes might result in greater minority representation and cuts to the costs of senate campaigns (1996). By contract, Michael Lind thinks "The best approach would be to sever the Senate from the states altogether" (2005, 318). He thinks that senators should "be elected by proportional representation, in national elections, and serve four years, concurrent with the president (318.).

See also Constitutional Convention of 1787; Entrenchment Clauses; Seventeenth Amendment.

For Further Reading:

Baker, Lynn A., and Samuel H. Dinkin. 1997. "The Senate: An Institution Whose Time Has Gone?" *Journal of Law & Politics* 13 (Winter): 21–95.

Bowman, Scott J. 2004. "Wild Political Dreaming: Constitution Reformation of the United States Senate." *Fordham Law Review* 72 (March): 1017–1051.

Fleming, James E. 2009. "Toward a More Democratic Congress?" *Boston University Law Review* 89 (April): 629–640

Lind, Michael. 2005. *The Next American Nation: The New Nationalism and the Fourth American Revolution.* New York: The Free Press.

Smith, Terry. 1996. "Rediscovering the Sovereignty of the People: the Case for Senate Districts." *North Carolina Law Review* 75 (November): 1–74.

CONGRESS, SIZE OF

Article I, Section 2 of the U.S. Constitution specifies that the membership of the House of Representatives "shall not exceed one for every thirty Thousand [people]," and Article I, Section 3 guarantees that each state will have at least two senators. The first of 12 amendments proposed by Congress in 1789 (10 of which were ratified as the Bill of Rights) would have provided that when membership in the House reached 100, there would be at least one representative for every 40,000 persons. It also would have mandated that when House membership reached 200, it should not fall below this number, nor should there be more than one representative for every 50,000 persons—requirements that, at some population stage, may well have been contradictory (Amar 1992, 1143). Unlike an accompanying provision that was putatively ratified as the Twenty-Seventh Amendment in 1992, the congressional representation amendment was not ratified and is today irrelevant.

There were 65 members in the first session of the House of Representatives. After the 1800 census, the number grew to 106, and by 1900, it reached 391. This led to concerns that the size of the House might become too unwieldy. Beginning with a proposal introduced by Anti-Democrat States' Rights senator James Barbour of Virginia in 1821, there were just over a dozen proposed amendments to cap the size of the House (with the proposed size gradually increasing) until 1911, when the number of House members was set by law at 435 (*Congressional Quarterly* 1991, 741–742).

Since 1911, there have been a few proposals to raise the number of House members to 450,

480, or 500. Columnist George W. Will has suggested that the number should be 1,000. However, members of Congress have also proposed reducing the size of such membership to 300, 350, or 400. There have also been some proposals to increase the size of the Senate by equally increasing the number of senators for all states or by increasing the number of senators apportioned to the more populous states. Unless all states approved the latter amendment, it would be in apparent violation of an entrenchment provision now in Article V that prohibits states from being deprived of their equal representation in the Senate without their consent.

See also Constitutional Amendments, Limits on; Entrenchment Clauses; Twenty-seventh Amendment.

For Further Reading:
Amar, Akhil R. 1992. "The Bill of Rights as a Constitution." *Yale Law Journal* 100 (Winter): 1131–1210.
Congressional Quarterly. 1991. *Guide to Congress.* 4th ed. Washington DC: Congressional Quarterly.
Will, George W. "Congress Just Isn't Big Enough." *Washington Post,* January 14, 2001.

CONGRESS, SPECIAL ELECTIONS

In the United Kingdom, which is typical of parliamentary systems, the people elect the prime minister and members of Parliament to five-year terms, but the prime minister may call an early election when the minister believes that an election will bolster party support. The prime minister may also call a new election after receiving a vote of "no confidence" in Parliament (Rasmussen and Moses 1995, 82). By contrast, the U.S. Constitution provides for fixed terms and makes no such provision for ad hoc congressional elections (except in the case of individual members who die).

Numerous proponents of incorporating one or more parliamentary features into the U.S. government have advocated allowing Congress or the president to call such special elections.

Populist senator William Peffer of Kansas introduced such a proposal in 1895, as did Republican representative Charles Potter of Michigan in 1951. The former was directed specifically at issues of finance and foreign relations. The latter resolution would have required Congress to hold a national election if requested to do so by a two-thirds vote of its members.

See also Parliamentary System.

For Further Reading:
Rasmussen, Jorgen S., and Joel C. Moses. 1995. *Major European Governments.* 9th ed. Belmont, CA: Wadsworth.

CONGRESS, TAXATION BY

See Sixteenth Amendment; Taxation entries.

CONGRESS, TERM LENGTHS

The Constitution sets the terms of members of the House of Representatives at two years and the terms of senators at six years. The terms of House members were designed to keep them especially close and accountable to the people; by contrast, the terms of senators were designed to give them greater independence.

Because all members of the House are elected every two years, there is a chance for a large turnover in presidential election years, and the president's party almost always loses seats in so-called off-year, or midterm, House elections that occur between presidential contests. By contrast, only one-third of senators run for election in presidential election years, and swings in nonpresidential election years tend to be less dramatic than those in the House.

A study completed in 1991 listed just over 200 proposals that had sought to alter House terms and just over 50 more that would have both altered such terms and limited the number of terms that an individual could serve (S. Richardson 1991, 72–80, 87–90). Proposals have ranged from those calling for yearly election of House members to those calling for terms of three, four, or six years. Similarly, from 1789 to 1991, 13 proposals were introduced to lower the terms of senators to three or four years or to raise them to eight years; another four would also have limited the number of terms (S. Richardson 1991, 91, 100). Some versions of the four- and eight-year terms have been designed so that such terms would be more closely tied to presidential fortunes and thus encourage greater party discipline and coherence.

By far, the most common proposal in regard to congressional term lengths has been to raise the terms of members of the House of Representatives to four years. Longer House terms would arguably give members greater independence and allow them to devote more time to legislating and less to fundraising. Critics argue that such terms would also put further distance between the representatives and their constituents.

At least one proposal introduced in 1989 to increase House terms to four years would also have required House members running for the Senate to vacate their seats (H.J. Res. 203). Individuals proposing raising the length of congressional terms have sometimes also advocated recall mechanisms.

See also Congress, Term Limits.

For Further Reading:

Richardson, Sula. 1991. *Congressional Terms of Office and Tenure: Historical Background and Contemporary Issues.* Washington DC: Congressional Research Service, Library of Congress.

Vile, John R. 2010. *A Companion to the United States Constitution and Its Amendments.* 5th ed. Westport, CT: Praeger.

CONGRESS, TERM LIMITS

In 1951, the states ratified the Twenty-Second Amendment, limiting presidents to two full terms. Ever since, proposals have periodically been introduced to limit the terms that members of Congress can serve. Between 1789 and 1991,

141 such proposals were introduced—most of them after 1950 (S. Richardson 1991, 45). Frequently, such proposals have been tied to calls for altering the length of congressional terms, but since the 1970s, the focus has shifted from term lengths to term limits (S. Richardson 1991, 39).

Neither idea, however, is new. The Articles of Confederation limited delegates to serving three one-year terms out of a possible six, and in the early history of the Constitution, Anti-Federalists pressed the idea of limiting the number of terms that members of the Senate could serve (Kesler 1990, 21). In recent years, however, the idea appears to have gained momentum. A number of presidents have supported the idea. Republican presidential candidates supported the idea in 1988 and 1992. In 1990, a lobby group called Americans to Limit Congressional Terms (ALCT) was formed to press for such an amendment, which was incorporated into the Republican Contract with America (S. Richardson 1991, 53). The House of Representatives voted 227 to 204 in March 1995 to limit service by members of the House and Senate to 12 years. By larger margins, it rejected proposals to limit service in the House to six years, to apply term limits retroactively, or to allow states to impose their own stricter limits. Although term-limit proposals had stronger support among Republicans than among Democrats, Republicans were far from united. Illinois Republican representative Henry Hyde voted against such limits, saying, "I just can't be an accessory to the dumbing-down of democracy" (Babson 1995, 918).

In large part, the movement for term limits, like the putative ratification of the Twenty-seventh Amendment, is tied to popular frustration with Congress. This has occurred with the increased professionalization of a body that now seems far removed from the idea of "citizen legislators" that many founders originally contemplated. Ironically, reelection rates for members of Congress have been quite high. People appear to like their own representatives while disliking the institution as a whole (Prinz 1992, 150). This may stem in part from members' focus on constituent service rather than on more controversial political issues. Members also gain name recognition and access to the media through their service and have privileges, such as frank-ing (free use of the mails), that are unavailable to other officeholders.

Advocates of term limits believe that they would help overcome such advantages and bring in "new blood" and new ideas—some amending proposals have been designated as the Citizen Representative Reform Act New Blood Provi-sion. Increased turnover would also decrease the role that seniority plays in congressional assign-ments and might encourage members to devote more time to issues. Opponents argue both that voters already have the power to impose term limits by refusing to reelect their representatives and that additional limitations are contrary to the spirit of democracy. Some also fear that term limits would weaken Congress as an institution and give greater power to unelected bureaucrats, many of whom would be able to serve longer than congressional representatives (S. Richard-son 1991, 39–41; also compare Frenzel 1992 with Mann 1992).

Those who have achieved leadership posi-tions in Congress (where seniority plays an important, albeit not dispositive, role) can hardly expect to favor a measure that would undercut their own power. Outside pressure for such an amendment might be exerted by state petitions to call an Article V constitutional con-vention on the subject, but to date, states have preferred to attempt to limit congressional terms through state laws and referendums (S. Richard-son 1989). After considerable academic debate (see, for example, Whitaker 1992), the Supreme Court declared in *U.S. Term Limits, Inc. v. Thornton* (1995) that the requirements for mem-bers of Congress listed in the Constitution are exclusive and that such state attempts were therefore unconstitutional; *Cook v. Gralike* (2001) subsequently prevented states from including notations on ballots as to how individ-uals in Congress voted on the subject of pro-posed term limit amendments.

Another obstacle to terms limits is that pro-ponents have not been united on precisely what limits are appropriate. Supporters of limits for the Senate have typically advocated from one to three terms. Proposals relative to the House of Representatives have varied from three to 10 terms; some proposals also advocate increasing House terms from two to four years, with a two- or three-term limit.

Proponents of term limits have frequently also suggested altering congressional terms, especially in the House of Representatives. Some have sought to limit the total number of terms an individual can serve, whereas others have focused on the total number of consecutive terms or the total number of years an individual can serve within a given time period (for exam-ple, 10 out of 12 years). Some proponents of term limits have attempted to limit the total num-ber of years that an individual can serve as pres-ident, vice president, a member of the cabinet, or a member of Congress—a proposal that could drastically affect the pool of candidates for these offices. Some proposals have also sought to limit the number of years that individuals can serve as ambassadors, judges, and justices.

Some advocates of term limits are now press-ing for a constitutional convention. Attempts to get an unprecedented national referendum (there is no constitutional provision for such a measure) on the subject in the 1996 elections failed. Some proponents of congressional term limits want a single, nationwide standard, whereas others simply want to reverse the U.S. Supreme Court decision in *U.S. Term Limits, Inc. v. Thornton* (1995) and allow states to spec-ify limits according to their own judgment.

See also Articles of Confederation; Con-stituent Instructions for Amending Constitu-tions; Contract with America; Twenty-second Amendment; *U.S. Term Limits, Inc. v. Thornton.*

For Further Reading:

Babson, Jennifer. 1995. "House Rejects Term Limits: GOP Blames Democrats." *Congressional Quarterly Weekly Reports* 53 (1 April): 918–919.

Cloud, David S. 1996. "Term Limits Stall in Sen-ate; GOP Blames Democrats." *Congressional Quar-terly* 54 (27 April): 1153–1154.

Frenzel, Bill. 1992. "Term Limits and the Immor-tal Congress." *Brookings Review* 10 (Spring): 18–22.

Kesler, Charles R. 1990. "Bad Housekeeping: The Case against Congressional Term Limits." *Policy Review* 53 (Summer): 20–25.

Mann, Thomas E. 1992. "The Wrong Medicine." *Brookings Review* 10 (Spring): 23–25.

Prinz, Timothy S. 1992. "Term Limitation: A Perilous Panacea." *The World & I* 7 (January): 143–153.

Richardson, Sula. 1991. *Congressional Terms of Office and Tenure: Historical Background and Contemporary Issues.* Washington DC: Congressional Research Service, Library of Congress.

CONGRESS, TRUTH-IN-LEGISLATION

See Truth-in-Legislation Amendment.

CONGRESS, VACANCIES IN

The Seventeenth Amendment provides that state governors may make appointments to fill vacancies in the U.S. Senate until the next general election. Because the Constitution makes no such provision for the House of Representatives, vacancies there continue to be governed by the provision in Article I, Section 2 that specifies that "when vacancies happen in the Representation from any State, the Executive Authority thereof shall issue Writs of Elections to fill such Vacancies." Thus, such vacancies can be filled only by special election (Clem 1989, 66). When there is less than a year left in a member's term, states may simply leave a House seat vacant until the next term.

Within a decade after ratification of the Seventeenth Amendment, a New Jersey representative proposed that state governors be permitted to make temporary appointments until House vacancies could be filled by election. This proposal came long before later concerns generated by nuclear weapons that have been reflected in more than a score of proposals to provide for the emergency functioning of Congress. Such concerns have been heightened after the terrorist attack of September 11, 2001, on the World Trade Center and the Pentagon and have generated new attention to the subject.

In the meantime, Congress has devoted increased attention to the provision allowing for gubernatorial appointment of Senators to vacant seats. Democrat Russ Feingold of Wisconsin was among those who proposed an amendment that would require elections after outgoing Illinois governor Rod Blagojevich (who was subsequently impeached and removed from office) appeared to have expected financial gain in return for an appointment to Barack Obama's Senate seat (Welna, February 20, 2009).

See also Congress, Emergency Functioning; Seventeenth Amendment.

For Further Reading:
Clem, Alan L. 1989. *Congress: Powers, Processes, and Politics.* Pacific Grove, CA: Brooks/Cole.

Welna, David. "Proposal Calls for Elections to Fill Senate Vacancies," NPR. http://www.npr.org/templates/story/story.php?storyId=100894656. Accessed March 9, 2009.

CONSENSUS AND THE AMENDING PROCESS

Because it embodies a system of separated powers, the U.S. Constitution requires an unusual consensus for the adoption of legislation. Legislation must be adopted in identical form by both houses of Congress and then either approved by the president or adopted by two-thirds congressional majorities over the president's veto. The requirements for the adoption of constitutional amendments, which alter the fundamental law of the land, are even more onerous and mimic, at least in part, the extraordinary consensus that was necessary to adopt the original Constitution. Article V requires two-thirds majorities to propose amendments and three-fourths majorities to ratify them. The framers clearly designed these requirements in part to assure that amendments are not adopted on behalf of narrow sectional interests. On a related matter, in *Dillon v. Gloss* (1921), the U.S. Supreme Court specifically noted that amendments are designed to reflect a contemporary consensus.

The later decision in *Coleman v. Miller* (1939) declaring that issues of timing were to be left to Congress, and the ratification of the Twenty-Seventh Amendment in 1992 over 200 years after it was first proposed, have somewhat called the issue of contemporary consensus into question. Many critics of both decisions have argued either that the Court was correct in *Dillon* and that it should therefore independently examine amendments to see whether they reflect a contemporary consensus, or, if the constitution does not assure such a consensus, that there should be some measure to assure that such amendments do reflect a consensus. Since the adoption of the Eighteenth Amendment (1919) providing for national alcoholic prohibition, Congress has usually included a time limit on the ratification of amendments either within the texts, where they are presumably self-enforcing, or in accompanying authorizing resolutions. During controversy over the ratification of the Equal Rights Amendment, Congress extended a deadline that it had included in its authorizing resolution, but this measure is still controversial.

Some critics of the amending process believe that it is too difficult and that it requires such an extraordinary consensus that it becomes almost impossible to use or that it invites change by other means. Some proposed alternatives to the amending process, like constitutional alterations brought about through judicial review, may not achieve the same consensus.

See also *Coleman v. Miller; Dillon v. Gloss;* Equal Rights Amendment; Time Limits on Amendments; Twenty-seventh Amendment.

For Further Reading:

Lieber, Benjamin, and Patrick Brown. 1995. "Our Supermajorities and the Constitution." *Georgetown Law Journal* 83 (July): 2347–2384.

CONSTITUENT INSTRUCTIONS FOR AMENDING CONSTITUTIONS

Between 1996 and 1998, 10 states adopted popular initiatives instructing their congressional representatives to support a constitutional amendment favoring term limits (Kobach 1999, 3). In *U.S. Term Limits, Inc. v. Thornton* (1995), the U.S. Supreme Court struck down state legislative attempts to limit the terms of members of Congress and ruled that such limits could be enacted only through a constitutional amendment. The states that provided for instructions to their representatives on the issue of term limits also provided that ballots would contain the words "Disregarded Voters' Instruction on Term Limits" in the cases of legislators who failed to comply (Kobach 1999, 3). In case after case in both state and lower federal courts, with one exception (the Supreme Court of Idaho), courts struck down such constituent "instructions" as unconstitutional infringements of Article V (Kobach 1999, 7–8).

At least two scholars have analyzed these decisions and their implications for republican, or representative, government. One scholar, Kris Kobach, believes that the decisions ignored a long history of constituent instructions to legislators beginning before the American Revolution and continuing through demands for independence from England, demands for the Articles of Confederations, demands for the Constitution itself, demands for the Bill of Rights, and demands for the Eleventh Amendment (Kobach 1999, 27–80). Kobach admits that such instructions began to decline in the late 19th century (and especially after the Seventeenth Amendment provided for the direct election of senators—who had previously been chosen by state legislatures—in 1913) but believes they were supplanted in part by popular initiatives during the Populist and Progressive Eras. He further argues that recent court decisions have been mistaken in ignoring this long history of instructions and that requiring notice to voters on ballots of candidates' failure to heed such instructions is valid.

A second writer, Vikram Amar (2000), distinguishes between what he considers to be permissible instructions by voters to their state legislators and what might be impermissible instructions to federal legislators. This author not only notes that the authors of the federal Bill of Rights specifically rejected an amendment to permit the people to instruct their federal legislators (a point that

Kobach takes simply as recognition that such power of instruction already existed), but that it might be inappropriate for voters from an entire state to try to dictate to representatives from specific districts (Amar 2000, 1090). Amar also argues that members of Congress have unique responsibilities to the nation as a whole and that such instructions might be seen as adding qualifications to those specified within the Constitution and thus violating the decision in *U.S. Term Limits, Inc. v. Thornton.*

In *Cook v. Gralike* (2001), the Supreme Court settled the issue by ruling that ballot notations were, like the provisions struck down in *U.S. Term Limits,* unconstitutional attempts to impose additional qualifications on individuals running for Congress and an impermissible intrusion on legislative discretion.

See also *Cook v. Gralike.*

For Further Reading:

Amar, Vikram David. 2000. "The People Made Me Do It: Can the People of the States Instruct and Coerce Their State Legislatures in the Article V Convention Amendment Process?" *William and Mary Law Review* 41 (March): 1037–1092.

Kobach, Kris W. 1999. "May 'We the People' Speak? The Forgotten Role of Constituent Instructions in Amending the Constitution." *University of California Davis Law Review* 33 (Fall): 1–94.

CONSTITUTION-21

Constitution-21 is a plan posted on the Internet for rewriting the U.S. Constitution for the 21st century. Its unidentified author, who claims to have been influenced in part by Stanley Tobin's *A Journey in Search of Justice* (1998) and *A Legacy Lost* (2005), thinks that the existing document has become antiquated. Constitution-21 proposes a draft of a new constitution, which is divided into 12 articles.

Article I declares that the United States is a republic and that the new government is divided into four branches, including a new electoral branch.

The legislative branch, which is outlined in Article II, divides Congress into a Senate and a House of Representatives, but the houses are quite different from the current ones. The new Senate would be reduced to 21 members, and the House increased to more than 850. The Senate would pass laws, approve treaties, and ratify appointments, whereas the house could propose and reject, albeit not amend, laws proposed by the Senate. Congressional terms would be their current length with maximum term limits of 24 (Senate) and 16 (House) years. Senate districts would be approximately equal and would span multiple states, and districts of representatives would be formulated to exclude "any history of voting patterns in an area."

Article III outlines the executive branch, which would continue to consist of a president and a vice president. The president would appoint heads of executive units subject to senatorial confirmation, but the attorney general, the head of the FBI, the CIA director, the chair of the Federal Reserve, and the IRS director would serve for fixed terms. The president would continue to be head of state and would have the power to set tariffs. Although the president could repel attacks on the United States, 14 Senators would be required to declare war.

Article IV outlines a judicial branch similar to that already in existence. Members would have to retire at a set age. The system would be designed "to suppress the demand for legal services."

Article V sets out the new electoral branch, which would consist of an electoral college and an electoral board. The former would consist of retired officeholders who would serve without pay, whereas the 10 members of the electoral college, who are chosen from the former, would be paid.

Article VI further outlines the process for nominations and elections. Primaries would be abolished. Federal Nominating Conventions consisting of state governors, state legislators, and member of Congress would divide into party caucuses to nominate presidents and senators. Members of the House would be nominated at the state level. Elections would be held each year on the first or second weekend of April, with House elections held in odd years and others in even years. The president would have to win a plurality of House districts. Campaigns would last from 11 to 132 weeks.

Article VII outlines the federal service and the pay and privileges of its members. Article VIII deals with federal finance, responsibility for which it divides between the legislative and executive branches. The president would have an item veto over pork barrel projects. Payroll and corporate income taxes would be eliminated. A value-added tax would be instituted, with the president have power to adjust rates, and individuals would pay "an income tax at progressive rates."

Constitution-21 is quite concerned with issues of federalism. Article IX outlines a host of congressional powers including power to establish "an independent central bank," to set minimum wages for businesses operating in interstate commerce, and to "stabilize, but not to subsidize . . . market prices." In a turnabout to the Tenth Amendment, states would have authority for matters "which are not reserved to the federal government." Duties would include the maintenance of "public order, safety, and sanitation," the definition of "family relationships and responsibilities," care for "the indigent, insane [and] incompetent," creation of public education systems, and so forth. Both sets of governments would strive to maintain "a minimum standard of living," with all persons "entitled to a basic level of health care" and environmental protections.

Article X provides for citizenship. It would establish English as the official language and would abrogate all treaties with Native Americans, who would now have "all attendant rights, privileges, and obligations, including liability to pay federal, state, and local taxes."

Article XI includes traditional limits on government powers found within Article I, Sections 9 and 10 and the Bill of Rights. It would specifically recognize a right of privacy.

Article XII provides that majority votes of either the electoral college or the House of Representatives could propose amendments, which would then have to be approved by "65% of the Representatives, 65% of the Electoral College, 16 Senators, and the President" before being submitted to the states for approval by a majority vote of the legislatures of half the states

within a year. If the states do not reject such amendments, they must be approved by "60% of the national vote and majority approval in 60% of the Representative Districts."

The author says that Constitution-21 is designed "as an on-line forum, a modern Constitutional Convention."

See also Constitutional Convention.

For Further Reading:

"Constitution-21," Homepage. http://www.constitution-21.com/Introduction.htm. Accessed June 24, 2008. Homepage provides link to document: http://www.constitution-21.com/printable.php.

Toobin, Stanley. 2005. *A Legacy Lost.* West Hartford, CT: The Graduate Group.

CONSTITUTIONAL AMENDMENTS, LIMITS ON

Article V of the Constitution establishes the formal procedures to amend the document and specifies two explicit limits (sometimes called entrenchment clauses) on the content of amendments. One such provision that has since expired was introduced on September 10, 1787, at the Constitutional Convention by South Carolina's John Rutledge and guarded a compromise between the North and the South by prohibiting any changes in Article I, Section 9 of the Constitution, which allowed for the importation of slaves until 1808 (Farrand 1966, 2:559).

The other, more permanent provision, which Pennsylvania's Gouverneur Morris introduced at the convention on September 15, provides "that no State, without its Consent, shall be deprived of its equal Suffrage in the Senate" (Farrand 1966, 2:631). This was designed to protect the Connecticut, or Great, Compromise, which Connecticut's Roger Sherman introduced at the Constitutional Convention. It was formulated to mediate the desires of the small states, which favored equal state representation, and those of the large states, which wanted to base representation on population. This compromise provided that representation in the House of Representatives would be based on population and that representation in the Senate would be apportioned equally among the states, each of which would have two senators. The convention had rejected an earlier proposal by Sherman that, in addition to guaranteeing equal state suffrage, would have prevented each state from being affected "in its internal police" without its consent (Farrand 1966, 2:630).

Just before the Civil War, congressmen introduced several amendments, including the Corwin Amendment, designed permanently to freeze the institution of slavery within the Constitution in an attempt to reassure the South and avert war. Abraham Lincoln indicated that he did not oppose such a compromise, but it was not adopted. Ironically, if ratified, this, rather than the amendment abolishing involuntary servitude, would have become the Thirteenth Amendment.

From the time of John C. Calhoun to the present, politicians and scholars have speculated as to whether there are any additional unstated limits on the substance of amendments to the Constitution. Conservative spokesmen such as Selden Bacon and William Marbury challenged the validity of the Fifteenth, Eighteenth, and Nineteenth Amendments on the grounds that they exceeded such implicit restraints. The Court ignored or rejected such arguments in *Myers v. Anderson* (1915), the *National Prohibition Cases* (1920), *United States v. Sprague* (1931), and *Leser v. Garnett* (1922).

A number of contemporary scholars, most notably Walter Murphy (1980) and John Rawls (Kelbey 2004), have argued that the Constitution embodies certain fundamental values, such as the protection of human dignity, that implicitly limit any conflicting changes. Such scholars have hypothesized that there are a number of conceivable amendments that would be unconstitutional. Similarly, Eric Isaacson (1992) and Jeff Rosen (1991) argued that the proposed amendment designed to prohibit flag burning would be unconstitutional and would be subject to judicial invalidation. Vile (1985) has argued that the explicit prohibitions in Article V were intended to be exclusive and that acceptance of other implicit limits would unduly elevate judicial powers.

See also Bacon, Selden; Corwin Amendment; Entrenchment Clauses; *Leser v. Garnett;* Marbury, William; Murphy, Walter F.; *Myers v. Anderson; National Prohibition Cases; United States v. Sprague.*

For Further Reading:

Cooley, Thomas M. 1893. "The Power to Amend the Federal Constitution." *Michigan Law Review* 2 (April): 109–120.

Farrand, Max, ed. 1966. *The Records of the Federal Convention.* 4 vols. New Haven, CT: Yale University Press.

Isaacson, Eric A. 1990. "The Flag Burning Issue: A Legal Analysis and Comment." *Loyola of Los Angeles Law Review* 23 (January): 535–600.

Kelbey, Charles A. 2004. "Are There Limits to Constitutional Change? Rawlson Comprehensive Doctrines, Unconstituional Amendments, and the Basis of Equality." *Fordham Law Review* 72: 1487–1536.

Linder, Douglas. 1981. "What in the Constitution Cannot Be Amended?" *Arizona Law Review* 23: 717–731.

Murphy, Walter F. 1980. "An Ordering of Constitutional Values." *Southern California Law Review* 53: 703–760.

Rosen, Jeffrey. 1991. "Was the Flag Burning Amendment Unconstitutional?" *Yale Law Review* 100: 1073–1092.

Vile, John R. 1985. "Limitations on the Constitutional Amending Process." *Constitutional Commentary* 2 (Summer): 373–388.

Wright, R. George. 1991. "Could a Constitutional Amendment Be Unconstitutional?" *Loyola University of Chicago Law Review* 22: 741–764.

CONSTITUTIONAL COMMISSIONS

One mechanism of state constitutional revision that has not been used at the national level is the constitutional commission. Although the legislative or executive branch sometimes creates such commissions individually, they generally have the support of both branches. Such commissions may propose constitutional reforms for legislative consideration and approval, or they may prepare amendments for a constitutional convention (Rich 1960, 89). Often, such commissions attract high-caliber individuals, but their work is usually at the mercy of the state legislatures. Because such commissions lack "the strong legal position and the dynamic character and drama of a convention," a student of the commission has concluded that such commissions are "no substitute" for conventions (Rich 1960, 99).

As the bicentennial of the Declaration of Independence approached, political scientist Conley Dillon (1974) proposed establishing a national constitutional commission to recommend needed changes. The Constitution mentions no such mechanism, but there appears to be no legal obstacle to the creation of such a body, as long as it is only advisory.

See also Dillon, Conley; States, Constitutional Revision.

For Further Reading:

Dillon, Conley. 1974. "Recommendation for the Establishment of a Permanent Commission of Constitutional Review." *Bureaucrat* 3 (July): 211–224.

Rich, Bennett M. 1960. *Major Problems in State Constitutional Revision,* ed. W. Brooke Groves. Chicago: Public Administration Service.

CONSTITUTIONAL CONVENTION OF 1787

Delegates to a convention that met in Philadelphia from May through September 1787 wrote the U.S. Constitution. Altogether, 55 delegates from 12 states (Rhode Island did not send any delegates) attended the convention, which elected George Washington as chairman and quickly began to focus on alternatives to the Articles of Confederation rather than attempting merely to amend that document. Many states were spurred to send delegates by Shay's Rebellion, a taxpayer revolt centered in Massachusetts in the winter of 1787–1788 that convinced many men of property that civil order was endangered.

Much of the deliberation at the Constitutional Convention centered on conflicts between the large states, the interests of which were initially represented in the Virginia Plan, and the small states, the interests of which were reflected somewhat later in the New Jersey Plan (Vile 2002, 15–16). These plans and other proposals and controversies also reflected tension between advocates of expanded national powers and those who wished to retain many of the states' prerogatives under the Articles of Confederation. Delegates adopted compromises to reconcile the conflicting interests of the slave and free states.

The Constitutional Convention initiated major changes in the government under the Articles of Confederation. In addition to expanding the powers of the national government vis-à-vis the states, convention delegates divided the legislative branch into two chambers, the House of Representatives and the Senate (the Congress under the Articles of Confederation had been unicameral) and created an independent executive, headed by a unitary executive, and a judicial branch headed by the U.S. Supreme Court, which eventually claimed the power, known as judicial review, to declare state and federal laws to be unconstitutional.

Most convention delegates, all of whom had lived through the Revolutionary War, agreed that a constitutional amending process was a necessary alternative to revolution. Delegates agreed that the unused provision for amendment under the Articles of Confederation that required unanimous state consent was too onerous.

The Virginia Plan's initial provision for an amending process was more a statement of intent than a viable mechanism, but it did specify that congressional assent should not be required for amendments. At the end of July, the five-member Committee of Detail proposed a scheme under which Congress would call a convention upon receiving petitions from two-thirds of the states (Farrand 1966, 2:159). Delegates debated these proposals during the last week of the convention, beginning on September 10. Elbridge Gerry of Massachusetts feared that the proposal did not protect minority state interests, Alexander Hamilton of New York thought that Congress should have a role in initiating amendments, and Virginia's James Madison was concerned about the vagueness of the convention mechanism (Vile 1992, 29). The response was a proposal introduced by Madison and seconded by Hamilton, allowing two-thirds majorities of Congress or two-thirds of the states to propose amendments, which would not become effective until three-fourths of the states ratified them. After an objection by South Carolina's John Rutledge, the delegates adopted a provision prohibiting the importation of slaves for 20 years.

The amending issue reemerged on September 15, when Virginia's George Mason objected that the amending mechanism was too much under the control of Congress. This objection resulted in the still unused provision allowing two-thirds of the states to propose a convention for amending the Constitution. One of Pennsylvania's representatives, Gouverneur Morris, returned to concerns raised by Connecticut's Roger Sherman; Morris successfully introduced a provision that states could not, without their consent, be deprived of their equal representation in the Senate. This remains the only entrenchment provision within the current amending clause.

The delegates to the Constitutional Convention exceeded their mandate to revise the Articles of Confederation. Moreover, new Article VII specified that the Constitution would be ratified by conventions rather than by state legislatures. The success of this ratification is attributable to the better organization of the supporters of the Constitution, the Federalists; to the fact that they were advocating a positive remedy to generally recognized ills; and to the strength of their arguments. To date, the formal amending process that the convention developed remains unchanged; it has been used to adopt 27 amendments.

See also Annapolis Convention; Articles of Confederation; Bill of Rights; Council of Revision; Federalists; Ratification of the Existing U.S. and/or Future U.S. Constitutions; Sherman, Roger.

For Further Reading:

Beeman, Richard. 2009. *Plain, Honest Men: The Making of the American Constitution*. New York: Random House.

Butzner, Jane, comp. 1941. *Constitutional Chaff—Rejected Suggestions of the Constitutional Convention of 1787 with Explanatory Argument*. New York: Columbia University Press.

Farrand, Max, ed. 1966. *The Records of the Federal Convention*. 4 vols. New Haven, CT: Yale University Press.

Solberg, Winton, ed. 1958. *The Federal Convention and the Formation of the Union*. Indianapolis, IN: Bobbs-Merrill.

Vile, John R. 2005. *The Constitutional Convention of 1787: A Comprehensive Encyclopedia of America's Founding*. 2 vols. Santa Barbara, CA: ABC-CLIO.

———. 2002. *A Companion to the United States Constitution and Its Amendments*. 3d ed. Westport, CT: Praeger.

———. 1992. *The Constitutional Amending Process in American Political Thought*. New York: Praeger.

CONSTITUTIONAL CONVENTIONS

Delegates from 12 states drafted the U.S. Constitution in Philadelphia, Pennsylvania, at the Constitutional Convention of 1787. Article VII specified that the new Constitution would not go into effect until delegates to conventions in nine or more states ratified it. The delegates also delineated two convention mechanisms in Article V, the amending article. One provided that amendments could, at congressional specification, be ratified by conventions in three-fourths of the states. To date, this mechanism has been used only in the case of the Twenty-first Amendment, repealing national alcoholic prohibition.

Fears of giving Congress a monopoly on the amending process led to a second convention mechanism outlined in Article V, which permitted two-thirds of the state legislatures to petition Congress to call a convention "for proposing Amendments." Although states have submitted hundreds of petitions for such a convention, to date, the necessary two-thirds of the states have not applied for either a general convention or a convention on a single specified topic (but see Van Sickle and Boughey 1990). In part because no Article V convention has ever been called, a host of unanswered questions continue to surround this process.

Two interrelated questions have dominated the discussion of the convention mechanism: whether a convention must be general or whether it can be restricted to a single topic, and if such a convention is not limited, whether it might become a "runaway" body (Vile 1993, 55–73). Those who believe that a convention cannot be limited believe that any other kind of convention would not be free to propose amendments in the manner that Article V appears to contemplate. Thus, they conclude that any state applications for a convention that are predicated on such limitations are invalid. As one such scholar argued, "Applications asking for something other than what is meant by Article V are nullities, and thirty-four times zero is zero" (C. Black 1979, 628). This position is bolstered by the fact that most 19th-century petitions for conventions contemplated a general convention rather than one limited to a specific topic.

Walter Dellinger has further argued against a limited convention on the basis that such conventions would allow states "to propose and ratify amendments that enhance their power at the expense of the national government" (Dellinger 1979, 1630), something that he believes is contrary to the intentions of those who wrote the Constitution. Dellinger argues,

> States were empowered under Article V to *ratify* amendments; the power to *propose* amendments was lodged in two national bodies, Congress and a convention. The proceedings suggest that the framers did not want to permit enactment of amendments by a process of state proposal followed by state ratification without the substantive involvement of a national forum (Dellinger 1979, 1630).

By contrast, a number of scholars have argued that an Article V convention could be limited. William Van Alstyne argued that

> [A] generous construction of what suffices to present a valid application by a state for consideration of a particular subject or of a particular amendment in convention, is far more responsive to the anticipated use of Article V than a

demanding construction that all but eliminates its use in response to specific, limited state dissatisfactions (Van Alstyne 1978, 1303).

Similarly, Grover Rees III (1986) argued that the Constitution designed the convention mechanism to facilitate state amendments, and an interpretation that would force the states to risk all or nothing would not meet such an objective. Reflecting some reservations, Russell Caplan concluded that "a national convention is in all likelihood constitutionally limited to proposing amendments described in the state applications that generated the call" (Caplan 1988, 157). Two other authors have concluded that there are various "political" safeguards, including the requirement that any proposed amendments be ratified by three-fourths of the state legislatures, that make a "runaway" convention unlikely (Weber and Perry 1989, 105–125).

Legislation proposed by Senators Sam Ervin and Orrin Hatch dealing with constitutional conventions has been predicated on the idea that states have the authority to call limited conventions. Such legislation has also attempted to address a variety of other questions, including the length of time that petitions calling for a convention are valid; whether states have the power to rescind such petitions; how states would be represented at a convention; whether a convention would vote by a simple majority or whether it would have to muster a two-thirds vote; and—related to whether conventions may be limited—whether Congress could refuse to submit amendments to the states for ratification, or whether courts might invalidate proposed amendments that appeared to exceed a limited convention call.

States frequently use conventions to revise constitutions or propose new ones. The lessons of such conventions, some of which are limited by state law, are not, however, necessarily applicable at the national level (F. Heller 1982).

Significantly, in recent years, a number of states have been concerned enough that Congress might feel obliged to call a convention upon the acceptance of a given number of state petitions that they have withdrawn their applications to Congress requesting such conventions, either on a specific topic (like the Balanced Budget Amendment) or for more generalized grievances (R. Lee 1999). There has not yet been a Supreme Court ruling as to whether such rescissions are valid.

See also Constitutional Convention of 1787; Jameson, John A.; Twenty-first Amendment.

For Further Reading:

Black, Charles L., Jr. 1979. "Amendment by a National Constitutional Convention: A Letter to a Senator." *Oklahoma Law Review* 32: 626–644.

Caplan, Russell L. 1988. *Constitutional Brinkmanship: Amending the Constitution by National Convention.* New York: Oxford University Press.

Dellinger, Walter. 1979. "The Recurring Question of the 'Limited' Constitutional Convention." *Yale Law Journal* 88: 1623–1640.

Heller, Francis H. 1982. "Limiting a Constitutional Convention: The State Precedents." *Cardozo Law Review* 3: 563–579.

Hensler, Louis W. III. 2003. "The Recurring Constitutional Convention: Therapy for a Democratic Constitutional Republic Paralyzed by Hypocrisy." *Texas Review of Law and Politics* 7 (Spring): 263–312.

Lee, Robert W. 1999. "Battling for the Constitution," 15 *The New American* (26 April), at http://www.thenewamerican.com/tna/1999/04/vol5no09_constitution.htm. Accessed April 24, 2002.

Rees, Grover, III. 1986. "The Amendment Process and Limited Constitutional Conventions." *Benchmark* 2: 67–108.

Rogers, James Kenneth. 2007. "The Other Way to Amend the Constitution: The Article V Constitutional Convention Amendment Process." *Harvard Journal of Law & Public Policy* 30 (Summer): 1005–1022.

Taylor, Arthur H. 2006. "Fear of an Article V Convention." *Brigham Young University Journal of Public Law* 20: 407–438.

Van Alstyne, William. 1978. "Does Article V Restrict the States to Calling Unlimited Conventions Only?—A Letter to a Colleague." *Duke Law Journal* 1978 (January): 1295–1306.

Van Sickle, Bruce M., and Lynn M. Boughey. 1990. "Lawful and Peaceful Revolution: Article V and Congress' Present Duty to Call a Convention for Proposing Amendments." *Hamline Law Review* 14 (Fall): 1–115.

Vile, John R. 1993. *The Theory and Practice of Constitutional Change in America: A Collection of Original Source Materials.* New York: Peter Lang.

Weber, Paul J., and Barbara A. Perry. 1989. *Unfounded Fears: Myths and Realities of a Constitutional Convention.* New York: Praeger.

CONSTITUTIONAL INTERPRETATION

The United States prides itself on a written Constitution that is unchangeable by ordinary acts of legislation, but far more changes have been effected in constitutional understandings through interpretations, especially by the judicial branch, than by constitutional amendment. This fact has even led one contemporary law professor to question the relevance of the constitutional amending process (Strauss 2001). Few areas have been more frequent or controversial subjects of inquiry in recent years than questions of constitutional interpretation. Some controversies center on the terminology, and others center on the hermeneutical, or interpretive, principles that should guide members of the judiciary or others who are called upon to apply the Constitution.

Terminologically, debate sometimes centers on a distinction between judicial activism and judicial restraint (Halpern and Lamb 1982; Wolfe 1991); at other times, it centers on a distinction between interpretivism and noninterpretivism (J. H. Ely 1980). Neither set of terms is altogether luminous.

When critics accuse judges of being too "activist," judges may well respond that they are simply enforcing the Constitution as they see it. Moreover, a judge might arguably exercise "restraint" by failing to heed constitutional mandates. This caveat noted, the term "activist" is frequently used to describe a judge who reaches out to deliver opinions in uncharted waters and gives little or no deference to past precedents or to legislative judgments. Such a jurist may argue that judicial activism is necessitated by the failure of the other two branches (A. Miller 1982). An advocate of judicial restraint, by contrast, would give issues maximum time to develop and would typically be respectful and deferential toward both precedents and determinations of constitutionality by other branches of the government. When the Warren Court was frequently criticized for being overly activist and, indeed, for judicially amending the Constitution, Justices Felix Frankfurter and John Marshall Harlan often counseled against getting unduly involved in "political questions" or unnecessarily overturning prior judicial or legislative judgments.

Another dimension in constitutional interpretation centers on the dichotomy between interpretivism and noninterpretivism. Interpretivists attempt to limit their decisions to those they can justify from within the confines of the constitutional text, refusing to give judicial solutions to questions that they do not believe the Constitution addresses. Frequently, interpretivists advocate the idea of "original intent." Although there are numerous versions of this principle, all ultimately attempt to answer questions of interpretation whenever possible by asking what the authors or ratifiers of a particular phrase in the Constitution understood or intended for it to mean. Noninterpretivists, by contrast, are likely to look beyond the text to considerations of policy, democracy, or justice, or with a view toward keeping the Constitution up to date. During the Reagan administration, there was a serious public debate on this subject between Attorney General Edwin Meese, an advocate of original intent, and Justice William Brennan, who thought that this interpretive principle was too narrow (see Rakove 1990). This debate also figured prominently in the confirmation hearings of Robert Bork, who, like Meese, was a strong advocate of original intent (Bork 1990; for a critique of original intent, see Levy 1988).

Knowing that an individual is an advocate of judicial activism or restraint, or that such an individual is an interpretivist or a noninterpretivist, does not always allow one to predict how this individual will decide a given case. This is because everyone has supplementary notions about how much weight to give to words and how to interpret them, about what the historical record of given clauses means, about constitutional structures and relationships, about the need to defer to past precedents (the principle of stare decisis), and the like (see Bickel 1986; Bobbitt 1992; L. Goldstein 1991; Tribe and Dorf 1991).

The difficulty of the constitutional amending process undoubtedly prods the judiciary to be more creative than it might be if the process were easier. Overly creative interpretations might, in turn, make authors of amendments nervous about including broad or vague language in constitutional additions. Fears that the judiciary would interpret and apply the amendment more radically than its authors intended generated some of the opposition to the Equal Rights Amendment.

See also Living Constitution; Relevance of Constitutional Amendments.

For Further Reading:
Bickel, Alexander. 1986. *The Least Dangerous Branch: The Supreme Court at the Bar of Politics.* 2d ed. New Haven, CT: Yale University Press.

Bobbitt, Philip. 2005. Rev. by Mark Graber. "Constitutional Interpretation." In *The Oxford Companion to the Supreme Court of the United States,* ed. Kermit L. Hall. 2d ed. New York: Oxford University Press, 211–218.

Bork, Robert H. 1990. *The Tempting of America: The Political Seduction of the Law.* New York: Free Press.

Ely, John Hart. 1980. *Democracy and Distrust.* Cambridge, MA: Harvard University Press.

Fallon, Richard H., Jr. 2001. *Implementing the Constitution.* Cambridge, MA: Harvard University Press.

Goldstein, Leslie F. 1991. *In Defense of the Text: Democracy and Constitutional Theory.* Savage, MD: Rowman and Littlefield.

Halpern, Stephen C., and Charles M. Lamb, eds. 1982. *Supreme Court Activism and Restraint.* Lexington, MA: Lexington Books.

Levy, Leonard W. 1988. *Original Intent and the Framers' Constitution.* New York: Macmillan.

Miller, Arthur S. 1982. *Toward Increased Judicial Activism: The Political Role of the Supreme Court.* Westport, CT: Greenwood Press.

Murphy, Walter F., James E. Fleming, and Sotirios A. Barber. 1995. *American Constitutional Interpretation.* 2d ed. Westbury, NY: Foundation Press.

Rakove, Jack N., ed. 1990. *Interpreting the Constitution: The Debate over Original Intent.* Boston: Northeastern University Press.

Strauss, David A. 2001. "Commentary: The Irrelevance of Constitutional Amendments." *Harvard Law Review* 114 (March): 1457–1505.

Tribe, Laurence H., and Michael C. Dorf. 1991. *On Reading the Constitution.* Cambridge, MA: Harvard University Press.

Wolfe, Christopher. 1991. *Judicial Activism: Bulwark of Freedom or Precarious Security?* Pacific Grove, CA: Brooks/Cole.

CONSTITUTIONS, PROPOSED NEW U.S.

See Alternative U.S. Constitutions, Proposed.

CONTRACT WITH AMERICA

In an attempt to derive a mandate from the 1994 midterm congressional elections, Republican candidates for the House of Representatives, led by Georgia Representative and soon-to-be Speaker of the House Newt Gingrich, drew up a Contract with America that outlined an ambitious program of legislative and constitutional reform (Wilcox 1995, 69–71; Gillespie and Schellhas 1994). Modeling their agenda on Franklin Roosevelt's broad program of an earlier day, the Republicans hoped to adopt many of these reforms within the first 100 days of their election. Proposals included adoption of a balanced budget amendment, a legislatively mandated line item presidential veto (rather than a constitutional amendment), and an amendment to provide for congressional term limits. Although not in the contract, Republicans also promised prompt consideration of an amendment to restore prayer in public schools. One critic subsequently noted that Congress faced a "glut of amendments" (Ornstein 1994, 5), and another referred to "amendment fever" (Sullivan 1995).

Although the 1994 election brought Republican control of the House of Representatives for the first time since 1952 (as well as control of the Senate, which Republicans kept until 2001, and regained in the elections of 2002), some observers question whether the Contract with America was responsible for this victory (Wilcox 1995, 211), and Republican victories in the House did not translate into a Republican victory in the subsequent 1996 presidential contest, when Bill Clinton was reelected. Moreover, once in power, Republicans realized that bold legislative initiatives often face considerable opposition and that constitutional amendments are particularly difficult to enact. Although they succeeded in getting the Balanced Budget Amendment through the House in the first 100 days, Republicans fell one vote short in the Senate. In the House itself, Republicans split over the appropriate length of time for limited congressional terms and whether the limit should apply to the total number of years or the number of consecutive years in office. The year after the Contract with America, the Christian Coalition proposed a Contract with the American Family (Reed 1995). Among other proposals, it advocated a Religious Equality Amendment. However, it focused on legislation rather than on an amendment as a way of limiting abortion. None of the amendments proposed in the Contract with America have yet been proposed by the requisite congressional majorities.

See also Abortion; Balanced Budget Amendment; Congress, Term Limits; Prayer in Public Schools; Presidency, Veto Power of; Religious Equality Amendment.

For Further Reading:

Armey, Dick. 2008. "Whatever Happened to the Contract with America?" *Imprints* 37 (May): 4-5.

Faulkner, Scott. 2008. *Naked Emperors: The Failure of the Republican Revolution.* Lanham, MD: Rowman & Littlefield Publishers.

Gillespie, Ed, and Bob Schellhas, eds. 1994. *Contract with America: The Bold Plan by Rep. Newt Gingrich, Rep. Dick Armey, and the House Republicans to Change the Nation.* New York: Random House.

Ornstein, Norman J., and Amy L. Schenkenberg. 1995. "The 1995 Congress: The First Hundred Days and Beyond." *Political Science Quarterly* 110 (Summer): 183–206.

Reed, Ralph. 1995. *Contract with the American Family: A Bold Plan by Christian Coalition to*

Strengthen the Family and Restore Common-Sense Values. Nashville, TN: Moorings.

Sullivan, Kathleen M. 1995. "Constitutional Constancy: Why Congress Should Cure Itself of Amendment Fever." *Record of the Bar of the City of New York* 50 (November): 724–735.

Wilcox, Clyde. 1995. *The Latest American Revolution? The 1994 Elections and Their Implications for Governance*. New York: St. Martin's Press.

CONTRACTS CLAUSE

Article I, Section 10 of the U.S. Constitution provides that "no State shall . . . pass any Law impairing the Obligations of Contracts." This was a much-litigated clause in early American history (B. Wright 1938). The Supreme Court under John Marshall strictly construed it to restrict state regulatory powers. Thus, in *Fletcher v. Peck* (1810), it prevented a state from renouncing a sale of land that had been influenced by fraud, and in *Dartmouth College v. Woodward* (1819), it declared that a college charter that the English king had granted prior to U.S. independence was a contract that a state could not abridge. The Supreme Court has interpreted the clause far more liberally in the 20th century (for example, in *Home Building and Loan Association v. Blaisdell* [1934], upholding the Minnesota Mortgage Moratorium Law suspending debt payments during the Great Depression).

From 1884 to 1889, a time during which the Supreme Court was beginning to rely increasingly on the idea of substantive due process rather than on the contracts clause to protect property rights, a Maryland representative, Louis McComas, introduced several proposals to circumvent the contracts clause. His amendment would have voided any promises a state may have made to a corporation exempting it from taxes.

Perhaps because some framers of the Constitution thought that the multiplicity of interests at the national level would serve as adequate protection, the contracts clause does not limit the national government. In 1871, New York Demo-

cratic representative Clarkson Potter offered an amendment prohibiting Congress from chartering corporations or impairing the obligation of contracts. Similarly, in 1982, Republican representative Robert Walker of Pennsylvania offered two resolutions prohibiting Congress from adopting any laws to abridge the right of citizens to enter into contracts, except when this was necessary to preserve vital and pressing governmental interests (H.J. Res. 466).

Martin J. Bailey, Jim Davidson, and Jack Durst are among libertarian advocates of recent proposals for new constitutions who have sought to strengthen the rights of contracting parties.

See also Bailey, Martin J., Davidson, Jim, and Durst, Jack; Marshall, John.

For Further Reading:

Wright, Benjamin F. 1938. *The Contract Clause of the Constitution*. Cambridge, MA: Harvard University Press.

COOK V. GRALIKE (2001)

This U.S. Supreme Court decision affirmed two lower federal court rulings by invalidating an amendment to the Missouri Constitution, enacted in the wake of the U.S. Supreme Court decision in *U.S. Term Limits, Inc. v. Thornton* (1995), where the Court had invalidated an Arkansas law keeping the names of congressional candidates off the ballot if they had served for two terms in the U.S. Senate or three terms in the U.S. House of Representatives. The contested Missouri amendment instructed its U.S. representatives to press for an amendment to the U.S. Constitution advocating term limits and provided that electoral ballots indicate either that such representatives had disregarded such instructions or had declined to support such limits. Justice John Paul Stevens wrote the majority decision of the Court on behalf of four other justices and himself (two others concurred in most parts of the opinion), but all other members of the Court concurred in the result in this case, leaving little likelihood of reversal in the near future.

Missouri had argued that it had exercised a power that the Tenth Amendment reserved to the states. It also argued that states could exercise under their power in Article I, Section 4, Clause 1 to regulate the "Times, Places and Manner of holding elections for Senators and Representatives." Justice Stevens rejected both arguments.

Acknowledging that states appeared to "instruct" their representatives in early American history, Stevens noted that none of these examples "was coupled with an express legal sanction for disobedience" (*Cook* 2001, 520). Moreover, absent evidence that states had previously exercised such "legally binding" instructions, this could not be a power that the Tenth Amendment had reserved to the states. Stevens further noted that, in formulating the First Amendment, Congress specifically rejected a proposal that would have allowed states "to instruct their representatives" (*Cook* 2001, 521).

Stevens also rejected the idea that states could exercise their control under their power to regulate the "times, places and manner" of elections. Citing *U.S. Term Limits,* he argued that these provisions were designed to enable states to assure the honesty and integrity of elections and not to dictate electoral outcomes or favor one class of candidates over another. Further citing lower court decisions that recognized the ballot statements to be "pejorative," Stevens ruled that such attempts to "dictate electoral outcomes" were simply "not authorized by the Elections Clause" (*Cook* 2001, 526).

There were a number of concurring opinions. Justice Anthony Kennedy indicated that legislators were responsible to the people of a state rather than to their state governments. State legislatures had the right to petition the people, but not to "instruct" them. Consistent with his dissent in *U.S. Term Limits, Inc. v. Thornton,* Justice Clarence Thomas indicated that, although Missouri had not rested its case on the issue, he still believed that states could add to the qualifications of their representatives. Chief Justice William Rehnquist, in an opinion joined by Sandra Day O'Connor, would have rested his decision on the First Amendment, claiming that a candidate has the right "to have his name appear [on a ballot] unaccompanied by pejorative language required by the State" (*Cook* 2001, 530–531).

See also Constituent Instructions for Amending Constitutions; First Amendment; Tenth Amendment; *U.S. Term Limits v. Thornton.*

For Further Reading:
Cook v. Gralike, 531 U.S. 510 (2001).
Jackson, Vicki C. 2001. "*Cook v. Gralike:* Easy Cases and Structured Reasoning." *Supreme Court Review* 299–345.

CORPORATIONS

U.S. economic development has rested in part on its legal recognition of corporations. Nonetheless, there has often been a perceived conflict in American history between the rights and privileges granted to corporations, which are not specifically mentioned in the U.S. Constitution, and those granted to ordinary citizens.

Persuaded of its constitutionality and utility by Secretary of the Treasury Alexander Hamilton, President Washington and the Federalist Congress incorporated a national bank. The U.S. Supreme Court upheld the constitutionality of the bank in *McCulloch v. Maryland* (1819). That same year, in *Dartmouth College v. Woodward,* the Court upheld a charter issued to Dartmouth College even before the American nation had been formed and recognized corporations as artificial persons with legal rights. However, in a popular decision in *Gibbons v. Ogden* (1824), the U.S. Supreme Court under John Marshall used the clause giving Congress control over interstate and foreign commerce to strike down a grant of a monopoly that New York had given to a steamboat company that would have impeded such commerce.

Although this was not its primary purpose, the ratification of the Fourteenth Amendment in 1868 created the possibility of renewed protection for corporations, which were becoming increasingly large and important to the development of the postbellum economy. In an unsubstantiated assertion, prominent attorney Roscoe Conkling argued in *San Mateo Co. v. Southern Pacific Railroad* (1885) that one of the intentions of the joint committee on which he had served in Congress to draft the amendment was to protect such corporations (Vile 2001, 131–132). Perhaps influenced by his arguments, in a companion case, *Santa Clara County v. Southern Pacific Railroad* (1886), the Supreme Court ruled that "[t]he court does not wish to hear argument on the question whether . . . the Fourteenth Amendment . . . applies to these corporations. We are all of the opinion that it does" (*Santa Clara County* 1886, 396).

Initially, most attempts to regulate corporations were initiated at the state level. This changed with the advent of the New Deal in Franklin Roosevelt's first administration. The Securities Act of 1933 and the Securities Exchange Act of 1934 introduced increased federal regulation of corporations, but much regulation also continues at the state level (R. Hamilton 1987, 8–9).

Members of Congress introduced four proposed amendments in the 1880s to enable states to tax corporations, even in cases in which such states had provided tax exemptions when granting corporate charters. Another proposal would have prohibited state grants or loans to such corporations. Several other amendments were introduced at the turn of the century, most by New Jersey Democratic representative Allan McDermott, to give Congress control over corporations.

The national government exercised such control in the New Deal period. Although the Supreme Court initially resisted such control, it eventually recognized increased federal powers under the commerce and taxing clauses. With post–New Deal latitudinarian constructions of such congressional powers, the national government has exercised increasing control over corporations. Such powers were widened to achieve expanded social objectives as diverse as "environmental protection, consumerism, minority employment, women's rights, and health and safety" (Mayer 1990, 601) during President Lyndon Johnson's "Great Society" initiatives in the 1960s and their aftermath. As federal regulations have multiplied, corporations have, in turn, increasingly used their status as legal "persons"

to claim protections under the Bill of Rights, most provisions of which have also been applied to the states via the due process clause of the Fourteenth Amendment.

Decrying this trend, which has shielded corporations from much legislation, consumer advocate and later third-party candidate for president Ralph Nader, along with Carl J. Mayer, then a Harvard law student, wrote an article in 1988 proposing an amendment to limit corporate use of such rights (Nader and Mayer 1988, 31). As a professor at Hofstra Law School, Mayer later suggested the following language:

> This Amendment enshrines the sanctity of the individual and establishes the presumption that individuals are entitled to a greater measure of constitutional protection than corporations. For purposes of the foregoing amendments, corporations are not considered to be "persons," nor are they entitled to the same Bill of Rights protections as individuals. Such protections may only be conferred by state legislatures or in popular referenda (Mayer 1990, 661).

Some recent proposals for new U.S. constitutions have included provisions that seek to trim both large corporations and expanding governments. A group called ReclaimDemocracy.org has proposed an amendment specifically labeled "to Preclude Corporations from Claiming Bill of Rights Protections." It would limit constitutional protections to "living human beings," and would prohibit corporations "from attempting to influence the outcome of elections, legislation or government policy through the use of aggregate resources or by rewarding or repaying employees or directors to exert such influence."

See also Banking; Fourteenth Amendment; Jefferson, Thomas; *McCulloch v. Maryland.*

For Further Reading:

Goodnow, Frank J. 1911. *Social Reform and the Constitution.* New York: Macmillan Co. Reprint, New York: Burt Franklin, 1970.

Hamilton, Robert W. 1987. *The Law of Corporations.* St. Paul, MN: West.

Mason, Alpheus T., and Donald Grier Stephenson Jr. 2002. *American Constitutional Law: Introductory Essays and Selected Cases.* 13th ed. Upper Saddle River, NJ: Prentice Hall.

Mayer, Carl J. 1990. "Personalizing the Impersonal: Corporations and the Bill of Rights." *Hastings Law Journal* 41 (March): 577–667.

Nader, Ralph, and Carl J. Mayer. 1988. "Corporations Are Not Persons." *The New York Times* (9 April), sect. 1, p. 31.

ReclaimDemocracy.org. "An Amendment to Preclude Corporations from Claiming Bill of Rights Protections." http://www.reclaimdemocracy.org/political _reform/proposed_constitutional_amendments. Accessed April 23, 2009.

Vile, John R. 2001. *Great American Lawyers: An Encyclopedia.* 2 vols. Santa Barbara: ABC-CLIO.

CORWIN AMENDMENT

From the election of President Abraham Lincoln in November 1860 through the session of the lame-duck Congress that met from December 1860 to March 1861, members introduced a large number of proposals to preserve the Union and avert war. These included a series of proposals known as the Crittenden Compromise. Also, the Washington Peace Convention met in February 1861 to accomplish the same end. The Corwin Amendment was the only compromise that the requisite majorities in Congress actually approved and is one of six amendments not subsequently ratified by the requisite number of states.

In December 1860, outgoing President James Buchanan proposed an "explanatory amendment" that consisted of a series of three proposals. It would give "express recognition of the right of property in slaves in the States where it now exists or may hereafter exist"; recognize the right to own slaves within the territories (thus legitimizing the 1857 decision in *Scott v. Sandford* that the incoming Republican president had opposed); and recognize slave owners' rights to have escaped slaves returned to them (J. Richardson 1908, 5:638).

The House of Representatives subsequently created a committee of 33 (one representative from each state), with Republican Thomas Corwin of Ohio as chairman, to address this issue. The Senate created a committee of 13, chaired by Democrat Lazarus Powell of Kentucky, with a similar aim (R. Lee 1961, 7–8). The Corwin Amendment originated in the latter committee and was apparently the product of New York Republican William Seward (soon to be Lincoln's secretary of state), who had access to the new president. The amendment was introduced in the House committee by Massachusetts Republican Charles Francis Adams, son of former president John Quincy Adams and a confidant of Seward's (R. Lee 1961, 17). In the final form proposed by Representative Corwin, the amendment provided for an entrenchment clause that would guarantee the existence of slavery within its contemporary limits: "No amendment shall ever be made to the Constitution which will authorize or give to Congress power to abolish or interfere, within any State, with the domestic institutions thereof, including that of persons held to labor or service by the laws of the said State" (R. Lee 1961, 22).

On the first try, on February 28, 1861, the House fell short of the necessary majority, voting 123 to 71 for the measure. The next vote, held the following day, was 133 to 65. The Senate proposed the amendment by a vote of 24 to 12 on March 3, 1861 (R. Lee 1961, 23–24). In a highly unusual move not required by the U.S. Constitution, outgoing President James Buchanan signed the amendment (Bernstein with Agel 1993, 91).

In his first inaugural address, President Lincoln (who was willing to permit slavery in the South but was adamantly opposed to its expansion in the territories, as the Crittenden Compromise would have allowed) indicated his support for the amendment. He said, "Holding such a provision to now be implied constitutional law, I have no objection to its being made express and irrevocable" (J. Richardson 1908, 6:11). One of his central concerns, shared by other congressional supporters of the amendment, was to keep border states, in which slavery was permitted, within the Union.

Ohio ratified the Corwin amendment in May 1861; Maryland and Illinois followed in January and February 1862. By then, however, Southern states had attempted to secede from the Union. The Thirteenth Amendment, which would be ratified after the war, did not protect the institution of slavery but abolished it. The Corwin Amendment continues to raise questions about whether there are any unstated substantive limits on what can be added to the Constitution (Brandon 1995).

See also Crittenden Compromise; Entrenchment Clauses; Peace Convention; Slavery, Protection for; Thirteenth Amendment.

For Further Reading:

Bernstein, Richard B., with Jerome Agel. 1993. *Amending America: If We Love the Constitution So Much, Why Do We Keep Trying to Change It?* New York: Random House.

Brandon, Mark E. 1995. "The 'Original' Thirteenth Amendment and the Limits to Formal Constitutional Change." In *Responding to Imperfection: The Theory and Practice of Constitutional Amendment,* ed. Sanford Levinson. Princeton, NJ: Princeton University Press.

Keogh, Stephen. 1987. "Formal and Informal Constitutional Lawmaking in the United States in the Winter of 1860–1861." *Journal of Legal History* 8 (December): 275–299.

Lee, R. Alton. 1961. "The Corwin Amendment in the Secession Crisis." *Ohio Historical Quarterly* 70 (January): 1–26.

Richardson, James E., ed. 1908. *A Compilation of the Messages and Papers of the Presidents, 1789–1908.* 11 vols. n.p.: Bureau of National Literature and Art.

COST-OF-LIVING ADJUSTMENTS

Automatic cost-of-living adjustments (COLAs) became popular during the inflationary 1960s and 1970s, and they were added to the Old Age and Survivors Insurance Program in 1972 (Watson 1985, 628). Although they help protect workers and pensioners against inflation, COLAs also contribute to increased prices. Democratic Representative Bill Burlison of

Missouri offered a proposal on June 13, 1977, (H.J. Res. 514) to prohibit automatic increases in the prices of goods or services under any law, contract, or other authority. Congress adopted a law in 1989 that extended relatively automatic COLAs to its members. Subsequent U.S. District Court and U.S. Circuit Court decisions in *Boehner v. Anderson* (1992, 1994) have declared that this law did not violate the Twenty-seventh Amendment, which provided that members of Congress could not give themselves a pay raise that applied before an intervening election.

See also *Boehner v. Anderson;* Twenty-seventh Amendment.

For Further Reading:

Watson, Richard A. 1985. *Promise and Performance of American Democracy.* 5th ed. New York: John Wiley & Sons.

COUNCIL OF CENSORS

When the U.S. Constitution was written, states with amending procedures used one of three means—legislative action, conventions, or a council of censors (Traynor 1927, 61–62). Pennsylvania and Vermont employed the third of these mechanisms. Thus, the Pennsylvania state constitution of 1776 called for a council consisting of two persons from each of the state's cities and counties to meet every seventh year "to enquire whether the constitution has been preserved inviolate in every part; and whether the legislative and executive branches of government have performed their duty as guardian of the people" (Meador 1898, 265). The council would also check into other matters of government and have the authority—the only such power specified in the constitution—to call a convention to propose constitutional amendments.

The Pennsylvania Council of Censors met as scheduled in 1783, but its deliberations were torn by partisan controversy (*Records of the Council of Censors* 1783–1784). A majority recommended establishing a bicameral rather than a unicameral legislature. It also proposed substituting a governor with veto power for the existing president and council, providing independence for state judges, and eliminating the council of censors mechanism (Meador 1898, 288). Because two-thirds of the council did not agree, however, no convention was called to accomplish these purposes.

The second Pennsylvania Council of Censors was scheduled to meet in 1790, but the year before, the legislature called for a constitutional convention. It proposed a constitution that incorporated most of the suggestions made by the earlier council. The new constitution, which was subsequently adopted, omitted the council of censors mechanism. A commentator noted that the citizens had "become wearied with so unwieldy a piece of political machinery" (Meador 1898, 298). The provision remained in the Vermont constitution until 1869 (Meador 1898, 266).

In *Federalist No. 50*, James Madison opposed plans for periodic appeals to the people for constitutional change that Thomas Jefferson had advocated, citing the experience of Pennsylvania. Madison observed that the state's council had been split into violent factions, consisting in part of individuals who had served in the very government they were called upon to assess. He concluded that "this censorial body, therefore, proves at the same time, by its researches, the existence of the disease, and by its example, the inefficacy of the remedy" (Hamilton, Madison, and Jay 1961, 320).

Despite Madison's negative assessment, a recent commentator has advocated creating a national council of censors every 12 years, consisting of one delegate elected from each state. He envisions that it "would convene periodically to assess whether the federal judiciary had properly interpreted the U.S. Constitution and to ensure that the judiciary had not exceeded its constitutional function" (Albert, 2007, 20). He suggests that the Council should have power by a two-thirds vote "to void a judicial decision" (21), thus adding a check on the current judiciary.

See also Jefferson, Thomas; Madison, James; States, Constitutional Revision.

For Further Reading:

Albert, Richard. 2007. "The Constitutional Imbalance." *New Mexico Law Review* 37 (Winter): 1–38.

Hamilton, Alexander, James Madison, and John Jay. 1787–1788. *The Federalist Papers*. Reprint, New York: New American Library, 1961.

Meador, Lewis H. 1898. "The Council of Censors." *Pennsylvania Magazine of History and Biography* 22: 265–300.

Records of the Council of Censors. 1783–1784. Journal vols. 1–3. Division of Archives and Manuscripts, Pennsylvania Historical and Museum Commission.

Traynor, Roger J. 1927. *The Amending System of the United States Constitution: An Historical and Legal Analysis*. PhD dissertation, University of California.

COUNCIL OF REVISION

One of James Madison's greatest disappointments at the Constitutional Convention of 1787 was his inability to get approval for a council of revision. This body, which would consist of the president and selected members of the federal judiciary, would have the power "to examine every act of the National Legislature before it shall operate, [and] every act of a particular [state] Legislature before a Negative thereon shall be final" (Farrand 1966, I, 21). Although the mechanism was used in New York until 1921, the Constitutional Convention of 1787 did not adopt this proposal, both because it seemed to violate separation of powers by mixing the executive and judicial branches and because it seemed to involve members of the judiciary in policymaking.

Concerned about the modern role of the judiciary, constitutional law scholar Richard Albert (who also thinks the idea of resurrecting a council of censors might be desirable), has suggested adopting such a council, which might be "elected or appointed by the President and confirmed by the Senate" (Albert 2007, 27). He suggests that such a council should "possess the power to either invalidate the bill—on grounds of unconstitutionality—or return it to the Congress with suggested amendments" (27). He further proposes that "A supermajority of both houses of the Congress could trump the Council's decision to invalidate a bill. The effect of the Council's blessing of legislation would be to shield the law from invalidation at the hands of the judiciary" (27–28).

See also Constitutional Convention of 1787; Council of Censors; Madison, James.

For Further Reading:

Albert, Richard. 2007. "The Constitutional Imbalance," *New Mexico Law Review* 37 (2007): 1–38.

Farrand, Max, ed. 1966. *The Records of the Federal Convention.* 4 vols. New Haven, CT: Yale University Press.

Hobson, Charles F. 1979. "The Negative on State Laws: James Madison, the Constitution, and the Crisis of Republican Government." *William and Mary Quarterly,* 3rd ser. 36 (April): 214–235.

COUNCIL OF STATE GOVERNMENTS

In *Baker v. Carr* (1962), the Supreme Court declared that it would no longer consider issues of state legislative apportionment to be "political questions." This decision stirred considerable controversy, including a drive for a constitutional convention led by Republican senator Everett Dirksen of Illinois. The Council of State Governments issued one of the strongest responses when the General Assembly of States, which it sponsored, proposed three amendments at its December 1962 meeting (Committee on Federal State Relations 1963; for further discussion, see Vile 1991c, 97–100).

The first proposal would have made the amending process easier by allowing two-thirds of the state legislatures to propose amendments by submitting identical texts of such amendments to Congress; this proposal would also have eliminated the convention method of ratifying amendments, thus leaving such power exclusively in the hands of state legislatures. The second proposal, clearly aimed at *Baker v. Carr,* would have declared that "no provision of this Constitution, or any amendment thereto, shall restrict or limit any state in the apportionment of representation in its legislature" (Com-

mittee 1963, 9). Much along the lines of the Eleventh Amendment, this proposal also would have restricted judicial jurisdiction over this issue. The third proposal would have created a Court of the Union consisting of the chief justice from each state. This court, the decisions of which would be final, would hear petitions from state legislatures concerning issues alleged to be reserved to the states.

The scholarly reaction to these proposals was quite negative. William Swindler (1963) of the College of William and Mary saw these proposals as an attempt to return to a government like that under the Articles of Confederation. Focusing on the proposed reform of the amending process, Yale's Charles Black called the amendments "A Threatened Disaster" (1963); Princeton's Alpheus Mason called the amendments the "'DisUnion' Amendments" (1964, 199). The title of a popular magazine article summarized such sentiments when it proclaimed, "Seventeen States Vote to Destroy Democracy as We Know It" (Morgan 1963).

Although the proposals by the Council of State Governments failed, and the principle of one person, one vote is now generally accepted, (matters arising from racial gerrymandering continue to receive attention), issues of federalism continue to stir controversy. By 1990, largely prompted by decisions in *Garcia v. San Antonio Metropolitan Transit Authority* (1985) and *South Carolina v. Baker* (1988), 15 states had adopted resolutions proposing amendments to redress the balance between the state and national governments (Tolchin 1990, A12).

In October 1995, states held a States' Federalism Summit in which they favorably considered a proposal that would have allowed for what are described as "state-initiated amendments." Such amendments would reverse the current amending process. Under this plan, three-fourths of the state legislatures, which are currently limited to proposing constitutional conventions, could propose amendments, which would then have to be ratified by two-thirds majorities in Congress. This proposal was discussed again at the 1997 National Conference of State Legislatures but was not adopted (Kincaid 2000, 15).

See also *Baker v. Carr;* Political Questions.

For Further Reading:

Black, Charles L., Jr. 1963. "The Proposed Amendment of Article V: A Threatened Disaster." *Yale Law Journal* 72 (April): 957–966.

Committee on Federal State Relations. 1963. "Amending the Constitution to Strengthen the States in the Federal System." *State Government* 10 (Winter): 10–15.

Kincaid, John. 2000. "Constitutional Proposals from the States." *Insights on Law & Society* 1 (Fall): 15.

Mason, Alpheus T. 1964. *The States' Rights Debate: Antifederalism and the Constitution.* Englewood Cliffs, NJ: Prentice Hall.

Morgan, Thomas J. 1963. "Seventeen States Vote to Destroy Democracy as We Know It." *Look* 27 (3 December): 76–88.

Swindler, William. 1963. "The Current Challenge to Federalism: The Confederating Proposals." *Georgetown Law Review* 52 (Fall): 1–41.

Tolchin, Mark. 1990. "Fifteen States Rally behind Calls for Amendment to Gain More Powers." *New York Times,* 26 June, A12, col. 3–6.

Vile, John R. 1991. *Rewriting the United States Constitution: An Examination of Proposals from Reconstruction to the Present.* New York: Praeger.

COURT OF GENERATIONS AMENDMENT

See Tonn, Bruce E.

COURT OF THE UNION

See Council of State Governments.

COURT-PACKING PLAN

One of the most dramatic confrontations between the presidency and the judiciary took place when President Franklin D. Roosevelt introduced his so-called court-packing plan in a fireside address in February 1937.

On May 27, 1935, or Black Monday as it came to be called, the Court had delivered three unanimous opinions that struck at various New Deal programs. In *Louisville Joint Stock Land Bank v. Radford,* it invalidated a bill providing mortgage relief to farmers; in *Humphrey's Executor v. United States,* it ruled that the president could not remove members of independent regulatory agencies; and in *Schechter Poultry Corporation v. United States,* it invalidated the National Industrial Recovery Act. The next year, the Court continued its attack on the New Deal, albeit by much closer votes, by invalidating the Agricultural Adjustment Act, the National Bituminous Coal Act, and a New York minimum wage law.

Working with Attorney General Homer Cummings (who, in turn, appears to have been influenced by Princeton political science professor Edwin S. Corwin), Roosevelt formulated a plan. Ironically, one of the sitting conservative justices, James McReynolds, had supported a central plank of this plan when he had served as Woodrow Wilson's attorney general (Leuchtenburg 1995, 120). This plan would have allowed the president to add an additional Supreme Court justice, up to 15 justices, for any justice with 10 years or more of service who did not retire at age 70. It also provided for additions to lower courts and for expediting judicial work.

Roosevelt justified his plan as a means of helping the aging justices (often contemporaneously referred to as "the nine old men") keep up with their work, but the political implications of the plan were too apparent to hide. In a March fireside chat, Roosevelt compared the three branches of the federal government to three horses, one of which was pulling in the wrong direction (R. Jackson 1941, 340–351). Chief Justice Charles Evans Hughes wrote a letter to Congress assuring its members that the Court was not falling behind in its work. The Senate Judiciary Committee subsequently issued a report critiquing the president's plan, and the unexpected death of Roosevelt's Senate floor leader, Joe Robinson, doomed it.

Within months of the proposal of the court-packing plan, however, the Court issued several decisions upholding New Deal measures. Thus, the decision in *West Coast Hotel v. Parrish* (1937) (which may have been written, although not issued, previous to the plan [G. White 2000, 201]), and the one coming two weeks later in *National Labor Relations Board v. Jones & Laughlin Steel Corp.*, appeared to mark a judicial shift—contemporaneously dubbed the "shift in time that saved nine." Justice Owen Roberts, always a swing vote, appears to have deserted the conservative "Four Horsemen of the Apocalypse" on the Court, and thereafter the Supreme Court upheld fairly expansive federal powers. Scholars still dispute whether the court-packing plan led to this shift.

Scholars continue to debate the consequences of Roosevelt's strategy. The changes signaled, if not inaugurated, by the Court's shift in 1937 and thereafter certainly seem as consequential as many that constitutional amendments had previously made. Bruce Ackerman (1996), who favors many of the developments that the New Deal initiated, argues that this shift marks one of three major "constitutional moments" in U.S. history. David Kyvig believes that Roosevelt overestimated the difficulty of the amending process and laments the lack of a "specific constitutional sanction" for the New Deal (1989, 481). Changes not incorporated within the constitutional text are generally more malleable than those that are so incorporated.

See also Ackerman, Bruce; Child Labor Amendment; Living Constitution.

For Further Reading:

Ackerman, Bruce. 1996. *We the People: Transformation.* Cambridge, MA: Harvard University Press.

Jackson, Robert H. 1941. *The Struggle for Judicial Supremacy.* New York: Vintage Books.

Kyvig, David E. 1989. "The Road Not Taken: FDR, the Supreme Court and Constitutional Amendment." *Political Science Quarterly* 104 (Fall): 463–481.

Lash, Kurt T. 2001. "The Constitutional Convention of 1937: The Original Meaning of the New Jurisprudential Deal." *Fordham Law Review* 70 (November): 459–525.

Leuchtenburg, William E. 1995. *The Supreme Court Reborn: The Constitutional Revolution in the Age of Roosevelt.* New York: Oxford University Press.

Ross, William G. 2005. "When Did the 'Switch in Time' Actually Occur?: Re-discovering the Supreme Court's 'Forgotten' Decisions of 1937–1937." *Arizona State Law Journal* 37 (Winter 2005): 1153–1220.

White, G. Edward. 2000. *The Constitution and the New Deal.* Cambridge, MA: Harvard University Press.

COURTS

See Judiciary entries.

CRAM, RALPH (1863–1942)

Ralph Cram proposed one of the 20th century's most iconoclastic schemes of constitutional reform (Vile 1992, 75–78) in a book entitled *The End of Democracy* (1937). Cram was a noted architect whose works, often patterned on medieval structures, included the Cathedral Church of St. John the Divine in New York City (Shand-Tucci 1975).

Cram was a critic of modern, or what he called "low," democracy. In its place, he proposed substituting a "high democracy" or an "aristocratic republic" (Cram 1937, 19), which is what he believed the American framers had intended. Indeed, by extending democracy and increasing governmental powers, the Fourteenth through Nineteenth Amendments had elevated the masses over individuals of character who could exercise true leadership. The result was "quite a new world where quantitative have taken the place of qualitative values and the tabloid type of man controls all things" (Cram 1937, 93). In such a situation, the solid middle class on which democracy should rest had become "the Forgotten Class" (Cram 1937, 94).

To restore this middle class, existing "*political* organization" needed to be replaced by a new "*functional* organization, representation and control" (Cram 1937, 120). Cram advocated a corporate state, which he described as "the substitution for professional politicians chosen on a partizan [sic] or territorial basis, of nonpolitical, non-partizen [sic] delegates or representatives made up of voluntary associations of the functional factors in society" (Cram 1937, 122). Elsewhere, Cram described a quaint scheme associating individuals in largely autonomous units of 500 families, each with their own farms, gardens, town halls, and professional personnel (Cram 1935, 201–222).

Concentrating more directly on the national government in *The End of Democracy,* Cram critiqued universal suffrage. Recognizing that it would now be difficult to abolish, he advocated restrictions for those convicted of crimes and for those applying for naturalization.

Cram favored rearranging Congress along functional representative lines. Although elsewhere in his book he criticized parliamentary systems, he borrowed a number of their features. He proposed that the president and Congress work together on a legislative budget. He favored repealing the Seventeenth Amendment so as to provide for a Senate known as "a body of men of high character, noble intelligence and wide vision; men of mature judgment, of scholarly attainments and of knowledge of the world" (Cram 1937, 166). Cram thought that such a body could best be chosen partly by appointment and partly by indirect election, with some appointments being made by the major secular and religious interests in society. Members would serve from 10 years to life. All laws would originate in the House of Representatives, a body that would apparently remain largely unchanged.

Cram, who admired Franklin Roosevelt, also liked the strong presidency that had developed in the United States. He would further strengthen this institution by providing that the president would be chosen for life, quite possibly by members of the House from among those in the Senate. Personally preferring that the president be designated as king, Cram settled on "His Highness the Regent of the Republic of the United States" (Cram 1937, 187). As head of state, the regent would appoint a prime minister, who would choose a cabinet. Like William Yandell Elliott, with whom he was familiar, Cram believed that the head of state should be able to dissolve the House of Representatives; unlike Elliott, Cram thought that the regent should appoint a new prime minister if the vote went against him.

Again drawing from Elliott, Cram opposed allowing the Supreme Court to invalidate federal laws except by an extraordinary majority. Cram favored unanimity. Like Elliott, he also believed that the Supreme Court should issue advisory opinions.

Continuing to draw from Elliott, Cram further advocated dividing the nation into five or six provinces or commonwealths and decentralizing administration. He wanted to create an order of nonhereditary knighthood, with recipients being designated as "Sir" as a means of recognizing the natural aristocracy. He also advocated expanding the civil service and creating a "Civilian West Point" (Cram 1937, 218). Suspicious of the existing exercise of such freedoms as those of speech and the press, Cram nonetheless recognized that the evils of state licensing might prove worse than current abuses. Here, as elsewhere, he favored placing "men of character, capacity, and intelligence in all positions, social, economic, political" (Cram 1937, 237).

See also Elliott, William Yandell; Seventeenth Amendment.

For Further Reading:
Cram, Ralph. 1937. *The End of Democracy.* Boston: Marshall Jones Company.
Shand-Tucci, Douglass. 1995. *Ralph Adams Cram: Life and Architecture.* Vol. I. Amherst: University of Massachusetts Press.

CRIMINALS, EARLY RELEASE

In recent years, citizens have been increasingly concerned about the threat of violent crime. Many states have increased the minimum sentences for violent criminals, whereas others have adopted recidivism legislation that expands jail terms for individuals who have committed three or more felonies. Such laws, following a baseball analogy, are often referred to as "three strikes and you're out" laws.

Somewhat in tension with such laws are periodic budget shortfalls during which governors and legislators sometimes propose releasing offenders from prison early in order to save state or federal tax dollars. Perhaps alarmed by this development, Florida Democratic congressman Robert Wexler proposed an amendment in March 1997 to prohibit such early release of violent criminals. Such laws would undoubtedly interest proponents of proposed victims' rights amendments.

See Also Victims' Rights.

For Further Reading:
Wooten, James. 1995. "Truth in Sentencing: Why States Should Make Violent Criminals Do Their Time." *Dayton Law Review* 20 (Winter): 779–792.

CRITICAL ELECTIONS

The amending process is often likened to a "safety valve" that provides an alternative to revolution, but elections perform a similar function on a more regularized basis. Just as some amendments—for example, the Fourteenth—are more far reaching than others, so too are some elections. Political scientists refer to these as critical, or realigning, elections.

There appear to have been at least five critical elections in the United States. They occurred in 1800, 1828, 1860, 1896, and 1932 (Burnham 1970, 1). Such elections are associated with "short-lived but very intense disruptions of traditional patterns of voting behavior"; they exhibit high intensity on the part of voters, are often associated with the rise or demise of minor parties, and tend to occur with fairly "uniform periodicity" (Burnham 1970, 6–10).

Amendments, like realigning elections, often have a generational dimension (Strickland 1989, 48–50). At least a few amendments appear to have resulted from realigning elections. The Twelfth Amendment remedied a flaw in the Electoral College that was highlighted by the election of 1800. The Civil War Amendments (Thirteen through Fifteen) were made possible by Republican gains in 1860 and 1864. Although the election of 1896 kept Republicans in control, a number of Progressive Era amendments reflected reform elements from that election. The election of 1932 manifested itself chiefly in changed judicial interpretations rather than in amendments (although the Twentieth and Twenty-first Amendments soon followed), but Professor Bruce Ackerman is among those who consider this to be a key "constitutional moment," equivalent to others that constitutional amendments have inaugurated (Ackerman 1991).

Because U.S. political parties have weakened in recent years, it has been difficult to establish whether there has been another realigning election; the 1994 midterm congressional elections, which were linked in part to the proposed Contract with America, have been the subject of special attention (Burnham 1995; Wilcox 1995). With a view toward recent ambiguity, a number of political scientists refer to a "dealigning" process (Rohde 1994), and other observers caution that apparent realignments are sometimes fairly transitory (Berke 1995, E3). Whatever the status of such elections, they serve as a reminder that political changes often occur in clusters (Silva 1970), and majorities that are successful in mustering support for one amendment often develop sufficient momentum to initiate others as well.

See also Ackerman, Bruce; Contract with America; Safety-Valve Analogy; Fourteenth Amendment; Progressive Era.

For Further Reading:
Ackerman, Bruce. 1991. *We the People: Foundations.* Cambridge, MA: Belknap.

Berke, Richard L. 1995. "Epic Political Realignments Often Aren't." *New York Times,* 1 January, E3.

Burnham, Walter D. 1995. "Realignment Lives: The 1994 Earthquake and Its Implications." In *The Clinton Presidency: First Appraisals,* ed. Colin Campbell and Bert Rockman. Chatham, NJ: Chatham House.

Rohde, David W. 1994. "The Fall Elections: Realignment or Dealignment." *Chronicle of Higher Education* 41 (14 December): B1–B2.

Silva, Edward J. 1970. "State Cohorts and Amendment Clusters in the Process of Federal Constitutional Amendments in the United States, 1869–1931." *Law and Society Review* 4 (February): 445–466.

Strickland, Ruth A. 1989. *The Ratification Process of U.S. Constitutional Amendments: Each State Having One Vote as a Form of Malapportionment.* PhD dissertation, University of South Carolina.

Wilcox, Clyde. 1995. *The Latest American Revolution? The 1994 Elections and Their Implications for Governance.* New York: St. Martin's Press.

CRITTENDEN COMPROMISE

The period between the election and the inauguration of Abraham Lincoln was marked by the introducing of a number of compromises to keep the Southern states from seceding. Among the most prominent, albeit ultimately unsuccessful, attempts was a series of unamendable amendments that Kentucky Unionist senator John J. Crittenden first introduced in the Senate on December 18, 1861. Crittenden's proposals, if accepted, would have marked the first attempt to settle the slavery issue by amendment rather than by ordinary acts of legislation (Kirwan 1962, 374). This was a logical approach, because the Southern movement for secession was stimulated in part by fears—raised much earlier by John C. Calhoun and accentuated by Lincoln's election and the growth of the free states—that majorities might one day use the amending process to abolish slavery throughout the nation.

Altogether, Crittenden proposed seven amendments. Tennessee senator (later president) Andrew Johnson also introduced a series of amendments designed in part to split the presidency, vice presidency, and membership of the Supreme Court between the North and the South (Dumond 1973, 159). Crittenden's proposals would have (1) restricted and extended the Missouri Compromise line to California, prohibiting slavery north and permitting it south of the line, with new states making their own choices as to whether they would be slave or free; (2) prohibited Congress from abolishing slavery on federal property within slave states; (3) prohibited Congress from abolishing slavery in the District of Columbia as long as it existed in Maryland or Virginia, and even if it did not, abolition would require consent of District residents and compensation; (4) prohibited Congress from interfering with interstate slave transit; (5) provided compensation for owners of fugitive slaves rescued by mobs; and (6) prohibited future amendments altering the three-fifths clause or the fugitive slave clause or interfering with slavery in the South (Kirwan 1962, 375). Crittenden's compromise also called on Congress to pass resolutions recognizing that (1) the fugitive slave laws were constitutional and should be enforced, (2) conflicting state laws should be repealed, (3) provisions of fugitive slave laws offensive to Northerners should be repealed, and (4) laws prohibiting the foreign slave trade should be strengthened (Kirwan 1962, 375–376).

Debates about these proposals occupied much of the lame-duck session of Congress. The Peace Convention meeting in February 1861 submitted proposals to Congress much like Crittenden's.

The Crittenden Compromise has been called "a Southern plan in search of Northern support" (Keogh 1987, 283). Outgoing President James Buchanan endorsed the plan. It failed because most Republicans, including incoming President Abraham Lincoln, balked at the provisions relating to slavery in the territories and decided instead to support the Corwin Amendment, which merely guaranteed that the national government would not interfere with slavery in those states where it already existed. Crittenden eventually allowed a similar set of proposals drafted by the Peace Convention to be substituted for his own. This substitute did not receive the two-thirds vote necessary to be placed on the House agenda, and the Senate voted it down on March 4, 1861, by a vote of 7 to 28 (Keogh 1987, 292).

Crittenden hoped to break the congressional logjam of opposition by having the people vote on the plan in a national plebiscite, or referendum. Unlike some modern advocates of such a provision, Crittenden recognized that such a vote would be extraconstitutional and hence nonbinding, but the Senate refused to send it to the people (Keogh 1987, 288).

See also Calhoun, John C.; Corwin Amendment; Lincoln, Abraham; Peace Convention; Slavery, Protection for.

For Further Reading:

Dumond, Dwight L. 1973. *The Secession Movement, 1860–1861.* New York: Octagon Books.

Keogh, Stephen. 1987. "Formal and Informal Constitutional Lawmaking in the United States in the Winter of 1860–1861." *Journal of Legal History* 8 (December): 275–299.

Kirwan, Albert D. 1962. *John J. Crittenden: The Struggle for the Union.* n.p.: University of Kentucky Press.

converted the democracy of the Constitution into "a golden hoard," which Croly intended to open directly to the people (Croly 1914, 237).

See also Amending Process, Proposals for Changing; Progressive Era; Rigid Constitution.

For Further Reading:

Croly, Herbert. 1914. *Progressive Democracy.* New York: Macmillan. Reprint, New Brunswick, NJ: Transaction Publishers, 1998.

————. 1909. *The Promise of American Life.* New York: Macmillan Company. Reprint, Indianapolis: Bobbs-Merrill, 1965.

CROLY, HERBERT (1870–1930)

Herbert Croly published *The Promise of American Life* in 1909 (1965) and went on to become editor of the *New Republic* from 1914 to 1928. Typical of intellectuals in the Progressive Era, Croly critiqued the amending process in *Progressive Democracy* (1914).

Arguing that the constitutional amending process was overly rigid, Croly agreed with Professor Munroe Smith in stating that "the first article of any sincerely intended progressive program must be the amendment of the amending clause of the Constitution" (Croly 1914, 230). Croly suggested that constitutional changes should be made by a majority of voters, with provisions for due "deliberation" and "territorial distribution of the prevailing majority" (Croly 1914, 231). Croly specifically commended Senator Robert La Follette's plan, whereby amendments could be proposed by a majority of both houses of Congress or one-fourth of the states and then be subsequently ratified by a majority of voters in a majority of states.

Croly perceived that the rigidity of the amending process had contributed to the role that the Supreme Court had assumed in interpreting and adapting the Constitution. Believing that the Court was beginning to defer more readily to legislative bodies, Croly argued that the power of the people was superior to both. The amending process had

CULTURAL AND LINGUISTIC RIGHTS

At a time of increasing calls for an amendment making English the official language of the United States, Representative Jimmy Hayes and Senator John Breaux, both Democrats from Louisiana (although Hayes subsequently switched parties), introduced a different amendment in 1989. Designated the Cultural Rights Amendment (Baron 1990, 24), it would enable people "to preserve, foster, and protect their historic, linguistic, and cultural origins" and see that no one is denied equal protection of the law for exercising such a right (H.J. Res. 408, 1989).

This proposal reflects Louisiana's interest in reviving and preserving its unique Acadian heritage, including its French language (J. Taylor 1976, 177–178). The 1921 Louisiana state constitution contained a compulsory English provision, and teachers of the day, from both French and English backgrounds, often humiliated children who continued to speak French in school (Estaville 1990, 116; Brasseau 1989, 11–12).

See also English Language Amendment.

For Further Reading:

Baron, Dennis. 1990. *The English-Only Question: An Official Language for America?* New Haven, CT: Yale University Press.

Brasseau, Carl A. 1989. "Four Hundred Years of Acadian Life in North America." *Journal of Popular Culture* 23 (Summer): 3–22.

Estaville, Lawrence E. 1990. "The Louisiana French Language in the Nineteenth Century." *Southeastern Geographer* 30 (November): 107–120.

Taylor, Joe Gray. 1976. *Louisiana: A Bicentennial History.* New York: W. W. Norton.

CUMMINGS, RICHARD (1938–)

When the U.S. Constitution was created, Anti-Federalist opponents of the document cited the Baron de Montesquieu to argue that democratic government was impossible over a large land area. James Madison countered in *Federalist No. 10* that representative, or indirect, democracy was not only possible over a large area but would serve the additional function of moderating political factions.

Although the new Constitution was adopted, many Americans continued to look to state and local governments for their most immediate needs. In the 1830s, Alexis de Tocqueville especially commended the New England town meetings. Southern states later attempted to preserve the institution of slavery by seceding from the larger union, but were defeated on the battlefield by those who believed that the Union was indissoluble.

In 1980, attorney, professor, and journalist Richard Cummings published a book entitled *Proposition Fourteen: A Secessionist Remedy.* Drawing from critics of American government from both the right and the left as well as from concerns expressed by discontented localities from throughout the nation, Cummings perceived the central problems of America to stem from its large size and the high taxes and unresponsive bureaucracies that this size generated. He believed that Americans needed to consider the idea of decentralization, or devolution of power. Specifically, he suggested amending Article IV, Section 4 of the U.S. Constitution so as to guarantee "a democratic" rather than a "republican" form of government (Cummings

1980, 94). Going beyond those who initiated the Civil War, Cummings was willing to allow not only individual states but also individual localities to secede and govern themselves.

Cummings did not go into great detail as to how such governments might function. He did suggest that "an alliance of small, well-disciplined and highly-motivated armies is the best possible defense for the country" (Cummings 1980, 98). He further believed that localities might be better able to provide for their own welfare, education, and social services. He thus observed that "if money were kept within a locality, it is probable that the area's inhabitants would be at least as compassionate as Congress, and probably more astute than civil servant social workers" (Cummings 1980, 99).

Cummings believed that new communities might be formed along the order of communes or New England towns, with "a single local tax" sufficing to meet local needs. Admitting that his idea sounded "utopian," he believed that such new communities might contribute to "life based on spiritual values; full integration of all age groups, with the old given positions of leadership and veneration, and the young, increased responsibility, a kind of continuing 'celebration of life'" (Cummings 1980, 103). Much like the French philosopher Jean-Jacques Rousseau, who had suggested that people might have to be "forced" to be free, Cummings further suggested that citizens might be mandated to participate in politics (Cummings 1980, 110).

Cummings realized that "the handmaidens of Big Business, Big Labor, and Big Government" (Cummings 1980, 118) would resist his proposals. Cummings, who had himself worked in the Democratic Party, favored abandoning the two major parties.

Not long before Cummings published his book, Howard Jarvis had led the fight for "Proposition 13" in California, an initiative ratified by the people and limiting property tax rates. Cummings thus titled his own proposal Proposition 14. Beginning with a list of grievances against the national government and the two-party system that supported it, Cummings's proposal provided that the people of local communities were reasserting their autonomy:

- To be free from the abuses of ever-increasing "government" in the form of usurpation of said communities' rightful functions;
- To end taxation beyond reasonable tolerance, and expenditures beyond any control;
- To end the imposition of any form of harmful technology without due regard to the consequences (Cummings 1980, 123).

They therefore "declare themselves to be self-governing by direct democracy, which is the only system to further mankind and to preserve the world" (Cummings 1980, 123).

Secession seems unlikely, but pleas for greater state and local autonomy, or devolution, and for national initiatives and referendums continue.

See also Initiative and Referendum; Naylor, Thomas H.

For Further Reading:

Cummings, Richard. 1980. *Proposition Fourteen: A Secessionist Remedy.* Sagaponack, New York: The Permanent Press.

CURRENCY

Article I, Section 8 of the U.S. Constitution invests Congress with power "to coin Money, [and] regulate the value thereof." During the Civil War, the government issued paper bills, known as "greenbacks," and subsequently passed a law, the Legal Tender Act of 1862, requiring that such currency be accepted in payment for debts. When initially challenged in *Hepburn v. Griswold* (1870), the Supreme Court held by a 4-to-3 vote that this law—at least as applied to preexisting contracts—violated both the due process clause of the Fifth Amendment and the contracts clause (J. W. Ely 1992, 84). The day the opinion was issued, President Grant appointed two new justices, and when the case was reargued the next year, the Court reversed itself in *Knox v. Lee* (1871)

in a 5-to-4 vote, again split along partisan lines (J. W. Ely 1992, 84).

Several amending proposals, undoubtedly motivated by these developments, would have made gold and silver the exclusive legal tender or would have limited the issuance of paper currency. Some proposals introduced in 1892 provided for issuing paper money in the amount of $20 per person and equalizing its value with that of gold and silver (Musmanno 1929, 110).

In *Norman v. Baltimore & Ohio Railroad Co., Nortz v. United States,* and *Perry v. United States* (the *Gold Clause Cases* of 1935), the Supreme Court endorsed broad congressional powers over currency. In these cases, it decided that the government could annul requirements in private contracts calling for payment in gold.

A number of proposed new constitutions have provided for additional denominations of existing monies or for the renaming of American currency. Michael Marx's proposed utopia is based on a gold and silver standard.

See also Marx, Michael.

For Further Reading:

Bancroft, George. 1888. *A Plea for the Constitution of the United States: Wounded in the House of its Guardians.* http://www.constitution.org/gb/gbplea.htm. Accessed September 28, 2008.

Ely, James W. 1992. *The Guardian of Every Other Right: A Constitutional History of Property Rights.* New York: Oxford University Press.

Musmanno, M. A. 1929. *Proposed Amendments to the Constitution.* Washington DC: U.S. Government Printing Office.

CUSTOMS AND USAGES

Although the text of the Constitution can be changed only by constitutional amendment, its interpretation can be altered in a variety of ways, the most common of which is judicial interpretation. Other customs and usages, however, may also develop as the elective branches make moves that serve as precedents for future actions. Conceptually, then, the "written" Constitution is surrounded by a larger "unwritten" constitution, more familiar in nations such as the United Kingdom that do not have a written constitution (Tiedeman 1890; W. Harris 1993; Vile 1994).

The most authoritative, albeit dated, discussion of U.S. customs and usages is found in a book published by British scholar, Herbert Horwill, in 1925. In describing the "Law of the Constitution," Horwill referred to the Constitution and its amendments, as well as to the "Statute Law" and "Common Law" surrounding it. He described other conventions that grew up around the Constitution as "customs and usages."

Among the customs that Horwill identified were practices that had democratized the electoral college, the precedent whereby a vice president who takes over for a president who has died takes his title rather than merely serving as an "acting president," the two-term presidential limit (in force when Horwill wrote, broken by Franklin D. Roosevelt, and later reestablished by the Twenty-second Amendment), the role of the president's cabinet, various customs regarding the appearance of cabinet officers before Congress, the appointment and removal powers, and the custom whereby members of Congress are expected to reside in their own districts. Horwill noted that customs and usages may change or be incorporated into the written Constitution. Thus, prior to the adoption of the Seventeenth Amendment, many state legislatures had already agreed to accept the popular choice for U.S. senators (Horwill 1925, 203–205). Similarly, Woodrow Wilson changed a custom that had been in force since Thomas Jefferson when he decided to read a presidential message before Congress (Horwill 1925, 199).

Similarly, a more recent British author noted the existence of certain "abeyances" in government. He describes such abeyances as contrasting with more determinable conventions and as representing "a form of tacit and instinctive agreement to condone, and even cultivate, constitutional ambiguity as an acceptable strategy for resolving conflict" (Foley 1989, xi). Noting that not all constitutional provisions receive equal scrutiny, other scholars have pointed to what they describe as "underenforced constitutional norms" (Sager 1978).

Although advocates of strict construction of the Constitution have frequently accused liberal justices on the Warren and Burger Courts of interpreting the U.S. Constitution by inventing concepts like "privacy" that are not specifically stated there, another scholar has noted that the more conservative justices, who proclaim adherence to constitutional literalism, also rely on certain unwritten norms, like state sovereign immunity and the doctrine that the national government cannot conscript state employees when interpreting the Constitution, and especially the Tenth and Eleventh Amendments (Rubenfeld 2001). A respondent notes that it is dangerous "to overestimate the importance of the most recent cases" and that "historically the Court spends most of its time oscillating within a fairly narrow band in the middle of the continuum [of constitutional interpretations that adhere closely to the text and those that rely on unwritten norms]; and there are institutional mechanisms that explain why it does and will continue to do so" (Vermeule 2001, 475).

Like the idea of customs and usages, the concepts of abeyances and underenforced constitutional norms demonstrate that, even in a nation that professes adherence to a written constitution, the text is interpreted in light of practices, both written and unwritten, that surround it. Reformers who ignore such surroundings are likely to misunderstand the operation of government, propose amendments that are not needed, or be frustrated by the effects of their own proposals.

See also Seventeenth Amendment; Superstatutes; Twenty-second Amendment.

For Further Reading:

Foley, Michael. 1989. *The Silence of Constitutions: Gaps, "Abeyances" and Political Temperament in the Maintenance of Government.* London: Routledge.

Gerhardt, Michael J. 2008. "Non-Judicial Precedent." *Vanderbilt Law Reivew* 61 (April): 713–784.

Harris, William F., II. 1993. *The Interpretable Constitution.* Baltimore: Johns Hopkins University Press.

Horwill, Herbert W. 1925. *The Usages of the American Constitution.* Reprint, Port Washington, NY: Kennikat Press, 1969.

Jenkins, David. 2003. "From Unwritten to Written: Transformation in the British Common Law Constitution." *Vanderbilt Journal of Transnational Law* 36 (May): 863–960.

Quirk, William J. 2008. *Courts and Congress: America's Unwritten Constitution.* New Brunswick, NJ: Transaction Publishers.

Rubenfeld, Jed. 2001. "The New Unwritten Constitution." *Duke Law Journal* 51 (October): 289–305.

Sager, Lawrence Gene. 1978. "Fair Measure: The Legal Status of Underenforced Constitutional Norms." *Harvard Law Review* 92: 1212–1264.

Tiedeman, Christopher G. 1890. *The Unwritten Constitution of the United States.* New York: G. P. Putnam's Sons.

Vermeule, Adrian. 2001. "The Facts about Unwritten Constitutionalism: A Response to Professor Rubenfeld." *Duke Law Journal* 51 (October): 473–476.

Vile, John R. 1994. *Constitutional Change in the United States: A Comparative Study of the Role of Constitutional Amendments, Judicial Interpretations, and Legislative and Executive Actions.* Westport, CT: Praeger.

Wilson, James G. 1992. "American Constitutional Conventions: The Judicially Unenforceable Rules That Combine with Judicial Doctrine and Public Opinion to Regulate Political Behavior." *Buffalo Law Review* 40 (Fall): 645–738.

CUTLER, LLOYD N. (1917–2005)

A prominent Washington attorney who was especially influential in the administration of President Jimmy Carter, and who continued to serve under President Bill Clinton, published an article in *Foreign Affairs* in 1980, which was subsequently reprinted in a book on the separation of powers. Cutler focused on what he believed to be "the structural inability of our government to propose, legislate, and administer a balanced program for governing." (1986, 1).

Whatever the initial merits of separation of powers, Cutler believed that the structure "almost guarantees stalemate today" (2). Comparing the difficulties that President Carter had experienced with greater successes of leaders in parliamentary systems with greater party discipline, Cutler believed that these difficulties showed the need to create a system "to govern more efficiently" (6). Although he acknowledged that there had been times of extraordinary consensus, such as the early days of the Franklin D. Roosevelt and Lyndon B. Johnson Administrations, he thought that most of the time the nation was likely to be "divided somewhere between 55-45 and 45-55 on each set of a wide set of issues," making it almost impossible for presidents to carry out their programs (11).

Cutler concluded that the only way to form such effective governments was to amend the Constitution. He offered a set of seven proposals that he thought would tilt the U.S. system closer to the parliamentary model.

Cutler's initial proposal called for increasing the terms of members of the House of Representatives from two years to four and requiring voters to cast straight-ticket votes for their representative, president, and vice president. He further suggested that it might be desirable to do the same with U.S. senators, which would reduce their terms from six years to four. Cutler's second proposal called for requiring the president to select half the members of the president's cabinet from the president's party in the House and Senate. Cutler believed this "would tend to increase the intimacy between the executive and the legislature and add to their sense of collective responsibility" (145). Cutler's third proposal would have allowed a president, albeit not more than once per term, "to dissolve Congress and call for new congressional elections" (14). He further opined as to whether such a president ought to have to run as well, but, perhaps reflecting his own frustration as a presidential advisor, acknowledged that "even then, the American public might be perverse enough to reelect all the Incumbents to office" (14). Cutler's fourth proposal suggested that perhaps two-thirds of both houses of Congress should be able to call for new presidential elections. Cutler's fifth proposal, which appears to clash with his first, suggested a six-year presidential term. Sensing this potential conflict, Cutler proposed combining his third, fourth, and fifth proposals, so that the president and all members of Congress would serve six-year terms, with the president having power to dissolve Congress at least once a term, and Congress having its own power to reverse the tables within 30 days. In either circumstance, Cutler would require that the entire cycle of state primaries and conventions, nominating conventions, and elections take place within a 120-day period. Cutler's seventh proposal provided that "Congress would first enact broad mandates, declaring general policies and directions and leaving the precise allocative choices, within a congressionally approved budget, to the president," to whom all such agencies would be responsible (16). Presidential actions would become law unless vetoed by both houses of Congress. Acknowledging that this "would turn the present process on its head," Cutler said that "it would bring much closer to reality the persisting myth that it is up to the president to govern—something he now lacks the constitutional power to do."

Skeptical that there would be support for a constitutional convention to enact such measures, Cutler favored "the appointment of a bipartisan presidential commission to analyze the issues, compare how other constitutions work, hold public hearings, and make a full report" (17) that might be incorporated in the Constitution through amendments. Two modern critics content that Cutler's proposals stemmed from his inability to recognize that the problems in the Carter administration were "the failure of a president" rather than "a failure of the system" (Lane and Oreskes 2007, 187).

Cutler subsequently served on the Committee on the Constitutional System, which issued a report in January 1987 that called for considerably less sweeping changes than those that he had advocated. Cutler also later served on the Continuity of Government Commission, designed to deal with the continuation of government after a catastrophic attack on the United States.

See also Committeee on the Constitutional System; Parliamentary Systems.

For Further Reading:

Cutler, Lloyd N. 1986. "To Form a Government," in *Separation of Powers—Does It Still Work?* ed. Robert A. Goldwin and Art Kaufman. Washington DC: American Enterprise Institute for Public Policy Research. Cutler's original essay was published under the same title in 1980, *Foreign Affairs* (Fall): 50:126–143. The rest of the Goldwin-Kaufman volume addresses many of the issues that Cutler raised.

Jasper, William F. August 25, 2003. "Who's Attacking the Constitution," *The New American.* http//www.thenewamerican.com/node/183. Accessed May 13, 2008.

Lane, Eric, and Michael Orekes. 2007. *The Genius of America: How the Constitution Saved Our Country—and Why It Can Again.* New York: Bloomsbury.

"Symposium: The Constitutional Structure of National Government in the United States: Is It in a State of Crisis?" 1995. *Administrative Law Journal* 9 (Spring): 1–42. (Note: participants included Lloyd Cutler.)

D

DAVIDSON, JIM

Jim Davidson has formulated a constitution for a "floating" concrete nation named "Oceania." This new Oceania was to be designed by architect Sten Sjostrand, located somewhere in the Caribbean, and based on libertarian ideals. In addition to an introduction and a set of definitions, the constitution of Oceania, which Davidson posted on the Internet, is divided into 10 articles.

The introduction likens the new government to that of a "peaceful dolphin" rather than to sharklike governments that use "force and fraud to extract wealth and labor from their citizens." The introduction specifically cites the U.S. Constitution as one that has been so "vague" as "to allow its government to pass laws clearly at odds with the spirit of liberty in which that once-free nation was founded." Unusual definitions in the constitution include a "child," who is identified as less than 16 years old, a "teen," who is between 16 and 18, and an "adult," who is 18 or older. All persons are referred to with non-gender-specific designations. Oceanians might be either "persons" or "entities."

The constitution for Oceania begins with "A Partial Listing of Rights." It would require a 95 percent vote to remove rights and a 66 percent vote to add new ones. Rights are categorized under the headings of "life," "liberty," "property," and "privacy." The right to life includes the right of a hospital to turn off life support for individuals whose families can no longer afford such care. The right to life also encompasses "the Right to keep and bear Weaponry," and even to set booby traps, if proper warnings are

posted. The right encompasses a "Right to Self-Sovereignty" that includes what individuals will put into or wear on their bodies, including using drugs and seat belts and helmets, as well as all kinds of consensual sexual conduct and participation in dangerous sports. The right to life also includes broad rights of free speech, employment, and religious freedom.

The right to liberty includes a prohibition of slavery, a right to travel, a right to assemble, a right to associate and discriminate, and a right to knowledge. This latter right includes the right to engage in insider trading. The right to liberty also includes the right to listen. The right to travel would be facilitated by providing that all land in Oceania "Must contain eight-meter-wide and eight-meter-high easements in a grid format of squares with eight kilometer sides on which there is an Entitlement to travel."

The right to property is based on the proposition that "taxation, civil forfeiture, [and] eminent domain" are all "forms of theft." Individuals would be permitted to sell body parts or engage in sex or medical experiments for money. The right to property includes permission for individuals to operate businesses without licenses. The government would be prohibited from requiring "minimum wage, family leave benefits, medical insurance, disability benefits, unemployment insurance, or workers' compensation." The right to property includes a right to negotiate contracts, including marriage, which appears open to combinations of both genders. The right to free enterprise is explicitly affirmed as is the right to free trade, and limited intellectual property rights. The right to privacy includes protections against warrantless searches, the "Right to Self-Identity," the "Right to Financial Privacy," the "Right to Encryption," the "Right to Secure Conversations," and privacy rights on government property and in the workplace. Unlike adults, children would be vested with certain entitlements to be provided by one or more parents, whom children would have a right to sue. Children and teens would have less-restricted rights than adults, and animals would be protected against "cruel and unusual mistreatment."

Having begun with rights, Article II of the Oceania Constitution deals with "Government Agencies and Power Structures." It outlines the judicial branch first. Denying the possibility of "victimless crimes" in Oceania, this Article would abolish the distinction between civil and criminal law. Judges of the supreme court and lower bodies would serve two- or four-year terms; judges would not require "lawyer licenses." To bring suit in an Oceanian court, individuals would have to obtain court membership, which is anticipated to be widespread. Membership would bring the "Right to Fair Prosecution," the right to a jury, "the Right to a Level Playing Field," the "Right to Fair Bail and Fines," the "Right to Presumption of Innocency," and other rights currently designated within the U.S. Bill of Rights. A statute of limitations for all crimes is set at 10 years. Prisoners would work in their prisons to support themselves or be the objects of charity.

The delineation of the executive branch begins by specifying that all major laws must "be decided by referendum." Presidents and vice presidents would serve for four-year terms and have the power to put referendums on the ballot and "sign minor Contracts and legislation." The president could sign treaties to which 75 percent or more of Oceania voters have agreed. Directors of the various departments of war would be selected through popular election and would contract for services with private militia. An "Anti-Law Department" would be responsible for helping to repeal unwanted laws.

The legislative branch replaces representative bodies with direct popular legislation, thereby eliminating lobbying. The people are given a restricted list of areas in which they might adopt laws. The provision relating to abortion provides for the possibility of restric-

tions "after three months gestation where the mother's life is not endangered." The Constitution expresses the hope that "Whenever a need or a problem arises, . . . Oceanians will not ask 'What law can we pass?' but 'What Business can we create?' Elections for elected offices would include designations for "None of the Above" and "Remove This Office."

With formal government so restricted, a section focusing on "The Power Structure of Oceania" deals primarily with the rights of restricted and unrestricted businesses. The constitution would strip governments of their powers to "issue or control currency," to generate power, to run a postal service, to finance art, to engage in traffic control, to inspect foods, to provide job training, or to finance scientific research or tourism. The constitution tersely notes that "Governmental charities are compassion at gunpoint." Employers and their employees would freely negotiate working conditions.

Article III further designates powers that would be denied to the government. These would include the right of taxation, of establishing businesses, of running embassies, of owning property or streets, of regulating banking, of running schools, of engaging in "Welfare and Humanitarian Activities" including Social Security, of funding scientific research, of funding police, and of providing fire protection, garbage disposal, public transit, and the like.

Article IV deals with national security. Except in cases of attack, wars would generally be declared by referendum. Oceania might join the United Nations, but such membership must be privately funded. The right to free trade would not include the right to export mind-altering drugs or weapons to nations on forbidden lists.

Article V repeats the earlier right of the people to regulate abortion by referendum after the first three months of gestation. Article VI deals with budgeting and requires agencies to publish a list of donors each year. Some budgets would be funded by user fees by losing parties in court cases.

Article VII identifies a housing development as "the most powerful governmentlike structure in Oceania." Such developments must be subdivided once they reach 5,000 persons. Article

VIII permits a county or local government to secede with a vote of 75 percent or higher. Article IX provides that the constitution requires ratification "by unanimous consent of the original Land Owners of Oceania." Article X ends with a list of "suggestions" that have "no Force of law." These include allowing animal rights groups to be plaintiffs in animal rights' cases; allowing armed forces to challenge one another to games of skill; and choosing English to be the official language.

The Constitution of Oceania attempts to spell out libertarian ideals in a single constitutional document. The project to build a concrete nation in the Caribbean in the near future appears to have dissolved. Indeed, in personal correspondence with the author, the chief architect of the project (who reports that he became a Christian in 1999 but still largely holds to his libertarian ideals) indicates that the author's purchase of *The Atlantis Papers,* outlining the proposed government, was the first "in about two years" (Davidson May 28, 2002). In this same letter, however, Davidson cites two newly proclaimed independent nations called Sealand, six miles east of the United Kingdom, and Awdal Free Port, in the Gulf of Aden near the Red Sea, and indicates that futurists Alvin and Heidi Toffler (discussed in an entry later in this volume) anticipated the development of as many as 5,000 new countries in the 21st century. He also notes that his constitution could be applied to "countries organized beyond the Earth" and reflects optimism that, "when the resources of our Solar System are at the disposal of our most creative and inventive minds, many of the problems here on Earth will fade to distant memories."

An article published on the Web in March 2009 reports that the Seasteading Institute has drawn up plans to construct at least one floating city off the coast of San Francisco and that a prototype might be available within three years. Patri Friedman, identified as a former Google engineer, is cited as saying that such cities "are the perfect places to experiment with new forms of government" (Erdman 2009). The article suggests that such cities might be modular, that they might allow for the use of marijuana, and that they might make "intellectual property communal."

See also Bailey, Martin J.; Marx, Michael; Toffler, Alvin and Heidi.

For Further Reading:

Erdman, Shelby. "City Floating on the Sea Could Be Just 3 Years Away," CNN.com/technology. http://www.cnn.com/2009/TECH/03/09/floating.cities.seasteading/index.html. Accessed March 10, 2009.

"Oceania—The Atlantis Project." At http://www.oceania.org/indexgif.html. Accessed April 29, 2002. All quoted materials above are taken directly from the Web site.

Davidson, Jim. May 28, 2002. Personal correspondence with the author.

Davidson, Jim, with Eric Klien, Norm Doering, and Lee Crocker. 1994. *The Atlantis Papers.* Houston, TX: Interglobal Paratronics, Inc.

DECLARATION OF INDEPENDENCE

One of the foremost documents in American history sets forth the reasons that the colonies declared their independence from Great Britain; it explains that the united colonies were resorting to revolution only after more conventional means of seeking legal change had failed. The Second Continental Congress delegated the task of writing this document to a committee of five men consisting of Thomas Jefferson, John Adams, Benjamin Franklin, Roger Sherman, and Robert Livingston. Jefferson did the initial drafting, and the document was subsequently debated and revised by Congress as a whole. Congress voted to accept the document on July 4, 1776, and delegates signed over the next several months.

The Declaration of Independence was firmly based on a philosophy of natural rights according to which men are created equal and are all entitled to the right to "life, liberty, and the pursuit of happiness." Governments are instituted to secure such rights. Accordingly, "whenever any form of government becomes destructive of these ends, it is the right of the people to alter or abolish it, and to institute new government, laying its foundation on such principles, and organizing its powers in such form, as to them shall seem most likely to effect their safety and happiness."

After arguing that humans were generally more inclined to suffer deprivation of rights than to alter their form of government, Jefferson argued that when faced with attempts to set up despotism, the people have both the "right" and the "duty" to "throw off such government, and to provide new guards for their future security." Much of the remainder of the Declaration focuses on specific colonial grievances against the English king.

The Declaration of Independence did not create a new government—that was the task accomplished with the writing of the Articles of Confederation and the U.S. Constitution. The Declaration did effectively articulate principles that continue to guide American government and inspire free peoples throughout the world. When delegates met at the Seneca Falls Convention in New York in 1848 to push for women's rights and begin the drive for women's suffrage that did not culminate until the adoption of the Nineteenth Amendment in 1920, they modeled their "Declaration of Sentiments" on the Declaration of Independence (Bernhard and Fox-Genovese 1995, 85–89).

The Constitution and the Bill of Rights gave life to many of the principles embodied in the Declaration of Independence. The eventual ratification of the equal protection clause of the Fourteenth Amendment was an especially important step toward governmental protection of equal rights to liberty. The constitutional amending process provides a viable "safety valve" against the necessity for revolution; changes in judicial interpretation and congressional and presidential practices also accommodate changes that may not be written into the constitutional text. In his original draft of the Bill of Rights, James Madison had proposed adding a prefix to the Constitution specifying "that all power is derived from the people, who have a right to reform or change their government whenever it is found inadequate" (Schwartz 1992, 166). In a similar vein, in July 1976, the bicentennial of the Declaration, Representative Robert Michel, a Republican from Illinois, introduced an amendment (H.J. Res. 1016) to incorporate certain principles of the Declaration of Independence into the preamble of the U.S. Constitution.

See also Fourteenth Amendment; Jefferson, Thomas; Madison, James; Safety-Valve Analogy; Seneca Falls Convention; Virginia Declaration of Rights.

For Further Reading:

Adler, Mortimer J. 1987. *We Hold These Truths: Understanding the Ideas and the Ideals of the Constitution.* New York: Macmillan.

Becker, Carl L. 1970. *The Declaration of Independence: A Study in the History of Political Ideas.* New York: Vintage Books.

Bernhard, Virginia, and Elizabeth Fox-Genovese, eds. 1995. *The Birth of American Feminism: The Seneca Falls Woman's Convention of 1848.* St. James, NY: Brandywine Press.

Gerber, Scott D. 1995. *To Secure These Rights: The Declaration of Independence and Constitutional Interpretation.* New York: New York University Press.

Maier, Pauline. 1997. *American Scripture: Making the Declaration of Independence.* New York: Alfred A. Knopf.

Schwartz, Bernard. 1992. *The Great Rights of Mankind: A History of the American Bill of Rights.* Madison, WI: Madison House.

Vile, John R. 2010. *A Companion to the United States Constitution and Its Amendments.* 5th ed. Westport, CT: Praeger.

Wills, Garry. 1978. *Inventing America: Jefferson's Declaration of Independence.* New York: Doubleday.

DEFAMATION

The First Amendment to the Constitution prohibits the national government from abridging freedom of speech and press. These protections have been extended via the due process clause of the Fourteenth Amendment to the states as well. The Supreme Court has ruled, however, that some forms of expression do not constitute free speech. These include "fighting words," obscenity, and libel. Libel refers to written communication that "is injurious to the reputation of another" (*Black's Law Dictionary* 1969, 824). Slander is defamation in spoken rather than written form.

Up to 1964, states enforced laws against libel. In *New York Times Co. v. Sullivan* (1964), however, state officials had attempted to use such laws to stifle criticism against them; in this case, an Alabama police commissioner who had taken action against civil rights protesters sued in response to an advertisement that had overstated some of his actions. Accordingly, the Supreme Court ruled that, in proving libel, public officials have a substantial burden of proof. They have to show that libelous statements made about them were made with "actual malice," that is, with knowledge that they were false or with "reckless disregard" to their truth or falsity. Subsequent rulings have extended this standard to other public figures who are not officials, but not to private individuals who are merely caught up in public controversy (*Gertz v. Robert Welch, Inc.* [1974]).

Although some individuals favor further liberalization of libel laws, others fear that current laws allow too much leeway to those who would abuse free speech. In April 1982, Democratic representative Bill Burlison of Missouri introduced an amendment to provide that nothing in the First Amendment "shall prevent the recovery by any person, including any person deemed newsworthy, of damages in a civil action, or the imposition of criminal penalties, in cases involving defamation of such persons" (H.J. Res. 1285). A provision called the "speech or debate clause" within Article I, Section 6 of the Constitution, which was designed to give members of Congress absolute freedom to criticize the government, provides that members of Congress shall not be "questioned in any other Place" "for any Speech or Debate in either House." Later amending proposals have expressed fear that members of Congress might use their protection under this clause to injure the reputations of private individuals without being amenable to the kinds of legal remedies that would be available for other defamatory speech.

See also First Amendment; Fourteenth Amendment.

For Further Reading:

Lewis, Anthony. 1991. *Make No Law: The Sullivan Case and the First Amendment.* New York: Random House.

Sack, Robert D., ed. 1999. *Sack on Defamation: Libel, Slander and Related Problems.* 3d ed. New York: Practicing Law Institute.

DELIBERATION AND THE AMENDING PROCESS

Fifty-five delegates who met in Philadelphia between May and September of 1787 contributed to the deliberations that resulted in the U.S. Constitution. The delegates took the task of writing a new constitution very seriously. They adopted a number of rules to enhance deliberation. One, which was rarely breached and which would be almost impossible if such a convention were to be held today, provided for the secrecy of convention deliberations. Another provided that votes would be listed by states rather than under individual names. A third provided that votes could be retaken, giving delegates a chance to change their minds if they came to different understandings during the course of debates.

The document that emerged from convention deliberations provided a number of mechanisms, including a bicameral Congress and a presidential "signature" (or a supermajority congressional override) to assure that legislation was the result of a deliberative process. Because amendments would involve alterations to the fundamental law, the framers rejected the idea of parliamentary, or legislative, sovereignty that had been dominant in Great Britain. The American framers chose to make the amending process more difficult, requiring supermajorities at both the proposal and ratification stages. One of the framers' major goals appears to be that of ensuring that amendments would not be adopted without adequate deliberation and without a consensus in their favor. In light of how few amendments have actually been adopted, some critics believe that the framers may have made the process too difficult, although most agree that there should be some distinction between the legislative process and the amending process.

Some proposals for constitutional initiatives and referendums could short-circuit the deliberative process that is currently involved in the amending process, but mechanisms (multiple votes, supermajorities, or specified passages of time between stages, for example) might be adopted to provide for such deliberation.

Although citizens and scholars alike may argue as to whether the current amending mechanism involves the ideal balance, most agree that the process should encourage both deliberation and consensus. The Citizens for the Constitution, the group which authored the Constitutional Amendment Initiative, have suggested that one criterion for an amendment should be that the amendment has had the opportunity for "full and fair debate." As part of this suggestion, the group proposed that no substantive changes to amendments should be offered on the floor of Congress that had not been fully vetted in committee.

See also Citizens for the Constitution, the Constitutional Amendment Initiative; Consensus and the Amending Process; Initiative and Referendum; Parliamentary Sovereignty.

For Further Reading:

Lieber, Benjamin, and Patrick Brown. 1995. "On Supermajorities and the Constitution." *Georgetown Law Review* 83 (July): 2347–2384.

DEMOCRACY AND CONSTITUTIONAL AMENDMENTS

When it was established in 1789, the U.S. Constitution provided for a more democratic system than those of most other nations of the world at the time, but James Madison argued in *Federalist* No. 10 that the system was a government of republican, or indirect, democracy. In part by such design, and in part because it was the product of compromises among rival interests, the resulting system of government not only moderated direct democracy but also contained a number of undemocratic features. The Constitution did not directly establish voting rights, but left this matter to the states, most of which denied such rights to blacks and women, and, in some cases, to individuals who did not own a specified amount of property. Similarly, although the Constitution did not mention the institution of slavery, it acquiesced to the institution by pro-

viding for the continuing importation of slaves for 20 years, by providing for a fugitive slave clause, and by specifying that slaves would be counted as three-fifths of a person for purposes of taxation and representation. In addition, the Constitution contained no definition of citizenship, leaving the status of free blacks and others to the whims of state law.

By requiring supermajorities both to propose and to ratify amendments, the amending provisions of the U.S. Constitution did not embody direct democracy, but in time, the provisions have done much to democratize this system. The first 10 amendments are concerned more with the protection of individual rights than with direct participation in government. Still, they include guarantees in the First Amendment for freedom of speech, press, assembly, and petition that are essential to democratic governance, and provisions in other amendments provide for due process rights and for jury trials. Depending on one's perspective on federalism, one could question whether the Tenth Amendment expands or narrows rights. Similarly, the Eleventh Amendment, and the doctrine of sovereign immunity that it has been said to embody, arguably makes state governments less accountable to citizens. By contrast, in curing one of the obvious defects of (while not eliminating) the Electoral College, the Twelfth Amendment made it more likely that the people, and not members of Congress, would decide who would be selected as president and vice president.

The three amendments adopted in the aftermath of the Civil War helped rid the nation of slavery, guarantee equal rights to all citizens, and (on paper) prohibit discrimination on the basis of race. The Fourteenth Amendment, in particular, embodied the sentiments of the Declaration of Independence within the Constitution.

The Progressive Era Amendments were also largely democratic in character. One could argue that the Sixteenth Amendment (providing for a national income tax) was not per se democratic or undemocratic and that the Eighteenth Amendment (providing for national alcoholic prohibition) enabled what proved to be a temporary majority the right to limit individual choice over a matter in which the government's role should have been more limited. However the Eighteenth Amendment is interpreted, it was subsequently repealed by the Twenty-first Amendment. The Seventeenth Amendment clearly extended democracy by providing that state voters rather than state legislatures would choose U.S. senators. Similarly, the Nineteenth Amendment significantly expanded the franchise by prohibiting discrimination in voting on the basis of sex.

A number of other amendments have provided for the expansion of voting rights. Thus, the Twenty-third Amendment provided for electoral votes for the District of Columbia, the Twenty-fourth Amendment eliminated the poll tax in federal elections, and the Twenty-sixth Amendment lowered the voting age to eighteen. Likewise, the Twentieth Amendment made members more accountable by reducing the terms of lame-duck members. The Twenty-second Amendment, limiting the number of terms that presidents may serve, narrowed popular choice of this branch—although only one previous president, Franklin D. Roosevelt, had been chosen to serve more than two terms. Similarly, the Twenty-fifth Amendment, while providing not only for a method for ascertaining presidential disability, but also for replacing vice presidents, embodies a method of indirect, rather than direct, democracy for doing so.

A scholar of the amending process has observed "a pattern of successive extensions of democracy" (Grimes 1978, 163). He argues that "twenty-one amendments may be said to affirm either the principle of democratic rights or that of democratic processes," whereas "only three amendments—the Tenth, Eleventh, and Twenty-fifth—would appear to be indifferent, or irrelevant, to democratic principles" (Grimes 1978, 166). He accordingly concludes that "the record of the twenty-six amendments to the Constitution is in a sense a record of democracy in America" (Grimes 1978, 167).

A number of caveats should be added to this analysis. First, many of the initial limitations on voting rights—for example, those based on property ownership or church membership—were liberalized at the state level, and periods of progress were sometimes punctuated with periods of backsliding (Keyssar 2000, 53).

Second, guarantees on paper were not always put into immediate operation. Federal courts did not apply the provisions of the Bill of Rights to state governments until well into the 20th century. In the early years of their operation, the Fourteenth and Fifteenth Amendments were notoriously ineffective in protecting the rights of newly freed slaves.

Third, by requiring supermajorities, the amending process gives a veto to minorities with strong views and is an obstacle to the immediate realization of many proposals that mere popular majorities may favor. Even though proposed by the required majorities in Congress, amendments providing for restricting child labor, equal rights for women, and congressional representation for the District of Columbia have all failed to be ratified. Nevertheless, child labor laws are now accepted by the courts, a place where women have also made substantial gains.

Fourth, a number of fairly important constitutional mechanisms remain that are not fully democratic (although many may embody indirect, or republican, democracy). These include the electoral college system that sometimes results in presidential and vice-presidential winners who did not carry the popular vote; the provision for equal state representation in the U.S. Senate; the system of selection of members of the House of Representatives through single member, winner-take-all districts rather than through a system of proportional representation, which is more common in other democratic nations; and the wide-ranging exercise of judicial review by unelected judges and justices (Dahl 2001). Similarly, the national constitution has no provisions for citizen initiatives, referendums, or recalls, which many states have adopted to make their constitutions more directly accountable to the people.

Proposals by Daniel B. Jeffs, Mike Gravel (the National Initiative for Democracy), Larry Sabato, and Sanford Levinson are among those that are designed to edge the United States much closer to a system of direct democracy.

See also Jeffs, Daniel B.; Levinson, Sanford; National Initiative for Democracy; Progress and the Amending Process; Sabato, Larry; Voting Rights, Constitutional Amendments Relating to.

For Further Reading:

Berns, Walter. 2006. *Democracy and the Constitution: Essays by Walter Berns.* Washington DC: AEI Press.

Dahl, Robert. 2001. *How Democratic Is the American Constitution?* New Haven, CT: Yale University Press.

Keyssar, Alexander. 2000. *The Right to Vote: The Constitutional History of Democracy in the United States.* New York: Basic Books.

Levinson, Sanford. 2006. *Our Undemocratic Constitution: Where the Constitution Goes Wrong (and How the People Can Correct It).* New York: Oxford University Press.

Macedo, Stephen. 2009. "Our Imperfect Democratic Constitution: The Critics Examined," 89 *Boston University Law Review* (April): 609–628.

Somin, Ilya, and Neal Devins. 2007. "Can We Make the Constitution More Democratic?" *Drake Law Review* 55 (Summer): 971–1000.

Vermeule, Adrian. "Second-Best Democracy." *Harvard Law & Policy Review* online. http://www.hlpronline.com/2006/11/vermeule_01.html. Accessed May 4, 2009.

DEROGATORY MATERIAL, TEACHING OF

In 1943 and 1945, Democratic Representative Jerry Voorhis of California introduced amendments to prohibit the teaching of derogatory materials about the government to citizens of the United States. Voorhis had been a member of the Dies Committee on Un-American Activities, but his appointment had come after he expressed opposition to what he considered to be improper investigatory and accusatory tactics that the committee was utilizing (Voorhis 1947, 207–231). Moreover, both on the committee and throughout his service in Congress, his was generally a liberal voice. Voorhis lost the election of 1946 to Richard Nixon, who campaigned against Voorhis's alleged liberalism.

For Further Reading:

Voorhis, Jerry. 1947. *Confessions of a Congressman.* Garden City, NY: Doubleday. Reprint, Westport, CT: Greenwood Press, 1970.

DILLON, CONLEY (1906–1987)

Political scientist Conley Dillon offered a number of proposals to revise the Constitution about the time of the bicentennial of the Declaration of Independence and the Constitution (Vile 1991c, 25–27). His proposals were closely tied to a resolution by the American Society for Public Administration (ASPA) (C. Dillon 1974). It proposed the establishment of the Permanent Commission for Constitutional Review consisting of 15 members appointed by the president, the president pro tempore of the Senate, and the speaker of the House of Representatives (C. Dillon 1977, 14).

Following the ASPA report, Dillon suggested nine areas of study for the commission:

(1) "the constitutional basis of our federal structure"; (2) the "selection, removal, and succession" of the president and vice president, as well as "executive branch accountability" and the possibility of "a modified parliamentary system"; (3) "the method of selecting and removing members of Congress, their terms of office, and the[ir] organization and procedures"; (4) the selection and removal of judges; (5) the "distribution and sharing" of powers among the three branches; (6) the "constitutional status and role" of political parties; (7) the "scope of individual and group freedoms and rights"; (8) the organization of a constitutional convention; and (9) ways to deal with loss of confidence in government (22).

Dillon also discussed other plans for constitutional change, including plans by Rexford Tugwell, the Reuss Resolution, and the proposal by James L. Sundquist to allow Congress to remove the president, dissolve itself, and call a new election. Dillon acknowledged that "a realistic assessment, however, does not promise action on constitutional review in the near future" (22).

See also Tugwell, Rexford; Sundquist, James.

For Further Reading:

Dillon, Conley. 1977. "American Constitutional Review: Are We Preparing for the 21st Century?" *World Affairs* 140 (Summer): 211–224.

Dillon, Conley. 1974. "Recommendation for the Establishment of a Permanent Commission of Constitutional Review." *Bureaucrat* 3 (July): 211–224.

DILLON V. GLOSS (1921)

This case, which highlighted the importance of contemporary consensus to the amending process, arose from a habeas corpus petition filed by a petitioner who had been convicted of transporting alcohol in violation of the National Prohibition Act (also known as the Volstead Act), adopted pursuant to the Eighteenth Amendment. The petitioner questioned the legitimacy of the seven-year time limit for ratification that had been incorporated into that amendment. He also claimed that the amendment, which contained a one-year implementation delay, had not been in effect when he was arrested because his arrest had been less than a year from the time the secretary of state had certified the amendment.

Noting that Article V of the Constitution did not specify a ratification time period, Justice Willis Van Devanter observed for a unanimous Court that, without such an understanding, four amendments would still be pending. Analyzing Article V, he concluded that because it treated proposal and ratification not "as unrelated acts, but as succeeding steps in a single endeavor, the natural inference" was that "they are not to be widely separated in time" (*Dillon* 1921, 374–375). He further concluded that

> [A]s ratification is but the expression of the approbation of the people and is to be effective when had in three-fourths of the states, there is a fair implication that it must be sufficiently contemporaneous in that number of states to reflect the will of the people in all sections at relatively the same period, which, of course, ratification

scattered through a long series of years would not do (*Dillon* 1921, 375).

Although the Constitution does not specify how long the ratification period should be, Van Devanter concluded that the seven-year span that Congress had established in the case of the Eighteenth Amendment was reasonable. Van Devanter further decided that the Eighteenth Amendment became effective when ratified by the requisite number of states and not when such ratification was certified 13 days later by the secretary of state.

The current status of *Dillon v. Gloss* is not clear. In *Coleman v. Miller* (1939), the Supreme Court ruled that the question of contemporaneousness was a "political question" for Congress to decide. Moreover, although *Dillon* suggested that it would be "quite untenable" (1921, 375) to consider an amendment proposed in 1789 without a specified time limit to be pending, Congress did exactly this when it voted in 1992 to accept ratification of the Twenty-seventh Amendment.

One contemporary author, who is concerned about the institution's failure to mention specific time limits for the ratification of proposed amendments, has argued that

> *Dillon*'s conclusion that Article V contains an implicit time limit is wrong, although its premise that such a time limit is necessary is right. Essentially, the Court in *Dillon* makes the mistake of assuming that because it is advisable from a policy perspective for Article V to contain a ratification time limit, that it therefore does contain such a limit (Hanlon 2000, 674–675).

See also *Coleman v. Miller;* Eighteenth Amendment; Ratification of Amendments; Secretary of State; Time Limits on Amendments; Twenty-seventh Amendment.

For Further Reading:

Dillon v. Gloss, 256 U.S. 368 (1921).

Hanlon, Michael C. 2000. "Note: The Need for a General Time Limit on Ratification of Proposed Constitutional Amendments." *Journal of Law & Politics* 16 (Summer): 663–698.

DIRECT DEMOCRACY

See Jeffs, Daniel B.; Initiative and Referendum.

DIRKSEN, EVERETT MCKINLEY (1896–1969)

Everett McKinley Dirksen of Illinois served in the U.S. House of Representatives from 1933 to 1949 and in the Senate from 1951 to 1969. In his Senate years, he was the minority leader during the heyday of President Johnson's Great Society years and the activism of the Warren Court. Dirksen often led the opposition to both. He is remembered for his deep, gravelly voice and for advocating making the marigold the national flower (Penney 1968, 91–92).

When first elected to the House, Dirksen was one of the few Republicans who ran on a platform to repeal the Eighteenth Amendment (Kyvig 1979, 168). He was subsequently a leading advocate of two proposed amendments. One would have overturned the Supreme Court's decision in *Engel v. Vitale* (1962) and permitted "voluntary participation by students and others in prayer." The other was designed to overturn *Baker v. Carr* (1962) and *Reynolds v. Sims* (1964) by allowing states to apportion at least one house of their state legislatures other than by population. After the apportionment amendment failed to pass in the Senate by a vote of 57 to 39, Dirksen formed the Committee for Government of the People (CGP) to call a national constitutional convention on the subject (Schapsmeier and Schapsmeier 1985, 180). This movement apparently came but a single state shy of the necessary two-thirds majority before faltering (*Proposals for a Constitutional Convention* 1979, 2).

See also *Baker v. Carr;* Prayer in Public Schools.

For Further Reading:

Bonfield, Arthur E. 1968. "The Dirksen Amendment and the Article V Convention Process." *Michigan Law Review* 66 (March): 949–1000.

Dirksen, Everett M. 1968. "The Supreme Court and the People." *Michigan Law Review* 66 (March): 837–874.

Proposals for a Constitutional Convention to Require a Balanced Federal Budget. 1979. Washington DC: American Enterprise Institute for Public Policy Research.

Schapsmeier, Edward L., and Frederick H. Schapsmeier. 1985. *Dirksen of Illinois: Senatorial Statesman.* Urbana, IL: University of Illinois Press.

DISTRICT OF COLUMBIA, REPRESENTATION FOR

Article I, Section 8 of the Constitution entrusts Congress with the power to legislate on behalf of the nation's capital. During the time of the Articles of Confederation, Congress was threatened by militiamen in Philadelphia who wanted to collect back pay (members of Congress temporarily moved to Princeton, New Jersey, during this crisis), and the experience persuaded the framers that the national government should control its own immediate surroundings (Report to the Attorney General 1987, 52–55). After states ratified the Constitution, the early capital moved from New York to Philadelphia to the current site. The selection of a spot ceded by Virginia and Maryland was one of the first examples of "logrolling": Southerners promoting the site got their wish in exchange for their support for Alexander Hamilton's plan to pay off Revolutionary War debts in full (Bernstein with Agel 1993, 144–145).

In 1802, Congress provided for a charter that allowed for a mayor and a city council for the new District of Columbia, a plan that continued until 1871. At that time, it was replaced by a territorial government. After a scandal, Congress took control in 1874 and governed the district through congressional committees until 1966. President Lyndon Johnson used an executive order to appoint a mayor—later elected by the district (Schrag 1985, 10–12). In 1971, Congress granted the district a nonvoting member in the House of Representatives, and Democrat Walter Fauntroy was elected to this post.

As early as 1825, Augustus Woodward proposed granting the district representation in Congress. More than 150 such proposals were introduced from the 1880s through 1978 (Report to the Attorney General 1987, 11). The Twenty-Third Amendment, ratified in 1961, granted the district representation in the Electoral College, but it still had no voting members in Congress. After a 289-to-127 vote in the House on March 1, 1978, followed on August 22 by a 67-to-32 vote in the Senate, a proposal was sent to the states to address this longstanding issue (Bernstein with Agel 1993, 146).

The amendment consisted of four parts. The first provided that "for purposes of representation in the Congress, election of the President and Vice President, and article V [the amending article] of this Constitution, the District constituting the seat of government of the United States shall be treated as though it were a State." Section 2 provided that "the exercise of the rights and powers conferred under this section shall be by the people of the District constituting the seat of government, as shall be provided by the Congress." Section 3 would have repealed the now redundant, and possibly contradictory, Twenty-Third Amendment, and Section 4 provided for a seven-year ratification deadline.

The District of Columbia subsequently held a convention to write a constitution for the state of New Columbia (Schrag 1985). This convention proved to be overly optimistic, and by the 1985 deadline, only 16 states had ratified. A key problem with the amendment was political—the District of Columbia was predominantly African American and Democratic, thus offering little to the Republican Party (Vose 1979; Horn 1990). Beyond that, some believed that the amendment violated the one remaining limit on Article V in that, by granting an entity that was not a state representation in the Senate, it would deprive the others of their equal representation therein and would thus require unanimity. Others were uncomfortable with the notion of treating an entity, still somewhat under congressional control, "as though it were a state."

Some have sought to add the district as a state through ordinary legislation. In early 2009, Congress thus reconsidered the constitutionality of the District of Columbia House Voting Rights Act of 2009 that would simply allocate a voting representative to the district. Given the district's constitutional status, there are doubts about the constitutionality of such a move (but see Raven-Hansen 1975; Ward and Grossman 2009). Another possibility is retrocession—giving the district, perhaps exclusive of federal enclaves, back to Maryland; Virginia's portion has already been so retroceded. Yet another possibility is to allow district residents to vote in Maryland elections, but it is by no means clear that Maryland would favor this move, which might also require the repeal of the Twenty-third Amendment, which grants existing district residents representation in the Electoral College. Finally, Congress could end charges of "no taxation without representation" by abolishing income taxes on District residents (Ward and Grossman 2009, 6).

In *Adams v. Clinton* (2000), with one dissenting vote, the U. S. District Court for the District of Columbia rejected a suit to provide for congressional voting representation in Congress. In this decision, later reaffirmed by the U.S. Circuit Court and the U.S. Supreme Court, the judges rejected both the argument that members of the District of Columbia could properly characterize themselves as "state" citizens and the argument that they had the right to vote in Maryland's elections of representatives as "residual" citizens of that state (although district members had been granted a continuing right to vote in state elections until Congress took complete control in 1801, the court found that this right ended with the complete cession of the territory to the United States).

The court also rejected arguments based on the equal protection and privileges and immunities clauses of the Fourteenth Amendment, on the due process clause of the Fifth Amendment, and on the guarantee of a "republican" form of government in Article IV. Looking at specific provisions in the Constitution for the District of Columbia and examining the history of these provisions, the court decided that the guarantee of "one person, one vote" did not apply to cases in which the U.S. Constitution had itself made exceptions. The court noted that "many courts have found a contradiction between the democratic ideals upon which this country was founded and the exclusion of District residents from congressional representation. All, however, have concluded that it is the Constitution and judicial precedent that create the contradiction" (*Adams* 2000, 120–121).

The district thus remains a constitutional anomaly. Although it remains the center of free government and its members pay federal taxes, its inhabitants are denied direct voting representation in the Congress that meets there and that taxes them.

See also Fourteenth Amendment; Twenty-Third Amendment; Woodward, Augustus.

For Further Reading:

Adams v. Clinton, 90 F. Supp. 2d 35 (2000), *appeal dismissed sub nom. Adams v. Bush,* 2001 U.S. App. LEXIS 25877 (D.D.C. 2001), *cert. denied* 2002 U.S. LEXIS 5485 (U.S. Oct. 7, 2002).

Bernstein, Richard B., with Jerome Agel. 1993. *Amending America: If We Love the Constitution So Much, Why Do We Keep Trying to Change It?* New York: Random House.

Best, Judith. 1984. *National Representation for the District of Columbia.* Frederick, MD: University Publications of America.

Bowling, Kenneth R. 1991. *The Creation of Washington, D.C.: The Idea and Location of the American Capital.* Fairfax, VA: George Mason University Press.

Hatch, Orrin G. 1979. "Should the Capital Vote in Congress? A Critical Analysis of the Proposed D.C. Representation Amendment." *Fordham Urban Law Journal* 7: 479–539.

Horn, Dottie. 1990. "Another Star for the Stripes?" *Endeavors* 8 (Fall): 4–6.

Raven-Hansen, Peter. 1975. "Congressional Representation for the District of Columbia: A Constitutional Analysis." *Harvard Journal of Legislation* 12: 167–192.

Report to the Attorney General. 1987. *The Question of Statehood for the District of Columbia.* 3 April. Washington DC: U.S. Government Printing Office.

Schrag, Philip G. 1985. *Behind the Scenes: The Politics of a Constitutional Convention.* Washington DC: Georgetown University Press.

Turley, Jonathan. 2008. "Too Clever by Half: The Unconstitutionality of Partial Representation of the District of Columbia in Congress." 76 *George Washington Law Review* (February): 305–374.

Vose, Clement E. 1979. "When District of Columbia Representation Collides with the Constitutional Amendment Institution." *Publius: The Journal of Federalism* 9 (Winter): 105–125.

Ward, Nathaniel, and Andrew M. Grossman. 2009. "Voting Representation for the District of Columbia: Violating the Framers' Vision and Constitutional Commands." Legal Memorandum published by the Heritage Foundation. February 19.

DIVIDED GOVERNMENT

One impetus for proponents of a parliamentary system alternative to U.S. government is divided government. Such a divided government occurs when one party captures the presidency and another captures a majority of one or both houses of Congress. This situation is made possible by a system of separation of powers. In parliamentary systems, a scheme of fused powers guarantees that the prime minister, who is chosen by parliament, heads the majority party or coalition. In the United States, by contrast, the president and Congress have different electoral bases. Thus, in the 44 years from 1946 to 1990, control was divided between Democrats and Republicans for 26 years (Mayhew 1991, 1). Democratic president Bill Clinton found himself facing both a Republican House and Senate. Republican George W. Bush's party lost control of both houses of Congress by the end of his term.

Critics of separation of powers contend that this system leads to needless controversy and to legislative gridlock. Defenders argue that divided government often reflects a popular unwillingness to invest either party with control over both branches and that such a division helps guard liberty and deter precipitous legislation. The author of an influential study that investigated the progress of lawmaking and the success of congressional investigations since the end of World War II concluded that "surprisingly, it does not seem to make all that much difference whether party control of American government happens to be unified or divided" (Mayhew 1991, 198). Another author critiquing the parliamentary model of fused powers has argued that legislative-executive party conflict can be healthy (Sargentich 1993, 707).

See also Parliamentary System.

For Further Reading:

Annenberg Democracy Project. 2007. *A Republic Divided.* New York: Oxford University Press.

Mayhew, David R. 1991. *Divided We Govern: Party Control, Lawmaking, and Investigations, 1946–1990.* New Haven, CT: Yale University Press.

Sargentich, Thomas O. 1993. "The Limits of the Parliamentary Critique of the Separation of Powers." *William and Mary Law Review* 34 (Spring): 679–739.

DODD, WALTER F. (1880–1960)

Walter F. Dodd, a professor at Johns Hopkins University, published an important book on amending state constitutions in 1910. Although many of the specifics of this work are obviously outdated, Dodd's book helps explain the development and early use of the constitutional convention mechanism and its relation to the state legislature.

Dodd noted that the development of this mechanism followed three steps: establishing "the distinction between the constitution and ordinary legislation"; developing the convention as a body distinct from the legislature; and submitting the constitution "to a vote of the people, after it has been framed by a constitutional convention" (Dodd 1910, 22). Of these steps, he viewed the first as fundamental and the others as "but the elaboration of machinery to carry out more clearly the distinction between constitutions and ordinary legislation" (Dodd 1910, 22).

In his classic work on constitutional conventions, Judge John Jameson (1887) argued that legislatures could control the constitutional convention mechanism. Believing that "the process of piecemeal amendment of state constitutions is absolutely under the control of the state legislatures except in the states that have adopted the popular initiative," Dodd instead argued that constitutional conventions were in a somewhat different category:

The calling of constitutional conventions is also to a large extent subject to legislative control, but the convention method of altering constitutions is the one more independent of the regular legislatures. . . . The convention loses a large part of its usefulness as an organ of the state if it be treated as strictly subject to control by the regular legislative body (Dodd 1910, 79).

On another issue, Dodd authored an article supporting the decision in the *National Prohibition Cases* (1920), which held that the Eighteenth Amendment was not unconstitutional. Dodd noted that an understanding that would permit the courts to void amendments "would introduce into American constitutional practice a highly undesirable type of judicial control" (Dodd 1921, 334).

See also Eighteenth Amendment; Jameson, John A.; National Prohibiton Cases.

For Further Reading:

Dodd, Walter F. 1921. "Amending the Federal Constitution." *Yale Law Journal* 30 (February): 321–354.

Dodd, Walter F. 1910. *The Revision and Amendment of State Constitutions.* Baltimore: Johns Hopkins University Press.

Jameson, John A. 1887. *A Treatise on Constitutional Conventions: Their History, Powers, and Modes of Proceeding.* 4th ed. Chicago: Callaghan and Company.

DODGE V. WOOLSEY (1856)

This case involved a suit by a bank stockholder contesting a new tax that Ohio had laid on a bank. This tax violated a prior act under the previous state constitution limiting such taxes on newly chartered banks to 6 percent.

In declaring that the new tax violated the contract clause, Justice James Wayne declared that the U.S. Constitution was supreme "over the people of the United States aggregately and in their separate sovereignties, because they have excluded themselves from any direct or immediate agency in making amendments to it, and have directed that amendments shall be made representatively for them" (*Dodge* 1856, 348) through the Article V amending process. Henry Monoghan has cited this decision in attempting to refute Akhil Reed Amar's contention that popular majorities have authority to amend the Constitution outside of Article V provisions (1996, 128).

See also Amar, Akhil Reed; Initiative and Referendum.

For Further Reading:
Dodge v. Woolsey, 59 U.S. (18 How.) 331 (1856).
Monaghan, Henry P. 1996. "We the People[s], Original Understanding, and Constitutional Amendment." *Columbia Law Review* 96 (January): 121–177.

DOLBEARE, KENNETH (1930–), AND JANETTE HUBBELL (1948–)

These two authors, self-described as "an eastern iconoclast who teaches politics at a small college and a southwestern populist who left elementary school teaching to launch a successful small business," published a wish list of constitutional reform couched in a fictional narrative set in the year 2012 (Dolbeare and Hubbell 1996, xiv). *USA 2012: After the Middle-Class Revolution* centers on a college student who reviews with his parents the developments that led to a successful middle-class revolution based on the concept of "economic nationalism" (Dolbeare and Hubbell 1996, xiii).

In the book's invented history, this program was instituted as a result of economic deterioration and a sense of middle-class outrage that resulted in the adoption of a new Declaration of Independence on July 4, 2000. The new Declaration aimed at the two-party system, at large corporations and banks (which come in for particularly intensive criticism by the authors), at the media, at special interests, and at the bureaucracy. The book also reflects concern about the effect of free trade policies, especially the General Agreement on Tariffs and Trade (GATT) and North American Free Trade Agreement (NAFTA) treaties, on workers.

The book describes how, after extensive debate and discussion, the American people of this fictional future decided to adopt four amendments to restore the United States to its prior prosperity. The first and most important of those amendments provided for quarterly popular referendums on major issues of public policy, which neither the president nor the Congress could veto (Dolbeare and Hubbell 1996, 118–119). This referendum mechanism allowed for a more direct democracy than is currently practiced and helped convert members of Congress into delegates of the people rather than independent decision makers.

The second amendment adopted by the people of the novel limited campaign contributions to $100 for any individual or group and mandated that television and radio stations make free time available to candidates. Campaigning was limited to 60 days prior to a primary election or 90 days prior to a general election.

The third amendment provided for proportional representation, both within the Electoral College and within Congress. This amendment, which also lifted existing restrictions on third parties, encouraged a multiparty system. This amendment also lifted voting registration requirements, extended voting to a two-day weekend, and allowed voters to cast their ballots for "None of the Above" (NOTA).

The fourth amendment was aimed at the judicial system and attempted to balance individual rights against public concerns. It specifically mandated consideration of "comparative liability and contributory negligence," allowed judges to review jury awards, and attempted to reduce litigation (Dolbeare and Hubbell 1996, 134).

Although the authors believe it important that the changes they propose in their fictional account be adopted by amendments, they offer their proposals as "discussion drafts" rather than as final products.

See also Campaign Contributions and Expenditures; Initiative and Referendums.

For Further Reading:
Dolbeare, Kenneth M., and Janette K. Hubbell. 1996. *USA 2012: After the Middle-Class Revolution.* Chatham, NJ: Chatham House Publishers.

DOMESTIC VIOLENCE, PROTECTION AGAINST

Article IV, Section 4 of the Constitution authorizes the United States to protect states against domestic violence when states petition it to do so. In *Luther v. Borden* (1849), the Supreme Court upheld a congressional law vesting the power to respond to such requests in the president.

Perhaps reacting to a speech in which outgoing President James Buchanan noted that Southern women retire at night "to apprehensions of civil insurrections" (J. Richardson 1908, 637), Democratic representative Thomas Florence of Pennsylvania introduced a series of proposals in 1861 to save the Union by recognizing that slavery was a matter of state option. He also provided, however, that the government had an obligation to come to a state's aid in suppressing slave insurrections (Ames 1896, 171).

In 1870, motivated by a far different concern, Republican senator Charles Drake of Missouri introduced another resolution entitling the national government to intervene in cases of Ku Klux Klan, violence even when not requested to do so by state governments (Ames 1896, 172). Klan violence remained a legislative concern well into the 20th century, with Southern white leaders successfully resisting national legislation in this area.

Congress attempted to address a much different issue in the Violence Against Women Act of 1994. The U.S. Supreme Court voided a portion of this act in *United States v. Morrison* (2000), when it decided that the federal claim of authority under the law exceeded congressional power under the commerce clause. Some observers viewed this decision as a victory for rights reserved to the states under the Tenth Amendment.

See also Tenth Amendment; *United States v. Morrison.*

For Further Reading:

Ames, Herman. 1896. *The Proposed Amendments to the Constitution of the United States during the First Century of Its History.* Reprint, New York: Burt Franklin, 1970.

Richardson, James E., ed. 1908. *A Compilation of the Messages and Papers of the Presidents, 1789–1908.* 11 vols. n.p.: Bureau of National Literature and Art.

DOUBLE JEOPARDY

The Fifth Amendment provides that no person shall "be subject for the same offense to be twice put in jeopardy of life or limb." Initially, this doctrine applied only to the national government; for a long time, the Supreme Court rejected its application to the states. In *Palko v. Connecticut* (1937), for example, the Court decided that this was not one of the rights implicit in a scheme of ordered liberty. The Court did not reverse course until *Benton v. Maryland* (1968), the last of the contemporary incorporation cases (Abraham and Perry 2003, 93–95). Contemporary understandings of the doctrine, however, do not prevent prosecution of individuals in cases involving the same set of facts in different jurisdictions (an individual declared not guilty of murder in a state court might later be tried and convicted of violating an individual's civil rights under federal law), nor do such understandings prohibit an individual (such as O. J. Simpson) who is acquitted of a criminal act from being successfully prosecuted for civil damages.

In 1958, South Carolina senator Strom Thurmond introduced a resolution to amend the Constitution so that when an individual appealed a criminal conviction and was granted a new trial, that individual could "be convicted of any crime of which he could have been convicted upon his former trial for such offense." In *Trono v. United States* (1905), the Supreme Court had established a similar rule—applied in the historic case of *Palko v. Connecticut* (1937), but it reversed course in *Green v. United States* (1957). In that case, an individual who successfully appealed a conviction for arson and second-degree murder was subsequently retried and convicted of first-degree murder. The Supreme Court voided this conviction, ruling that when an individual files a criminal appeal, conviction of a lesser offense bars subsequent prosecution of a greater offense, even if the conviction is later reversed on appeal (Sigler 1969, 71–72).

See also *Palko v. Connecticut.*

For Further Reading:

Abraham, Henry J., and Barbara Perry. 2003. *Freedom and the Court: Civil Rights and Liberties in the United States.* 8th ed. New York: Oxford University Press.

Sigler, Jay A. 1969. *Double Jeopardy: The Development of a Legal and Social Policy.* Ithaca, NY: Cornell University Press.

DOUGLASS, FREDERICK (1817–1895)

Few Americans have had more inspirational lives or so influenced thinking about the U.S. Constitution, and especially about voting rights, as did Frederick Douglass. Born in Maryland in 1817 as a slave (of a white father and African American mother) under the name Frederick Augustus Washington Bailey, Douglass was taught by his slave owner's wife to read as a youth. After being trained as a ship caulker in Baltimore, he escaped in September 1838 to New York City, where he married and proceeded to New Bedford, Connecticut. Initially serving as a laborer, Douglass attended an Antislavery Society meeting in Massachusetts, where he was asked to address the group. He had a commanding presence and a powerful story, and he was eventually employed as an agent for the Massachusetts Antislavery Society (Du Bois 1928–1936). In 1845, Douglass published an influential account of his life known as the *Narrative of the Life of Frederick Douglass,* but, having thus identified his origins and put his continuing freedom in jeopardy, he left for England until he could return with enough money to buy his freedom from his former master.

After his return to the United States, Douglass founded a newspaper entitled the *North Star,* which he edited for 17 years. Douglass attended the Seneca Falls Convention in New York in 1848, and it was largely through his insistence and that of Elizabeth Cady Stanton that the Convention resolutions included one on behalf of women's suffrage, which at the time was considered to be a novel idea and subject to considerable ridicule. In the years ahead, U.S. women were in the forefront of the abolitionist movement. Unlike some abolitionists who viewed the U.S. Constitution as a "covenant with death, an agreement with hell," Douglass chose to interpret that document in a more generous manner (McFeely 1991, 204–207) that did not permanently embody slavery.

Douglass strongly supported the Northern war effort during the Civil War and encouraged African Americans to sign up to support the Union cause; two of his own sons joined the conflict. Initially less concerned with the amendment designed to outlaw slavery (the Thirteenth) or to guarantee equal rights (the Fourteenth), Douglass focused most of his efforts on black suffrage (what became the Fifteenth Amendment), believing, in the words of a current historian, "that only suffrage would provide African Americans with the power necessary to make themselves truly free" (Vorenberg 2001, 85).

Douglass's support for the Fifteenth Amendment led, at least initially, to a rift with some of the key leaders of the women's rights movement, including Susan B. Anthony and Elizabeth Cady Stanton, who sometimes appealed to the perceived superiority of white women over black men in arguing that suffrage for the two groups should go hand in hand. The Civil War had been so clearly fought on behalf of African Americans and suffrage for women was still such a novel idea that Douglass and many other supporters of the Fifteenth Amendment did not believe they could take the chance of risking suffrage for black men by coupling it with that for women. Douglass was sympathetic to the plight of both groups, but he thought that the plight of blacks was far worse, and hence their need for the franchise was far greater than it was for women. Writing to a supporter of women's suffrage, Douglass thus said,

> I am now devoting myself to a cause [if] not more sacred, certainly more urgent, because it is one of life and death to the long enslaved people of this country, and

this is: negro suffrage. While the negro is mobbed, beaten, shot, stabbed, hanged, burnt and is the target of all that is malignant in the North and all that is murderous in the South, his claims may be preferred by me without exposing in any wise myself to the imputation of narrowness or meanness towards the cause of woman. As you well know, woman has a thousand ways to attach herself to the governing power of the land and already exerts an honorable influence on the course of legislation. She is the victim of abuses, to be sure, but it cannot be pretended I think that her cause is as urgent as . . . ours (Quoted in McFeely 1991, 268–269).

Shortly after adoption of the Fifteenth Amendment, however, Douglass advocated an amendment to enfranchise women (McFeely 1991, 269) and he continued his support for such an amendment thereafter, joining Anthony and Stanton at suffrage events and even attending a convention for women's suffrage on the day that he died in 1895 (Du Bois 1928–1936).

Given the setbacks to voting rights that African Americans faced in the aftermath of the adoption of the Thirteenth Amendment, Douglass was undoubtedly disappointed that the promise of black suffrage did not become the immediate reality for which he hoped. Douglass himself lived to be an honored figure, serving as secretary of a commission to Santo Domingo, a marshal and recorder of deeds in Washington DC, and, finally, as U.S. minister to Haiti (Du Bois 1928–1936). Although not initially enforced with much effectiveness, the Fifteenth Amendment reemerged in the 1960s and thereafter as a means of guaranteeing that African Americans could use the political process to help themselves.

See also Abolitionists; Anthony, Susan Brownell; Fifteenth Amendment; Fourteenth Amendment; Seneca Falls Convention; Stanton, Elizabeth Cady; Thirteenth Amendment.

For Further Reading:
Du Bois, W. E. Burghardt. 1928–1936. "Frederick Douglass." In *Dictionary of American Biography,* American Council of Learned Societies, at http://www.galenet.com. Accessed November 26, 2002.

Douglass, Frederick. 1845. *Narrative of the Life of Frederick Douglass: An American Slave.* Boston: Anti-Slavery Office. Reprint, New York: Signet Books, 1968.

McFeely, William S. 1991. *Frederick Douglass.* New York: W. W. Norton & Company.

Vorenberg, Michael. 2001. *Final Freedom: The Civil War, the Abolition of Slavery, and the Thirteenth Amendment.* Cambridge, UK: Cambridge University Press.

DUELING

In the 18th and 19th centuries, gentlemen—especially in the South—sometimes resolved matters of personal honor by engaging in duels. These were closely bounded by recognized social norms (Stowe 1987, 5–49; Wyatt-Brown 1948, 350–361). It was in such a duel that Aaron Burr, a vice president, killed Alexander Hamilton, a former secretary of the treasury. Prior to becoming president, Andrew Jackson also engaged in such duels.

In 1828, the year Jackson was elected president, an amendment was introduced to prohibit dueling. In February 1838, William Graves, a Whig congressman from Kentucky, killed Jonathan Cilley, a Democratic congressman from Maine, in a duel. Graves was censured, but the House rejected a committee report calling for his expulsion (Seitz 1966, 278). Similarly, two resolutions that would have excluded individuals who participated in such duels from holding office came to naught. Over time, state laws and public sentiment combined to eliminate this vestige of feudal aristocracy.

For Further Reading:
Seitz, Don C. 1929. *Famous American Duels: With Some Account of the Causes That Led Up to Them and the Men Engaged.* Reprint, Freeport, NY: Books for Libraries Press, 1966.

Stowe, Steven M. 1987. *Intimacy and Power in the Old South: Ritual in the Lives of the Planters.* Baltimore: Johns Hopkins University Press.

Wyatt-Brown, Bertram. 1948. *Southern Honor: Ethics and Behavior in the Old South.* New York: Oxford University Press.

DURST, JACK

Although he does not identify himself on his Web site, Jack Durst responded to the author's query by indicating that as of May 2002 he was a "22 year old undergraduate student" at the University of Nevada (Reno) where he is working on a "prelaw criminal justice degree with a minor in casino management." He also indicates that he is active in local Democratic politics, that he became involved in political theory when he saw the movie *People v. Larry Flynt,* that he tries to understand things, including languages, "by building models of them," and that his draft of a new constitution entitled a "Constitution of the Republic" was his "seventh and final draft" (e-mail correspondence with the author dated May 22, 2002).

On the Web site, Durst indicates that "the writing of a new constitution" is "perhaps the greatest protest possible against the current organization of one's country," and says that his work, which was not yet completed as of May 18, 2002, was done "over the course of 2000" ("Constitution of the Republic" 2000). The preamble announces the constitution's intention to "establish an entirely new system of self-government" and to establish a law "which is fair, just, and honorable" ("Constitution" 2000). Durst's detailed table of contents outlines eight articles, the first five of which appear to have been completed. Durst lists a variety of theorists, including a number of libertarians who have guided his thinking, but it is difficult to put his rather extensive proposal into a single pigeonhole.

Durst's first article begins with a declaration of rights. The rights of expression, the first to be listed, include a prohibition on government ownership of any media outlet "with the exception of a single printing office for the printing of laws and records." The article also includes a specific protection for "academic freedom of any institution of higher education, public or private, in the republic except to the extent that it may require certain courses for license to practice some professions, may require that civics and/or political science classes be taught, and shall, by law, insure the requirement that all human experimental subjects give informed consent" ("Constitution" 2000). Durst includes a provision that states that "the expectation of privacy in the body, the home and its surrounds is absolute." This right also includes confidentiality of conversations with lawyers, doctors, and other professionals, makes provision for "the dignity of all persons," and prohibits the government from denying a passport "without a finding of good cause by a judge of the trial courts." Durst includes "rights of noninterference" ("Constitution" 2000). These include individuals' ownership of their own bodies and the right of "consenting adults in private" to engage in "their own sexual and reproductive decisions," "the rights to grow, possess in reasonable quantity, and use any psychoactive substance," and the "right to work in any lawful profession" ("Constitution" 2000). Durst also includes "freedom of religion and culture," exempting conscientious objectors from military service and guaranteeing all individuals "the right to participate in their culture and to enjoy and preserve their cultural heritage" ("Constitution" 2000). Property and corporate rights include the rights not to have taxes levied against savings, to form corporations, and to "form unions or employer's associations, bargain collectively, participate in any organization, or strike" ("Constitution" 2000).

Durst balances rights with eight duties that include obedience to law, participation in government, voting, seeking to change laws with which one disagrees, protecting the republic, being informed, paying taxes, and honoring contracts.

Article II outlines the basic form of the proposed government. Its three branches would consist of "a Republic Council who execute the laws, a judiciary which interprets them, and a Parliament [sic] which causes to be made and approves them." The republic council has 12 members who serve three-year terms; it is presided over by the prime minister. Parliament will apparently be a unicameral rather than a bicameral body, and will consist of 100 members who are elected yearly; a supreme court of from three to seven members will head the judiciary. The prime minister will be elected by the parliament and will "serve as liaison between the Council, the Parliament, and the ministers." Durst goes into an elaborate description of elections and voting under his system, a right that may be exercised by individuals as young as 15 who can demonstrate "the ability to make an informed and reasoned political choice" ("Constitution" 2000). Individuals will be limited to national elective offices for no more than 10 years, with candidates selected in "partisan caucuses" and subject to election according to systems that take voters' first, second, and third choices into account. States appear to be replaced by a set of 20 geographically contiguous but shifting districts, each of which has five seats in parliament. Trial judges will serve three-year terms, appellate judges 10-year terms, and members of the supreme court during good behavior. The system of lawmaking is as complicated as that for voting. The parliament and the council may call consensus committees on topics of their own choosing and on topics about which voters have petitioned. Courts will maintain the power of judicial review, but the parliament will be able to overrule decisions dealing with the interpretation of statutes by a three-fifths vote. "Omnibus bills" are forbidden, and provisions are made for legislation by initiative. Laws made by "cities and local cabinets" are mentioned but not by states or by the districts from which members of parliament are elected. The council has the power to impose taxes, but the total tax on any given item or income is limited to 30 percent. A new common currency, designated the "shilling," shall be established, initially to be "worth .07 of a Swiss Franc," a standard for which there is no explanation. The council has the power to declare war, but the parliament will make laws regarding the military; it will also be able to adopt emergency laws when needed. The supreme court will have power to decide on the constitutionality of wars, and the prime minister, with authority from the council, will have power to declare martial law. Cabinet ministers

will serve four-year terms. All ministries shall be similar to those like the ministry of justice/police, which Durst describes in detail. Created by the council, it shall be based on "a uniform police force and prosecutor throughout the republic, divided geographically into departments, with oversight by the legislative and judicial branch and control by the executive" ("Constitution" 2000). A chief prosecutor shall head each police department. He and other heads of local ministries may "form a local cabinet, to govern and coordinate the actions of the executive branch in their area of mutual geographical jurisdiction with the advice and consent of the citizen's advisory board" ("Constitution" 2000).

In Article III, Durst discusses the authorization of laws. He lists 24 separate powers of the government including the protection of workers and consumers, the regulation of businesses, the protection of property and civil rights, environmental protection, "fair distribution of inheritances," care "for idiots and the insane," education, "access for all citizens to food, housing, and other necessities," and so forth ("Constitution" 2000). No crimes, except for a few designated "felonies," will carry a penalty of more than one year in prison.

Article IV describes the judiciary and due process rights. The first statement provides that "[t]he judiciary shall insure that children within the republic have access to safe, modern schools which provide knowledge relevant to their futures and useful as citizens" ("Constitution" 2000). The judiciary will include both trial and appellate courts, and Durst specifically recognizes the government's obligation to provide counsel for criminal defendants unable to afford it. In addition to a variety of rights of criminal defendants already recognized in the current U.S. Constitution, Durst provides that "the responsible party shall be liable to compensate all persons wrongly or illegally arrested for actual damages" ("Constitution" 2000). He also incorporates the standard of "beyond a reasonable doubt" in criminal cases and specifies that all references to a jury are "to a jury of 12." Durst would outlaw capital punishment and provide each prisoner "with a rulebook . . . which shall be strictly and unerringly enforced, and shall contain all regulations placed on prisoners which are not placed on ordinary citizens" ("Constitution" 2000). Durst provides that "all adults with equal bargaining power have absolute freedom to make any contract except one for illegal acts and/or services" ("Constitution" 2000). He also outlaws discrimination by law or by any organization tied to the government on the basis of "a. Race, color, ethnicity, or genetic makeup; b. Condition of current or former drug use; c. Gender, marital status, gender or sexual preference; d. Religion; e. Political beliefs; [or] f. Physical disability" ("Constitution" 2000). Article IV further provides that "[t]his constitution is to be broadly construed in such a manner that the greatest liberty is afforded the citizen, the least power and the greatest obligation consistent with that power to the government and to incorporate the long-standing traditions developed under it" ("Constitution" 2000).

Article V specifies that council members may propose amendments after receiving petitions of 10 percent of the voters. A two-thirds majority of the council will then send the amendment to a consensus committee, and the amendment, if proposed by a two-thirds majority vote of parliament, will then have to be approved by three-fifths of the people. Such an amendment will be in effect for 10 years, after which it will be made permanent, or may be extended as a nonpermanent amendment for an additional 10 years. Durst specifies, however, that "No amendment may be made to this constitution which substantially alters the form of the government or the powers of its branches except by singular addition or subtraction of powers, nor may any amendment be made which addresses more than one basic topic" ("Constitution" 2000). He specifies a number of provisions that cannot be amended, but also provides that those provisions that can be amended can be altered by convention. Durst provides that no constitution shall be adopted without a provision specifying that "After 10 years, all citizens shall vote on whether to retain this constitution or return to the previous constitution as amended. If a majority votes to return to the previous constitution this constitution shall become null and void" ("Constitution" 2000).

Although included in his detailed table of contents, implementation of his plan is not something that Durst elaborates on. Neither does he specify the "Name, Flag, and Location" of the new government, nor the names of its signatories.

Durst's plan is closer to a parliamentary than to the current presidential model of government. Listing more rights than the current document, Durst's proposal does not go as far as some libertarian proposals in limiting governmental powers. Most fascinating is Durst's apparent (and seemingly unexplained) dismissal of existing state governments and their replacement by districts of shifting dimensions.

See also Bill of Responsibilities; Parliamentary Systems.

For Further Reading:

Durst, Jack. 2000. "Constitution of the Republic." http://spynx_jd.tripod.com/constitution/CS-1-A. html. Accessed October 22, 2008.

DUTIES

See Tariffs; Taxation, Export.

DYER V. BLAIR (1975)

John Paul Stevens, who subsequently became a U.S. Supreme Court justice, wrote this U.S. district court decision involving Illinois's ratification of the Equal Rights Amendment. Members of the legislature had sued Robert Blair, speaker of the Illinois House of Representatives, for declaring state ratification of the amendment dead after it failed to achieve the three-fifths vote that the legislature and the state constitution had mandated for such amendments (Vile 1993b, 28–30).

Despite the Supreme Court's decision in *Coleman v. Miller* (1939), Stevens declared that this particular amending issue was not a "political question." Citing *Powell v. McCormack*

(1969), Stevens argued that, however difficult, this case involved "no more than an interpretation of the Constitution" (*Dyer* 1975, 1301). As to the requisite vote for ratification, Stevens concluded that although Article V of the Constitution does not require an extraordinary majority by ratifying state legislatures, it also does not prohibit states from adopting such a majority.

Citing *Hawke v. Smith* (*I*) (1920) and the *National Prohibition Cases* (1920), which had decided that a state could not require ratification of amendments by popular referendum, Stevens struck down a provision in the Illinois state constitution that required the election of a new legislature before a vote was taken on a constitutional amendment. Stevens further ruled that because states were performing a federal function when they ratified amendments, any language in a state's constitution regarding a supermajority requirement would be "precatory" (*Dyer* 1975, 1308) or recommendatory only.

This case suggests that caution is in order in interpreting earlier cases, such as *Coleman v. Miller* (1939), that seem to withdraw the courts from consideration of key amending issues.

See also *Coleman v. Miller; Hawke v. Smith; National Prohibition Cases;* Political Questions.

For Further Reading:

Dyer v. Blair, 390 F. Supp. 1291 (1975).

Vile, John R. 1993. *The Theory and Practice of Constitutional Change in America: A Collection of Original Source Materials.* New York: Peter Lang.

EDUCATION, ESTABLISHMENT OF A NATIONAL UNIVERSITY

Each of the first six presidents favored a national university to train public servants, but some, including Thomas Jefferson, had reservations about congressional authority to establish such an institution (Ambrose 1966, 11, 17). James Madison, Charles Pinckney, and James Wilson suggested a measure at the Constitutional Convention of 1787 that would have entrusted such power to Congress, but it was not adopted (Eidelberg 1968, 27). As president, both Thomas Jefferson and James Monroe proposed in annual messages that such an amendment be adopted, and one was introduced in Congress in 1825 (Ames 1896, 274–275).

Although Jefferson had argued as Washington's Secretary of State that Congress had no authority to establish a military academy, he supported the establishment of West Point during his presidency (Ambrose 1966, 18–19). This and other military academies are the only universities currently operated by the national government. Other U.S. universities, including the University of Virginia, which Jefferson founded after leaving the presidency, are either state or privately funded and operated.

Throughout American history, however, the federal government has encouraged the creation of colleges and universities throughout the nation. The Morrill Acts of 1862 and 1890 were especially important in the creation of land grant institutions—so-called because they were funded by revenues from the sale of federal lands (Carleton 2002, 27–40, 53–62). More recently, the Higher Education Act of 1965 was used to funnel increased federal funds to colleges and universities (Carleton 2002, 147–159).

In an apparent revival of the idea of a national university, educators Chris Myers Asch and Shawn Raymond have proposed a U.S. Public Service Academy that would serve 5,100 students, who would be nominated and selected, much like members of current military academies, and who would repay the government for their education with four years of public service. Asch and Raymond are seeking to initiate the Academy, which would probably be located in Washington DC, through congressional legislation (former New York senator Hillary Clinton was one of the co-sponsors) rather than through constitutional amendment (http://uspublicservice academy.org, accessed May 25, 2008).

See also Jefferson, Thomas.

For Further Reading:

Ambrose, Stephen E. 1966. *Duty, Honor, Country: A History of West Point.* Baltimore: Johns Hopkins University Press.

Ames, Herman. 1896. *The Proposed Amendments to the Constitution of the United States during the First Century of Its History.* Reprint, New York: Burt Franklin, 1970.

Carleton, David. 2002. *Student's Guide to Landmark Congressional Laws on Education.* Westport, CT: Greenwood Press.

Eidelberg, Paul. 1968. *The Philosophy of the American Constitution: A Reinterpretation of the Intentions of the Founding Fathers.* New York: Free Press.

EDUCATION, RIGHT TO

When the U.S. Supreme Court outlawed the system of de jure racial segregation in public schools in *Brown v. Board of Education* (1954), it recognized that education was increasingly important to success. However, the Constitution, which confines itself largely to the delineation of political rights, does not specifically list a right to education. Although today's national government continues to give increasing aid to education, Supreme Court decisions since *Brown* have refused to recognize that the right to an education is a "fundamental right," subject to heightened judicial scrutiny.

Whereas in *San Antonio Independent School District v. Rodriguez* (1973) the Court decided not to invalidate a Texas system of education in which funding varied from one district to another depending on local property taxes, some state courts have subsequently ruled that their own constitutions required greater equality in state educational funding. In an article written in 1864, when public education was especially meager in the South, journalist E. L. Godkin (editor of *The Nation*) argued that one area in which the U.S. Constitution should be changed was in the area of education. Specifically pointing to the myriad of problems that he thought stemmed from inadequate education, Godkin asked,

> Would it not be wiser, as well as juster and more humane, to give it [the national government] the power, and not only this, but to make it its duty, to establish schools whenever the State governments, through indolence or indifference, false economy or sheer malevolence, fail to do so? If, in short, the safety of the nation depends on the education of the people, ought not the education of the people to be made a national concern (Godkin 1864, 143)?

Although the national government helped establish schools for freedmen after the Civil War, the Constitution was never amended to mention the right to an education. Court decisions in *Meyer v. Nebraska* (1923) and *Pierce v.*

Society of Sisters (1925) did respectively recognize the right of a school to teach a modern foreign language and the right of parents to send their children to parochial schools.

Individuals who believe that the modern Constitution should include social and economic rights often include the right to an education. Congressman Jesse L. Jackson Jr. (D-IL) has proposed an amendment to the Constitution that would guarantee that "[a]ll citizens of the United States shall enjoy the right to a public education of equal high quality" (Jackson with Watkins 2001, 330). Undoubtedly, the devil would be in the details of such a broadly worded right.

Typifying the fact that education is often viewed primarily as a state and local issue, all 50 states currently have some provisions in their constitutions relative to education (Dayton and Dupre 2004, note 13 at 2356). Studies of attempts to improve funding of schools on the basis of such provisions indicate that results have been mixed and that "as many decisions have upheld challenged funding systems as have declared them unconstitutional (Dayton and Dupre, 2405).

See also *Brown v. Board of Education;* Jackson, Jesse L., Jr.; Social and Economic Rights.

For Further Reading:

Dayton, John, and Anne Dupre. 2004. "School Funding Litigation: Who's Winning the War?" *Vanderbilt Law Review* 57 (November): 2351.

Godkin, E. L. 1864. "The Constitution and Its Defects." *North American Review* 99 (July): 117–143.

Jackson, Jesse L., Jr., with Frank E. Watkins. 2001. *A More Perfect Union: Advancing New American Rights.* New York: Welcome Rain Publishers.

EIGHTEENTH AMENDMENT

The Eighteenth Amendment mandated national alcoholic prohibition. It represents the only time that sumptuary legislation has been incorporated into the Constitution and is the only amendment to have been repealed. The first prohibition amendment to be introduced in Congress was offered by Republican representative Henry Blair of New Hampshire in 1876; amendments were introduced sporadically thereafter until 1913. That year, the Anti-Saloon League decided to focus its energy on a national amendment. After this decision, dozens of proposals were introduced until the amendment was adopted in 1919.

Dr. Benjamin Rush was among the American founders who expressed concern over the health effects of alcohol, and politicians (including Abraham Lincoln, who signed an abstinence pledge) and religious reformers subsequently encouraged temperance. Maine established statewide prohibition in 1851 (Grimes 1978, 83), but the primary waves of prohibition at the state level occurred in 1864–1865, in the 1880s, and beginning in 1907. During the last of these waves, the focus of reform moved from the state to the national level. By 1917, 23 states had prohibition laws, although only 13 were completely dry (U.S. Senate 1985).

Scholars continue to debate the weight to assign to various motivations behind Prohibition. Some supporters (especially those in the influential Women's Christian Temperance Union) were motivated by religious beliefs, some by medical evidence of the detrimental effects of alcohol use, and some by the belief in moral reform and progress so characteristic of the Progressive Era, during which a constitutional amendment was finally adopted (Timberlake 1970).

More negative cultural forces also played a part. Many people viewed the saloon as "a political brothel in which corrupt liaisons were formed between foreign-born voters and political bosses" (Grimes 1978, 84), and the Anti-Saloon League became a major focus for prohibition. Reformers were disproportionately rural white Protestants of northern European ethnic stock, and such reformers sometimes saw prohibition as a means of controlling or reforming Catholics, immigrants, African Americans, Indians, and poor whites. With the advent of World War I, some reformers also found that prohibition and anti-German sentiment went well together because Germans were frequently associated with breweries.

Many advocates of temperance opposed the idea of prohibition as unwarranted state interference in personal decision-making and saw national prohibition as an improper interference with states' rights. Others pointed to the injustice of shutting down what had previously been legitimate businesses. Opponents also pointed out that it was possible for a minority of the people to adopt an amendment that the majority did not support.

Proponents nonetheless insisted on the evils of alcohol. A preface to an amending resolution introduced in Congress in 1914 explained their views:

> Exact scientific research has demonstrated that alcohol is a narcotic poison, destructive and degenerating to the human organism, and that its distribution as a beverage or contained in foods lays a staggering economic burden upon the shoulders of the people; lowers to an appalling degree the average standard of character of our citizenship, thereby undermining public morals and the foundations of free institutions; produces widespread crime, pauperism, and insanity; inflicts disease and untimely death upon hundreds of thousands of citizens and blights with degeneracy their children unborn, threatening the future integrity and the very life of the Nation (U.S. Senate 1985, 50).

As early as 1890, Congress adopted the Wilson Act, subjecting imported liquor to state regulation. But in *Leisy v. Hardin* (1890), the Supreme Court said that such alcohol was not subject to state regulation as long as it remained in its "original package" (Musmanno 1929, 228–229). The Webb-Kenyon Act of 1913 further strengthened federal control over interstate shipment of alcohol, but proponents of prohibition obviously wanted more.

In 1914, the House of Representatives defeated a prohibition amendment, but support for such an amendment increased as war loomed. In 1917, Congress adopted the Lever Food Control Act, restricting the importation of alcohol and prohibiting the use of foodstuffs in its production. That same year, Democratic Texas senator

Morris Sheppard reintroduced the Prohibition Amendment, which the House and the Senate subsequently adopted in December.

As amended, the proposal had a number of unique features. The first paragraph provided for a one-year transitional period, probably to allay concerns about putting people out of work. Although it prohibited "the manufacture, sale, or transportation of intoxicating liquors within, the importation thereof into, or the exportation thereof for beverage purposes," the amendment left open the possible use of alcohol for medicinal and other purposes and did not explicitly outlaw the purchase of alcohol. The second paragraph of the amendment rather ambiguously provided that the state and national governments would have "concurrent power" to enforce the amendment. The third paragraph was the first to contain a seven-year ratification deadline. Republican senator (later president) Warren G. Harding initially proposed a somewhat shorter deadline in the unrealized hope of undermining the amendment. The amendment was adopted despite arguments by Idaho's Republican senator William Borah that the deadline provision was unconstitutional (Grimes 1978, 87).

The amendment was ratified in just over a year. In 1919, Congress overrode President Woodrow Wilson's veto to adopt the Volstead Act, which defined as intoxicating any beverage—including beer and wine—that contained more than 0.5 percent alcohol.

In *Hawke v. Smith (I)* (1920), the Supreme Court ruled that a state could not require approval of this or other amendments by referendum, thus creating the impression in the public mind that the amendment did not have majority support. That decision might also have paved the way for the decision to ratify the Twenty-first Amendment through state conventions rather than by state legislatures. In the *National Prohibition Cases* (1920) and again in *United States v. Sprague* (1931), the Supreme Court rejected arguments that the Eighteenth Amendment exceeded implicit limitations alleged to inhere in Article V. The *National Prohibition Cases* also defined concurrent powers to allow the state and national governments to enforce their own provisions and upheld the definition of alcohol in the Volstead Act.

The prohibition movement and the Eighteenth Amendment appear to have reduced but not eliminated alcohol consumption (Kyvig 1985, 13). Although it sanctioned increased governmental power over individuals, Prohibition was widely flouted, and the Eighteenth Amendment probably contributed to the rise of organized crime by providing it with a profitable source of illegal revenue. In 1932, the Twenty-first Amendment repealed the Eighteenth Amendment.

See also Anti-Saloon League; *Hawke v. Smith;* National Prohibiton Cases; Twenty-first Amendment; *United States v. Sprague;* Women's Christian Temperance Union.

For Further Reading:

Grimes, Alan P. 1978. *Democracy and the Amendments to the Constitution.* Lexington, MA: Lexington Books.

Kyvig, David E., ed. 1985. *Alcohol and Order: Perspectives on National Prohibition.* Westport, CT: Greenwood Press.

Musmanno, M. A. 1929. *Proposed Amendments to the Constitution.* Washington DC: U.S. Government Printing Office.

Timberlake, James H. 1970. *Prohibition and the Progressive Movement, 1900–1920.* New York: Atheneum.

U.S. Senate Committee on the Judiciary, Subcommittee on the Constitution 1985. *Amendments to the Constitution: A Brief Legislative History.* Washington DC: U.S. Government Printing Office.

EIGHTH AMENDMENT

The first congress proposed the Eighth Amendment, which the states ratified in 1791 as part of the Bill of Rights. It provides that "excessive bail shall not be required, nor excessive fines imposed, nor cruel and unusual punishments inflicted." The prohibition against excessive fines has roots in the English Magna Carta, whereas the provisions against excessive bails and cruel and unusual punishments originated in the Massachusetts Body of Liberties and the

Virginia Declaration of Rights (Lutz 1992, 53). Both the Virginia and the North Carolina ratifying conventions called for amendments against cruel and unusual punishments, and James Madison linked this guarantee to the provisions against excessive bail and fines when he presented his proposal for a bill of rights before Congress.

Debates in Congress were limited but prescient. William Smith of South Carolina thought that the words "cruel and unusual" were "too indefinite" (Kurland and Lerner 1987, 5:377). Samuel Livermore of New Hampshire positively noted that "the clause seems to express a great deal of humanity," but doubted its necessity or clarity: "What is meant by the terms excessive bail? Who are to be the judges? What is understood by excessive fines? It lies with the courts to determine. No cruel and unusual punishment is to be inflicted; it is sometimes necessary to hang a man, villains often deserve whipping, and perhaps having their ears cut off; but are we in the future to be prevented from inflicting these punishments because they are cruel?" (Kurland and Lerner 1987, 5:377). Acknowledging that the legislature should adopt as limited a punishment as proved useful, Livermore said, "we ought not to be restrained from making necessary laws by any declaration of this kind" (Kurland and Lerner 1987, 5:377). Despite his objections, the provision passed overwhelmingly.

Generally, the courts have granted legislatures flexibility in deciding whether fines and bail are excessive. Most contemporary controversy about the Eighth Amendment has centered on the provision prohibiting "cruel and unusual punishments." In *Furman v. Georgia* (1972), the Supreme Court declared that the death penalty as then administered was unconstitutional, but subsequent cases have allowed for such punishment when juries consider aggravating and mitigating circumstances and when trials are bifurcated so that the determination of guilt or innocence is separated from the fixing of a penalty. Numerous amendments have been proposed that would either permit or outlaw capital punishment.

On May 1, 2001, Indiana Democratic representative Julia Carson introduced an amendment to modify the Eighth Amendment by inserting a provision after "cruel and unusual punishments" that would have read "(including incarceration, before or after trial, for minor traffic offenses)." This amendment appears to have been provoked by a U.S. Supreme Court decision in *Atwater v. City of Lago Vista* (2001), in which the Court decided in a 5-to-4 majority decision written by David Souter that the arrest of a Texas mother in front of her children and her short incarceration at a cell in the police station for the failure of any of them to be wearing seatbelts was not an unreasonable search and seizure in violation of the Fourth Amendment.

On a related matter, a majority of the Supreme Court has apparently reversed course on earlier rulings that declared that the Eighth Amendment was intended, in noncapital cases, to outlaw punishments that are disproportionate to the crimes they are designed to punish. Thus, in a decision authored by Justice Antonin Scalia, the Court refused in *Harmelin v. Michigan* (1991) to overturn a sentence of life without parole for a man convicted of possession of more than 650 grams of cocaine; Scalia argued that if the framers had intended the Eighth Amendment to outlaw disproportionate punishments, they would have specifically said so. Scalia thought that legislators, rather than judges, should determine such matters.

Scalia was on the losing side in *Atkins v. Virginia* (2002), when six of nine justices led by Justice John Paul Stevens decided that the cruel and unusual provision of the Eighth Amendment prohibited application of the death penalty to individuals who are retarded, but he agreed with the decision in *Ring v. Arizona* (2002) requiring that a jury, rather than a judge, decide whether the aggravating circumstances were such as to warrant the death penalty.

See also Capital Punishment.

For Further Reading:

Atwater v. City of Lago Vista, 532 U.S. 318 (2001).

Hoffmann, Joseph L. 1993. "The 'Cruel and Unusual Punishment' Clause: A Limit on the Power to Punish or Constitutional Rhetoric?" In *The Bill of Rights in Modern America,* ed. David J. Bodenhamer and James W. Ely Jr. Bloomington, IN: Indiana University Press.

Kurland, Philip B., and Ralph Lerner, eds. 1987. *The Founders' Constitution.* 5 vols. Chicago: University of Chicago Press.

Lutz, Donald S. 1992. *A Preface to American Political Theory.* Lawrence: University Press of Kansas.

For Further Reading:

Eiselen, Malcolm R. 1941. "Can We Amend the Constitution?" *South Atlantic Quarterly* 40 (October): 333–341.

Eiselen, Malcolm R. 1937. "Dare We Call a Federal Convention?" *North American Review* 244 (Autumn): 27–28.

EISELEN, MALCOLM R. (1902–1965)

Historian Malcolm Eiselen used the sesquicentennial of the U.S. Constitution to argue for a second constitutional convention (Vile 1991c, 74–75). Altogether, he suggested about a dozen changes, including abolishing the Electoral College, changing the president's tenure of office, clarifying the power of judicial review, considering the federal initiative and referendum, allowing cabinet members to be seated in Congress, nominating presidents more democratically, clarifying issues of presidential disability, making the process of constitutional amendment easier (see Eiselen 1941), abandoning the requirement that treaties be ratified by two-thirds majorities, redistributing powers between state and national governments, and providing mechanisms to avoid "national bankruptcy and financial chaos" (Eiselen 1937, 29–33). Eiselen was particularly concerned about federal spending and suggested longer terms for the president and members of Congress and adopting the item veto and the executive budget as possible remedies (Eiselen 1937, 32).

Eiselen proposed that members of the convention should be a mixture of elected and appointed delegates, with the American Bar Association, the American Political Science Association, and the American Economic Association among the groups making appointments (Eiselen 1937, 34). Eiselen cautioned that delegates should avoid the temptation to create a document too lengthy or detailed. He recognized that, like the document of 1787, any new constitution would have to embody compromises making it acceptable to the people.

See also Constitutional Conventions.

ELECTIONS, DATES OF

Article II, Section 1 of the Constitution provides that Congress shall determine a uniform day for choosing presidential electors. For a time, Congress merely specified that such elections should be made 34 days prior to the first Wednesday in December (Ames 1896, 114). Before Congress acted in 1845 to set the Tuesday after the first Monday in November for such elections, it received a number of petitions for an amendment setting a uniform date or allowing for more than one day during which elections would be held. Two proposals offered in 1888 to prevent state elections on the same day as federal contests were apparently motivated by concerns that political parties were trading votes for the two sets of offices (Ames 1896, 111). Many individuals who are concerned about low voting rates in the United States have proposed that the day for national elections be on a Saturday or be declared a national holiday, but neither action would require a constitutional amendment.

See also Congress, Powers of.

For Further Reading:

Ames, Herman. 1896. *The Proposed Amendments to the Constitution of the United States during the First Century of Its History.* Reprint, New York: Burt Franklin, 1970.

ELECTIONS, DISPUTED

Article I, Section 5 specifies that "each House shall be the Judge of the Elections, Returns, and

Qualifications of its own members." Deciding whom to seat in closely contested elections can become a highly partisan decision.

Prompted by the contested election of five New Jersey representatives, States' Rights Democratic representative Richard Habersham of Georgia introduced an amendment in 1840 to specify the kinds of evidence Congress could consult in deciding which individuals to seat (Ames 1896, 57). To date, Congress still has no specific constitutional guidelines to follow. When the 104th Congress convened in January 1995, Congress seated four members whose seats were contested, pending further investigation (MacPherson 1995, 28).

In the disputed presidential election of 1876, a commission consisting of a number of U.S. Supreme Court justices ultimately awarded disputed electoral votes that resulted in the selection of Republican Rutherford B. Hayes over Democrat Samuel B. Tilden (Robinson 1996). The Supreme Court took an even more direct role in the election of 2000, when its decision in *Bush v. Gore* (2000) ultimately halted vote recounting in the pivotal state of Florida because the Court decided that it was standardless and thus violated the equal protection clause of the Fourteenth Amendment. The decision resulted in George W. Bush's victory over Al Gore. Scholars continue to debate the merits of this decision (compare Ceaser and Busch 2000 with Gillman 2001).

See also Electoral College Reform.

For Further Reading:

Ames, Herman. 1896. *The Proposed Amendments to the Constitution of the United States during the First Century of Its History.* Reprint, New York: Burt Franklin, 1970.

Bush v. Gore, 531 U.S. 98 (2000).

Ceaser, James W., and Andrew W. Busch. 2001. *The Perfect Tie: The True Story of the 2000 Presidential Election.* Lanham, MD: Rowman & Littlefield.

Gillman, Howard. 2001. *The Votes That Counted: How the Court Decided the 2000 Presidential Election.* Chicago: University of Chicago Press.

MacPherson, Peter. 1995. "Contested Winners Seated; Challengers in Pursuit." *Congressional Quarterly Weekly Report* 53 (7 January): 28.

Robinson, Lloyd. 1996. *The Stolen Election, Hayes versus Tilden—1876.* New York: Forge.

ELECTIONS, PRIMARY

In *Newberry v. United States* (1921), the Supreme Court ruled that Article I, Section 4 did not give Congress power to regulate party primaries. Shortly thereafter, Oklahoma Republican representative Manuel Herrick introduced an amendment extending federal election laws to primaries as well as to general elections.

Subsequently, in *United States v. Classic* (1941), the Court allowed regulation of state primaries when such primaries were tied to the process of choosing candidates for federal office. In later outlawing the all-white primary in *Smith v. Allwright* (1944), the Court specifically overturned the *Newberry* decision. Significantly, in outlawing poll taxes in federal elections, the Twenty-fourth Amendment specifically mentioned "any primary or other [federal] election."

In recent decades, primary elections have played an increased role in the selection of presidential nominees.

See also Twenty-fourth Amendment; Voting Rights, Constitutional Amendments Relating to.

For Further Reading:

Gangala, Thomas. 2007. *From the Primaries to the Polls: How to Repair America's Broken Presidential Nomination Process.* Westport, CT: Praeger.

ELECTORAL COLLEGE REFORM

No amendment effort has been more consistent than that for reform of the Electoral College, which is used to select presidents and vice presidents. More than 850 proposals have been offered in Congress, making this topic second in overall numbers only to the Equal Rights

Amendment. The Twelfth Amendment and the Twenty-third Amendment have both formally modified the Electoral College. The former requires that electors differentiate between their votes for president and vice president (thus eliminating the possibility of a tie between them, which occurred in the election of 1800). The latter grants representation in the Electoral College to the District of Columbia equivalent to that of the smallest state—currently, three votes.

Operation

The Electoral College system is a complicated scheme, which delegates to the Constitutional Convention of 1787 formulated. Under this system, each state has a number of votes equivalent to its representation in the House and the Senate. States then select electors, who meet in the state's capital. Since the Twelfth Amendment, each elector casts one vote for president and another for vice president, with at least one such vote going to an out-of-state candidate. Such votes are then reported to Washington DC and opened in a joint session of Congress.

If no candidate receives a majority of the Electoral College—currently 270 out of 538 possible votes—then the election for the president goes to the House of Representatives and that of the vice president to the Senate. The House chooses from among the top three candidates (prior to adoption of the Twelfth Amendment, it voted from among five candidates in such circumstances), with each state's delegation getting a single vote. Similarly, the Senate, which previously had no role except in the case of a tie between the runners-up, chooses between the top two candidates for vice president. Typically, the Electoral College exaggerates the votes of the winner, thus providing the appearance of greater support for an incoming president and arguably making fraud within one or two states less likely to affect the outcome than if all votes were counted (for a more complete discussion of the operation of the electoral system, see Berns 1992), but on occasion the system gives the election to an individual who did not get the highest popular vote.

Foundation and Development

When the Constitutional Convention first considered presidential elections, it contemplated that Congress would choose the president. Members feared, however, that this method would undercut separation of powers and presidential independence. Similarly, a system of direct election would have been difficult to implement at a time when transportation and communications were slow. Moreover, such a system would have effectively stripped the small states of any real influence in presidential selection. The system adopted, by contrast, reinforced federalism by incorporating the agreement that already lay at the base of the Connecticut, or Great, Compromise (Hardaway 1994, 82). That is, the smallest states would get at least three votes, because each state was guaranteed at least one member in the House of Representatives and two senators. (For an argument questioning the Electoral College's effect on federalism, see "Rethinking the Electoral College Debate" 2001.)

Most of the operation of the Electoral College has developed by usage rather than by constitutional mandate. Thus, all states now choose their electors by popular vote, but neither the original Constitution nor the Twelfth Amendment mandates this. Similarly, all states except Maine and Nebraska now use a winner-take-all system. Scholars debate whether the constitutional framers expected electors to exercise independent judgment, but with a few flukes (so-called faithless electors), most follow the pledges that the parties now require of them.

Criticism

The use of the Electoral College system raises the possibility that the winner of the electoral vote may not be the winner of the popular vote; to many, this departure from direct democracy is unjustifiable. Until recently, the only election in which such a result clearly happened was the election of 1888, in which Benjamin Harrison amassed 230 electoral votes to President Grover Cleveland's 168, even though Cleveland (who would be reelected in the next presidential election) had received about 100,000 more popular votes. In 2000, however, Republican candidate

George W. Bush, who did particularly well in less-populated western states, narrowly won the Electoral College despite falling approximately half a million votes nationwide behind his Democratic opponent, Albert Gore Jr. Moreover, there continues to be vigorous debate about whether Bush or Gore actually won the greater number of votes in the pivotal state of Florida, where there were problems with voting machines and vote counting. The Supreme Court eventually brought recounts to an end in *Bush v. Gore* (2000), arguing that Florida officials were not utilizing consistent standards for equal protection of the law under the Fourteenth Amendment. Journalists and scholars authored numerous books chronicling and debating the election and the accompanying court decisions (see Ceaser and Busch 2001; Correspondents of *The New York Times* 2001; Dershowitz 2001; Dionne and Kristol 2001; Gillman 2001; Political Staff of *The Washington Post* 2001).

Some critics would also include the elections of 1824, 1876, and 1960 as examples in which the winner of the Electoral College may not have won the popular vote. In the election of 1824, Andrew Jackson received more popular votes than John Quincy Adams, who was selected by the House of Representatives as the winner. However, there were four candidates, and in the initial voting, none gained a majority of either the electoral or the popular vote. Similarly, there is evidence that Samuel Tilden may have captured more votes in the election of 1876 than his opponent, Rutherford B. Hayes. Hayes, however, was declared the eventual winner after an electoral commission, appointed by the House of Representatives to resolve disputed electoral votes in three states, voted along party lines to give all the votes to Hayes. Corruption was so rampant on both sides in this contest that it is not clear that the Electoral College system should be held responsible for the outcome (Hardaway 1994, 128–137). The dispute over who won the popular vote in the election of 1960, in which John F. Kennedy received the greater number of electoral votes, centers on whether he should have been credited with the votes cast for unpledged delegates in Alabama.

Critics of the Electoral College argue that the system advantages particular types of states or minority groups that may hold the balance of power. The winner-take-all feature of the system certainly encourages candidates to go for majorities in the most populous states, whereas the three votes cast by the smallest states are more than they would be entitled to have, judged purely by population. Critics also charge that the winner-take-all feature of the current system effectively "wastes" the votes of minorities within each state and thus decreases voter turnout. Critics further highlight the possibility of faithless electors, like the Washington DC elector who cast a blank ballot in the 2000 election in protest over the district's failure to have voting representatives in Congress ("Electoral College" 2001), or the resolution of disputed elections in the House of Representatives.

The District Plan

Several reforms have dominated recent discussion of the electoral college system. A popular proposal dating back to 1800 favors modifying the system along the order of a district plan. Some proposals have called for dividing each state into a number of districts equal to its total number of electors and giving each district a single elector. Others call for using existing congressional districts, with each state electing two electors on an at-large basis. Such a plan was proposed by a 22-to-9 vote in the Senate in 1813, and again in 1819 by a vote of 28 to 10. The House did not act on the first proposal, and in 1820, its vote of 92 to 54 was just shy of the required two-thirds majority.

Missouri's senator Thomas Hart Benton supported the district plan, as did Andrew Johnson. In the 1870s, Indiana senator Oliver P. Morton supported the plan, and in the 1940s and 1950s, New York representative Frederic R. Coudert Jr. and South Dakota senator Karl E. Mundt supported it. Other supporters of this plan have included South Carolina senator Strom Thurmond, Arizona senator Barry Goldwater, and President Harry Truman. Democratic senators Paul Douglas of Illinois and John F. Kennedy of Massachusetts opposed it.

Whatever its merits, the district system still allows a candidate to win a majority of votes within a state and not win a majority of its electoral votes. Indeed, this plan might still have resulted in George W. Bush's election in 2000 ("Electoral College" 2001). The district plan does little to deal with the problem of "wasted" votes within districts, and it still leaves open the possibility that a president would be elected with less than a majority of popular votes (Peirce 1968, 152–168). Such a system might also encourage gerrymandering of individual districts (Hardaway 1994, 144–145).

The Proportional Plan

A second plan frequently introduced is the proportional plan, which would allocate a state's electoral votes in proportion to its popular votes. First introduced in 1848, the original plan awarded only whole delegates, but subsequent plans have carried this out to the nearest one-thousandth.

Supporters of a proportional plan have included Nebraska senator George W. Norris, Massachusetts senator Henry Cabot Lodge, and Texas representative Ed Gossett. In 1950, the Senate approved such a plan by a vote of 67 to 27, but the House defeated it by a vote of 134 for and 210 against. In 1956, the Senate subsequently voted 48 to 37 for a substitute offered by Price Daniel of Texas that would allow states to choose between the direct and the proportional plan.

Although the proportional plan takes care of the "wasted" vote problem, it does not guarantee a president elected by a majority. In the 1940s and 1950s, some opponents also feared that it would give an advantage to noncompetitive one-party states, especially those in the South, where Democrats typically racked up large majorities.

The Automatic Plan

A third alternative to the current electoral college system is often called the automatic system and appears to have been first contemplated by Thomas Jefferson. This system would eliminate the individual electors and give each state's votes to candidates who captured a majority there.

In 1934, the Senate voted 42 to 24 for such a plan, thus falling short of the required two-

thirds. President Lyndon Johnson later supported this plan, as did Indiana Democratic senator Birch Bayh, before he became a supporter of the direct popular vote mechanism. The automatic plan would constitute a relatively minor change in the current system, and some may have opposed this scheme for fear that it would be an obstacle to more serious reforms (Peirce 1968, 177–181).

Direct Popular Election

By far the most popular alternative to the current electoral college system is that of the direct popular vote suggested at the Constitutional Convention of 1787 and first proposed in Congress in 1816. Andrew Jackson has been designated "the spiritual godfather of the direct vote movement" (Peirce 1968, 183). Many observers believe that such a plan would lead to participation by an increased number of political parties. Most such plans have accordingly called for a runoff election in the event that no candidates receive 40 percent or more of the votes. Variations of such plans have called for voters to rank candidates, or give "yes" votes to all candidates they think are acceptable, giving the candidate with the highest number of such votes the election ("Electoral College" 2001).

The Chamber of Commerce and the American Bar Association supported a popular election plan in the 1960s, and Senator Birch Bayh, who was a key proponent of the Twenty-fifth Amendment providing for cases of presidential disability and the Twenty-sixth Amendment lowering the voting age to 18, became a prominent supporter. The House of Representatives adopted such a proposal in 1969 by a vote of 338 to 70 (Longley and Braun 1972, 152), but the Senate killed it, twice falling short of the number needed to invoke cloture of debates intended to defeat the measure.

Other Proposals

Other plans have been introduced to give electoral representation to Guam, Puerto Rico, or other U.S. possessions; to allow the U.S. Supreme Court to resolve disputed elections; to allow both houses of Congress—rather than the

House of Representatives alone—to resolve elections in which no candidate receives a majority; to require a vote of electors; to require a runoff in cases in which no presidential candidate receives a majority of the popular vote; and so forth. Connecticut Federalist senator James Hillhouse once suggested that U.S. senators should serve for three-year terms, with retiring senators drawing balls from a box, and the one drawing the colored ball to serve as president for a year (Peirce 1968, 194). Other plans have called for alternating presidents between the North and the South or requiring candidates to get a majority of electors in each of four sections of the nation.

Another plan, supported by Jesse Jackson's Rainbow Coalition, calls for majority preference voting (MPV). Under such a system, voters rank candidates in their order of preference, with the votes of last-place candidates being redistributed until one candidate has a clear majority (Richie 1995). Such a plan might well encourage third-party candidates.

In the aftermath of the 2000 presidential election, historian Arthur Schlesinger Jr. proposed creating 102 "superelectors," whose votes would go to the winner of the popular vote, but there are questions about how many such delegates would be appropriate ("Electoral College" 2001). If the number is very large, it would simply seem easier to abolish the current system altogether.

Obstacles to Reform

The diversity of reform proposals has served in part as an obstacle to change, because it has made achieving consensus on an alternative difficult. Moreover, whereas critics charge that the current system is archaic, many defenders of the current system believe that it has been vital to achieving governmental consensus by discouraging third parties. Defenders also believe that the current system is a bastion of federalism that has worked remarkably well. It appears that it would take sustained leadership or another election like that of 1800 or 1824 to inaugurate major reform of the current system. A number of Democratic members of Congress, including former New York senator Hillary Rodham Clinton, proposed abolishing or altering the Elec-

toral College in the aftermath of the presidential election of 2000. Most Americans, however, accepted the legitimacy of a president who gained office without winning the popular vote, and some scholars continue to defend this institution (Gregg 2001). Thus, to date, most of the reforms stimulated by the presidential election of 2000 have focused on changing the types of voting machines and ballots used rather than on reform or abolition of the Electoral College.

Prior to the adoption of the Seventeenth Amendment, providing for direct election of U.S. senators, a number of states helped the process along by pledging to select the popular vote winners in their states; most such senators, in turn, felt obligated to support popular election. Drawing from this experience, a law professor from Northwestern University has recently suggested that a relatively small number of large states could effectively provide for direct election of the president by pledging their electors to cast their votes for the winner of the national electoral vote (Bennett 2001).

In February 2006, the National Popular Vote (NPV) organized to promote such national popular vote legislation. Supporters have introduced this legislation in California, Illinois, New York, Missouri, Colorado, and Louisiana and have actually succeeded in getting it passed in California, only to have it vetoed by Governor Arnold Schwarzenegger on September 30, 2006 (Chang, 2007, 215–216). One critic thinks such laws might conflict with provisions of the Voting Rights Act that are designed to protect minority interests and describes the law as "an end run around the Constitution," which "should be struck down by the Court for this reason alone" (Gringer 2008, 223).

See also Hillhouse, James; Seventeenth Amendment; Twelfth Amendment; Twenty-third Amendment.

For Further Reading:
Bennett, Robert W. 2001. "Popular Election of the President without a Constitutional Amendment." *Green Bag* 2d 4 (Spring): 241–246.
Berns, Walter., ed. 1992. *After the People Vote: A Guide to the Electoral College.* Rev. ed. Washington DC: AEI Press.

Bush v. Gore, 531 U.S. 98 (2000).

Ceaser, James W., and Andrew E. Busch. 2001. *The Perfect Tie: The True Story of the 2000 Presidential Election.* Lanham, MD: Rowman & Littlefield.

Chang, Stanley. 2007. "Updating the Electoral College: The National Popular Vote Legislation." *Harvard Journal on Legislation* 44 (Winter): 205–229.

Correspondents of *The New York Times.* 2001. *36 Days: The Complete Chronicle of the 2000 Presidential Election Crisis.* New York: Henry Holt.

Dershowitz, Alan M. 2001. *Supreme Injustice: How the High Court Hijacked Election 2000.* New York: Oxford University Press.

Dionne, E. J., and William Kristol, eds. 2001. *Bush v. Gore: The Court Cases and the Commentary.* Washington DC: The Brookings Institution.

Edwards, George C., III. 2004. *Why the Electoral College is Bad for America.* New Haven, CT: Yale University Press.

Gillman, Howard. 2001. *The Votes That Counted: How the Court Decided the 2000 Presidential Election.* Chicago: University of Chicago Press.

Gregg, Gary L., II, ed. 2001. *Securing Democracy: Why We Have an Electoral College.* Wilmington, DE: ISI Books.

Gringer, David. 2008. "Why the National Popular Vote Plan is the Wrong Way to Abolish the Electoral College." *Columbia Law Review* 108 (January): 182–230.

Hardaway, Robert M. 1994. *The Electoral College and the Constitution: The Case for Preserving Federalism.* Westport, CT: Praeger.

Longley, Lawrence D., and Alan G. Braun. 1972. *The Politics of Electoral College Reform.* New Haven, CT: Yale University Press.

Peirce, Neal R. 1968. *The People's President: The Electoral College in American History and the Direct-Vote Alternative.* New York: Simon and Schuster.

Political Staff of *The Washington Post.* 2001. *Deadlock: The Inside Story of America's Closest Election.* New York: Public Affairs.

"Rethinking the Electoral College Debate: The Framers, Federalism, and One Person, One Vote." 2001. *Harvard Law Review* 114 (June): 2526–2549.

Richie, Robert. 1995. "Democracy and Majority Preference Voting." *Rainbow* 3, no. 30 (27 July).

"The Report of the National Symposium on Presidential Selection." 2001. The Center for Governmental Studies at the University of Virginia. http://www.goodpolitics .org/reform/report/electoral.htm. Accessed November 29, 2002.

ELEVENTH AMENDMENT

The Eleventh Amendment was the first amendment that overturned a Supreme Court decision and the only adopted amendment ever directly to address the judicial branch of government. The amendment has spawned numerous cases that have both expanded and narrowed its apparent scope.

Origins

Article III of the Constitution extends judicial power to controversies "between a State and Citizens of another State." In arguing on behalf of the new Constitution, however, leading Federalists responded to Anti-Federalist critics by contending that this clause would not undermine the doctrine of sovereign immunity, according to which a sovereign—in this case, a state government—could not be sued without its consent; they apparently thought such cases could only go to federal courts when initiated by the states themselves.

Despite such assurances, in *Chisholm v. Georgia* (1793), the Supreme Court upheld a suit brought against Georgia by the executor of the estate of a South Carolina merchant for payment for goods delivered during the Revolutionary War. The success of this suit not only threatened state sovereignty, but may have threatened other states with significant debts. The lower house of the Georgia legislature subsequently passed a bill providing that any federal marshal attempting to enforce the Court's judgment would be "hereby declared guilty of felony, and shall suffer death, without the benefit of the clergy, by being hanged" (cited by Jacob 1972, 57).

Congress proposed the Eleventh Amendment in 1794; the necessary number of states ratified the amendment in 1795, but the secretary of state did not promulgate it until 1798, which is sometimes incorrectly cited as the official ratification date. The amendment provides that "the Judicial power of the United States shall not be construed to extend to any suit in law or equity, commenced or prosecuted against one of the United States by Citizens of another State, or by Citizens or Subjects of any Foreign State." Professor Kurt T. Lash has observed that the language "shall not be construed" is identical to that in the Ninth Amendment, which he believes served a similar function in protecting state sovereignty (2009, 133). In *Hollingsworth v. Virginia* (1798), the Court ruled that the original congressional resolution did not require the president's signature for the amendment to be valid and gave the amendment retrospective application.

Early History and Reconstruction Period

The Eleventh Amendment does not appear to have barred many suits during its early history. This was largely because Chief Justice John Marshall ruled in *Osborn v. Bank of the United States* (1824) that the Eleventh Amendment did not bar suits against officers of a state. Moreover, in *Cohens v. Virginia* (1821), Marshall ruled that the amendment did not bar appeals to federal courts in cases in which the states themselves initiated the suits.

By the end of Reconstruction, however, a number of Southern states were repudiating debts, and after resolution of the disputed presidential election of 1876, there was little federal will to enforce such debts by force of arms. Thus, in 1883, the Supreme Court ruled in *Louisiana ex rel. Elliott v. Jamel* that shareholders could not sue Louisiana for interest on bonds. In 1890, Justice Joseph P. Bradley, the same justice whose vote on the electoral commission had resulted in the election of fellow Republican Rutherford B. Hayes, authored the decision in *Hans v. Louisiana* (1890) that reinterpreted and extended the scope of the Eleventh Amendment.

Extending the literal language of the Eleventh Amendment to cover suits brought by a state citizen against its own state, Bradley broadly interpreted the Eleventh Amendment as a restatement of what he believed to be the original constitutional understanding that states

could not be sued without their consent. *Ex parte New York* (1921) subsequently extended the breadth of the Eleventh Amendment to forbid admiralty cases (not technically considered cases in "law or equity") against a state without its consent. *Monaco v. Mississippi* (1934) applied the same principle to cases brought against a state by foreign governments (Orth 1987, 139–141).

Limitations of Amendment

State immunity has, however, been somewhat modified by *Ex parte Young* (1908), which effectively reaffirmed *Osborn v. Bank of the United States* (1824) by permitting state officials, as opposed to states themselves, to be sued. Moreover, in *Lincoln County v. Luning* (1890), the Court decided that state immunity was not extended to state subdivisions. Other rulings have held that federal jurisdiction in the area of interstate commerce and in enforcement of the Fourteenth Amendment (the ratification of which came after that of the Eleventh Amendment) may override traditional state immunities. Ironically, the concept of sovereign immunity has become so much "part of the United States unwritten constitution" that it has often predominated over "the language of the Amendment" (Orth 1987, 152).

There have been at least two attempts to amend the Eleventh Amendment, one introduced in 1883 and the other in 1913. The former provided that Congress could make provision "by appropriate legislation for the enforcement of contracts entered into by any of the States of the Union" (quoted in Orth 1987, 70). The latter called for an unspecfied amendment to the provision.

Recent Interpretations

Some recent cases have called renewed attention to the Eleventh Amendment. In *Seminole Tribe v. Florida* (1996), the Supreme Court reaffirmed the broad reading of the amendment given in *Hans v. Louisiana* (1890) by deciding, in a 5-to-4 ruling, that the Eleventh Amendment precluded Indian tribes' suing of states without their consent for failing to negotiate in good faith over the establishment of gambling casinos on Indian lands (Greenhouse 1996). In *Alden v. Maine* (1999), the Court decided that a group of state probation officers did not have standing to sue Maine without its consent for violations of the Fair Labor Standards Act. Similarly, in *Kimel v. Florida Board of Regents* (2000), the Supreme Court decided that states could not be subjected to provisions of the Age Discrimination in Employment Act of 1967, as amended, without their consent.

A 5-to-4 majority of the Court decided in *Federal Maritime Commission v. South Carolina State Ports Authority* (2002) that states could not be sued for failure to berth a gambling cruise ship at their ports. The majority decision, written by Justice Clarence Thomas, specifically noted that "Dual sovereignty is a defining feature of our Nation's constitutional blueprint." Thomas observed that "the Eleventh Amendment does not define the scope of the States' sovereign immunity; it is but one particular exemplification of that immunity." Thomas further cited an earlier case to say that "[w]e have understood the Eleventh Amendment to stand not so much for what it says, but for the presupposition of our constitutional structure."

Taken together with recent rulings regarding states' rights under the Tenth Amendment, contemporary Supreme Court decision-making regarding the Eleventh Amendment reveals a desire by a majority of members of the U.S. Supreme Court to allow states to exercise increased prerogatives. This could ultimately prove to be the central legacy of the Rehnquist Court.

See also *Chisholm v. Georgia;* Fourteenth Amendment; *Hollingsworth v. Virginia;* Ninth Amendment; Supreme Court Decisions Reversed by Constitutional Amendments; Tenth Amendment.

For Further Reading:

Federal Maritime Commission v. South Carolina State Ports Authority, 535 U.S. 743 (2002).

Greenhouse, Linda. 1996. "Justices Curb Federal Power to Subject States to Lawsuits." *New York Times* 115 (28 March): A1, A12.

Jacob, Clyde E. 1972. *The Eleventh Amendment and Sovereign Immunity.* Westport, CT: Greenwood Press.

Lash, Kurt T. 2009. *The Lost History of the Ninth Amendment.* New York: Oxford University Press.

Orth, John V. 1987. *The Judicial Power of the United States: The Eleventh Amendment in American History.* New York: Oxford University Press.

ELLIOTT, WILLIAM YANDELL (1896–1979)

Harvard political scientist William Yandell Elliott published a book entitled *The Need for Constitutional Reform* (1935) during Franklin Roosevelt's first term in office. Elliott advocated a number of reforms designed primarily to strengthen both executive and legislative power and to overcome problems that Elliott perceived in the existing system of separated powers (Vile 1991c, 72–74).

Elliott offered a number of small steps that could be taken to achieve this end. These included a presidential item veto and a prohibition of riders that were not germane to the aims of a bill. The linchpin of Elliott's plan, however, was his proposal for a constitutional arrangement, borrowed from parliamentary systems, under which the president would have the power, at least once during a term, to force members of the House of Representatives to stand for election. If such an election upheld Congress over the president, the president could resign (with Congress then choosing his successor), but the president would not, as in most parliamentary systems, be required to do so.

Elliott desired to cut the power of the Senate, which he associated with special interests, and he advocated taking from that body "the power over bills appropriating money or raising revenue" (Elliott 1935, 32). Ideally, states would be reorganized into districts designated as "commonwealths," similar to those used for the Federal Reserve System. Elliott suggested that there might be 12 such regions, each electing eight senators. The president would be able to add 15 prominent individuals to the Senate; losing presidential candidates would also serve in this body. The vote needed to approve treaties would be changed from two-thirds of the Senate to a simple majority of both houses.

Representation in the House would continue to be based on population, but members would be elected from the new commonwealths rather than from existing states. Elliott favored a form of proportional representation for the House, with up to five representatives per district. He believed that this would help overcome the power of existing interest groups. A continuing committee of both houses would be in "perpetual residence" in Washington DC. (Elliott 1935, 37).

Elliott favored a new system for selecting the president. Under his plan, a joint House and Senate committee would nominate presidential candidates, and the House would choose two of these to run in a national election. The president would be selected by majority popular vote. The president would choose an executive vice president or an assistant president who would also head the administrative cabinet.

Elliott believed that, although the system of judicial review was needed in the current system, such power might be modified if the legislative and executive branches were more responsible. In such a situation, he believed that the Supreme Court should be required to vote by a two-thirds vote before invalidating legislation. Generally, battles "over social reform should be fought out in party politics, not in the courts" (Elliott 1935, 179). Elliott feared that existing protections for criminal defendants—such as the prohibition against double jeopardy—were working to "aid gangsters and racketeers" (Elliott 1935, 204). He also suggested that the Supreme Court should choose the attorney general.

Elliott would strengthen the positions of governors in the new commonwealths. Elliott would grant them the power to dissolve the legislature (now to be unicameral) once during their four-year terms. Elliott would also create governors' councils and legislative steering committees. Like the president, state governors would originate the budget and would be subject to override on money bills only by a two-thirds majority.

Elliott advocated a number of administrative reforms. He wanted to create a civil service head for each department and a permanent cabinet secretariat "to propose and document Cabinet meetings" (Elliott 1935, 203). Elliott also proposed adding an advisory committee to each department consisting of "all the great interests with which it comes into normal contact" (Elliott 1935, 203), and he favored allowing cabinet members to have seats in the Senate and to appear before the House.

Elliott recognized that some of his proposals could be implemented on a piecemeal basis, but he believed that the more substantial changes—especially in regard to the Senate—could best be initiated by a constitutional convention.

See also Constitutional Conventions; Parliamentary System.

For Further Reading:

Elliott, William Y. 1935. *The Need for Constitutional Reform: A Program for National Security.* New York: Whittlesey House.

ELLIS, FREDERICK, AND CARL FREDERICK

Frederick Ellis and Carl Frederick have presented their ideas for constitutional change in *The Oakland Statement,* which they describe as *A Political Adventure Novel.* Ellis, a graduate of Villanova and Armstrong University (MBA) left his brokerage firm to become involved in civil rights and worked for Senator Eugene McCarthy in 1968 and for George McGovern in 1972. He now lives in Costa Rica, where he says "the idea was born to write a political adventure novel presenting a progressive vision for *real solutions* by creating two new constitutional amendments to the Bill of Rights, resulting in a *popular political economy* for all the people" (Ellis and Frederick 2002, inside back cover). Carl Frederick, who earned his MBA at the University of Chicago, also began in business before writing a bestselling book entitled *Est: Playing the Game the New Way* (1975). After traveling the world, he also settled in Costa Rica.

The overriding political agenda arguably detracts from the merits of *The Oakland Statemen* as fiction. In the wake of the September 11, 2001 attack on the World Trade Centers and the Pentagon, the book might also suffer from poor timing. Published in 2000, its storyline is based on a leaderless revolution that begins with patriotic terrorists blowing up power stations throughout the nation. Rather miraculously, no one ever appears to be actually killed, and the patriotic terrorists are all eventually pardoned for the great good they have done in calling attention to the nation's problems. Moreover, the result is the convening of a second constitutional convention presided over by former vice president Al Gore Jr. that adds amendments twenty-eight and twenty-nine to what is described as the Bill of Rights.

In the novel, all this occurs between October 2000 and March 2005. The story describes the election of president Veronica Lake, who beats out George W. Bush for the Republican nomination, chooses Senator John McCain as a running mate, and gives Patrick Buchanan a prominent place in her new administration. By 2005, newly elected Democratic President Paul Wellstone (who, in reality, was killed in a 2002 plane crash), who narrowly beats out Lake and Jesse Ventura, issues his amnesty to the patriots whose violence concentrated the nation's attention on the two amendments. In between, Eugene McCarthy, George McGovern, John Anderson, Jesse Jackson, Jerry Brown (in one of the more creative moments of the book appearing complete with an 800 number "2 RATIFY" [Ellis and Frederick 2000, 245]), and other progressives play cameo roles, with Ross Perot commended on a number of occasions for his role in calling attention to existing problems. Former president Jimmy Carter ends up sidelined by a fall from a horse, while former president Clinton, who has become "a total sex hound since Hillary divorced him," apparently largely ignores the reform movement as he travels the world in search of illicit sex (151).

Three aspects of this book deserve scholarly attention. They are the Oakland Statement, in which the middle-class revolutionaries announce their philosophy; the mechanism chosen for constitutional reform; and the two amendments that the book describes as succeeding.

The Oakland Statement begins by observing that "our citizens are voting less and less, while our economic wealth is being concentrated rapidly into the hands of fewer and fewer people" (Ellis and Frederick 2000, 3). Tying itself to earlier movements for the U.S. Constitution, the Bill of Rights, the Civil War, and the battle for "labor rights and civil rights," the statement goes on to announce that extraordinary action is necessary to accomplish two objectives. The first would "guarantee the absolute right of the people to enjoy the most equitable methods of a representative electoral system," including "pro-

portional representation, preference voting, cumulative voting and referendums at every level of government" (4). The second would "guarantee the absolute right of the people to participate in the creation of the national wealth," which would be achieved "primarily through the establishment of majority employee owned enterprises and progressive labor organizing" (4). The Oakland Statement goes on to provide a "rationale" for "extraordinary action" including violence. Specifically, it proposes "the formation of other small (3 to 5 people) autonomous ATTACK UNITS, with the specific purpose of inflicting maximum damage on electrical power while minimizing loss of life" (6).

The Oakland Statement further expresses the hope that this action will lead states, as it does in the novel, to call a limited constitutional convention specifically to consider these and only these amendments. Although many citizens in the novel question the violent methods used to get public attention, the citizens eventually realize the importance of the two amendments. As a result, two-thirds of the states petition Congress to call a constitutional convention, which proposes two amendments that are subsequently proposed and ratified by the necessary number of state conventions. Afterwards, Puerto Rico, the Virgin Islands, and the District of Columbia join as new states (the last apparently by congressional resolution rather than by constitutional amendment), and overtures are made to other Caribbean and Central American nations, including Haiti and Cuba, to join.

The texts of both amendments that are eventually proposed and adopted are longer than any current constitutional amendments. Both amendments contain some provisions that are quite specific and others that are quite general. This approach appears to be quite deliberate. The revolutionaries note at one point in the book that "the amendments themselves would have to be in very general language" (93). Referring to a proposal, similar to one later adopted, providing that "[t]he people shall have the absolute right to enjoy the *most equitable methods* of a representative electoral system," they explain, "If the various branches of government failed to change the electoral process to what citizens believed to be 'most equitable,' then suits could be filed in various courts, challenging the process and at the same time, demanding specific remedies" (93–94). The authors express little concern over judicial accountability.

The Twenty-Eighth Amendment has eight sections. The first provides for mandatory voting for all, except for those with conscientious objections to the practice. Section 2 provides that elections "shall be conducted using the most equitable methods as determined by each level of state, district, territory, and local governments utilizing the process of referendums" (224) and allows citizens to go to court to obtain this right. Section 3 provides for the election of the president through "preference voting." In the process, existing provisions providing for the Electoral College are repealed (224–225). Section 4 further provides for "an open referendum process" (225). Section 5 would increase the number of U.S. Representatives by assuring that no district had more than 250,000 individuals, and Section 6 would accordingly guarantee each state at least three votes. Section 7 provides for the public financing of elections, except for individual contributions limited to no more than $250 each. Section 8 concludes by allowing respective entities to limit the length of electoral campaigns, but also gives citizens the right to challenge such time limits in court.

The Twenty-ninth Amendment has seven sections and is designed to institute a system similar to that which Marshall Tito employed in Yugoslovia after World War II. It is difficult to assess whether this amendment can better be considered to be based upon, or whether it is better viewed as a substitute for, utopian principles. In an earlier section of the book discussing this amendment, aspiring revolutionaries refer both to the failure of the world's great religions and of modern ideologies to create a "new man." One revolutionary notes,

> Maybe, in the distant future, if we last that long, men will come to the conclusion that the high ideals of religions and communitarian practices is not only a better way to live, but might be the only way to survive, as the world population increases exponentially. But, as material beings, right now we gotta look at *real* economic systems that are based on both individualism and collectivism (48).

Section 1 guarantees all citizens from age 18 to 60 or older the right "to participate in the creation of the national wealth" (235). Section 2 further indicates that this will be done "by the majority-employee ownership of conditional and certified enterprises," these categories being determined by the number of employees of each. Section 3 provides governmental charters and licenses for all "private, conditional, and certified enterprises as businesses for profit" (235). Section 4 specifically guarantees the right to organize "democratic labor unions, supervisor and management employee organizations" (235). Section 5 provides that the federal government "shall be the employer of last resort for able-bodied and mentally capable citizens" under retirement age (235). Section 6 proceeds to guarantee further social and economic rights by providing for "the right to free education to the highest levels available, based upon scholastic qualifications" (235). Section 7 further provides all citizens with "the right to free complete medical and mental health insurance coverage," including "[a]ll prescription drugs and dental costs, except nonaccidental cosmetic, medical, and dental expenses" (236).

In the novel, the ratification of the two amendments by 40 states begins a series of additional reforms at state and local levels, including in the city of Oakland, where the original manifesto was written. This work is among the few books that anticipates or portrays acts of violence as the necessary catalyst to an Article V convention.

See also Constitutional Conventions; Social and Economic Rights; Voting Rights entries.

For Further Reading:

Ellis, Frederick, with Carl Frederick. 2000. *The Oakland Statement: A Political Adventure Novel.* Miami, FL: Synergy International of the Americas, Ltd.

EMANCIPATION PROCLAMATION

Abraham Lincoln often declared that although he opposed slavery, his primary goal in prosecuting the Civil War was to preserve the Union.

As the war continued, Lincoln became convinced that it could best be prosecuted and the future of the Union best be guaranteed by abolishing slavery. He officially issued the Emancipation Proclamation on January 1, 1863, but Lincoln had announced his intention to do so in September of 1862 (Anastaplo 1995, 138). A war measure taken under executive authority, this proclamation declared all slaves in states adhering to the Confederacy to be free. This amounted to 74 percent of all slaves in the United States (Paludan 1994, 155).

Although Lincoln also proposed amendments containing plans for more gradual emancipation for other slaves, the momentum generated by the Emancipation Proclamation made this virtually impossible. The proclamation was extended and placed on firmer constitutional authority when, in 1865, the Thirteenth Amendment to the Constitution, which Lincoln also supported, abolished involuntary servitude throughout the nation.

See also Lincoln, Abraham; Thirteenth Amendment.

For Further Reading:

Anastaplo, George. 1995. *The Amendments to the Constitution: A Commentary.* Baltimore: Johns Hopkins University Press.

Guelzo, Allen C. 2005. *Lincoln's Emancipation Proclamation: The End of Slavery in America.* New York: Simon and Schuster.

Paludan, Phillip S. 1994. *The Presidency of Abraham Lincoln.* Lawrence: University Press of Kansas.

EMBARGOES, ARMS, LOANS, AND FOREIGN AID

In 1934, Republican Senator Gerald P. Nye of North Dakota held hearings indicating that bankers and manufacturers of munitions had made huge profits from their sales to the Allies in World War I (Cole 1962, 79–97). These revelations about the so-called merchants of death increased isolationist sentiment in the United States and led many to suspect that U.S. participation in the war had been engineered to continue such profit-making.

Even before the hearings, Democratic representative Ross Collins of Mississippi had introduced a resolution that would have prohibited making or renewing loans to nations engaged in war, unless the United States itself was engaged in such a war as an ally. Collins repeatedly introduced this resolution in the late 1930s, during which time Congress adopted a number of neutrality acts to prevent the United States from trading with belligerent nations or taking passage on their ships (DeConde 1971, 567). Some such laws had a "cash and carry" exemption or allowed the president some discretion whether to impose the embargo on one or both sides of a conflict. President Franklin D. Roosevelt arranged a "lend-lease" arrangement with Great Britain prior to U.S. entry into World Ward II that enable the United States to exchange arms for access to military bases. The Japanese attack on Pearl Harbor in 1941 ended U.S. isolationism.

During the Cold War, the United States used foreign aid as a tool of foreign policy making, but critics charged that such aid was wasteful. In 1949, Republican senator William Langer of North Dakota offered an amendment restricting foreign aid to times of war. Republican representative Noah Mason of Illinois introduced similar resolutions in 1957 and 1959, extending the prohibition on foreign aid to international organizations as well as to foreign governments.

See also War, Proclamation of.

For Further Reading:

Cole, Wayne S. 1962. *Senator Gerald P. Nye and American Foreign Relations.* Minneapolis: University of Minnesota Press.

DeConde, Alexander. 1971. *A History of American Foreign Policy.* 2d ed. New York: Charles Scribner's Sons.

EMBARGOES, TRADE

When Thomas Jefferson was president, he asked Congress to declare an embargo on trade with Great Britain and France rather than risk war over the seizure of American vessels and the impressment of American seamen. Such power could be justified either as an exercise of congressional power over foreign commerce or as a means of national defense. Initially defensive in nature, in time embargo became a method, albeit a fairly unsuccessful one, of exerting pressure on belligerents (Mayer 1994, 217). The embargo, which lasted from December 1807 to March 1809, was especially resented in the New England states, which were dependent on such commerce. Both during this embargo and later at the Hartford Convention that met during the War of 1812, these states issued calls to limit congressional embargo powers. The Hartford Convention called for a 60-day limit (Vile 1993, 186).

In modern times, the United States has declared embargoes against Iran, Iraq, and Cuba. The United States also boycotted the Olympics after the Russian invasion of Afghanistan. The U.S. Supreme Court ruled in *Crosby v. National Foreign Trade Council* (2000) that states cannot declare embargoes or other sanctions against foreign nations (in this case Burma, or Myanmar) that are not supported by the national government.

See also Congress, Powers of; Hartford Convention; Jefferson, Thomas.

For Further Reading:

Mayer, David N. 1994. *The Constitutional Thought of Thomas Jefferson.* Charlottesville: University Press of Virginia.

Vile, John R. 1993. *The Theory and Practice of Constitutional Change in America: A Collection of Original Source Materials.* New York: Peter Lang.

EMERGENCY, NATIONAL

See Congress, Emergency Functioning.

EMPLOYMENT OPPORTUNITY

Unemployment has prompted governmental intervention in the form of job creation and training programs as well as unemployment insurance. Franklin Roosevelt's New Deal and Lyndon Johnson's War on Poverty were high points in the national government's efforts. There continue to be sharp debates over what role the government—as opposed to private enterprise—should play in reducing unemployment and over the effectiveness of specific governmental programs (Baumer and Van Horn 1985).

At least seven times since 1983, Representative Major Owens, a Democrat from Brooklyn, New York, has introduced an amendment to guarantee the right to employment opportunity to everyone and to give Congress power to enforce the amendment with appropriate legislation. More recently, Representative Jesse Jackson Jr. (D-IL) has proposed a "full employment" amendment to guarantee that every citizen "has a right to work" and assuring that each will get "just and favorable remuneration for themselves and their family, an existence worthy of human dignity, and supplemented, if necessary, by other means of social protection" (Jackson with Watkins 2001, 252). Recent welfare reforms point less toward work as a governmentally guaranteed right and more toward work as a duty to be performed in return for welfare and other benefits.

See also Jackson, Jesse L., Jr.; Social and Economic Rights.

For Further Reading:

Baumer, Donald C., and Carl E. Van Horn. 1985. *The Politics of Employment.* Washington DC: Congressional Quarterly Press.

Jackson, Jesse L., Jr., with Frank E. Watkins. 2001. *A More Perfect Union: Advancing New American Rights.* New York: Welcome Rain Publishers.

ENFORCEMENT CLAUSES IN AMENDMENTS

Most congressional powers are specified, or implied, in Article I, Section 8 of the U.S. Constitution. Many amendments also limit congressional powers. To take one of the more obvious examples, the First Amendment provides that "Congress shall make no law . . ."

related to certain designated matters. In *Barron v. Baltimore* (1833), Chief Justice John Marshall decided that this and subsequent provisions in the Bill of Rights limited only the national government and not the states, although later Supreme Court decisions applied most such provisions to the states via the due process clause of the Fourteenth Amendment.

Beginning with the three amendments adopted after the Civil War, many amendments have included specific authorizations for congressional enforcement that echo the necessary and proper clause. The end of Article I, Section 8 grants power to Congress "[t]o make all Laws which shall be necessary and proper for carrying into Execution the foregoing Powers, and all other Powers vested by this Constitution in the Government of the United States, or in any Department or Officer thereof."

The provision in Section 2 of the Thirteenth Amendment specifying that "Congress shall have power to enforce this article by appropriate legislation" is fairly typical. There are similar provisions in Section 5 of the Fourteenth Amendment and in Section 2 of the Fifteenth Amendment. The central text of the Sixteenth Amendment (providing for an income tax) specifically grants Congress "power to lay and collect taxes," so there is no separate enforcement provision. The Eighteenth Amendment, providing for national alcoholic prohibition, is somewhat unique in that its second section vests "concurrent" enforcement power in both Congress and the states, with the Twenty-first Amendment providing for the Eighteenth Amendment's repeal, reiterating state powers to restrict importation of alcohol. Rather than a separate section, the Nineteenth Amendment, prohibiting denial of voting on the basis of sex, vests Congress with enforcement authority in its second sentence. Section 2 of the Twenty-third Amendment, which grants Electoral College representation to the District of Columbia, is another example of an enforcement clause. There is a similar provision in Section 2 of the Twenty-fourth Amendment, which abolished the poll tax in federal elections, and in Section 2 of the Twenty-sixth Amendment, which lowered the voting age to 18. Many proposed amendments contain similar enforcement provisions.

Given the necessary and proper clause, additional enforcement clauses have a kind of "belt-and-suspenders" quality to them (an analogy suggested in e-mail correspondence by Professor Brannon Denning). However, in a number of cases interpreting the Thirteenth, Fourteenth, and Fifteenth Amendments, the Supreme Court has referred to the enforcement clauses to allow Congress to outlaw practices that, while not unconstitutional in and of themselves, might prove to be unconstitutional obstacles to the rights of equality and voting. Thus, in *Jones v. Alfred H. Mayer Co.* (1968), the Court upheld a provision of the Civil Rights Act of 1866 barring private discrimination in the sale of housing on the basis that it fell within congressional enforcement authority in abolishing slavery. Similarly, in *South Carolina v. Katzenbach* (1966), the Court upheld the congressional suspension of literacy tests in states where they appeared to be serving as significant obstacles to voting. In *City of Boerne v. Flores* (1997) and other more recent cases dealing with the free exercise clause of the First Amendment as applied to the states through the due process clause of the Fourteenth Amendment, however, the Court has made it clear that congressional enforcement of amendments does not give Congress free rein to define and expand the content of such amendments, especially in the face of contrary judicial interpretations.

Joseph Blocher, who notes various congressional efforts to use the exceptions clause in Article III to withdraw various contentious issues from appellate judicial review, has suggested that future amendments might include a provision saying either that "The Supreme Court shall have appellate jurisdiction over cases arising under this amendment" or that "The Supreme Court shall have appellate jursidiction over cases arising under this amendment" (2008, 1026). Noting that amendments often require judicial enforcement but rarely say anything "about federal courts' duty to enforce them," he observes that "This deafening silence regarding judicial power contrasts with the increasingly loud expansions of congressional power in constitutional amendments passed since the Civil War" (1027).

See also Eighteenth Amendment; Fifteenth Amendment; First Amendment; Fourteenth Amendment; Judiciary, Jurisdiction of; Nineteenth Amendment; Sixteenth Amendment; Thirteenth Amendment; Twenty-first Amendment; Twenty-fourth Amendment; Twenty-sixth Amendment.

For Further Reading:

Banks, Christopher. 2003. "The Constitutional Politics of Interpreting Section 5 of the Fourteenth Amendment." *Akron Law Review* 36: 425–471.

ENGEL V. VITALE (1962)

Few decisions have stirred more calls for a constitutional amendment than this ruling by the Supreme Court authored by Justice Hugo L. Black. At issue was a short nondenominational prayer mandated by the New York State Board of Regents for public school children to recite at the beginning of each school day. A number of parents objected on the basis that the prayer constituted an undue establishment of religion in violation of the First Amendment as applied to the states by the due process clause of the Fourteenth Amendment.

Black agreed with the challengers. Viewing the prayer as a distinctively "religious activity" (*Engel* 1962, 424), he noted that England had been torn by controversy over the Book of Common Prayer and that Americans, especially Thomas Jefferson and James Madison, were aware of the dangers of unifying church and state. Black argued that the voluntary nature of the prayer was irrelevant. The key was the fact that "a union of government and religion tends to destroy government and to degrade religion" (*Engel* 1962, 431).

Justice William O. Douglas's concurrence emphasized that because the schools in question were funded by the government, the state would be financing a religious exercise. In his dissent, Justice Potter Stewart argued that the New York exercise fell short of an establishment of religion and cited a variety of other connections between church and state that were accepted in modern America.

The majority decision in *Engel* was vigorously denounced. New York Republican congressman Frank Becker called it "the most tragic decision in the history of the United States" (Becker and Feeley 1973, 24). The decision prompted 53 representatives and 22 senators to introduce anti-*Engel* amendments in the 87th Congress, and the Senate Judiciary Committee held hearings on the subject (Becker and Feeley 1973, 25–26). Congressional opposition was even more pronounced after the Court's subsequent decision extending *Engel*'s prohibitions to Bible reading in *Abington School District v. Schempp* (1963).

To date, the Court has not backed down. In *Wallace v. Jaffree* (1985), it struck down an Alabama law specifically designed to designate school prayer as an option during a moment of silence—a decision that may not, however, apply to moment-of-silence laws that do not put prayer in a privileged position. In *Lee v. Weisman* (1992), the Court extended the ban to prayers delivered by members of the clergy at junior high school graduations, a decision extended in *Santa Fe Independent School District v. Doe* (2000) to student-led prayers at football games. Pressures for an amendment to establish prayer in schools continue. Some, but not all, versions of the Religious Equality Amendment appear aimed at restoring this practice.

See also Black, Hugo Lafayette; First Amendment; Prayer in Public Schools; Religious Equality Amendment.

For Further Reading:

Becker, Theodore L., and Malcolm M. Feeley, eds. 1973. *The Impact of Supreme Court Decisions: Empirical Studies.* 2d ed. New York: Oxford University Press.

Dierenfield, Bruce J. 2007. *The Battle Over School Prayer: How* Engel v. Vitale *Changed America.* Lawrence: University Press of Kansas.

Engel v. Vitale, 370 U.S. 421 (1962).

ENGLISH BILL OF RIGHTS

The U.S. Bill of Rights was largely modeled on declarations of rights within state constitutions.

However, an earlier model was adopted as statutory law by the English Parliament in 1689 and accepted by William of Orange and his wife Mary. They became king and queen in place of James II, who had fled the country after disputes with Parliament over perceived abuses of power.

After a series of indictments against James II that resemble Jefferson's later charges against George III in the Declaration of Independence, the English Bill of Rights proceeded to guarantee 13 rights. These include the "right of the subjects to petition the King" (a provision similar to one, *sans* king, later included in the First Amendment of the U.S. Constitution); the prohibition against raising taxes without parliamentary consent; prohibitions against a "standing army"; the right, limited to Protestants, to "have arms for their defence suitable to their conditions, and as allowed by law" (a provision that may cast light on the U.S. Second Amendment); the right to freedom of speech and debate for members of parliament; a requirement (quite similar to the latter language of the U.S. Eighth Amendment) "that excessive bail ought not to be required, nor excessive fines imposed, nor cruel and unusual punishments inflicted"; and a provision for impaneling jurors (quoted in Kurland and Lerner 1987, 5:2) The English Bill of Rights also outlined the right of future succession, a perpetual problem in monarchies.

The English Bill of Rights has been described as "one of the great constitutional documents of English history and one of the great charters of the rights and liberties of the subjects under English law" (Walker 1980, 132). It differs from the U.S. Bill of Rights in that, being adopted in a nation with an "unwritten constitution," it was enacted by, and could be undone by, statute rather than by constitutional amendment.

See also Bill of Rights; Eighth Amendment; First Amendment; Second Amendment.

For Further Reading:

Kurland, Philip B., and Ralph Lerner, eds. 1987. *The Founders' Constitution.* 5 vols. Chicago: University of Chicago Press.

Walker, David M. 1980. *The Oxford Companion to Law.* Oxford, UK: Clarenden Press.

ENGLISH LANGUAGE AMENDMENT

The issue of language is often tied to sentiments connected with nationality and race (Baron 1990, xiv). Moreover, people who speak the dominant language sometimes regard those who do not as unpatriotic. Since 1981, members of Congress have introduced a score of proposals to make English the official language of the United States. California Republican senator Samuel I. Hayakawa, a nationally recognized linguist, introduced the first such amendment. Both the Senate (*The English Language Amendment* 1985) and the House (*English Language Constitutional Amendments* 1989) held hearings. The Senate version of this amendment was fairly general, whereas the House version prohibited the use of languages other than English except as a means of teaching language proficiency. Some believe that such an amendment could be used to restrict "multilingual tests, forms and ballots, as well as translators for legal and emergency services" (Baron 1990, 24–25). Some states have adopted English language laws (Baron 1990, 201), but the impact of such legislation has varied from state to state.

Laws against teaching foreign languages have sometimes reflected nativist sentiments. In *Meyer v. Nebraska* (1923), the Supreme Court invalidated a Nebraska law prohibiting the teaching of languages other than English, which the state had enforced against a parochial school teacher teaching from a German text. Similarly, in *Pierce v. Society of Sisters* (1925), the U.S. Supreme Court voided an Oregon law, supported in part by the Ku Klux Klan, that required parents of children between eight and 16 to send their children to public (and not private or parochial) schools.

In *Katzenbach v. Morgan* (1966), the Supreme Court upheld a provision of the Voting Rights Act of 1965 that struck down literacy tests for otherwise eligible voters who had completed the sixth grade in an accredited school in Puerto Rico. In *Lau v. Nichols* (1974), the Supreme Court ruled that a school system had to provide a program to deal with some 1,800 Chinese students who knew no English. The Court noted that "[t]here is no equality of treatment merely by providing students with the same facilities, textbooks, teachers, and curriculum; for students who do not understand English are effectively foreclosed from any meaningful education" (*Lau* 1974, 566). This decision provoked considerable controversy over bilingual education. However, with California's adoption of initiative 227 in 1998, which shifted the emphasis in that state from bilingual education to programs of English immersion (Carleton 2002, 167), most such programs are now designed to enable students to make a transition to English (Baron 1990, 11).

Since the adoption of the Bilingual Education Act of 1968, Congress has provided local school districts with funds for bilingual education. As of 1990, it is believed that English is now spoken "by more than 97 percent of the people in the nation" (Baron 1990, 177). Although some individuals see the English language amendment as a way of promoting national unity, others fear that it could be used to discriminate against people for whom English is a second language.

See also Cultural and Linguistic Rights; Illegal Immigration.

For Further Reading:

Baron, Dennis. 1990. *The English-Only Question: An Official Language for America?* New Haven, CT: Yale University Press.

Carleton, David. 2002. *Student's Guide to Landmark Congressional Laws on Education.* Westport, CT: Greenwood Press.

Lau v. Nichols, 414 U.S. 563 (1974).

Tatalovich, Raymond. 1995. *Nativism Reborn? The Official English Language Movement and the American States.* Lexington: University Press of Kentucky.

ENTRENCHMENT CLAUSES

The U.S. Constitution makes it more difficult to adopt constitutional amendments than to adopt other legal changes. Entrenchment clauses make specified changes even more difficult to amend. Article V of the U.S. Constitution contains two entrenchment provisions. It provides that "no Amendment which may be made prior to the Year One thousand eight hundred and eight shall in any Manner affect the first and fourth Clauses in the Ninth Section of the first Article; and that no State, without its Consent, shall be deprived of its equal Suffrage in the Senate." The first clause reflected a sectional compromise between the North and South at the Constitutional Convention that limited control of, or taxation of, slaves for 20 years. By specification, this clause had a set termination date. The second clause, reflecting conflicts between the large and small states at the Convention that resulted in the Great Compromise providing for equal state representation in the U.S. Senate, does not establish an absolute prohibition of changing state representation in the Senate, but, by requiring that no state can be deprived of such equal suffrage without its consent, provides "'de facto entrenchment,' because no state would willingly surrender its equal suffrage" (Schwartzberg 2007, 116).

The Corwin Amendment, proposed just before the beginning of the Civil War, would have prohibited constitutional alterations that "would authorize or give to Congress power to abolish or interfere, within any State, with the domestic institutions thereof, including that of persons held to labor or service by the laws of the said State" (R. Lee 1961, 22). Fortunately, the Thirteenth Amendment abolishing slavery, and not the Corwin Amendment, was ultimately added to the Constitution.

Advocates of implicit limits on constitutional amendments (based on constitutional structure and/or philosophy) are essentially arguing that there are implicit entrenchment clauses in the Constitution in addition to the two listed. The constitutions of a number of nations, including those of France and Germany, prohibit certain changes in the fundamental principles of their constitutions, and in India, the supreme court has limited the kinds of amendments that can be added. California and Delaware likewise require that major constitutional revisions can be adopted only through the convention mechanism (Katz 1996, 282–285); Spain has a similar provision.

Entrenchment clauses might appear desirable for rights generally regarded as fundamental, but, as the unsuccessful Corwin Amendment suggests, such proposals could also be unwisely used to freeze into place undesirable institutions. Melissa Schwartzberg has further argued that such entrenchment "does not exclude the possibility of constitutional change" but takes this power "out of the hands of assemblies and grants it to judges." However necessary the compromise providing for equal state suffrage was to the ratification of the U.S. Constitution, this compromise remains one of the most undemocratic aspects of the document, giving equal weight in the Senate (and to a lesser extent in the Electoral College) to states with drastically different populations.

Elai Katz has suggested that, although the text of Article V does not specifically require it, Congress should distinguish between mere amendments and more important revisions to basic principles. He thus argues that in cases where legislators propose to alter a fundamental part of the Constitution, for example, the First Amendment, they should consider doing this by convention proposal and ratification (Katz 1996, 291). Similarly, he suggests that entrenched provisions should not be absolute but should "explicitly require that subsequent amendments to the proposed amendment be proposed using the convention method" (Katz 1996, 291–292). Jason Mazzone has advanced a similar argument (2005).

See also Constitutional Amendments, Limits on; Constitutional Convention of 1787; Corwin Amendment; Equal Suffrage Clause; Thirteenth Amendment.

For Further Reading:

Da Silva, Virgilio Afonso. 2004. "A Fossilized Constitution?" *Ratio Juris* 17 (December) 454–473.

Elster, Jon. 2000. *Ulysses Unbound.* Cambridge: Cambridge University Press.

Katz, Elai. 1996. "On Amending Constitutions: The Legality and Legitimacy of Constitutional Entrenchment." *Columbia Journal of Law and Social Problems* 29 (Winter): 251–292.

Lee, R. Alton. 1961. "The Corwin Amendment in the Secession Crisis." *Ohio Historical Quarterly* 70 (January): 1–26.

Mazzone, Jason. 2005. "Unamendments." *Iowa Law Review* 90 (May): 1747–1855.

Schwartzberg, Melissa. 2007. *Democracy and Legal Change.* New York: Cambridge University Press.

Schwartzberg, Melissa. 2004. "Athenian Democracy and Legal Change." *American Political Science Review* 98 (May): 3121–3325.

ENVIRONMENTAL PROTECTION

The text of the U.S. Constitution is silent about a number of contemporary concerns, including the right to an education and the right to a clean environment. Increasing concern over the environment in the 1960s led to a number of proposals late in that decade and thereafter to provide environmental protection.

Typical was a proposal introduced by Democratic representative Richard Ottinger and Republican representative Theodore Kupferman (both from New York) in 1968. They described their proposal as "a conservation bill of rights" (*Congressional Record* 1968, 17116). The first section of their proposal broadly guaranteed "the right of the people to clean air, pure water, [and] freedom from excessive noise and [that] the natural, scenic, historic and esthetics qualities of their environment shall not be abridged." The second section called on Congress to draw up a national inventory of "the natural, scenic, esthetics and historic resources of the United States." A third section would have prohibited action by state or federal agencies adversely affecting this heritage "without first giving reasonable notice to the public and holding a public hearing thereon" (*Congressional Record,* 17116–17117). Whereas most existing constitutional provisions offer "negative protection for individuals from government action" (Hoban and Brooks 1987, 169), Section 1 of the proposed amendment would commit the government to a more affirmative role (also see Schlickeisen 1994). Other proposals, including one by Democratic representative Morris Udall of Arizona, whose brother served as secretary of the interior in the Kennedy and Johnson administrations, followed language of the Declaration of Independence in proposing to make environmental rights "inalienable" (H.J. Res. 1205, 1970).

Members of 37 state legislatures petitioned Congress in the 1990s to adopt an Environmental Quality Amendment providing that

The natural resources of the nation are the heritage of present and future generations. The right of each person to clean and healthful air and water, and to the protection of other natural resources of the nation, shall not be infringed by any person (Cited in Ruhl 1999, 247).

Futurist Bruce E. Tonn included environmental concerns when he wrote an article in 1991 proposing an amendment to create a "Court of Generations" (Tonn 1991). Similarly, Representative Jesse Jackson Jr. (D-IL) has called for an amendment declaring that "[a]ll citizens of the United States shall enjoy the right to a clean, safe, and sustainable environment" (Jackson with Watkins 2001, 371). In addition to doubting whether there is a democratic consensus on behalf of such an amendment, a law professor has cited this proposal as an example of a symbolic and aspirational amendment that cannot be reducible to binding legal principles and that is not sufficiently clear so as to avoid unanticipated consequences (Ruhl 1999, 254).

In 1970, the National Environmental Policy Act (NEPA) heralded an anticipated "environmental decade," in which environmental legislation and litigation both increased immensely (Winner 1982, 1). Congress has adopted most of this legislation under its authority to regulate interstate commerce. Judicial decisions In *United States v. Lopez* (1995) and *United States v. Morrison* (2000) have subjected congressional exercises of power under this clause to greater scrutiny. Mindful of the possible effects of such interpretations on future environmental regulations and also cognizant of criticisms that earlier proposed environmental quality amendments were largely aspirational in nature, Dan Gildon, a Berkeley law professor, has proposed an amendment empowering Congress to "preserve, protect, and promote the environment" (2005, 855). Gildor likens his proposal to the Sixteenth Amendment, which legitimized the national income tax. He believes his proposed amendment "would legitimize existing federal environmental laws," while freeing environmental legislation "from the shackles of economic considerations" (860), which stem from its current ties to the commerce clause. Continuing concerns over global warming and other potential environmental catastrophes could add to the impetus for such an amendment.

See also Jackson, Jesse L., Jr.; Sixteenth Amendment; Tonn, Bruce E.

For Further Reading:

Gildor, Dan L. 2005. "Preserving the Priceless: A Constitutional Amendment to Empower Congress to Preserve, Protect, and Promote the Environment." *Ecology Law Quarterly* 32: 821–861.

Hoban, Thomas M., and Richard O. Brooks. 1987. *Green Justice: The Environment and the Courts.* Boulder, CO: Westview Press.

Jackson, Jesse L., Jr., with Frank E. Watkins. 2001. *A More Perfect Union: Advancing New American Rights.* New York: Welcome Rain Publishers.

Rosenberg, Gerald N. 1991. *The Hollow Hope: Can Courts Bring about Social Change?* Chicago: University of Chicago Press.

Ruhl, J. B. 1999. "The Metrics of Constitutional Amendments: And Why Proposed Environmental Quality Amendments Don't Measure Up." *Notre Dame Law Review* 74 (January): 245–281.

Schlickeisen, Rodger. 1994. "Protecting Biodiversity for Future Generations: An Argument for a Constitutional Amendment." *Tulane Environmental Law Journal* 8 (Winter): 181–221.

"The Conservation Bill of Rights." *Congressional Record,* 90th Cong., 2d sess., 13 June 1968, Vol. 114, pt. 13: 17116–17117.

Tonn, Bruce E. 1991. "A Court of Generations: A Proposed Amendment to the U.S. Constitution." *Futures* 21: 413–431.

Wenner, Lettie M. 1982. *The Environmental Decade in Court.* Bloomington: Indiana University Press.

EQUAL RIGHTS AMENDMENT

Members of Congress have proposed the Equal Rights Amendment (ERA) more than any other. From its first introduction in 1923, three years after ratification of the Nineteenth Amendment, the amendment has been sponsored several hundred times.

Proposals in Congress

The first time Congress actually voted on the amendment was in 1946, when it garnered a 38 to 35 vote in the Senate. In 1950, the amendment achieved the needed two-thirds majority with a Senate vote of 65 to 19; in 1953, the Senate proposed it again by a vote of 73 to 11. In both the 1950 and the 1953 votes, the Senate accepted what was known as the Hayden rider, sponsored by Democratic senator Carl Hayden of Arizona. This rider provided that the amendment "shall not be construed to impair any rights, benefits, or exemptions now or hereafter conferred by law upon members of the female sex" (Boles 1979, 38). In 1970, a discharge petition effectively pried the amendment from the House Judiciary Committee, where Democratic chairman Emanuel Celler had previously kept it bottled up (Boles 1979, 38). That same year, a House majority of 252 to 15 approved the amendment with no riders. In 1972, the House again adopted the amendment, this time by a 354-to-24 vote, and the Senate followed suit in 1972 by a vote of 84 to 8 (Boles 1979, 13–16).

As finally approved, the Equal Rights Amendment contained a seven-year deadline in its authorizing resolution. Although the amendment came out of the congressional starting gate fast, at the end of seven years, it was still three states shy of the 38 needed for ratification. Accordingly, in 1979, the House voted 233 to 189 and the Senate 60 to 36 to extend the deadline until June 30, 1982 (Berry 1986, 70), but at the end of this time, no new states had ratified, and some of these had attempted to rescind their ratifications. In January 1983, the amendment was reintroduced in the House, but the 278-to-147 vote fell shy of the required two-thirds majority (Mansbridge 1986, 187). Subsequently, the amendment has not been voted on by either house.

Content of the ERA

The Equal Rights Amendment proposed by Congress had three sections. Its heart was Section 1, which provided simply that "equality of rights under the Law shall not be denied or abridged by the United States or by any State on account of sex." The second section invested enforcement power in Congress, and the third provided for a transitional period of two years after its ratification.

Debates over the ERA

Such differences in wording and proposed alterations indicate some of the tensions that surrounded the Equal Rights Amendment debate. When it was initially proposed, the National Woman's Party, a "militant" wing of the forces that had pushed for the Nineteenth Amendment (Boles 1979, 40), was one of the few organizations that actively supported the amendment. More moderate organizations such as the League of Women Voters opposed it. They had been working for protective legislation such as minimum wage and maximum hour legislation for women and feared that an equal rights amendment might be used to undermine such gains. Over time, many more groups joined the cause, but differences in emphasis remained, as did ambiguity about precisely what results the amendment would have.

Once proposed by Congress, the ERA was initially received quite positively; 21 of 32 legislatures in session in 1972 ratified with hardly any delays (Boles 1979, 61). In time, 35 of the needed 38 states would ratify, but by then, the anti-ERA forces had effectively mobilized, and some states that had given their approval attempted to rescind their ratifications. Conservative activist Phyllis Schlafly, founder of the Eagle Forum, appears to have been particularly successful with her Committee to Stop ERA, as was Senator Sam Ervin Jr. of North Carolina, a constitutional expert who achieved prominence during the Senate investigation of the Watergate scandal.

Judicial Decisions and the ERA

Ironically, progressive judicial decisions on behalf of women's rights may have undercut the impetus for the ERA (L. Goldstein 1987). In the 19th century, the Court had been unsympathetic to the issue. At just about the time that Congress proposed the ERA, however, the Court began to use the equal protection clause of the Fourteenth

Amendment to liberalize women's rights. In *Reed v. Reed* (1971), for example, a unanimous Court held that a state could not select the administrator of an estate on the basis that one candidate was a man and the other a woman. Similarly, in *Frontiero v. Richardson* (1973), the Court struck down a military law that presumed that married women depended on their husbands, who were thus automatically entitled to extra monetary allowances, but made women prove that their husbands were dependent on them. Perhaps more importantly, four of the justices declared that they considered gender to be a "suspect category," thus mandating the Court's most stringent level of scrutiny (the majority of the Court later settled on an intermediate standard for gender-based classifications). In the same year as *Frontiero,* the Court declared in *Roe v. Wade* that the right of privacy gave fairly broad leeway to women in obtaining abortions.

These decisions on behalf of women's rights enabled opponents of the ERA to argue that it was no longer needed. At the same time, the abortion decision enabled them to raise fears that the courts might expand interpretations of the amendment in unforeseen directions that might bring about greater changes in social relationships than many Americans, who were committed to equality in theory, actually wanted in practice (Mansbridge 1986). Some argue that a key reason the ERA failed to muster the required congressional majorities in 1983 stemmed from fears that it might require states to fund abortions (Craig and O'Brien 1993, 148). ERA supporters arguably played into the hands of such critics by suggesting, in their attempts to get the ERA adopted, that the amendment would bring about greater changes than it actually would have.

Yale law professor Reva B. Siegal (2005–2006) believes that, even though the ERA failed to be adopted, it nonetheless changed cultural understandings in a manner that supports these and other decisions that have expanded women's rights.

Controversies over the ERA Extension

As the seven-year ratification deadline approached, proponents asked for more time,

and in 1979, Congress extended the deadline for another three years. This led to controversy over whether the action was legal and whether the vote should have required a two-thirds majority (Freedman and Naughton 1978).

Lower courts addressed ERA issues in two cases, both of which challenged the idea, set forth in *Coleman v. Miller* (1939), that issues concerning the amending process were "political questions" inappropriate for judicial resolution. In *Dyer v. Blair* (1975), Judge—later Supreme Court Justice—John Paul Stevens ruled that the Illinois state legislature could require a three-fifths vote for ratification of the amendment. In *Idaho v. Freeman* (1981), Judge Marion Callister decided that Idaho had a right to rescind ratification of the ERA, that Congress had no power to extend the ERA deadline, and that, in any case, such a vote would have required a two-thirds majority. Although it was appealed to the Supreme Court, this case was mooted when the ERA failed to be ratified within the extension that Congress had granted.

Perhaps heartened by the belated ratification of the Twenty-seventh Amendment (which, however, had no designated ratification limit) in 1992, more than 200 years after it was first proposed by Congress, a number of representatives introduced a resolution in May 1995 requiring that the House of Representatives verify ratification of the Equal Rights Amendment if and when it received an additional three ratifications from the states. Indeed, Representative Robert E. Andrews of New Jersey and 22 cosponsors reintroduced this idea again in 2007. A number of scholars have weighed in on the matter. Supporters of such belated ratification processes, who generally rely on both what they consider to be the desirability of the ERA and on the Twenty-seventh Amendment precedent, have included Held (1997) and Baker (1999). Opponents, who focus chiefly on the two specified deadlines that have already gone unmet, on the ambiguity of what the amendment would do, and on attempts by states that have ratified to withdraw their ratifications, therefore undermining the idea that the amendment represents an ongoing consensus, have included Denning and Vile (2000).

A number of states have added equal rights amendments to their own constitutions (Gammie

1989). In the meantime, the U.S. Supreme Court continues to expand protections for women's rights. Ruth Bader Ginsburg, who had distinguished herself as a lawyer by defending women's rights before being appointed a judge and a justice, wrote the U.S. Supreme Court decision in *United States v. Virginia* (1996), declaring that gender classifications must be "exceedingly persuasive," and finding that Virginia's defense of its all-male Virginia Military Institute in Lexington, Virginia, failed to meet this standard and that the school was thus obligated to admit women if, as it chose, it continued to remain a state institution.

See also *Coleman v. Miller; Dyer v. Blair;* Ervin, Sam, Jr.; Fourteenth Amendment; *Idaho v. Freeman;* Nineteenth Amendment; Ratification of Amendments; Rescission of Ratification of Pending Amendments; Schlafly, Phyllis; Seneca Falls Convention; Twenty-seventh Amendment.

For Further Reading:

Baker, Debra. 1999. "The Fight Ain't Over," American Bar Association Journal 85 (August): 52.

Baldez, Lisa, Lee Epstein, and Andrew D. Martin. 2006. "Does the U.S. Constitution Need an Equal Rights Amendment?" *The Journal of Legal Studies* 35 (January): 243–283.

Boles, Janet K. 1979. *The Politics of the Equal Rights Amendment: Conflict and the Decision Process.* New York: Longman.

Craig, Barbara H., and David M. O'Brien. 1993. *Abortion and American Politics.* Chatham, NJ: Chatham House.

Critchlow, Donalt T., and Cuynthia L. Stachdei. 2008. "The Equal Rights Amendment Reconsidered: Politics, Policy, and Social Mobilization in a Democracy." *Journal of Policy History* 20: 156–176.

Denning, Brannon P., and John R. Vile. 2000. "Necromancing the Equal Rights Amendment." *Constitutional Commentary* 17 (Winter): 593–602.

Freedman, Samuel S., and Pamela J. Naughton. 1978. *ERA: May a State Change Its Vote?* Detroit, MI: Wayne State University Press.

Gammie, Beth. 1989. "State ERA's: Problems and Possibilities." *University of Illinois Law Review* 1989: 1123–1159.

Goldstein, Leslie F. 1987. "The ERA and the U.S. Supreme Court." In *Research in Law and Policy Studies,* ed. Stuart S. Nagel. Greenwich, CT: JAI.

Held, Allison L., Sheryl L. Herndon, and Danielle M. Stager. 1997. "The Equal Rights Amendment: Why the ERA Remains Legally Viable and Properly before the States." *William and Mary Journal of Women and Law* 3: 113.

Hoff-Wilson, Joan, ed. 1986. *Rights of Passage: The Past and Future of ERA.* Bloomington: Indiana University Press.

Mansbridge, Jane J. 1986. *Why We Lost the ERA.* Chicago: University of Chicago Press.

Siegal, Reva B. "Constitutional Culture, Social Movement Conflict and Constitutional Change: The Case of the de facto ERA." 2005–2006 Brennan Center Symposium Lecture. *California Law Review* 94 (October): 1323–1419.

EQUAL SUFFRAGE CLAUSE

Article V of the Constitution, the amending article, contains two entrenchment clauses. The first, protecting the right to import slaves for 20 years, has expired. The provision providing that "no State, without its Consent, shall be deprived of its equal Suffrage in the Senate" remains.

At the Constitutional Convention of 1787, one of the key compromises between the least and most populous states provided that the former be equally represented in the Senate, even as the House of Representatives was apportioned according to population. The equal suffrage clause poses a near insuperable obstacle to altering this arrangement. In *Dodge v. Woolsey* (1855), the Supreme Court referred to the clause as a "permanent and unalterable exception to the power of amendment" (348). Benjamin Lieber and Patrick Brown have called this provision an "Equal Protection Clause for states" (1995, 2366).

Lieber and Brown have further argued that the clause points to the unconstitutionality of rules adopted in the 104th Congress providing for a three-fifths vote to enact tax increases because it "implements a supermajority voting requirement on a substantive issue without requiring, as a condition of implementation, that a supermajority of the body approve of the rule" (2355). By contrast, they believe that Senate

Rule XXII, requiring a vote of 60 Senators to end debate, encourages, rather than forestalls debate and therefore does not violate the clause.

See also Constitutional Convention of 1787; *Dodge v. Woolsey;* Entrenchment Clauses.

For Further Reading:

Lieber, Benjamin, and Patrick Brown. 1995. "On Supermajorities and the Constitution." *Georgetown Law Journal* 83 (July): 2347–2384.

ERVIN, SAM J., JR. (1896–1985)

Sam J. Ervin Jr. of North Carolina served in the U.S. House of Representatives from 1946 to 1947 and in the Senate from 1954 to 1974. Ervin's most visible public role occurred when he chaired the Senate Watergate Committee, which held televised hearings about abuses in the Nixon administration. Although he had a law degree from Harvard, Ervin was known for his down-home country charm, and he was passionately devoted to the U.S. Constitution.

Ervin participated in a number of controversies involving the constitutional amending process. Perhaps most notably, in the wake of the attempt led by fellow Senator Everett Dirksen of Illinois to call a convention to overturn Supreme Court decisions involving state legislative apportionment, Ervin introduced legislation to govern such Article V conventions. Ervin did not believe that such a convention would have to be an open, or general, convention. He believed that Congress, faced with the necessary number of applications, had a mandatory obligation to call such a convention. Ervin believed that states should be able to rescind calls for such a convention prior to a two-thirds majority or to rescind amendment ratifications prior to a three-fourths majority. Ervin proposed that state requests for a convention should be valid for four years. As to representation at a convention, Ervin proposed that a delegate be selected from each congressional district, with two at-large delegates, bringing each state's representation to

its strength in the Electoral College. Although he originally advocated following the precedent of 1787 by giving each state delegation a single vote, he later modified this view, proposing to allow each delegate to vote individually (Ervin 1968; Kauper 1968). Ervin's legislation was not adopted, but it might still serve as a model if an Article V convention is ever convened.

Especially in the field of criminal justice, Ervin believed that the activist Warren Court had usurped the role of the amending process. He argued that there was a rather clear line between amending and interpreting the Constitution: "The power to amend is the power to change the meaning of the Constitution, and the power to interpret is the power of determining the meaning of the Constitution as established by the Founding Fathers" (Ervin 1984, 123).

As a senator, Ervin supported an amendment to permit voluntary confessions and limit federal habeas corpus review of criminal convictions. A strong proponent of separation of church and state, Ervin opposed the amendment that would have restored voluntary prayer in public schools (Ervin 1984, 237–248). Ervin also opposed the Equal Rights Amendment. He proposed revisions that would have allowed laws that protected women, kept child-support laws in force, protected personal privacy, maintained existing definitions of sexual offenses, recognized physiological and functional differences between males and females, and exempted women from military service (Ervin 1984, 265–266).

Summarizing his view of the sanctity of the Constitution, Ervin observed:

> Constitutional amendments are "for keeps." Unlike ordinary laws, they cannot be easily repealed. Once adopted, they can be removed from the Constitution only by means of the amendatory process created by Article V. . . . Congress and the States should act cautiously, advisedly, soberly, and without emotion when they are asked to add an amendment to the Constitution. They should never adopt an amendment unless it is calculated as well as intended to promote the general welfare of the United States (Ervin 1984, 273).

See also Confessions; Constitutional Conventions; Equal Rights Amendment; Prayer in Schools.

For Further Reading:

Ervin, Sam J., Jr. 1984. *Preserving the Constitution: The Autobiography of Sam J. Ervin Jr.* Charlottesville, VA: Michie.

Ervin, Sam J., Jr. 1968. "Proposed Legislation to Implement the Convention Method of Amending the Constitution." *Michigan Law Review* 66 (March): 875–902.

Kauper, Paul G. 1968. "The Alternate Amending Process: Some Observations." *Michigan Law Review* 66 (March): 903–920.

EXECUTIVE OFFICES, EXCLUSION FROM

The president selects executive branch officials, including members of the cabinet, with the advice and consent of the Senate. The original Virginia Plan that was introduced at the Constitutional Convention of 1787 included a provision specifying that members of Congress would be ineligible for appointments to the executive or judicial branches, but this disqualification was later applied only to offices that were created or whose salaries were increased during the term of a legislator (Sundquist 1986, 37–38). In contrast to many parliamentary systems where individuals may serve in both the legislative and executive branches, the U.S. Constitution specifies that members of Congress appointed to other offices must resign their seats, but they are, in such circumstances, permitted to accept cabinet or other posts.

Especially in the nation's first 100 years, members of Congress introduced numerous amending resolutions to minimize risks that governmental offices would be awarded simply as political favors. Proposals included exclusion of general contractors, members of Congress, relatives of members of Congress, officeholders in general, and individuals who had served as representatives in the Electoral College. Periodically, proposals also surfaced to elect postmasters, district attorneys, and other federal functionaries.

Many proposals were introduced after the presidential election of 1824. In that election, there were four candidates: Andrew Jackson, John Quincy Adams, William Crawford, and Henry Clay. None received the majority of electoral votes necessary for election, and under the terms of the Twelfth Amendment, the House of Representatives had to choose among the top three candidates. Although he had come in last in the balloting, Henry Clay had considerable influence in the House of Representatives, where he was Speaker. He used this influence to support John Quincy Adams, who won on the first ballot, despite the fact that he had received fewer popular and electoral votes than Jackson.

Jackson and his followers were furious when, three days after Adams's selection, he appointed Clay as his secretary of state. Jackson charged that a "corrupt bargain" had been struck (Boller 1984, 35–37). In his first annual message after being elected president in 1828, Jackson proposed reforming the Electoral College system to exclude members of the House who had participated in presidential selection from executive offices (J. Richardson 1908, 2:448).

See also Cabinet; Electoral College; Twelfth Amendment.

For Further Reading:

Boller, Paul E., Jr. 1984. *Presidential Campaigns.* New York: Oxford University Press.

Richardson, James E., ed. 1908. *A Compilation of the Messages and Papers of the Presidents, 1789–1908.* 11 vols. n.p.: Bureau of National Literature and Art.

Sundquist, James L. 1986. *Constitutional Reform and Effective Government.* Washington DC: Brookings Institution.

EXTRACONSTITUTIONAL MEANS OF CHANGE

Since the U.S. Constitution was ratified in 1789, it has been formally amended only 27 times. In part, the paucity of amendments stems from the fact that the U.S. Constitution is a relatively brief document that deals primarily with matters of governmental structure rather than with day-to-day policies (Lutz 1994, 357). A contemporary scholar has also hypothesized that "a low amendment rate associated with a long average constitutional duration strongly implies the use of some alternate means of revision to supplement the formal amendment process" (Lutz 1994, 358).

In the United States, it is not always easy to decide which issues are "constitutional" and which are not. Some changes can be made only by constitutional amendments, whereas others may or may not require such amendments, largely depending on the attitude of those who occupy the government. Judicial decisions, especially those by the Supreme Court, have a major impact on constitutional interpretation. Laws and executive orders can also modify constitutional understandings and practices. The constitutional amending process, the legislative process, and executive orders each have advantages and disadvantages and often act synergistically (Vile 1994a, 111).

Two contemporary scholars have directed renewed attention to extraconstitutional changes. Focusing on the founding period, the Civil War, and the New Deal—the last of which was implemented without the use of any constitutional amendments—Bruce Ackerman has argued that periods of "higher lawmaking" may be effected by actions taken by the political branches that are later codified by the Supreme Court (Ackerman 1991, 266–267).

Working from the premise of popular sovereignty, Akhil Reed Amar has argued that an Article V convention could specify that its proposals be ratified by a majority of the people. Alternatively, in a position that is very close to that advocated by supporters of a referendum amendment, Amar has argued "that Congress would be constitutionally obliged to convene a proposing convention, if a bare majority of American voters so petitioned Congress" (Amar 1988, 1065; for critique, see Vile 1990–1991; also see Torke 1994).

Partly because of the role that extraconstitutional changes have played in U.S. constitutional history, a scholar has published an article that questions the continuing "relevancy" of the constitutional amending process (Strauss 2001). Formal constitutional amendments can, however, reverse constitutional changes, including judicial decisions, that have grown up outside the Constitution (Denning and Vile, 2002–2003), and the rate at which members of Congress continue to propose amendments suggests that they believe such amendments are important.

David Orentlicher of the Indiana University School of Law has argued that extraconstitutional means of change might be especially appropriate in cases where existing actors face potential conflicts of interest. He suggests that it might be particularly difficult to get members of Congress to support term limits or campaign finance reform through existing mechanisms in Article V.

See also Ackerman, Bruce; Amar, Akhil Reed.

For Further Reading:

Ackerman, Bruce. 1991. *We the People: Foundations.* Cambridge, MA: Belknap.

Amar, Akhil Reed. 1988. "Philadelphia Revisited: Amending the Constitution outside Article V." *University of Chicago Law Review* 55 (Fall): 1043–1104.

Denning, Brannon P., and John R. Vile. 2002. "The Relevance of Constitutional Amendments: A Response to David Strauss." *Tulane Law Review* 77 (November): 247–282.

Lutz, Donald S. 1994. "Toward a Theory of Constitutional Amendment." *American Political Science Review* 88 (June): 355–370.

Orentlicher, David. 2002. "Conflicts of Interest and the Constitution." *Washington and Lee Law Review* 59 (Summer): 713–766.

Strauss, David A. 2001. "Commentary: The Irrelevance of Constitutional Amendments." *Harvard Law Review* 114 (March): 1457–1505.

Torke, James W. 1994. "Assessing the Ackerman and Amar Theses: Notes on Extratextual Constitutional Change." *Widener Journal of Public Law* 4: 229–271.

Vile, John R. 1994. *Constitutional Change in the United States: A Comparative Study of the Role of Constitutional Amendments, Judicial Interpretations, and Legislative and Executive Actions.* Westport, CT: Praeger.

———. 1990–1991. "Legally Amending the United States Constitution: The Exclusivity of Article V's Mechanisms." *Cumberland Law Review* 21: 271–307.

FAILED AMENDMENTS

Only six of the 33 amendments that Congress has proposed by the necessary two-thirds majorities have subsequently failed to be ratified by three-fourths of the states (Keller 1987; for texts, see Anastaplo 1989, 298–299).

The Bill of Rights that Congress proposed in its first session originally contained 12 amendments. The second became the Twenty-seventh Amendment when it was ratified in 1992. By contrast, states never ratified the first proposal, dealing with the size of Congress and the ratio of representation to population.

Two amendments proposed by the required congressional majorities in the 19th century failed to be adopted. In 1810, the so-called Reed Amendment, or Phantom Amendment, was introduced to strip citizenship from individuals who accepted titles of nobility from foreign governments. Although it was mistakenly printed in one edition of the U.S. Statutes as though it had been ratified, this amendment actually fell two states short of such ratification, before the entry of additional states made the margin even wider. The Corwin Amendment, proposed in 1861 on the eve of the Civil War, made far less progress. It attempted to reassure the South to stay in the Union by prohibiting future amendments that might interfere with slavery. There was at least one proposal introduced in Congress to repeal this amendment, which, of course, became a nullity with the adoption of the Thirteenth Amendment.

Congress proposed three amendments in the 20th century that the states failed to ratify. One was the Child Labor Amendment proposed in 1924; decisions by the Supreme Court now permit the kind of restrictions of child labor that this amendment was designed to approve. A second was the Equal Rights Amendment for women; many of its objectives have also been achieved through legislation and judicial decision-making giving stricter scrutiny to sex-based classifications. The third such proposal, adopted by Congress in 1978, would have treated the District of Columbia as a state for purposes of congressional representation, presidential and vice presidential selection, and the amending process; the goals of this amendment remain unfulfilled.

The Equal Rights Amendment contained a ratification deadline, subsequently extended, in the congressional authorizing resolution but not in the text; the amendment dealing with representation for the District of Columbia had an internal deadline of seven years. Although none of the other amendments had internal deadlines, none presently appear to be a likely candidate for an attempt at ratification similar to the one that resulted in the Twenty-seventh Amendment.

See also Child Labor Amendment; Congress, Size of; Corwin Amendment; District of Columbia, Representation for; Equal Rights Amendment; Titles of Nobility; Twenty-seventh Amendment.

For Further Reading:

Anastaplo, George. 1995. *The Amendments to the Constitution: A Commentary.* Baltimore: Johns Hopkins University Press.

Keller, Morton. 1987. "Failed Amendments to the Constitution." *The World & I* 9 (September): 87–97.

Lynch, Michael J. 2001. "The Other Amendments: Constitutional Amendments That Failed." *Law Library Journal* 92 (Spring): 303–310.

FAIR CONSTRUCTION AMENDMENT

Karl Spence, a journalist from San Antonio, has written a book and created a Web site advocating what he calls a Fair Construction Amendment. The purpose of the amendment is to reign in what Spence believes to be an "imperial judiciary" that has substituted its judgments for those of the Founding Fathers. By contrast, Spence cites Chief Justice John Marshall's dictum that "There is a fair construction which gives to language the sense in which it is used, and interprets an instrument according to its true intention."

Spence is particularly upset with decisions that have expanded the rights of criminal defendants, questioned the constitutionality of the death penalty, expanded protections for pornography, sanctioned reverse discrimination, provided constitutional protections for abortion, and the like. He thinks it unlikely that even judges who are appointed as strict constructionists will be able to resist "the temptation to 'grow' into the liberal establishment's good graces and cross over to the activist side" (www.fairamendment.us).

Spence has proposed an amendment of five sections, which he includes on his Web site. The first section provides that "The Judiciary of the United States shall not presume to exercise nonjudicial power." His hope is to elevate the written words over judicial interpretations. Section 1 continues:

> This Constitution is changed only by an explicit and authentic act of the whole people. The sense in which it was accepted and ratified by the nation shall be the guide in expounding it, precedents to the contrary notwithstanding. Its provisions are neither to be restricted into insignificance nor extended beyond the natural and obvious meaning contem-

plated by the plain understanding of the people at the time of its adoption. Any faults it may contain are to be corrected by amendment as prescribed in Article V, not by usurpation.

Section 2 further specifies impeachment as a method of enforcement.

Section 2 recognizes the importance of judicial interpretations relative to the rights of equal protection. It provides that "No one in the United States shall be either subject to or entitled to discrimination in education, employment, housing, or public accommodations on account of race."

Section 3 provides that "The provisions of this Constitution's first article of amendment shall apply to the states as well as to the United States"; he does not think that the founders intended for the amendment to protect libel and pornography. He thus adds that "in every other respect, they shall be expounded according to the rules set forth in Section 1 of this article."

By contrast, Section 4 provides that in order "that the perpetrators of violent crimes may meet with swift and certain retribution, the courts' effort to protect them in their rights shall not be perverted into permitting any mere technicality to avert or delay their punishment."

Section 5 further provides for congressional enforcement. In his book, Spence indicates that he does not believe that returning to "original" intent will mean that courts always have to interpret the Constitution as "literal" (181).

See also Marshall, John.

For Further Reading:

Spence, Karl. 2006. *Yo! Liberals! You Call This Progress?: Crime, Race, Sex, Faith, Law and the Culture War.* Converse, TX: Fielding Press. www.fairamendment.us.

FAIRCHILD V. HUGHES (1922)

In this companion case to *Leser v. Garnett* (1922), the Supreme Court rejected a challenge to the constitutionality of the Nineteenth

Amendment by a plaintiff taxpayer and member of the American Constitutional League. The Court declared that a general citizen, in this case one who was not an elected official and who resided in a state (New York) where women already had the right to vote, had no standing "to secure by indirection a determination whether a statute if passed, or a constitutional amendment about to be adopted, will be valid" (*Fairchild* 1922, 130).

See also *Leser v. Garnett;* Nineteenth Amendment.

For Further Reading:
Fairchild v. Hughes, 258 U.S. 126 (1922).

FAIRMAN, CHARLES (1897–1988)

In *Adamson v. California* (1947) and subsequent cases, Justice Hugo L. Black cited speeches by John Bingham and other supporters of the Fourteenth Amendment to argue that they had intended to overturn *Barron v. Baltimore* (1833) and incorporate all the provisions of the Bill of Rights and apply them to the states.

Fairman, a professor of law and political science at Stanford University, authored a seminal article designed to refute Black's view. Fairman drew on evidence from records of congressional debates over the Fourteenth Amendment and contemporary civil rights legislation, as well as from debates in the states over ratification of this amendment, observations about contemporary state constitutions, and judicial interpretations contemporary with the amendment's ratification (Fairman 1949). Arguing that contemporaries had not been as clear about their intention as Black attempted to portray them, Fairman ultimately concluded that Benjamin Cardozo's interpretation of the due process clause of the Fourteenth Amendment in *Palko v. Connecticut* (1937) came close to the framers' understanding of the privileges and immunities clause. In that case, Cardozo had argued that the due process clause was designed to protect only those provisions

of the Bill of Rights "implicit in the concept of ordered liberty," a view often labeled "selective incorporation."

Fairman's study, like Black's own thesis, continues to be the subject of lively scholarly debate (see Yarbrough 1988; Curtis 1986; Morrison 1949). Over the course of time, the U.S. Supreme Court has incorporated most, but not all, provisions of the Bill of Rights into the Fourteenth Amendment.

See also *Adamson v. California; Barron v. Baltimore;* Bill of Rights; Bingham, John A.; Black, Hugo LaFayette; Fourteenth Amendment; Incorporation; *Palko v. California.*

For Further Reading:
Curtis, Michael K. 1986. *No State Shall Abridge: The Fourteenth Amendment and the Bill of Rights.* Durham, NC: Duke University Press.

Fairman, Charles. 1949. "Does the Fourteenth Amendment Incorporate the Bill of Rights? The Original Understanding." *Stanford Law Review* 2 (December): 5–139.

Morrison, Stanley. 1949. "Does the Fourteenth Amendment Incorporate the Bill of Rights? The Judicial Interpretation." *Stanford Law Review* 2 (December): 140–173.

Yarbrough, Tinsley E. 1988. *Mr. Justice Black and His Critics.* Durham, NC: Duke University Press.

FAMILIES

See Federal Marriage Protection Amendment; Marriage and Divorce Laws.

FEDERAL MARRIAGE PROTECTION AMENDMENT

States have traditionally regulated marriage and family matters through the police powers that they exercise under the Tenth Amendment. Most states have, in turn, relied on definitions of marriage that originated in English common law (which was largely derived from judicial precedents) and involved monogamous relationships between a man and a woman.

This consensus was challenged in the 19th century by polygamists, typically associated with the early Mormon Church. Federal courts permitted prosecution of polygamous relationships, the Mormon Church reversed course, and the adoption of state and federal laws opposing polygamy undercut the movement for constitutional amendments. Prosecutors sometimes applied the Mann Act, also known as the White Slave Act, which Congress adopted chiefly to prevent interstate "white slavery," or prostitution, to individuals engaged in polygamous relationships (Langum 1994).

Members of Congress proposed three amendments in the late 19th and early 20th centuries to prevent interracial marriages. Although courts initially upheld such laws, in time, the U.S. Supreme Court decided in *Loving v. Virginia* (1967) that they violated the equal protection clause of the Fourteenth Amendment.

Between 1884 and 1906, members of congress proposed 30 amendments that Cardozo law professor Edward Stein calls "jurisdictional amendments," relative to marriage and designed to provide for uniformity among states relative to marriage and divorce. Both amendments and federal legislation were stymied by disputes between conservatives and liberals as to whether divorce laws should be relaxed or stiffened (Stein 2004, 634–640).

In addition to *Loving,* however, other Supreme Court decisions have subsequently also affected state laws relative to marriage, family, and sexuality. In *Griswold v. Connecticut* (1965), the Court recognized a constitutional right to privacy in invalidating a state law that limited birth control, and in *Eisenstad v. Baird* (1972), it extended similar protection to unmarried individuals. *Roe v. Wade* (1973) struck down most laws restricting access to abortion, and *Zablocki v. Redtail* (1978) struck down a state law forbidding a noncustodial parent who was delinquent in child support from remarrying. In *Bowers v. Hardwick* (1986), the Supreme Court upheld a Georgia law that was applied to consensual acts of sodomy, but in *Romer v. Evans* (1996), it struck down an amendment that voters had added to the Colorado state constitu-

tion that would have prohibited the government from acting to protect individuals based on their sexual orientation or lifestyle, and in *Lawrence v. Texas* (2003), it reversed its decision in *Bowers.* Dissenting in the latter two cases, Justice Antonin Scalia argued that the Court was unnecessarily involving itself in modern cultural wars.

Such conflicts are now playing out over the issue of same-sex marriage. Shortly after some gay rights advocates began to press for legal recognition of same-sex marriage, in *Baker v. Nelson,* 409 U.S. 810 (1972), the U.S. Supreme Court dismissed a challenge to Minnesota's marriage law "for want of a substantial federal question." This did not prevent subsequent state cases. In 1994, the Hawaii Supreme court decided in *Baehr v. Miike,* 852 P.2d 44, that prohibitions on same-sex marriage violated the state's equal rights amendment. Although state voters subsequently changed the state constitution to overturn this interpretation (George 2001, 33), the case created fears that other states might have to accept the validity of such unions. Congress accordingly adopted the Defense of Marriage Act (DOMA) in 1996. Defining marriage under federal law as the union of a male and a female, the law, adopted under a perceived congressional authority to make exceptions under the full faith and credit clause, prevents states from having to recognize same-sex marriages performed in other states.

In the meantime, the Vermont Supreme Court ruled in *Baker v. State,* 744 A.2d 864 (Vt. 1999), that the state would have to extend rights, albeit not the designation of marriage, to same-sex couples. Similarly, the Supreme Court of Massachusetts ruled in *Goodridge v. Department of Public Health,* 798 N.E. 2d 941 (Mass 2003), and the California Supreme Court ruled in the *In Re Marriages Cases* (2008), that their states would have to recognize gay marriage. Although state voters overturned the California ruling in the 2008 elections, this and other rulings continue to stimulate proposed federal constitutional amendments.

Supported by a broad-based group known as the Alliance for Marriage that is headed by Matt Daniels, who lists a J.D. from the University of Pennsylvania and a PhD from Brandeis University, Democratic Representative Ronnie Shows of Mississippi introduced the first Federal Marriage Protection Amendment in May 2002. Supported by five co-sponsors, it provided that "Marriage in the United States shall consist only of the union of a man and a woman. Neither this Constitution or the constitution of any State, nor state or federal laws, shall be construed to require that marital status or the legal incidents thereof be conferred upon unmarried couples or groups" (Quoted in Wardle 2006, 442). The amendment was introduced the following year by Republican Marilyn Musgrave of Colorado. The original five so-sponsors swelled to more than 125 after the U.S. Supreme Court decision in *Lawrence v. Texas* and the Massachusetts Supreme Court decision in *Goodridge v. Department of Public Health,* and Republican senator Wayne Allard introduced a similar resolution in the upper house (Wardle 2006, 443).

After hearings in 2004, another version of the amendment was proposed that altered the second sentence to read, "Neither this Constitution, nor the constitution of any State, shall be construed to require that marriage or the legal incidents thereof be conferred upon any union other than the union of a man and a woman." President George W. Bush supported the amendment, but the Senate failed by a vote of 48 to 50 (60 votes were needed) to invoke cloture on the rule, and the House of Representatives supported it by a vote of 227 to 186, which still fell short of the two-thirds needed (Wardle 2006, 444). There were similar results in another congressional vote on this amendment in 2006, when the House voted 236 to 187 for this amendment, and the Senate voted 49 to 48 for it. By contrast, as of 2007, 45 states had enacted some kind of ban on gay marriages, and six of seven states that voted on the matter in the 2006 elections voted affirmatively (Wilson 2007, 568).

Members of Congress have introduced several subsequent versions of this amendment. Thus, in 2005, California Republican representative Daniel Lungren introduced an amendment, the second section of which provided that "No court of the United States or of any States shall have jurisdiction to determine whether this Constitution or the constitution of any State requires that the legal Incidents of marriage be conferred upon any union other than a legal union between one man and one woman." A third section reads like a state DOMA, in that it prevents the states from having "to give effect" to any such laws of another state. Senator Sam Brownback of Kansas proposed a simpler version, which simply added a second section, similar to provisions that have appeared in the Thirteenth Amendment and in some that have followed, to grant Congress power to enforce the definition of marriage as the union of one man and one woman "by appropriate legislation" (Wardle 2006, 445–446).

Supporters of proposed amendments have variously argued that they are needed to preserve morality and the traditional family and to protect children. Some further argue that the amendment is consistent with provisions in other national constitutions and will help to reign in activist judicial decisions and preserve federalism (Wardle 2007).

Supporters of a Federal Marriage Amendment have sometimes disagreed over whether an amendment should allow states to permit domestic partnerships or civil unions that are not classified as marriages. Then magazine reporter Tim Graham noted that some defenders of traditional marriage "argue that if you preserve the word marriage for its traditional definition, but allow 'civil unions' that accomplish a similar objective, what have you won?" Ken Connor of the Family Research Council has thus observed that "If you back a counterfeit solution, it depreciates the value of the real things" (Graham 2002, 17).

Opponents of the amendment, in addition to expressing fears that an amendment might, in fact, erode health care benefits and other rights that states have given to same-sex couples, argued that the amendment is discriminatory, unnecessary, or would erode the rights that states now have to decide this issue for themselves. Some have also argued that attempts to define marriage are attempts to incorporate a religious definition of marriage into the Constitution, which they think the establishment clause of the First Amendment should otherwise forbid (Wilson 2007).

See also First Amendment; Fourteenth Amendment; *Griswold v. Connecticut;* Intermarriage; Polygamy; Tenth Amendment.

For Further Reading:

George, Robert P. 2001. "The 28th Amendment: It Is Time to Protect Marriage and Democracy in America." *National Review* 53 (July 23): 32–34.

Graham, Tim. 2002. "Preenuptial Disagreement." *World* 17 (June 8): 14–18.

Langum, David J. 1004. *Crossing Over the Line: Legislating Morality and the Mann Act.* Chicago: University of Chicago Press.

Stein, Edward. 2004. "Past and Present Proposed Amendments to the United States Constitution Regarding Marriage." *Washington University Law Quarterly* 82 (Fall): 611–685.

Wardle, Lynn D. 2007. "Lessons from the Bill of Rights about Constitutional Protection for Marriage." *Loyola University Chicago Law Review* 38 (Winter): 279–322.

Wardle, Lynn D. 2006. "Federal Constitutional Protection for Marriage: Why and How." *Brigham Young University Journal of Public Law* 20: 439–485.

Wilson, Justin T. 2007. "Preservationism, or the Elephant in the Room: How Opponents of Same-Sex Marriage Deceive Us into Establishing Religion." *Duke Journal of Gender Law & Policy* 14 (January): 561–679.

FEDERALISM AND THE AMENDING PROCESS

Before it became a nation, the United States started out as 13 colonies. These colonies retained many of their powers under the Articles of Confederation. Supermajorities of nine of 13 states were required under that system for Congress to adopt most important pieces of legislation. Constitutional amendments required the unanimous consent of the states. Although the sizes of their delegations varied, states had an equal vote in the Confederation Congress. Aside from Rhode Island, which chose not to send any delegates, states were equally represented at the Constitutional Convention of 1787.

At the Convention, the delegates replaced the existing confederal system with a federal system that strengthened the powers of the national government without eliminating the states (which would have resulted in a unitary government). Under this system, both state and national governments have their own constitution and can operate directly on their own citizens. The Convention provided that states would be represented according to population in the House of Representatives and equally in the U.S. Senate.

Article IV of the U.S. Constitution provides various protections for the states. It also lists their obligations to one another. The Tenth Amendment soon thereafter provided that powers not delegated to the national government would be reserved to the states. The Eleventh Amendment strengthened the states by seeming to recognize the doctrine of state sovereign immunity.

By contrast, the Fourteenth Amendment secured various rights against state abridgement and eventually became the means by which the U.S. Supreme Court applied most of the provisions in the Bill of Rights to limit the states. Similarly, the Seventeenth Amendment, while democratizing the process by which U.S. senators were selected, undercut federalism by making senators more accountable to the needs of their individual constituents than to the states as political and geographical entities.

Still, the original design at the Constitutional Convention continues to have a major effect on the amending process. Article V specifies that two-thirds majorities of both houses of Congress are required to propose amendments, or, in an alternate method never used to date, two-thirds of the states can petition Congress to call a constitutional convention. Such proposals do not become part of the Constitution unless three-fourths of the states ratify them. Article VII of the new Constitution did not follow the Articles of Confederation in requiring unanimous consent, but it did specify that the new Constitution would not go into effect until nine or more states ratified it, and no states would be bound in the new union until they consented to join.

The Article V requirements related to the constitutional amendment process implicate federalism in a number of ways. By requiring supermajorities in both the proposal and ratification phases, the process gives groups of states, or their representatives in the Senate, the power to block amendments that they do not favor.

Thus, it is unlikely that amendments will be adopted that go against the interest of more than one-fourth of the states, whether they be large or small. If the states in opposition are small ones, this effectively means that a small percentage of the population could thwart amendments that a much larger majority favors. Similarly, a relatively small number of states with the majority of the nation's population might be unable to get amendments that their citizens favor adopted.

All kinds of mathematical models can and have been constructed to estimate what percentage of the population could, under the most adverse circumstances, conceivably block an amendment, but such models rarely play out in the real world, where states often find themselves bound together, or divided by, interests other than size (Livingston 1956, 242). Still, many of the elements (most notably equal state representation in the U.S. Senate) that ensure that Congress does not operate completely according to democratic principles also ensure that the amending process is not altogether democratic.

The supermajorities required in both stages of the amending process enhance the likelihood that amendments that are adopted will have a broad national consensus. The two-step process is further designed to promote deliberation in more than one forum. Some proposed changes in the amending process, most notably those that call for the adoption of constitutional amendments through a referendum process, could significantly diminish the current effects that the federal structure has on this process, although some such proposals would require ratification by a majority or more of the voters in a majority of the states. States often seek to protect what they consider to be their prerogatives through proposed amendments. The proposal to overturn the Supreme Court's reapportionment decisions in the 1960s, although ultimately unsuccessful, is one such example.

See also Articles of Confederation; Consensus and the Amending Process; Constitutional Convention of 1787; Deliberation and the Amending Process; Eleventh Amendment; Entrenchment Clauses; Fourteenth Amendment; Initiative and Referendum; Seventeenth Amendment; Supermajorities; Tenth Amendment.

For Further Reading:

Aroney, Nocholas. 2006. "Formation, Representation and Amendment in Federal Constitutions." *American Journal of Comparative Law* 54 (Spring): 277–336.

Ishikawa, Brendon T. 1996. "Toward a More Perfect Union: The Role of Amending Formulae in the United States, Canadian, and German Constitutional Experiences." *Journal of International Law & Policy* 2 (Spring): 267–294.

Livingston, William S. 1956. *Federalism and Constitutional Change.* Oxford, UK: Clarendon Press.

FEDERALIST PAPERS

See Federalists.

FEDERALISTS

Soon after Congress forwarded the U.S. Constitution from the Constitutional Convention to the states for ratification, the nation split into two camps. Those who supported the document called themselves Federalists and designated their opponents as Anti-Federalists. The respective sides argued their cases in the state ratifying conventions that subsequently approved the new constitution (see Gillespie and Lienesch 1989). The most famous product of the Federalist/Anti-Federalist debates was a series of articles defending the Constitution that were initially published in a New York newspaper and shortly thereafter collected in a book known as *The Federalist Papers.* Alexander Hamilton, James Madison, and John Jay authored these essays under the pen name of Publius. A number of their essays addressed issues related to the constitutional amending process (Vile 1992, 34–41).

Federalist No. 40 was devoted primarily to demonstrating that the authors of the Constitution were justified in proposing a new constitution. Although admitting that the original purpose of the Constitutional Convention had been to revise the Articles of Confederation rather than to propose a new government, Madison noted that the delegates had also been commissioned to make such alterations as were necessary "to render the Constitution of the federal government adequate to the exigencies of the Union" (Hamilton, Madison, and Jay 1961, 247). Such a goal, he argued, had proved impossible to achieve by mere revisions, and the delegates had therefore pursued their higher duty, subject to approval or disapproval by the people.

In *Federalist Nos. 39* and *43,* Madison defended the amending process as a moderate mechanism. *Federalist No. 39* noted that the amending mechanism is "neither wholly federal nor wholly national" (246). Similarly, *Federalist No. 43* argued that the amending mechanism "guards equally against that extreme facility, which would render the Constitution too mutable, and that extreme difficulty, which might perpetuate its discovered faults" (278). Madison further defended the mechanism for allowing either the states or the national government "to originate the amendment of errors" (278).

In *Federalist Nos. 49* and *50,* Madison explained why the Constitution did not embody two contemporary amending proposals. In the first essay, Madison critiqued a proposal that Thomas Jefferson had advanced in his *Notes on the State of Virginia* (Jefferson 1964, 204–205), whereby two branches of government could call a constitutional convention. Madison objected that frequent conventions would prove destabilizing and would undermine faith in the document. He also believed that such conventions would stir popular passions and would aggrandize the legislative branch, whose members would be more numerous and better connected within the population. In *Federalist No. 50,* Madison further opposed Pennsylvania's scheme for periodic reviews of the Constitution by a council of censors. His discussion leads into the defense of separation of powers that is found in the subsequent and better-known essay.

A key Anti-Federalist objection to the Constitution was the absence of a bill of rights. Hamilton addressed this issue in *No. 84,* the penultimate *Federalist* essay. Arguing that such a bill of rights was unnecessary and might even prove dangerous, Hamilton argued in the final essay that a second convention would be unwise and that amendment would be much easier and more prudent after adoption of the new Constitution.

Faced with increasing calls for a bill of rights and frightened by the prospect that a second convention might undo the work of the first (Levinson 1990b; Weber 1989; Lash 1994), key Federalists agreed to push for a bill of rights once the Constitution was ratified. James Madison subsequently led the fight in the First Congress for what became the first 10 amendments to the Constitution.

Opposition to the Constitution dissipated relatively soon after its ratification. Almost everyone supported the new constitution, but newly created political parties quickly divided on how the new document should be interpreted. One of the first two political parties, organized largely by Alexander Hamilton and advocating strong powers for the national government, subsequently took the Federalist label. James Madison, by contrast, identified with the Democratic-Republican Party that he and Thomas Jefferson organized and that (echoing many of the themes of the original Anti-Federalists) was more suspicious of national power.

See also Anti-Federalists; Bill of Rights; Council of Censors; Federalism and the Amending Process; Hamilton, Alexander; Jefferson, Thomas; Madison, James.

For Further Reading:

Gillespie, Michael L., and Michael Lienesch, eds. 1989. *Ratifying the Constitution.* Lawrence: University Press of Kansas.

Hamilton, Alexander, James Madison, and John Jay. 1787–1788. *The Federalist Papers.* Reprint, New York: New American Library, 1961.

Jefferson, Thomas. 1861. *Notes on the State of Virginia.* New York: Darby. Originally published as part of Vol. VIII of *The Writings of Thomas Jefferson,* ed. H. A. Washington. Reprint, New York: Harper and Row, 1964.

Lash, Kurt T. 1994. "Rejecting Conventional Wisdom: Federalist Ambivalence in the Framing and Implementation of Article V." *American Journal of Legal History* 38 (April): 197–231.

Levinson, Sanford. 1990. "'Veneration' and Constitutional Change: James Madison Confronts the Possibility of Constitutional Amendment." *Texas Tech Law Review* 21: 2443–2461.

Meyerson, Michael. 2008. *Liberty's Blueprint: How Madison and Hamilton Wrote the Federalist, Defined the Constitution, and Made Democracy Safe for the World.* New York: Basic Books.

Vile, John R. 1992. *The Constitutional Amending Process in American Political Thought.* New York: Praeger.

Weber, Paul. 1989. "Madison's Opposition to a Second Convention." *Polity* 20 (Spring): 498–517.

Wills, Garry. 1981. *Explaining America: The Federalist.* Garden City, NY: Doubleday.

FIFTEENTH AMENDMENT

Before the adoption of the Fifteenth Amendment, the matter of suffrage was purely a matter for the states. Once the Fifteenth Amendment prohibited deprivation of voting rights on the basis of "race, color, or previous condition of servitude," however, a number of other amendments—most notably the Nineteenth and Twenty-sixth—have protected the franchise.

The first resolutions in Congress on African American suffrage were introduced in 1860 and 1861 as a way of averting war. In contrast to amendments that would be introduced after the Civil War, these amendments would have excluded blacks from voting or holding office. One of the supporters of such an amendment was Democratic senator Stephen A. Douglas of Illinois, who had participated in the famous Lincoln-Douglas debates.

After the war, there was considerable, albeit far from universal, sentiment among Republicans to guarantee that the franchise would not be denied on the basis of race. In addition to racist sentiment, there were also concerns that a national guarantee of voting rights would erode the American scheme of federalism. Largely as the result of compromise, Section 2 of the Fourteenth Amendment did not actually forbid disenfranchisement of blacks, but it did give Congress the right to reduce representation in states that did so. This provision was never enforced.

After ratification of the Fourteenth Amendment in 1868, there was continuing concern about voting rights for African Americans. Idealistic principles mixed with more partisan Republican concerns that the black vote might be crucial to the party's continuing electoral success. Congress adopted laws granting suffrage to blacks in the District of Columbia and in the federal territories, and it conditioned the admission of Nebraska into the Union and the seating of Southern state congressional delegates on those states' extending the right to vote to African Americans. Ironically, this legislation left the Northern and border states as the only ones in which such suffrage had not been so guaranteed (U.S. Senate 1985, 36).

Radical Republicans preferred the statutory route, because they wanted to assert congressional power over the area of voting rights; more moderate Republicans feared that rights obtained via legislation would lack the security that an amendment could provide (Maltz 1990, 146). Republican electoral victories in the 1868 elections gave special impetus to such efforts, which probably could not have been enacted under other circumstances.

The debates over the Fifteenth Amendment became quite complex. In the House, the original proposal introduced by Massachusetts Republican George Boutwell prohibiting abridgment of the right to vote "by reason of race, color, or previous condition of slavery" was met with unsuccessful calls to guarantee universal suffrage, thus invalidating literacy, property, and any other voting qualifications (Maltz 1990, 147–148). At least one proposal was offered to exclude "Chinamen and Indians not taxed" from the provisions of this amendment; another proposal would have prohibited any restriction of the voting rights of anyone 12 years of age or older (cited in Ames 1896, 230).

For its part, the Senate, mindful of Georgia's attempt to exclude black officeholders from the state legislature, voted on a proposal by Nevada Republican senator William Stewart that would protect both the right to vote and the right to hold office. The Senate also considered limitations on property and literacy requirements. As initially passed, the amendment also sought to guarantee the popular election of electors for president (Maltz 1990, 149).

After the House rejected this plan, a conference committee drafted the current language of the Fifteenth Amendment. This dropped all references to office-holding rights and to qualifications other than race, color, or previous condition of servitude and included a separate enforcement section. The House approved this amendment on February 25, 1869, by a vote of 144 to 44 (35 not voting); the Senate followed the next day by a vote of 39 to 13 (U.S. Senate 1985, 37). The amendment was ratified by February 1870. A controversy over New York's attempted rescission of its ratification was nullified by an additional ratification by Nebraska and a number of other states. Georgia, Texas, Virginia, and Mississippi were required to ratify as a condition of readmission into the Union (Grimes 1978, 58). Advocates of woman's suffrage were disappointed that the Fifteenth Amendment did not prohibit discrimination against women.

The Fifteenth Amendment was evaded by numerous strategies, legal and otherwise. These included adoption of grandfather clauses, literacy tests, understanding clauses (often enforced in a highly arbitrary manner), poll taxes (later invalidated by the Twenty-fourth Amendment), the all-white primary, and physical intimidation. These mechanisms proved so effective that Goldwin Smith (1898, 267) suggested at the turn of the century that the amendment had become a dead letter and should be repealed. From a somewhat different vantage point, attorneys Arthur Machen (1910) and William Marbury argued that the Fifteenth Amendment violated implicit limits on the amending process. The Supreme Court ignored such arguments in voiding Maryland's grandfather clauses in *Myers v. Anderson* (1915).

Despite evasion and slack enforcement of the Fifteenth Amendment, an amending proposal was introduced as early as 1877 to restrict its application. Moreover, members of Congress from the South introduced numerous proposals from 1900 to 1915 to repeal the amendment. Perhaps they realized that, although it was being narrowly interpreted at the time, it had the potential for expansive interpretation in the future. Some revival of the amendment occurred with the Supreme Court's decision in *Smith v. Allwright* (1944), invalidating the all-white primary. The amendment subsequently served as a justification for expansive voting rights legislation in the 1960s and thereafter. In cases like *South Carolina v. Katzenbach* (1966), the Supreme Court has sometimes allowed Congress to use its enforcement powers in Section 2 of the amendment to invalidate legislation, such as literacy tests, that would otherwise be constitutional.

See also: Enforcement Clauses in Amendments; Fourteenth Amendment; Marbury, William; *Myers v. Anderson;* Nineteenth Amendment; Twenty-fourth Amendment; Twenty-sixth Amendment.

For Further Reading:

Ames, Herman. 1896. *The Proposed Amendments to the Constitution of the United States during the First Century of Its History.* Reprint, New York: Burt Franklin, 1970.

Grimes, Alan P. 1978. *Democracy and the Amendments to the Constitution.* Lexington, MA: Lexington Books.

Maltz, Earl M. 1990. *Civil Rights, the Constitution, and Congress, 1863–1869.* Lawrence: University Press of Kansas.

Mathews, John M. 1909. *Legislative and Judicial History of the Fifteenth Amendment.* New York: Da Capo Press, 1971 reprint.

Smith, Goldwin. 1898. "Is the Constitution Outworn?" *North American Review* 166 (March): 257–267.

United States Senate, Subcommittee on the Constitution, Committee on the Judiciary. 1985. *Amendments to the Constitution: A Brief Legislative History.* Washington DC: U.S. Government Printing Office.

FIFTH AMENDMENT

The Fifth Amendment was proposed by the First Congress and ratified in 1791 as part of the Bill of Rights. The amendment outlines a variety of guarantees, most of which are directed toward the rights of individuals who are accused of crimes.

The multiple guarantees of this amendment were found in several different parts of the bill of rights that James Madison originally presented to Congress and remained separated until the Senate combined them. Madison's original proposals specified that no one would be subject "to more than one trial or one punishment" (Kurland and Lerner 1987, 5:262) rather than to be "twice put in jeopardy." Madison's original proposal also had a broader self-incrimination provision; the limitation to criminal cases was made during House debates.

Grand Jury Indictment

The Fifth Amendment contains five basic guarantees. The first such guarantee requires indictment by a grand jury in "capital" (death penalty) or other "infamous" cases, with an exception for personnel in the armed services. The grand jury is distinct from the petit jury guaranteed in the Sixth Amendment. Whereas petit juries award judgments or decide on guilt or innocence and determine penalties in criminal cases, a grand jury simply ascertains whether a prosecutor has sufficient evidence to proceed with a trial. Such juries are designed to guard against prosecutorial vindictiveness. The purpose of the so-called double-jeopardy provision that follows is similar. If an initial finding of innocence were not considered final, then a prosecutor could simply wear down a defendant with repeated prosecutions for the same offense.

Grand jury proceedings have traditionally been secret, both in order to encourage witnesses to make free disclosure and in order to protect the innocent. Some concern has been expressed that the USA Patriot Act of 2001, passed in the aftermath of the terrorist attacks of September 11, 2001, might erode such privacy by its provisions for sharing intelligence gathered through grand juries with a wide variety of governmental agencies (Whitehead 2002, 1113–1115). The grand jury provision is the only one in the Fifth Amendment that the Supreme Court has not applied to the states, some of which continue to indict "by information."

The Provision against Self-incrimination

No provision in the Fifth Amendment is better known, or more controversial, than the provision against self-incrimination. A similar guarantee was found in a number of early state constitutions and in proposals offered by the Virginia and North Carolina ratifying conventions (Lutz 1992, 160; for earlier origins, see Levy 1968). One scholar has identified three major purposes of this provision: "(1) maintaining a responsible accusatorial system, (2) preventing cruel and inhumane treatment of suspects, and (3) offering protection for personal privacy" (D. O'Brien 2000a, 974).

Modern judicial decisions have extended the meaning of this clause beyond that of prohibiting physical coercion to forbid mental coercion as well. In its famous decision in *Miranda v. Arizona* (1966), the Supreme Court extended this guarantee from the courtroom to the station house by ruling that police have to inform suspects of their right to remain silent. The U.S. Supreme Court reaffirmed this decision in *Dickerson v. United States* (2000).

The Due Process Clause

No clause in the Fifth Amendment has been more important than the due process clause. Due process obviously relates to procedural fairness, but there are times when the Court has given this clause, and its companion clause in the Fourteenth Amendment (the primary vehicle through which most limitations in the Bill of Rights, which once applied exclusively to the national government, are now also applied to the states), a substantive content as well. In the late nineteenth and early twentieth century, this provision was sometimes used to void economic regulations. In *Bolling v. Sharpe* (1954), it was used to outlaw forms of racial segregation at the federal as well as at the state level (the latter is covered under the equal protection clause of the Fourteenth Amendment). Although all provisions of the Constitution are subject to judicial interpretation, this one seems to allow greater leeway than many less open-ended clauses.

The Takings Clause

Unlike the other provisions in the amendment, the last provision of the Fifth Amendment, usually dubbed the takings clause, does not deal with the rights of suspected criminals. Instead, it provides that the government cannot take private property without justly compensating its owners. The right of the government to condemn private property for public use, the so-called right of eminent domain, is thus assumed rather than directly stated. Significantly, in *Chicago, Burlington & Quincy Railway Co. v. Chicago* (1897), the takings clause was the first to be applied to the states via the due process clause of the Fourteenth Amendment. In *Kelo v. City of New London,* 545 U.S. 469 (2005), the Supreme Court decided that states could use their power of eminent domain to condemn well-maintained houses for private economic development. This decision led to a flurry of proposed amendments, many of which have been adopted at the state level.

Attempts to Repeal the Fifth Amendment

There have been attempts to repeal various provisions in the Fifth Amendment. In 1958, Senator Strom Thurmond of South Carolina introduced an amendment designed to alter the provision against double jeopardy. In the next year, a book questioned whether courts had properly interpreted the self-incrimination provision of the amendment and suggested that the principle should not apply to pretrial investigations (although there should be protections against police use of "third degree" tactics) and that the right should apply only to an accused and not to other witnesses called to testify at a trial (Mayers 1959, 229–231). Similarly, a federal judge writing in 1968 offered an amendment designed to change a number of judicial interpretations of the self-incrimination clause (Friendly 1968, 721–722). Some amendments have also been offered that would suspend the prohibition against the taking of private property without compensation during times of war.

See also Fourteenth Amendment; Grand Jury; Self-Incrimination; Substantive Due Process; Takings Clause.

For Further Reading:

Bodenhamer, David J. 1992. *Fair Trial: Rights of the Accused in American History.* New York: Oxford University Press.

Friendly, Henry J. 1968. "The Fifth Amendment Tomorrow: The Case for Constitutional Change." *University of Cincinnati Law Review* 37 (Fall): 671–726.

Levy, Leonard W. 1968. *Origins of the Fifth Amendment: The Right against Self-Incrimination.* New York: Oxford University Press.

Lutz, Donald S. 1992. *A Preface to American Political Theory.* Lawrence: University Press of Kansas.

Mayers, Lewis. 1959. *Shall We Amend the Fifth Amendment?* New York: Harper and Brothers.

O'Brien, David M. 2000. *Civil Rights and Civil Liberties.* Vol. 2 of *Constitutional Law and Politics.* 4th ed. New York: W. W. Norton.

Whitehead, John W. 2002. "Forfeiting 'Enduring Freedom' for 'Homeland Security': A Constitutional Analysis of the USA Patriot Act and the Justice Department's Anti-Terrorism Initiatives." *American University Law Review* 51 (August): 1081–1133.

Yandle, Bruce. 1995. *Land Rights: The 1990s' Property Rights Rebellion.* Lanham, MD: Rowman & Littlefield.

FINER, HERMAN (1898–1969)

Political scientist Herman Finer offered far-ranging reforms of U.S. government in a book published in 1960. Finer focused primarily on the presidency, believing that the job had become too onerous for one individual to handle, but he also believed that differing terms of office for the president and members of Congress contribute to the problem.

Finer offered nine major reforms of the existing system. His first and most important proposal was that the president would run on a ticket with 11 vice presidents to be named by national nominating conventions without any instructions from primaries. The president and his cabinet would serve four-year terms, and the two-term limit found in the Twenty-second Amendment would be eliminated. Vice presidents would, like current cabinet members, head executive departments, although some would not have such responsibility but "would be available as deputies to the President and concerned with the main lines of policy as well as general counseling" (Finer 1960, 304).

Finer's second proposal called for making the terms of the president, members of the House, and members of the Senate equal. He favored a four-year term but would accept a five-year stint. He believed that if the executive and legislative candidates ran at the same time and for the same term, this would promote a common platform and would serve to strengthen U.S. political parties.

The third aspect of Finer's plan provided that, to be eligible for president or vice president, an individual "must be presently a member of the House of Representatives or the Senate or must have served at least four years in either house" (Finer 1960, 309). Those elected to the cabinet would be replaced through special elections; individuals on the losing ticket "could be regarded as elected to Congress by the fact of their appearance on the presidential ticket; and they could choose in which house they wished to serve" (312).

Finer's fourth proposal called for the president to name his first vice president and designate an order of succession among the others. His fifth proposal provided that the president would assume the general direction of policy while allowing each vice president to "conduct the business of his department independently and on his own responsibility" (314).

Finer's sixth proposal would give the president the authority to dismiss and replace his vice presidents. Finer also indicated that the president and his cabinet would sit in the House of Representatives and "participate in congressional business—through messages, through debates, [and] through answering the questions" (315). Finer proposed reducing the powers of the Senate. It would lose its power to confirm appointments and ratify treaties and would no longer share power with the House in overriding presidential vetoes. Finer's seventh proposal called for maintaining the presidential veto but allowing a 55-percent vote of the House of Representatives to override it.

Although Finer did not believe that Congress should be able to oust the president and his cabinet, he did think that the president and his cabinet should be able to resign, thus necessitating new elections for both the legislative and the executive branches. This was his eighth proposal. His ninth would have eliminated patronage and spoils, allowing civil servants to continue in office regardless of party affiliation as long as they served the government faithfully and competently.

See also Parliamentary System.

For Further Reading:
Finer, Herman. 1960. *The Presidency, Crisis and Regeneration: An Essay in Possibilities.* Chicago: University of Chicago Press.

FINLETTER, THOMAS (1893–1980)

Thomas Finletter, attorney and special assistant to the secretary of state, authored a book advocating constitutional reform just as World War II was coming to an end (Finletter 1945). Like Alexander Hehmeyer, Finletter was concerned about the government's ability to function effectively once the war was over (Vile 1991c, 91–93). Finletter was especially concerned about what he perceived to be the lack of fit between governmental means under a system of checks and balances and expanded governmental ends.

Finletter dedicated much of his book to a historical overview designed to show that the existing governmental system resulted in excessive legislative-executive conflict and often led to paralysis. He favored the establishment of more executive-legislative bodies; an institution like the British question hour, where representatives of the administration could explain and justify their policies; and reform of the congressional committee system and its use of seniority. He also advocated establishment of "a joint executive-legislative cabinet" (Finletter 1945, 88). Such a cabinet would be composed of nine congressional leaders from the majority party and nine members of the executive cabinet. Finletter also believed that a majority of both houses of Congress should be able to ratify treaties.

Finletter opposed a parliamentary system, largely because he believed that the American people (and not Congress) had a right to choose their chief executive directly. Finletter believed, however, that the system of fixed election dates should be altered. He proposed that the president and members of both houses of Congress be elected for six-year terms. The president would, in turn, be able to dissolve Congress and call new elections. Finletter believed that such a system would restore unified government, strengthen party discipline, and make parties more responsible. Finletter favored eliminating the residency requirement for members of Congress so that parties could run candidates for office outside their districts.

Finletter recognized that formidable forces of "inertia and of satisfaction with things as they are" blocked the path to reform, but he thought that without reform, the conflict between the legislative and executive branches would eventually destroy self-government in the United States (Finletter 1945, 145–147).

See also Divided Government; Hehmeyer, Alexander; Parliamentary Systems.

For Further Reading:

Finletter, Thomas K. 1945. *Can Representative Government Do the Job?* New York: Reynal and Hitchcock.

FIRST AMENDMENT

The First Amendment was proposed by the First Congress and ratified in 1791 as part of the Bill of Rights. The amendment contains two clauses related to religion. One provides that "Congress shall make no law respecting an establishment of religion." The other forbids Congress from "prohibiting the free exercise thereof." The amendment also provides protection for freedom of speech, press, peaceable assembly, and petition. Without the latter rights, a republican, or representative, form of government would be quite precarious. Although it was originally the third of 12 proposed amendments (the first two of which were not initially ratified), there is some rightful symbolism in the fact that this important amendment now heads the Bill of Rights.

Background

The First Amendment is a distillation of proposals that James Madison submitted to Congress after consulting state constitutions and requests from the state ratifying conventions. In the area of religion, Madison proposed that "the civil rights of none shall be abridged on account of religious belief or worship, nor shall any national religion be established, nor shall the full and equal rights of conscience be in any manner, or on any pretext, infringed" (Kurland and Lerner 1987, 5:25). In attempting to protect freedom of speech and the press, Madison proposed that "the people shall not be deprived or abridged of their right to speak, to write, or to publish their sentiments; and the freedom of the press, as one of the great bulwarks of liberty, shall be inviolable." Similarly, Madison proposed that "the people shall not be restrained from peaceably assembling and consulting for their common good; nor from applying to the Legislature by petitions, or remonstrances, for redress of their grievances" (Kurland and Lerner 1987, 5:25). Madison also proposed that "no State shall violate the equal rights of conscience, or the freedom of the press, or the trial by jury in criminal cases" (Kurland and Lerner 1987, 5:25).

It appears that Madison's wording prohibiting Congress from establishing a "national" religion was dropped largely out of concern that it would imply that the new government was "national" rather than "federal" (Kurland and Lerner 1987, 5:93). A similar concern for states' rights apparently led to the deletion of Madison's guarantee against state invasions of individual rights by the states.

Religion

No provisions of the First Amendment have provoked greater controversy than the first two clauses dealing with religion. There may well be implicit tension between the idea that government should not establish religion and the guarantee that it should not interfere with its free exercise. Thus, attempts to guarantee free exercise may further religion, whereas attempts to prevent an establishment may infringe on religious exercise. Congress continues to discuss a Religious Equality Amendment that might better clarify this balance.

The most notable cases before the Supreme Court involving the establishment clause have involved public prayer and Bible reading in public schools. In *Engel v. Vitale* (1962), the Supreme Court ruled that the recitation of a prayer composed by the New York State Board of Regents constituted an impermissible establishment of religion that violated the rights of nonbelievers. Similarly, in *Abington v. Schempp* (1963), the Court struck down daily devotional Bible readings and recitations of the Lord's Prayer in school. Although courts appear to be more receptive toward the idea of a moment of silence during which prayer is not mandated but may take place, the earlier Court decisions continue to bring calls for a constitutional amendment. A decision of the U.S. Court of Appeals for the Ninth Circuit in 2002 that the pledge of allegiance could not be recited in public schools because of its inclusion of the words "under God" although eventually mooted, led to a number of proposed amendments.

Under its interpretations of the establishment clause, the Supreme Court has struck down most forms of direct governmental aid to parochial schools. In so doing, it formulated the three-pronged *Lemon* test, named after the case *Lemon v. Kurtzman* (1971), in which it was first formulated. This test requires that, to pass constitutional muster, a law must have a secular legislative purpose; must not, as its primary effect, either advance or inhibit religion; and must avoid excessive entanglement between church and state. On occasion the Court has decided that government funding that promotes student or parental participation in parochial schools is not unconstitutional. Thus, the Supreme Court has permitted tax write-offs for parents who send children to parochial schools (*Mueller v. Allen* [1983]); vocational assistance monies for use by a blind student attending a religious college (*Witters v. Washington Department of Services for the Blind* [1986]); use of a publicly funded sign language interpreter for a deaf student attending a Catholic high school (*Zobrest v. Catalina Foothills School District* [1993]); the use of public school teachers to teach remedial classes in parochial school settings (*Agostini v. Felton* [1997]); and, most recently, the use of state vouchers to private schools (*Zelman v. Simmons-Harris* [2002]).

Sometimes the Court ignores the *Lemon* test. Thus, in *Marsh v. Chambers* (1983), it permitted continuation of the practice of a chaplain leading prayers at the beginning of a state legislative session; in *Lynch v. Donnelly* (1984), it permitted the display of a religious crèche on public property because this crèche was part of a much larger secular display (see Swanson 1990). These decisions interpreted the establishment clause to permit accommodation between the government and religion; others have taken a view of strict separation of church and state, and still others attempt to enforce complete neutrality (for one view, see Monsma 1993; for another, see Levy 1986).

The free exercise clause intended to guarantee a wide range of religious freedoms, but questions remain as to the degree to which it should exempt religious people from criminal laws. In *Employment Division v. Smith* (1990), the Supreme Court ruled that state employees fired from their jobs for ingesting peyote as part of a Native American religious ceremony were not entitled to unemployment compensation. The outcry over the decision, which appeared to contradict some earlier cases in which the Court had taken a more sympathetic stance toward actions, albeit not typically illegal ones, motivated by religious beliefs, led to the Religious Freedom Restoration Act. It attempted to ensure that the Court did not override free exercise claims except in cases in which the government was able to establish a compelling state interest. The Supreme Court overturned this law in *City of Boerne v. Flores* (1997), deciding that it exceeded congressional powers under Section 5 of the Fourteenth Amendment, granting power to "enforce" but not to "reinterpret" the provisions of that amendment. This decision has led to renewed calls for a Religious Equality Amendment, some versions of which would require that courts strike down laws with differential impacts on amendments that do not have a "compelling state interest."

Speech

Freedom of speech is essential to the democratic process, but speech can be so related to action that the First Amendment's seemingly absolute prohibition on governmental infringement of the former has been subject to numerous judicial qualifications. In an early case, *Schenck v. United States* (1919), Justice Oliver Wendell Holmes noted that even the most stringent protection of speech would not protect an individual falsely shouting "fire" in a crowded theater and causing a panic. Although there has been much subsequent discussion and eventual judicial repudiation of Holmes's "clear and present danger" test, the notion that even speech has limits has remained. In *Brandenburg v. Ohio* (1969), the Court indicated that it would suppress the expression of pure speech only when it was likely to lead to imminent lawless action (Wirenius 1994).

The Court has been willing to accept reasonable restrictions on the time, place, and manner of speech, but it has been wary of laws that single out speech on the basis of its content. In recent years, the Court has also extended protection to symbolic speech. Its two most controversial cases have been *Texas v. Johnson* (1989) and *United States v. Eichman* (1990), wherein the Court respectively struck down a state law and a federal law designed to prohibit desecration of the American flag. Numerous amendments have been introduced to overturn these decisions, and support in the states is strong for such an amendment. During the Cold War, amendments were also introduced to ban certain types of speech thought likely to lead to subversion of the government.

There are a number of special areas related to freedom of speech that the Supreme Court has treated somewhat differently from others. For example, the Supreme Court has never regarded obscenity as speech. In *Miller v. California* (1973), it identified three criteria for defining obscenity. Under these criteria, speech can be judged obscene if the average person applying contemporary community standards would find that a work taken as a whole appeals to a prurient (lustful) interest in sex; if a work depicts or describes in a patently offensive way sexual conduct specifically defined by law; and if such a work lacks serious literary, artistic, political, or scientific value. These criteria still leave considerable room for judicial judgment. In a number of recent decisions, the U.S. Supreme Court

has struck down laws designed to protect children from obscene materials on the Internet. Although concerned about children, the Court insists that laws designed to protect children cannot be so broad that they would deny legitimate rights to adults.

Libel, or defamatory writing, is another special area. Since *New York Times Co. v. Sullivan* (1964), the Court has applied the standard of "actual malice" to cases involving "public figures." This is a stringent test designed to encourage robust criticism of such individuals. Under this test, such figures can collect libel awards only when they are able to demonstrate that information was published with knowledge that it was false or with "reckless disregard" for its veracity (see Lewis 1991).

Although it is an extremely narrow category, the Supreme Court also ruled in *Chaplinsky v. New Hampshire* (1942) that so-called fighting words are not protected by the First Amendment. Such words are derogatory words spoken in close proximity to another person and likely to evoke physical violence rather than reasoned discussion. Similarly, the Court will not protect "true threats" of violence to others.

The U.S. Supreme Court has generally concluded that the First Amendment protects symbolic expression. Thus in *Tinker v. Des Moines Independent Community School District* (1969), it upheld the right of junior high school students to wear black armbands to school in protest of the Vietnam War. In some cases in which speech has been combined with illegal action, the Court has permitted regulation. In *United States v. O'Brien* (1968), for example, it upheld a law prohibiting individuals from burning their draft cards, which were considered to be government property essential to the national selective service system.

Press

Freedom of the press is a corollary to freedom of speech (Powe 1991), and the two rights often overlap, as in the Internet and libel cases mentioned above. Traditionally, the core of freedom of the press was identified as the prohibition against prior restraint of publication. Although it strongly affirmed this core content in *Near v.*

Minnesota (1931), the Supreme Court also insisted that the freedom was wider than this. In *New York Times Co. v. United States* (1971), the Pentagon Papers case, the Supreme Court overruled an injunction against the *Times* and other newspapers and permitted them to publish a classified story critical of American participation in the Vietnam conflict (see Unger 1972). Members of the press have used the First Amendment to assert privileges against being called before grand juries, but, to date, they have had more success in receiving protection through legislation (known as shield laws) than through judicial decisions. Courts have been generally wary of extending protections, such as exemption from grand jury testimony, to members of the official press that it does not extend to all—see *Branzburg v. Hayes, In re Pappas,* and *United States v. Caldwell* (1972).

Assembly and Petition

The guarantees for peaceable assembly and petition have not been adjudicated as frequently as others in the First Amendment, but like the other guarantees, they are critical to the functioning of democratic institutions, including petitions for desired constitutional amendments. In recent years, the Supreme Court has held that these and related clauses guarantee a constitutional right of association. In *Griswold v. Connecticut* (1965), Justice William O. Douglas cited the First Amendment, and this right of association, as one of the foundations of the constitutional right to privacy. More recently, in *Boy Scouts of America v. Dale* (2000), the U.S. Supreme Court limited the application to the Boy Scouts of a New Jersey law forbidding discrimination against homosexuals, on the basis that the Scouts composed a private association, whose views were at odds with homosexual behavior.

All the provisions of the First Amendment have been applied to the states via the due process clause of the Fourteenth Amendment. Although interpretations by the U.S. Supreme Court serve as a floor below which state standards may not fall, states may extend higher degrees of protection to First Amendment freedoms under their own individual constitutions.

See also *Abington v. Schempp; Engel v. Vitale;* Flag Desecration; Madison, James; Obscenity and Pornography; Prayer in Schools; Religious Equality Amendment; Religious Freedom Restoration Act; *Texas v. Johnson.*

For Further Reading:

Branzburg v. Hayes, In re Pappas, and *United States v. Caldwell,* 408 U.S. 665 (1972).

Kurland, Philip B., and Ralph Lerner, eds. 1987. *The Founders' Constitution.* 5 vols. Chicago: University of Chicago Press.

Levy, Leonard W. 1986. *The Establishment Clause and the First Amendment.* New York: Macmillan.

Lewis, Anthony. 1991. *Make No Law: The Sullivan Case and the First Amendment.* New York: Random House.

Monsma, Stephen V. 1993. *Positive Neutrality: Letting Religious Freedom Ring.* Westport, CT: Greenwood Press.

Powe, Lucas A., Jr. 1991. *The Fourth Estate and the Constitution: Freedom of Press in America.* Berkeley, CA: University of California Press.

Swanson, Wayne R. 1990. *The Christ Child Goes to Court.* Philadelphia: Temple University Press.

Unger, Sanford J. 1972. *The Paper and the Papers.* New York: E. P. Dutton.

Vile, John R., David L Hudson Jr., and David Schultz. 2009. *Encyclopedia of the First Amendment.* Washington DC: CQ Press.

Wirenius, John F. 1994. "The Road to *Brandenburg:* A Look at the Evolving Understanding of the First Amendment." *Drake Law Review* 43: 1–49.

FISHER, PAUL (1913–2006)

Paul Fisher, the founder and owner of Fisher Pen and sometime candidate for political office, who once spent some time in jail rather than permit a warrantless search of his business that he thought violated the Fourth Amendment, published a book in 1988, the year after a major stock market decline, which he designed to apply scientific thinking to politics, and especially to economics. In a book sprinkled with personal experiences, and newspaper reports about them, Fisher proposed an amendment of

15 sections, which he believed would address major issues confronting the nation.

The opening sections dealt with taxes. Section 1 of the amendment would apply all tax laws "uniformly to all individuals, partnerships, trusts, clubs, foundations, corporations, churches, unions, schools, and all other organizations including all governments and their agencies" (331). Section 2 would repeal the Sixteenth Amendment and repeal "all income, payroll, inheritance, gift and sales taxes (except Federal excise taxes)" (331). By contrast, Section 3 would provide for a tax on "all assets in excess of $100,000 which are owned or controlled by any individual or by any organization" (331). Rates would vary from 0.5% on assets from $100,000 to $1,000,000 to 1.2% on assets in excess of $5,000,000,000. Futher paragraphs elaborate details, including a provision by which "state and local governments may also levy a graduate tax on all assets provided the state and local governments' total combined taxes on any asset does not exceed 60% of these initial federal rates" (332). Section 4 would create a cabinet position of controller of the budget. The controller would be charged with reducing the federal debt "to less than $200 billion" and with balancing the federal budget and reducing federal expenditures to "less than 10% of the nation's Gross National Product" within three years (333). Similarly, Fisher's Section 5 would require the treasury secretary to purchase the Federal Reserve System and regulate "all financial institutions, including insurance companies, with over $50 million in total assets" (333). Section 6 would vest the secretary of state with power to maintain a "fair balance of trade and credit with each foreign nation" (334). The secretary would have power to raise and lower tariffs and interest rates to accomplish this objective.

Section 7 proposed structural changes in government. Section 7 would provide for all new legislation to be written and endorsed by the cabinet and recommended by the president. It would require two-thirds majorities for adoption. Four-fifths majorities of Congress would be able to replace the president, vice president, and cabinet members. Section 8 further proposed repealing the Seventeenth Amendment and choosing members of the House for four-year terms, to be served along with the president.

Section 9 would require 12 or more citizens to endorse an individual before such an individual could vote. Section 10 would further attempt to control constitutional interpretation by providing that "No decision nor opinion by any court may be used to justify alteration of the literal, accurate meaning of the Constitution or any other governmental law."

Section 11 would limit governmental licensing with exceptions for transportation that results in pollution. Section 12 would further limit the dissemination of untruths or harmful services. Section 13 would require that courts settle cases within a year. Section 14 would require governments to subsidize private schools to the same extent that they do public ones, and Section 15 would provide for the new amendment to go into effect "on the second January 1 following its ratification" (337).

See also Fourth Amendment; Seventeenth Amendment; Sixteenth Amendment.

For Further Reading:

DeBartolo, Anthony. "Having Perfected the Ball-Point, Paul Fisher Wrote a Plan to Save the World," http://www.hydeparkmedia.com/fisher.html. Accessed November 17, 2008.

Fisher, Paul. 1988. *The Plan to Restore the Constitution and Help Us All Get Out of Debt.* Boulder City, NV: Paul Fisher Campaign for Scientific Government.

FISHER, SIDNEY GEORGE (1809–1875)

Philadelphia lawyer Sidney George Fisher published a critique of the U.S. Constitution titled *The Trial of the Constitution* in 1862 (Vile 1992, 97–105). Largely prompted by Fisher's perception that the rigidity of the formal constitutional amending process had been an obstacle to the satisfactory resolution of the issues that led to the Civil War, Fisher's analysis is remarkable for at least two reasons. First, in contrast to almost all previous commentators other than the Anti-Federalists, Fisher questioned the adequacy of the formal amending process. Second, Fisher proposed the British model of legislative sovereignty, which he also associated with caution and incremental change, as an alternative.

Joseph Story, the prominent U.S. Supreme Court justice and constitutional commentator, had praised the amending process in Article V as an effective safety valve. Fisher argued that this safety valve had been ineffective in preventing revolutionary violence and that "the [constitutional] boiler has burst" (Fisher 1862, 27). Instead, Fisher proclaimed that Article V had become "an iron fetter" (33). In Fisher's judgment, the irony of the amending process was that it was most likely to be used at the very time when its operation was likely to be most dangerous: "To put its cumbrous machinery in motion, the people must be roused, and as the most important organic changes are generally connected with the interests of sections or of classes, the people are very likely to be roused by them, to be divided into parties, to be influenced by passion" (34).

Having concluded that the existing mechanism for constitutional change was essentially unusable, Fisher proceeded to advocate a system whereby Congress would institute constitutional change subject to popular appeal at the ballot box. In this manner, the people of the current generation rather than those of the American founding would govern. Such a scheme required a substantial limitation of judicial power. Fisher would limit federal judicial review to correcting "unintentional" violations of the Constitution, to controlling state courts, and to "criminal usurpations of power by the Executive or Legislative, or a conspiracy by both to overturn the Government" (Fisher 1862, 79).

Although the legislative and executive branches both demonstrated by their actions in the Civil War that the Constitution was a grant of power as well as a list of restraints, Fisher's proposal for a system of legislative sovereignty was not accepted. Fisher's book was published toward the end of the longest period in U.S. history (1804–1865) during which no constitutional amendments were adopted. Ironically, the very process that Fisher criticized for its ineffec-tiveness was successfully utilized to adopt the Thirteenth through Fifteenth Amendments from 1865 to 1870. This period was, however, followed by more than a generation before another amendment was adopted. This period, especially the early Progressive Era, also witnessed criticism of the adequacy of the constitutional amending process.

See also Rigid Constitution; Safety-Valve Analogy; Story, Joseph.

For Further Reading:

Fisher, Sidney G. 1862. *A Philadelphia Perspective: The Diary of Sidney George Fisher Covering the Years 1834–1871.* Reprint, Philadelphia: Historical Society of Pennsylvania, 1967.

Riker, William H. 1954. "Sidney George Fisher and the Separation of Powers during the Civil War." *Journal of the History of Ideas* 15 (June): 397–412.

Vile, John R. 1992. *The Constitutional Amending Process in American Political Thought.* New York: Praeger.

FLAG DESECRATION

In *Texas v. Johnson* (1989), the U.S. Supreme Court overturned the conviction of Gregory Johnson under the Texas Venerated Objects Law. Johnson had burned an American flag in front of the Dallas City Hall during the Republican National Convention in 1984. In an intensely argued decision, five of nine Supreme Court justices of diverse ideological leanings ruled that Johnson's action was a form of "symbolic speech," which the First Amendment protected. Both the House and the Senate passed resolutions expressing their concern about and disappointment with this decision, and they subsequently debated a constitutional amendment on the subject.

History of Flag Desecration Laws and Judicial Decisions

Although the decision in *Texas v. Johnson* initiated a firestorm, concern for protecting the flag dates quite far back in U.S. history. The flag's importance as a national symbol increased during the U.S. Civil War. Legislation designed to protect the flag was favorably voted on by the House of Representatives in 1890 and by the Senate in 1904 and 1908. Moreover, between 1897 and 1905, 34 states adopted flag desecration laws, with most of the remaining states following suit in the period during and immediately after World War I (Goldstein 1990, 38). Many of these laws dealt not only with desecration of the flag but also with improper commercial usage. Thus, in *Halter v. Nebraska* (1907), the U.S. Supreme Court upheld the conviction of a businessman who sold beer bottled with flag emblems. However, in *Stromberg v. California* (1931), the Court invalidated a California law prohibiting the display of red flags as too vague.

The next two cases to reach the Supreme Court dealt not with flag desecration but with flag salutes. Before the U.S. entry into World War II, many states adopted compulsory flag salute laws to encourage patriotism. The Court upheld such a law in *Minersville School District v. Gobitis* (1940). Jehovah's Witnesses, who interpreted the flag salute as worship of a graven image, opposed these laws. In the aftermath of the Court's decision, mobs victimized Jehovah's Witnesses, and schools expelled as many as 2,000 Witness children (Goldstein 1990, 46). Subsequently, the Supreme Court used Flag Day in 1943 to reverse itself in *West Virginia Board of Education v. Barnette,* and declare that the First Amendment protected individuals' rights not to violate their consciences by mouthing salutes they did not believe. The Ninth Circuit Court of Appeals has subsequently ruled in *Newdow v. U.S. Congress* (2002) that the flag salute cannot be said in public schools because its use of the words "under God" (added by congressional legislation in 1954) constitutes an unlawful establishment of religion contrary to the First Amendment, but the U.S. Supreme Court decided that Newdow, a noncustodial parent, lacked proper standing to bring the case.

The Vietnam War and a televised incident of flag burning in Central Park in April 1967 brought renewed attention to the flag and precipitated the first federal legislation on the subject. This law, adopted in 1968, provided a penalty of up to $1,000, a year in jail, or both for anyone who "knowingly cast[s] contempt upon any flag of the United States by publicly mutilating, defacing, defiling, burning, or trampling upon it" (cited in Goldstein 1990, 49). Shortly thereafter, members of Congress introduced proposals to guard voluntary flag salutes in public schools and buildings and to allow Congress to protect the flag from desecration.

In *Street v. New York* (1969), the Court overturned the conviction of a man who burned a flag in the aftermath of civil rights leader James Meredith's assassination. The Court feared that Street's conviction might have resulted from what he said when burning the flag rather than from the act itself. In *Spence v. Washington* (1974), the Court overturned the conviction of an individual who had taped a peace symbol to the flag. That same year, in *Smith v. Goguen,* the Supreme Court declared void for vagueness a Massachusetts law that the state had applied to an individual who had worn a flag patch on the seat of his pants. The Supreme Court issued no further decisions on the subject between 1974 and 1989 (Goldstein 1990, 63).

Reactions to *Texas v. Johnson*

Scores of amendments were introduced in the wake of the Court's 1989 decision in *Texas v. Johnson;* interestingly, a number of these amendments also sought to exclude campaign spending from First Amendment restraints, thus arguably overturning the Supreme Court's 1976 decision in *Buckley v. Valeo.* President George Bush Sr. went to the Iwo Jima Monument to announce his support for an amendment introduced by Republican representative Robert Michel of Illinois. This amendment provided that "the Congress and the states shall have power to prohibit the physical desecration of the Flag of the United States" (Vile 1989, 169).

During hearings on the proposed amendment, some members of Congress—relying on some equivocal language in the Court's opinion and on the testimony of some prominent law professors, including Laurence Tribe of the Harvard Law School—concluded that Congress could overturn the decision in *Texas v. Johnson* by legislation. The Senate defeated the flag desecration amendment by a vote of 51 to 48 (Goldstein 1990, 28). That same year, however, Congress adopted the Flag Protection Act to punish anyone who "knowingly mutilates, physically defiles, burns, maintains on the floor or ground, or tramples upon any flag of the United States." The law exempted "any conduct consisting of the disposal of a flag when it has become worn or soiled" (Goldstein 1990, 85).

Accepting expedited review of the law, the Supreme Court struck it down in a 5-to-4 decision in *United States v. Eichman* (1990). As many supporters of the law appeared originally to have hoped, however, both public and congressional sentiment had cooled since the earlier decision. Faced with arguments that an amendment would protect the flag at the cost of sacrificing the principles for which it stood and that it would be unwise to set the first precedent of restricting the Bill of Rights, Congress could not garner the required two-thirds majorities in 1990 (the votes for an amendment were 254 to 177 in the House and 58 to 42 in the Senate), but the issue has refused to die. In June 1995, the House voted 312 to 120 in favor of an anti–flag desecration amendment, but the Senate could muster only 63 (of a needed 67) votes in December of that year. The House achieved the requisite majorities in June 1997, but senators kept the issue from reaching the floor. The House voted 305 to 124 to adopt such an amendment in June 1999, but the Senate again mustered only 63 votes when it voted on the issue in March 2000 (Dorsen 2000, 430–433). The House reapproved a flag desecration amendment in July 2001, in June 2003, and in June 2005, but the only full Senate vote on the measure in June 2006 (66 to 34) fell one vote shy of the necessary two-thirds required for proposal. Many states have indicated that they will support this amendment if the necessary congressional majorities propose it.

Issues Raised by the Flag Desecration Amendment

The flag desecration amendment has revived arguments that there might be limits on the amending process. Thus, one scholar argued that such an amendment would violate rights protected by the Ninth Amendment and could be adopted only if language were included specifically indicating that the American people no longer considered flag burning to be a natural right (Rosen 1991). Another author argued that because the First Amendment prohibits Congress from making any law abridging the freedom of speech, such an amendment would have to be adopted by the unused convention route (Isaacson 1990; for critiques of Rosen and Isaacson, see Vile 1993, 136–143).

If a constitutional amendment is adopted, the courts would have to decide precisely what representations are defined as flags. For example, would representations of flags in newspapers or magazines count? There is also the ironic possibility that an amendment specifically prohibiting flag desecration would actually widen protection for other forms of symbolic speech (Vile 1989).

See also Campaign Contributions and Expenditures; Constitutional Amendments, Limits on; First Amendment; Flag Salute; Ninth Amendment; *Texas v. Johnson.*

For Further Reading:

Bates, Stephen. 1991. "Deconstructing the Flag-Burning Debate." *This World & I* 7 (July): 523–529.

Curtis, Michael K., ed. 1993. *The Constitution and the Flag.* Vol. 2. *The Flag Burning Cases.* New York: Garland.

Dorsen, Norman. 2000. "Flag Desecration in Courts, Congress, and Country." *Thomas M. Cooley Law Review* 17 (Michaelmas Term): 417–442.

Dry, Murray. 1991. "Flag Burning and the Constitution." In *The Supreme Court Review, 1990,* ed. Gerhard Casper et al. Chicago: University of Chicago Press.

Goldstein, Robert J. 2000. *Flag Burning and Free Speech.* Lawrence: University Press of Kansas.

———. 1996. *The American Flag Desecration Controversy: A Collection of Documents from the Civil War to 1990.* Kent, OH: Kent State University Press.

———. 1995. *Burning the Flag: The Great 1989–1990 American Flag Desecration Controversy.* Kent, OH: Kent State University Press.

———. 1994. *Saving "Old Glory": The History of the American Flag Desecration Controversy.* Boulder, CO: Westview.

Isaacson, Eric A. 1990. "The Flag Burning Issue: A Legal Analysis and Comment." *Loyola of Los Angeles Law Review* 23 (January): 535–600.

Kaplan, Morton A. 1991. "Freedom of Speech: Its Constitutional Scope and Function." *This World & I* 7 (July): 531–541.

McBride, James. 1991. "'Is Nothing Sacred?': Flag Desecration, the Constitution and the Establishment of Religion." *St. John's Law Review* 65: 297–324.

Rosen, Jeff. 1991. "Was the Flag Burning Amendment Unconstitutional?" *Yale Law Review* 100: 1073–1092.

Tushnet, Mark. 1990. "The Flag-Burning Episode: An Essay on the Constitution." *University of Colorado Law Review* 61: 39–53.

Vile, John R. 1993. *Contemporary Questions Surrounding the Constitutional Amending Process.* Westport, CT: Praeger.

———. 1989. "How a Constitutional Amendment Protecting the Flag Might Widen Protection of Symbolic Expression." *Louisiana Bar Journal* 37 (October): 169–172.

FLAG SALUTE

The words by which individuals salute the American flag were first written in 1892 by Francis Bellamy, an American Baptist minister, and published in the *Youth's Companion.* In 1924, the words "My Flag" were changed to "the flag of the United States of America," and, apparently influenced in part by sermons that Rev. George M. Docherty delivered at the New York Avenue Presbyterian Church in Washington DC ("Pastor who helped" 2008), Congress added the words "under God" in 1954 (Fineman 2002, 24). In *West Virginia State Board of Education v. Barnette* (1943), the U.S. Supreme Court reversed an earlier decision and ruled that students could not be forced to salute the American flag in public schools if such a salute conflicted with their religious convictions. Many Americans were nevertheless stunned when two of three judges on the Ninth U.S. Circuit Court of Appeals (with jurisdiction over California and other western states) handed down a decision in *Newdow v. U.S. Congress* on June 26, 2002, indicating that it was

unconstitutional for school children to recite the pledge of allegiance in public schools. The court held that because the pledge contained the words "under God" in a public school setting where students might feel undue compulsion when the salute was led by a teacher, it constituted an impermissible violation of the establishment clause of the First Amendment by sending a message to nonbelievers in monotheistic religion that they were second-class citizens.

The morning following the ruling, members of Congress lined up collectively to repeat the pledge in the legislative chambers. In addition, some members of Congress offered amendments on the same day specifically stating that it is not an establishment of religion for school students to make such a recitation. Some versions of the amendment specifically identify the current pledge, with the words "under God," which were added by congressional legislation in the Eisenhower administration in 1954. If such an amendment is adopted, it would be the first direct mention of a deity in the U.S. Constitution, thus partially fulfilling the wishes of those who advocated what was known as the Christian Amendment. At least one proposed amendment introduced in the Senate relative to the constitutionality of the flag salute would also permit reference to God on U.S. currency; the words "In God We Trust" were added during the U.S. Civil War. In time, the U.S. Supreme Court ruled that Newdow, a noncustodial parent, did not have standing to bring the case, and dismissed the Ninth Circuit Court of Appeals decision.

See also Christian Amendment; First Amendment; Flag Desecration.

For Further Reading:

Fineman, Howard. 2002. "One Nation, Under . . . Who?" *Newsweek* 140 (July 8): 20–25.

"Pastor Who Helped Get 'God' in U.S. Pledge Dies," Associated Press. http://www.msnbc.msn.com/Id/27968211/. Accessed November 29, 2008.

FORFEITURE OF OFFICE

See Offices, Forfeiture of, or Ineligibility for.

FOURTEENTH AMENDMENT

The Fourteenth Amendment, which sought to extend national rights to citizens regardless of their race, has been the most litigated provision in the U.S. Constitution. It was proposed by the necessary congressional majorities in June 1866 and ratified in July 1868. The Fourteenth Amendment was wedged between two other amendments that were adopted contemporaneously soon after the Civil War, and an understanding of the dilemmas faced after the war does much to explain it.

Background

The Thirteenth Amendment eliminated involuntary servitude, except as a form of punishment for crimes. Because slaves had previously counted as only three-fifths of a person for determining a state's representation in the House of Representatives and the Electoral College, emancipation presented the possibility that the states of the ex-Confederacy might actually gain representation in the government. In such circumstances, those who had led the rebellion might actually increase their political power, gaining in Congress what they had been unable to achieve on the battlefields. Moreover, almost as soon as the slaves were freed, many of the states that had permitted slavery enacted restrictive Black Codes that effectively stripped the former slaves of their freedom.

Congress reacted by adopting the 1866 Civil Rights bill, which effectively ignored the Supreme Court's decision in *Scott v. Sandford* (1857) by recognizing the citizenship of all native-born Americans (except some Native Americans) and attempting to protect their rights. Congress also adopted the Freedmen's Bureau Bill of 1866, which authorized military trials for those violating civil rights (U.S. Senate 1985, 30). Both bills were adopted over President Andrew Johnson's vetoes and in the face of arguments that they were unconstitutional. Although the Thirteenth Amendment had abolished slavery, doubts remained as to whether it provided adequate authority for the protection of other civil and political rights that had traditionally rested with the states.

Content

The Fourteenth Amendment is divided into five sections. It is the longest, the most complex, and arguably the most significant amendment to have been added to the Constitution. Congressman Robert Dale Owen has been credited with the idea of binding together a variety of proposals in a single amendment with the idea of increasing the likelihood of congressional adoption and state ratification. In this respect, the Fourteenth Amendment differed from the Bill of Rights where, with some notable exceptions (consider the takings clause of the Fifth Amendment), "various propositions [or groups of propositions] were offered as separate amendments to be decided upon individually" (Kyvig 1996a, 166). It has been noted that

> Instead of demanding a supermajority committed to a single measure, the Owen approach brokered inclusion of individual elements for willingness to accept the other parts of the package. Whether because of the difficulty of assembling such a coalition, failure to recognize it as an effective strategy, or perceived undesirability of an approach that compromised the terms of amendment, the Owen method of designing an amendment has not been used again, despite its effectiveness when first employed (Kyvig 1996a, 167).

Section 1 of the Fourteenth Amendment overturned *Scott v. Sandford* (1857) by extending citizenship to all persons "born or naturalized in the United States and subject to the jurisdiction thereof." It also forbade states to abridge the privileges and immunities of such citizens. More broadly, it prohibited states from denying persons "due process of law" or "equal protection of the law."

Section 2 repealed the three-fifths clause and, in a provision that was never enforced, sought to reduce representation for states restricting the franchise "in the proportion which the number of such male citizens shall be to the whole number of citizens twenty-one years of age in such State." This section was very upsetting to advocates of women's rights such as Susan B. Anthony and Elizabeth Cady Stanton, who had hoped that suffrage for women would be granted along with suffrage for African Americans. Disappointed by both the Fourteenth and the Fifteenth Amendments, they had to wait until 1920 for the adoption of the Nineteenth Amendment granting suffrage to women.

The last three sections of the amendment dealt with incidental matters. Section 3 prohibited office-holding by those who, having taken an oath to uphold the U.S. Constitution, subsequently supported the Confederacy, but it provided that a two-thirds vote of Congress could remove such a disability, and it soon did so. Section 4 guaranteed the Union debt while repudiating that of the Confederacy and denied all claims by former slaveholders for compensation for their slaves. Finally, Section 5, like Section 2 of the Thirteenth Amendment, granted Congress power to enforce the amendment.

Ratification

The ratification of the Fourteenth Amendment was almost as controversial as the debates over its proposal (Fernandez 1966; Suthon 1953). Although the amendment met with favor in the North, most Southern states rejected it. In 1867, Congress subsequently adopted the Military Reconstruction Act, providing that states of the former Confederacy could be readmitted to the Union without military rule if they ratified the Fourteenth Amendment, an irregular, if not necessarily illegal, procedure (Harrison 2001). Several subsequently did so. At about that time, New Jersey and Ohio attempted to rescind their ratifications. Secretary of State William Seward presented the facts to Congress, which declared the amendment adopted (James 1984, 288–299). At least one other state appears to have ratified the amendment prior to the congressional votes, and other ratifications followed before any judicial decisions based on the amendment. Moreover, Congress had not previously found it necessary to take a separate step to "promulgate" an amendment.

Interpretation

Ratification of the Fourteenth Amendment was just the beginning of the controversy over its meaning. Especially difficult to resolve is the question of the extent to which the guarantees in the Fourteenth Amendment were designed to harmonize with, or supersede, earlier understandings of federalism (compare Nelson 1988 and Richards 1993). Much contemporary debate has also centered on the question of whether the due process clause or the privileges and immunities clause in Section 1 of the amendment was designed to overrule *Barron v. Baltimore* (1833) and apply the provisions of the Bill of Rights to the states. Senator Hugo L. Black later advocated this view based on his reading of the congressional debates on the subject.

The Supreme Court majority did not initially take this position. Indeed, its decisions in the 19th century gave restrictive readings to most provisions of the amendment. In the *Slaughterhouse Cases* (1873), the Court narrowly read the privileges and immunities of Section 1 of the amendment. In the *Civil Rights Cases* (1883), the Court overturned the Civil Rights Act of 1875, which had attempted to prohibit discrimination in places of public accommodation. In a distinction that has never been repudiated, the Court reasoned that the Fourteenth Amendment applied only to state action and not to actions by individuals. Finally, in *Plessy v. Ferguson* (1896), the Supreme Court upheld racial segregation and Southern Jim Crow laws by formulating the "separate but equal" doctrine, justifying segregation as long as facilities for races were equal.

Although limiting the scope of the Fourteenth Amendment in the area of civil rights, the Court increasingly embraced the idea of substantive due process, by which it imposed limits on governmental regulation of businesses (Cortner 1993; Gillman 1993). In 1886, the U.S. Supreme Court unanimously decided in *Santa Clara County v. Southern Pacific Railroad* that corporations were legal "persons," subject to the protections of the Fourteenth Amendment (a judgment later questioned by Justices Hugo Black and William O. Douglas). Indeed, in the late 19th and early 20th centuries, the Fourteenth Amendment was often more successfully utilized to protect corporate rights than to protect the rights of former slaves and their descendants. In a case often thought to epitomize judicial thinking during this era, *Lochner v. New York* (1905), the Supreme Court ruled that a New York law regulating the hours that bakers could work was an infringement of their "liberty of contract" under the Fourteenth Amendment. Only in 1937, after Roosevelt introduced his "court-packing" plan, did the Supreme Court retreat from this area, but the Court continues to recognize corporations as legal persons entitled to a variety of rights under the Fourteenth Amendment.

Indeed, although the heyday of economic due process ended in 1937, the 20th century witnessed the progressive expansion of the civil rights provisions of the Fourteenth Amendment. Through a process of selective incorporation, the Supreme Court gradually applied most provisions of the Bill of Rights to the states via the due process clause of the Fourteenth Amendment. Indeed, in *Griswold v. Connecticut* (1965) and *Roe v. Wade* (1973), it ruled that additional penumbral rights of privacy not specifically stated in the Bill of Rights also apply to the states through the due process clause. In *Baker v. Carr* (1962), *Reynolds v. Sims* (1964), and subsequent cases, the Court has also expanded the equal protection clause to cover matters of state and congressional legislative apportionment, generating numerous pleas for an amendment to curb the Court's interpretation. In *Brown v. Board of Education* (1954), the Court overturned *Plessy v. Ferguson* (1896) and gave a broad reading to the equal protection clause (Jackson 1992). Although such interpretations have recently been narrowed, in past cases, the Court has given similarly broad readings to the congressional enforcement provisions in Section 5 of the Fourteenth Amendment. Although this does not appear to have been the intent of the amendment (Farnsworth 2000), the Supreme Court has also used the Fourteenth Amendment to limit discrimination based on gender. In *Romer v. Evans* (1996), the Court used the amendment to invalidate a Colorado constitutional provision that limited legislation on behalf of homosexuals. The Fourteenth Amendment has also been applied to classifications based on legitimacy and mental retardation but has been applied only loosely to classifications based on wealth (for example, differences in funding of state educational districts) or age, where it continues to allow states to use relatively arbitrary cutoffs for positions such as police officers and judges.

Some of the most controversial areas of modern public policy—including questions about affirmative action and school busing—continue to center on the meaning of the Fourteenth Amendment.

Proposals for Amendment or Repeal

From 1903 to 1920, several proposals were introduced—most by Southern representatives—to eliminate all but the first sentence of Section 2 of the Fourteenth Amendment. Although Congress had never acted to reduce representation for states that restricted voting rights, the threat was apparently still of concern. In 1920, Democratic senator James Phelan of California introduced an amendment restricting citizenship by birth to those who were white, African, or American Indian, presumably with the intention of excluding those of Asian backgrounds. The 1930s witnessed at least three attempts to repeal Section 1 of the Fourteenth Amendment, one by Senator William Borah of Idaho.

In March 1957, the Georgia General Assembly sent a memorializing resolution to Congress to declare both the Fourteenth and Fifteenth Amendments invalid on the basis of alleged irregularities in the procedures by which they were adopted. A supporter of this resolution argued for an amendment repealing the Fourteenth and Fifteenth Amendments, adding the word "expressly" to the Tenth Amendment, and limiting citizenship to whites. This latter provision provided in relevant part,

> No person shall be a citizen of the United States unless he is a non-Hispanic White of the European race, in whom there is no ascertainable trace of Negro blood, nor more than one-eighth Mongolian, Asian, Asia Minor, Middle Eastern, Semitic, Near Eastern, American Indian, Malay or other non-European or nonwhite blood, provided that Hispanic whites, defined as anyone with an Hispanic ancestor, may be citizens if, in addition to meeting the

aforesaid ascertainable trace and percentage tests, they are, in appearance, indistinguishable from Americans whose ancestral home is the British Isles or Northwest Europe. Only citizens shall have the right and privilege to reside permanently in the United States (Pace 1986, 99).

The most recent attempt to repeal the Fourteenth Amendment appears to have been made by Democratic representative John Rarick of Louisiana in 1973.

See also Affirmative Action; *Barron v. Baltimore;* Bingham, John A.; Black, Hugo Lafayette; Civil Rights Cases; Corporations; Enforcement Clauses in Amendments; Equal Rights Amendment; Federalism and the Amending Process; Fifteenth Amendment; Incorporation; Lieber, Francis; Nineteenth Amendment; Promulgation of Amendments; Thirteenth Amendment.

For Further Reading:

Bryant, Douglas H. 2002. "Unorthodox and Paradox: Revisiting the Ratification of the Fourteenth Amendment." *Alabama Law Review* 53: 555–581.

Cortner, Richard C. 1993. *The Iron Horse and the Constitution: The Railroads and the Transformation of the Fourteenth Amendment.* Westport, CT: Greenwood Press.

Farnsworth, Ward. 2000. "Women under Reconstruction: The Congressional Understanding," *Northwestern University Law Review* 94 (Summer): 1229–1295.

Fernandez, Ferdinand F. 1966. "The Constitutionality of the Fourteenth Amendment." *Southern California Law Review* 39: 378–407.

Flack, Horace E. 1908. *The Adoption of the Fourteenth Amendment.* Baltimore: Johns Hopkins. Reprint, Gloucester, MA: Peter Smith 1965.

Gillman, Howard. 1993. *The Constitution Besieged: The Rise and Demise of Lochner Era Police Powers Jurisprudence.* Durham, NC: Duke University Press.

Harrison, John. 2001. "The Lawfulness of the Reconstruction Amendments." *University of Chicago Law Review* 68 (Spring): 375–462.

James, Joseph B. 1984. *The Ratification of the Fourteenth Amendment.* Macon, GA: Mercer University Press.

James, Joseph B. 1956. *The Framing of the Fourteenth Amendment.* Urbana: University of Illinois Press.

Kyvig, David E. 1996. *Explicit and Authentic Acts: Amending the Constitution, 1776–1995.* Lawrence: University Press of Kansas.

Maltz, Earl M. 1990. *Civil Rights, the Constitution, and Congress, 1863–1869.* Lawrence: University Press of Kansas.

Nelson, William E. 1988. *The Fourteenth Amendment: From Political Principle to Judicial Doctrine.* Cambridge, MA: Harvard University Press.

Pace, James O. 1986. *Amendment to the Constitution: Averting the Decline and Fall of America.* Los Angeles: Johnson, Pace, Simmons and Fennell.

Perry, Michael J. 1999. *We the People: The Fourteenth Amendment and the Supreme Court.* Oxford, UK: Oxford University Press.

Richards, David A. J. 1993. *Conscience and the Constitution: History, Theory, and Law of the Reconstruction Amendments.* Princeton, NJ: Princeton University Press.

Suthon, Walter J., Jr. 1953. "The Dubious Origin of the Fourteenth Amendment." *Tulane Law Review* 28: 22–44.

United States Senate, Subcommittee on the Constitution, Committee on the Judiciary. 1985. *Amendments to the Constitution: A Brief Legislative History.* Washington DC: U.S. Government Printing Office.

Virginia Commission on Constitutional Government. 1967. *The Reconstruction Amendments Debates.* Richmond: Virginia Commission on Constitutional Government.

FOURTH AMENDMENT

The First Congress proposed the Fourth Amendment in 1789, and the states ratified it in 1791 as part of the Bill of Rights. The Amendment provides that "the right of the people to be secure in their persons, houses, papers, and effects, against unreasonable searches and seizures, shall not be violated, and no Warrants shall issue, but upon probable cause, supported by Oath or affirmation, and particularly describing the place to be searched, and the persons or things to be seized."

Origins

Like the amendment that precedes it, the Fourth Amendment was largely motivated by abuses of the British when they ruled America. They had used general warrants, or so-called writs of assistance, in tracking down customs violations in the colonies. A number of states subsequently adopted provisions against such warrants, and ratifying conventions in Maryland, Virginia, and North Carolina all proposed amendments dealing with the subject (Lutz 1992, 57).

The proposed bill of rights that James Madison submitted to the House of Representatives contained a provision that is quite similar to what became the Fourth Amendment. One difference was that Madison's version referred to "other property" rather than to "effects." Madison's version also specified that the people's rights "shall not be violated by warrants issued without probable cause," whereas the text of the current Fourth Amendment leaves a greater disjunction between the prohibition against unreasonable searches and seizures and the warrant requirement (see Kurland and Lerner 1987, 5:25, 237).

The final version of this amendment presents an interpretive ambiguity—namely, that of establishing the relationship between unreasonable searches and seizures and warrants. The amendment clearly outlaws searches conducted pursuant to warrants that are not supported by probable cause, that are not supported by oath or affirmation, or that do not particularly describe the person or place to be seized. What courts have had to flesh out is precisely what, if any, kinds of warrantless searches are considered to be reasonable and what kinds are "unreasonable" and therefore unconstitutional.

Exceptions to Warrant Requirements

Currently, the courts recognize a number of circumstances in which warrantless searches are considered to be reasonable. These include cases involving "hot pursuit" of suspects, "exigent circumstances" in which evidence is in imminent danger of destruction, stop and frisk searches incident to arrest (an exception created in *Terry v. Ohio* [1968]), and searches of objects in "plain view" or in "open fields" (O'Brien 2000a, 2:829–837). Moreover, because automo-

biles are mobile, giving criminals unique opportunities to escape or destroy evidence, courts have fashioned a whole host of exceptions related to them (O'Brien 2000, 2:859–883).

In *Skinner v. Railway Labor Executives' Association* (1989), the Court permitted drug tests of railroad employees involved in accidents and, in *National Treasury Employees Union v. Von Raab* (1989), of customs officials dealing with drugs. As of June 2002, it has also permitted random drug-testing not only of student athletes (searches that had been approved in an earlier 1995 decision in *Vernonia School District 47J v. Acton*) but also of students involved in other extracurricular activities.

Electronic Surveillance

The framers of the Fourth Amendment could not have contemplated the problems of wiretapping and other forms of electronic surveillance, but such surveillance arguably poses a threat that is equal to or greater than that which the framers did anticipate. In *Olmstead v. United States* (1928), the Supreme Court initially decided against applying the Fourth Amendment to this issue, but Congress adopted legislation prohibiting most such surveillance, and the Court subsequently reversed course in *Katz v. United States* (1967) and ruled that such surveillance, like other searches, requires a warrant.

There is ongoing debate about the impact of the Foreign Intelligence Surveillance Act (FISA) of 1978 and the USA Patriot Act of 2001 on the Fourth Amendment. Both acts have made it easier for the government to conduct electronic surveillance of individuals suspected of being foreign agents or conspiring to commit terrorist activities. The former law established a special Foreign Intelligence Surveillance Court to review such surveillance, whereas the latter provided for roving wiretaps, for installation pen registers that record the number of all outgoing calls from specific sources, and for expanded disclosures of business records (Whitehead 2002, 1101–1109). A group known as the Electronic Privacy Information Center in Washington DC posted an epitaph on its Web site over the Fourth Amendment, "1789–2001," after passage of the USA Patriot Act, but some scholars have argued that provisions in the law for obtaining court approval for pen registers actually recognize some protections that were not previously incorporated into the law (Cohen 2002, B9). After a judge on the Foreign Intelligence Surveillance Court (FISC) questioned whether the United States could intercept electronic communications from U.S. soil, Congress adopted the Protect America Act of 2007, which permitted such surveillance of persons residing outside the United States (Seamon 2008, 463)

The Exclusionary Rule

Although the Fourth Amendment outlaws unreasonable searches and seizures and sets some basic guidelines for issuing warrants, it does not specify what will happen if the government proceeds to conduct illegal searches. Over time, the Court has formulated the exclusionary rule, which excludes such illegally obtained evidence from trials. First applied to the national government in *Weeks v. United States* (1914) but not to the states in *Wolf v. Colorado* (1949), this rule was subsequently extended to the states in *Mapp v. Ohio* (1961). Recent cases, however, have recognized some exceptions—for example, the "good faith" exception established in *United States v. Leon* (1984) and the "inevitable discovery" exception established in *Nix v. Williams* (1984). Courts have extended other provisions of the Fourth Amendment to the states via the due process clause of the Fourteenth Amendment.

One Basis for a Right to Privacy

In the Connecticut birth control case *Griswold v. Connecticut* (1965), Justice William O. Douglas cited the Fourth Amendment as one of the sources of the right of privacy. No amendments have been introduced in Congress to repeal the Fourth Amendment, but there are continuing criticisms of judicial interpretations of this amendment (Rothwax 1996), and many proposed new constitutions have suggested language to incorporate existing interpretations of it, including the exclusionary rule.

See also Bill of Rights; Fourteenth Amendment; *Griswold v. Connecticut;* Madison, James; Privacy, Right to.

For Further Reading:

Cohen, Patricia. 2002. "9/11 Law Means More Snooping? Or Maybe Less?" *The New York Times,* 7 September, B9.

In re: Sealed Case No. 02–001. Consolidated with 02–002. Decision by United States Foreign Intelligence Surveillance Court of Review. Decided November 18, 2002. http://www.fas.org/irp/agency/doj/fisa/fiscr111802.html. Accessed November 29, 2002.

Kurland, Philip B., and Ralph Lerner, eds. 1987. *The Founders' Constitution.* 5 vols. Chicago: University of Chicago Press.

Lutz, Donald S. 1992. *A Preface to American Political Theory.* Lawrence: University Press of Kansas.

O'Brien, David M. 2000. *Civil Rights and Civil Liberties.* Vol. 2 of *Constitutional Law and Politics.* 5th ed. New York: W. W. Norton.

Rothwax, Harold J. 1996. *Guilty: The Collapse of Criminal Justice.* New York: Random House.

Seamon, Richard Henry. "Domestic Surveillance for International Terrorists: Presidential Power and Fourth Amendment Limits." *Hastings Constitutional Law Quarterly* 35 (Spring 2008): 449–504.

Whitehead, John W. 2002. "Forfeiting 'Enduring Freedom' for 'Homeland Security': A Constitutional Analysis of the USA Patriot Act and the Justice Department's Anti-Terrorism Initiatives." *American University Law Review* 51 (August): 1081–1133.

FREE ENTERPRISE

The Constitution of the United States contains several protections for private property. These include protections for inventors and writers in Article I, Section I; the contracts clause in Article I, Section 10; the takings, or just compensation, clause of the Fifth Amendment; and the due process clauses of the Fifth and Fourteenth Amendments.

The Constitution does not specifically prohibit the government from creating or purchasing private enterprises. Chief Justice John Marshall's decision in *McCulloch v. Maryland* (1819) authorized the establishment of a national bank as a legitimate means of carrying out other constitutional powers—a means consistent with and not elsewhere prohibited by the Constitution. Although socialism has never been especially popular in the United States—with the Socialist Party suffering a significant decline since the 1930s (Shannon 1967, ix)—the national government has occasionally taken on projects, such as the Tennessee Valley Authority, that could be undertaken by private industry. From time to time, reformers have called on the government to take over the operation of one or another industry, with railroads being a special concern toward the end of the 19th century.

From 1952 to 1978, members introduced more than a dozen amending proposals in Congress to prohibit the national government from engaging in any private business not specified in the Constitution (thus presumably exempting the post office) that would compete with private enterprise. A number of these proposals also called for repeal of the Sixteenth Amendment (which legitimized the national income tax) and estate or gift taxes, an area in which Congress has recently enacted legislation abolishing the so-called death tax.

Constitutions proposed by libertarian advocates like Michael Marx and Jim Davidson often significantly limit the functions that the national government could perform. Some would even turn over such basic services as postal delivery, highway construction and maintenance, and even police protection to private firms, with expenses being paid through user fees and neighborhood associations. Some individuals who have proposed new constitutions have also envisioned significant new ownership by government of industries that are now private, or significantly reduced governmental roles even in such traditional areas as the provision of postal services, police protection, and public roadways.

See also Davidson, Jim; Fifth Amendment; Marx, Michael; *McCulloch v. Maryland;* Sixteenth Amendment.

For Further Reading:

Shannon, David A. 1967. *The Socialist Party of America: A History.* Chicago: Quadrangle Books.

FREE TRADE

Dr. James M. Buchanan, a Nobel laureate in economics, has proposed what he calls a "Natural Liberty" amendment. Specifically aimed at what he believes to have been the unjustified growth of the federal government under the commerce clause, Buchanan explains that the clause should be interpreted to prevent interferences with "voluntary exchanges and should not extend to the prohibition, or the coercive dictation of the terms, of such exchanges." He adds, "Nor should any differentiation be made between exchanges within the domestic economy and those made with others outside the political jurisdiction." He adds that "The Constitution have proved effective in insuring that the large American market be open inside national boundaries; it has not operated to insure freedom of trade beyond these limits" (2005).

Responding to anticipated critics, Buchanan argues that such an amendment "does not, in any way, amount to the constitutionalization of a particular economic theory, as sometimes alleged." Instead, he believes that the requirement "is little more than explicit acknowledgement that persons possess the natural liberty to enter into and exit from agreements, without concern for collectively imposed constraints" (2005). This is why he labels his proposal the "Natural Liberty" amendment.

Buchanan, who proposed this amendment along with a balanced budget amendment and an amendment prohibiting political discrimination, is not particularly sanguine about the chances for its adoption. He observes that "even die-hard classical liberals may bridle at constitutional prohibition of governmental regulatory activity" (2005).

See also Congress, Powers of; Congress, Private Bills; Public Choice and Constitutional Amendment.

For Further Reading:

Buchanan, James M. December 5, 2005. Cato Unbound. "Three Amendments: Responsibility, Generality, and Natural Liberty." http://www

.cato-unbound.org/2005/12/05james-m-buchanan/three-amendments/

FREEDMEN, REDISTRIBUTION OF

Democratic senator Garrett Davis of Kentucky, who largely blamed New England "Puritans" rather than Southern slaveholders for the Civil War (Vorenberg 2001, 95), offered two of the most bizarre amendment proposals during debates over the Thirteenth Amendment that abolished involuntary servitude, thus creating a large class of former slaves, often called freedmen (one of the federal bureaus designed to help these individuals would later be known as the Freedman's Bureau).

Davis first proposed requiring that slaves be removed from slave states before being given their freedom. His second proposal suggested distributing freedmen throughout the country proportionally to the white population.

Davis's proposals are a reminder that, as early as Thomas Jefferson, many observers thought that the past history of black-white relations in America would make it difficult for the two races to coexist if African Americans were granted freedom (Jefferson 1964, 132). Moreover, as late as Abraham Lincoln, politicians advocated slave recolonization, with Lincoln using his second annual address to advocate an amendment proposing such recolonization, albeit one that would have rested on the consent of those being recolonized (Richardson 1908, 6:140).

See also Jefferson, Thomas; Lincoln, Abraham; Thirteenth Amendment.

For Further Reading:

Jefferson, Thomas. 1964. Notes on the State of Virginia. New York: Harper & Row.

Richardson, James E., ed. 1908. *A Compilation of the Messages and Papers of the Presidents, 1789–1908.* 11 vols. n.p.: Bureau of National Literature and Art.

Vorenberg, Michael. 2001. *Final Freedom: The Civil War, the Abolition of Slavery, and the Thirteenth Amendment.* Cambridge, UK: Cambridge University Press.

FUTURIST PROPOSALS FOR CONSTITUTIONAL REFORM

See Toffler, Alvin and Heidi; Tonn, Bruce E.

G

GARCIA V. SAN ANTONIO METROPOLITAN TRANSIT AUTHORITY (1985)

Garcia v. San Antonio Metropolitan Transit Authority is one of the most important contemporary judicial interpretations of the Tenth Amendment. At issue was whether the San Antonio Metropolitan Transit Authority (SAMTA) was subject to the wage and overtime provisions of the Fair Labor Standards Act that Congress enacted under its authority to regulate commerce. *Garcia* overturned *National League of Cities v. Usery* (1976). In that 5-to-4 decision, which Justice William Rehnquist authored, the Supreme Court had cited concerns about federalism, the chief concern of the Tenth Amendment, in exempting traditional state and local governmental activities (as opposed to private enterprises) from such federal regulations.

After reviewing the history that had transpired since *Usery*, Justice Harry Blackmun wrote the 5-to-4 decision in *Garcia* arguing that the Court had been unable to distinguish with any degree of consistency between those governmental functions that were traditional, and should be left to state control, and those that were not, and should be subject to federal regulation. He therefore concluded that this judicial attempt to shield states from federal regulation should be abandoned. Blackmun argued that federal appropriations to SAMTA and other state programs demonstrated that the states had clout in influencing federal decisions. He argued that the structure of the federal system—and especially the guarantee of equal state suffrage in the Senate—rather than judicial oversight would be sufficient to protect state interests.

Justices Lewis Powell, Warren Burger, William Rehnquist, and Sandra Day O'Connor dissented, emphasizing the importance of the Tenth Amendment as a limit on federal power. Justice Powell noted that "the States' role in our system of government is a matter of constitutional law, not of legislative grace" (*Garcia* 1985, 567). Appealing to "the spirit of the Tenth Amendment," Justice O'Connor, a former Arizona state legislator, noted a number of changes, including the direct election of senators, that had increased the need for judicial vigilance in protecting states' rights (584–585).

Congress reacted to *Garcia* by adopting a bill allowing states to substitute compensatory time off for overtime pay (Rossum and Tarr 1999, 217). Several amendments were also advocated to overturn or limit *Garcia* (see Advisory Commission on Intergovernmental Relations 1986, 43–48). Recent discussions of unfunded federal mandates and other issues may indicate renewed concern over state power, and recent Supreme Court decisions relative to federal commerce powers in *United States v. Lopez* and *United States v. Morrison* have directed renewed attention to the Tenth Amendment. The constitutional allocation of powers between state and national governments thus continues to be a key concern.

See also Seventeenth Amendment; Tenth Amendment; Unfunded Federal Mandates.

For Further Reading:

Advisory Commission on Intergovernmental Relations. 1986. *Reflections on Garcia and Its*

Implications for Federalism. February. Washington DC: ACIR.

Garcia v. San Antonio Metropolitan Transit Authority, 469 U.S. 528 (1985).

GARDINER, WILLIAM (1885–?)

Born in Missouri, William Gardiner worked as a teacher and department store credit supervisor before earning an Ed.D. in 1942. Gardiner may well have been the oldest individual ever to offer a new U.S. constitution for consideration when he published *A Proposed Constitution for the United States of America* in 1973. His plan included an odd mix of prescription and commentary, of existing constitutional provisions and innovations.

Under Gardiner's plan, Congress would continue to be bicameral, but the House would have 200 members serving for four-year terms. Moreover, members of the House would elect the president and vice presidents, who would also serve as cabinet members. Senators would serve eight-year terms and would be selected, as they were prior to the adoption of the Seventeenth Amendment, by state legislatures. Legislators in such bodies, like members of the House of Representatives when choosing executive officials, would have to pledge not to consult beforehand about such choices. Strict attendance would be kept by page boys and girls (to whom Gardiner's constitutional proposal makes several references), and members could be removed for missing twice in one month or three times in a year.

The president and eight vice presidents would serve for four-year terms, and the Justice Department would be elevated to a more prominent watchdog role. The Supreme Court would consist of 11 members serving to age 70. Other officials in government would be required to attend special academies.

In contrast to the existing Constitution, Gardiner's describes the organization of state governments in great length. All counties would have to adopt a county commissioner form of government, with the number of commissioners being based on each county's population. Gardiner listed specific state officials and their methods of selection. Under his plan, local school boards would be replaced by parent-teacher associations. Schools would work with industries to provide jobs to keep juveniles from delinquency.

Gardiner proposed prohibiting political parties and lobbying. He would also eliminate campaign managers, speechwriters, and most congressional staff.

Constitutional amendments could be proposed in four ways and ratified in five; they would have a five-year deadline. Gardiner further suggested that a president who made himself a temporary dictator might put his plan in place.

Gardiner's greatest innovations would have been in the area of civil liberties. He would permit a speaker to lecture or pray in public schools, "provided he does not boost or condemn any church organization, or question the validity of the Bible" (Gardiner 1973, 9). He would eliminate freedom of the press so that "spoken or printed words that have a deteriorating influence on the morals and stability of the people shall be prohibited" (Gardiner 1973, 15). Gardiner specified that "any mawkish person or news medium that criticizes an apprehending officer for a justifiable killing shall be prosecuted" (Gardiner 1973, 17). Gardiner proposed to eliminate both grand and petit juries and to replace trials with "criminal proceedings" without Fifth Amendment guarantees against self-incrimination, confrontation of witnesses, and private defense attorneys. Capital punishment would be prescribed for a litany of offenses. Individuals who had received "free food" or other relief over the past four years would be prohibited from voting (Gardiner 1973, 27). Guns and other concealed weapons would be registered but not prohibited. In place of the current Bill of Rights, people would be assured of being "treated fairly and squarely" (Gardiner 1973, 43).

See also Bill of Rights.

For Further Reading:
Gardiner, William. 1973. *A Proposed Constitution for the United States of America.* Summerfield, FL: William Gardiner.

GARRISON, WILLIAM LLOYD
(1805–1879)

William Lloyd Garrison was the controversial leader of the American abolitionist movement against slavery. He lived when the views of individuals in the North and South increasingly diverged and hardened on the issue of slavery, and few views were more radical than his own. Born in Massachusetts in 1805, Garrison was apprenticed to a printer and began in 1826 to edit the *Free Press,* which subsequently went bankrupt. He honed his editorial skills at the *National Philanthropist,* where he advocated a variety of reforms, which, after his association with Benjamin Lundy, began to focus chiefly on the evils of slavery.

Garrison began his editorship of the antislavery *Liberator* in 1831 and continued until the end of 1865, after the Thirteenth Amendment was adopted. In his first issue, Garrison announced "I am in earnest—I will not equivocate—I will not excuse—I will not retreat a single inch—and *I will be heard*" (quoted in Fuess, 1928–1936). Garrison advocated the doctrine of "immediatism," which would abolish slavery immediately without any compensation to slave owners, but he had few ideas about how abolition would take place. He was a pacifist who rarely voted but relied on the moral force of his ideas and writings to bring about change. He did help organize the New England Anti-Slavery Society in 1831, and, after returning from a trip to the United Kingdom in 1833, helped found the American Anti-Slavery Society and author its Declaration of Sentiments. It declared

> That all those laws which are now in force, admitting the right of slavery, are . . . before God utterly null and void, being an audacious usurpation of the Divine prerogative, a daring infringement on the law of nature, a base overthrow of the very foundations of the social compact, a complete extinction of all the relations, endearments and obligations of mankind, and a presumptuous transgression of all the holy commandments—and that therefore they ought to be instantly abrogated (Pease and Pease 1965, 68).

Garrison, whose rhetoric was always forceful, was jailed for libel in 1830 and dragged through the streets of Boston with a rope around his neck in 1835. On the latter occasion, he might very well have been lynched had the city mayor not intervened on his behalf (Fuess, 1928–1836). Although the issue of slavery and states' rights eventually led the Southern states to attempt secession, Garrison had long argued that the Northern states should secede rather than tolerate continuing association with slavery (further demonstrating that extreme views of states' rights are not confined to one area of the nation, some Federalist New Englanders had taken a similar stance, albeit over different issues, at the Hartford Convention of 1815).

Unlike the ex-slave and abolitionist Frederick Douglass who interpreted the U.S. Constitution as a document that looked toward the eventual abolition of slavery, Garrison, who admired the sentiments in the Declaration of Independence, publicly declared in 1843 that the U.S. Constitution was "a covenant with death and an agreement with hell" that should be abrogated. Garrison often found himself in conflict with more orthodox religious believers, whom he believed had compromised with slavery. Garrison riveted public attention in 1854 when he publicly burned a copy of the U.S. Constitution at a gathering on July 4, 1854, at Framingham, Massachusetts.

Initially cool toward Abraham Lincoln, Garrison supported him after Lincoln issued the Emancipation Proclamation and later supported the Thirteenth Amendment. In April 1865, Garrison visited Charleston, South Carolina, laid his hand on the gravestone of former senator and slavery advocate John C. Calhoun, and announced that "Down into a deeper grave than this slavery has gone, and for it there is no resurrection" (quoted in Fuess, 1928–1936). Although the American Anti-Slavery Society did not, as he wanted, dissolve in 1865, Garrison continued to support a variety of reform causes, including alcoholic prohibition and women's rights.

See also Abolitionists; Calhoun, John C.; Douglass, Frederick; Emancipation Proclamation; Fourteenth Amendment; Hartford Convention; Lincoln, Abraham; Thirteenth Amendment.

For Further Reading:

Fuess, Calude Moore. 1928–1936. "William Lloyd Garrison." *Dictionary of American Biography, Base Set.* American Council of Learned Societies. Accessed through www.galenet.com on November 14, 2002.

Mayer, Henry. 2008. *All on Fire: William Lloyd Garrison and the Abolition of Slavery.* New York: W. W. Norton.

GAY MARRIAGES

See Marriage, Divorce, and Parenting.

GENERAL WELFARE

Article I, Section 8 of the Constitution grants Congress power to lay taxes "to pay the Debts and provide for the Common Defense and general Welfare of the United States." Because this general welfare clause is linked to the taxing power, Congress has "no general power" to legislate for the general welfare but only to tax for this purpose (Peltason 1994, 71).

In *United States v. Butler* (1936), however, although it voided the provision of the Agricultural Adjustment Act it was examining through an interpretation of the Tenth Amendment, the Supreme Court ruled that the taxing and spending powers may be exercised in addition to other grants of power in Article I, Section 8. The Court thus upheld the view originally advanced by Alexander Hamilton over the rival view advocated by James Madison, which would have limited taxing and spending powers to carrying out other specific constitutional grants.

Faced with quite restrictive judicial readings of congressional power over economic issues, members of Congress introduced amendments in 1935, 1936, and 1937 to expand congressional power to legislate on behalf of the general welfare. President Franklin Roosevelt considered support of a proposal that had originally been introduced as part of the Virginia Plan at the Constitutional Convention of 1787. It would have allowed Congress to "legislate in all cases for the general interests of the union, and also in those in which the states are separately incompetent, or in which the harmony of the United States may be interrupted by the exercise of individual legislation" (cited in Kyvig 1989, 471). Beginning with *West Coast Hotel v. Parrish* (1937), its historic "switch in time that saved nine," the Supreme Court interpreted congressional powers under the commerce clause more liberally. Proposals to expand such powers via a new general welfare clause subsequently ceased although subsequent proposals have sometimes called for expanding federal powers in one or more areas not currently enumerated.

See also Hamilton, Alexander; Madison, James; Tenth Amendment.

For Further Reading:

Engdahl, David E. 1994. "The Spending Power." *Duke Law Journal* 44 (October): 1–109.

Kyvig, David E. 1989. "The Road Not Taken: FDR, the Supreme Court and Constitutional Amendment." *Political Science Quarterly* 104 (Fall): 463–481.

Peltason, Jack W. 1994. *Corwin and Peltason's Understanding the Constitution.* 13th ed. Fort Worth, TX: Harcourt Brace College Publishers.

GERRYMANDERING

Gerrymandering is a term named after Governor Elbridge Gerry of Massachusetts that describes the process of drawing district boundaries to favor the election of certain individuals. Typically employed by incumbent legislators to help ensure their reelection, districts may also be gerrymandered to make it easier for members of the dominant race, for racial and ethnic minorities, or for members of a particular political party to be elected.

In recent years, the U.S. Supreme court has begun to subject racial gerrymandering to heightened scrutiny. The state of Florida is considering a pair of constitutional amendments that would limit such gerrymandering.

Michael Lind has proposed replacing the current system of single-member districts that is used in the U.S. House of Representatives with a system of proportional representation to eliminate all "partisan and racial gerrymandering" (315). He points out, however, that Congress could do this through legislation (316).

See also Congress, District Representation.

For Further Reading:

Lind, Michael. 1995. *The Next American Nation: The New Nationalism and the Fourth American Revolution.* New York: The Free Press.

"Proposed Amendments Would End Gerrymandering," *Bay News* 9, Saturday, July 19, 2008. http://www.baynews9.com/content/36/2008/7/19/366545.thml.

GILLMAN, STEVE

Steve Gillman, of Canon City, Colorado, (listed as 44 years old in 2008) is chiefly known for his blogs on a host of subjects that range from the outdoors to politics. He has posted ideas for "A New Constitution," possibly at or near his publication of an online article on September 13, 2008, entitled "A Better U.S. Constitution?"

Pointing in that article to antiquated features of the Constitution, Gillman recognizes the danger of creating "an entirely new constitution" but is especially interested in seeing a system with "an electoral process that is less based on geography and more on citizens['] political beliefs." In a proposed preamble in his site on "A New Constitution," Gillman proposes limiting governmental powers to those "specified in the constitution." He thinks that the government's sole function is that of protecting rights and believes that the government should adhere to these standards both at home and abroad.

In implementing a revised constitution, Gillman proposes voiding all existing laws within two years. He thinks each law should address a single issue and should require a two-thirds vote of both houses and the consent of the president, who should be able to exercise an item veto.

Gillman would allow individuals to run for office once they get a designated percentage of signatures from registered voters. They could be party members but could not run under party labels. Voters would be able to vote for multiple candidates.

Gillman wants to limit the House of Representatives to 200 members, who would serve four-year terms and would no longer be geographically based. Senators would serve terms of eight years.

Recognizing the sketchy nature of his proposals, Gillman is open to other ideas. He notes that he favors proposals "that create a true limit to the power of government, and a clear vision of its purpose," which he considers to be protecting "the rights of individuals" who live within it.

See also: Congress, Representation in; Congress, Size of.

For Further Reading:

Gillman, Steve. "A Better U.S. Constitution?" http:www.webraydian.com/content/view/1048/1/. Accessed October 18, 2008.

Gillman, Steve. "A New Constituiton." http://www.999ideas.com/new-constitution.html. Accessed October 18, 2008.

GOLD STANDARD

See Currency.

GOVERNORS, ROLE IN THE AMENDING PROCESS

Observers have sometimes questioned whether state governors need to approve either state ratifications of amendments or states' applications for a constitutional convention. Although no Supreme Court decision has addressed this issue directly (in 1939, in *Coleman v. Miller*, the U.S. Supreme Court declared itself "equally divided" as to whether a lieutenant-governor could cast a deciding vote in a state legislature), the answer appears to be negative (Edel 1981, 107–108). This does not, of course, prevent a governor from urging members of his or her state legislature to support or oppose pending amendments.

At the national level, the Supreme Court decided in *Hollingsworth v. Virginia* (1798) that the president's approval was not required for ratification of an amendment. In *Hawke v. Smith (I)* (1920), the Court further indicated that the "legislature" mentioned in Article V was the lawmaking body. Democratic North Carolina senator Sam Ervin convincingly argued that "the term 'legislature' should have the same meaning in both the application clause and the ratification clause of Article V" (Ervin 1968, 889). Legislation that he and Utah Republican senator Orrin Hatch proposed to deal with Article V conventions did not require such gubernatorial approval of convention recommendations.

See also *Coleman v. Miller;* Ervin, Sam, Jr.; *Hawke v. Smith; Hollingsworth v. Virginia.*

For Further Reading:

Edel, Wilbur. 1981. *A Constitutional Convention: Threat or Challenge?* New York: Praeger.

Ervin, Sam J., Jr. 1968. "Proposed Legislation to Implement the Convention Method of Amending the Constitution." *Michigan Law Review* 66 (March): 875–902.

GRAND JURY

The Fifth Amendment to the U.S. Constitution specifies that "no person shall be held to answer for a capital, or otherwise infamous crime, unless on a presentment or indictment of a grand jury." This provision remains one of the few in the Bill of Rights that has not been applied to the states as well as to the national government (*Hurtado v. California* [1884]; *Gyuro v. Connecticut* [1968]). Today, less than half of the states have grand jury systems. The remaining states rely on a system of indictment by "information" that is offered in an affidavit by a prosecutor to a judge (Abraham and Perry 2003, 100).

Whereas a petit jury decides on guilt or innocence, a grand jury decides whether there is sufficient evidence for a prosecutor to bring an individual to trial. The grand jury developed in England to shield individuals from overzealous or vindictive prosecutors, who might bring unwarranted indictments. Federal grand juries typically consist of 23 individuals, with 12 or more needed for an indictment. Proceedings are held in secret, without many of the due process safeguards required in an actual trial. Given the dominance that prosecutors sometimes exercise over grand juries, law professors often say that prosecutors could get an indictment against a ham sandwich if they wished; the protection thus may not always perform the function for which it was instituted.

In 1973, Republican congressman Charles Wiggins of California introduced an amendment to modify the existing Fifth Amendment requirement to allow Congress to specify whether indictments would proceed by grand jury or by use of information. Several such resolutions have subsequently been introduced, and the House of Representatives held hearings on the subject in 1976 and 1977.

In introducing his amendment, Wiggins noted that most grand jury proceedings were "dominated by the prosecutor." He further observed that "in modern society grand jurors do not ordinarily possess either the skills or the training to conduct the complex investigations that a truly independent evaluation would require" (Wiggins 1973, 125).

See also Fifth Amendment; Incorporation.

For Further Reading:

Abraham, Henry J., and Barbara A. Perry. 2003. *Freedom & the Court: Civil Rights and Liberties in the United States.* 8th ed. Laurence: University Press of Kansas.

Wiggins, Charles. 1973. "A Constitutional Amendment Concerning Information Proceedings and Grand Jury Indictments." *Congressional Record.* 93rd Cong. 1st sess., 1973, Vol. 119, pt. 25: 32911–32912.

GRISWOLD V. CONNECTICUT (1965)

The scope of judicial interpretation influences the degree to which legislative action or constitutional amendment will be needed to strike down unwise laws. Few modern cases have sparked more intense debate on the subject than this case involving a longstanding state law prohibiting the use of prescription of birth control devices.

Justice William O. Douglas's majority opinion striking down the law was apparently strongly influenced by Justice William Brennan (Garrow 1994, 245–249). Douglas argued that, although the Constitution did not specifically mention the right to privacy, the First, Third, Fourth, Fifth, and Ninth Amendments all had "penumbras, formed by emanations from those guarantees which help give them life and substance" (*Griswold* 1965, 484). The majority found that such penumbras, as applied to the states by the due process clause of the Fourteenth Amendment, protected the right of marital privacy.

Justice Arthur Goldberg's concurring opinion emphasized the hitherto largely neglected Ninth Amendment, arguing that it provided a textual basis for the judicial protection of unenumerated rights. In his concurring opinion, Justice John Marshall Harlan argued that the due process clause of the Fourteenth Amendment "stands . . . on its own bottom" (*Griswold* 1965, 478) rather than being intended to incorporate one or more specific provisions in the Bill of Rights. In another concurring opinion, Justice Byron White stated that prohibitions on the use of contraceptives by married couples did not deter illicit sexual activity.

In dissent, Justice Hugo Black reiterated his long-held belief, previously articulated in *Adamson v. California* (1947), that the authors of the due process clause of the Fourteenth Amendment intended to apply the specific guarantees of the Bill of Rights to the states, but no more. As such, the amendment did not authorize the Court to strike down legislation simply because it was unwise. Those who desired to keep the Constitution "in tune with the times" needed to use the amending process (*Griswold* 1965, 522). In his dissent, Justice Potter Stewart agreed that the Court had no power to invalidate a law simply because it was silly or unwise.

Griswold prepared the way for the 1973 decision in *Roe v. Wade,* invalidating most state laws on abortion. This decision has prompted numerous calls for a right-to-life amendment, which have in turn prompted countercalls for amendments protecting reproductive freedom.

See also Abortion; Black, Hugo Lafayette; Fifth Amendment; Ninth Amendment; Privacy, Right to; Right to Life; *Roe v. Wade.*

For Further Reading:

Garrow, David J. 1994. *Liberty and Sexuality: The Right to Privacy and the Making of* Roe v. Wade. New York: Macmillan.

Griswold v. Connecticut, 381 U.S. 479 (1965).

Johnson, John W. 2005. Griswold v. Connecticut: *Birth Control and the Constitutional Right of Privacy.* Lawrence: University Press of Kansas.

GUARANTEE CLAUSE

One of the most elusive provisions of the Constitution is the clause in Article IV, Section 4 providing that "the United States shall guarantee to every State in this Union a Republican Form of Government." It further provides that the United States "shall protect each of them against Invasion; and on Application of the Legislature, or of the Executive (when the Legislature cannot be convened) against domestic Violence." The first part of this guarantee is the only specific restriction in the Constitution "on the form or structure of state governments" (Wiecek 1972, 1). A scholar of this clause has noted that "it was designed to allow the states great flexibility to alter their optional characteristics." He further noted that "The first draft of the Clause was rejected precisely because it could be read to freeze existing state forms and laws into the U.S. Constitution" (Natelson 2002, 830). By providing for change, in a sense, the guarantee clause thus did for state governments what Article V (the amending article) did for the national government.

Throughout most of U.S. history, this clause has been what one-time Massachusetts senator Charles Sumner called "a sleeping giant" (Wiecek 1972, 290). Although some Republicans relied on this clause to reconstruct the South after the Civil War (others had anticipated that its authority might serve as a substitute for a constitutional amendment abolishing slavery), its inherent ambiguity has made it difficult to apply.

Two amending proposals have related to the guarantee clause. A proposal introduced in 1861 to give each state control over slavery within its territories also stipulated that the national government could still aid states faced with slave insurrections. In 1870, a much different proposal, aimed at Klan violence against African Americans, would have allowed Congress to authorize intervention even when a state did not apply for aid (Ames 1896, 171–172).

In *Luther v. Borden* (1849), the Supreme Court decided that the question of whether a state government was republican or not was a "political question," for Congress to resolve when it decided whether to seat a state's representatives. Alternatively, a president might make such a determination when deciding whether to send aid to a government facing domestic violence, as John Tyler had done in the case of Rhode Island.

For many years, the guarantee clause stood as an obstacle to judicial intervention in matters involving state legislative apportionment. When the Supreme Court eventually decided in *Baker v. Carr* (1962) that this issue was justiciable, it did so on the basis of the equal protection clause of the Fourteenth Amendment rather than the guarantee clause.

If either the Supreme Court or Congress ever gave an expanded meaning to the guarantee clause, the results could be as politically far-reaching as the adoption of any amendment ratified to date.

Natelson has argued that the guarantee clause would permit a state to substitute initiative and referendum mechanisms for state legislatures, albeit not for executive and judicial branches (2002), but it is difficult to know how states without a legislative branch could constitutionally ratify federal amendments. In *Hawke v. Smith* (*I*) (1920), the U.S. Supreme Court required that amendments be approved either through state legislatures or conventions.

See also *Baker v. Carr;* Fourteenth Amendment; *Hawke v. Smith* (*I*); Political Questions.

For Further Reading:

Ames, Herman. 1896. *The Proposed Amendments to the Constitution of the United States during the First Century of Its History.* Reprint, New York: Burt Franklin, 1970.

Natelson, Robert G. 2002. "A Republic, Not a Democracy? Initiative, Referendum, and the Constitution's Guarantee Clause." *Texas Law Review* 80 (March): 807–857.

Wiecek, William. 1972. *The Guarantee Clause of the U.S. Constitution.* Ithaca, NY: Cornell University Press.

GUN CONTROL

See Second Amendment.

HAMILTON, ALEXANDER (1755–1804)

A brilliant and ambitious immigrant from the Leeward Islands, Hamilton immigrated to the United States in 1772, where he attended King's College (now Columbia) and quickly became active in the American revolutionary movement. During the war, he served as an aide-de-camp to George Washington and commanded an infantry regiment in the battle of Yorktown. After the war, Hamilton went into practice as an attorney. An admirer of the English system of government, Hamilton favored a strong national government with an equally strong executive. He quickly recognized the weaknesses of the Articles of Confederation and was one of the forces behind the Annapolis Convention that led to the Constitutional Convention of 1787, and was selected to this convention as a delegate from New York.

At the convention, Hamilton favored a stronger national government than most other delegates. This, combined with the fact that the New York delegation was split between those who favored change and those who opposed it, meant that Hamilton did not have as important an influence on the document as did some other members of the convention. He did, however, have some input into the amending process. By September 10, 1787, the delegates were considering a proposal for Congress to call a convention to propose amendments after receiving requests from two-thirds of the states. After Elbridge Gerry objected that states might propose amendments that would unfairly bind other states, Hamilton expressed a different concern, namely that "[t]he State Legislatures will not apply for alterations but with a view to increase their own powers" (Farrand 1966, 2:558). He therefore proposed that

> The National Legislature will be the first to perceive and will be most sensible to the necessity of amendments, and ought also to be empowered, whenever two-thirds of each branch should concur to call a Convention—There could be no danger in giving this power, as the people would finally decide in the case (Farrand 1966, 2:558).

The substance of Hamilton's proposal is embodied in the current amending provision in Article V of the U.S. Constitution, whereby two-thirds majorities of both houses of Congress propose amendments. To date, all amendments that have been adopted have gone through this procedure.

After the Constitution was proposed, Hamilton was one of three authors of *The Federalist Papers* (the other two were James Madison and John Jay), who urged constitutional ratification. Although Hamilton mentioned the subject in *Federalist No. 85,* Madison wrote the chief essays relating to the constitutional amending process. Hamilton was a strong advocate of judicial review, the process by which American courts can strike down legislation they consider to be unconstitutional, and he addressed this subject in *Federalist No. 78* and in other essays. Such judicial interpretations of the document have made the Constitution much more flexible than it otherwise would have been, arguably obviating the need for many amendments that might otherwise be necessary.

As the first secretary of the treasury, Hamilton urged President George Washington to establish a national bank. In so doing, he argued for a broad reading of congressional powers under the "necessary and proper clause" at the end of Article I, Section 8. This interpretation has also made the adoption of new formal amendments less necessary. Hamilton further argued for a restrictive reading of the Tenth Amendment, an amendment that reserved powers to the states. Hamilton's restrictive reading was largely incorporated into Chief Justice John Marshall's decision in *McCulloch v. Maryland* (1819), which interpreted federal powers broadly.

A founder of the Federalist Party, Hamilton often quarreled with fellow party members and worked at cross-purposes with Federalist John Adams. Thomas Jefferson, a fellow cabinet member (the first secretary of state) and the founder of the Democratic-Republican Party often opposed Hamilton's programs. However, Hamilton supported the selection by the U.S. House of Representatives of Thomas Jefferson when Jefferson and Aaron Burr (Jefferson's putative running mate whom Hamilton trusted even less than Jefferson) tied in the Electoral College in the presidential election of 1800. This election eventually led to adoption of the Twelfth Amendment. Burr killed Hamilton in a duel in 1804.

See also Annapolis Convention; Article V of the U.S. Constitution; Articles of Confederation; Constitutional Convention of 1787; Federalists; Jefferson, Thomas; McCulloch v. Maryland; Tenth Amendment; Twelfth Amendment.

For Further Reading:

Chernow, Ron. 2004. *Alexander Hamilton.* New York: Penguin.

Farrand, Max, ed. 1966. *The Records of the Federal Convention.* 4 vols. New Haven, CT: Yale University Press.

McDonald, Forrest. 1979. *Alexander Hamilton: A Biography.* New York: W. W. Norton.

Rossiter, Clinton. 1964. *Alexander Hamilton and the Constitution.* New York: Harcourt, Brace and World.

HAMILTON, HUGH L.

Hugh L. Hamilton presented one of the most thorough and systematic plans for a new constitution in a book in 1938. Likening the Constitution to a jigsaw puzzle, Hamilton concluded that "thirty-one pieces are rotted and have to be thrown away; forty-four of them are badly in need of repair; thirty-seven of them have to be repainted; and we have to make eighteen new pieces to complete the picture. Only thirty-seven of the original pieces are left intact" (H. Hamilton 1938, 5).

Hamilton does not appear to have been motivated by a consistent ideology, but many of the changes he proposed addressed prominent issues of the time. His goals were fairly conventional, and he suggested that the main goal of contemporaries was "contentment—congenial occupation, adequate leisure, an absorbing hobby, a pleasant home, and wholesome recreation" (H. Hamilton 1938, 102).

Section I of his new constitution addressed general provisions. Innovations included allowing adjustments on state boundaries, with the proviso that the number of states would not be reduced below 30. Hamilton also proposed a provision—similar to contemporary neutrality legislation—limiting travel on ships of belligerent nations and restricting loans to or trade with such countries. His constitution further specified that most jobs would be filled through a civil service commission.

Section II of the proposed constitution was the bill of rights. It would deny citizenship "to the insane, the criminal, the illiterate, the non-English speaking and those who fail to comprehend the nature of our government" (H. Hamilton 1938, 112). Freedom of the press would include a provision "prohibiting control of the press in any part of the United States by individuals or groups which tends to abridge their freedom" (H. Hamilton 1938, 113). The current Fourth Amendment would have been modified to make government officials responsible for unreasonable searches and seizures or from "publicity, initiated by their order or performed by them" (H. Hamilton 1938, 113). Hamilton would have permitted the use of sworn testimony by dead witnesses, outlawed capital punishment, and eliminated the due process clause, which he considered to be ambiguous.

Section III outlined states' rights and limitations. It would have required state executives to extradite criminals who had fled to their states.

Congress would be renamed the National Assembly and be divided into a Senate and a Congress; members would receive salaries of $9,000 a year and actual travel expenses. Congress would consist of from 100 to 200 members chosen for a maximum of two six-year terms. The Senate would be of similar size. Instead of representing states, senators would be chosen by "representatives of the professions, finance, service, agriculture, manufacturing, construction, trade, communication and transportation, apportioned according to the census" (H. Hamilton 1938, 122). Senators would serve a single 12-year term. The National Assembly would have power over child labor, with a provision allowing work by those over age 13 that was not injurious to their health or schooling. The National Assembly would have control over commerce but not over manufacturing. In a measure similar to some modern proposals for a balanced budget amendment, Hamilton would have required all laws mandating expenditures to "specify the method of raising said funds" (H. Hamilton 1938, 120).

The president would be directly elected by the people to a single six-year term and would be paid $75,000 a year. The vice president would serve as postmaster general and would be a member of the president's cabinet.

The number of Supreme Court justices would be specified at nine. Judges would be required to retire at age 80. The power of judicial review would be spelled out, but when the Supreme Court declared a law to be unconstitutional, Hamilton provided that it "shall include the wording of a Constitutional Amendment which would validate the legislation" (H. Hamilton 1938, 132). Hamilton would eliminate the provisions of the current Eleventh Amendment and allow a two-thirds majority of the Supreme Court to impeach the president "for non-adherence to this Constitution" (H. Hamilton 1938, 133).

Amendments would be proposed by two-thirds of both houses of the National Assembly and ratified by the electors. Every 25 years, the president could call a constitutional convention. Hamilton specified that "no amendment which would prohibit the electorate from changing any part of this Constitution by methods prescribed therein shall ever be proposed or ratified" (H. Hamilton 1938, 134).

Hamilton remains an elusive figure. Several academic journals reviewed his work, but it appears to have "faded into near oblivion" (Boyd 1992, 153).

For Further Reading:

Boyd, Steven R., ed. 1992. *Alternative Constitutions for the United States: A Documentary History.* Westport, CT: Greenwood Press.

Hamilton, Hugh L. 1938. *A Second Constitution for the United States of America.* Richmond, VA: Garrett and Massie.

HANS V. LOUISIANA (1890)

Hans v. Louisiana continues to influence interpretation of the Eleventh Amendment. A Louisiana citizen brought suit against that state to recover money that it owed him on bonds that he had purchased.

In *Chisholm v. Georgia* (1793), the Supreme Court accepted jurisdiction over a similar case involving a suit brought against a state by a citizen of another state. The Eleventh Amendment was adopted in response. It stated that the judicial power of the United States would not be interpreted to extend to suits "commenced or prosecuted against one of the United States by Citizens of another State, or by Citizens or Subjects of any Foreign State."

Granting that the words of the Eleventh Amendment did not specifically cover the contingency in *Hans* involving a state's own citizens, Justice Joseph Bradley upheld what he believed to be the popular understanding of the Constitution prior to *Chisholm,* according to which a state, as a sovereign, could not be sued without its consent. He thereby effectively accepted Justice James Iredell's dissenting opinion in *Chisholm* over the majority ruling. Justice John Marshall Harlan agreed with the result in *Hans* but did not accept the Court's analysis of *Chisholm v. Georgia*.

Hans in effect viewed the Eleventh Amendment as a restatement rather than a true amendment of the original Constitution (Orth 1992, 251). In so doing, it specifically widened the application of the literal words of the amendment. The Court has continued to utilize this approach in decisions like *Seminole Tribe v. Florida* (1996) and *Kimel v. Florida Board of Regents* (2000), broadly interpreting the Eleventh Amendment not only as to what it actually says but according to what the Court considers to be its wider purpose.

See also *Chisholm v. Georgia;* Eleventh Amendment.

For Further Reading:

Hans v. Louisiana, 134 U.S. 1 (1890).

Orth, John V., revised by Susan A. Bandes. 2005. "Eleventh Amendment." In *The Oxford Companion to the Supreme Court of the United States*, ed. Kermit L. Hall. New York: Oxford University Press, 290–291.

HARDIN, CHARLES (1908–1997)

Political scientist Charles Hardin introduced his plans for governmental reform in the midst of the Watergate crisis of the early 1970s. His objective was summarized in the title of his book, *Presidential Power and Accountability,* but he also described his plans as covering "presidential leadership and party government" (Hardin 1974, 2). After an analysis designed to show that existing limits on the president were inadequate and that the bureaucracy was out of control, Hardin advanced nine proposals, each designed to lead to greater governmental accountability and direction (Hardin 1974, 183–185).

First, Hardin proposed that the president and members of the House and Senate be elected at the same time to four-year terms, with this calendar being interrupted if the government dissolved and new elections were called.

Second, Hardin proposed supplementing existing single-member House districts with at-large seats—the party winning the presidency would get 100 extra seats and the losing party 50, provided that the winning party retained a majority. Party committees would select the at-large members, with the minority "shadow cabinet" having input into its party's slate of candidates.

Third, Hardin proposed that members of the House would nominate presidential candidates. These members would also replace a president who was disabled. As part of this proposal, Hardin would eliminate the vice presidency. Fourth, Hardin would significantly reduce the power of the Senate. It would neither confirm nominees to office nor ratify treaties. Moreover, if the House of Representatives waited at least 60 days and repassed a bill that the Senate had rejected, it would still go to the president for his signature.

Hardin's fifth proposal allowed for the override of a presidential veto by a majority of House votes and for only limited participation by the Senate.

Sixth, Hardin would allow members of Congress to serve in other offices, especially the president's cabinet. Seventh, the defeated presidential candidate would have a seat in the House and other privileges (including an official residence). Like the president, such individuals could be removed by the party committee that nominated them.

Hardin's eighth proposal provided that the presidency would go to the party winning the national plurality of votes.

His ninth called for repeal of all conflicting constitutional provisions as well as of the two-term presidential limit in the Twenty-second Amendment.

Other than his last proposal, Hardin was fairly vague about how to implement his ideas (see Vile 1991c, 117). Indeed, at one point, he suggested that it would be better to allow some features of a new system to "develop by convention than to stipulate them in advance" (Hardin 1974, 182). Hardin reissued his call for reform in 1989, at which time he reiterated the need to replace "the separation of powers between the executive and the legislature by a separation between the government and the opposition" (Hardin 1989, 201).

See also Parliamentary System.

For Further Reading:

Hardin, Charles M. 1974. *Presidential Power and Accountability: Toward a New Constitution.* Chicago: University of Chicago Press.

Vile, John R. 1991. *Rewriting the United States Constitution: An Examination of Proposals from Reconstruction to the Present.* New York: Praeger.

HARPER V. VIRGINIA STATE BOARD OF ELECTIONS (1966)

In 1964, the states ratified the Twenty-fourth Amendment. Applying to both primary and general elections for national offices, it prohibited the imposition of a poll tax as a condition of voting. In *Harper v. Virginia State Board of Elections,* Justice William O. Douglas wrote an opinion for the Supreme Court extending the poll tax prohibition to state elections. He relied on the equal protection clause of the Fourteenth Amendment and on his judgment that, as a fundamental right, voting should not be dependent on one's ability to pay a fee.

Justice Hugo Black wrote a striking dissenting opinion, in which he stated that the Court should have upheld its earlier decisions in *Breedlove v. Suttles* (1937) and *Butler v. Thompson* (1951). Acknowledging his own personal opposition to the imposition of a poll tax, he argued that such a tax could have a rational basis. Moreover, he argued that, in making its decision, the Court was usurping the amending power:

> If basic changes as to the respective powers of the state and national government are needed, I prefer to let those changes be made by amendment as Article V of the Constitution provides. For a majority of this

Court to undertake the task . . . amounts . . . to an exercise of power the Constitution makers with foresight and wisdom refused to give to the Judicial Branch of the Government (*Harper* 1966, 676).

Citing the "concept of a written constitution," Black further suggested that "when a 'political theory' embodied in our Constitution becomes outdated," the Court was less qualified to come up with a new one "than the people of this country proceeding in the manner provided by Article V" (*Harper* 1966, 678). Black believed that Congress could, under its enforcement authority in Section 5 of the Fourteenth Amendment, outlaw the poll tax if it found that this tax was "being used as a device to deny voters equal protection of the laws" (*Harper* 1966, 679).

Justices John Marshall Harlan and Potter Stewart also dissented. They argued that the majority decision was based on "current egalitarian notions of how a modern democracy should be organized" rather than on any constitutional mandates (*Harper* 1966, 686).

See also Black, Hugo Lafayette; Fourteenth Amendment; Twenty-Fourth Amendment.

For Further Reading:

Ackerman, Bruce, and Jennifer Nou. 2009. "Canonizing the Civil Rights Revolution: The People and the Poll Tax." Northwestern University Law Review 103 (Winter): 63–148.

Harper v. Virginia State Board of Elections, 383 U.S. 663 (1966).

Lawson, Steven F. 1976. Black Ballots: Voting Rights in the South, 1944–1969. New York: Columbia University Press.

HARTFORD CONVENTION

Early American history witnessed numerous disputes about the respective authority of the state and national governments. In the Virginia and Kentucky Resolution of 1798, James Madison and Thomas Jefferson asserted the right of states to "interpose" themselves on behalf of civil liberties, in this case, by opposing the federal Alien and Sedition Acts, the latter of which they believed to be in conflict with the First Amendment. Other southerners later developed this doctrine into the doctrines of nullification and secession.

States' rights sentiment was not, however, confined to the South. Such sentiment became especially strong in New England in the years leading up to and including the War of 1812. Jefferson's proclamation of an embargo, as well as the war itself, interfered substantially with New England commerce and led to resentment, culminating in a meeting of representatives of five states from December 15, 1814, to January 5, 1815, known as the Hartford Convention. This convention, which was not called by Congress under provisions of Article V, proposed seven amendments.

The first two resolutions reflected the continuing split between free and slave states. Delegates proposed eliminating the clause whereby slaves were counted as three-fifths of a person; they also favored requiring a two-thirds vote in both houses of Congress for the admission of new states, thus making the admission of additional slave states less likely. The third and fourth resolutions would have limited Congress's power to impose embargoes to 60 days and would have required a two-thirds vote to do so. The fifth proposal would have required a two-thirds vote for Congress to declare war, absent the need for immediate defense. The sixth proposal would have prevented naturalized citizens from serving in Congress or holding other civil offices, and the seventh would have limited the president to one term (Ford 1898, 688–689).

Delegates from the Hartford Convention arrived in Washington, D.C., as residents were celebrating news of the American victory at the Battle of New Orleans and the signing of a peace treaty with Great Britain (Vile 1993b, 186). The close association of the Federalist Party with the Hartford Convention led to its demise, but a number of the convention's ideas continued to be topics of discussion. Abolitionist leader William Lloyd Garrison was among those who later urged Northern states to secede from the Union rather than continuing their association with slave states.

Later conventions of state delegates that met to discuss possible laws and amendments included the Nashville Convention of 1850 and the Peace Convention of 1865. Neither averted the eventual secession, albeit not of the states of the North but of those of the South. The idea of Southern secession is generally considered to be a logical extension of earlier ideas of state nullification, which South Carolina Senator John C. Calhoun had advocated.

See also Calhoun, John C.; Garrison, William Lloyd; Nashville Convention; Peace Convention; Virginia and Kentucky Resolutions.

For Further Reading:

Banner, James M., Jr. 1970. *To the Hartford Convention: The Federalists and the Origins of Party Politics in Massachusetts, 1789–1815.* New York: Alfred A. Knopf.

Ford, Paul L., ed. 1898. *The Federalist.* New York: Henry Holt.

Vile, John R. 1993. *The Theory and Practice of Constitutional Change in America: A Collection of Original Source Materials.* New York: Peter Lang.

HAWES, ROBERT F., JR. (1973–)

The American Liberty Alliance Web site describes Robert F. Hawes Jr. as a native Virginian, who graduated from Pensacola Christian College in 1995 and is working in the IT field in South Carolina. A self-described "Jeffersonian," he has written for *The Libertarian Enterprise.* In a 2006 book, Hawes examined the doctrine of secession and concluded that Abraham Lincoln had been wrong and that states do have a right to secede from the Union.

Concerned both that the nation was becoming increasingly divided and that it was denying civil liberties because of concerns about terrorism, Hawes proposed 14 "potentially helpful constitutional amendments" that might be considered to be "a 21st Century bill of rights" (2006, 295). The first would limit presidential war powers by providing that the president would need the "consent of two-thirds of Congress" before employing "armed forces in any purely offensive, pre-emptive, 'peace-keeping,' or punitive operation on foreign soil." The second would limit the time during which citizens could be imprisoned without a suspension of the writ of habeas corpus for such citizens. The third limited the use of martial law, the fourth prohibited suspension of the Constitution, and the fifth would curb the use of executive orders outside the executive department. The sixth would tighten search and seizure requirements, the seventh would provide greater security against invasions of privacy, and the eighth would allow one-half of the state legislatures to invalidate any act of the president, Congress, or the Supreme Court.

This ninth proposal would prohibit the U.S. Supreme Court from considering foreign law when making its rulings, and the tenth would require three-fourths of the state legislatures to ratify treaties. The eleventh would prohibit international bodies from adopting laws or regulations for the states. The twelfth would amend congressional powers under the commerce clause "to actual exchanges of goods and services and related monies between persons and/or entities of differing states." The thirteenth would forbid inheritance taxes, and the fourteenth would prohibit Congress from "regulating the private or public behavior of individuals; domestic institutions and civil unions; reproductive concerns; minor child rights and status; or private business contracts and practices, where interstate commerce is not involved" (295–299).

For Further Reading:

American Liberty Alliance. http://american libertyalliance.org/index/php?option=com-contract &Itemid=3. Accessed June 20, 2008.

Hawes, Robert F., Jr. 2006. *One Nation, Indivisible? A Study of Secession and the Constitution.* n.p.: Fultus Books.

HAWKE V. SMITH (I) (1920)

This case stemmed from a petition to enjoin the Ohio secretary of state from printing ballots for voter approval of the state legislature's ratification of the Eighteenth Amendment, which provided for national alcoholic prohibition. Ohio had added such referendum provisions to its constitution in November 1918. In January 1919, Ohio's governor sent copies of the state's legislative ratification of the Eighteenth Amendment to the U.S. secretary of state, who included Ohio's ratification in his count.

Writing for a unanimous Court, Justice William Day decided that, in specifying legislative ratification of amendments, the Constitution clearly had in mind "the representative body which made the laws of the people," rather than the people themselves (*Hawke* [*I*] 1920, 227). Referring to the precedent in *Hollingsworth v. Virginia* (1798), Day argued that, when ratifying amendments, states were performing a federal rather than a legislative function. Perhaps partly motivated by concern about the possible rescission of amendments, Day noted that "any other view might lead to endless confusion in the manner of ratification of federal amendments" (*Hawke* [*I*] 1920, 230).

Hawke leaves open Congress's option to specify that states ratify amendments by conventions, as in the case of the Twenty-first Amendment, which repealed the Eighteenth. Indeed, the decision in *Hawke* led some observers to believe that the Eighteenth Amendment would never have been enacted had it required popular approval; this view, in turn, encouraged Congress to seek repeal of this amendment by the hitherto untried state convention method.

A U.S. circuit court opinion in *Kimble v. Swackhamer* (1978) permits purely advisory referendums on constitutional amendments, but in *Cook v. Gralike* (2001), the U.S. Supreme Court decided that states could not give binding instructions to their representatives as to how they had to vote on amendments or make negative notations on the ballots of those who refused to support such amendments.

See also *Cooke v. Gralike;* Eighteenth Amendment; *Hollingsworth v. Virginia;* Initiative and Referendum; *Kimble v. Swackhamer;* Twenty-fourth Amendment.

For Further Reading:

Hawke v. Smith (*I*), 253 U.S. 221 (1920).

Walroff, Jonathan L. 1985. "The Unconstitutionality of Voter Initiative Applications for Federal Constitutional Conventions." *Colorado Law Review* 85: 1525–1545.

HAWKE V. SMITH (II) (1920)

A companion case to *Hawke v. Smith* (*I*), this ruling concerned the submission of the Nineteenth Amendment (prohibiting restrictions on women's suffrage) rather than the Eighteenth Amendment (providing for national alcoholic prohibition) to state voters. In a two-paragraph decision, Justice William Day ruled that, in accord with the companion opinion, the provision of Ohio's constitution requiring approval of amendments by referendum was unconstitutional.

See also *Hawke v. Smith* (*I*); Nineteenth Amendment.

For Further Reading:
McLaughlin, Michael. 2008. "Direct Democracy and the Electoral College: Can a Popular Initiative Change How a State Appoints its Electors?" *Fordham Law Review* 76 (May): 2943–3000.

HAZLITT, HENRY (1894–1993)

Journalist Henry Hazlitt offered his proposal for a parliamentary system in a book first published in 1942 and subsequently reissued, in somewhat reduced form, in 1974. Throughout this period, Hazlitt continued to blame the nation's inflexible Constitution for many of its ills. He favored a parliamentary system, whereby the Congress could vote no confidence in a premier, who could, in turn, dissolve Congress and call for new elections.

Hazlitt believed that the first step toward change should be reform of the amending process. He favored adoption of a system like that in Australia. Under such a plan, amendments would be proposed by absolute majorities in both houses of Congress and submitted to the people through a referendum. Ratification would require a majority of voters in a majority of states (Hazlitt 1942, 11–12).

The central reform that Hazlitt advocated was to fuse legislative and executive powers. To this end, he favored significantly reducing the power of the Senate, ending the system of fixed terms of office, and eliminating the president's veto and related powers. Hazlitt concentrated on Congress. One of his more novel suggestions was his proposal to deprive officeholders of voting rights during their tenure; alternatively, their votes could be segregated at separate polling booths so that the public could see how their positions influenced their votes. Hazlitt thought that the House of Representatives should have about 150 members. Their first task would be to choose a premier. The president would make the ultimate selection, but only after congressional balloting. The premier would, in turn, select a cabinet of 10 to 12 persons; like the premier, they would not necessarily have to be selected from Congress.

Members of the cabinet would continue to head executive departments, but undersecretaries would do the actual administration so that cabinet members could focus on policy issues. The cabinet would formulate major bills. These would then be submitted to a legislative council of about a dozen individuals representing the entire legislature. Bills would then go to standing congressional committees (where seniority would have been eliminated), whose power would be that of revising and overseeing rather than formulating legislative measures (Hazlitt 1942, 140). The cabinet would subsequently set the legislative agenda, with the legislature weighted, when needed, to give the largest party a majority.

Rejecting the initiative except for amendments designed to reduce "the powers, terms or number of legislators or changing the method of election" (Hazlitt 1942, 159), Hazlitt favored the referendum mechanism only as a way of ratifying constitutional amendments. House members would serve four-year terms, subject to dissolution and new elections or to individual recall.

Ideally, Hazlitt favored a Senate of two dozen people chosen for eight-year terms by the House of Representatives, but he realized that this would conflict with the Article V provision that no state be deprived of its equal representation without its consent. He was therefore willing to settle for a Senate with a reduced role, enabling it to delay and reconsider, but not block, House legislation.

Although he would take away the president's power to veto and to execute laws, make treaties, and direct military policy (Hazlitt 1942, 105), Hazlitt wanted to preserve the president as head of state. The president could perform ceremonial functions, advise the premier, and, on extraordinary occasions, dissolve the legislature (Hazlitt 1942, 111). The president would be chosen for a five- to ten-year term by both houses of Congress.

Recognizing that such major changes would be difficult to adopt, Hazlitt proposed a number of less drastic expedients. These included amendments to limit the president to two terms (later adopted with the ratification of the Twenty-second Amendment), to give the president an item veto, to eliminate the requirement that members of Congress reside in the states that select them, to specify that judges retire at 70 or 75 years of age, to fix the membership of the Supreme Court, and to allow Congress to remove up to one judge a year for usurping congressional functions. Other proposed reforms included allowing both houses of Congress to approve treaties by majority vote, eliminating the vice presidency, and reforming congressional rules (Vile 1991c, 86). In his 1974 book, Hazlitt also proposed preventing the president from serving consecutive terms and allowing state governors to appoint one member of the Supreme Court (Vile 1991c, 94 n.2). In an essay first published in 1983, Hazlitt reaffirmed his support for a presidential item veto and sought to prevent the Senate from increasing appropriations approved by the House (Hazlitt 1987).

See also Parliamentary System; Twenty-second Amendment.

For Further Reading:

Hazlitt, Henry. 1987. "A Proposal for Two Constitutional Amendments." In *A Nation in Debt: Economists Debate the Federal Budget Deficit,* ed. Richard H. Fink and Jack H. High. Frederick, MD: University Publications of America.

Hazlitt, Henry. 1974. *A New Constitution Now.* New Rochelle, NY: Arlington House.

Hazlitt, Henry. 1942. *A New Constitution Now.* New York: Whittlesey House.

Vile, John R. 1991. *Rewriting the United States Constitution: An Examination of Proposals from Reconstruction to the Present.* New York: Praeger.

HEHMEYER, ALEXANDER (1910–1993)

Attorney Alexander Hehmeyer originally prepared his proposals for constitutional revision as part of a study of domestic political reform anticipating the end of World War II (Hehmeyer 1943). He hoped to use the sense of urgency generated by the war to stimulate interest in reform (Vile 1991c, 90–91). Recognizing that all a convention could do was to propose changes, Hehmeyer favored convening a constitutional convention by a concurrent resolution of Congress.

Hehmeyer anticipated a convention of 97 members: 48 to be named by the states, 16 by Congress, 16 by the president, 16 by the chief justice, and a chair appointed by Congress (Hehmeyer 1943, 38–40). He foresaw four areas where such a convention should concentrate: relations between the president and Congress, the balance between the nation and the states, liberalization of the amending process, and a reexamination of the Bill of Rights.

In reassessing Congress, Hehmeyer concluded that plans for a parliamentary system were impractical and concentrated instead on seeking "to make Congress more responsive to the President and to make the President more responsive to Congress and to do this without departing radically from existing institutional forms" (Hehmeyer 1943, 64). Initially suggesting a three-year presidential term, Hehmeyer instead recommended a plan by which members of the House of Representatives would serve four-year terms.

Hehmeyer advocated extensive cabinet reform. He proposed reorganizing the cabinet so that it would have eight members: a "Secretary Without Portfolio, Secretary for Administration, Secretary for Legislation, Secretary for International Affairs, Secretary for National Defense, Secretary for Law, Secretary of the Economy, [and a] Secretary for National Welfare" (Hehmeyer 1943, 77). Most such secretaries would not have to run departments; that task would be given to full-time administrators. The secretary of legislation would have the power to initiate legislation in Congress and participate in debates. The president could make changes in the cabinet on the basis of midterm elections. Administrators of agencies could be selected through the civil service system.

Hehmeyer proposed a number of congressional reforms, including the establishment of automatic vote recorders, more efficient parliamentary procedures, better staffing, and a joint legislative council. This council would include three presidential representatives to coordinate legislation between the two houses. Hehmeyer would also reduce the number of standing committees, eliminate the seniority rule, and alter the system of appropriations. He further advocated that treaties be proposed by a majority of both houses of Congress rather than by a two-thirds vote of the Senate.

Hehmeyer believed that there was considerable room to develop regional authorities and consolidate local governments. He also favored eliminating tax duplication and resolving conflicts between state and national taxing authorities.

Hehmeyer respected the Bill of Rights and thought that consideration should be given to including economic and social rights. He also favored a more liberalized amending process. He suggested introducing amendments in one of five ways: "by a majority of the elected membership of both Houses of Congress"; "by a two-thirds majority of either House if approved in two (or perhaps three) consecutive sessions"; "by a majority of the State legislatures if within a period of five years, they approve the identical proposal"; "by a convention to be convened by Congress either on its own initiative or if requested within a period of five years by a majority of the State legislatures"; or, in a proposal reminiscent of Thomas Jefferson, "by a Convention to be convened regularly every thirty years upon the call of the President" (Hehmeyer 1943, 163–167). Such amendments would be ratified "(a) By two-thirds of the State legislatures acting within four years or (b) By a majority of the voters in two-thirds of the States and a major-

ity of all those voting in the nation at a special election held within two years from the date of the proposal or at the next succeeding election for Representatives" (Hehmeyer 1943, 169).

Hehmeyer admired the role of the Supreme Court in applying constitutional guarantees to modern times and suggested that it might render advisory opinions. He also wanted to fix the number of Supreme Court justices at nine and eliminate federal jurisdiction in diversity of citizenship cases. Under miscellaneous reforms, Hehmeyer included such proposals as having ex-presidents serve for life in the Senate, giving the president an item veto, allowing for the postponing of national elections in times of emergency, abolishing the electoral college and the vice presidency, and abolishing state residency requirements for members of Congress.

For Further Reading:

Hehmeyer, Alexander. 1943. *Time for Change: A Proposal for a Second Constitutional Convention.* New York: Farrar and Rinehart.

HENDERSON, YANDELL
(1873–1974)

Yandell Henderson was a professor of physiology at Yale University and an active member of the newly formed Progressive Party, under whose banner he ran unsuccessfully for Congress (Vile 1991c, 54–55). He advocated three major reforms in an article in the *Yale Review* (Henderson 1913).

First, Henderson favored either fusing or otherwise bringing the legislative and executive branches into closer cooperation. He even suggested that, at the state level, legislators might be replaced by a board of directors presided over by the governor. Second, Henderson proposed that the people should be able to "recall" judicial decisions by voting on whether to give sanction to laws that the courts invalidated. Henderson suggested that this would be "a far more sensible method of amending the old and of gradually building up a new set of principles and institutions than the present method of effecting constitutional amendments" (Henderson 1913, 89).

Third, Henderson proposed to "establish a real nation and a real national government instead of a Union of States and a Federal Government" (Henderson 1913, 89). Henderson favored calling a national constitutional convention to achieve these goals.

For Further Reading:
Henderson, Yandell. 1913. "The Progressive Movement and Constitutional Reform." *Yale Review* n.s. 3: 78–90.

HIGHWAYS

Few states are more closely associated with the automobile than California. The state's clogged freeways are daily reminders of the importance of the car to the state's lifestyle. In 1952, the California legislature petitioned Congress to call a convention relative to the use of federal highway taxes. The proposed amendment specified that

> all money, collected from any taxes now or hereafter imposed by the United States upon motor vehicles or the operation thereof, and upon the manufacture, sale, distribution, or use of motor vehicle fuels, supplies and equipment . . . shall be apportioned by the Congress to the several States and shall be used by the States exclusively for the construction and maintenance of highways in the manner prescribed by Congress ("Assembly Joint Resolution 8" 1952, 4003).

In 1956, the national government created the Highway Trust Fund, which earmarked monies from user taxes for highway construction, including the interstate highway system. The fund succeeded in insulating expenditures on highways from competition with projects in the general budget (I. Rubin 1990, 131–141).

For Further Reading:
"Assembly Joint Resolution 8." 1952. *Congressional Record,* 82nd Cong., 2d sess. 1952, Vol. 98, pt. 3: 4003–4004.

Rubin, Irene S. 1990. *The Politics of Public Budgeting: Getting and Spending, Borrowing and Balancing.* Chatham, NJ: Chatham House.

HILLHOUSE, JAMES (1754–1832)

This Federalist lawyer, who served in the Revolutionary War, and subsequently in both the U.S. House of Representatives (1791–1796) and Senate (1796–1810), offered seven related amendments in the latter body in 1808. In addition to his service in Congress, Hillhouse was the longtime treasurer of Yale College and served from 1810 to 1825 as the director of the Connecticut school fund, which had been funded by the sale of Connecticut's western lands.

The seven proposals that Hillhouse introduced in the Senate in 1808 called for fairly substantial changes in presidential elections, presidential powers, and presidential and congressional terms. Although he incorrectly identifies Hillhouse as a New Yorker, Richard H. Hansen observed that Hillhouse was the first member of congress to offer an amendment in Congress "to alter the method of nominating and electing the President" (1962, 178).

Hillhouse accompanied his proposals with a speech to the Senate in which he contrasted his own proposals, which sought "a radical cure," to some of the piecemeal proposals that had preceded them (1808b, 4).

Hillhouse's first two proposals called for shortening the terms of members of the House of Representatives to one year and of Senators from six to three years. Hillhouse reasoned that "frequent elections are a complete antidote" to popular fears of entrusting such legislators with power over a more sustained period (12).

Hillhouse's third proposal was his most radical. Beginning in 1813, so as not to affect the immediate presidential contest, Hillhouse proposed choosing the president by lot from among the class of Senators who were serving in what would now be their last year. This seat would then become vacant and would be filled by the requisite state legislature (the procedure in place prior to adoption of the Seventeenth Amendment, providing for direct popular election of Senators). This proposal expressed great faith in the state legislatures responsible for selecting Senators, who would effectively be the nation's new electors, and discounted the need for extraordinary presidential leadership. Hillhouse reasoned that, although it had taken genius "to organize and put in operation a new government . . . now that our government is *under way,* and furnished with *laws* and well digested systems, which are the *compass* and *charts* of the political pilots . . . a number of men may be found in every state fully competent to take the helm" (22). Perhaps taking a dig at Democratic-Republican leaders Thomas Jefferson and James Madison, Hillhouse observed that the new system might be more likely to produce "*practical*" men rather than "men formed for *science* and abstruce learning."

Hillhouse's third proposal stemmed from his fear that the president was too powerful and that the contest for the office, and the hope of patronage that presidential appointments brought with it, inflamed party passions. He thus observed that "Party spirit is the *demon* which has engendered the factions that have destroyed most free governments." (27) He further opined that "State or local parties will have but a feeble influence on the general government. It is regular, organized parties, extending from the northern to the southern extremity of the U. States, and from the Atlantic, to the utmost western limits, which threaten to shake this UNION to its *centre*" (27).

Hillhouse further observed that the existing Electoral College was working almost opposite of what its author intended:

> And to secure his [the president's] election, it will be required that every person before he shall receive a vote or an appointment as an elector, shall pledge himself to support such nomination; and thus the *president* will in *fact* be made to *choose* the *electors,* instead of the *electors choosing the president.* (30)

He further observed that if the method of electing the president were not changed, it might

be necessary "to strip the office of *royal* prerogatives" (31). This observation coincided with Hillhouse's fourth proposed amendment to cap the president's annual salary (then set at $25,000) at $15,000.

With a president serving for such a shortened term, Hillhouse further proposed to eliminate the vice presidency and to provide for the Senate to choose its own speaker. More importantly, in his sixth proposal, Hillhouse would have subjected presidential appointments to confirmation not by the Senate, as under the existing Constitution, but by both houses. In his seventh proposal, he further advocated reversing the practice giving the president the power to dismiss such appointees by providing that such termination would also require the consent of both houses.

Recognizing that some would think that the time the nation was facing "danger from abroad" and "party dissensions at home" (50) was inauspicious for amendments, he argued that "the time of danger is the only time when public attention can be universally excited" (50). Significantly, Hillhouse later participated in the Hartford Convention of 1815, which was also notable for considering amendments to the U.S. Constitution.

The author of a short biography of Hillhouse noted that, 20 years after he proposed his amendments in Congress, Hillhouse corresponded with some notable statesmen to garner their opinions as to the merits of his proposals. James Madison opposed the changes as too sweeping, but Chief Justice John Marshall expressed some support for "some less turbulent and less dangerous mode of choosing the chief magistrate" (Quoted in Bacon 1860, 27). Similarly, New York's Chancellor Kent thought that popular election of the president "is that part of the machine of our government that I am afraid is doomed to destroy us," and William Crawford of Georgia, while agreeing that great talents were unnecessary for a president, was "not certain that the nation is prepared for such an amendment" (quoted in Bacon 1860, 28).

See also Congress, Term Lengths; Electoral College Reform; Hartford Convention; Madison, James; Marshall, John.

For Further Reading:

Bacon, Leonard. 1860. *Sketch of the Life and Public Services of Hon. James Hillhouse of New Haven; with a Notice of His Son Augustus Lucan Hillhouse.* New Haven, CT: n.p.

Hansen, Richard H. 1962. "Barriers to a National Primary Law," *Law and Contemporary Problems,* 27 (Spring): 178–187.

Hillhouse, James. 1808a. *Amendments to the Constitution of the United States Submitted for Consideration by Mr. Hillhouse.* April 12, 1808. Printed by Order of the Senate. 7 pp.

Hillhouse, James. 1808b. *Propositions for Amending the Constitution of the United States Submitted by Mr. Hillhouse to the Senate on the Twelfth Day of April, 1808, with his Explanatory Remarks.* U.S. Senate. 52 pp.

HISTORY OF CONSTITUTIONAL AMENDMENTS IN THE UNITED STATES

Since the U.S. Constitution was ratified in 1789, only 27 amendments have been proposed and ratified by the necessary majorities, and 10 of these (known collectively as the Bill of Rights) were adopted practically contemporaneously with the U.S. Constitution. The process is difficult but not impossible, and an historical overview of all the amendments illumines points that might not be obvious by reviewing each amendment individually.

The Ideas behind Amending Provisions

The idea of balancing constitutional stability with the need for change is old. It was put into relief both when the British system proved unresponsive to the demands that led to the Revolutionary War and when the American founders decided to abandon the idea of parliamentary sovereignty for a written Constitution that would delineate governmental powers and limits and that would be unchangeable by ordinary legislative means. The prototype for such mechanisms had already been established in a number of colonial charters that provided that basic freedoms could only be altered, if at all, by extraordinary majorities, as well as in state constitutions that states began writing at the time of the American Revolution. Most states had designed mechanisms, especially the constitutional convention and subsequent popular ratification mechanisms, to assure that their constitutions had firmer foundations and were less subject to change than ordinary legislation. In this manner, such constitutions served as fundamental law, or "higher law."

The Articles of Confederation, the government adopted in 1781 that emphasized state sovereignty, took the principle of constitutional stability to extremes. The adoption of most legislation required the consent of nine or more states. The Articles further provided that amendments would have to be proposed by Congress and be unanimously ratified by the states. A number of proposals had strong support, but none ever achieved the unanimous consensus required for an amendment. Frustration with this mechanism contributed to calls for a constitutional convention. Initially called together to rewrite the Articles, delegates ultimately decided instead to consider a whole new scheme of government that substituted a system of separation of powers and checks and balances. The system that emerged established a bicameral legislature, a president, and a system of courts in place of the single unicameral Congress under the Articles. Legislation required the consent of both houses of Congress and the president, subject to a two-thirds congressional override or a presidential veto.

The U.S. Constitutional Convention

At the Constitutional Convention, the framers designed a two-step process of proposal and ratification of amendments that they incorporated in Article V. It specified that two-thirds majorities of both houses of Congress would propose amendments, which would then have to be ratified by three-fourths of the states; an alternative mechanism allowing for two-thirds of the state legislatures to propose amendments through a constitutional convention was adopted but has never been used. Highlighting the importance of the Great Compromise, whereby states were represented according to population in the House of Representation and equally in the Senate, the framers provided that no state could be deprived of its equal suffrage in the latter house without its own consent; delegates also agreed that no amendment could prohibit slave importation for the succeeding 20 years. The framers of the new Constitution bypassed the amending provision in the Articles of Confederation, as well as existing state legislatures (which stood to lose some power under the new government), by providing in Article VII that the Constitution would go into effect when ratified by special conventions in nine or more of the states.

The Constitutional Convention of 1787 had barely adjourned before the nation split into rival Federalist and Anti-Federalist factions, the former supporting, and the latter opposing, ratification of the new document. Anti-Federalists feared that the new national government would threaten the rights of the states and of individuals. They increasingly focused in debates on the need for a bill of rights, such as was found in many state constitutions of the day (where they were sometimes called declarations of rights). Initially, most Federalists argued that a bill of rights was unnecessary because the national government could only exercise a limited set of powers. Federalists further argued that such a list might even prove dangerous if the authors of a bill of rights inadvertently omitted an important right. In time, however, many Federalists agreed that a bill of rights could do no harm and might even help. They also decided that such a bill was needed to head off a second convention, which might reverse the gains made at the first. Thomas Jefferson, then a U.S. ambassador to France, was among those who helped persuade James Madison (often identified as the father of the U.S. Constitution and the Bill of Rights) of the desirability of such a bill of rights.

Proposal and Ratification of the Bill of Rights

Federalists succeeded in ratifying the Constitution with the understanding that they would support adoption of a bill of rights. In the first Congress, Virginia representative James Madi-

son led the way in crafting a bill of rights from provisions within existing state constitutions and from the many proposals that states had submitted for constitutional change along with their ratifications. Fortunately, no states had approved the Constitution contingent upon the adoption of a single provision or set of provisions or the convening of a second convention. Despite arguments from his congressional colleagues for delay, Madison persuasively argued that the credibility of the new government rested largely on its ability to adopt a bill of rights in an expeditious fashion. Madison was unable to get one of his favorite proposals included—a provision providing for the rights of conscience that would have limited both state *and* national governments—but he did succeed in getting Congress to propose 12 amendments, 10 of which were ratified in 1791 as the Bill of Rights. These rights, like subsequent amendments, were added to the end of the document, where they have come to have increasing importance.

The provisions in the Bill of Rights were listed as judicially enforceable provisions rather than as mere aspirations. The amendments did not prove particularly important during the first century of the nation's existence for two reasons. First, the national government was relatively small and had little occasion to regulate daily life, and second, as the Supreme Court indicated in *Barron v. Baltimore* (1833), the provisions in the Bill of Rights limited only on the national government and not the states. Nonetheless, these amendments remained a vital symbol of some of the nation's highest ideals.

The First Amendment prohibited the establishment of religion; provided for its free exercise; and provided for freedom of speech, freedom of the press, and the right of peaceable assembly and petition. The Second Amendment provided for the right to bear arms and is still the object of fierce debate. (Was it primarily intended to identify an individual or a collective right?) The Third Amendment, responding to a grievance that the colonists had against the British, limited the quartering of troops within individual homes without the owner's consent.

The Fourth Amendment also responded to the system of general warrants, or writs of assistance, that the British had used to search colonial houses and businesses. This amendment limited unreasonable searches and seizures. It further provided that warrants would not issue except upon probable cause and unless they described with particularity the person, place, or thing intended to be searched and/or seized.

The Fifth Amendment followed with a series of rights for those accused of crimes or on trial for such crimes. These included a provision for grand jury indictment, a prohibition against double jeopardy or compulsory self-incrimination, and a provision specifying that individuals could not be deprived of their "life, liberty, or property, without due process of law." The Fifth Amendment further forbade the government from taking private property for public use without "just compensation."

The Sixth Amendment delineated additional rights for the accused, adding the right "to a speedy and public trial, by an impartial jury," the right of defendants to be informed of charges against them, and the right to confront adversary witnesses and compel witnesses to come to court, as well as the right to counsel. The Seventh Amendment extended the right of jury trials to civil cases. The Eighth Amendment prohibited excessive bail, excessive fines, and cruel and unusual punishments.

The Ninth and Tenth Amendments are more elusive. The Ninth Amendment was an apparent response to Anti-Federalist arguments that listing rights could prove to be dangerous. It indicated that the listing of rights did not "deny or disparage others retained by the people." The Tenth Amendment further specified that powers not delegated to the national government remained with the states or the people.

The Eleventh and Twelfth Amendments and the Quiet Interlude that Followed

During debates over ratification of the Constitution, some Federalists had given assurances that, in accord with the generally accepted doctrine of sovereign immunity then current, states would not be sued without their consent. Consequently, there was a strong outcry when the U.S. Supreme Court upheld such a suit against a state in *Chisholm v. Georgia* (1793). States fairly quickly adopted the Eleventh Amendment, which overturned this decision.

The complicated electoral college mechanism to elect a president encountered trouble with the development of the two-party system. Under the original electoral college system, each elector cast two votes for president, with the individual receiving the highest number of votes becoming the president and the individual with the second highest becoming the vice president. Not only did this system sometimes result in a president from one party and a vice president from another (as in the election of 1796, when the electors selected Federalist John Adams as president and Democratic-Republican Thomas Jefferson as vice president), but in the election of 1800, all the Democratic-Republican electors who voted for Jefferson also voted for Aaron Burr, leading to a tie in the Electoral College that had to be resolved in the U.S. House of Representatives, where outgoing Federalists still had a vote. The Twelfth Amendment was accordingly ratified in 1804. It provided that future electors would cast separate ballots for the president and vice president, with the House of Representatives choosing from among the top three candidates in cases (such as the election of 1824) when no individual received a majority.

The period from 1804 to 1865 was a period of great constitutional struggles over tariffs, slavery, and the relationship between the national government and the states, during which no amendments were ratified. In 1819, Congress did propose an amendment that would have stripped individuals who accepted foreign titles of nobility of their citizenship, but the requisite number of states never ratified this amendment. Similarly, Congress proposed the Corwin Amendment in 1861 to avert the Civil War by guaranteeing the continuing existence of slavery in states where it was already established. This proposal became more and more irrelevant with the beginning of war and Abraham Lincoln's eventual issuance of the Emancipation Proclamation.

Three Post–Civil War Amendments

Three amendments were proposed and ratified from 1865 to 1870. The Thirteenth Amendment eliminated the institution of slavery and gave Congress appropriate enforcement authority. This did not prevent a number of Southern states from enacting restrictive Black Codes regulating the freedom of former slaves.

The Fourteenth Amendment was much more extensive, containing a total of five sections. Most important was the first sentence. It overturned the Supreme Court decision in [*Dred*] *Scott v. Sandford* (1857), which had ruled that blacks were not and could not be American citizens. By contrast, the Fourteenth Amendment declared that all persons who were born or naturalized in the United States were citizens. Section 1 further reaffirmed early principles articulated in the Declaration of Independence by guaranteeing that all citizens would be entitled to the privileges and immunities of U.S. citizens; that none would be deprived of life, liberty, or property without due process of law (a provision modeled on that in the Fifth Amendment); and that all would be accorded equal protection of the laws. The due process clause later served as the constitutional basis for the doctrine that key provisions in the Bill of Rights that once limited only the national government would also apply to the states. Section 2 of the amendment effectively overturned the three-fifths clause, which had provided that slaves would be counted as "three-fifths of a person" for purposes of taxation and representation, and, in a provision that was never enforced, allowed for diminished representation for states that did not extend the vote to male voters over the age of 21; this was a serious disappointment to women's rights advocates, many of whom had also worked hard for the rights of African Americans. Section 3 disqualified Confederate supporters from office, subject to requalification by a congressional supermajority. Section 4 repudiated Confederate debts, and Section 5 provided for congressional enforcement of the amendment. Congress refused to recognize Southern governments until they adopted this amendment, assuring its passage but also leaving some states feeling that they had been blackmailed and possibly encouraging future evasion of the amendment's provisions. Initial Supreme Court interpretations of this amendment were quite restrictive. *The Slaughterhouse Cases* (1873)

gave a narrow reading to the privileges and immunities clause; the *Civil Rights Cases* of 1883 limited governmental intervention to cases involving state, rather than private, action, and *Plessy v. Ferguson* (1896) eventually sanctioned the system of Jim Crow laws under the doctrine of "separate but equal" (a decision later reversed by the Supreme Court's 1954 decision in *Brown v. Board of Education*). Ironically, while the application of the Fourteenth Amendment was being narrowed in the field of civil rights, its provisions were increasingly used to strike down economic legislation that the Supreme Court believed to be in violation of the rights of due process. In *Santa Clara County v. Southern Pacific Railroad* (1886), the Court specifically recognized corporations as legal "persons" entitled to protection under this amendment.

The last of the trio of amendments adopted after the Civil War, the Fifteenth, was initially the least effective. It prevented states from denying the vote to individuals on the basis of race. States evaded the amendment through poll taxes, literary tests, grandfather clauses, registration requirements, all-white primaries, and even physical violence. Over time, the U.S. Supreme Court struck down many of these mechanisms, and in 1965, Congress used the enforcement mechanism in Section 2 of this amendment to enact a tough Voting Rights Act, which has subsequently been extended in a number of other acts.

The Progressive Era Amendments

Although constitutional disputes continued, Congress did not propose any new constitutional amendments by the necessary majorities for the next 40 years. However, the states ratified four such amendments from 1913 to 1920, a period generally known as the Progressive Era and dominated by movements for direct democracy and other reforms.

The Sixteenth Amendment, adopted in 1913, overturned a Supreme Court decision in *Pollock v. Farmers' Loan & Trust Co.* (*II*) (1895), in which the Supreme Court had declared that the income tax was unconstitutional. The amendment provided revenues for an expanding national government that would soon be involved in a world war and also offered a means of equalizing wealth. The Seventeenth Amendment further democratized the Constitution by providing that members of the U.S. Senate would now be selected by direct popular vote rather than being chosen by their state legislatures, some of which had already begun appointing popular vote winners. Most controversial was the Eighteenth Amendment, which provided for national alcoholic prohibition. Partly fueled by the obvious harms of excessive alcohol consumption, which were often associated with immigrants (often Roman Catholics from Eastern and Southern European nations), and partly as a patriotic way of saving foodstuffs in a time of war, the Amendment was interpreted not only to outlaw hard liquors but also beers and wines that were much lower in alcoholic content. This attempt to use the Constitution to enact social policy was widely evaded and led to a significant increase in organized crime. It remains the only amendment ever to have been specifically repealed, with the adoption of the Twenty-first Amendment in 1933, shortly after the election of Franklin D. Roosevelt, who had opposed prohibition in his party's platform.

The Nineteenth Amendment brought to fruition hopes of women's suffrage that dated to the Seneca Falls Convention of 1848. Numerous women's organizations had fought for this amendment in the interim, and President Wilson had eventually supported it, in part to achieve unity during World War I. A proposed amendment by Congress in 1924 to overturn Supreme Court decisions by allowing Congress to prohibit child labor was never ratified by the required majority of the states, although changes in judicial interpretation of the commerce clause eventually permitted child labor laws.

The New Deal and Thereafter

Although the New Deal is associated with many changes in the role and function of government, the only amendments that it left in its wake were the Twenty-First Amendment repealing alcoholic prohibition and the Twentieth Amendment (also adopted in 1933) moving up the times that newly elected presidents and members of Congress assumed office. This reduced the time period during which so-called lame-duck representatives, who had not been reelected to office, could propose and adopt legislation. The amendment also provided for cases in which a president or vice president died between election and inauguration. Franklin Roosevelt's threat to "pack" the Supreme Court in 1937 was followed by a turnaround in judicial doctrine— "the switch in time that saved nine"—that made many proposed amendments approving the increased national powers associated with the New Deal unnecessary.

Democrat Franklin D. Roosevelt was the first president to break the tradition that limited a president to two terms, and Republicans were especially frustrated and outraged by the long period of Democratic dominance. In a move that some later regretted in the aftermath of the popular presidencies of Republicans Dwight D. Eisenhower and Ronald Reagan, Republicans succeeded in getting the Twenty-second Amendment ratified in 1951. It limited future presidents to two full terms or no more than 10 years in office.

Ever since the adoption of the Fourteenth Amendment, there had been questions about which provisions of the Bill of Rights were intended to apply to the states. During the 1960s, the Supreme Court nearly completed the job of applying all these provisions (especially those related to the rights of individuals accused of crimes) to the state governments. Three additional amendments were ratified in the 1960s. The Twenty-third Amendment, adopted in 1961, granted representation to the District of Columbia in the Electoral College, equivalent to that of the smallest states and raising the total number of electoral votes to 538. The Twenty-fourth Amendment, ratified in 1964, abolished the poll tax in national elections. With increased concern over dangers to presidential life and health at a time when presidents could have to decide whether to respond to attacks through use of nuclear weapons, the Twenty-fifth Amendment, ratified in 1967, further provided for cases of presidential disability and for the replacement of vice presidents who died in office.

The Twenty-sixth Amendment, given impetus by the war in Vietnam, where many American young people were serving and dying, was adopted in 1972. It lowered the voting age to 18. In a previous decision in *Oregon v. Mitchell* (1970), the U.S. Supreme Court had decided that the portion of a congressional law seeking to lower the voting age in state as well as in federal elections was unconstitutional. If uniformity were to be attained, this amendment thus became a virtual necessity.

The requisite number of states did not ratify amendments proposed from this time period to provide equal rights for women (1972) or to grant the District of Columbia voting representation in Congress (1978). In the former case, the proposal failed even after Congress extended its original seven-year deadline. Women proceeded to make dramatic legal gains through the adoption of other legislation at both the state and national levels and through more generous judicial constructions of their rights under the equal protection clause of the Fourteenth Amendment.

No deadline had accompanied one of the 12 amendments originally proposed as the bill of rights (the other, which dealt with the size of Congress, has never been adopted). Largely through the efforts of a Texas student named Gregory Watson, this amendment was resurrected and ratified in 1992 as the Twenty-seventh Amendment in a time of growing distrust of Congress. Dispute continues as to whether it was appropriate for states to add their ratifications to an amendment that many had assumed to have been dead, but no states attempted to rescind their ratifications during the long period throughout which it was subject to ratification. This amendment provided that laws varying the compensation of members of Congress could not go into effect without an intervening election.

Individual members of Congress have proposed more than 11,000 amendments since the writing of the U.S. Constitution. The states have never succeeded in calling a constitutional convention to propose amendments, and Congress has proposed only 33 amendments by the requisite two-thirds majorities of both houses. The 27 amendments that have been adopted stand as testimony to the fact that amendments are difficult but not impossible to enact. The difficulty of this mechanism arguably cautions against incorporating unduly prescriptive provisions with short-lived goals within the Constitution. This difficulty has also undoubtedly encouraged other branches, particularly the courts, to interpret the Constitution as a broad charter of government that gives adequate powers to Congress and to other branches of the government, while still recognizing the existence and importance of key individual rights.

See also Individual amendments, for example, First Amendment and Second Amendment.

For Further Reading:

Kyvic, David. 1996. *Explicit and Authentic Acts: Amending the Constitution, 1776–1995.* Lawrence: University Press of Kansas.

Vile, John R. 1991. "American Views of the Constitutional Amending Process: An Intellectual History of Article V." *The American Journal of Legal History* 35 (January): 44–69.

HOLLINGSWORTH V. VIRGINIA (1798)

Hollingsworth v. Virginia arose when stockholders of the Indiana Company attempted to stop Virginia from selling lands that the company had claimed after ratification of the Eleventh Amendment limiting such suit. They therefore asked the Court to declare that the amendment had not been properly ratified. Opponents argued that the orders, resolutions, and votes clause in Article I, Section 7, requiring that "every order, resolution, or vote to which the concurrence of the Senate and House of Representatives may be necessary (except on a question of adjournment) shall be presented to the President of the United States," applied to amendments and that the president had not signed this measure. Opponents also asked the Court to rule that, if the amendment had been ratified, it should have only a prospective effect, and not apply to cases that had been brought before its adoption.

The Court unanimously rejected both arguments, with Justice Samuel Chase responding to attorneys' arguments by saying that the presidential veto applied "only to the ordinary cases of legislation" and that the president "has nothing to do with the proposition, or adoption, of amendments to the Constitution" (*Hollingsworth* 1798, 382).

Professor David Currie noted that, in dismissing a suit seemingly still authorized by Section 13 of the Judiciary Act of 1789 (now thought to be superseded by the Eleventh Amendment), the Court anticipated the exercise of judicial review of federal legislation that is more commonly traced to the Supreme Court's 1803 decision in *Marbury v. Madison* (Currie 1985, 22). In arguing that an extension of the Equal Rights Amendment ratification deadline required a two-thirds vote of Congress and presidential approval, Yale's Charles Black (1978) warned against any further extension of the *Hollingsworth* precedent regarding the need for presidential signatures.

Although his signature was not required, President James Buchanan signed the proposed (but ultimately unsuccessful) Corwin Amendment, which was designed to head off civil war by guaranteeing the continuing existence of slavery in those states that still wanted it. This may have been the reason that Abraham Lincoln later signed the Thirteenth Amendment abolishing slavery. Complaining that it had not been submitted to him for signature, President Andrew Johnson proclaimed the validity of the Fourteenth Amendment (Ishikawa 1997, 590). President Lyndon Johnson later had a special ceremony in which he signed as a witness that the Twenty-fifth Amendment, relating to presidential disability and vice-presidential succession, had been ratified, and President Jimmy Carter signed the resolution extending the ratification deadline for the Equal Rights Amendment (Ishikawa 1997, 590). Other presidents who did not formally sign documents have, of course, worked for the adoption of amendments that have been proposed and/or ratified. In one such dramatic act, President Woodrow Wilson addressed Congress on behalf of the adoption of the Nineteenth Amendment.

See also Corwin Amendment; Eleventh Amendment; Equal Rights Amendment; *Marbury v. Madison;* Thirteenth Amendment; Twenty-fifth Amendment.

For Further Reading:

Hollingsworth v. Virginia, 3 U.S. (3 Dall.) 379 (1798).

Ishikawa, Brendon T. 1997. "Everything You Always Wanted to Know about How Amendments Are Made, but Were Afraid to Ask." *Hastings Constitutional Law Quarterly* 24 (Winter): 545–597.

Tillman, Seth Barret. 2005. "A Textualist Defense of Article I, Section 7, Clause 3: Why *Hollingsworth v. Virginia* Was Rightly Decided, and Why *INS v. Chadha* Was Wrongly Reasoned." *Texas Law Review* 83 (April): 1265–1372.

HOPKINS, CASPAR (1826–1893)

Caspar Hopkins was a "pioneer, businessman, author, and former president of the California Immigration Union" (Vile 1991c, 38). He published an article in 1885 advocating a series of 10 constitutional amendments (Hopkins 1885).

In Hopkins's first two proposals, he called for authorizing Congress to legislate on civil matters such as "marriage, divorce, inheritance, probate proceedings, modes and subjects of taxation, education, the tenure of real estate, and the collection of debts" (Hopkins 1885, 388). He also proposed to clarify congressional jurisdiction "over interstate commerce and communication, and the exclusive regulation of banks, insurance companies, and all other corporations which transact business in more than one State or Territory" (Hopkins 1885, 388). Similarly, state powers would be curtailed in these areas.

Hopkins's third proposal called for increasing federal judicial jurisdiction over all claims against the United States. He would also invest courts with the power to settle contested elections or cases involving the qualifications of legislators. His fourth proposal called for restricting congressional authority to the adoption of general or public measures, thus eliminating private bills.

Like Woodrow Wilson, Hopkins favored allowing the president to appoint cabinet members from the majority party in Congress. This was his fifth proposal. His sixth would have required legislators to undergo special education in colleges specifically designed for the purpose.

Although sentiment was already growing for a system of direct election of senators (which would eventually result in the adoption of the Seventeenth Amendment), in his seventh proposal, Hopkins took a different approach. He advocated recognizing the inevitable influence of wealth by limiting the right to vote for senators to those who had paid taxes on $100,000 or more of their incomes.

Hopkins's eighth and ninth proposals dealt with immigrants and Native Americans. He favored limiting immigration to foreigners with a certain level of education, skills, or property and limiting voting to natural-born citizens. Hopkins wanted to abolish programs that treated American Indians differently from other groups.

Finally, Hopkins proposed a number of changes relative to terms of office. Under his scheme, senators would serve for 10 years, the president for eight, and members of the House for six. No executive officers—presumably including the president—with the power of patronage would be eligible for reelection. Hopkins would further eliminate the Electoral College and establish two or three vice presidents in case both the president and the first vice president were disabled.

Hopkins believed that the weight of inertia was working against his proposals. He feared that a convention would be "full of peril and probabilities of failure," in part because "the country is full of communists, socialists, advocates of woman suffrage, agrarians, and cranks, whose every effort would be concentrated upon such an opportunity to realize their peculiar views in the fundamental law" (Hopkins 1885, 898).

See also Seventeenth Amendment.

For Further Reading:
Hopkins, Caspar T. 1885. "Thoughts toward Revising the Federal Constitution." *Overland Monthly* n.s. 6 (October): 388–398.

Vile, John R. 1991. *Rewriting the United States Constitution: An Examination of Proposals from Reconstruction to the Present.* New York: Praeger.

HOUSING

Unlike many constitutions that were formulated in the two centuries that followed its adoption, the U.S. Constitution confines itself to protecting political rights and leaves economic and social rights largely to the political process. Although both state and national governments have attempted to provide housing for those in need, the right to housing has never been considered to be an entitlement (Salins 1987, 176).

In July 1993, Democratic representative Charles Rangel of New York introduced an amendment designed to guarantee "that all U.S. citizens shall have a right to decent and affordable housing, which shall not be denied or abridged by the United States or any State" (H.J. Res. 64). Representative Jesse Jackson Jr. has since supported a similar proposal.

See also Jackson, Jesse L., Jr.; Social and Economic Rights.

For Further Reading:
Salins, Peter D., ed. 1987. *Housing America's Poor.* Chapel Hill: University of North Carolina Press.

HUBBELL, JANETTE

See Dolbeare, Kenneth, and Janette Hubbell.

IDAHO V. FREEMAN (1981)

This case emerged from the controversy over the proposed Equal Rights Amendment (ERA). Judge Marion Callister from the U.S. District Court in Idaho delivered the verdict in *Idaho v. Freeman.*

A number of Idaho and other state legislators argued that Idaho's rescission of its prior ratification of the ERA was constitutional, that Congress had no right to extend the ERA deadline, and that, in any case, such an extension would have required a two-thirds rather than a simple majority vote. Callister agreed with all three contentions. His ruling was, however, stayed by the U.S. Supreme Court and eventually mooted by the failure of the necessary number of states to ratify the ERA, despite the deadline extension.

The most extended portion of Callister's decision, which relied heavily on the district court decision written by John Paul Stevens in *Dyer v. Blair* (1975), had to do with whether the questions the legislators raised were political questions and therefore inappropriate for judicial resolution. In *Coleman v. Miller* (1939), the Supreme Court had suggested that many amending issues, and specifically the matter of whether amendment ratifications were made contemporaneously, were committed to congressional, rather than judicial, resolution. After reviewing the criteria established in *Baker v. Carr* (1962) for deciding whether issues were political questions, Callister decided that they were not present in this case. He argued that the Constitution had divided amending powers between Congress and the states rather than granting them exclusively to

the former. Moreover, he decided that precedents surrounding the adoption of the Fourteenth Amendment had not yet established the right of a state to rescind ratifications. Callister believed that such issues "must be interpreted with the kind of consistency that is characteristic of a judicial, as opposed to political [congressional] decision making" (*Idaho* 1981, 1139).

Callister settled on a contemporary consensus model similar to the one the Court had articulated in *Dillon v. Gloss* (1921), but arguably since called somewhat into question by the belated ratification of the Twenty-seventh Amendment. Under this contemporary consensus model, he decided that, prior to ratification by three-fourths of the states, a state's last action—whether ratification or rescission—should prevail. Callister further ruled that, although Congress was not required to set a ratification deadline, once it did so, it would have to abide by it, because states may have ratified an amendment contingent on their understanding that other states would have to ratify within that limit. In any case, Callister believed that the congressional extension of the ERA deadline had been unconstitutional because Congress could act in such circumstances only in its Article V rather than in its Article I capacity, and Article V referred only to actions by two-thirds of that body. Although this decision hardly settles the issues addressed, *Idaho v. Freeman,* like *Dyer v. Blair,* could undercut *Coleman v. Miller* by providing precedents for judicial resolution of amending issues.

See also *Coleman v. Miller; Dyer v. Blair; Equal Rights Amendment.*

For Further Reading:

Carroll, John. 1982. "Constitutional Law: Constitutional Amendment. Rescission of Ratification. Extension of Ratification Period. *State of Idaho v. Freeman.*" *Akron Law Review* 14 (Summer): 151–161.

Idaho v. Freeman, 529 F. Supp. 1107 (1981).

IMMIGRATION, ILLEGAL

Article I, Section 8 of the Constitution vests Congress with the power "to establish a uniform Rule of Naturalization." It is also responsible for protecting American borders. States often complain that federal failures in this area lead them to bear the burden of caring for illegal aliens. In *Plyler v. Doe* (1982), the U.S. Supreme Court specifically provided that states could not deny educational benefits to children of illegal aliens. Concern over illegal immigrants was especially pronounced in the Republican presidential primary contests in 2008.

The previous year, Glenn McConnell, the Senate president pro tem of South Carolina, announced his intention to call a convention to grant states power to deny benefits to illegal aliens and to expel them from the country. He observed that "It's really an act of frustration. The state is bearing the burden because of the power failure in Washington." He further observed that "If Congress continues to refuse to act, then states would have the ability to act in order to protect themselves and their pocketbooks." McConnell was especially concerned that illegal immigrants were contributing to the state's high unemployment rates. At the time it was proposed, McConnell's proposal was the only call for a convention on this subject on record (Wenger 2007).

See also Birthright Citizenship Amendment; Constitutional Convention.

For Further Reading:

Wenger, Yvonne. "Sen. McConnell Calls for US Constitutional Convention to Stop Illegal Immigration," *The Post and Courier,* October 5, 2007.

http://scsenategop.com/sen-mcconnell-calls-for-us-constitutional-convention-to-sto-illegal-immigration.htm. Accessed May 23, 2008.

IMPEACHMENT

Like the constitutional amending process, the impeachment power, that is, the power to bring charges against the president, vice president, and select appointed officials, is a device for "protecting the Constitution" (Kyvig 2009, vii). Article I, Section 2 of the U.S. Constitution vests this power in the House of Representatives. Article II, Section 4 specifies "Treason, Bribery, or other high Crimes and Misdemeanors" as the exclusive grounds for impeachment. Article I, Section 3 further provides that trials of impeachment take place before the Senate; if the president is on trial, the chief justice presides. Conviction of any officer requires a two-thirds vote and results in removal from office.

In ratifying the U.S. Constitution, New York proposed to widen the court for impeachment to include not only members of the Senate but also Supreme Court justices and senior judges of the highest courts of each state. Egbert Benson of New York would further have allowed federal judges to be tried within their states by U.S. Senators, Supreme Court justices, and judges of general judicial courts.

As of 2000, 17 persons, including 12 lower federal judges, one Supreme Court justice, one cabinet member, one senator (whom the Senate decided not to try), and two presidents have been impeached (Grossman and Yalof 2000, 7). Obviously, not all have been convicted. In the most comprehensive book on the subject, David Kyvig notes that the late–20th century became something of an "age of impeachment," with the unsuccessful attempts to impeach Chief Justice Earl Warren and Justices William O. Douglas and Abe Fortas preceding more high-profile successful impeachments that followed.

The meaning of the term "high Crimes and Misdemeanors" remains the subject of popular and scholarly discussion, with most scholars believing that the term refers either to illegal or quasi-illegal acts, typically involving abuse of power. A number of amendments have attempted to alter or clarify this process. Two proposals were introduced in 1913 by Ohio congressmen. One, offered by Democrat Atlee Pomerene, would have provided for a method other than impeachment for removing civil officers other than the president, the vice president, and members of the Supreme Court. A second, proposed by Republican Leonard Howland, would have allowed for trials of all except top officials by 12 senators. In 1945, Republican senator William Langer of North Dakota proposed that a vote by a majority of senators present should be sufficient for an impeachment conviction.

Former Democratic senator Howell Heflin of Alabama introduced a number of amendments on the subject. One would have allowed Congress to remove judges from office for inability to perform their duties, as well as for infractions of the law; this proposal would also have suspended officers indicted for felony offenses. A more detailed proposal offered by Heflin would have provided for a seven-member judicial inquiry commission to discipline judges guilty of violating canons of judicial ethics and to suspend or place on senior status judges unable to perform their duties. A number of recent proposals have also provided that judges would lose their offices immediately upon conviction of a crime.

Such proposals may have been prompted in part by late–20th-century cases of impeachment involving U.S. District Judges Harry E. Claiborne, Alcee L. Hastings, and Walter L. Nixon (Abraham 1998, 48–49; Volcansek 1993). Claiborne refused to resign after being convicted of felonies and imprisoned. Hastings was elected to the House of Representatives after being impeached and convicted. Like Claiborne, Nixon refused to resign from office after being convicted, in his case, of perjury. Nixon objected to the procedure by which a committee of the Senate heard his case in 1989 before the full Senate voted to convict him. In *Nixon v. United States* (1993), the Supreme Court upheld the Senate conviction on the basis that Article I, Section 3 of the Constitution vested the Senate with "the sole Power to try all Impeachments,"

thus implying that matters of procedure were "political questions" for the Senate to resolve. In June 2009, the House impeached U.S. District Judge Samuel Kent of Texas on four counts of sexual assault and lying after he refused to resign from the bench after being sent to prison.

Although President Richard M. Nixon resigned from the presidency after it became clear that the House of Representatives was likely to accept charges of obstruction of justice, abuse of powers, and failure to turn over papers to investigators that would lead to his conviction in the Senate, only two presidents, Andrew Johnson and Bill Clinton, have actually been impeached. The impeachment of Johnson was largely partisan and the charges against him (falling a single vote shy of the necessary two-thirds needed to convict in the U.S. Senate) did not rise to the level of "high crimes and misdemeanors."

Debate continues to swirl around the appropriateness of the charges that were brought against President Clinton, but for which he was not convicted and removed from office. The president's defenders claim that he was targeted by right-wing opponents simply for improper sexual behavior with a White House intern. Opponents claimed that this offense against propriety had been compounded by attempts to cover the matter up (thus obstructing justice) and lying to a grand jury. One contemporary author has suggested that future impeachment prosecutions for sexual matters might be avoided if the Constitution were to be amended so as to include the four words in the original draft of the Constitution—"against the United States"—after the words "high crimes and misdemeanors" (Germond and Witcover 1999, 296).

Two other authors, concerned about ambiguities and problems that appeared during the Clinton impeachment, have proposed a far more complex amendment divided into seven sections, some of which incorporate existing language and others of which plough new ground (Grossman and Yalof 2000). The first section would exempt members of Congress, who may already be removed from office by a two-thirds vote of their colleagues, from impeachment and would limit charges to "serious abuses of official power that undermine their conduct of office and threaten the integrity and legitimacy of the government. Such abuses include treason, bribery, and other serious crimes, as well as actions that are not criminal in nature" (Grossman and Yalof 2000, 17). The second section, which would continue to require the chief justice to preside in the case of a trial of the president (but would, by omission, apparently leave open the possibility that a vice president could continue to preside over his or her own trial), would require conviction of two-thirds of the entire Senate membership and would limit impeachments to a biennial Congress and prevent them from taking place "between a general election and the convening of a new Congress" (17). Section three, reacting to the Supreme Court's decision in *Clinton v. Jones* (1997) permitting the president to be sued in office for alleged sexual harassment he had committed as a state governor, would further prohibit the president from being the subject of a civil suit while in office but would allow Congress to lengthen the statute of limitations in such cases. Section four would allow Congress power "[t]o censure, rebuke, or otherwise publicly condemn official misconduct" and would further allow it to "devise alternative means, other than impeachment, for dealing with the disability, misconduct, or failure to maintain good behaviour, of federal judges other than justices of the Supreme Court" (17). Section five would prevent the president from issuing a self-pardon. Section 6 would somewhat modify the decision in *Nixon v. United States* by allowing the Supreme Court to exercise its original jurisdiction to review, prior to a Senate trial, "a petition submitted by an impeached president, the procedures employed in, and the constitutional basis of, articles of impeachment voted against the president by the House of Representatives" (17). Section seven would extend power to Congress to enforce this provision.

See also Judiciary, Removal of Members.

For Further Reading:

Abraham, Henry J. 1998. *The Judicial Process: An Introductory Analysis of the Courts of the United States, England, and France.* 7th ed. New York: Oxford University Press.

Berger, Raoul. 1973. *Impeachment: The Constitutional Problems.* Cambridge, MA: Harvard University Press.

Committee on Federal Legislation of the Bar Association of the City of New York. n.d. *The Law of Presidential Impeachment.* New York: Harrow Books.

Germond, Jack W., and Jules Witcover. 1999. "After the Trial, Revisions Are in Order." *National Journal* 31 (January 30): 296.

Grossman, Joel B., and David A. Yalof. 2000. "The Day After: Do We Need a 'Twenty-Eighth' Amendment?" *Constitutional Commentary* 17 (Spring): 7–17.

Kyvig, David E. 2008. *The Age of Impeachment: American Constitutional Culture since 1960.* Lawrence: University Press of Kansas.

Posner, Richard A. 1999. *An Affair of State: The Investigation, Impeachment, and Trial of President Clinton.* Cambridge, MA: Harvard University Press.

Volcansek, Mary L. 1993. *Judicial Impeachment: None Called for Justice.* Urbana: University of Illinois Press.

IMPLEMENTATION DATES OF AMENDMENTS

Amendments are generally forward looking, but some, like the Thirteenth and the Eighteenth, which respectively make slavery and the sale or consumption of alcohol illegal, prohibited widespread conduct that was previously considered legal, if not always acceptable. The Articles of Confederation, which required unanimous consent, were proposed in 1777 but did not go into effect until Maryland ratified in 1781. Although they did not designate a specific date, the writers of the U.S. Constitution specified in Article VII that it would go into effect when ratified by nine of the states. Article V now specifies that amendments proposed by two-thirds majorities in Congress or by conventions do not become law until ratified by three-fourths of the states. With problems of implementation in view, the authors of a number of amendments have designated the time period when they would go into effect.

Although, when adopted, the Thirteenth Amendment did not provide for a phase-in period for the elimination of slavery, many of the framers of the Constitution appeared to hope that the institution would die out on its own, and a number of previous writers on the subject of slavery had specified a period, often a generation or two in the future, when abolition might go into effect. The Seventeenth Amendment, which provided for the direct election of U.S. senators, specified that it "shall not be so construed as to affect the election or term of any Senator chosen before it becomes valid as part of the Constitution." The Eighteenth Amendment, providing for national alcoholic prohibition, specified that it would take effect "[a]fter one year from the ratification of this article . . ." (by contrast the Twenty-first Amendment, which repealed the Eighteenth, apparently went into effect immediately). The Twentieth Amendment, relating to terms of Congress, specified that those provisions would "take effect on the 15th day of October following the ratification of this article." The Twenty-second Amendment, which limited presidential terms, provided that it would not "apply to any person holding the office of President when this Article was proposed by the Congress" (at that time, Harry Truman was president) and that it would "not prevent any person who may be holding the office of President, or acting as President, during the term within which this Article becomes operative from holding the office of President or acting as President during the remainder of such term." Perhaps anticipating that the amendment might require fairly significant changes in legislation, the proposed Equal Rights Amendment specified that it "shall take effect two years after the date of ratification." Many versions of the Balanced Budget Amendment that were proposed in the 1990s provided that it would go fully into effect either two years after ratification or after 2002, whichever came later. Similarly, the proposed Victims' Rights Amendment provides that it would take effect "on the 180th day after the ratification of this article," presumably to give the national government and the states, as well as prosecutors' offices, time to take appropriate implementing actions.

In *United States v. Chambers* (1934), the U.S. Supreme Court decided that once an amendment (in this case the Eighteenth) was repealed,

no prosecutions or sentencing could occur on legislation on which it was based.

See also Eighteenth Amendment; Seventeenth Amendment; Thirteenth Amendment; Twentieth Amendment; Twenty-first Amendment; Twenty-second amendment; *United States v. Chambers*; Victims' Rights.

IMPLIED POWERS

See *McCulloch v. Maryland.*

INCORPORATION OF THE BILL OF RIGHTS

The "incorporation" of prominent provisions of the Bill of Rights into the due process clause of the Fourteenth Amendment, where they now apply to the states as well as to the national government, was one of the most prominent developments in 20th-century constitutional interpretation. Prior to the Civil War, Chief Justice John Marshall ruled in *Barron v. Baltimore* (1833) that the provisions in the Bill of Rights only limited the national government.

The language of the Fourteenth Amendment, however, was directed to the states, which were now prohibited from denying the privileges and immunities, the due process rights, or the equal protection rights of their citizens. Most prominently in the *Slaughterhouse Cases* (1873), the Supreme Court initially gave a narrow reading to these clauses, especially the privileges and immunities provision. In 1884, however, Justice John Marshall Harlan wrote a dissent in *Hurtado v. California* (1884), arguing that the due process guarantees in the Fourteenth Amendment intended to apply provisions of the Bill of Rights—in this case, the provision for indictment by grand jury—to the states. With the possible exception of Fifth Amendment property rights (*Missouri Pacific Railway Co. v. Nebraska* [1896] and *Chicago, Burlington & Quincy Railway Co. v.*

Chicago [1897]), the Court majority rejected Justice Harlan's stand. In 1925, however, the Court declared in *Gitlow v. New York* that freedom of speech did apply to the states, and it recognized several other exceptions in subsequent years.

In *Palko v. Connecticut* (1937), Justice Benjamin Cardozo provided an organizing principle to distinguish those guarantees in the Bill of Rights that were applicable to the states from those—like the Fifth Amendment guarantee against double jeopardy at issue in this case—that were not. He articulated the idea of selective incorporation, ruling that those guarantees in the Bill of Rights that were "implicit in the concept of ordered liberty" would apply to the states, but others would not.

Few cases better exemplify the varied views on incorporation than *Adamson v. California* (1947). At least four different views were articulated there. In refusing to overrule a decision on a case in which a prosecutor had commented on a defendant's failure to testify in his own defense (forbidden in federal cases by the self-incrimination provision of the Fifth Amendment), Justice Stanley Reed restated the view of selective incorporation for the Supreme Court majority. In a concurring opinion, Justice Felix Frankfurter articulated the view that the due process clause required "fundamental fairness" and that such fairness could not be mechanically ascertained simply by determining whether a provision was or was not in the Bill of Rights. Justice Hugo Black, like Justice Harlan before him, argued for total incorporation. As a former U.S. senator, he based his conclusion on his own reexamination of the debates over the Fourteenth Amendment—an argument that Charles Fairman (1949) and other scholars have since disputed, albeit not without generating questions about their own scholarship. Justices Frank Murphy and Wiley Rutledge articulated the view of total incorporation plus—that is, the idea that there may be rights in addition to those in the first 10 amendments that apply to the states. This view became even more prominent in the Connecticut birth control case *Griswold v. Connecticut* (1965). Rounding out the picture is the position of "selective incorporation plus" (Abraham and Perry 2003, 100).

Although the view of selective incorporation has dominated most Supreme Court decision-making, over the course of time, the Supreme Court has incorporated more and more guarantees from the Bill of Rights into the due process clause. Today, only five guarantees have not yet specifically been given judicial protection. They are the Second Amendment right to bear arms, the Third Amendment's guarantee on quartering troops, the Fifth Amendment's guarantee of a grand jury indictment, the Seventh Amendment's right to a jury trial in a civil case, and the Eighth Amendment's guarantee against excessive fines and bail (O'Brien 2000a, 311). The last case to incorporate a new provision in the Bill of Rights was the decision to apply the protection against double jeopardy in *Benton v. Maryland* (1968).

See also *Adamson v. California; Barron v. Baltimore;* Black, Hugo Lafayette; Fairman, Charles; Fourteenth Amendment; *Griswold v. Connecticut; Palko v. Connecticut.*

For Further Reading:

Abraham, Henry J., and Barbara Perry. 2003. *Freedom and the Court: Civil Rights and Liberties in the United States.* 8th ed. Lawrence: University Press of Kansas.

Fairman, Charles. 1949. "Does the Fourteenth Amendment Incorporate the Bill of Rights? The Original Understanding." *Stanford Law Review* 2 (December): 5–139.

O'Brien, David M. 2000a. *Civil Rights and Civil Liberties.* Vol. 2 of *Constitutional Law and Politics.* 4th ed. New York: W. W. Norton.

INDIANS

See Native Americans.

INITIATIVE AND REFERENDUM

In *Federalist No. 10*, James Madison distinguished a direct, or pure, democracy from an indirect, or representative, democracy (Hamilton, Madison, and Jay 1961, 81–82). Although he defended the latter, subsequent advocates of more direct democracy have favored the initiative and referendum. The initiative allows citizens to initiate legislation or constitutional amendments through petitions, and the referendum permits citizens to approve or disapprove legislation; sometimes both mechanisms are classified under the single term "referendum" (Schmidt 1989, 3). Such mechanisms are often linked to the recall, by which voters may petition to remove officeholders with whom they are dissatisfied.

Types of Referendums

Referendums can effect either legislative or constitutional change. The first American referendum was the 1788 Massachusetts referendum on the state constitution, and although the U.S. Constitution makes no such provision, many American states and foreign nations have subsequently adopted a requirement for popular approval of constitutions or of amendments to them. In early 1861, the Senate apparently came but one vote shy of accepting a proposal for a national plebiscite on a series of compromises offered by Senator John J. Crittenden of Kentucky to avoid the Civil War (Shermer 1969, vii).

Direct Democracy's Three Periods of Popularity

Thomas Cronin has identified three periods during which direct democracy was particularly popular at the national level. These are "the populist and progressive movements (1890–1912); . . . the isolationist and peace movements (1914–1940); and . . . the issue activism both of the left and the right (1970–1988)" (1989, 164).

The Populist and Progressive Eras

The movement for the initiative and referendum in the Populist and Progressive Eras began in the states. South Dakota adopted this mechanism in 1898, and 17 other states had followed by 1917 (Musmanno 1929, 173). Perhaps because other representative institutions were less developed, this movement was successful primarily in the West and Midwest—a breeding ground for other

Progressive Era amendments (Grimes 1978, 65–100). Four-fifths of the states adopting the mechanism were west of the Mississippi River (Schmidt 1989, 10).

As early as 1895, Populist Kansas senator William Peffer introduced a national amendment to submit important matters to the people upon petition by one-fifth of the voters or one-fourth of the state legislatures (Musmanno 1929, 173). Other contemporary proposals varied the number of voters required to initiate such a petition—a proposal by Wisconsin Democratic Representative Lucas Miller permitted such action by as few as 1,000 inhabitants. Republican Senator Joseph Bristow of Kansas proposed allowing the president to go over the head of Congress by placing measures that he favored, but that Congress failed to enact, on the ballot (Musmanno 1929, 175). The National Direct Legislative League was formed in the 1890s to push for a national referendum. This idea was often favored by Prohibitionists and other third-party representatives. Theodore Roosevelt and Woodrow Wilson both indicated support for such measures (Cronin 1989, 50).

The Isolationist and Peace Movements

The most popular referendum proposal from 1914 to 1940 was the war referendum, or the Ludlow Amendment (after Democratic representative Louis Ludlow of Indiana). The idea actually appears to have originated during the Civil War in a book by Robert E. Beasley (1864), in which he advocated taking a vote on whether the war should be continued. The idea was subsequently stimulated by hopes of keeping the United States out of World War I and by disillusionment with that war and suspicions that it had been engineered by arms dealers.

Such proposed amendments usually specified that, except in cases of invasion, Congress could not declare war or draft citizens until the people approved. Influential supporters included Democratic and Populist presidential candidate and secretary of state William Jennings Bryan and Republican senator Robert La Follette of Wisconsin. Both, however, subsequently supported Wilson's decision to enter World War I without such a vote (Cronin 1989, 165). In the 1930s, the movement for a war referendum received support from 65 college and university presidents, the National Education Association, historian Charles Beard, and even Republican congressman Everett Dirksen of Illinois (Cronin 1989, 169–170).

In 1938, the House of Representatives voted 209 to 188 not to discharge this amendment from committee. Franklin D. Roosevelt's opposition and the approach of World War II pretty much ended this proposal, although Oregon Republican senator Mark Hatfield introduced a variant during the Vietnam War.

Issue Activism of the Right and Left

The 1960s and 1970s witnessed renewed support for the idea of a national initiative and referendum from representatives of both the political right and the political left. The movement received support in 1977, when Roger Telschow and John Forster, who had worked with such measures at the state level, founded a lobby group called Initiative America. Democratic senator James Abourezk of South Dakota and Democratic representative James Jones of Oklahoma introduced an amendment supported by at least 50 members of Congress. It would have permitted 3 percent of citizens (including at least 3 percent of the voters in 10 or more states) to initiate a referendum that would take effect when subsequently ratified by a majority (Cronin 1989, 159). Supporters included consumer advocate Ralph Nader, New York Republican representative Jack Kemp, columnist Patrick Buchanan, then Democratic (later Republican) Texas congressman Phil Gramm, California Republican congressman Barry Goldwater Jr., Oregon Republican senator Mark Hatfield, economist Arthur Laffer, and a majority of the American people as measured in public opinion polls (Cronin 1989, 173–175). A fair number of scholars also favored this proposal (Berg, Hahn, and Schmidhauser 1976, 190–201; Barber 1984, 281–289). There was wide variation as to what percentage or regional representation would be needed to propose or approve referendums, with 3 and 8 percent being the most common numbers suggested for proposing a referendum.

Most referendum proposals would have exempted issues of constitutional reform or warmaking matters, thus somewhat distancing

advocates of this period from those of the preceding one. Many proposals would have prevented Congress from modifying laws adopted by referendum for two years, except by an extraordinary majority of two-thirds or three-fourths. Congress held hearings on the subject in 1977.

National Initiative for Democracy

A more recent attempt at national initiative, the National Initiative for Democracy, which is led by a nonprofit organization, Philadelphia II, is designed to allow the public to propose both laws and constitutional amendments. This movement is predicated on the assumption that the American people are already sovereign and that they have the right to bypass both the regularized processes of adopting legislation and amendments.

Concerns of Initiative and Referendum Supporters

Advocates of the initiative and referendum often see these mechanisms as a way to bypass politicians who have lost touch with the people. The same concern has been shared by advocates of congressional term limits. Perhaps illustrating this tie, in 1993 and 1994, Republican representative Peter Hoekstra of Michigan offered a bill to provide for a national advisory referendum on term limits for members of Congress.

States continue to experiment with initiative and referendum measures. Such state experiences—for example, the successful movement led by Howard Jarvis in 1978 to adopt Proposition 13 to limit California state property taxes and Coloradans' more recent vote (voided in *Romer v. Evans* [1996]) to prohibit all state and local legislation that protects homosexuals (Baker 1995a)—have led to speculation about whether conservatives or liberals would be most likely to gain if such mechanisms were adopted. Austin Ranney found that the advantage tends to shift from one side to the other, depending on the issue. He therefore concluded that "the referendum is neither an unfailing friend nor an implacable enemy of either left or right" (1978, 85).

See also Beasley, Robert; Congress, Recall of Members; Crittenden Compromise; Democracy and Constitutional Amendments; Judiciary entries; National Initiative for Democracy, Removal of Members; President, Vote of No Confidence.

For Further Reading:

Barber, Benjamin. 1984. *Strong Democracy.* Berkeley: University of California Press.

Beasley, Robert. 1864. *A Plan to Stop the Present and Prevent Future Wars: Containing a Proposed Constitution for the General Government of the Sovereign States of North and South America.* Rio Vista, CA: Robert Beasley.

Berg, Larry L., Harlan Hahn, and John R. Schmidhauser. 1976. *Corruption in the American Political System.* Morristown, NJ: General Learning Press.

Cronin, Thomas E. 1989. *Direct Democracy: The Politics of Initiative, Referendum, and Recall.* Cambridge, MA: Harvard University Press.

Fisch, William B. 2006. "Constitutional Referendum in the United States of America." *The American Journal of Comparative Law* 54 (Fall): 485–504.

Grimes, Alan P. 1978. *Democracy and the Amendments to the Constitution.* Lexington, MA: Lexington Books.

Ku, Raymond. 1995. "Consensus of the Governed: The Legitimacy of Constitutional Change." *Fordham Law Review* 64 (November): 535–586.

Musmanno, M. A. 1929. *Proposed Amendments to the Constitution.* Washington DC: U.S. Government Printing Office.

Ranney, Austin. 1978. "The United States of America." In *Referendums: A Comparative Study of Practice and Theory,* eds. David Butler and Austin Ranney. Washington DC: American Enterprise Institute for Public Policy Research.

Schmidt, David D. 1989. *Citizen Law Makers: The Ballot Initiative Revolution.* Philadelphia: Temple University Press.

Sullivan, J. W. 1893. *Direct Legislation by the Citizenship.* New York: Nationalist Publishing Company.

INSURANCE

From 1905 through 1933, members of Congress introduced proposals either to allow that body to insure the lives of U.S. citizens or to regulate the insurance industry. The latter proposals were undoubtedly stimulated by the unique position that insurance has occupied in relation to other industries.

Because of the nation's commitment to free enterprise, most life insurance and many other types of insurance are handled by private companies. Initially, states were responsible for most regulation of the insurance industry, and such governments often discriminated against companies with headquarters located in other states. Such regulations were challenged as a violation of the federal commerce power in *Paul v. Virginia* (1869), but the U.S. Supreme Court rejected this challenge, deciding that insurance policies were not interstate transactions, and state regulation continued until 1944.

In *United States v. South-Eastern Underwriters Association* (1944), in a close 4-to-3 decision, which Justice Hugo Black wrote, the Supreme Court reversed course and applied the Sherman Antitrust Act (a federal law) to insurance companies that operated across state lines. The following year, Congress responded by passing the McCarran Act. This law left insurance regulation to the states, absent adoption of congressional laws specifically addressed to the insurance industry. The insurance industry thus rather anomalously continues to be exempt from most of the regulations affecting other industries that operate across state lines.

INTERMARRIAGE

North American laws against interracial marriage, or miscegenation, date back to colonial times, and President Andrew Johnson was among those who feared that the proposed Fourteenth Amendment, which provided equal protection for all citizens, might invalidate them. States ratified that amendment in 1868, and three years later, Missouri Democratic representative Andrew King introduced an amendment to extend the ban on miscegenation throughout the nation. Although Congress never proposed the amendment, a large majority of states did limit interracial marriages, and most courts that examined such state laws found them to be constitutional.

In 1912, an African American boxer (the first African American world heavyweight champion) named Jack Johnson was charged with abducting a 19-year-old white woman, Lucille Cameron, after the suicide of Johnson's first white wife, Etta Duryea. Cameron refused to substantiate the charges against Johnson and subsequently married him on December 3, after he was acquitted of the charge. In what many believe to have been a case of injustice (Arizona senator John McCain has sought a pardon), Johnson was later convicted, and served time, under the Mann Act, of having transported another white woman he had dated years earlier across state lines for immoral purposes.

The same year that Johnson was charged with abducting Lucille Cameron, Democratic representative Seaborn Roddenbery of Georgia introduced an amendment to prohibit interracial marriage, which he described as "a debasing, ultra-demoralizing, un-American and inhuman leprosy" (quoted in Gilmore 1973, 32). His amendment would have defined "negroes and persons of color" as persons with "any trace of African or Negro blood" (cited in Stein 2004, 630). Other legislators proposed such laws in states that did not have them and in Congress itself (Gilmore 1973, 33).

Representative Coleman Blease of South Carolina proposed another antimiscegenation amendment in 1928. It was notable for requiring that Congress establish a punishment for individuals engaged in such marriages (Stein 2004, 630).

Law professor Edward Stein reports that 30 states had antimiscegenation laws in the time period from 1887 to 1948 (2004, 628). In the last year, the California Supreme Court ruled in *Perez v. Lippold,* 198 P.2d 17 (Cal. 1948), that its state's law violated the equal protection clause of the Fourteenth Amendment. Thirteen states repealed their prohibitions on interracial marriage between then and 1967, when the U.S. Supreme Court ruled in *Loving v. Virginia* that laws against interracial marriage violated the equal protection clause of the Fourteenth Amendment.

See also Fourteenth Amendment; Marriage, Divorce, and Parenting.

For Further Reading:

Gilmore, Al-Tony. 1973. "Jack Jackson and White Women: The National Impact." *The Journal of Negro History* 58 (January): 18–38.

Schaffner, Joan. 2005. "The Federal Marriage Amendment: To Protect the Sanctity of Marriage or Destroy Constitutional Democracy?" *American University Law Review* 54 (August): 1487–1526.

Stein, Edward. 2004. "Past and Present Proposed Amendments to the United States Constitution Regarding Marriage." *Washington University Law Quarterly* 82 (Fall): 611–685.

INTERNAL IMPROVEMENTS

Under the general welfare clause in Article I, Section 8 of the Constitution, Congress may tax and spend for the general welfare. In early American history, Republicans who feared excessive national powers often interpreted this and other constitutional provisions quite restrictively. Their reading led many to question the legitimacy of federal expenditures on projects such as roads or canals. Presidents Thomas Jefferson, James Madison, James Monroe, Andrew Jackson, and James Polk all either recommended an amendment specifically to authorize federal expenditures of this nature or vetoed congressional laws for such improvements that they thought were directed chiefly to state rather than national interests (Ames 1896, 260–263). On occasion, as in Jackson's veto of the Maysville Road bill (extending a road from Maysville, Kentucky, to Henry Clay's hometown of Lexington), they were also tied to partisan considerations (Urofsky 1988, 280). However, few early presidents took the position of John Quincy Adams, who argued for an expansive list of federal domestic expenditures (McDonald 1982, 71).

In the first half of the 19th century, a number of congressmen, including future president Martin Van Buren, introduced constitutional amendments to legitimize federal expenditures on internal improvements; others, including Henry Clay and Abraham Lincoln, took the position consistent with the doctrine of implied powers that Chief Justice John Marshall had established in *McCulloch v. Maryland* (1819), that such an amendment was unnecessary because the existing Constitution already permitted such expenditures. With the expansion of federal powers over the last century and a half, the issue of federal aid to the states appears to have become chiefly a prudential rather than a constitutional issue.

See also General Welfare; *McCulloch v. Maryland.*

For Further Reading:

Ames, Herman. 1896. *The Proposed Amendments to the Constitution of the United States during the First Century of Its History.* Reprint, New York: Burt Franklin, 1970.

Chen, Paul. 2006. "The Constitutional Politics of Roads and Canals: Inter-branch Dialogue Over Internal Improvements, 1800–1828." *Whittier Law Review* 28 (Winter): 625–662.

McDonald, Forrest. 1982. *A Constitutional History of the United States.* New York: Franklin Watts.

Urofsky, Melvin I. 1988. *A March of Liberty: A Constitutional History of the United States.* New York: Alfred A. Knopf.

INTERNET

Recent years have witnessed increased use of, and reliance upon, communications through the Internet. Courts have had to decide the extent to which their jurisdiction extends under this new medium, the reach of which often extends across state, and even national, divisions. Indeed, Internet jurisdiction has been likened to that of admiralty law (Ban 1998). In *Reno v. American Civil Liberties Union* (1997), the Supreme Court struck down an attempt to regulate children's access to obscenity under the Communications Decency Act of 1996 as being so broad as to interfere with the legitimate First Amendment rights of adults.

In addition to the possibility of disseminating pornographic materials, the Internet may present unique opportunities for fraud and for copyright infringements. An author addressing these and related matters has suggested that, although Congress can currently exercise regulations under its power to control interstate commerce, such control could be eroded "if future technological breakthroughs make it possible to distinguish between interstate Internet transmissions and purely intrastate Internet transmissions" (Ban 1998, 539). He has proposed that the adoption of an amendment "may be the most impregnable basis upon which to establish such a jurisdiction" (540).

The advent of the Internet has provided a new forum for individuals to publicize proposals to either amend or rewrite the U.S. Constitution.

See also Alternative U.S. Constitutions, Proposed; First Amendment; Obscenity and Pornography.

For Further Reading:

Ban, Kevin K. 1998. "Does the Internet Warrant a Twenty-Seventh Amendment [sic.] to the United States Constitution?" *The Journal of Corporation Law* 23 (Spring): 521–540.

Reno v. American Civil Liberties Union, 521 U.S. 844 (1997).

ITEM VETO

See Presidency, Veto Power of.

J

❖

JACKSON, JESSE L., JR. (1965–)

Representative Jesse L. Jackson Jr. was elected from the Second Congressional District of Chicago, Illinois, in 1995 and has served in that capacity ever since. The son of civil rights leader Jesse Jackson, he graduated from North Carolina A & T State University and earned a degree from the Chicago Theological Seminary and from the Illinois College of Law at Urbana-Champaign.

In a book written with the help of his press secretary, Frank Watkins, Jackson comments on American history from the dual perspectives of race and federalism—the relation between the national government and the states. Jackson further proposes eight constitutional amendments, which he has persistently introduced in Congress. In contrast to existing constitutional provisions, most of Jackson's proposals center on economic and social, rather than purely political, rights.

Jackson regards his proposal for a full employment amendment to be his "most controversial" and "the most important" (Jackson 2001, 253). It is based on the 23rd article of the United Nations Universal Declaration of Human Rights and would likely require considerable governmental expenditures. The amendment contains five sections. The first provides that "Every citizen has the right to work, to free choice of employment, to just and favorable conditions of work, and to protection against unemployment" (Jackson 2001, 252). The second section focuses on nondiscrimination and on "equal pay for equal work." Section 3 is

designed to see that each citizen receives fair remuneration that provides for that worker and the worker's family. Section 4 provides for an explicit right to form and join trade unions (Jackson opposes "right to work" laws that enable individuals not to join unions at their places of employment, thus permitting individuals who are not members to get benefits that the unions have won). Section 5 is a congressional enforcement mechanism that Jackson includes with each of his proposals (Jackson 2001, 252).

Jackson's second proposal calls for provision of "health care of equal high quality" for all American citizens (Jackson 2001, 285). Again, Jackson believes the government should be willing to commit substantially more resources to health care than it currently does. Jackson believes the details of this and other amendments would have to be left to political processes, but his next proposal for "decent, safe, sanitary, and affordable housing without discrimination" does not contain a similar equality clause (300). The proposal for a "right to a public education" does specify that it should be "of equal high quality" (330), although by way of explanation, Jackson suggests that the amendment would provide for "a high minimum state floor" rather than a ceiling (348).

Jackson also proposes an equal rights amendment, to go into effect two years after being ratified (Jackson 2001, 350). Jackson proposes an environmental amendment that would guarantee each citizen the right to enjoy "a clean, safe, and sustainable environment" (371), and he includes a copy of The People's Earth Charter as an appendix to his book.

The Sixteenth Amendment to the U.S. Constitution permits an income tax but does not require that it tax incomes of individuals with higher incomes at higher percentages. Jackson's next proposal would change this. It provides that "The Congress of the United States shall tax all persons progressively in proportion to the income which they respectively enjoy under the protection of the United States" (Jackson 2001, 385). Jackson is very concerned about current disparities in income and wealth in the United States, and he believes this amendment is part of the remedy. Jackson's commentary suggests that the amendment would also apply to state taxation, which he regards as more regressive than that at the federal level (403).

Jackson's longest amendment, with five sections, is his proposed voting rights amendment. The first section guarantees the right to vote in public elections to all who are 18 years of age or older. The second section provides that Congress will establish electoral standards to be reviewed each year. Section 3 would provide for "the opportunity to register and vote on the day of any public election." Section 4 provides for election by majority vote within each state or district, and Section 5 is the familiar enforcement provision (Jackson 2001, 425). Jackson uses the 2000 presidential election as an example of what can happen when votes are cast and counted without adequate federal safeguards and supervision, although he does not call for an outright rejection of the current Electoral College system. Jackson does think that a system of proportional representation, which would give representation to minor parties, would be preferable to a system like that of the current U.S. House of Representatives, which is composed of single-member districts. He also favors instant runoff voting (IRV), in which individuals indicate their second and third choices for office, allowing votes cast for third-party candidates to be aggregated with those at the top of the ticket in the major parties. Jackson is also concerned about the large number of ex-felons who are currently excluded from voting in many of the states and thinks the Democratic Party would profit from running an African American candidate for vice president.

Jackson favors aspirational amendments that would give increased power to federal courts to intervene on behalf of those who are not currently treated equally. His proposals are among the most comprehensive set of social and political rights to be offered by any modern American writer.

See also Education, Right to; Environmental Protection; Social and Economic Rights.

For Further Reading:

Bentley, Curt. 2007. "Constrained by the Liberal Tradition: Why the Supreme Court Has Not Found Positive Rights in the American Constitution." *Brigham Young University Law Review*: 1721–1765.

Jackson, Jesse L., Jr., with Frank E. Watkins. 2001. *A More Perfect Union: Advancing New American Rights.* New York: Welcome Rain Publishers.

Michen, Jeff. 2005. "Beyond the Voting Rights Act: Why We Need a Constitutional Right to Vote." August 8. http://reclaimdemocracy.org/political_reform/right_to_vote.html. Accessed April 23, 2009.

JAMESON, JOHN A. (1824–1890)

John Jameson practiced law in Chicago and served for 18 years as a judge in the chancery division of Cook County (Malone 1961, 5:601). In 1867, he published the first edition of a work on constitutional conventions, released in a number of subsequent editions (Jameson 1887), that proved to be extremely influential. Stimulated in part by the movement for Southern secession and in part by claims by leaders of state conventions that such bodies were sovereign, Jameson was intent on establishing that a constitutional convention was subject to legal restraints.

Jameson identified four types of conventions: "the spontaneous convention, or public meeting"; "the ordinary legislative convention, or general assembly"; "the revolutionary convention"; and the "constitutional convention" (Jameson 1887, 3–4). Jameson was especially concerned with distinguishing the revolutionary convention, or the provisional government that bridges the gap from one form of government to another, from the constitutional convention, which, he argued, was "subaltern" and "never governs" (10). Thus domesticated, a constitutional convention was unlikely to pose a threat to existing governments.

Jameson related the constitutional convention to other forms of change. Arguing that amending mechanisms were "in the nature of safety valves," he argued that such provisions needed "to reconcile the requisites for progress with the requisites for safety" (Jameson 1887, 549). Jameson believed that the methods of proposing amendments by conventions and by general assemblies were "of about equal authority," although he speculated that "as our Constitutions become riper and more perfect with time and experience, the necessity of employing the more expensive mode by Conventions will be found to be less and less" (551–552). Jameson also suggested that the convention method was more suitable for major revisions and the method of legislative proposal more appropriate for less drastic alterations. He further argued that Sidney George Fisher had been mistaken in believing that a system of legislative sovereignty would have prevented the Civil War (567).

Jameson suggested that states had the power to ratify amendments they had previously rejected but not to rescind ratifications once given. Arguing that "an alteration of the Constitution has relation to the sentiments of today," he said, however, that if not ratified in a timely fashion, an amendment "ought to be regarded as waived, and not again to be voted upon, unless a second time proposed by Congress" (Jameson 1887, 634). On this basis, Jameson questioned Ohio's 1873 ratification of what, in 1993, putatively became the Twenty-seventh Amendment.

See also Constitutional Conventions; Fisher, Sidney George.

For Further Reading:

Jameson, John A. 1887. *A Treatise on Constitutional Conventions: Their History, Powers, and Modes of Proceeding.* 4th ed. Chicago: Callaghan and Company.

Malone, Dumas, ed. 1961. *Dictionary of American Biography.* 10 vols. New York: Charles Scribner's Sons.

JEFFERSON, THOMAS (1743–1826)

Born in Albemarle County, Virginia, in 1743, Thomas Jefferson was more receptive to the idea of both constitutional and revolutionary change than most Americans and did much to bring both about. Jefferson was the chief author of the Declaration of Independence, the nation's first secretary of state, its second vice president, and its third president.

In the Declaration of Independence, Jefferson advocated a moderate view of revolution to be implemented after "a long train of abuses and usurpations" and not "for light and transient causes." Jefferson expressed faith both in the people's ability to make constitutional changes and in the existence of natural rights that were morally beyond majority control. In authoring his Bill for Establishing Religious Freedom, Jefferson noted that a declaration of irrevocability would not be legally binding. He nonetheless declared that "the rights hereby asserted are of the natural rights of mankind, and . . . if any act shall be hereafter passed to repeal the present or to narrow its operations, such act will be an infringement of natural rights" (Jefferson 1905, 2:441).

Jefferson was serving as a diplomat in France during the Constitutional Convention of 1787. Although he subsequently favored the Constitution as a whole, he strongly believed that a bill of rights was needed to complete the framers' work. His correspondence with Madison on the subject is often credited with helping to persuade the latter of the advisability of such protections. Madison later repeated some of Jefferson's arguments when advocating the Bill of Rights on the floor of the House of Representatives (Mason and Stephenson 2002, 421–423). One of Jefferson's arguments for such a bill of rights was that, by being placed in the Constitution, such rights would be enforced by the judiciary. Later, however, Jefferson became concerned that John Marshall and his Federalist allies on the Supreme Court were using such power to sap democratic institutions. When the Federalists adopted the Alien and Sedition Acts of 1798, the latter of which restricted freedom of speech, Jefferson took action. Jefferson helped author the Kentucky Resolution (Madison had authored a corresponding Virginia Resolution) urging states to "interpose" themselves against unconstitutional federal legislation, and arguably helped pave the way for the more extreme views of states' rights that would follow.

Jefferson respected those who had authored his state's constitution during the Revolution, but he warned against looking at this or any other such constitutions "with sanctimonious reverence" or deeming them to be "too sacred to be touched" (Jefferson 1905, 12:11). Jefferson also feared that judges could modify the Constitution by liberal construction rather than by appeals directly to the people.

In the controversy over the constitutionality of the national bank, which had been advocated by Treasury Secretary Alexander Hamilton, approved by George Washington, and later confirmed by the U.S. Supreme Court decision in *McCulloch v. Maryland* (1819), Jefferson relied heavily on the as yet unratified Tenth Amendment, which spoke of powers reserved to the states. He took the view that because such a power was not listed among the powers of Congress, it could not be created under the existing Constitution.

The election of 1800 helped trigger the Twelfth Amendment, which modified the Electoral College. Because presidential electors did not initially distinguish between their choices for president and vice president, Jefferson and his running mate Aaron Burr tied the electoral college vote in the presidential election of 1800 (Vile 2002b, 30). This tie was not resolved until 36 ballots had been cast in the lame duck Congress, and not until his longtime adversary Hamilton had supported Jefferson over Burr—who later killed Hamilton in a duel. The Twelfth Amendment, adopted during Jefferson's first term, provided that electors would subsequently cast separate ballots for president and vice president, with the House of Representatives choosing from the top three candidates in case no candidate received a majority.

Because of his stance against broad constructions of national powers, Jefferson's opponents chastised him for the most daring and farsighted act of his administration—namely the purchase of the Louisiana Territory, which also required deficit spending (Adams 1974, 1:165–172). The Constitution did not directly sanction this purchase, and Jefferson preferred to get approval from an amendment for his action, but he feared that the delay might scuttle the deal, and he proceeded without such specific constitutional authorization.

Of all of Jefferson's writings, none has provided more support for would-be constitutional reformers than a phrase he coined in a letter to James Madison in 1789. There, Jefferson introduced the principle "'*that the earth belongs in usufruct to the living*'; that the dead have neither powers nor rights over it" (Jefferson 1905, 6:3–4). Jefferson suggested that every debt, and indeed every constitution, should be renewed every 19 years.

The more sober-minded Madison, concerned about the effect that frequent changes might have on popular appreciation for the Constitution, subjected this proposal to withering criticism, some of which found its way into *Federalist* No. 49. Despite this critique, Jefferson continued to advocate his view. In a letter in 1813, Jefferson repeated his idea that each generation "has . . . a right to choose for itself the form of government it believes most promotive of its own happiness" and that, accordingly, "for the peace and good of mankind . . . a solemn opportunity of doing this every nineteen or twenty years should be provided by the constitution" (Jefferson 1905, 12:13). In this letter, Jefferson noted that "we might as well require a man to wear still the coat which fitted him when a boy, as civilized society to remain ever under the regimen of their barbarous ancestors" (12:12). Consistent with such views, Louis Hensler III (2003) has suggested that the nation should consider having a constitutional convention once every generation to update the Constitution and correct perceived flaws.

At the national level, Madison's view of cautious constitutional change has dominated. Purposely or otherwise, many states have come closer to the idea that each generation should be able to incorporate its own views into, or indeed to rewrite, its own constitution (Vile 1992, 72–74).

Jefferson died at Monticello on July 4, 1826, 50 years to the day after the adoption of the Declaration of Independence and on the same day as his co-revolutionary, John Adams.

See also Bill of Rights; Constitutional Convention of 1787; Declaration of Independence; Louisiana Purchase; Madison, James; *McCulloch v. Maryland;* Tenth Amendment; Twelfth Amendment; Virginia and Kentucky Resolutions.

For Further Reading:

Adams, Henry. 1974. *The Formative Years,* ed. Herbert Agar. 2 vols. Westport, CT: Greenwood Press.

Cunningham, Noble E. 1987. *The Pursuit of Reason: The Life of Thomas Jefferson.* Baton Rouge: Louisiana State University Press.

Foner, Eric, and John A. Garraty, eds. 1991. *The Reader's Companion to American History.* Boston: Houghton Mifflin Company.

Hensler, Louis W., III. 2003. "The Recurring Constitutional Convention: Therapy for a Democratic Constitutional Republic Paralyzed by Hypocrisy." *Texas Review of Law and Politics* 7 (Spring): 263–312.

Jefferson, Thomas. 1905. *The Works of Thomas Jefferson,* ed. Paul Leicester Ford. 12 vols. New York: G. P. Putnam's Sons, Knickerbocker Press.

Knowles, Robert. 2003. "The Balance of Forces and the Empire of Liberty: States' Rights and the Louisiana Purchase." *Iowa Law Review* 88 (January): 343–419.

Mason, Alpheus T., and Donald G. Stephenson Jr. 2002. *American Constitutional Law: Introductory Essays and Selected Cases.* 13th ed. Englewood Cliffs, NJ: Prentice Hall.

Mayer, David N. 1994. *The Constitutional Thought of Thomas Jefferson.* Charlottesville: University Press of Virginia.

Samaha, Adam M. 2008. "Dead Hand Arguments and Constitutional Interpretation." *Columbia Law Review* 108 (April): 606–680.

Vile, John R. 2002a. *A Companion to the United States Constitution and Its Amendments.* 3d ed. Westport, CT: Praeger.

———. 2002b. *Presidential Winners and Losers: Words of Victory and Concession.* Washington, DC: Congressional Quarterly.

———. 1992. *The Constitutional Amending Process in American Political Thought.* New York: Praeger.

JEFFS, DANIEL B.

Daniel B. Jeffs outlined his view on direct democracy and direct education in a book titled *America's Crisis,* which chiefly outlines what he regards as the flaw of existing American governments. Jeffs portrays himself as a modern-day Thomas Paine, and his book is a follow-up to an earlier pamphlet, "The Truth: the 28th Amendment," published under the name "John Citizen" and advocating interactive television ties to voters, homes (see Jeffs 2000, 36–37 for further description). The back cover of *America's Crisis,* which chiefly focuses on problems in contemporary American government, identifies Jeffs as the founder of The Direct Democracy Center with "an extensive investigative background in the criminal justice system" who has run for local office and "holds a law degree and teaching credentials." The text of the book itself indicates that Jeffs "was a career cop." He says that, although "I worked with prosecutors, and then defense attorneys, . . . I simply could not be one of them" (Jeffs 2000, 35).

Jeffs has created a Web site, *www.realdemocracy.com,* in which he has proposed both a 12-section amendment to implement his plans and a petition whereby individuals "petition" and "demand" that their representatives work toward this plan. On his Web site, Jeffs notes that, "In the tradition of the simplicity of the U.S. Constitution, it would be simple to amend a constitution by just writing: 'The government of the United States, and the several states, shall be a nonpartisan direct democracy through established voting networks connected to voters' homes.'" He immediately adds, however, that "Unfortunately, if left to the Congress, the Presidency and the Supreme Court, they would soon dilute it out of existence in the same ways they have perverted the U.S. Constitution." Jeffs's amendment is labeled the "Nonpartisan Direct Representative Democracy Government Electorate Voting Networks and Education Networks." The first section of the amendment specifies that the national government and that of the states should be "nonpartisan direct representative democracy government" embodied "through the equality of citizenship." The section states Jeffs's intention "for the electorate to have and maintain absolute control of government and education" and to require "truth and accountability to the electorate from all elected representatives and all government employees."

Section 2 provides that, within four years after ratification, a system of "direct representative democracy" will be established using "electorate voting networks of interactive electronic devices between elected representatives of all levels of government and the homes of the electorate." This section further specifies that "all elected representatives shall be nonpartisan," and it provides for annual confirmation or rejection "by majority vote of the electorate."

Section 3 would further enhance direct democracy by allowing the electorate "to instruct, direct and control all levels of government through their elected representatives by majority vote," with "all elections, recall elections, initiatives and referendums" to "be conducted by means of the electorate voting network."

Section 4 extends direct democracy to members of all U.S. courts and to all cabinet posts and agency heads at both state and national levels. Section 5 repeals the Twelfth Amendment (and presumably other provisions of the Constitution that helped establish the Electoral College) and provides for annual direct confirmation or rejection of the president and vice president. Section 6 further repeals the Sixteenth Amendment and the national income tax, which his book identifies as "the gravest mistake the American people ever made" (Jeffs 2000, x).

Section 7 provides that "All matters of public policy and taxation shall require a two-thirds majority of the electorate voting." The electorate would also be vested with amending both state and national constitutions by a two-thirds majority vote. Judges would also be subject to electoral recall.

Section 8 moves to Jeffs's second emphasis, namely education. All citizens will be provided with "direct education by interactive electronic devices" in their homes. Section 9 further provides that this education, initially conducted by the government, will subsequently be contracted out to private institutions. It also provides that "quality choice in education shall be provided to all citizen students through means tested vouchers," and that "no student shall be excluded for lack of funds" from education to include the first four years of college. Section 10 further provides that the federal Department of Education "under the direction and control of the electorate" shall set minimum national standards, which states will be free to raise if they choose. The Federal Communications Commission would be entrusted with "the public communication function of direct education."

Section 11 provides that the amendment will supersede any conflicting provisions of the Constitution. Section 12 further specifies that, within four years of establishing voting networks, the government will give the people the opportunity of either confirming or repealing "each law, or group of laws, by majority vote." (This section is missing from Jeffs's book, where the text of the amendment is found on pages 304–307.)

Jeffs's is one of a number of new voices calling for more direct democracy in the United States; significantly, his Web site contains links to "Philadelphia II" and its plans for "Direct Democracy" as well as to other sites advocating the initiative and fair taxation.

See also Education, Right to; Initiative and Referendum; Madison, James; Sixteenth Amendment.

For Further Reading:

Jeffs, Daniel B. 2000. *America's Crisis: The Direct Democracy and Direct Education Solution.* Amherst Junction, WI: The Hard Shell Word Factory.

"The Direct Democracy Center." At www.realdemocracy.com. Accessed November 26, 2002.

JOINT RESOLUTION

Although members of Congress occasionally introduce amendments in the form of simple resolutions in a single house, members introduce the great majority of amendments in both houses as joint resolutions. This joint resolution mechanism reflects the fact that amendments require approval by a two-thirds vote of both houses of Congress before they are sent to the states, three-fourths of which are required for ratification.

Although it often deals with somewhat narrower matters, a joint resolution has been described as "for all intents and purposes the same as a bill" (Schneier and Gross 1993, 125). Unlike other joint resolutions, resolutions proposing amendments do not require the president's signature (*Hollingsworth v. Virginia* [1798]). Joint resolutions are designated as H.J. Res. or S.J. Res. and are numbered consecutively in each house in the order they are introduced within each two-year congressional session (Kravitz 1993, 139).

See also *Hollingsworth v. Virginia.*

For Further Reading:

Kravitz, Walter. 1993. *American Congressional Dictionary.* Washington, DC: Congressional Quarterly.

Lathan, Darren R. 2005. "The Historical Amendability of the American Constitution: Speculations on an Empirical Problematic." *American University Law Review* 55 (October): 145–264.

Schneier, Edward V., and Bertram Gross. 1993. *Legislative Strategy.* New York: St. Martin's Press.

JUDICIAL INTERPRETATION

See Constitutional Interpretation.

JUDICIARY, ADVISORY OPINIONS BY

Ever since the first Supreme Court headed by John Jay declined President Washington's request to define rights under a U.S. treaty, U.S. constitutional courts have declined to issue such advisory opinions. Early in the New Deal, the Supreme Court exercised a fairly obstructionist role, voiding a number of Franklin D. Roosevelt's major programs. Two members of Congress introduced resolutions in 1935, one of which was reintroduced in 1937, that would

have required the Supreme Court, when so requested by the president or a set majority of Congress, to issue such an opinion.

In 1934, Congress had already adopted the Federal Declaratory Judgment Act, permitting the Court to issue declaratory judgments in some cases. Like advisory opinions, such judgments are nonbinding, but unlike advisory opinions, they involve real disputes between specific individuals. Professor Henry J. Abraham observed that "the line between advisory opinions and declaratory judgments is a thin one" (1998, 393).

See also Judiciary, Exercise of Judicial Review by.

For Further Reading:

Abraham, Henry J. 1998. *The Judicial Process: An Introductory Analysis of the Courts of the United States, England, and France.* 7th ed. New York: Oxford University Press.

JUDICIARY, AGE LIMITS FOR MEMBERS

The judicial branch is the only one for which the U.S. Constitution makes no provision for a minimum age (Vile and Perez-Reilly 1991). Moreover, because federal judges are appointed "during good behavior," they may serve until they are quite old without ever facing voters' judgment of their competency for continued service.

Members of Congress have introduced a few proposals that would have required a minimum age for judges and justices (often from 30 to 40). Others would have required that judges have a minimum number of years of legal practice or experience in other courts. Members have typically introduced such provisions as parts of amendments designed to change the current method of judicial selection.

Members of Congress have introduced many more proposals (often as part of amendments that also would have applied to members of Congress and other officeholders) to limit the age of sitting judges or require a mandatory retirement age. This practice is followed in many states and has been upheld against equal protection claims by the U.S. Supreme Court in *Gregory v. Ashcroft* (1991). The most frequently proposed ages range from 65 to 75. A proposal advanced in 1937 to require retirement of Supreme Court justices at the age of 75 had scholarly and congressional support and might have been adopted had it not been opposed by President Franklin D. Roosevelt, who was concerned with more immediate problems and was pushing for his own "court-packing" plan. Roosevelt's plan, designed to get the Supreme Court to line up behind the New Deal, called for adding one new justice (up to 15) for every justice over the age of 70 who remained on the Court (Garrow 2000, 1019–1026). Congress rejected this plan, which would also have enabled the president to appoint additional judges to the lower courts, but it did provide a generous retirement package so that judges would not have to continue in office simply for financial reasons.

The American Bar Association, supported by former Supreme Court Justice Owen J. Roberts, launched another such proposal designed to insulate the Supreme Court from future political conflicts (including congressional attempts to trim its appellate jurisdiction), from 1946 to 1955. The U.S. Senate voted positively on this proposal by a vote of 58 to 19 in 1954. However, this effort was stymied by intense opposition among some members of Congress to the Supreme Court's decision in *Brown v. Board of Education* (1954) mandating desegregation in the field of education (Garrow 2000, 1028–1043). Yet another campaign for an amendment or bill that would have provided for judicial removal or impeachment in cases of mental incapacity was launched, with support from Georgia Democratic senator Sam Nunn, from 1974 to 1980, but it too proved unsuccessful (Garrow 2000, 1057–1065).

Mandatory retirement limits might have a significant impact on the composition of the courts, many of whose members continue to serve until reaching an advanced age. Thus, of the 100 Supreme Court vacancies from 1789 to 1994, 48 were created by death in office (Abraham 1998, 44). Moreover, other justices have retired from the Court only after extensive periods of disability (Cooper and Ball 1996, 354–368). Modern commentators are divided as to whether a constitutional amendment is needed, with David Garrow favoring an amendment and pointing to numerous cases throughout American history where he believes justices have served while they were mentally impaired, and David Atkinson and Warn Farnsworth believing that stories of judicial impairment have been exaggerated and that this is a problem that justices can handle on their own (Atkinson 1999).

See also Court-Packing Plan.

For Further Reading:

Abraham, Henry J. 1998. *The Judicial Process: An Introductory Analysis of the Courts of the United States, England, and France.* 7th ed. New York: Oxford University Press.

Atkinson, David N., 1999. *Leaving the Bench: Supreme Court Justices at the End.* Lawrence: University Press of Kansas.

Cooper, Phillip, and Howard Ball. 1996. *The United States Supreme Court from the Inside Out.* Upper Saddle River, NJ: Prentice Hall.

Farnsworth, Ward. 2005. "The Regulation of Turnover on the Supreme Court." *University of Illinois Law Review*: 407–453.

Garrow, David J. 2000. "Mental Decrepitude on the U.S. Supreme Court: The Historical Case for a 28th Amendment." *University of Chicago Law Review* 67: 995–1087.

Gregory v. Ashcroft, 501 U.S. 452 (1991).

Mauro, Tony. 2001. "The Age of Justice." *American Lawyer* 23 (March): 67.

Vile, John R., and Mario Perez-Reilly. 1991. "The U.S. Constitution and Judicial Qualifications: A Curious Omission." *Judicature* 74 (December–January): 198–202.

JUDICIARY, COMPENSATION OF MEMBERS

In an attempt to preserve executive independence, Article II, Section 1 of the Constitution prevents Congress from increasing or diminishing a president's pay during his or her term of office. The Twenty-seventh Amendment now prevents congressional salaries from being raised or lowered prior to an intervening election.

Because judges serve "during good behavior," which effectively means until they die, retire, or are impeached and convicted, their salaries could be eroded by inflation during their service. Article III, Section 1 of the Constitution thus allows Congress to raise, but not to lower, the salaries of judges during their terms of office. In the process of ratifying the Constitution, Virginia and North Carolina proposed that periodic increases or decreases in judicial salaries be enacted as part of more general salary regulations (Ames 1896, 153). No subsequent proposals have addressed this topic, although the subject of judicial raises is periodically the focus of political disputes. In *Atkins v. United States* (1976), the Supreme Court denied review of a lower court decision that had dismissed a claim that the salaries of judges had been unconstitutionally reduced because salaries had not kept up with inflation, but it subsequently ruled in *United States v. Will* (1980) that, while Congress could withhold promised pay raises, it could not roll back such raises that had already been given.

Also see Twenty-seventh Amendment.

For Further Reading:

Ames, Herman. 1896. *The Proposed Amendments to the Constitution of the United States during the First Century of Its History.* Reprint, New York: Burt Franklin, 1970.

JUDICIARY, COURT OF THE UNION

Although the issue of judicial review of congressional legislation receives the majority of scholarly attention, the Supreme Court's exercise of judicial review of state laws might be even more important. The Supreme Court exercised this power as early as 1810 (*Fletcher v. Peck*), and it often met with stiff resistance from proponents of states' rights.

One of the problems, particularly during the Marshall Court, was that proponents of states' rights thought that the Supreme Court was biased toward federal powers, just as state courts might be biased toward their own. There were a handful of proposals in the 19th century, at least

two during the period of Reconstruction, to create a special tribunal to resolve questions of conflict between state and national powers. A proposal introduced in 1821, apparently stimulated by the Supreme Court's nationalistic opinion in *Cohens v. Virginia* of that year (Levy 1995, 435), would have had the Senate, whose members were then appointed by state legislatures, serve as the appellate review body for such cases. A proposal submitted in 1867 would have vested this power in a court consisting of one member from each state (Ames 1896, 163).

Reaction to decisions by the Warren Court—especially regarding state legislative apportionment—stimulated renewed attention to this issue in the early 1960s. The December 1962 meeting of the General Assembly of States, sponsored by the Council of State Governments, adopted a resolution to create a Court of the Union composed of the chief justices of each state's highest court. This court would hear appeals when requested to do so by five noncontiguous states and would be authorized by majority vote to reverse Supreme Court decisions relative to the rights reserved to the states under the Tenth Amendment.

Alabama, Arkansas, Florida, South Carolina, and Wyoming subsequently requested a constitutional convention to deal with the topic, and at least 15 proposals for an amendment were introduced in Congress from 1963 to 1981. South Carolina senator Strom Thurmond appears to have been the first to introduce this proposal. This, and other proposals by the Council of State Governments, riled scholars, one of whom called a Court of the Union as "patently absurd" (Black 1963, 957).

See also Council of State Governments; Tenth Amendment.

For Further Reading:

Ames, Herman. 1896. *The Proposed Amendments to the Constitution of the United States during the First Century of Its History.* Reprint, New York: Burt Franklin, 1970.

Black, Charles L., Jr. 1963. "The Proposed Amendment of Article V: A Threatened Disaster." *Yale Law Journal* 72 (April): 957–966.

Levy, Leonard W. 1995. *Seasoned Judgments: The American Constitution, Rights, and History.* New Brunswick, NJ: Transaction Publishers.

JUDICIARY, EMERGENCY REPLACEMENT OF MEMBERS

The president appoints all federal judges and justices subject to confirmation or rejection by the U.S. Senate. Supreme Court justices have been relatively unknown to the general public, and no Supreme Court justice has ever been assassinated, but, as in the case of Congress, the threat of terrorism always poses the possibility that multiple members could be killed or disabled simultaneously. Panels considering the replacement of multiple members in an emergency similar to the terrorist attacks of 2001 have also considered the possibility of multiple judicial replacements.

See also Congress, Emergency Functioning.

For Further Reading:

Zuckerman, Edward. 1984. *The Day after World War III.* New York: Viking Press.

JUDICIARY, EXERCISE OF JUDICIAL REVIEW BY

Judicial review is the most important power that U.S. courts exercise. This power enables them to declare state or federal laws or actions taken by the executive or governmental agencies to be unconstitutional, and hence void. The Constitution does not specifically state the power of judicial review, but Chief Justice John Marshall forcefully asserted this power in *Marbury v. Madison* (1803) and defended it as a way of ensuring the supremacy of the written constitution over popular willfulness. Such review distinguishes the U.S. system from systems of parliamentary sovereignty, under which decisions of the legislative branch are final.

Although the power of judicial review is consistent with a system providing for checks and balances, it pits the judgment of the only unelected branch of the government against the judgment of the people's elected representatives. This presents what constitutional scholar Alexander Bickel described as "the counter-majoritarian difficulty" (Bickel 1986, 16–22). Judicial review also continues to spark controversy over the appropriate level of judicial activism or restraint—generally interpreted to mean deference to legislative judgments (Halpern and Lamb 1982; Wolfe 1991)—and helps fuel continuing controversies over questions of constitutional interpretation.

Many of the amending proposals that were introduced in the 19th century relative to the judiciary dealt with judicial jurisdiction. The Eleventh Amendment, which limited suits against the states, was the most visible and, to date, the only successful proposal designed specifically to limit judicial jurisdiction. A member of Congress introduced a proposal in the December–January session of the 1846–1847 Congress to take away the Court's power to declare laws unconstitutional, but proposals aimed specifically at judicial review are more characteristic of the 20th century. The Progressive Era, the years surrounding the Court's historic "switch in time that saved nine" in 1937, and the 1960s and 1970s mark the greatest activity in this area. Most proposals did not call for the complete elimination of judicial review but would have limited its exercise by requiring supermajorities of the Supreme Court to act before it invalidated laws. In 1912, Republican representative Fred Jackson of Kansas further proposed that when any U.S. court declared a law to be invalid, three-fourths of the state legislatures should then decide on the law's validity (H.J. Res. 351). Numerous proposals have also been introduced to allow Congress to override judicial exercises of its review power.

At least three proposals introduced during the Progressive Era would have required the concurrence of all but two of the Supreme Court justices to declare laws to be unconstitutional. Another proposal from this period would simply have vested Congress with the power to specify the majority on the Court that would be necessary to invalidate such legislation. Republican senator Joseph Bristow of Kansas introduced another proposal that would have submitted exercises of judicial review to voters, who would be able to reverse such decisions by a majority referendum.

A far greater number of proposals emerged during the New Deal, especially around the time of Franklin D. Roosevelt's court-packing plan. These ranged from giving explicit constitutional recognition to the right to judicial review, to eliminating the power altogether, to providing (as in proposals from the Progressive Era) for supermajority votes, most commonly set at two-thirds.

Beginning in 1958 and reaching a peak in the late 1960s, members of Congress again began introducing amendments to limit judicial review. Louisiana Democratic representative John Rarick introduced a proposal in 1967 (H.J. Res. 384) that would have limited the power of judicial review to the Supreme Court. It would further have required a unanimous verdict in cases in which the Court decided to void a law. Far more common were proposals to require a two-thirds vote either of the Supreme Court's entire membership or of those voting in a given case. A variation introduced by Republican representative Jesse Younger of California (H.J. Res. 173) in 1967 would have allowed a two-thirds majority of Congress to limit the power of judicial review. More recently, professor John Kincaid has proposed that the Supreme Court should have to muster a three-fourths vote to "void a state law or local ordinance" (Kincaid 1989, 36). Kincaid believed that such a change—it is not altogether clear whether he thought this would or would not require a constitutional amendment—was necessary to preserve federalism against erosion.

In a related vein, former Judge Robert Bork, who is known for his conservatism, has proposed an amendment that would make "any federal or state court decision subject to being overruled by a majority vote of each House of Congress" (1997, 117). Mark Tushnet, a noted law professor known for being on the liberal side of the political spectrum, has gone even further by proposing what he calls an End Judicial Review Amendment (EJRA). It would provide that "Except as authorized by Congress, no court of the United States or of any individual state shall have the power to review the constitutionality of statutes enacted by Congress or by state legislatures" (2005, 59). Tushnet believes that such an amendment would vest more power in the people and that progressives should be able to persuade majorities of the desirability of their proposals without expecting the judiciary

to intervene on behalf of such liberal causes. Scholar James MacGregor Burns recently suggested that a president should be willing to defy a U.S. Supreme Court decision invalidating legislation that Congress had adopted and that the president has signed (2009).

See also Congress, Overriding Judicial Decisions; Constitutional Interpretation; Court-Packing Plan; Eleventh Amendment; Marshall, John.

For Further Reading:

Bickel, Alexander. 1986. *The Least Dangerous Branch: The Supreme Court at the Bar of Politics.* 2d ed. New Haven, CT: Yale University Press.

Bork, Robert. 1977. *Slouching Towards Gomorrah: Modern Liberalism and American Decline.* New York: Harper Perennial.

Burns, James MacGregor. 2009. *Packing the Court: The Rise of Judicial Power and the Coming Crisis of the Supreme Court.* New York: Penguin Press.

Halpern, Stephen C., and Charles M. Lamb, eds. 1982. *Supreme Court Activism and Restraint.* Lexington, MA: Lexington Books.

Kincaid, John. 1989. "A Proposal to Strengthen Federalism." *The Journal of State Government* 62 (January/February): 36–45.

Sloan, Cliff, and David McKean. 2009. *The Great Decision: Jefferson, Adams, Marshall, and the Battle for the Supreme Court.* New York: Public Affairs.

Tushnet, Mark. 2005. "Democracy versus Judicial Review." *Dissent.* 52 (Spring): 59–62.

Wolfe, Christopher. 1991. *Judicial Activism: Bulwark of Freedom or Precarious Security?* Pacific Grove, CA: Brooks/Cole.

JUDICIARY, JURISDICTION OF

Article III, Section 2 of the Constitution outlines the jurisdiction of—that is, the types of cases to be heard by—the federal courts. In a few cases, the Supreme Court exercises original jurisdiction and hears cases for the first time, but in most instances, its jurisdiction is appellate. In such cases, it reviews the judgments of lower federal courts or decisions reaching a state's highest court that involve questions of federal law or constitutional interpretation (Abraham 1998, 189–192).

From the beginning, many advocates of states' rights feared the exercise of federal judicial power and sought to curb it. After the Supreme Court's decision in *Chisholm v. Georgia* (1793), the states succeeded in adopting the Eleventh Amendment, which modified Article III so as to preclude the Court from accepting cases brought against a state by citizens of another state without the defendant state's consent. Members of Congress introduced a number of other proposals designed to clip federal jurisdiction from 1800 to 1810, but apart from a few proposals designed to provide for an alternative tribunal to adjudicate cases between the states and the national government, the remaining amending proposals— including one that would have repealed the Eleventh Amendment—actually sought to expand federal jurisdiction.

Twentieth-century proposals to alter judicial jurisdiction have varied. They include an attempt in 1901 to extend jurisdiction to matters involving the use of water, attempts in the second decade to limit federal jurisdiction over matters involving corporations (considered to be citizens under the terms of the Fourteenth Amendment), and limits on the Court's exercise of judicial review of state and federal legislation. Democratic representative Robert Sikes of Florida introduced a resolution in 1959 (H.J. Res. 201) prohibiting the Supreme Court from being able to "overrule, modify, or change any prior decision of that Court construing the Constitution or Acts of Congress promulgated pursuant thereto."

From a somewhat different perspective, individuals who fear that congressional power might undermine individual rights have proposed to limit congressional authority under Article III to make exceptions to and provide regulations for the Supreme Court's appellate jurisdiction. One proponent of the latter amendment was onetime Supreme Court Justice Owen Roberts (Smith 1987, 268).

In recent years, members of Congress have introduced measures to withdraw judicial jurisdiction from such issues as flag burning, school prayer, and gay marriage as well as many less controversial subjects (Quirk 2008, 213–281).

The author of a recent law review article has suggested that subsequent amendments, especially the First and Fourteenth, may limit the scope of such jurisdiction (Blocher 2008).

See also Eleventh Amendment; Judiciary, Court of the Union; Judiciary, Exercise of Judicial Review by.

For Further Reading:

Abraham, Henry J. 1998. *The Judicial Process: An Introductory Analysis of the Courts of the United States, England, and France.* 7th ed. New York: Oxford University Press.

Blocher, Joseph. 2008. "Amending the Exceptions Clause." *Minnesota Law Review* 92 (April): 971–1030.

Ernst, Morris L. 1973. *The Great Reversals: Tales of the Supreme Court.* New York: Weybright and Talley.

Quirk, William J. 2008. *Courts & Congress: America's Unwritten Constitution.* New Brunswick, NJ: Transaction Publishers.

Smith, Rodney K. 1987. *Public Prayer and the Constitution: A Case Study in Constitutional Interpretation.* Wilmington, DE: Scholarly Resources.

JUDICIARY, LIMITS ON TAXING POWER

On April 20, 1990, Missouri Republican senator John Danforth introduced an amendment (S.J. Res. 295) with more than 25 co-sponsors. It was designed to prohibit federal courts from ordering the laying or increasing of taxes. The Senate conducted hearings on the subject in June 1990, and the amending proposal was reintroduced in 1991 and 1992.

Senator Danforth and others were prompted by a Supreme Court decision rendered on April 18, 1990, in *Missouri v. Jenkins,* a desegregation case. The supervisory U.S. district court had initially ordered the Kansas City, Missouri, school district to double property taxes to pay for the construction of magnet schools designed to hasten desegregation. The U.S. Court of Appeals subsequently ruled that, rather than ordering this levy itself, the court could simply order a lifting of state restrictions on such taxes and let the

Kansas City school district come up with its own funding.

In upholding this less intrusive approach, the Supreme Court rested its decision on comity, or respect for state and local initiatives, rather than on constitutional grounds. Writing for the five-person majority, Justice Byron White asserted, however, that "a court order directing a local government body to levy its own taxes is plainly a judicial act within the power of a federal court" (*Missouri* 1990, 55). In a vigorous opinion concurring in the result, Justice Anthony Kennedy disagreed. He argued that "today's casual embrace of taxation imposed by the unelected, life-tenured Federal Judiciary disregards fundamental precepts for the democratic control of public institutions" (*Missouri* 1990, 58–59).

One of the last-minute modifications to the Senate version of the Balanced Budget Amendment, which came but a single vote shy of adoption in March 1995, was a provision that Democratic senator Sam Nunn of Georgia introduced that would have provided that "the judicial power of the United States shall not extend to any case or controversy arising under this Article except as may be specifically authorized by legislation adopted pursuant to this section." Nunn's concern suggests that the issue raised by *Missouri v. Jenkins* is still viable.

For Further Reading:

Friedman, Barry. 1992. "When Rights Encounter Reality: Enforcing Federal Remedies." *Southern California Law Review* 65 (January): 735–780.

Missouri v. Jenkins, 495 U.S. 33 (1990).

JUDICIARY, NUMBER OF SUPREME COURT JUSTICES

Article III of the U.S. Constitution does not specify how many justices shall sit on the Supreme Court. In the Judiciary Act of 1789, Congress set this number at six, but the number alternated between five and 10 before Congress settled on nine justices in 1869 (Barnum 1993, 202). In his court-packing plan of 1937, Franklin Roosevelt proposed adding one justice (up to 15) for each justice who remained on the Court over the age of 70. Ultimately defeated in Congress, this plan prompted a score of proposals from 1937 through the 1950s to set the number of justices permanently at nine.

Such proposals sometimes contained other provisions mandating the retirement of justices at a certain age or requiring an extraordinary majority to declare laws unconstitutional. In the 83rd Congress (1953–1954), the Senate voted 58 to 19 to accept a proposal sponsored by Republican senator John Marshall Butler of Maryland (S.J. Res. 44) to fix the number of justices at nine, to set a compulsory retirement age of 75, to make justices ineligible to run for president or vice president, and to prevent Congress from altering the appellate jurisdiction of the Supreme Court, but the House of Representatives did not concur. ("Composition and Jurisdiction" 1953, 1106).

See also Court-Packing Plan.

For Further Reading:

Barnum, David G. 1993. *The Supreme Court and American Democracy.* New York: St. Martin's Press.

"Composition and Jurisdiction of the Supreme Court—Proposed Constitutional Amendment." 1953. In *Congressional Record.* U.S. Senate, 16 February, 1106–1108.

JUDICIARY, OFFICEHOLDING BY MEMBERS

The framers of the Constitution may have anticipated fairly close ties between the executive and judicial branches of government. Thus, although Article I, Section 6 prohibits members of Congress from holding other offices, it contains no such prohibition for judges and justices (Scigliano 1994, 278).

In early American history, members of the judiciary were sometimes appointed to serve on diplomatic missions or asked to perform other public duties. In the 20th century, Justice Robert Jackson served as the chief U.S. prosecutor at the Nazi war crime trials in Nuremberg, and Chief Justice Earl Warren headed the commission that bore his name and that investigated the assassination of President John F. Kennedy. Justice Abe Fortas's continuing service as an adviser to President Lyndon Johnson was, however, one of the factors that ultimately led to his resignation from the Court (Murphy 1988, 114–140), and experience suggests that modern justices are likely to keep informal contacts with the executive at arm's length.

Some justices have harbored presidential aspirations. John McLean, who served on the Supreme Court from 1830 to 1861, was called the "politician on the Supreme Court" and was mentioned as a possible presidential candidate for more than 30 years (Gatell 1969, 535). Charles Evans Hughes, who served as an associate Supreme Court justice from 1910 to 1916 and as chief justice from 1930 to 1941, resigned as an associate justice in 1916 to challenge Woodrow Wilson for the presidency. William Howard Taft was appointed chief justice of the Supreme Court after having served a term as president—the only individual to serve in both positions. More recently, in a letter released to the public, Franklin D. Roosevelt listed Justice William O. Douglas as a possible vice presidential running mate in 1944 (McCullough 1992, 304–307).

After President Washington appointed Chief Justice Oliver Ellsworth as a commissioner to France, congressmen introduced two proposals in 1800 to restrict judges from serving in dual offices. In the 1870s and again in 1916—the year Justice Hughes ran unsuccessfully for president—proposals were made to prevent justices from running for president. In the 1950s, the Senate voted positively on an amendment that would have included a prohibition on justices running for president or vice president, among other provisions designed to guarantee judicial independence.

See also Congress, Members' Eligibility for Other Offices.

For Further Reading:
Gatell, Frank O. 1969. "John McLean." In *The Justices of the United States Supreme Court, 1789–1969: Their Lives and Major Opinions.* Vol. 1, ed. Leon Friedman and Fred L. Israel. New York: R. R. Bowker.

McCullough, David. 1992. *Truman.* New York: Simon and Schuster.

Murphy, Bruce A. 1988. *Fortas: The Rise and Ruin of a Supreme Court Justice.* New York: William Morrow.

Scigliano, Robert. 1994. "The Two Executives: The President and the Supreme Court." In *The American Experiment: Essays on the Theory and Practice of Liberty,* ed. Peter A. Lawler and Robert M. Schoefar. Lanham, MD: Rowman and Littlefield.

JUDICIARY, ORGANIZATION OF

On a few occasions, members of Congress have introduced amendments to reorganize the federal judiciary. However, short of abolishing the Supreme Court, an institution for which the Constitution makes explicit provision, there are few alterations in the judicial system that cannot be made by ordinary acts of legislation. Article III, which describes the judiciary, is the briefest of the three distributing articles, and it does not even specify the number of Supreme Court justices.

Much of the current structure of the federal judicial system was established in a series of judiciary acts that were adopted from 1789 to 1925 (Hall 2005, 544–550). President Franklin D. Roosevelt's court-packing plan was a good example of a proposal to alter the judiciary that failed. So too was the Court of the Union, which the Council of State Governments proposed in 1962 to hear petitions from the state legislatures in regard to federal matters.

See also Council of State Governments; Court-Packing Plan.

For Further Reading:
Hall, Kermit L., ed. 2005. *The Oxford Companion to the Supreme Court of the United States.* 2d ed. New York: Oxford University Press.

JUDICIARY, QUALIFICATIONS OF MEMBERS

Although possession of the L.L.B. or J.D. degree is "neither a constitutional nor a statutory requirement for appointment" to the federal bench, "custom would automatically exclude from consideration anyone who did not have them" (Abraham 1998, 55). At least one modern scholar has suggested that individuals with other types of professional training should be considered for the Supreme Court (Miller 1982, 286). Moreover, there is considerable scholarly debate as to whether prior judicial experience ought to be required of federal judges or Supreme Court justices. Of the first 110 justices, 42, including such luminaries as John Marshall, Joseph Story, Louis Brandeis, and Felix Frankfurter, had no prior judicial experience at all (Abraham 1998, 56–61). The last of these justices was a particularly vocal advocate of the view that such previous experience should not be a prerequisite.

In addition to periodic proposals to require that judges be elected, serve for fixed terms, be subject to Senate reconfirmation, or retire at a certain age, the 1960s and 1970s witnessed a number of proposals that would have mandated judicial qualifications. Some such proposals would have required a specified minimum number of years of prior judicial experience. At least one would have required that judges be natural-born citizens, 30 years of age or older, with a law degree (see, for example, H.J. Res. 325, 1973); another attempted to guarantee partisan balance on the Supreme Court.

In 1971, Democratic representative Charles Griffin of Mississippi reintroduced a proposal (H.J. Res. 95) that he had also advocated in 1968 and 1969, prohibiting two justices from the same state from serving on the Supreme Court. Griffin may have been responding to President Nixon's 1970 appointment of Harry Blackmun, who, like Chief Justice Warren Burger (whom Nixon had appointed the previous year), was from Minnesota. Nixon nominated Blackmun after failing to get two southerners, Clement F. Haynesworth Jr. and Harold Carswell, confirmed.

For Further Reading:

Abraham, Henry J. 1998. *The Judicial Process: An Introductory Analysis of the Courts of the United States, England, and France.* 7th ed. New York: Oxford University Press.

Miller, Arthur S. 1982. *Toward Increased Judicial Activism: The Political Role of the Supreme Court.* Westport, CT: Greenwood Press.

JUDICIARY, RECALL OF MEMBERS

One of the mechanisms associated with the Progressive Era was the recall, by which voters could remove an official by popular vote. Former President Theodore Roosevelt called for such an amendment when he ran as a Progressive (Bull Moose) candidate in the election of 1912 (Gerhardt 2002, 591). Although recalls are more common for elected officials, several members of Congress have introduced amendments providing for the recall of federal judges—as has Daniel B. Jeffs, the author of a recent book proposing to make the U.S. government more accountable to the electorate. All federal judges are currently appointed and serve "during good behavior," or for life, but since the Jacksonian era, many states' judges have been elected to fixed terms and subject to reelection or rejection. Plans for judicial recall might increase popular accountability of judges still further but would also likely erode their independence and possibly their willingness to uphold unpopular constitutional provisions.

See also Jeffs, Daniel B.; Judiciary, Removal of Members; Progressive Era.

For Further Reading:

Gerhardt, Michael J. 2002. "The Rhetoric of Judicial Critique: From Judicial Restraint to the Virtual Bill of Rights." *William and Mary Bill of Rights Journal* 10 (April): 585–641.

JUDICIARY, REMOVAL OF MEMBERS

Currently, the only legal mechanism that is available for removing sitting federal judges is that of impeachment by the House of Representatives and conviction by a two-thirds vote of the Senate. Article II, Section 4 of the Constitution limits impeachable offenses to "Treason, Bribery, or other high Crimes or Misdemeanors." Although this provision guards judges against being removed for political reasons, it leaves no legal means to remove judges who are incompetent.

Throughout U.S. history, members of Congress have introduced proposals to liberalize this process. The first such plan was introduced by Virginia's flamboyant representative John Randolph, who had helped lead the unsuccessful impeachment effort against Justice Samuel Chase. Randolph's proposal would have enabled the president to remove judges, provided he gave a joint address to both houses of Congress to justify his actions. Members of Congress introduced several other proposals in the next 30 years, with others following in 1850 and 1867.

Members of Congress introduced at least three proposals for removing judges in 1912. Democratic senator Henry Ashurst of Arizona appeared to be influenced by contemporary interest in the recall. Tennessee Democratic representative Cordell Hull introduced the other two resolutions, providing for the removal of inferior court judges by concurrent resolution in Congress.

Proposals for removing judges have been introduced at a fairly steady pace since 1941. Some such proposals would apply only to lower court judges, and others have been directed specifically to members of the Supreme Court. Louisiana Democratic representative John Rarick introduced a proposal in 1968 (H.J. Res. 1094) that would allow 1 percent or more of the voters of two-thirds of the states to petition for the removal of a Supreme Court justice, which action would be effected by a majority vote at the next congressional election. Florida Republican Louis Frey introduced a resolution in 1976 (H.J. Res. 912) that would have allowed the Senate, with House concurrence, to remove a justice who was unable to perform his or her duties "by reason of a personal mental or physical disability," including "habitual intemperance." This proposal came within a year of the retirement of Justice William O. Douglas, who had remained on the Supreme Court after suffering a debilitating stroke.

Other proposals from this period would have delegated removal powers to the courts themselves, usually subject to review by the U.S. Supreme Court. Still others would have vested this power directly in the High Court.

Many states now provide for disciplinary commissions, often consisting of fellow judges and laypersons, as well as recall elections for judges thought to be incompetent or out of touch (Jacob 1995, 195–196). In 1980, Congress adopted the Judicial Councils Reform and Judicial Conduct and Disability Act. It permits judicial councils in the 13 federal circuits to discipline, but not to remove, lower court judges (Abraham 1998, 44–45).

See also Impeachment; Judiciary, Recall.

For Further Reading:
Abraham, Henry J. 1998. *The Judicial Process: An Introductory Analysis of the Courts of the United States, England, and France.* 7th ed. New York: Oxford University Press.

Jacob, Herbert. 1995. *Law and Politics in the United States.* 2d ed. New York: HarperCollins College Publishers.

JUDICIARY, SELECTION OF MEMBERS

The judicial branch is the only branch of the national government whose members are not elected. Instead, under the terms of Article II, Section 2 of the Constitution, the president appoints judges with the advice and consent, or approval, of the Senate. Although the framers designed this mechanism to insulate judges from the political process, judicial selection and confirmation can be an extremely political process (Massaro 1990), and nomination is certainly no guarantee of confirmation. Thus, as of the end of the Clinton administration, 30 of 144 nominees to the Supreme Court had failed to be confirmed by the Senate (Abraham 1999, 28).

In contrast to the national government, many states either elect judges or use a mechanism, such as the Missouri and California Plans, that combines a system of appointment and electoral confirmation (Abraham 1999, 35–39). The movement for judicial accountability was especially prominent in the Jacksonian period and again in the Progressive Era (Tarr 1994, 69).

Despite the former movement, there were only four proposed changes in the method of selecting federal judges in the nation's first 90 years (Ames 1896, 146). Since then, there have been more than 65 such proposals; many coincide with periods in which there was intense opposition to the Court as an institution or strong concern over controversial rulings (Nagel 1965).

The most common proposal calls simply for the election of federal judges and other appointed officeholders, for example, district attorneys, clerks, marshals, revenue collectors, and postmasters. Such elections may be proposed only for members of the Supreme Court, only for members of lower U.S. district and circuit courts, or for both the Supreme Court and the lower courts. Such proposed elections are also frequently tied to judicial terms of from four to 12 years and are sometimes phrased in terms of a recall.

Most proposals calling for the election of Supreme Court justices appear to foresee the creation of nine electoral districts in the United States for such elections. This might increase the role that geographic representation now plays in such appointments, although it might also reduce minority representation on that body. Some proposals also call for changing the current practice by which the president designates the chief justice (Vile 1994b), specifying instead that the justices would choose their own chief (as is the case in many states).

Other proposals, especially prominent in the 1950s and 1960s, would have allowed the president to appoint Supreme Court justices from a list of five nominees selected by the chief justices of state supreme courts. Some other proposals have called for including members of the House of Representatives in the confirmation process. One of the most innovative such proposals, a kind of congressional court-packing plan, was introduced in 1946 by Democratic senator James Eastland of Mississippi. It would have provided that no president could appoint more than three justices to the Supreme Court and would have required the retirement of any beyond three that had been so appointed. Such vacancies would have been filled by the U.S. House of Representatives, with the representatives of each state having a single vote.

Recent controversies over nominees to the Supreme Court (and long delays in considering nominees to lower federal court positions in both the Bill Clinton and George W. Bush administrations) have rekindled controversies about possible changes in Senate rules, many of which have grown informally over the course of time (Denning 2001), or constitutional alternatives to the current process. Among proposals that would require an amendment are those providing for judicial term limits, for judicial elections, or for raising the current requirement for Senate confirmation to a two-thirds majority of that body (Carter 1994, 195–203).

The author of a recent article suggests than an amendment might help remedy the current method of judicial selection. He thinks it should require the president to consult with Senate leaders before making appointments, should limit the use of executive privilege to withhold information that Congress seeks, should require the Senate Judiciary Committee to report all nominations to the full Senate, and should limit filibusters to "extraordinary circumstances" (Becker 2007).

For Further Reading:

Abraham, Henry J. 1999. *Justices, Presidents, and Senators: A History of the U.S. Supreme Court Appointments from Washington to Clinton.* Lanham, MD: Rowman & Littlefield Publishers, Inc.

Ames, Herman. 1896. *The Proposed Amendments to the Constitution of the United States during the First Century of Its History.* Reprint, New York: Burt Franklin, 1970.

Becker, Ryan T. 2007. "The Other Nuclear Option: Adopting a Constitutional Amendment to Furnish a Lasting Solution to the Troubled Judicial Confirmation Process." *Pennsylvania State Law Review* 111 (Spring): 981–1008.

Carter, Stephen L. 1994. *The Confirmation Mess: Cleaning Up the Federal Appointments Process.* New York: Basic Books.

Denning, Brannon P. 2001. "Reforming the New Confirmation Process: Replacing 'Despise and Resent' with 'Advice and Consent.'" *Administrative Law Review* 53 (Winter): 1–44.

Massaro, John. 1990. *Supremely Political: The Role of Ideology and Presidential Management in Unsuccessful Supreme Court Nominations.* Albany, NY: State University of New York Press.

Nagel, Stuart S. 1965. "Court-Curbing Proposals in American History." *Vanderbilt Law Review* 18: 925–944.

Tarr, G. Alan. 1994. *Judicial Process and Judicial Policymaking.* St. Paul, MN: West.

Vile, John R. 1994. "The Selection and Tenure of Chief Justices." *Judicature* 78 (September–October): 96–10.

JUDICIARY, TERMS OF OFFICE

The president appoints federal judges and justices with the "advice and consent," or approval, of the Senate. Such judges and justices serve "during good behavior," which means that they continue in office until they die or resign or until the House of Representatives impeaches and the Senate convicts them of an impeachable offense. By contrast, many state judges are elected by the people or serve fixed terms of office (Glick 1988, 86–98).

Proposals to limit the terms of federal judges date back to 1808 and have been introduced in almost every subsequent decade. Such proposals are often tied to mandatory retirement ages, typically somewhere between 65 and 75. In the 1850s and 1860s, Andrew Johnson was a prominent proponent of a 12-year judicial term (Ames 1896, 152).

Proposals for fixed judicial terms have been especially popular from the late 1960s to the present (with close to 200 proposals being introduced in this period), but their specific provisions have varied substantially. Some such proposals would apply only to Supreme Court justices, others only to lower federal judges, and still others to both. Although some call for a one-term limit, the overwhelming majority would allow judges to be reappointed or reelected to office. The process of presidential renomination and Senate reconfirmation appears to be the most popular.

As in recent controversies on congressional term limits, no consensus has emerged as to how long such terms should be. Proposals have varied from four to 18 years (Ross 1990; Levinson 1992; DiTullo and Schochet 2004; Calabresi and Lindgren 2006). As part of a package of term limits for members of the House and Senate, Democratic representative Andrew Jacobs Jr. of Indiana introduced a proposal in 1967 to prohibit federal judges from serving more than 10 out of any 12 years (H.J. Res. 868).

Senate confirmations of Supreme Court justices have become increasingly public affairs (Carter 1994), and Justice Clarence Thomas likened his own confirmation to a type of death (Danforth 1994). In such circumstances, there is likely to be substantial opposition to the idea of Senate reconfirmation of sitting judges and justices.

See also Judiciary, Age Limits for Members.

For Further Reading:

Ames, Herman. 1896. *The Proposed Amendments to the Constitution of the United States during the First Century of Its History.* Reprint, New York: Burt Franklin, 1970.

Calabresi, Steven G., and James Lindgren. 2006. "Term Limits for the Supreme Court: Life Tenure Reconsidered." *Harvard Journal of Law and Public Policy* 29 (Summer): 769–877.

Carter, Stephen L. 1994. *The Confirmation Mess: Cleaning Up the Federal Appointments Process.* New York: Basic Books.

Danforth, John C. 1994. *Resurrection: The Confirmation of Clarence Thomas.* New York: Viking.

DiTullo, James E., and John B. Schochet. 2004. "Saving This Honorable Court: A Proposal to Replace Life Tenure on the Supreme Court with Staggered, Nonrenewable Eighteen-Year Terms." *Virginia Law Review* 90 (June): 1093–1149.

Glick, Henry R. 1988. *Courts, Politics, and Justice?* 2d ed. New York: McGraw Hill.

Levinson, Sanford. 1992. "Contempt of Court: The Most Important 'Contemporary Challenge to Judging.'" *Washington and Lee Law Review* 49 (Spring): 339–343.

Ross, William G. 1990. "The Hazards of Proposals to Limit the Tenure of Federal Judges and to Permit Judicial Removal without Impediment." *Villanova Law Review* 35 (November): 1063–1138.

JURY TRIALS

Article III of the Constitution provides that "the trial of all crimes, except in cases of impeachment; shall be by jury." The Sixth Amendment also guarantees "an impartial jury" in federal criminal cases, and the Seventh Amendment extends this right to federal civil cases involving more than $20. Applying its incorporation doctrine, the Supreme Court has ruled that the Sixth Amendment right to a jury trial in criminal cases applies to the states via the due process clause of the Fourteenth Amendment (*Duncan v. Louisiana,* 391 U.S. 145 (1968)), but it has not extended the Seventh Amendment right in civil trials. With roots deep in English common law, the jury is thought to guarantee fairness; commentators have also long argued that service on a jury provides an education in citizenship (Tocqueville 1969, 270–276; Abramson 1994).

The fact that only a few amending proposals have been introduced relative to the jury system probably indicates that, despite periodic scholarly criticism (Frank 1969, 108–125), the system continues to be held in general favor. Several proposals introduced around the time of the Civil War would have provided jury trials for escaped slaves. In 1948, a proposal was introduced to permit juries of fewer than 12 members in certain cases.

The Constitution does not specify the number of individuals who must sit on a jury, and the Supreme Court has upheld the use of six-member juries in noncapital cases (*Williams v. Florida,* 399 U.S. 78 (1970)). In *Ballew v. Georgia* (1978), however, the Supreme Court struck down the use of a five-person jury. In *Johnson v. Louisiana* (1972) and *Apodaco v. Oregon* (1972), it upheld nonunanimous jury verdicts in noncapital criminal cases, and in *Burch v. Louisiana* (1979), it ruled that six-member juries must vote unanimously to convict. The judiciary has thus arguably adapted, or enabled the jury mechanism to adapt, to modern exigencies.

See also Seventh Amendment; Sixth Amendment.

For Further Reading:

Abramson, Jeffrey. 1994. *We the Jury: The Jury System and the Ideal of Democracy.* New York: Basic Books.

Frank, Jerome. 1969. *Courts on Trial: Myth and Reality in American Justice.* New York: Atheneum.

Tocqueville, Alexis de. 1835, 1840. *Democracy in America,* ed. J. P. Mayer. Reprint, Garden City, NY: Anchor Books, 1969.

K

KIMBLE V. SWACKHAMER (1978)

Acting as a circuit justice, Chief Justice William Rehnquist upheld a 4-to-1 Nevada Supreme Court decision by refusing to enjoin the placement of an advisory referendum concerning the Equal Rights Amendment on the upcoming Nevada ballot. Rehnquist said that *Leser v. Garnett* (1922) and *Hawke v. Smith* (*I*) (1920) "stand for the proposition that the two methods for state ratification of proposed constitutional amendments set forth in Art. V of the United States Constitution are exclusive" (*Kimble* 1978, 1387). Rehnquist noted, however, that this referendum was advisory only and thus was little different from a representative seeking advice from his constituents. By contrast, in *Cook v. Gralike* (2001), a majority of the U.S. Supreme Court led by Justice John Paul Stevens decided that a state did not have authority to "instruct" its representatives in the House of Representatives as to how to vote on an amendment or to put a notation on the ballot as to which representatives had followed such instructions.

See also *Cook v. Gralike; Hawke v. Smith; Leser v. Garnett.*

For Further Reading:
Kimble v. Swackhamer, 439 U.S. 385 (1978).
Woalcoff, Jonathan L. 1995. "The Unconstitutionality of Voter Initiative Applications for Federal Constitutional Conventions." *Colorado Law Review* 85: 1525–1545.

KIRSTEIN, HERBERT C.

Herbert Kirstein, identified as a former employee of the Central Intelligence Agency, a staff member of the U.S. Senate, and an employee of the U.S. Department of Health and Human Services, published his proposal for a new constitution in his book *U.S. Constitution for 21st Century and Beyond.* He also maintains a Web site, where this book and various other proposals are available. (Page numbers cited in this essay are taken from the more accessible Web site rather than from the printed text, from which it now diverges at some points.)

Kirstein's Web site lists 10 objectives of his government. These include a "stronger 'voice' for citizens; knowledgeable national-global leadership; effective management of government; futurized Congress for the 21st Century; law enforcement, security, and justice; tax laws to accelerate economic progress; monetary policy to finance future; stewardship of national resources; accelerated science and technology; and [a] new 'Voice of USAMERICA.'" He describes and explains each of these objectives on his Web site in detail, often accompanied by sharp criticisms of elements of corruption and inefficiency that Kirstein believes pervade the current system.

Kirstein divides his constitution into eight articles. It is considerably more complex than the Constitution of 1787. Article I describes the "Powers of the Citizens." To existing rights of election, Kirstein adds the right of the voters to "enact laws by a national referendum" and "to instruct, remove, or impeach" elected officials"

(Kirstein 1994, 14). Citizenship requires an oath or affirmation to abide by the Constitution. Voting is considered to be a duty as well as a right, and citizens can be fined up to $10 an election for not voting. Kirstein believes that the people need to be better educated. Article I thus includes a proposed "Universal Academy for Freedom and Democracy," which will educate candidates.

Article II deals with legislative powers. In addition to the existing two houses of Congress, Kirstein wants to create what he calls the "Office of the Premiere Legislative Coordinator of Congress" (Kirstein 1994, 16). Elected to office by a plurality of the people from among those who have attained "one (1) of the four (4) highest scores in the National Knowledge Examination for Premiere Legislative Coordinator of Congress," this individual would establish legislative goals and priorities, enhance legislative management, and exercise veto powers over legislation that are currently exercised by the president. The coordinator would serve for renewable six-year terms (17–18). Senators and members of the House of Representatives would be expected to pass national examinations, and the length of House terms would be raised to four years (21). Kirstein further specifies that "[a]ll proposed amendments or other modifications of legislative proposals shall be required to be germane to the subject matter" (22). Kirstein lists 43 separate powers that Congress would be able to exercise (24–28).

Article III describes executive and administrative powers. The president would become the "Chief Executive Officer of the National Executive and Administrative Service" (28). Like members of Congress, the president would have to qualify by attaining a certain score on the National Knowledge Examination. Once presidents and vice presidents are so qualified, their terms would be raised to six years, but they would remain limited to two terms. The president would direct the National Council for Progress and Security, which is divided into a number of departments, many of which are renamed cabinet departments (31). These would include a Department for Legislative Affairs; a Department of National Economic Development and Progress (along with a Directorate for

[the] National Monetary System [which Kirstein believes needs serious reform], a Directorate for [the] National Banking System, a Directorate for National Value and Pricing Systems, a Directorate for National Investment Policy and Systems, and a Directorate for Market Economy and Enterprise Systems); a Department for National Human Work Force and Automated and Robotic Systems (the former Department of Labor, which will in turn be divided into a number of directorates); a Department for Agriculture, Aquaculture, and other Food-production Systems; a Department for Natural Resources; a Department for Environmental Protection, Preservation, and Enhancement; a Department for Advancing Science and Technology; a Department for International Policy and Global Affairs; a Department for Extraterrestrial and Outer Universe Exploration and Developments Programs (formerly NASA); a Department for Advancing the Status of Citizens (with Directorates for profiling population, providing food and nutrition, furnishing health and medical care, and for Education and Enlightenment—providing, among other things, for tuition-free education); a Department for National Intelligence and Citizen-Information Systems; a Department for Natural Disaster-Recovery Systems; as well as a number of existing departments, for a total of 20 main departments with many subdirectorates. These departments and directorates are described in great detail; in addition, Kirstein indicates his view that the provision of governmental services will often require the use of "quasigovernmental enterprises" (38).

Article IV describes judicial powers. It would create a National Judicial System for Law and Justice that would be headed by a Supreme Judicial Minister, qualified like other officeholders by examination, and winning a plurality of votes in a national election (Kirstein 1994, 52–53). This minister would serve renewable six-year terms. The minister would be responsible for nominating members of the judiciary, but they would continue to be subject to Senate confirmation. The judicial branch would include a Ministry for Law Enforcement and Citizen Security that would replace the current Department of Justice. The minister of this Department would be nominated by the Supreme Judicial Minister and confirmed by a majority of Supreme Court justices with the aim of making this individual less political than the current attorney general. The minister "shall be a permanent, career appointment" (55).

Kirstein would also establish a "National Societal-Clone Prison System," which, except for its population, would mirror the institutions of the large society and would be expected to be self-supporting. The judicial branch would also include a Ministry of Justice to be composed of members of the U.S. Supreme Court and other courts. The minister of justice would be nominated by the supreme judicial minister for law and justice and confirmed by majority vote of U.S. Supreme Court Justices (57). In addition to passing tests establishing their knowledge, most judges would be required to have at least "10 years of experience in the U.S. judicial system" (57). U.S. Supreme Court justices would be nominated by the supreme judicial officer of the National Judicial System for Law and Justice and be confirmed by the Senate. Their terms would be limited to 30 years (58). Standards would be established for individuals who serve as jurors, with special exams, as for other officeholders. Kirstein would provide for a National Council for Constitutionality of Law (59). This council would review congressional laws "prior to implementation" (60). If the council decided that such laws were unconstitutional, then Congress would have to reconsider them, the Supreme Court would have to review and approve them, or, if the Supreme Court came to a contrary verdict, they would "remain inoperable" (60).

Article V of Kirstein's constitution deals with general provisions and includes a phrase making the new Constitution the "supreme law of the land" (61). Article VI deals with ratification of the constitution. Kirstein proposes that this be done by a national referendum approved by two-thirds or more of the voters. This article includes a provision prohibiting amendments during the first three years that the new constitution is in operation.

Article VII provides a right of citizens to alter their government. Amendments may be proposed by congressional legislation or by leg-

islation or referendum in two-thirds of the states. Amendments would be ratified, like the constitution, "by 2/3 or more of citizens voting in a national referendum" (62).

Article VIII is labeled "Citizen Rights, Obligation, and Rewards" (63). It contains the previously mentioned citizen oath of allegiance. Among other things, it pledges citizens to obey the law, to vote, to respect the rights of others, and to serve their nation for one or two years upon reaching the age of 18. This article also includes what Kirstein calls the "Golden Chronicle of Citizen Rights" (63), which includes many provisions in the existing U.S. Constitution as well as some that are not. The rights in Kirstein's constitution include freedom; democracy; entitlements to basic needs like "food, housing, health and medical care, education, and acceptable standards of living" (64); the right to own property, including firearms; freedom to communicate; freedom of assembly; equal status under law "without regard to race, creed, nationality, ethnic origin, gender, ideology, religion, economic status, or other factor or value" (64); due process of law; protections for private life; protections against exploitation and economic servitude by persons, organizations, and governments; protection against discrimination; the right to worship; the right to present grievances to government without the improper use of money to influence politicians; the sharing of resources; separation of religion and government (with provisions to tax religious groups that use more than 10 percent of their income for nonreligious purposes); human rights; "truth in public communications"; and a provision guaranteeing "general rights and privileges" (65).

Kirstein's complex plan is unique in its attempt to combine both elements of increased popular participation with increased education of individuals who hold office. If adopted, Kirstein's plan would appear to reduce the power of the presidency by taking away the president's current veto and by effectively giving each of the other two branches a single head.

In 1992, Kirstein published the *Ideology of Freedom and Democracy,* which is described as a "Master Plan for FREEDOM, DEMOCRACY, HUMAN RIGHTS, PROGRESS, SECURITY, and PEACE on Planet EARTH." There he advocated supplanting the United Nations with a more effective world organization and promoting democracy throughout the world.

For Further Reading:

Kirstein, Herbert C. 1994. *U.S. Constitution for 21st Century and Beyond.* Alexandria, VA: Realistic IDEALIST Enterprise.

Kirstein, Herbert C. 1992. *Ideology of Freedom and Democracy.* Alexandria, VA: Realistic IDEALIST Enterprise.

"U.S. Constitution for the 21st Century and Beyond." At http://www.newusconstitution.org/usc21a. html. Accessed June 28, 2000.

KRUSCH, BARRY (1958–)

In 1992, Barry Krusch of New York offered one of the most ambitious plans for a new U.S. constitution in a book entitled *The 21st Century Constitution* (1992). An extensive opening chapter detailed current faults in the U.S. system. Krusch attributed most of these to separation of powers, to the fact that the Constitution was written prior to the modern information age, and to the fact that actual practices (what he calls the empirical constitution) no longer match the written document. In the rest of his book, Krusch outlined an alternative constitution. His alternative was, however, built around the current constitutional outline. Krusch wanted to make the constitution more responsive to public wishes and more adaptable to modern technologies, but he also expressed great faith in the power of experts to guide legislative decision making and identify national interests.

Under Krusch's plan, Congress would continue to consist of two branches, but with somewhat different functions. Members of both branches would be prohibited from being members of political parties and would be limited to eight years of service. Members of the new House of Representatives, consisting of a minimum of 1,000 members, would serve one-year terms and would be required to be graduates of a federal academy (also responsible for proposing congressional rules). Each state would continue to have two senators, but they would serve two-year terms. The Senate's primary function would be governmental oversight. A federal committee of 50 senators would administer "the National Database, the National Poll, the National Objectives, the National Initiative, the National Referendum, and the National Recall" (Krusch 1992, 128). The committee would also nominate candidates for the House of Representatives and the presidency, making sure that their nominees were "representative of the population . . . with regard to sex, race, national origin and other factors" (Krusch 1992, 129). The Senate would be responsible for setting up a legislative review board of nine members, serving for single three-year terms, that would compile "performance ratings" for representatives according to the degree to which they voted for bills that served the national interest. The Senate would also commission polls to ascertain the public will.

The majority necessary to pass bills—and the determination of whether a bill would need to pass one or both houses and/or be signed by the president—would be based on the evaluation that the bills received from the legislative review board. Any income taxes would have to apply to at least three-fourths of the population, with the highest tax bracket limited to 50 percent and the lowest at least half that amount (Krusch 1992, 158). Borrowing would require a sanction by a two-thirds vote of both houses and the voters. Krusch would permit the legislative veto, which the Court declared unconstitutional in *Immigration and Naturalization Service v. Chadha* (1983) (Krusch 1992, 165). Congress would create and regulate a national academy, a department of rights enforcement, and a federal election commission, with all electoral campaigns to be publicly financed.

The right to an education would be granted, a national database would be created to disseminate information to the citizens, and a national television channel would educate people, with "one-half of the programming" to "reflect the Will of the People as determined by the June National Poll" (Krusch 1992, 179). Current principles regarding freedom of speech, religion, and other rights in the Bill of Rights would be set forth in greater detail that better reflects current case law. One fascinating provision allows for penalties for those distorting "those aspects of reality which have been or can be objectively verified as true" (Krusch 1992, 183).

The president and vice president would be selected by majority vote, with the national recall taking the place of presidential impeachment. Presidential powers to commit troops without congressional authorization would be clipped.

Nine nonpartisan judges representative of the population would serve staggered nine-year terms. Although judges would no longer have the power of judicial review, they would not be obligated to enforce laws that they considered to be unconstitutional.

The current federal arrangement of the government would undergo few changes, but a majority of both houses of two-thirds of the people would be able to propose amendments. Two-thirds of the people or state legislatures could also call for a convention. Amendments would be ratified by two-thirds of the state legislatures or conventions or by three-fifths of the electorate. In a provision similar to one that Thomas Jefferson made, every 25 years, the people would be asked whether they wanted another convention (Krusch 1992, 236).

The main articles of the new constitution would be augmented by supplements that could be altered more easily. Krusch would also include a rule of constitutional construction that "strict terms such as 'no' or 'all' shall be strictly construed, and broad terms such as 'liberty' and 'justice' shall be broadly construed" (Krusch 1992, 247).

A Second Federal Convention Act would provide the rules for constitutional ratification. Krusch anticipated a convention of 1,200 delegates to write or affirm the constitution, with members of no single profession to compose more than 5 percent of its members (Krusch 1992, 249). The people would choose from among three to six such documents.

Krusch's resume identifies him as a Web designer and indicates that he earned a bachelor's degree in psychology in 1980 and a master's degree in education in 1996 (http://www.krusch.com/resume.html, accessed June 2, 2008). His book included an address for people who are interested in serving as delegates to a mock constitutional convention.

See also Constitutional Conventions.

For Further Reading:

Krusch, Barry. 1992. *The 21st Century Constitution: A New America for a New Millennium.* New York: Stanhope Press.

L

LABOR, CONVICT

At least one proposal was introduced in 1883 and two in 1886 that would prohibit states from contracting out convict labor. This practice, almost exclusively applied to African Americans (and often involving slave-like conditions similar to those that the Thirteenth Amendment had outlawed), was especially widespread at the time in the South. In 1891, this system led to violence in Tennessee, when miners attempted to stop this source of competition. Although no such amendment was adopted, fears by free laborers of unfair competition continue to limit the tasks that states assign to convicts. In the 1990s, however, Alabama and Arizona reinstituted the chain gang as a way of saving state money and deterring crime (Gavzer 1995, 6).

See also: Thirteenth Amendment.

For Further Reading:
Gavzer, Bernard. 1995. "Life behind Bars." *Parade Magazine* 13 August, 4–7.

LABOR, HOURS OF

From 1884 to 1937, members of Congress introduced more than 30 proposals to give that body power to regulate the hours of labor. Some such resolutions applied specifically to factories; some proposed "uniform" hours of labor; and some combined proposals about hours of labor with power over minimum wages, the prevention of unfair labor practices, child labor, or other aspects of working life.

Proposals for reform coincided with a period during which the federal courts often struck down state and federal regulatory legislation that they perceived to have a class bias (Gillman 1993). The due process clause of the Fourteenth Amendment—which the Supreme Court interpreted as embodying "freedom of contract"—was the tool that the courts used most frequently to accomplish this objective. The best known of these decisions was *Lochner v. New York* (1905), in which the Supreme Court struck down a New York state law regulating the hours of bakers (Kens 1990). Decisions in which the Court upheld such laws usually involved industries considered to be particularly dangerous, such as mining in *Holden v. Hardy* (1898), or individuals the Court thought were in need of special state protection, such as women in *Muller v. Oregon* (1908).

Although the analysis has arguably been overdrawn, *West Coast Hotel v. Parrish* (1937) and *National Labor Relations Board v. Jones & Laughlin Steel Corp.* (1937) are often cited as the cases in which the Supreme Court made an historic "switch in time that saved nine," in response to Franklin D. Roosevelt's court-packing plan, and began interpreting existing congressional powers under the commerce and taxing provisions generously enough to uphold most labor-related legislation. Such interpretations negated the need for a constitutional amendment, and members of Congress ceased introducing them, but some libertarian proponents of a new U.S.

constitution would leave such matters to be regulated only by the market place.

See also Child Labor Amendment; Court-Packing Plan; Fourteenth Amendment; *Lochner v. New York.*

For Further Reading:

Gillman, Howard. 1993. *The Constitution Besieged: The Rise and Demise of Lochner Era Police Powers Jurisprudence.* Durham, NC: Duke University Press.

Kens, Paul. 1990. *Judicial Power and Reform Politics: The Anatomy of* Lochner v. New York. Lawrence: University Press of Kansas.

LABUNSKI, RICHARD

Richard Labunski, a journalism professor at the University of Kentucky with both a PhD and J.D., wrote a book titled *The Second Constitutional Convention* (2000). Labunski begins his introduction by noting that many contemporary Americans share "Disappointment, disillusionment, and distrust." His book is divided into four parts. The first discusses the current Constitution and recent perceived abuses, particularly in the areas of campaign financing and congressional resistance to term limits and other proposed changes, as well as judicial limitations in bringing about wholesale reform, that he thinks make a second convention necessary.

The second section of his book discusses how meetings leading to a national "preconvention," and precipitating states to call a real convention, can be organized. The third describes 10 amendments that he thinks a constitutional convention should consider, whereas the fourth attempts to square his proposals with the eight guidelines for amendments advanced by the Citizens for the Constitution. This entry examines the second and third of Labunski's objectives.

Drawing in part from the unsuccessful Peace Convention that preceded the U.S. Civil War, as well as from a National Issues Convention held in 1996 in Austin, Texas, that was designed to educate a group of more than 900 participants

on contemporary political issues, Labunski outlines a plan that he hopes will eventually result in sufficient petitions from the states to call a second constitutional convention. Labunski envisions meetings beginning at the county or congressional district level, perhaps attended by no more than two or three dozen people. They would in turn generate publicity about the possibility of another convention, seek to inform and engage the public (using state-of-the-art interactive Internet technology), discuss key constitutional issues and possible solutions, and elect representatives to state conventions, to be composed of 52 or fewer delegates (Labunski 2000, 199). Ideally, all state conventions would take place on the same day, but Labunski thinks that at the least they should take place within a 30- to 60-day period. Each convention would select two delegates to a national preconvention in Washington DC. This preconvention would identify "the *problems* that will be addressed by constitutional amendments"; identify "the specific *sections* of the Constitution that will be considered for revisions"; and suggest "in *general terms* language that may be appropriate for the new amendments" (220–221).

After this preconvention, the work would begin attempting to convince state legislatures to petition Congress for a second constitutional convention. Labunski thinks that the Internet can be used to generate enthusiasm for this project and devotes an entire chapter to this subject. Noting that no previous amendment "has been designed to limit congressional power" (Labunski 2000, 273), Labunski further explores previous attempts by Congress to legislate on the subject of conventions, as well as the fairly limited role that courts have played in overseeing this process in recent years.

Labunski labels his 10 amending proposals from "A" to "J." Labunski phrases each proposed amendment as a legislative petition; each further specifies how long after ratification it would go into effect, contains a built-in seven-year deadline for ratification, and requires ratification by state conventions.

Consistent with Labunski's critique of current American government, Amendment "A" deals with campaign finance reform and would overturn parts of the U.S. Supreme Court decision in

Buckley v. Valeo (1976). Labunski would permit regulations of both campaign contributions and expenditures. He would also require that candidates for Congress raise at least half their funds from within their respective district or state. Labunski would grant both Congress and state legislatures power to limit expenditures per voters within districts, limits that would apply both to direct candidate expenditures and to less direct "soft money" expenditures. He would also provide for "comprehensive disclosure of campaign contributions and expenditures" and would authorize Congress and the states to "study a plan by which elections are publicly financed" (Labunski 2000, 294).

Amendment "B" is an expanded version of the Equal Rights Amendment. Addressing one of the issues that originally divided supporters of women's rights, Labunski specifically provides that "This amendment shall not be construed to invalidate legislation, administrative regulations, or other acts of Congress or the states that have benign effects on the economic or political status of women" (Labunski 2000, 315), but he does not specifically address the equally provocative issue of women in the military. Undoubtedly with the precedent of *United States v. Morrison* (2000) in view, Labunski further provides that "[t]he interstate commerce clause of Article I, Section 8, shall not be construed by any federal or state court as inhibiting congressional authority to enact laws related to gender-motivated violence" (316).

Amendment "C" advances the cause of victims' rights. These would include "the right to be present in all public proceedings to determine release from custody, acceptance of a plea agreement, or a sentence; the right to be informed of and to offer written or oral testimony at parole hearings; the right to reasonable notice of release or escape from custody of the defendant; and the right to compensation for crimes in amounts fixed by federal and state law" (Labunski 2000, 338). Labunski's proposal would extend a "civil right of action" against crime perpetrators and waive state immunity (thus presumably modifying existing interpretations of the Eleventh Amendment) in cases in which the conduct of public officials resulted "in gratuitous harm to the crime victim, and

where the conduct of such officials is reckless or malicious" (338).

Labunski groups Amendments "D," "E," and "F" together. Amendment "D" addresses the issue of congressional term limits. Members of the House would be limited to four two-year terms and senators to two six-year terms, with similar overall limits in effect if the term of senators were reduced to four years, as Amendment "E" proposes. On a related noted, Amendment "F" provides for allowing the Senate to ratify treaties by majority vote rather than by the current two-thirds majority.

Amendment "G" is devoted to eliminating the Electoral College and replacing it with a system of direct election. Labunski further specifies that voters would designate their first, second, and third choices for president. If, when adding second and third choice votes, no candidate got 40 percent or more of the electoral vote, then the electoral outcome would be resolved by an assembly of both houses of Congress, with each member having a single vote (the Twelfth Amendment currently provides for resolving presidential contests by giving each state a single vote in the House).

Amendment "H" is designed to protect the judiciary. It does so by specifying that Congress "shall not have the power to alter, modify, restrict, or enhance the appellate jurisdiction of the federal courts" (377).

Amendment "I" would alter the amending process by providing for three methods. First, amendments could be proposed and ratified by 60 percent majorities of Congress and of the states. Second, Congress would be obligated to call a constitutional convention within 90 days of receiving "petitions from 50 percent of state legislatures requesting that Congress call a constitutional convention" (388). Third, Congress would be obligated to call such a convention after receiving petitions from 50 percent of state secretaries of states who had in turn received petitions from 10 percent or more of those voting in the last general election (388). Convention delegates would be elected by the people, and once states had ratified an amendment, such ratifications could not be rescinded.

Labunski's final proposal, Amendment "J," calls for the repeal of the Second Amendment.

Noting current controversies over whether this amendment protects individual or group rights (Labunski leans to the latter view), he thinks the best thing to do would be simply to repeal the amendment and allow for state and national gun control laws.

In addition to writing a book about a new constitution, Labunski has published a book on James Madison's role in the adoption of the Bill of Rights.

Labunski's proposal provides one of the most elaborate mechanisms for building the momentum that might be required to get states to petition Congress to call another constitutional convention, and his proposal for a preconvention is especially fascinating. His proposals are not easily classified under a single rubric but appear to mix concerns expressed by a number of contemporary groups.

See also Constitutional Conventions; Peace Convention.

For Further Reading:

Labunski, Richard. 2006. *James Madison and the Struggle for the Bill of Rights.* New York: Oxford University Press.

Labunski, Richard. 2000. *The Second Constitutional Convention: How the American People Can Take Back Their Government.* Versailles, KY: Marley and Beck Press.

LAME DUCK AMENDMENT

See Twentieth Amendment.

LAND, DIVISION OF

A number of amendments that have been proposed to grant or expand the national government's power over agriculture have included grants of power to tax or otherwise regulate land. Henry George (1839–1897) promoted a single-tax movement on land with the 1871 publication of his essay "Our Land and Land Policy," which subsequently became the basis of his influential *Progress and Poverty* (1938).

Democratic representative John Randolph Thayer of Massachusetts offered perhaps the most drastic proposal to alter land distribution by amendment in January 1904 (H.J. Res. 83). Thayer would have allowed the national government to take land from anyone with more than 12 acres and redistribute it so that everyone would have at least eight contiguous acres. Similar distributions were to be made after each census (Musmanno 1929, 1903).

See also Agriculture.

For Further Reading:

George, Henry. 1938. *Progress and Poverty: An Inquiry into the Cause of Industrial Depressions and of Increase of Want with Increase of Wealth, the Remedy.* 50th anniversary ed. New York: Robert Schalkenback Foundation.

LAWRENCE, WILLIAM B. (1800–1881)

American diplomat and international law specialist William B. Lawrence published an article in 1880 in which he advocated substantial changes in the U.S. Constitution (Vile 1991c, 32–34). He was especially concerned about the treatment the South had received during Reconstruction and by the irregularities of the disputed presidential election of 1876. He also considered the power of the presidency to be a special threat to republican government.

Lawrence directed the majority of his article to historical critique and review rather than to suggested changes, but the suggestions he offered were major. Lawrence favored allowing Congress to select the president and anticipated that such a system would lead to greater legislative-executive harmony and would entrust the decision to those who were most knowledgeable. Lawrence believed that it was "impossible to conceive of any worse political machinery" than the national nominating convention (Lawrence 1880, 407).

Lawrence also called the vice presidency "altogether objectionable," noting that vice presidents were often selected "without regard to the possible succession" and that the office had been largely created so that each member of the Electoral College could cast two votes (406). Lawrence argued that a powerful executive was dangerous in a heterogeneous nation, where he could "influence legislation, as well as the administration of the Government, in favor of his section to the prejudice of others" (408).

Lawrence favored establishing a parliamentary system. Passing over more familiar models, Lawrence commended the Swiss form. As he described it, this system vested executive authority in a federal council of seven members from different geographic areas who the legislature would select for three-year terms. This legislature chose the president and vice president annually, but neither officer had substantially more powers than members of the council, a majority of which was necessary "to sanction every deliberation" (408–409).

See also: Parliamentary Systems.

For Further Reading:

Lawrence, William B. 1880. "The Monarchical Principle in Our Constitution." *North American Review* 288 (November): 385–409.

LAWYERS

Lawyers have long been critical to the implementation of American laws, and judges, as well as many legislators at both the state and national level, are drawn from their ranks (Vile 2001). Although most individuals profess confidence in their own lawyers, citizens often blame lawyers as a class for injustices, or perceived injustices, in the legal system. One contemporary, albeit farfetched, interpretation of the titles of nobility, or the Reed Amendment proposed by Congress in 1812—which, had it been adopted, would have been the Thirteenth—is that it would bar attorneys from holding public office.

Gosta H. Lovgren, on a Web site titled "A Constitutional Amendment Banning Lawyers from Public Office" at http://www.spectacle .org/797lgosta.html, and who is not otherwise identified, has suggested an amendment providing that "No Person who holds, or has held, a license to practice law; nor any person who has represented any entity (other than himself) in a court of law in these United States, may be elected to any public office." Lovgren's proposal is based on the idea that lawyers already control two of the three branches of government, that they are "amoral by definition," that they try to complicate matters, that criminal law "has become more of an auction block than a system of justice," and that lawyers help their clients evade personal responsibility.

See also Titles of Nobility.

For Further Reading:

Lovgren, G. H. "A Constitutional Amendment Banning Lawyers from Public Office." At http:// www.pectacle.org1797/gosta.html. Accessed November 25, 2002.

Vile, John R. 2001. *Great American Lawyers: An Encyclopedia.* 2 vols. Santa Barbara: ABC-CLIO.

LAZARE, DANIEL (1950–)

Lazare, a freelance journalist, authored a stinging critique of modern American government, *The Frozen Republic: How the Constitution Is Paralyzing Democracy* (1996), in which he argues that most American social problems result from an antiquated constitution that stresses checks and balances and separation of powers and produces gridlock rather than governmental accountability. In almost every area he examines, Lazare finds European parliamentary systems to be better, and he condemns what he regards as American worship of a written constitution. He even compares those who admire the American founders, the Constitution, and Federalist justifications of it to "Iranian mullahs waving copies of the Koran" (Lazare 1996, 284).

Lazare argues that Article V is the "dangling thread" (297) that could eventually unravel the existing system that he so criticizes. Lazare imagines a situation in which California threatens to secede unless the current system of equal state apportionment in the Senate is ended. In arguments similar to those that Akhil Reed Amar has advanced elsewhere, Lazare suggests that the House of Representatives could respond in an extraconstitutional manner by voting by a simple majority to abolish equal representation in the Senate and then allowing the American people to ratify its decision in a referendum.

Although he does not go into detail about the new system this would initiate, he does say that it would not only embody the principle of legislative sovereignty but also "reduce the president to semi-figurehead status" and "effectively rob the judiciary of much of its power" (293–94). Lazare further notes that "not just the Constitution would be toppled, but so would checks and balances, separation of powers, and the deeply inculcated habit of deferring to the authority of a group of eighteenth-century Country gentlemen. Instead of relying on previous generations' judgment and analysis, the people would have no choice than to rely on their own" (295).

Lazare has extended his criticism of the U.S. Constitution in another book published in 2001.

See also Reverence for the Constitution.

For Further Reading:

Lazare, Daniel. 1996. *The Frozen Republic: How the Constitution Is Paralyzing Democracy.* New York: Harcourt Brace & Company.

Lazare, Daniel. 2001. *The Velvet Coup: The Constitution, the Supreme Court, and the Decline of American Democracy.* New York: Verso.

LEGISLATION PROPOSED ON CONSTITUTIONAL CONVENTIONS

To date, Congress has not adopted legislation to guide a possible convention, which two-thirds of the states can call under Article V of the Constitution to propose constitutional amendments. One prominent and active supporter of such legislation was Democratic senator Sam Ervin of North Carolina, who introduced the Federal Constitutional Convention Act in 1967. At that time, he and Republican senator Everett Dirksen of Illinois were working for a convention to repeal the Supreme Court's reapportionment decisions. The other most prominent supporter of such legislation has been Republican senator Orrin Hatch of Utah, who first presented his Constitutional Implementation Act in 1979 and has been advocating it ever since. The Ervin bill passed the Senate in 1971 and 1973, but the House of Representatives never acted on it. Hatch's bill has been approved by the Senate Judiciary Committee but not by either house of Congress (Caplan 1988, 77).

Both Ervin and Hatch believed that Congress has the power to adopt such legislation under the necessary and proper clause. Both also argued that neutral legislation should be passed to apply to any issue rather than being tailor-made to specific conventions. Although both senators believed that states can call either a limited or an open convention, their legislation applied only to the former.

The Ervin and Hatch bills were quite similar. The Ervin bill originally proposed that applications for a convention would be valid for seven years, but Ervin subsequently reduced this period to four years (Ervin 1968, 891). The Hatch bill provides a period of no longer than seven years but allows state applications to specify a shorter period (Hatch 1991, S561). Because no such deadline is now specified, the Hatch bill would give an additional two-year life (absent state rescission) to proposals introduced in the last 16 years (Hatch 1991, S561). The Hatch bill also encourages, but does not require, states to list other state applications that they believe cover the same topic.

Both the Ervin and the Hatch legislation would permit Congress to specify the time, place, and (consistent with state petitions) the general subject matter of the convention. The original Ervin bill gave each state a number of delegates equal to its representation in the House but required that state delegates vote as a bloc ("Proposed Legislation" 1972, 1625). The revised bill followed the model of the Electoral College in giving each state a number of votes equal to its total number of U.S. senators and representatives and allowed for majority rule. The Ervin bill provided that such delegates would be elected in the states. Hatch apparently favors such popular election but would not require it (Hatch 1991, S562). Like the Ervin bill, the Hatch bill would apportion delegates in the same manner as does the Electoral College.

The Ervin bill explicitly provided that the convention could propose amendments by a majority rather than by a two-thirds vote; the Hatch bill appears to contemplate this but does not explicitly say so. Although Hatch opposed the amendment designed to treat the District of Columbia as a state for purposes of representation in Congress, his proposal explicitly provides that "the people of the District of Columbia shall elect as many delegates as the whole number of Senators and Representatives to which said District would be entitled in the Congress if it were a State" (Hatch 1991, S564).

Both Ervin and Hatch accepted the doctrine of contemporary consensus as articulated in *Dillon v. Gloss* (1921). Accordingly, in addition to limiting the time span during which convention petitions were valid, both would permit states to rescind petitions for a convention or to rescind ratification of a proposed amendment up to the point where two-thirds of the states had ratified it. If adopted as legislation, such a rule might well apply to all amendments and not simply to those that were proposed by a convention.

Although both Ervin and Hatch believed that Congress was obligated to call a convention when it received the necessary number of applications, both sought to guard against a so-called runaway convention by allowing Congress to refuse to report amendments to the states that were proposed by a convention that exceeded its mandate. The Ervin bill was criticized for attempting to preclude judicial review of important questions related to this legislation ("Proposed Legislation" 1972, 1635–1644). In contrast, the Hatch legislation specifically recognizes such judicial authority. Hatch thus rejects the notion that such matters are political questions beyond judicial cognizance.

If adopted, legislation on the constitutional convention would, like constitutional statutes in the United Kingdom, be considered "quasi-organic" legislation (Ervin 1968, 880). Even if never adopted by Congress, such proposals might be consulted in the event that states mustered sufficient petitions to call a convention. Absent adoption of such legislation, such decisions will likely be made on an ad hoc political basis.

See also: Constitutional Conventions; *Dillon v. Gloss;* Ervin, Sam.

For Further Reading:

Caplan, Russell L. 1988. *Constitutional Brinkmanship: Amending the Constitution by National Convention.* New York: Oxford University Press.

Ervin, Sam J., Jr. 1968. "Proposed Legislation to Implement the Convention Method of Amending the Constitution." *Michigan Law Review* 66 (March): 875–902.

Hatch, Orrin. 1991. "Constitutional Convention Implementation Act." *Congressional Record,* U.S. Senate, 15 January, S559–S565.

"Proposed Legislation on the Convention Method of Amending the United States Constitution." 1972. *Harvard Law Review* 85: 1612–1648.

LEISURE, RIGHT TO

In contrast to some constitutions (those of Bangladesh and the Peoples' Republic of China, for example), the text of the U.S. Constitution does not guarantee social and economic rights. At least one writer, after first exploring the possibility that a right to leisure might be discovered in the penumbras of the Thirteenth and/or Fourteenth Amendments, has toyed with the idea of adding a constitutional amendment to guarantee a right to leisure. He ultimately concluded both that the amending process was too difficult to accomplish this objective and that such an amendment would face the further obstacles posed by "the American worship of work and the power of large corporations, most of which would probably lobby as hard as they could to sink this proposed addendum" (Kramer 2001, 67).

See also Social and Economic Rights.

For Further Reading:
    Kramer, Daniel C. 2001. "The Constitution and the Right to Leisure." *The Good Society* 10: 64–67.

LESER V. GARNETT (1922)

In a test of contemporary arguments that there were limits on the amending process, Oscar Leser and other Maryland voters brought suit to strike the names of women from the voting list in Baltimore despite the adoption of the Nineteenth Amendment. In rejecting this attempt, the Supreme Court addressed three arguments.

The first argument was that the Nineteenth Amendment exceeded implicit constitutional limitations by altering the electorates of even those states that had not ratified the amendment, such as Maryland. Justice Louis Brandeis responded by noting the similarities in the language of the Fifteenth (which prohibited voting discrimination against African Americans) and Nineteenth Amendments. He argued that the former could not be valid and the latter invalid. In so ruling, Brandeis rejected the contention that the former amendment was a war measure "validated by acquiescence" (*Leser* 1922, 136) rather than through legitimate amending procedures.

A second argument was that some of the states included in the secretary of state's compilation of ratifying states should not have been counted because of provisions in their constitutions preventing such ratification. Brandeis responded by noting that "the function of a state legislature in ratifying a proposed amendment to the Federal Constitution, like the function of Congress in proposing the amendment, is a federal function derived from the Federal Constitution; and it transcends any limitations sought to be imposed by the people of a State" (*Leser* 1922, 137). Brandeis cited both *Hawke v. Smith* cases (1920) and the *National Prohibition Cases* (1920) to buttress this argument.

The third argument was that ratifications by Tennessee and West Virginia were illegal because they violated the states' own rules of legislative procedure. Brandeis responded that "official notice to the Secretary, duly authenticated," that they had ratified "was conclusive upon him, and, being certified by his proclamation, is conclusive upon the courts" (*Leser* 1922, 137).

See also Constitutional Amendments, Limits on; Fifteenth Amendment; Nineteenth Amendment.

For Further Reading:
    Leser v. Garnett, 258 U.S. 130 (1922).
    Siegel, Riva B. 2002. "She the People: The Nineteenth Amendment, Sex Equality, Federalism, and the Family." *Harvard Law Review* 115 (February): 947–1046.

LEVINSON, SANFORD (1941–)

A Texas law professor who has, for many years, published thoughtful commentaries on the U.S. Constitution as a whole and on the amending process in particular, like Professors Richard Labunski and Larry Sabato, Sanford Levinson has recently published a book calling for another constitutional convention to rectify defects in the U.S. Constitution. Like Robert Dahl (2001), Levinson believes that the U.S. Constitution is too undemocratic, and he wants the American people to vote on the following proposal:

> Shall Congress call a constitutional convention empowered to consider the adequacy of the Constitution and, if thought necessary, to draft a new constitution that, upon completion, will be submitted to the electorate for its approval or disapproval by majority vote? Unless and until a new constitution gains popular approval, the current Constitution will continue in place" (2006, 11).

Levinson begins his critique of the current constitutional system with the legislative branch. He believes that the system has over-emphasized bicameralism, and he is especially critical of equal state representation in the Senate and its denial of voting representation to the District of Columbia. Levinson thinks that the presidential veto gives the president too much power in the legislative process, and he thinks that the time between elections and the seating of new members of Congress is too long.

The subtitle of his next chapter encapsulates his critique of the presidency. "Too-powerful presidents, chosen in an indefensible process, who cannot be displaced even when they are manifestly incompetent" (79). Levinson is particularly critical of the Electoral College. He also believes there is too much time between a presidential election and the presidential inauguration. He expresses additional concerns over recess appointments, presidential exercises of the pardon power, the rigidity of presidential terms of office, and the office of vice president.

In examining the judiciary, Levinson questions life tenure for Supreme Court justices. Levinson further argues that the age requirements for public office-holders "are indefensible in our contemporary world" (143). He thinks residency requirements provide a *"bias toward localism"* (147) and thinks that it is unfair to require that a president be a natural-born citizen and that presidents be limited to two terms.

Levinson believes the Article V amending processes constitute "an iron cage with regard to changing some of the most important aspects of our political system" (165). Levinson believes this stunts constitutional imagination: "Because it is so difficult to amend the Constitution—it seems almost utopian to suggest the possibility, with regard to anything that is truly important—citizens are encouraged to believe that change is almost never desirable, let alone necessary" (165).

What then should be done? Levinson believes that some amendments providing, for example, for the continuity of government after an attack on the United States or permitting immigrants to run for president, could be done through the amending process. He thinks others may need to be initiated through a constitutional convention. Like Akhil Reed Amar, Levinson believes that "a new convention could legiti-

mately declare that its handiwork would be binding if ratified in a national referendum where each voter had equal power" (177). Levinson thinks that use of "deliberative polling," whereby people discuss issues for several days before deciding what to do about them, might be a way to get such a convention off the ground. He opines that "if a critical mass does indeed agree that our Constitution is seriously defective, then a campaign would have the potential to capture national attention and forge a new consciousness" (180).

See also Amar, Akhil Reed; Constitutional Conventions; Labunski, Richard; Sabato, Larry.

For Further Reading:

Dahl, Robert. 2001. *How Democratic is the American Constitution?* New Haven, CT: Yale University Press.

Gerken, Heather K. 2007. "The Hydraulics of Constitutional Reform: A skeptical Response to our Undemocratic Constitution." *Drake Law Review* 55 (Summer): 925–943.

Levinston, Sanford. 2006. *Our Un-Democratic Constitution: Where the Constitution Goes Wrong (And How We the People Can Correct It)*. New York: Oxford University Press.

———. 1996. "The Political Implications of Amending Clauses." *Constitutional Commentary,* 13 (Spring): 107–123.

———. ed. 1995. *Responding to Imperfection: The Theory and Practice of Constitutional Amendments*. Princeton, NJ: Princeton University Press.

LIEBER, FRANCIS (1800–1872)

Lieber was a German-born immigrant. He came to the United States after obtaining his doctorate in Germany, fighting as a volunteer in the Greek revolt against Turkey, visiting Rome, and being imprisoned in Prussia for his political writings and republican sympathies. Arriving in the United States in 1827, after a brief stint in the United Kingdom (whose legal system he especially admired), he began working on editing the 13-volume *Encyclopedia Americana,* which appeared from 1829 to 1833. He became a citizen and took a post as professor of history and political economy at South Carolina College (now the University of South Carolina), where he served from 1832 to 1856. Lieber took a similar post in 1857 at Columbia College in New York, where he taught—transferring to the law school in 1865—until his death in 1872 (see Lieber 1881, 144).

Lieber was a prolific scholar whose works included the widely read and respected two-volume *Manual of Political Ethics* (1838), *Legal and Political Hermeneutics* (1839), and *Civil Liberty and Self-Government,* published in two volumes in 1853. Lieber also wrote the *Instructions for the Government of the Armies of the United States,* issued by the army secretary in 1863 and later embodied into international law. Despite having taught in South Carolina, Lieber was a longtime defender of the Union against radical theories of states' rights and secession. He served as president of the Loyal Publication Society of New York, for which he wrote in 1865 a pamphlet proposing a series of constitutional amendments, some ideas of which paralleled provisions in the forthcoming Thirteenth, Fourteenth, and Fifteenth Amendments of the U.S. Constitution.

In offering his proposals, Lieber included a long justification for amendments in which he stressed that, however wise the American founders had been, laws and constitutions are organic and need to change in order to preserve themselves. The Civil War had brought certain problems into relief that required resolution, especially the matters of slavery and states' rights. Lieber thought the idea of the nation should be paramount to that of state sovereignty, and his proposals reflected this idea. Interestingly, Lieber did not regard the time in which he was writing as propitious for a constitutional convention (Lieber 1865, 35), preferring to "build additions to the mansion we dwell in" rather than demolishing the edifice and beginning anew. Moreover, although he indicated that he favored a six-year term for the president, an item veto, changes in the constitutional provisions related to "direct" taxes, laws against polygamy, and consideration of an amendment allowing cabinet officers to appear in Congress—a provision of

which he doubted the actual necessity (Lieber 1865, 31–33)—he decided to limit his own proposals to more urgent concerns for which he proposed seven amendments.

First, Lieber proposed an amendment requiring allegiance from each American native-born and naturalized citizen and guaranteeing to each citizen the government's "full protection" (Lieber 1865, 36). Second, Lieber proposed extending the definition of treason to include attempts to separate any state from the Union. His third proposal would have made armed resistance to the United States a "high crime," and his fourth would have permitted trials for treason outside a state or a district during times of war or rebellion. His fifth and most critical amendment would (like the eventual Thirteenth Amendment ratified the same year as his proposal) have abolished slavery forever. Interestingly, in similarly proposing to eliminate the three-fifths clause, Lieber based the number of representatives, as would Section 2 of the Fourteenth Amendment, on the "respective number of male citizens of age" rather than on the number of all adults (Lieber 1865, 38). Lieber's sixth proposed amendment would classify participation in the slave trade as piracy, and his seventh would provide for the "privileges" of all citizens, including those recently freed (39). His commentary on the last proposal indicated that he was especially concerned to see that the courtroom testimony of whites and blacks was treated equally, a comment that could possibly shed light on the use of the "privileges and immunities" clause that found its way into the Fourteenth Amendment.

In 1867, Lieber published an additional essay on changes he thought were needed in the New York State Constitution of 1846 (Lieber 1888, 183–219).

See also: Fifteenth Amendment; Fourteenth Amendment; Thirteenth Amendment.

For Further Reading:

Lieber, Francis. 1888. *Manual of Political Ethics, Designed Chiefly for the Use of Colleges and Students at Law.* 2d ed. Philadelphia: Lippincott.

———. 1881. *Reminiscences, Addresses, and Essays,* ed. Daniel G. Gilman. 2 vols. Philadelphia: J. B. Lippincott & Co.

———. 1865. *Amendments of the Constitution Submitted to the Consideration of the American People.* New York: Loyal Publication Society.

Vile, John R. 1998. "Francis Lieber and the Constitutional Amending Process." *The Review of Politics* 60 (Summer): 524–543.

LIMITS ON CONSTITUTIONAL AMENDMENTS

See Constitutional Amendments, Limits on.

LIMITS ON WEALTH AND INCOME

Early in the 20th century and again during the Great Depression, some members of Congress proposed amendments to limit personal wealth or income. In 1933, Washington Democratic congressman Wesley Lloyd introduced an amendment to limit annual incomes to $1 million (Pizzigati 1992, 55), and Pennsylvania Democrat John Synder introduced an amendment to limit the amount of income derived from capital. The idea was especially appealing among socialists, as well as among utopian thinkers. Edward Bellamy's widely read novel *Looking Backward* (1968), first published in 1888, foresaw a world in the year 2000 in which there was a relative equality of wealth. Some proponents of the progressive income tax were as motivated by the redistributive possibilities of such a tax as by its potential to raise revenue.

Once the Sixteenth Amendment was adopted, it was more common to propose use of the tax code to effect equalization of wealth or income than to propose amendments to this end. Thus, in his book *My First Days in the White House,* Louisiana's flamboyant senator Huey P. Long speculated that the Supreme Court would uphold his own Share the Wealth Program (Long 1935, 134–135). Although Long's plans went through several alterations, he proposed limiting individual fortunes to $5 million and annual income or inheritance to $1 million. Long also proposed a guaranteed national income of $2,000 to $3,000 a year, "homesteads" for all Americans, and free college education for deserving youth (Williams 1970, 693). Share the Wealth Clubs advocating Long's ideas were quite popular for a time, although they were largely concentrated in the South (Williams 1970, 701). Pressure from Long's followers is believed to have pushed Franklin Roosevelt's own ideas on progressive taxation leftward (Christman 1985, xiv).

In recent years, the gap between the rich and the poor in the United States appears to have widened (Bradsher 1995, 1). Labor journalist Sam Pizzigati, concerned about this increasing gap, has advanced a "10 times rule," or maximum wage. Under such a system, individuals would be limited to earning 10 times the minimum wage, with incomes above that amount being paid in taxes. Pizzigati believes that, in such circumstances, people would donate or distribute assets above that needed to generate the maximum income and that such redistribution would result in a number of societal advantages. Pizzigati advocated beginning a campaign for such a program at the state level and then using those states as a base to call for a constitutional amendment to that end (Pizzigati 1992, 134–136).

See also: Sixteenth Amendment.

For Further Reading:

Bellamy, Edward. 1888. *Looking Backward.* Reprint, New York: Magnum Books, 1968.

Bradsher, Keith. 1995. "Gap in Wealth in U.S. Called Widest in West." *New York Times,* 17 April, 1, C4.

Christman, Henry M., ed. 1985. *Kingfish to America: Share Our Wealth: Selected Senatorial Papers of Huey P. Long.* New York: Shocken Books.

Long, Huey P. 1935. *My First Days in the White House.* Harrisburg, PA: Telegraph Press.

Pizzigati, Sam. 1994. "Salary Caps for Everyone!" *New York Times,* 28 August, 15.

———. 1992. *The Maximum Wage: A Common-Sense Prescription for Revitalizing America—By Taxing the Very Rich.* New York: Appex Press.

Williams, T. Harry. 1970. *Huey Long.* New York: Alfred A. Knopf.

LINCOLN, ABRAHAM (1809–1865)

The election in 1860 of Abraham Lincoln as the United States' 16th president helped precipitate the Civil War. The Republican platform of that year described slavery as immoral and opposed its expansion. Southern states feared that their cherished institution of slavery would be jeopardized if they remained in the Union.

In the Lincoln-Douglas debates, Lincoln had questioned the finality of the Supreme Court's decision in *Scott v. Sandford* (1857), which had ruled that the Missouri Compromise was illegal and thus allowed for the expansion of slavery into the territories (Johannsen 1965, 64–66). Prior to his inauguration, Lincoln worked behind the scenes with congressional Republicans to oppose the Crittenden Compromise, which would have recognized slavery in the territories. Lincoln did, however, support the Corwin Amendment, which would have guaranteed Southern states that slavery would not be abolished there without their consent.

In his first inaugural address, Lincoln distinguished between the "constitutional" right of amending the Constitution and the "revolutionary" right of dismembering it (J. Richardson 1908, 6:10). He further expressed support both for the Corwin Amendment and for the possibility of a constitutional convention that might propose amendments to the Constitution.

On January 1, 1863, Lincoln issued the Emancipation Proclamation, freeing slaves in states that remained loyal to the Confederacy. Lincoln had announced his intention to issue this proclamation in September, after the Union victory at Antietam Creek in Maryland. In his annual message of 1862, Lincoln also proposed three amendments. They would have compensated slave owners in states abolishing the institution before 1900, given perpetual freedom to all slaves freed by the war and compensated owners loyal to the Union, and provided for vol- untary slave colonization abroad (J. Richardson 1908, 6:136). Congress largely ignored these plans (Paludan 1994, 164).

The changes wrought by the Emancipation Proclamation made such gradualism impossible. In January 1864, Democratic senator John Henderson of Missouri offered the first amendment in Congress to abolish slavery. Soon a passage from the Northwest Ordinance of 1787 had been formulated into the Thirteenth Amendment (Paludan 1994, 300). Lincoln strongly supported this amendment (Donald 1995, 553–554). Contrary to the custom that had been followed with all amendments other than the Corwin Amendment, this amendment was sent to him for his signature before being sent to the states for their eventual ratification. Lincoln may have signed partly "to wipe out the memory of the Corwin Amendment" (Bernstein with Agel 1993, 100), which President Buchanan had signed.

Lincoln did not live to see the intense controversy generated by the Reconstruction of the South (1865–1877) and the proposal and ratification of the Fourteenth and Fifteenth Amendments, which grew, like the Thirteenth, out of the Civil War. Lincoln might have particularly favored the provision in the Fourteenth Amendment reversing the [*Dred*] *Scott* decision and providing for equal protection of the laws; Lincoln had often argued that the Constitution needed to be understood and interpreted in light of the Declaration of Independence, which had announced that "all men are created equal."

After John Wilkes Booth assassinated Lincoln at Ford's Theater in April 1865, the presidency fell into the far less capable hands of his vice president, Andrew Johnson.

See also Corwin Amendment; Declaration of Independence; Emancipation Proclamation; *Scott v. Sandford;* Thirteenth Amendment.

For Further Reading:

Bernstein, Richard B., with Jerome Agel. 1993. *Amending America: If We Love the Constitution So Much, Why Do We Keep Trying to Change It?* New York: Random House.

Donald, David H. 1995. *Lincoln.* New York: Simon & Schuster.

Johannsen, Robert W., ed. 1965. *The Lincoln-Douglas Debates of 1858.* New York: Oxford University Press.

Paludan, Phillip S. 1994. *The Presidency of Abraham Lincoln.* Lawrence: University Press of Kansas.

Richardson, James E., ed. 1908. *A Compilation of the Messages and Papers of the Presidents, 1789–1908.* 11 vols. n.p.: Bureau of National Literature and Art.

LIVERMORE V. WAITE (1894)

Livermore v. Waite is a California case that is frequently cited in discussions of the amending process. It is especially relevant to the issue of whether a constitution can be changed other than by its own procedures, as well as to possible limits on the amending process. The case involved an amendment ratified by the California state legislature for approval by state voters to transfer the state capital from Sacramento to San Jose. Adoption was to be contingent upon receipt of a donation of a minimum of 10 acres (of a site approved by the governor, secretary of state, and attorney general) and $1 million.

The California Supreme Court distinguished the two methods of amendment provided in the California constitution. The power of a constitutional convention to revise the constitution was declared to be limited only by the U.S. Constitution. By contrast, the court declared the procedure by which amendments were proposed by two-thirds majorities of both houses of the state legislature and subsequently sent to the people for ratification to be a delegated power "to be strictly construed under the limitations by which it has been conferred" (*Livermore* 1894, 117–118). The court observed that the state's constitution "can be neither revised nor amended except in the manner prescribed by itself, and the power which it has conferred upon the legislature in reference to proposed amendments, as well as to calling a convention, must be strictly pursued" (117).

In this case, the court struck down the proposed amendment because it did not become operational, as the California constitution

appeared to require, upon popular approval but upon considerations not specified there. The court concluded that "the amendment proposed substitutes for, or rather superadds to, the will of the people another will or judgment, without which its own will can have no effect" (123).

Stauss v. Horton, the 2009 decision by the California Supreme Court upholding Proposition 8, the state initiative that had altered the state constitution so as to overturn an earlier court decision that had allowed gay unions to be designated as marriages, relied heavily on the distinction in *Livermore* between amendment and revision. The Court thought that voters had the power to enact such a change through initiative rather than through the convention mechanism.

See also Constitutional Amendments, Limits on.

For Further Reading:

Colantuono, Michael G. 1987. "The Revision of American State Constitutions: Legislative Power, Popular Sovereignty, and Constitutional Change." *California Law Review* 75 (July): 1473–1512.

Livermore v. Waite, 102 Cal. 113 (1894).

LIVING CONSTITUTION

Judges and scholars who agree that the U.S. Constitution is a living document may mean quite different things by such a statement. For some, the very presence of an amending process that can and has been utilized is testimony to the fact that the Constitution is a "living" document that can be adapted to changing circumstances. Such individuals are likely to believe that the Constitution should be adapted to technologies unknown to the framers (railroads, steamships, and airplanes, for example) but that major constitutional principles remain the same and that constitutional innovations should await the proposal and ratification of formal amendments. For others, the idea of a "living" Constitution requires that legislators and/or judges apply and interpret the Constitution expansively and/or attempt to adapt it to the times.

Although the debate has been renewed in modern exchanges between those who advocate concentrating on the framers' intent and those who point either to the elusiveness of this quest or the need to take modern developments into consideration, this debate is hardly new. An analyst of the New Deal period (White 2000) notes that debates over the living Constitution were prominent in the period immediately before this time and were reflected in works on the Constitution written by James M. Beck (1922) and Howard Lee McBain (1927). Beck stressed the idea, consistent with earlier views, that "constitutional adaptivity involved the restatement of universal first principles in new contexts" (White 2000, 206). By contrast, McBain and other commentators were

> beginning to treat constitutional adaptivity as signifying something quite different: that constitutional principles themselves could be modified in response to the demands of modern American life. The latter conception of adaptivity illustrated a radically different set of assumptions about the nature of constitutional interpretation (White 2000, 206).

To the degree that such actors alter what were once considered to be fixed constitutional meanings, formal amendments might be far less necessary. By the same token, overly expansive judicial and political interpretations might erode the value of a fixed text and might well lead to calls for amendments to reverse decisions that are thought to lack adequate constitutional foundation or that conflict with what are considered to be original fundamental principles.

Some constitutional provisions are fairly specific and appear to leave little room for judicial interpretation. By contrast, provisions calling for the prohibition of "cruel and unusual punishments" (the Eighth Amendment), for "due process of law" (the Fifth and Fourteenth Amendments), or for "equal protection of the law" (the Fourteenth Amendment) require considerably more leeway. Makers and proponents of constitutions and amendments must be cognizant of the possibility, if not the likelihood, that broadly stated principles might be more expansively interpreted than more narrowly specified procedures. Some hope, and others fear, that such concerns can impact popular willingness to ratify new amendments, especially those that appear to be broadly or vaguely worded, for example, the Equal Rights Amendment or broad pronouncements about social and economic rights.

See also Constitutional Interpretation; Equal Rights Amendment.

For Further Reading:

Beck, James M. 1922. *The Constitution of the United States.* New York: G. H. Doran Co.

Friedman, Barry, and Scott B. Smith. 1998. "The Sedimentary Constitution." *University of Pennsylvania Law Review* 147 (November): 1–90.

Gillman, Howard. 1997. "The Collapse of Constitutional Originalism and the Rise of the Notion of the 'Living Constitution' in the Course of American State-Building." *Studies in American Political Development* 11 (Fall): 191–247.

McBain, Howard Lee. 1927. *The Living Constitution: A Consideration of the Realities and Legends of Our Fundamental Law.* New York: Macmillan.

Rehnquist, William H. 1976. "The Notion of a Living Constitution," *Texas Law Review* 54: 693–706.

White, G. Edward. 2000. *The Constitution and the New Deal.* Cambridge, MA: Harvard University Press.

LOCHNER V. NEW YORK (1905)

Few cases have more epitomized an era of Supreme Court decision making or indicated the potential scope of Supreme Court decisions in interpreting (and thus effectively amending) the written Constitution than did this 1905 decision. At issue was a New York law limiting the work hours of bakers to 10 hours a day and six days a week.

Lochner, who operated a bakery, argued that the law violated his liberty of contract as protected by the due process clause of the Fourteenth Amendment. Writing for a 5-to-4 majority, Justice Rufus Peckham upheld this idea of substantive due process. Rejecting arguments that the baking industry was unhealthy and thus in need of special legislative solicitude, Peckham found that the state had exceeded its police powers in legislating for adults who were capable of protecting their own interests. He referred to New York's laws as "mere meddlesome interferences with the rights of the individual" (*Lochner* 1905, 61).

Justice John Marshall Harlan wrote a dissenting opinion arguing that courts should defer to legislative judgments in cases in which policymakers might disagree and that the Court's interpretations unduly widened the scope of the Fourteenth Amendment. Referring to a notable contemporary proponent of laissez-faire economics, Justice Oliver Wendell Holmes's dissent observed that "the Fourteenth Amendment does not enact Mr. Herbert Spencer's Social Statics" (*Lochner* 1905, 75).

In subsequent cases, the Supreme Court expanded on the idea of substantive due process to strike down laws providing for minimum wages and prohibiting child labor. These rulings prompted numerous proposals to amend the Constitution, but after Franklin Roosevelt introduced his court-packing plan in 1937, the Court shifted course and allowed such legislation to be adopted through ordinary legislative means.

See also Child Labor Amendment; Court-Packing Plan; Fourteenth Amendment; Substantive Due Process.

For Further Reading:

Gillman, Howard. 1993. *The Constitution Besieged: The Rise and Demise of Lochner Era Police Powers Jurisprudence.* Durham, NC: Duke University Press.

Kens, Paul. 1990. *Judicial Power and Reform Politics: The Anatomy of* Lochner v. New York. Lawrence: University Press of Kansas.

Lochner v. New York, 198 U.S. 45 (1905).

LOCKWOOD, HENRY C. · (1839–1902)

Henry Lockwood wrote a book in 1884 that has been described as "a bestseller and an essential reference work for publicists of his time" (Pious 1978, 4). Although the title of the book, *The Abolition of the Presidency,* focused on the institution that Lockwood thought needed the most reform, he also proposed sweeping reforms of the Senate and of state governments. Like other prominent would-be reformers of his day, Lockwood's model was the English constitution, the workings of the executive of which Lockwood described as "nearer to the ideal of a representative government than any upon the face of the earth" (Lockwood 1884, 278).

Lockwood devoted much of his book to noting the flaws in the presidency and in those who had been elected to that office. Lockwood believed that the presidency was an unwelcome vestige of monarchy. He outlined his proposals in his last three chapters. Opposed to the idea of state sovereignty, Lockwood placed himself squarely on the side of nationalism. As such, he suggested that the Senate should be abolished, both because it was "the strongest fulcrum of the 'residuary sovereignty' of the States" (Lockwood 1884, 283) and because he did not think that the advantages of a bicameral system outweighed its disadvantages. Moreover, Lockwood saw no need for the existence of states from which the senators were chosen. He thus cited with approval the proposal that David Brearly had made at the Constitutional Convention of 1787 to abolish the existing states and to divide the country into 13 equal parts (Lockwood 1884, 282–283).

In his last chapter, Lockwood advanced plans for abolishing the presidency, adding the Articles of Confederation to Great Britain as a model. Lockwood's plan involved replacing the presidency with an executive council chosen by Congress and headed by the secretary of state. Members would have seats in Congress, where they would be entitled to debate and to initiate legislation. The council could also dissolve Congress and appeal to the people when the government was deadlocked on an important issue. Congress would, in turn, have the right to remove cabinet members. Lockwood's anticipated result would be "responsible Council Government" (Lockwood 1884, 305).

Lockwood's system would make Congress sovereign. Accordingly, he therefore favored eliminating judicial review, thus limiting courts to expounding and interpreting the laws (Lockwood 1884, 308).

Lockwood also favored other reforms. Thus, in critiquing the current system, Lockwood noted that "church property is not taxed, [and] religious laws deface the statute-books" (Lockwood 1884, 313). Similarly, he noted the "tendency towards moneyed aristocracy" and the fact that the secret ballot "opens the door to stupendous frauds." Lockwood specifically pointed to the virtual disenfranchisement of African Americans in the South (Lockwood 1884, 313–314).

See also: Judiciary, Exercise of Judicial Review by; Parliamentary Systems.

For Further Reading:

Lockwood, Henry C. 1884. *The Abolition of the Presidency.* New York: R. Worthington. Reprint, Farmingdale, NY: Darbor Social Science Publications, 1978.

Pious, Richard M. 1978. "Introduction." In *The Abolition of the Presidency.* Farmingdale, NY: Darbor Social Science Publications.

LOTTERIES

One senator and two members of the House of Representatives introduced amendments from May 1890 to January 1892 to prohibit lotteries. State-sponsored lotteries have been prominent during three periods in U.S. history—the colonial period to the early 19th century, after the Civil War, and from 1964 to the present (Clotfetter and Cook 1989, 42).

Apart from a lottery in 1776 to support the Continental Army and lotteries operated to finance projects in Washington DC from 1792 to 1842, such activity has been sponsored by the states *rather* than by the national government (Clotfetter and Cook 1989, 36). The 1890s marked a period of revulsion against lotteries that was stimulated by abuses associated with the Louisiana Lottery Company, which had been established in 1868.

Although Congress never adopted an amendment, in 1890, it prohibited use of the mails to promote lotteries, and in 1895, it outlawed interstate transportation of lottery tickets. The Supreme Court upheld the latter law in *Champion v. Ames* (1903). Recent years have witnessed a rebirth of numerous state-sponsored lotteries and privately established casinos, with the desire for state revenues (sometimes specifically designated for education or other desirable social programs) and employment opportunities often overcoming objections based on morals and concerns about the creation by the states of social problems like gambling addiction and poverty.

For Further Reading:

Clotfetter, Charles T., and Phillip Cook. 1989. *Selling Hope: State Lotteries in America.* Cambridge, MA: Harvard University Press.

Mason, John Lyman, and Michael Nelson. 2001. *Governing Gambling.* New York: The Century Foundation Press.

LOUISIANA PURCHASE

The U.S. purchase of the Louisiana Territory in 1803 added nearly a million square miles that lay from the Mississippi River to the Rocky Mountains. The purchase was effected through the adoption of a treaty. Ironically, Thomas Jefferson, a Democratic-Republican known for being a strict constructionist authorized the purchase. He initially favored adoption of a constitutional amendment to grant the national government the right to purchase such new territory and admit the new states into the Union.

American westerners relied heavily on the Mississippi River for navigation and were concerned about the occupation of the port of New Orleans by foreign powers. Jefferson had sent James Monroe and Robert Livingston to negotiate the purchase of this port. Napoleon decided to offer the Louisiana Territory to the U.S. negotiators, who eventually settled on a price of $15 million.

Spain was displeased that France had sold the territory that Spain had only recently ceded to it, and Jefferson feared that delay might provide a pretext for the French to back out of the deal. Jefferson's decision aided U.S. expansion to the West Coast but has been variously interpreted as wise statesmanship or as an abandonment of his own principles. Federalist John Quincy Adams proposed an amendment in Congress to allow for incorporating acquired territory into the Union, but it garnered only three votes (Knowles 2003, 296).

Robert Knowles has argued that the Louisiana Purchase was unconstitutional because it tipped the federal balance without giving input to existing states. New Englanders were particularly concerned about the addition of new slave states. Knowles believes that the purchase "paved the way for further re-interpretations of the Constitution outside the Article Five amendment process" and "set a precedent for expansion of federal power, and the corresponding reduction of states' rights, through federal actions that failed to give the states a voice in constitutional change" (401). Knowles further believes that the Louisiana Purchase "triggered Article's [sic] V's fall into disuse," although he acknowledges that the Supreme Court's assertion of judicial review in *Marbury v. Madison* (1803) probably also contributed to reliance on methods of constitutional change outside of Article V (414).

See also Jefferson, Thomas.

For Further Reading:

Hitchcock, Ripley. 1903. *The Louisiana Purchase, and the Exploration, Early History and Building of the West.* Boston: Ginn & Company, Publishers.

Knowles, Robert. 2003. "The Balance of Forces and the Empire of Liberty: States' Rights and the Louisiana Purchase." *Iowa Law Review* 88 (January): 343–419.

LUDLOW AMENDMENT

At least since Robert E. Beasley published a pamphlet entitled *A Plan to Stop the Present and Prevent Future Wars* (1864), some individ-

uals have surmised that citizens might be able to exert pressure on their leaders to avert war. In 1935, Indiana Democrat Louis Ludlow, who had served as a newspaper correspondent before being elected to Congress, introduced an amendment that provided that, except in cases of invasion or direct attack on the U.S. or its territories, no congressional declaration of war would go into effect unless ratified through referendum by a majority of voters throughout the nation. Ludlow continued to introduce this provision through 1941.

President Franklin D. Roosevelt sent a letter to the speaker of the U.S. House of Representatives on January 6, 1938, opposing this amendment. He expressed fear that the amendment "would cripple any President in his conduct of our foreign relations" and "encourage other nations to believe that they could violate American rights with impunity." His letter appears to have helped derail what was an otherwise popular proposal ("Ludow Amendment" January 1938).

See also Beasley, Robert E.; Initiative and Referendum; War, Declaration of.

For Further Reading:

"Ludlow Amendment (Jan. 1938)." http://www.cusdi.org/ludlow-1938.htm. Accessed May 30, 2008.

LUTHER V. BORDEN (1849)

Luther v. Borden was an important Supreme Court case, both in addressing the relationship between constitutional and revolutionary change and in developing the political question doctrine. Chief Justice Roger B. Taney wrote the majority decision. The case arose when Martin Luther brought a suit against Luther Martin for trespassing. Luther Martin had entered Martin Luther's house under authority of a declaration of martial law issued by the original charter government of Rhode Island. This declaration had been prompted by the establishment of a new government, under the direction of Thomas W. Dorr, which Martin Luther supported.

The problem arose because the Rhode Island charter, which the colonists had decided to continue with only minor modifications at the time of the American Revolution, did not specify any means of constitutional change. Although the charter government had severely limited the franchise, and Dorr's government may well have had the support of a majority of the citizens of Rhode Island, the Dorr government had come into being through extralegal means, and the charter government did not recognize its legitimacy. Thus, Daniel Webster argued on Luther Martin's behalf that, although American government was built upon the consent of the people, such government also secured itself "against sudden changes by mere majorities," and such government "does not draw any power from tumultuous assemblages" (*Luther* 1849, 31).

In deciding the case, Taney focused on the guarantee clause in Article IV, Section 4 of the Constitution. He ruled that this clause delegated to Congress the power to determine whether a state government was republican and whether to render military assistance to a state government. Congress, in turn, had delegated the latter power to the president. In this case, although the president (John Tyler) had not actually rendered aid, his declaration of support for the charter government had caused the Dorr government to fold. Taney thus decided that some matters "turned upon political rights and political questions," and it was the Court's duty "not to pass beyond its appropriate sphere of action, and to take care not to involve itself in discussions which properly belong to other forums" (*Luther* 1849, 47).

In *Coleman v. Miller* (1939), the Supreme Court decided that certain questions surrounding the amending process were political questions, but the current status of this opinion is in some doubt. In *Baker v. Carr* (1962), the Supreme Court agreed that the issue of whether a government was or was not republican continued to be a political question. It also ruled that the issue of a state's legislative apportionment could be decided on the basis of the equal protection clause of the Fourteenth Amendment.

The Dorr Rebellion warns both of the ways that constitutions without amending processes can become fossilized and of the kinds of revolutionary actions that they can precipitate. Its development of the political questions doctrine provides a hedge against inappropriate exercises of judicial review, but its subsequent application to questions raised under Article V of the Constitution remains disputed.

See also *Baker v. Carr; Coleman v. Miller;* Colonial Charters; Fourteenth Amendment; Guarantee Clause; Political Questions.

For Further Reading:
Dennison, George M. 1976. *The Dorr War: Republicanism on Trial, 1831–1861.* Lexington: University Press of Kentucky.
Luther v. Borden, 48 U.S. (7 How.) 1 (1849).

LYNCHING

Mobs lynched over 5,000 people, most of whom were black, from the 1890s through the 1950s, often with the complicity of state and local officials (Ferrell 1986, 1). The U.S. House of Representatives spent substantial time debating antilynching legislation from 1918 to 1921, and it adopted an antilynching law in 1921 that died the following year in the Senate (Ferrell 1986, 110–300).

A key objection to such legislation centered on the issue of whether Congress had sufficient authority under the Thirteenth and Fourteenth Amendments to adopt such legislation or whether such laws interfered with state police powers under the Tenth Amendment. Republican representative Henry Emerson of Ohio introduced an amendment in March 1919 explicitly to recognize federal power in this area. Courts have subsequently recognized substantially broader congressional powers over a variety of subjects. Even in the absence of federal legislation, in cases such as *Moore v. Dempsey* (1923), they were able to rule that mob-dominated trials violated the due process clause of the Fourteenth Amendment.

In recent years, Courts have applied most of the provisions in the Bill of Rights relative to criminal procedures, once applied solely to the national government, to the states via the due process clause of the Fourteenth Amendment through the doctrine of incorporation. There has, however, been renewed attention as to whether it would be desirable to pass national legislation aggravating penalties for so-called hate crimes that are motivated by the race, gender, sexual orientation, or the like, of victims. Once again, conflict has emerged between those who believe that this kind of legislation should be left to the states and those who believe that national legislation is warranted.

See also Fourteenth Amendment; Thirteenth Amendment.

For Further Reading:

Curriden, Mark, and Leroy Phillips Jr. 1999. *Contempt of Court: The Turn-of-the-Century Lynching That Launched 100 Years of Federalism.* New York: Faber and Faber.

M

MACDONALD, DWIGHT
(1906–1982)

On *Esquire's* 35th anniversary in 1968, its editors asked journalist Dwight Macdonald to draw up a set of proposals to bring the Constitution up to date. His article was a mix of serious proposals and hyperbole.

Macdonald began by proposing that the presidency should be abolished in favor of a chair to be chosen, as in a parliamentary system, by the majority party in Congress. This chairman would serve for six years or until the chair's party lost a major vote in Congress. This same proposal would have eliminated the Electoral College, the vice presidency, and the system of primaries. Macdonald also hoped that it would serve to clip the power and pretensions of the chief executive—and the temptation to assassinate him. Macdonald proposed lengthening the terms of members of the House of Representatives to five years and eliminating the requirement that members of the House or the Senate be residents of the states that elected them.

Macdonald proposed a number of social reforms. He favored conscripting all males between the ages of 18 and 30 for to two years' service either in the military or in "nonmilitary Work of Social Value"—the draftees' choice (Macdonald 1968, 145). The government would establish a negative income tax to bring all citizens up to a "minimum Health & Decency Standard"; this tax would be paid "without regard to Work, Moral Character or any other Consideration except Need" (*Id.,* 146). Macdonald would establish tribunes, or ombudsmen, in each congressional district. He would also set up history

preservation and nature preservation commissions to protect historical and environmental sites, limit the number of U.S. soldiers overseas to one-fourth of 1 percent of the population (except by a four-fifths vote of both houses of Congress), and limit military expenditures to 3 percent of the gross national product. Macdonald favored abolishing the space program and reconfiguring cities and states into more functional units.

An accompanying piece on the Bill of Rights by Karl E. Meyer was an eclectic mix of reforms that would not, like Macdonald's, require changes in governmental structure. He thought that the government should be responsible for providing a number of social and economic rights, such as access to dramatic performances, public parks, meals, and public transit. He also favored eliminating electronic eavesdropping and supersonic aircraft and curtailing the right to bear arms.

See also: Parliamentary Systems; Second Amendment; Social and Economic Rights.

For Further Reading:
Macdonald, Dwight. 1968. "The Constitution of the United States Needs to Be Fixed." *Esquire* 70 (October): 143–146, 238, 240, 243–244, 246, 252.

Meyer, Karl E. 1968. "So Does the Bill of Rights." *Esquire* 70 (October): 147–148.

MACDONALD, WILLIAM
(1863–1938)

Journalist and college professor William Mac-Donald offered his proposals for constitutional reform shortly after the Wilson administration (MacDonald 1921, 1922). His chief aim was to establish responsible parliamentary government, and toward this end, he offered a critique and a comprehensive plan of reform intended to reconfigure the federal system and all three branches of the federal government (Vile 1991, 57–59).

McDonald favored significantly altering the presidency, with the president responsible for designating a member of Congress to form a cabinet and, if successful, to be premier. The premier and the premier's cabinet would exercise most governmental powers, and they would resign when they lost congressional support. In cases in which a new cabinet could not be formed, the president would dissolve Congress and call for new elections.

MacDonald proposed to delete the requirement that the president be natural born, to replace the Electoral College with direct election, to transfer the directorship of the military forces and the negotiation of treaties to the cabinet, to eliminate the president's power of appointment and removal, and to take away the president's power to recommend legislation. MacDonald also favored vesting the power to execute laws in the cabinet, eliminating the presidential veto, providing for new elections in cases of presidential vacancy, and formulating a provision to deal with presidential disability (MacDonald 1922, 69–89).

MacDonald would maintain a bicameral Congress but would fix uniform four-year terms and a minimum age of 25 years for members of both houses. He would eliminate the custom whereby representatives must be residents of their districts, abolish secret congressional sessions, allow both the Senate and the House to ratify treaties, and create a more structured budget system in which both bills raising revenue and those appropriating money would originate in the House. He would grant Congress expanded powers over corporations, immigration and naturalization, education, marriage and divorce, the budget, economic control (including possible nationalizations), and internal improvements, and subject members to recall (MacDonald 1922, 90–116). MacDonald also favored a system of uniform requirements for voting in federal elections and wanted the House to represent both population and occupations and professions. MacDonald also favored the proliferation of political parties.

MacDonald wanted the Constitution to delineate more clearly the respective roles of the state and national governments. He thought that Congress should be able to ascertain whether a state government is republican and deny it representation, and he thought that state citizens should have a right to petition Congress on the subject (MacDonald 1922, 155). He wanted to guarantee protections for freedom of religion, assembly, and petition, and for the right to bear arms against abridgments by the states as well as by the national government. He also favored eliminating the anachronistic state militias. Interestingly, MacDonald believed that the Eighteenth Amendment (prohibition) was an undue infringement on state police powers.

Under MacDonald's scheme, the premier and the cabinet would appoint judges who would be subject to removal not only by impeachment but also at the request of both houses (MacDonald 1922, 181). He wanted to create a system of administrative courts. He also wanted to control the exercise of judicial power over receiverships, cut back on the use of injunctions, and officially recognize the rights of the courts to declare a law to be unconstitutional.

MacDonald proposed that Congress should pass a resolution favoring a constitutional convention and inviting states to send petitions to this end (MacDonald 1922, 224). Alternatively, arguing that the provisions in Article V might "properly be viewed as permissive and selective, not as exclusive" (MacDonald 1922, 227), he suggested that Congress could call a constitutional convention on its own.

See also Parliamentary Systems.

For Further Reading:

MacDonald, William. 1922. *A New Constitution for a New America.* New York: B. W. Heubsch.

Vile, John R. 1991. *Rewriting the United States Constitution: An Examination of Proposals from Reconstruction to the Present.* New York: Praeger.

MADISON, JAMES
(1751–1836)

Few individuals have had as profound an influence on the formation and understanding of the U.S. Constitution and the Bill of Rights as James Madison, the nation's fourth president. Madison also wrote and thought profoundly about the constitutional amending process.

In addition to taking the most complete notes of the proceedings of the Constitutional Convention of 1787, the physically diminutive Madison, who received his education at Princeton, was one of the guiding forces behind the Virginia Plan, the first major plan to be proposed there. This plan, which differed significantly from the existing Articles of Confederation, proposed three branches of government and a bicameral legislature representing states according to their population and exercising significantly wider powers. This plan indicated that provision should be made for "amendment of the Articles of Union whensoever it shall seem necessary." It further specified that the consent of Congress should not be necessary, but it was otherwise nonspecific (Vile 1992, 27). Madison subsequently supported a proposal, however, to funnel amendments through the national legislature, apparently opposing the state-requested convention mechanism largely for practical reasons (Weber 1989, 36).

Although he did not achieve all that he wanted at the Convention, Madison was one of the three authors of the *Federalist Papers,* who wrote under the name of Publius to defend the new constitution. In *Federalist No. 43,* Madison argued that the amending process "guards equally against that extreme facility, which would render the Constitution too mutable; and that extreme difficulty, which might perpetuate its discovered faults" (Hamilton, Madison, and Jay 1961, 278).

Federalist Nos. 49 and 50 may well constitute Madison's deepest and most original thinking on the idea of constitutional change. In *Federalist* No. 49, Madison opposed Thomas Jefferson's suggested plan that would enable two of three branches of the government to call a convention for altering the Constitution. Focus-ing on the advantages of stability, Madison honed in on the stabilizing advantages of inculcating "veneration" for the Constitution (Levinson 1990b). Madison noted that "as every appeal to the people would carry an implication of some defect in the government, frequent appeals would, in great measure, deprive the government of that veneration which time bestows on everything, and without which perhaps the wisest and freest governments would not possess the requisite stability" (Hamilton et al. 1961, 314). Madison offered similar arguments in private correspondence in regard to Jefferson's idea that the Constitution should be rewritten each generation (Vile 1992, 64–65). Likewise rejecting periodic appeals to the people in *Federalist* No. 50, Madison drew largely from the negative experiences that Pennsylvania had encountered with the Council of Censors. In *Federalist* No. 51 Madison further praised the system of checks and balances that the new Constitution had established.

The most persistent criticism of the new Constitution was that it lacked a bill of rights. Subsequently elected to the House of Representatives, Madison took the lead in formulating, advocating, and shepherding the Bill of Rights through the First Congress. He thought that adoption of such a bill was essential to securing popular approval of the Constitution. Madison structured the Bill of Rights so that it would focus primarily on individual rights rather than on possible structural changes to the yet untried national government. The Bill of Rights limited the national government and recognized some reserved powers for the states; Madison did not succeed in adopting an amendment that would have limited the states, which at the time he thought were more likely to abuse civil liberties.

As power shifted in the new government to political opponents in the Federalist Party, who were not always sensitive to the protection of individual rights (the party adopted the Sedition Act, limiting speech, in 1798), Madison often joined with Jefferson and other Democratic-Republicans in defending states' rights and opposing broad interpretations of federal powers like those announced in *McCulloch v. Maryland* (1819), which upheld the constitutionality of the national bank that Madison had initially opposed. Madison helped author the Virginia Resolution that suggested (along with Jefferson's Kentucky Resolution) that states might "interpose" themselves against unconstitutional legislation like the Sedition Act. Madison also served as Thomas Jefferson's secretary of state and was one of the parties in *Marbury v. Madison* (1803), in which Chief Justice John Marshall asserted the courts' power of judicial review.

As president, Madison recommended an amendment to permit the national government to undertake internal improvements. When no such amendment was adopted, he vetoed such legislation. By the same token, during his term, Madison approved the reestablishment of the national bank that he had previously argued was unconstitutional; he argued that established precedents, as well as necessities demonstrated during the War of 1812, were more important here than his own initial judgment as to the people's thoughts on the subject. Significantly, Madison saw that his notes of the Constitutional Convention of 1787 would not be published until after his death, when most precedents would already be established.

In 1829–1830, Madison participated in the convention that met to redraw the Virginia state constitution. His final words to his country were an appeal that "the Union of States be cherished and perpetual" (Meyers 1973, 576). At his death in 1836, Madison was the only surviving member of the Constitutional Convention of 1787.

See also Bill of Rights; Constitutional Convention of 1787; Federalists; Jefferson, Thomas; *McCulloch v. Maryland*; Internal Improvements.

For Further Reading:

Banning, Lance. 1995. *The Sacred Fire of Liberty: James Madison and the Founding of the Federal Republic.* Ithaca, NY: Cornell University Press.

Finkelman, Paul. 1991. "James Madison and the Bill of Rights: A Reluctant Paternity." In *The Supreme Court Review, 1990.* Chicago: University of Chicago Press.

Hamilton, Alexander, James Madison, and John Jay. 1787–1788. *The Federalist Papers.* Reprint, New York: New American Library, 1961.

Labunski, Richard. 2006. *James Madison and the Struggle for the Bill of Rights.* New York: Oxford University Press.

Levinson, Sanford. 1990b. "'Veneration' and Constitutional Change: James Madison Confronts the Possibility of Constitutional Amendment." *Texas Tech Law Review* 21: 2443–2461.

Matthews, Richard K. 1995. *If Men Were Angels: James Madison and the Heartless Empire of Reason.* Lawrence: University Press of Kansas.

Meyers, Marvin, ed. 1973. *The Mind of the Founder: Sources of the Political Thought of James Madison.* Indianapolis, IN: Bobbs-Merrill.

Miller, William Lee. 1992. *The Business of May Next: James Madison and the Founding.* Charlottesville: University Press of Virginia.

Morgan, Robert J. 1988. *James Madison on the Constitution and the Bill of Rights.* New York: Greenwood Press.

Rutland, Robert A. 1987. *James Madison: The Founding Father.* New York: Macmillan.

Sheehan, Colleen A. 2009. *James Madison and the Spirit of Republican Government.* New York: Cambridge University Press.

Vile, John R. 1992. *The Constitutional Amending Process in American Political Thought.* New York: Praeger.

Vile, John R., William Pederson, and Frank Williams, eds. 2008. *James Madison: Philosopher, Founder, and Statesman.* Athens: Ohio University Press.

Weber, Paul. 1989. "Madison's Opposition to a Second Convention." *Polity* 20 (Spring): 498–517.

MAGNA CARTA

The contrast between the "unwritten" English Constitution and the written Constitution of the United States is not completely accurate. Not only does the English constitution rest in part on written documents, but the United States has also adopted many extraconstitutional customs and usages that influence how the document is applied and interpreted.

The Magna Carta is one of the most significant milestones in the history of English liberty. Extracted by the English barons from King John at Runnymede in 1215 (and later reaffirmed by a number of subsequent monarchs), the document, consisting of a preamble and 63 clauses, was designed to limit perceived abuses of the barons and their subjects by the king. The document provided for the writ of habeas corpus and for a variety of procedural rights that Americans today associate with the Bill of Rights, and, more particularly, with the due process clauses of the Fifth and Fourteenth Amendments. By creating a council to assure that the document would be followed, the Magna Carta also marked one of the steps in the development of parliament, which became the prototype for U.S. state legislatures and the Congress.

The English jurist and commentator Edward Coke used the Magna Carta to argue against royal prerogatives. In their dispute with Great Britain that led up to the Revolutionary War, the American colonists who initially considered themselves to be English citizens with accompanying rights, in turn, utilized Coke's arguments to strike out against the doctrine of parliamentary sovereignty, which most British legal commentators were then embracing. The colonial rejection of parliamentary sovereignty led in turn to their espousal of the doctrine of "no taxation without representation."

The Magna Carta serves both as a foundation for the idea of a written constitution and for the idea that such constitutions should protect individual rights. The document also shows that written words can have in rallying individuals to protect their liberties.

See also: Customs and Usages; Parliamentary Sovereignty.

For Further Reading:

Holt, J. C. 1992. *Magna Carta.* New York: Cambridge University Press.

Walker, David M. 1980. "Magna Carta." In *The Oxford Companion to Law.* Oxford, UK: Clarenden Press, pp. 795–797.

MARBURY, WILLIAM (1762–1835)

During the Progressive Era, Maryland attorney William Marbury was one of the most prominent proponents of the argument that there were inherent limits on the power to amend the U.S. Constitution (Vile 1992, 157–171). Marbury presented his arguments in at least two law review articles questioning the legitimacy of the Eighteenth and Nineteenth Amendments (Marbury 1919, 1920; for response, see Frierson 1920). He also served as an attorney for the state of Maryland in *Myers v. Anderson* (1915)—unsuccessfully seeking to uphold the constitutionality of the state's grandfather clause against provisions of the Fifteenth Amendment, which denied discrimination in voting on the basis of race—and *Leser v. Garnett* (1922), also unsuccessfully questioning the legitimacy of the Nineteenth Amendment, denying discrimination on the basis of sex.

Marbury's arguments, like those of contemporary Selden Bacon, were built partly on views of state sovereignty. In recent years, the idea that there might be judicially enforceable inherent limitations on the amending process has been revived by individuals such as Walter Murphy, who are more concerned about the protection of individual rights than with state sovereignty.

See also Bacon, Selden; Eighteenth Amendment; Fifteenth Amendment; Murphy, Walter; Nineteenth Amendment.

For Further Reading:

Frierson, William. 1920. "Amending the Constitution of the United States: A Reply to Mr. Marbury." *Harvard Law Review* 33 (March): 659–666.

Marbury, William L. 1920. "The Nineteenth Amendment and After." *Virginia Law Review* 7 (October): 1–29.

———. 1919. "The Limitations upon the Amending Power." *Harvard Law Review* 33 (December): 223–235.

MARBURY V. MADISON (1803)

In Britain, Parliament is considered to be supreme. Because it exercises such legislative sovereignty and because the country has no single written constitution, a formal amendment process is not necessary. By contrast, in the United States, the Constitution is supreme over ordinary acts of legislation. If Congress wishes to alter the Constitution, it must proceed via the Article V amending processes.

In large part, this system emerged because of the extraordinarily important decision that Chief Justice John Marshall authored in *Marbury v. Madison* (1803). Marbury brought his case to the Supreme Court after Thomas Jefferson's new secretary of state, James Madison, refused to deliver a commission to Marbury, a prominent Georgetown businessman whom the outgoing administration of John Adams had appointed as a justice of the peace.

Marshall agreed that Marbury was entitled to his commission and that laws provide a remedy in such circumstances. Marshall decided, however, that the remedy was not a writ of mandamus, a judicial order issued to an executive official issuing from the Court. He reasoned that the provision of the Judiciary Act of 1789 that appeared to grant this power to the Court was flawed because Article III of the Constitution clearly limited the original jurisdiction of the Supreme Court to certain circumstances, of which this was not one. In deciding that the Court had the responsibility of exercising judicial review and of striking down this provision of the law, Marshall, a Federalist appointee, thus avoided a direct confrontation with the new Democratic-Republican administration.

In outlining his case for judicial construction of the Constitution, Marshall noted that the creation of a constitution was "a very great exertion," not "to be frequently repeated" (*Marbury* 1803, 176). He further said that the Constitution was "either a superior paramount law, unchangeable by ordinary means, or it is on a level with ordinary legislative acts, and like other acts, is alterable when the legislature shall please to alter it" (*Marbury* 1803, 177). Arguing that it was "emphatically the province and duty of the judicial department to say what the law is" (*Marbury* 1803, 177), Marshall thus ruled that he must be bound by the Constitution rather than by the Judiciary Act.

In assuming a power not directly stated in, but arguably implied by, the Constitution, Marshall at once limited changes that Congress could make in constitutional understandings and ensured that the judicial branch would play a big role in interpreting that document. If some institution in government did not have this power of interpretation, it might be necessary to resort to the constitutional amending process far more frequently.

See also Madison, James; Marshall, John; Judiciary entries; Parliamentary Sovereignty.

For Further Reading:

Alfange, Dean, Jr. 1994. "*Marbury v. Madison* and Original Understandings of Judicial Review: In Defense of Traditional Wisdom." In *The Supreme Court Review,* 1993. Chicago: University of Chicago Press.

Clinton, Robert L. 1989. Marbury v. Madison *and Judicial Review.* Lawrence: University Press of Kansas.

Marbury v. Madison, 5 U.S. (1 Cranch.) 137 (1803).

Sloan, Cliff and David McKean. 2009. *The Great Decision: Jefferson, Adams, Marshall, and the Battle for the Supreme Court.* New York: Public Affairs.

MARDUKE, P. G.

In 1970, P. G. Marduke (otherwise unidentified) published a hand-typed brochure titled *The CASCOT System for Social Control of Technology.* Marduke's thought that although many individuals feared technology, it could actually be a potent force for change at a time when the world was in crisis and greater democratic participation was desirable. Marduke devoted separate chapters to different areas of concern.

Marduke proposed that the political system be changed from a "system of 'power politics' to a system of 'people politics'" (Marduke 1970, 37). One specific proposal was the initiation of a system of Touch-Tone voting whereby citizens could vote on pending legislation. Marduke also advocated abolishing the Senate, with its malapportionment, and granting public officials "a lifetime salary" while prohibiting all other income and investment (Marduke 1970, 43). Marduke proposed conducting nominations by telephone computer system, requiring that the media give candidates opportunity to talk to the public, and limiting campaign spending to a fixed amount of money. Marduke also favored eliminating independent regulatory agencies and expanding the congressional representative's role as ombudsman. Marduke would replace the presidency with an elected National Council of five officials, each heading an agency (international affairs, environment, commerce, public welfare, and administration) consisting of five persons, each, in turn, responsible for a single technical area.

Considering the existing economic system to be seriously flawed, Marduke proposed some far-reaching changes also based on the application of modern technology. These included replacing the system of currency with electronic transactions, recording all capital assets over $25 in value, imposing limits on individual net worth as well as a minimum below which no one should be permitted to fall, and redistributing wealth according to public vote. The system would also be designed to provide "whatever amount of credit the people wanted" (Marduke 1970, 70–71).

Marduke favored establishing parallel public and private health systems. Marduke advocated hiring a network of foreign agents pledged to stop their nations from "the first use of atomic, biochemical or other mass-murder weaponry" (Marduke 1970, 94). The ultimate goal was a "cosmopolitan system where people, not nations or institutions, are the essential ingredients" (Marduke 1970, 95). In a chapter on international relations, Marduke thus proposed opening the doors "to any and every other nation that cares to enter the system" (Marduke 1970, 98). This would involve sharing economic resources as well as political ideals and would begin with pressure exerted by refusing to import goods from foreign nations.

In analyzing sex and morals, Marduke worked from the premise that "sex is fun" (Marduke 1970, 105) and argued that technological advances made traditional prohibitions against premarital sex outdated. Marduke favored establishing a fairly permissive "code for what is legally and morally prohibited," as well as a nonbinding code for "what is socially encouraged and discouraged" (Marduke 1970, 110). The latter would involve polling the public on attitudes about "dating, drinking and drugs; fashion, fads and fornication" (Marduke 1970, 111). Marduke further suggested a "random-sample-censorship" for media productions (Marduke 1970, 112) and the establishment of social centers to distribute drugs to addicts.

In order to deal with environmental problems, Marduke advocated the creation of mass-transit systems. Marduke also advocated banning all chemicals "applied to soil or vegetation for any purpose" (Marduke 1970, 126), creating sewage treatment plants in every city, ending offshore oil drilling, declaring minerals to be the property of all people, and making birth control available on a voluntary basis, with the possibility of a compulsory system if this did not work.

Marduke wanted to replace the existing welfare system with social centers for mass feeding and care. Marduke also advocated more extensive consumer education and examinations for people in the repair business. Marduke favored extensive educational reform. Education would be divided into four levels, with the first levels oriented toward practical training and consumer education.

Marduke criticized the legal system for preoccupation with money and favored devising a legal system with three levels consisting of a public arbitrator, three-person investigatory boards, and an appeals investigatory board. Criminal sanctions would be designed not to punish but to motivate better behavior or to isolate the criminal from society.

Clearly, Marduke's proposals called for extensive change involving not only the Constitution but the entire social structure. Accordingly, Marduke recognized that "the most difficult problem will be to keep the change on an evolutionary, rather than a revolutionary scale" (Marduke 1970, 163). Marduke hoped to run CASCOT candidates in the 1972 elections. Senatorial candidates would be pledged to abolish that institution. Marduke also favored modifying the amending process sometime before 1980 so that a majority of the House could propose amendments to be approved by popular majorities. That change would be followed by "the chain of amendments necessary to establish the popular voting system and the economic system and the form of government that can effectively deal with the world's crisis" (Marduke 1970, 170).

For Further Reading:

Marduke, P. G. 1970. *The CASCOT System for Social Control of Technology.* Silver Spring, MD: Citizens' Association for Social Control of Technology.

MARRIAGE AND DIVORCE LAWS

In a study examining proposed amendments relative to marriage in the United States, Edward Stein has divided them into three main types. Some proposed prohibiting interracial marriages, others were designed to limit polygamy, and still others were designed to provide uniformity among state marriage and divorce laws (2004, 625). Some proposals combined one or more of these objectives.

Stein observes that Rev. Samuel Dike formed the New England Divorce Reform League in 1881. Concerned about the rising number of divorces, this league succeeded in getting Congress to authorize a national study. Members of Congress proposed 30 amendments to grant Congress power to adopt uniform laws on the subject between 1884 and 1906 (Id. at 637). Others pushed states to adopt uniform laws on the subject. Stein observes that advocates of uniformity faced conflict between "liberals and women's rights activists" (these included Susan B. Anthony and Elizabeth Cady Stanton, who were working for women's suffrage) who "wanted to weaken the requirements for divorce, in part to give women more freedom to get out of unhappy marriages" and between conservatives who feared "that national marriage and divorce laws would mean it would become easier for couples in many states to get divorced" (Id. at 639). As a consequence, no amendment was adopted, and few states adopted uniform laws on the subject suggested by The National Conference of the Commissioners on Uniform State Laws (NCCUSL (White, 1991).

Although states continue to enforce different requirement for both marriage and divorce, a number of federal court decisions have some-what limited state regulation of domestic matters, usually on either privacy or equal protection grounds. The most notable cases have been *Griswold v. Connecticut* (1965), which recognized a right of marital privacy and provided access to contraceptives; *Loving v. Virginia* (1967), which struck down state restrictions on interracial marriage; *Roe v. Wade* (1973), which struck down most laws restricting access to abortion; and *Zablocki v. Redhail* (1978), which struck down a state law forbidding a noncustodial parent who was delinquent in child support from remarrying. Similarly, in *Roemer v. Evans* (1996), the Supreme Court used the equal protection clause of the Fourteenth Amendment to overturn Colorado's Amendment 2, a provision Colorado voters had adopted in a referendum that would have prohibited the government from taking action to protect individuals based on their sexual orientation or lifestyle. In *Lawrence v. Texas* (2003), the Court further overturned *Bowers v. Hardwick* (1986) and decided that state anti-sodomy laws violated the right to privacy.

In recent years, the most prominent movement for uniformity of marriage laws has been that on behalf of the Federal Marriage Protection Amendment. Reacting to developments whereby some states have recognized homosexual marriages, proponents favor an amendment that would limit marriage to that between one man and one woman.

See also Anthony, Susan B.; Federal Marriage Protection Amendment; Intermarriage; Parental Rights Amendment; Polygamy; Privacy; Stanton, Elizabeth Cady.

For Further Reading:

Stein, Edward. 2004. "Past and Present Proposed Amendments to the United States Constitution Regarding Marriage." *Washington University Law Quarterly* 82 (Fall): 611–685.

Thomas, Tracy A. 2005. "Elizabeth Cady Stanton on the Federal Marriage Amendment: A Letter to the President." *Constitutional Commentary* 22 (Spring): 137–159.

White, James J. 1991. "One Hundred Years of Uniform State Laws: *Ex Proprio Vigore,*" *Michigan Law Review* 89 (August): 2096–2133.

MARSHALL, JOHN
(1755–1835)

No one has had a greater impact on the interpretation of the U.S. Constitution than John Marshall. Marshall fought during the Revolutionary War and served as a delegate to the Virginia ratifying convention. As a prominent Federalist, Marshall served as John Adams's secretary of state before Adams appointed him to the Supreme Court, where he was chief justice from 1801 to 1835.

Marshall significantly enhanced the prestige of the Supreme Court. During his long tenure, it became customary for the Court to issue majority opinions (most of which he authored) rather than, as previously, for each justice to write separately. Much to the frustration of the Democratic-Republicans, Marshall was generally able to mass even their appointees behind his decisions supporting strong national powers—for example, *Cohens v. Virginia* (1821)—and establishing the authority of the Court.

One of Marshall's most important contributions was in the area of judicial review. By asserting the right of the judiciary "to say what the law is" and to invalidate federal laws in *Marbury v. Madison* (1803), Marshall made it possible on many occasions for the Court to initiate changes in constitutional interpretation and to apply the Constitution to new circumstances without the need for constitutional amendments (Cahn 1954, 19). Indeed, in *Marbury*, Marshall specifically noted that the creation of a new government "is a very great exertion, nor can it, nor ought it, to be frequently repeated." His justification for judicial review rested largely on the proposition that, in invalidating a law, the Supreme Court was not exerting its own will but simply enforcing written agreements already embodied within the Constitution. In *Cohens v. Virginia*, Marshall noted that "The people made the constitution, and the people can unmake it. It is the creature of their own will, and lives only by their will" (quoted in Kyvig 1996a, 486).

Marshall believed that the Constitution should be interpreted expansively. In upholding the constitutionality of the national bank in *McCulloch v. Maryland* (1819), Marshall followed Alexander Hamilton in using the necessary and proper clause in Article I, Section 8 to argue for a broad interpretation of the Constitution and to refute the notion that the Tenth Amendment precluded the congressional exercise of implied powers. In so doing, he distinguished such a broad charter intended to endure for generations from more prolix legal codes that should be interpreted more strictly. Without such an interpretation, the Constitution would have required many more amendments than it has received for Congress to exercise its current powers.

Marshall was a strong proponent of vested property rights, most notably in cases such as *Fletcher v. Peck* (1810) and *Dartmouth College v. Woodward* (1819), in which he gave a broad reading to the contract clause. Similarly, Marshall upheld broad national authority over interstate commerce, especially in *Gibbons v. Ogden* (1824), where he used the grant of a federal license to a steamship to strike down a conflicting state monopoly over navigation in its waters.

Although Marshall generally chartered a bold course in constitutional interpretation, his decision in *Barron v. Baltimore* (1833) limited the application of the Bill of Rights to the national government. This interpretation stood until 1868, when the adoption of the Fourteenth Amendment led to renewed questions about the scope of such rights, most of which courts have subsequently applied to the states via the due process clause of this amendment.

Marshall's vigorous tenure on the Court prompted numerous amending proposals to clip the federal judiciary, but like the efforts to convict Marshall's colleague Justice Samuel Chase on charges of impeachment, they failed. When Marshall left the Court, it was well situated as a coordinate branch of the national government, with power to interpret the law and to invalidate laws it judged to be in conflict with the Constitution.

See also *Barron v. Baltimore;* Fourteenth Amendment; Hamilton, Alexander; *Marbury v. Madison; McCulloch v. Maryland;* Tenth Amendment.

For Further Reading:
Baker, Leonard. 1974. *John Marshall: A Life in Law.* New York: Macmillan Publishing Company.

Beveridge, Albert J. 1916. *The Life of John Marshall.* 4 vols. Boston: Houghton Mifflin.

Cahn, Edmond. 1954. "An American Contribution." In *Supreme Court and Supreme Law.* Bloomington: Indiana University Press.

Kyvig, David E. 1996a. *Explicit and Authentic Acts: Amending the Constitution, 1776–1995.* Lawrence: University Press of Kansas.

Newmyer, R. Kent. 1968. *The Supreme Court Under Marshall and Taney.* New York: Thomas Y. Crowell.

Smith, Jean Edward. 1996. *John Marshall: Definer of a Nation.* New York: Henry Holt and Company.

White, G. Edward. 1991. *The Marshall Court and Cultural Change 1815–1835.* New York: Oxford University Press.

MARX, MICHAEL

Michael Marx is an author who writes and markets his own novels door-to-door, one of which is titled *Justus—A Utopia.* According to a resume posted on his Web site, he earned a B.A. in political science from Hobart College, an MFA in filmmaking at New York University, worked for a time on a master's degree in English at Indiana State University in Terre Haute where he also taught classes, and now lives in Del Mar, California.

Although his novel is utopian, it represents principles that he clearly thinks would be worth adopting and that might influence individuals seeking constitutional change within the United States. His proposals are based chiefly on laissez-faire economics, but also have a moralistic emphasis and look forward to the abolition of nuclear weaponry.

The novel itself describes the life of Michael Justus, a child who appears on the doorstep of Professor Eric Greenfield, wrapped in a priceless Renoir painting. The child turns out to be a prodigy. Fearful of an impending nuclear attack, the two buy property from the sale of the Renoir in a remote area of Mexico, cover it with radioactive protective material that Michael invents, figure out how to get static electricity from the air to produce power, and invite people to live in a tax-free society that survives a nuclear catastrophe that kills 95% of the world's population by 2000. Justus subsequently leads an army that eliminates nuclear weapons but is eventually lost at sea. The city-state that he and his father founded is destined to last half a millennium or longer.

The novel includes a constitution of 40 articles, which serves as the fundamental law for Justus. Citizens adopt all laws through petitions; amendments require petitions with 80% or more of the votes. "Since every citizen can vote for or against (by not signing) every petition of law in the Sate of Justus, there is no need for legislative or executive branches" (Marx, 184).

Article 2 of the Constitution is adamant that Justus will be "a tax-free democracy." It emphatically states that "there is no such thing as a good tax" (187). By contrast, property and ownership are sacrosanct— "In Justus, the property owner is king" (189). Individuals, and not corporations, will own property. Article 6 observes that "contracts of all types . . . shall be enforced to the letter" (194). The "free market," and not minimum or maximum wage laws will prevail with each citizen retaining "the right to be paid in gold and/or silver coin at the end of each work day for that day's labor" (195). Gold and silver will constitute the only form of currency. English will be the official language, and nuclear weapons will be prohibited.

To become citizens individuals must be 18 years of age, must have 10 or more ounces of gold, must be screened for disease, and must pass a test on the Constitution.

Although Marx's novel says that the gods abandoned the earth, Justus both prohibits religious establishments and permits free exercise. Churches and private individuals will provide all education, and individuals who do not set aside money for their own retirement or medical care will end up "destitute" (210).

Although the constitution provides for free speech, it also allows for punishment of lying, the use of filthy language, and pornography. Children under the age of 18 are prohibited from all sexual activity, including that which is "self-induced" (215). Individuals are expected to protect themselves by owning firearms. Drugs are forbidden, and those who are caught using them will be exiled to "a neutered sexual existence on Violent Criminal Island" (217).

Individuals may walk off their jobs, but unions and collective bargaining are prohibited. Citizen-elected judges will oversee search warrants and will be paid through fines. There shall be one elected police officer for every 200 citizens. All criminals will be punished in the same manner that they treated their victims: "Each individual determines his own punishment in the State of Justus by receiving the exact same punishment that he put upon another human being" (237).

Since Justus applies "universal moral law," ignorance will be no excuse for violations (245). Those who burn the flag will be exiled. Human rights will be placed above animal rights, and medical doctors will take the original Hippocratic Oath. All children will be raised in two-parent heterosexual homes, and if parents divorce (something they have to do elsewhere) their children will be put up for adoption. Unwed mothers cannot keep their children unless they get married before they are born. Abortion will be considered as murder and be punished by death. Homosexuals will not be permitted to visit or attain citizenship. Those committing rape or having sex with children will be castrated.

Clearly the founding of Justus depends on a founder with money and genius. Such a nation might also be more likely to survive in a world devastated by nuclear catastrophe than by one where rival nations might envy and seek the nation's wealth. The flyleaf of the book tells readers that, by reading the tome, they can "learn the means to create your own utopia."

Marx's work shares some similarities with Jim Davidson's proposed Oceania (set on an artificial island rather than in Mexico) and Jeremy Miller's proposed libertarian reconstruction of the U.S. Constitution.

See also: Davidson, Jim; Miller, Jeremy.

For Further Reading:

Marx, Michael. *Justus — A Utopia: Formation of a Tax Free Constitutional Democracy.* Flat Rock, IL: Marx & Marx, 1999.

http://www.michaelmarx.com/resume.htm. Accessed 5/20/2008.

MASON, GEORGE (1725–1792)

This Virginia planter, often incorrectly thought to be a lawyer, perhaps because of his role as a commissioner of the peace in Fairfax County, Virginia, played an important part in the development of American constitutionalism. A long-time neighbor and friend of George Washington, Mason was the chief author of the Virginia Declaration of Rights, which later served as a model of other bills of rights, and Virginia's revolutionary constitution. Although, largely for reasons of poor health and impatient temperament, Mason refused most public offices, he did attend the Constitutional Convention of 1787 as a delegate from Virginia. He was a strong advocate of an amending provision. Early in the convention, just after the Virginia Plan had been introduced, Mason noted that:

> The plan now to be formed will certainly be defective, as the Confederation has been found on trial to be. Amendments therefore will be necessary, and it will be better to provide for them, in an easy, regular and Constitutional way than to trust to chance and violence. It would be improper to require the consent of the Natl. Legislature, because they may abuse their power, and refuse their consent on that very account. (Farrand 1966, 1:202–203)

Two days before the Constitution was signed, Mason objected to the amending mechanism that then relied solely on congressional proposal and state ratification. Arguing that "no amendment of the proper kind would ever be obtained by the people, if the Government should become oppressive, as he verily believed would be the case" (Farrand 1966, 2:629), Mason's objection became the basis for the addition of the still unused provision that enables two-thirds of the states to petition Congress to call a constitutional convention to propose amendments.

Although he owned slaves, Mason believed that slavery was morally wrong, he expressed this opinion at the Constitutional Convention, and he was disappointed that the new Constitution did nothing to address the problem. Concerned that the Constitution "had been formed without the knowledge of the idea of the people," Mason suggested toward the end of the Constitutional Convention that "[a] second Convention will know more of the sense of the people, and be able to provide a system more consonant to it" (Farrand 1996, 2:632). Mason also argued that the Constitution should contain a bill of rights. Because it did not, he was one of three remaining delegates to the Constitutional Convention (the others were Elbridge Gerry and Edmund Randolph) who refused to sign the document. Mason continued his opposition to the point of alienating himself from George Washington. Eventually, Federalist supporters of the Constitution relented on one key point, and the first 10 amendments (the Bill of Rights) were proposed and ratified in 1791.

See also Constitutional Convention of 1787; Virginia Declaration of Rights.

For Further Reading:

Broadwater, Jeff. 2006. *George Mason: Forgotten Father.* Chapel Hill: University of North Carolina Press.

Farrand, Max, ed. 1966. *The Records of the Federal Convention.* 4 vols. New Haven, CT: Yale University Press.

Senese, Donald J. 1989. *George Mason and the Legacy of Constitutional Liberty: An Examination of the Influence of George Mason on the American Bill of Rights.* Fairfax County, VA: Fairfax County Historical Commission.

McGRATH, PATRICK J.
(1960–)

Patrick J. McGrath published a book in 2000 advocating "responsible," or "parliamentary" government. He has also posted the draft of the Constitution he included in the book on the Internet.

According to the back cover of his book, McGrath has degrees from Rockland Community College, Buffalo State College, and Iowa

State University and "works in public relations for a small nonprofit company in New York City." In explaining "why change is needed," McGrath identifies the current American constitutional structure as "the worst possible imaginable," and points to a "better way" based on the idea that "Responsibility is singular. Division of responsibility results in no responsibility." Here, and in the introductory chapters that follow, McGrath quotes extensively from Woodrow Wilson's *Congressional Government* and notes that he has been enamored with parliamentary government since being a high school exchange student with New Zealand (p. 6). McGrath's book includes a model state constitution as well as one for the national government, which this entry will describe.

McGrath's preamble is almost identical to that of the existing Constitution.

Article I of the new constitution outlines its "structure and functions," focusing on Congress, defined as consisting of "the President of the United States, the College of States' Legates, and the House of Representatives." It begins with a quotation from the Declaration of Independence affirming a right "to institute new government . . . as to them shall seem more likely to effect their safety and happiness" (38). The president is designated as the head of state; every seventh year, legates, sitting in convention, will select from two to five presidential candidates, and the people will choose among them in a popular election. Candidates are forbidden from being members of a political party, from ever having been a party committee member, from being lobbyists, from having contributed more than $500 to any candidate or from holding political office. Candidates would be limited to spending $500,000 each. The president shall be the commander-in-chief, "but will act in this capacity only on the advice of the appropriate Minister of State" (40). The president is vested with power to "ratify Treaties, upon the advice of the appropriate Ministers of State," and to make appointments (41). The president may also dissolve the House" on the advice of the Prime Minister" (42). The president is also designated as "Grand commander of the Order of Honor," as "Grand Commander of the Order of Freedom," and as

"Grand commander of any order of Honor" that Congress might establish (42).

The College of Legates is organized like the current senate, with members serving five-year terms unless previously dissolved. Such legates will be nominated, by state legislatures, which shall also pay them. Members are forbidden from being members of parties. Candidates may spend no more than $20,000 each. The College will nominate presidential candidates, appoint members of Boundary Commissions to draw up nonpartisan House districts, and make a number of appointments. It may pass resolutions, but they will have no force of law.

The House of Representatives will serve much like the House of Commons in England, with 625 to 650 members (47). Its members will serve for four-year terms unless dissolved earlier. McGrath provides that "It shall not be lawful for the House to adopt or pass any Vote, Resolution, Address, or bill for Appropriation of any Part of the Public Revenue, or of any Tax or Impost, to any purpose that has not been recommended by Message of the President in the Session" (49). The House will have the powers that Article I, Section 8 currently vests in Congress.

The executive power of Congress is vested in an Administration, which consists of "the Prime Minister and such other Ministers of State as the President, on the advice of the Prime Minister, shall appoint" (53). The head of the Administration will be designated as the Prime Minister. The Leader of the Loyal Opposition has power to propose a vote of no-confidence in the Administration, which would trigger another election.

Article II of the proposed constitution deals with "restrictions upon government," and celebrates "the self-evident truth that all human beings 'are endowed by their Creator with certain inalienable rights'" (54). It compiles and lists restrictions on governments currently found within Article I, Sections 9 and 10 and the Bill of Rights.

Article III outlines the judicial branch, which does not structurally vary significantly from that of the current constitution. The courts would have the power to examine a law before the president signs it to determine whether it is constitu-

tional, but it must speak with one voice, and may publish no dissents.

Article IV provides that the president may propose amendments on the advice of his administration or on recommendations by the College of Legates or on the application of two-thirds of the state legislatures. Amendments would require ratification by a majority of voters and "majorities of the votes cast in more than one-half of the states" (63).

Article V provides for miscellaneous matters, most reaffirming existing obligations of the states to one another. The Article further provides that the document come into force "on the second January 2 or July 1 following approval of this Constitution by the people, whichever is the later of the two" (65). It also provides for transitory laws to assist in the transition from one constitution to the other.

The appendixes to the book include references to the governments of the United Kingdom, Canada, Australia, New Zealand, Ireland, India, and other parliamentary systems.

See also: Parliamentary Systems.

For Further Reading:

McGrath, Patrick J. 2000. *The Way to Responsible Government: The Constitutional Re-Structuring America Needs.* San Jose: Writer's Showcase.

MCCULLOCH V. MARYLAND (1819)

McCulloch v. Maryland remains one of the most important decisions that Chief Justice John Marshall authored. By establishing the doctrine of implied powers and the principle of broad constitutional construction, this decision did much to obviate the need for many amendments that have been introduced to expand congressional powers. By the same token, by recognizing the broad reach of such powers, the decision has arguably enhanced the importance of explicit restraints on such powers, such as those found in the Bill of Rights and elsewhere in the Constitution.

McCulloch arose when Maryland attempted to levy a tax on a branch of the national bank established in Baltimore, which the teller McCulloch refused to pay. The Supreme Court had to decide whether the bank, which was first established after vigorous debate between Alexander Hamilton and Thomas Jefferson in the George Washington administration and subsequently reestablished during James Madison's presidency, was constitutional. The second issue centered on the legitimacy of Maryland's attempt to tax the bank.

In sanctioning the bank, Marshall developed the idea of implied powers. Although the Constitution had not specifically granted the power to incorporate a bank, neither had it prohibited one. In reserving powers to the states, the Tenth Amendment omitted the word "expressly," thus specifying that the powers "not delegated to the United States, nor prohibited to the States, are reserved to the States or to the people," and thus not precluding the idea of implied powers. Moreover, the right to create a corporation such as a bank was not an end in itself but a means to other ends, or powers, that were designated in the Constitution.

Specifying that under Article I, Section 8 of the Constitution Congress could exercise all powers that were "necessary and proper," Marshall argued that the framers had intended to expand rather than restrict such authority. In context, the word "necessary" neither denoted absolute necessity nor limited Congress to the most restrictive means. As Marshall observed, "The provision is made in a constitution intended to endure for ages to come, and, consequently, to be adapted to the various *crises* of human affairs (*McCulloch* 1819, 415). In justifying the creation of the bank, Marshall wrote, "Let the end be legitimate, let it be within the scope of the constitution, and all means which are appropriate, which are plainly adapted to that end, which are not prohibited, but consist with the letter and spirit of the constitution, are constitutional" (*McCulloch* 1819, 421).

In upholding national sovereignty over state sovereignty, Marshall ruled that Maryland had no right to tax the bank. Such a power would inappropriately give parts of the Union, the states, the power to destroy the whole, the Union.

Virginia's John Taylor of Caroline and Judge Spencer Roane severely criticized *McCulloch,* and the state proposed an amendment to create an institution other than the Supreme Court for resolving conflicts between the national government and the states (Levy 1995, 428). Today the Court continues to interpret constitutional powers broadly enough that the most important restrictions on such powers continue to be explicit constitutional restrictions rather than the lack of explicit constitutional grants of power.

See also Marshall, John; Necessary and Proper Clause; Tenth Amendment.

For Further Reading:

Ellis, Richard E. 2007. *Aggressive Nationalism: McCulloch v. Maryland and the Foundation of Federal Authority in the Young Republic.* New York: Oxford University Press.

Levy, Leonard W. 1995. *Seasoned Judgments: The American Constitution, Rights, and History.* New Brunswick, NJ: Transaction Publishers.

McCulloch v. Maryland, 17 U.S. (4 Wheat.) 316 (1819).

MCKEE, HENRY S. (1868–1956)

California businessman Henry McKee presented his plans for political, economic, and educational reform in a book published in 1933. Like Karl Marx, with whom he otherwise shared little in common, McKee predicted that without reform, the next economic depression was likely to lead to complete political breakdown. McKee drew many of his political solutions from earlier thinkers such as Woodrow Wilson and Gamaliel Bradford.

McKee opposed government by committee and favored strong executive power. Like Wilson, McKee believed that by forcing individuals to articulate and defend their views publicly, a parliamentary system would attract men of greater talents. Accompanying a strengthened cabinet would be a type of "question hour," during which members of the cabinet would have to defend their views before Congress. McKee believed that such debates would expose demagogic appeals and flawed programs, in which category he placed the progressive income tax and inheritance taxes.

McKee favored more centralized governmental control over economic problems, subject again to the increased scrutiny and accountability that a parliamentary system would bring. McKee favored creating a single national bank in place of the system of 12 federal reserve institutions. The central bank should, in turn, be headed by a governor, "not by a Board or Committee" (McKee 1933, 91). McKee also favored establishing a cabinet department to head transportation and a similar cabinet office to deal with retailing and extractive industries. He believed that businesses would welcome such control, as long as it was accountable.

Although it would not have required a constitutional amendment, McKee's solution to the problems of poverty and unemployment was perhaps his most novel. He viewed both problems as essentially moral problems, resulting from poor personal finance. He therefore proposed that public schools should teach children to keep expenditures within income and to save at least 10 percent of their income a year. As has been observed elsewhere (Vile 1991, 72), however modern his views of increased governmental control might seem, McKee took a dim view of the values of modern consumer society, stressing instead more traditional values of saving and thrift.

See also: Parliamentary Systems.

For Further Reading:

McKee, Henry S. 1933. *Degenerate Democracy.* New York: Thomas Y. Crowell.

Vile, John R. 1991. *Rewriting the United States Constitution: An Examination of Proposals from Reconstruction to the Present.* New York: Praeger.

MEDICAL CARE

Among advanced industrial nations, the United States is one of the few that relies primarily on private medical insurance rather than on government-financed health care. Moreover, although the Constitution guarantees many political rights, it makes no explicit provision for social and economic rights.

The 1940s, the 1970s, and the early 1990s all witnessed attempts to adopt national health insurance, but each effort failed (Laham 1993, 1–6). President Lyndon Johnson did succeed in 1965 in getting Congress to adopt programs for the poor (Medicaid) and the elderly (Medicare), and President Barack Obama has made health care reform a major project of his administration. In October 1991 and again in February 1993, Democratic Representative Pete Stark of California, chair of the Health Subcommittee of the Ways and Means Committee, introduced an amendment to grant U.S. citizens a right to health care and grant Congress power to enforce this right. Although health care has not been so established as a constitutional right, current obstacles to national health insurance are political rather than legal. Such barriers have not stopped Representative Jesse Jackson Jr. (D-IL) from proposing a constitutional amendment specifying that "[a]ll citizens of the United States shall enjoy the right to health care of equal high quality" (Jackson with Watkins 2001, 285).

See also Jackson, Jesse, Jr.; Social and Economic Rights.

For Further Reading:

Jackson, Jesse L., Jr., with Frank E. Watkins. 2001. *A More Perfect Union: Advancing New American Rights.* New York: Welcome Rain Publishers.

MERRIAM, CHARLES
(1874–1953)

Charles Merriam was a political science professor at the University of Chicago who served from 1924 to 1925 as president of the American Political Science Association. In 1931, he published a book titled *The Written Constitution and the Unwritten Attitude.* In this book, he discussed the process of constitutional change as well as several concrete contemporary proposals for such alterations (Vile 1991, 65–66).

Merriam argued that constitutional provisions were often ineffective if not supported by public opinion. The chief threat to modern government was not in "*lack of stability, but lack of mobility,* failure to make prompt adjustments to the new era in industry and science" (Merriam 1931, 25). Merriam was particularly impressed by the growth of cities, whose increases in population often were not reflected in state apportionment schemes. He also thought that states had lost significant power to the national government and suggested the feasibility of recognizing certain large cities as states.

Merriam was receptive to the idea of further alterations in the relation between the nation and the states. Although he thought that there was little chance that the United States would adopt a parliamentary system, he suggested that there were no obstacles to allowing members of the cabinet to appear before, or participate in debates within, Congress (Merriam 1931, 74). At a time prior to *United States v. Classic* (1941), when the Supreme Court limited federal oversight over primary elections (*Newberry v. United States* (1921)), Merriam favored an amendment to provide greater uniformity in such elections (Merriam 1931, 81). In a theme prominent in the wake of the Senate rejection of U.S. participation in the League of Nations, Merriam also favored altering the two-thirds vote required for the Senate to ratify treaties.

For Further Reading:

Merriam, Charles E. 1931. *The Written Constitution and the Unwritten Attitude.* New York: Richard R. Smith.

Vile, John R. 1991. *Rewriting the United States Constitution: An Examination of Proposals from Reconstruction to the Present.* New York: Praeger.

MERTENS, JOHN

John Mertens, the author of *The Second Constitution for the United States of America,* first printed in 1990 and subsequently reissued in 1991 and 1997, is otherwise unidentified, but also appears to have been the author of a 1998 novel titled *The Fall of America.* Mertens described his Constitution as "a fantasy of which some should not be taken too seriously" (title page), but the publishers noted that they were releasing the volume because "we believe that some of the propositions and ideas put forth in the *Second Constitution* will become realities at some time in the future."

What seems to distinguish the *Second Constitution* from fantasy (although the author of this essay does not believe this to be the case, there is an outside chance that some or all sections are intended to be ironic or satiric) is the fact that it takes the form of a written constitution, containing six articles and multiple sections, much like the U.S. Constitution of today. Considerably longer, the *Second Constitution* is remarkable for combining such diverse ideas as population limitation, concern about the environment and dependence on foreign resources, a desire to limit government to those of European descent, sexual equality, limitations on wealth, and massive governmental involvement and intrusion in many issues currently left to private enterprise. The *Second Constitution,* consisting of 57 printed pages, includes no commentary but, at least initially, follows the general outline of the current document.

Article I would establish a legislative department consisting of an altered House and Senate. Nominees for members of both houses would initially be selected at random from among previous state legislators and would have to be "third-generation citizens" (Mertens 1997, 2–3). Elections would be radically shortened, and all campaign contributions would be forbidden, with states reimbursing candidates for "reasonable travel expenses incurred during the campaign" (*Id.,* 2). The House would consist of 300 members and the Senate of one from each state; House members would serve four-year terms and senators for three years. While serving in office, members would be considered on leave from their regular jobs and receive similar compensation (*Id.,* 5). All bills would be voted on in joint session. Budgets would be strictly limited, and a one-time tax on assets and incomes would be used to pay off the national debt within three years (*Id.,* 7). Congressional powers would be similar to those of today, with some novel provisions—allowing, for example, for use of the armed forces in eradicating "the drug traffic and organized crime worldwide" (*Id.,* 9). State officers would be selected much like federal officials with state legislatures nominating candidates for governor (*Id.,* 13).

Article II proposed to divide the presidency into three parts. The executive president would command the military, with co-presidents supervising foreign and domestic affairs. Presidents would serve six-year terms and would rotate offices every two years. All three would have adjoining offices and live within a short distance of the White House.

Like other branches, the judiciary would be split equally between men and women. Supreme Court justices would serve 10-year terms. Each of six identified regions would have an appellate court. The Supreme Court would have the power to grant pardons (a power transferred from the president) by a unanimous vote. The Court would also appoint an ad hoc commission to create a uniform code of laws, "which the Supreme Court shall review, amend, or change as they deem proper" (Mertens 1997, 19). Provisions related to the rights of criminal defendants in the U.S. Bill of Rights are moved to this section of the Constitution. Mertens provides that prisoners "shall work for their keep, at hard labor, and be incarcerated in remote areas at minimum comfort" with more serious offenders being sterilized (*Id.,* 21).

Section IV provides for states, which Mertens would group into six designated regions. U.S. territories would become independent nations. No new states could be admitted to the Union, although Mertens later indicates that there would be a total of 58 of them.

Section V combines the treatment of rights, privileges, and responsibilities. The voting age would apparently be set at 21 (thus overturning the Twenty-sixth Amendment), and voting and "equality of rights" would not be abridged "on account of race, color, or sex" (Mertens 1997, 23). Indeed, "Men and women shall be equal in all respects." Citizens would be guaranteed free health care as well as a right of privacy. Duties

would include giving at least one year in the National Labor Service and one in the military, limiting offspring to no more than two per family (unmarried couples would be forbidden from reproducing), and maintaining "personal and family health."

Section VI of the *Second Constitution* it sets forth 17 "critical goals" for the United States, including reducing the population to 200 million and distributing it equally among 58 states (Mertens does not appear to identify the source of the additional eight states), "eliminating the causes of inflation," "reducing oil consumption to three million barrels a day," building "a national electrified rail transport system," eliminating welfare, establishing national health care and "an effective national education system," preserving the environment, and the like (Mertens 1997, 26–27). These tasks would be effected by councils and subcouncils.

Attempts to control and relocate populations would include compulsory sterilizations and the provision of "minimal health care for illness caused by consumption of tobacco, drugs, alcohol, and overeating" (Mertons 1997, 28). Population density would be limited to "two hundred persons per square mile" (*Id.,* 30), with citizens of cities and states larger than this encouraged or forced to relocate. The Council for an Integrated Economy would limit an individual's accumulation of wealth to $5 million, although a subsequent amendment appears to raise this amount to $750 million for those engaged in production. Corporate bonds would be exchanged for U.S. stocks, with the national government either taking over or directing most major industries. The Council for the Conservation, Generation, and Consumption of Energy would abolish busing in favor of neighborhood schools of no more than 300 students, build windmills for the milling of grain, and replace fossil fuel plants with nuclear reactors. The Council for Transport would plan and build electrified mass-transit systems and consolidate and operate airlines "as a single national fleet" (*Id.,* 37). The Council for Education would limit or reduce college enrollment to no more than 5,000 students while increasing the number of doctors. A Council for Production and Distribution of Food could forbid the service of fast foods that were found to "lack nutritional and health benefits" (*Id.,* 41). A Council for Healthcare and Care for Senior Americans would take control of all hospitals and nursing homes and create orphanages. The Council for the Protection of the Environment would establish a 200-mile offshore fishing limit, abolish clear-cutting of forests, phase out "internal combustion engines running on fossil fuels or their derivatives," and see that half of the U.S. land area was devoted to national parks, on which environmentally friendly farming could be conducted (*Id.,* 49). A Council for Racial Affairs would offer "immigrants of non-European origin who have entered the United States of American since 1945" incentives to "return to the country of their origin with their descendants" (*Id.,* 54). The United States would further engage in an exchange with South Africa whereby the United States would buy property from whites there, and American blacks would migrate there and South African whites would migrate here (*Id.,* 55).

A Council for Religious Affairs would guarantee that churches were independent of foreign control. They would also monitor church affairs "for deliberate acts of mismanagement, embezzlement or fraud involving their organization's assets" (Mertens 1997, 55).

Three amendments round out the document. One is the previously mentioned $750 million limit on individual accumulations. The second would provide for distributing $50 million each year to 100 of the nation's best scientists and teachers. The third would establish two juries, the first of which would monitor television advertising and the second of which would monitor other types.

There is no implementing article for the *Second Constitution* and thus no discussion of how it might be adopted (the Preamble, at p.1, does refer to "We, the majority of the people of the United States"). And, as indicated above, there is no indication of its provenance and even some question about its complete seriousness. Apart from the provision allowing the Supreme Court to amend the code of laws, the document appears to have no formal amending process. Many provisions are aspirational in quality, and those provisions that state specific goals do not specify how they would be implemented, other than through massive new assumptions of governmental powers.

For Further Reading:

Mertens, John. 1997. *The Second Constitution for the United States of America.* Cottonwood, CA: Gazelle Books.

MIGRATORY BIRDS

In June 1911 Republican Senator George McLean of Connecticut introduced an amendment to give Congress power to protect migratory birds. Even without such explicit constitutional authority, in March 1913 Congress adopted legislation that McLean sponsored to regulate migratory birds (Lofgren 1975, 79). U.S. district court decisions in *United States v. Shauver* (1914) and *United States v. McCullagh* (1915) found that such legislation infringed on powers reserved to the states by the Tenth Amendment, and the federal government decided not to appeal to the Supreme Court.

Congress then entered into a treaty with Great Britain in 1916, providing for the protection of birds flying between the United States and Canada, and adopted legislation implementing this treaty in 1918. In a decision written by Justice Oliver Wendell Holmes Jr., the Court upheld the constitutionality of this treaty and accompanying legislation in *Missouri v. Holland* (1920). This decision, based in part on a distinction (probably initially inserted to guarantee that the new government would continue to honor its treaties) in Article V between laws "made in Pursuance" of the Constitution and treaties "under the Authority of the United States," contributed to concerns, reflected in many versions of the Bricker Amendment, that Congress might by treaty deny or abridge rights that it would be unable to deny or abridge under ordinary laws.

Although the Supreme Court has subsequently qualified the treaty-making power in cases such as *Reid v. Covert* (1957), it has generally given more expansive readings to congressional authority under the commerce clause, which are adequate to justify continued congressional regulation of migratory birds.

See also Bricker Amendment; *Missouri v. Holland;* Tenth Amendment.

Further Reading:

Borchers, Patrick J. 1998. "Could a Treaty Trump supreme Court Jurisdictional Doctrine? Judgments, Conventions, and Minimum Contacts." *Albany Law Review* 61: 1161–1176.

Lofgren, Charles A. 1975. "*Missouri v. Holland* in Historical Perspective." *The Supreme Court Review.* Chicago: University of Chicago Press.

MILITIA

When they ratified the Constitution, a number of states proposed amendments calling for the prohibition of standing armies or for state regulation of the militia. Despite such pleas, the only mention of militias in the Bill of Rights is contained in the Second Amendment in connection with the right to bear arms.

After some New England states declined to allow their militias to participate in the War of 1812, Ohio Representative (and later President) William Henry Harrison introduced amendments to give Congress power concurrent with the states to provide militia training (Ames 1896, 270–271). In 1864, Democratic Senator Willard Saulsburg of Delaware introduced a series of proposals to permit slavery to continue in the South. One provision stated that the people should have certain rights against the militia.

Today the central arguments around a militia continue to center on the meaning of the word in the context of the Second Amendment. Does the reference to the militia provide a rationale for restricting gun ownership only to those officially registered in such bodies, or their equivalents, or may all citizens, or at least all who are law abiding, be regarded as constituting this body and thus be considered entitled to their firearms?

See also Second Amendment.

Further Reading:

Romana, John. 2005. "State Militias in the United States: Changed Responsibilities for a New Era." *The Air Force Review* 56: 233–247.

MILLER, ARTHUR S. (1917–1988)

Arthur Miller, while a professor emeritus at George Washington University, presented his ideas for major constitutional change in a book published in the year of the bicentennial of the U.S. Constitution (A. Miller 1987). This book reflected views presented in an earlier article (A. Miller 1984). Miller argued that there was an increasing disjunction between the United States' formal written constitution and the "secret" constitution by which it was actually governed. Much like critics from the Progressive Era, Miller believed that propertied elites wielded true power in American society (Vile 1991c, 143–145).

Miller began his chapter on proposed reforms by listing five major proposals. First, he wanted Congress to have the power to make all laws needed "to provide for and maintain an environment conducive to the attainment of a sustainable society." This would include the power "to achieve an optimum population, to control and diffuse the threat of nuclear war, and to control environmental degradation" (A. Miller 1987, 105). Second, Congress should have authority "to provide for and maintain the reasonable satisfaction of human needs and fulfillment of human desires." Specifically, Miller wanted Congress to be responsible for providing "sufficient meaningful job opportunities for all who are able to work" (*Id.*). Third, Congress should be able to check excessive presidential and bureaucratic power. To this end, Miller wanted to establish a council of state with which the president would have to discuss his decisions; Miller also advocated increased use of the legislative veto. Fourth, Miller wanted to expand the Supreme Court's original jurisdiction so that any voter could bring a suit to "determine the validity of allegations that Congress had failed in any of its duties" (*Id.*). Fifth, Miller proposed rewriting the Constitution so that it applied not only to the government but also "to any societal group that exercises substantial power over individuals." Such groups would include "the supercorporations, the major trade unions, churches, farmers' leagues, [and] professional associations" (*Id.,* 106). Miller, who was highly critical of nationalism, also wanted the Constitution altered so as to recognize the United States' close relations with other nations.

Believing that the idea of a parliamentary system was meritorious, Miller made six additional proposals. He favored making Congress a unicameral body of 100 members; dividing the presidency into a separate head of government and head of state; strengthening political parties so that they would have greater control over members of Congress; substituting 10 or 12 regional governments for the existing 50 states; recognizing "supercorporations" in the Constitution and bringing greater power to bear against them; and, consistent with his earlier pleas for judicial activism (A. Miller 1982), expanding the role of the Supreme Court to take cases against both the two political branches and "private governments" (A. Miller 1987, 123). Miller hoped to transform the Constitution from a collection of negative prohibitions into a set of more affirmative guarantees.

See also: Parliamentary Systems; Social and Economic Rights.

For Further Reading:
Miller, Arthur S. 1987. *The Secret Constitution and the Need for Constitutional Change.* Westport, CT: Greenwood Press.
————. 1984. "The Annual John Randolph Tucker Lecture: Taking Needs Seriously: Observations on the Necessity for Constitutional Change." *Washington and Lee Law Review* 41 (Fall): 1243–1306.
————. 1982. *Toward Increased Judicial Activism: The Political Role of the Supreme Court.* Westport, CT: Greenwood Press.

MILLER, JEREMY M. (1954–)

In the year the nation celebrated the bicentennial of the U.S. Constitution, Jeremy M. Miller, a professor at Western State University College of Law, wrote an article offering a new constitution for consideration (J. Miller 1987). In the essay accompanying this proposal, Miller argued that the Constitution should embody natural law and that, consistent with libertarian principles, it should avoid "paternalistic legislation" (J. Miller 1987, 221). Miller also argued that the Constitution should further the values of truth, dignity, equality, and fundamental fairness.

Such values were incorporated into Miller's expanded preamble, which explicitly included a number of the principles of the Declaration of Independence and specifically invoked "the Supreme Judge of the World" (J. Miller 1987, 226). Article I of Miller's constitution was an expanded version of the Bill of Rights that applied limits to "federal, state, and municipal governments" (*Id.*). Much more detailed than the current Bill of Rights, the provisions for religious freedom would specifically prohibit either the use of "government monies for" or "government endorsement of any religion" (*Id.,* 227). It also distinguished between religious belief and religious conduct and specified that "a short prayer to God, as 'God,' is not a government endorsement of religion" (*Id.,* 227). Similarly, provisions for freedom of speech prohibited "prior licensing" but allowed reasonable "time, place, and manner restrictions" (*Id.,* 227). The right to bear arms included the right to own and carry "non-automatic pistols and non-automatic rifles" (*Id.,* 228). Traffic regulations were to be entrusted to unarmed personnel; most abortions, dissections of the dead, and mechanical organ transplants were to be limited; judicial procedures and warrant requirements were to be made much more detailed; and juries were to be composed of seven persons.

Article II outlined citizen duties. These included the duty of males aged 17 and older to be subject to the military draft, the duty of families to find "gainful employment" (J. Miller 1987, 232), and the duty of losing plaintiffs to pay double a defendant's attorney's fees. Amendment procedures were also included in this section. All laws were to be open to such alterations. The exclusive method of change was to be for two-thirds of the states to call conventions (each state supplying a single delegate), proposals from which would subsequently become part of the Constitution when ratified by a majority of those voting in two-thirds of the states—a provision that appears to allow amendments to be adopted by less than a majority.

Article III outlined the three branches of government, "executive, parliamentary, and judicial" (J. Miller 1987, 233). The president would serve a three-year term, to be followed by possible reelection to a six-year term and subsequent two-year terms. The president would be elected by popular vote (with a runoff required when no one received a majority) and would share the power to nominate federal judges with the two houses of Congress and the Constitutional Court. Given increased powers over the budget, the president would have an item veto, power to hold a national lottery when bankruptcy threatened, and instructions to keep income taxes from 2 to 15 percent of individual income.

The parliament, like today's Congress, would consist of a House and a Senate, each state to have one senator and from one to three representatives, depending on its population. Members of the House would serve a maximum of two three-year terms. A four-fifths vote of both houses would be required to overturn decisions by the Constitutional Court on matters of constitutional interpretation, and majorities of both houses would ratify treaties.

The judicial system would be organized like the current one, with membership on the Constitutional Court specifically set at nine members, and judges serving 12-year terms. Given power to interpret the Constitution, the Constitutional Court was to be "bound by its letter and by its spirit" (J. Miller 1987, 237).

Miller included neither federal protections for voting rights nor an equal protection clause, and he has been criticized for writing a constitution that, because of "the undue specificity of some sections," was too much like a legal code (Knipprath 1987, 253–254). By the same token, his proposal omits a number of powers (for example, over the post office and copyrights) currently entrusted to Congress. Noting this, a critic said that Miller's plan "looks like a patchwork quilt, not a balanced, patterned tapestry" (*Id.,* 256). Another critic suggested that part of the problem is that because Miller presented his ideas in an article rather than a book, he did not, like authors of numerous other proposed constitutions, have adequate space both to outline and to justify his numerous additions to and departures from the current Constitution (Vile 1991c, 148).

See also: Parliamentary Systems.

For Further Reading:

Knipprath, Joerg W. 1987. "To See the Trees, but Not the Forest in Constitution Making: A Commentary on Professor Miller's Proposed Constitution." *Southwestern University Law Review* 17: 239–256.

Miller, Jeremy. 1987. "It's Time for a New Constitution." *Southwestern University Law Review* 17: 207–237.

Vile, John R. 1991c. *Rewriting the United States Constitution: An Examination of Proposals from Reconstruction to the Present.* New York: Praeger.

MINIMUM WAGES

Like the related problem of child labor, minimum wages were often associated with the so-called sweating system, under which large factories employed laborers for subsistence wages in unsanitary conditions. Such issues came into prominence with the rise of U.S. industrialization. Because of their position in the economy, women were inordinately affected by such conditions (Hart 1994, 64).

The first attempts to remedy the evils of the sweating system centered on limiting the number of hours that employers could require individuals to work. This movement faced a setback with the Supreme Court's decision in *Lochner v. New York* (1905), which declared that New York's regulation of bakers' work hours violated the bakers' freedom of contract. In *Muller v. Oregon* (1908), however, future Supreme Court Justice Louis Brandeis—who had been hired by the National Consumers League (NCL)—successfully argued on behalf of a Washington state law that limited women's work to 10 hours a day. Brandeis relied chiefly on evidence, presented in his historic "Brandeis brief," showing that women were especially vulnerable to such exploitation, and the Supreme Court responded with a unanimous decision upholding the legislation.

A number of states, often prodded by the Women's Trade Union League, subsequently adopted legislation providing minimum wages for women and children. Such a policy sometimes split feminist ranks. It pitted those who argued that half a loaf was better than none against those who disfavored any gender-specific legislation—an issue that would also emerge with the first introduction of the Equal Rights Amendment in Congress in 1923 (Hart 1994, 111).

In the same year that a member of Congress first introduced the Equal Rights Amendment, the Supreme Court issued a decision in *Adkins v. Children's Hospital* (1923). Justice George Sutherland authored this five-to-three decision for a divided Court. The Court struck down a minimum-wage law for women on the basis that although the Constitution permitted regulation of "incidents of employment" such as hours and working conditions, the due process clause mitigated against interferences with the "heart of the contract," that is, with wages. Interestingly, Sutherland relied in part on the equalizing effect that he thought the ratification of the Nineteenth Amendment had on women's ability to enter into their own contracts.

Even prior to the decision, at least one member of Congress had proposed an amendment to establish governmental powers to set minimum wages. However, most such amendments—some seeking to vest such powers in the states, some in Congress, and some in both—were introduced between 1925 and 1937, when Supreme Court decisions based on substantive due process were at their peak. As late as 1936, in *Morehead v. New York ex rel. Tipaldo,* the Court continued to strike down minimum-wage legislation.

In *West Coast Hotel v. Parrish* (1937), a narrow Court majority led by Chief Justice Charles Evans Hughes overturned *Adkins* and upheld a Washington state minimum-wage law for women. This case is often called the "switch in time that saved nine," because many believe that it was a political reaction to Franklin D. Roosevelt's court-packing plan introduced earlier in the year.

Congress subsequently adopted the Fair Labor Standards Act in 1938, providing for minimum wages and maximum hours for both men and women in industries affecting interstate commerce. The Supreme Court upheld this law in *United States v. Darby* (1941), thus overturning its earlier decision in *Hammer v. Dagenhart* (1918) and sanctioning the regulation of this issue by the national government.

Calls for amendments on the subject have subsequently ceased, although renewed attention was spurred by the decision in *Garcia v. San Antonio Metropolitan Transit Authority* (1985), in which such minimum wage laws were applied to state governments. In the United States, minimum-wage laws now apply to most industries. By contrast, in Britain, the minimum wage never applied beyond a few basic industries and was eliminated altogether in 1993. A student of the subject concluded that, despite claims for the flexibility of the British constitution, written constitutional guarantees ultimately strengthened U.S. minimum-wage policies in a positive direction (Hart 1994, 182). Debates periodically erupt about how high the minimum wage should be and whether it is adequate to support a family. Conservative economists have argued that higher minimum wages contribute to higher unemployment rates, but other scholars believe that higher wages actually pump more money into local economies and thus result in more employment.

See also Child Labor Amendment; Court-Packing Plan; Equal Rights Amendment; Labor, Hours of; Nineteenth Amendment.

For Further Reading:

Hart, Vivien. 1994. *Bound by Our Constitution: Women, Workers, and the Minimum Wage.* Princeton, NJ: Princeton University Press.

MINNESOTA BOUNDARY

Amendments are sometimes proposed not so much to get a policy adopted as to draw attention to a problem. There are few better illustrations of this than an amendment that Minnesota Democrat Collin C. Peterson introduced in Congress in March 1998. Peterson proposed that Congress should relinquish claims to that portion of Minnesota above the 49th parallel. At issue was the small Northwest Angle of Minnesota, a peninsula north of the 49th parallel that belongs to the United States and is considered a part of Minnesota, even though it borders completely on Canada and juts into the Lake of the Woods. Under a fishing treaty being worked out between the United States and Canada, individuals who camped on fishing resorts on the American land were to be given the right to keep fewer fish from the Lake of the Woods than those who camped on Canadian resorts that bordered the lake. Peterson, who had no desire to part with territory belonging either to his state or his nation, introduced his proposal to gain the attention of the U.S. trade representative negotiating for America. He succeeded in getting enough attention to gain more favorable treatment than under the original terms of the agreement. (Telephone interview by John R. Vile with Bill Black, Legislative Assistant for Congressman Collin C. Peterson of Minnesota, conducted 04/29/02). This amendment is likely the only one ever introduced specifically to protect the rights of American fishermen.

MINOR V. HAPPERSETT (1875)

Minor v. Happersett marked the defeat of a strategy called the New Departure, which advocates of women's suffrage pursued from 1869 through 1875 whereby they sought to achieve women's rights through judicial interpretation of the Fourteenth Amendment rather than by seeking a woman's suffrage amendment (Balkin, 2005, 37). Declaring in *Bradwell v. Illinois* that "the law of the Creator" mandated that "the paramount destiny and mission of woman are to fulfill the noble and benign offices of wife and mother" (1873, 141), the Supreme Court refused to overturn the decision of the Illinois bar to exclude Myra Bradwell from the practice of law simply because she was a woman. Simi-

larly, speaking through Chief Justice Morrison Waite in Mino*r v. Happersett* (1875), the Court unanimously upheld a registrar's refusal to allow Virginia Minor to vote in the presidential election of 1872. Susan B. Anthony had asserted a similar privilege, but her case had not made it to the Supreme Court (Basch 1992, 57).

Minor and her husband cited a number of constitutional arguments, all of which the Court rejected. It recognized that women were citizens of the United States both before and after adoption of the Fourteenth Amendment. However, in an interpretation similar to that which the *Slaughterhouse Cases* (1873) had advanced, it rejected the argument that the right to vote was among the privileges and immunities guaranteed to all citizens by the Fourteenth Amendment. The Court noted that voting qualifications had been set, up to that point, by individual states. No state that had refused to grant suffrage to women had been considered to lack a "republican" government because of this omission. The Court further noted that Section 2 of the Fourteenth Amendment specifically mentioned males and that the Fifteenth Amendment did not extend the right to vote to females. Moreover, if that right had been included among the privileges and immunities protected by the Fourteenth Amendment, then the Fifteenth Amendment would have been unnecessary.

The reference to males in the Fourteenth Amendment, as well as the effect of *Minor v. Happersett,* was overturned with the adoption of the Nineteenth Amendment in 1920.

See also Anthony, Susan B.; Fifteenth Amendment; Fourteenth Amendment; Nineteenth Amendment.

For Further Reading:
Balkin, Jack M. 2005. "How Social Movements Change (or Fail to Change) the Constitution: The Case of the New Departure." *Suffock University Law Review* 39 (January): 27–65.

Basch, Norma. 1992. "Reconstructing Female Citizenship: *Minor v. Happersett.*" In *The Constitution, Law, and American Life: Critical Aspects of the Nineteenth Century Experience,* ed. Donald G. Nieman. Athens: University of Georgia Press.

Minor v. Happersett, 88 U.S. (21 Wall.) 162 (1875).

MISSOURI V. HOLLAND (1920)

Political scientist Louis Henkin called this case "perhaps the most famous and most discussed case in the constitutional law of foreign affairs" (1972, 144). At issue was the constitutionality of a law passed under authority of a treaty with Great Britain whereby the U.S. government set rules for the protection of migratory birds between the United States and Canada. U.S. district courts had previously voided legislation adopted in the absence of such a treaty on the basis that such laws were a federal invasion of powers reserved to the states by the Tenth Amendment.

Writing on behalf of the Court, Justice Oliver Wendell Holmes Jr. upheld the legislation. He said that "there may be matters of the sharpest exigency for the national wellbeing that an act of Congress could not deal with but that a treaty followed by such an act could" (*Missouri* 1920, 433). Holmes further advanced the view that the Constitution was "an organism" whose life "could not have been foreseen completely by the most gifted of its begetters" (*Missouri* 1920, 322). Although Holmes cautioned that treaties could not "contravene any prohibitory words to be found in the Constitution" (*Missouri* 1920, 433), his opinion raised fears that the Constitution might be effectively amended by treaty rather than by constitutional amendment (Lofgren 1975, 93).

In the 1950s such fears helped fuel support for the Bricker Amendment, a proposal designed in part to limit the reach of federal treaties. Ironically, after 1937 the Supreme Court had already given a broad reading to other constitutional sources of federal power— especially the commerce clause and the taxing and spending clause—that seems to have undermined the importance of *Missouri v. Holland* as a source of federal authority (Lofgren 1975, 122). The Court qualified *Missouri v. Holland* in *Reid v. Covert* (1957). American commitments to international trade organizations like the World Trade Organization (WTO) and the ratification of the North American Free Trade Agreement (NAFTA) through expedited "fast track" congressional votes could renew questions about the possible effects of international agreements on matters of domestic policy (see Thomas 2000).

See also Bricker Amendment; Migratory Birds; Tenth Amendment.

For Further Reading:

Henkin, Louis. 1972. *Foreign Affairs and the Constitution.* Mineola, NY: Foundation Press.

Lofgren, Charles A. 1975. "*Missouri v. Holland* in Historical Perspective." In *The Supreme Court Review.* Chicago: University of Chicago Press.

Missouri v. Holland, 252 U.S. 416 (1920).

Thomas, Chantal. 2000. "Constitutional Change and International Government." *Hastings Law Journal* 52 (November): 1–46.

MOMENT OF SILENCE

See Prayer in Public Schools.

MONEY

See Currency.

MONOPOLIES AND TRUSTS

Among the restraints that Thomas Jefferson wanted to include in a national bill of rights was a "restriction against monopolies" (Mason and Baker 1985, 285). Such a resolution was introduced in the Senate in March 1793 but was subsequently tabled, possibly in the belief that such matters were more appropriate for state control. One of the Marshall Court's most popular decisions was in *Gibbons v. Ogden* (1824) when it utilized congressional authority over interstate commerce to strike down New York's grant of a steamboat monopoly.

Concern over monopolies was renewed as the United States industrialized and industries began to combine into giant trusts. Members of Congress introduced at least 18 amendments from 1889 to 1913 to give Congress power to regulate such combinations. In 1890, Congress adopted the Sherman Antitrust Act, which was followed by the Clayton Act of 1914 and the Federal Trade Commission Act of the same year (J. May 1992, 34). Initially, however, the Supreme Court interpreted the Sherman Antitrust Act narrowly. Thus, in *United States v. E. C. Knight Co.* (1895), the Court ruled that Congress could not control the acquisition of sugar refineries that led to a near monopoly because the acquisitions took place within a state and were a matter for state control under the Tenth Amendment.

In 1900, the House of Representatives debated an amendment submitted by Republican George Washington Ray of New York. It provided that "Congress shall have power to define, regulate, prohibit, or dissolve trusts, monopolies, or combinations, whether existing in the form of a corporation or otherwise." The unsuccessful House vote of 154 to 132 in favor of the measure has been attributed to the Republicans' inclusion of a provision, of great concern to states' rights advocates, that "the several States may continue to exercise such power in any manner not in conflict with the laws of the United States" (Musmanno 1929, 116–119). Also, many members of Congress believed that existing laws could be written and additional laws adopted to address the problem. Today, few doubt that congressional powers extend to this domain.

See also Jefferson, Thomas; Marshall, John; Tenth Amendment.

For Further Reading:

Mason, Alpheus T., and Gordon E. Baker. 1985. *Free Government in the Making: Readings in American Political Thought.* 4th ed. New York: Oxford University Press.

May, James. 1992. "Antitrust." In *The Oxford Companion to the Supreme Court of the United States,* ed. Kermit L. Hall. New York: Oxford University Press.

Musmanno, M. A. 1929. *Proposed Amendments to the Constitution.* Washington, DC: U.S. Government Printing Office.

MORRIS, GOUVERNEUR (1752–1816)

Gouverneur Morris, originally a New Yorker, was a delegate to the Constitutional Convention from Pennsylvania, where he had established his law practice. A large man with a wooden leg (he had lost his in an accident in his twenties), Morris advocated a strong national government and spoke more frequently than any other delegate to the convention. He is perhaps best known for being the individual who gave the final "polish" to the wording of the Constitution that the convention proposed. Although he was largely an advocate of the interests of the large states at the convention, Morris proposed on September 15, 1787 that no state could be deprived of its equal suffrage in the Senate without its consent (Farrand 1966, 2:631). The states unanimously adopted this entrenchment clause, perhaps in recognition of the importance that the Connecticut Compromise (providing for this equal Senate representation) had contributed to consensus at the convention. Many critics of the modern U.S. Constitution regard this compromise as an unfortunate concession that will forever stand in the way of more democratic alternatives.

See also Constitutional Convention of 1787: Entrenchment Clauses.

For Further Reading:

Bradford, M. E. 1994. *Founding Fathers: Brief Lives of the Framers of the United States Constitution.* 2d ed. Lawrence: University Press of Kansas.

Farrand, Max, ed. 1966. *The Records of the Federal Convention.* 4 vols. New Haven, CT: Yale University Press.

MORRIS, HENRY O.

Little is known about Henry Morris other than his authorship of the novel *Waiting for the Signal* (1897) and its publication by a socialist-leaning press (Boyd 1992, 106–109). The novel's main characters, Wesley Stearns and John McDermott, are reporters for the Chicago *Biograph,* owned by Adam Short. Short is sympathetic to the woes of the working class and gives his reporters the opportunity to report on the increasing gap between rich and poor and on the moral degradation of the plutocrats, especially those who live in New York City.

During the course of the novel, set shortly after the election of William McKinley in 1896 (Morris appears to have detested Cleveland and McKinley—and Mark Hanna—about equally but supported William Jennings Bryan's advocacy of a silver standard), workers initiate a revolution. The revolution results in little bloodshed except in New York City, which is almost completely burned by those trying to take advantage of the chaos.

A convention is subsequently held in Chicago, where Ignatius Donnelly heads a committee that writes a new declaration of independence. The convention also writes a new constitution, and William J. Lyon of Nebraska is nominated and subsequently elected president, replacing the military leader who oversaw the revolution. Adoption of the constitution leads to a new era of national peace and prosperity that haunts European plutocrats, who fear that their own revolutions will result in greater loss of life.

In his draft of a new constitution, Morris largely keeps the structure of the existing government in place, although he does propose some changes. He would guarantee each state at least three members in the House of Representatives, and the Speaker—Morris had particular disdain for Speaker Thomas B. Reed— would lose power to retard the progress of legislation (H. Morris 1897, 338). Morris would limit members of Congress to 12 years in office. Although the president would continue to have a veto power, both houses of Congress would be able to override this veto by majority vote. In anticipation of the Sixteenth Amendment, Congress would have the power to levy income and other taxes, and, in anticipation of the Seventeenth Amendment, senators would be elected by popular vote. The president, also elected by popular vote, would serve a single eight-year term.

Morris's constitution embodied a number of socialist elements. The national government would take over most means of production, destroy monopolies and trusts, and (in the novel) limit individual wealth.

Congress would establish uniform codes of civil and criminal procedure. Indians would be treated like other citizens, and foreign immigration would be restricted to "the healthy, moral, intelligent and self-supporting" (Morris 1897, 344). Morris's novel indicates that he was generally suspicious of both Jews and foreigners. The people would vote on whether they wanted an initiative and referendum.

Morris would expand most constitutional rights, and his constitution devotes special attention to freedom of speech and of the press. Judicial powers to issue injunctions would be limited, and no one could be imprisoned for violating a court order except after a jury trial.

In Morris's plan, a majority of both houses of Congress would be able to propose amendments or call a constitutional convention. Amendments would be ratified by a majority of the state legislatures.

In a preface to the third edition, Morris notes that he had been "deluged with letters" asking when the revolution would occur. He answered that he did not know the date but that "the revolution is sure to come—it is on the way. I leave the reader to guess when the storm will burst" (Morris 1897, ix).

For Further Reading:

Boyd, Steven R., ed. 1992. *Alternative Constitutions for the United States: A Documentary History.* Westport, CT: Greenwood Press.

Morris, Henry O. 1897. *Waiting for the Signal, a Novel.* Chicago: Schulte.

MOTT, LUCRETIA COFFIN (1793–1880)

Lucretia Coffin Mott was a Quaker minister and political reformer. She provided leadership in the movement for the abolition of slavery that eventually led to the Thirteenth Amendment and in the movement for women's rights that eventually resulted in the Nineteenth Amendment.

Mott, the mother of six children, helped found the Philadelphia Female Anti-Slavery Society in the 1830s and helped establish Swarthmore College in 1864. With Elizabeth Cady Stanton, Mott helped organize the Seneca Falls Convention of 1848, where the idea of women's suffrage first emerged as an important concern. The proposed Equal Rights Amendment was often called the Lucretia Mott amendment in her honor.

See also Equal Rights Amendment; Nineteenth Amendment; Seneca Falls Convention; Thirteenth Amendment.

For Further Reading:

Sterling, Doroghy. 1999. *Lucretia Mott.* New York: The Feminist Press at CUNY.

MURDER AND KIDNAPPING

In the U.S. federal system, states handled most matters of criminal law. A number of members of Congress have proposed amendments to give Congress power to punish criminals for felonies such as murder, kidnapping, lynching, or polygamy or to invest the trials for such offenses in federal courts.

The notorious kidnapping of pilot Charles Lindbergh's baby occurred in March 1932. The baby's body was found on May 12, 1932 (Knappman 1994, 386), and a week later, Illinois Democratic Representative Charles Karch introduced a resolution to give Congress power to punish murder and kidnapping. Although states retain primary jurisdiction over these offenses, Congress exercised its power under the commerce clause to adopt the Lindbergh Act, making it a crime to transport a victim across state or national lines and creating a presumption that such transit has occurred when a victim is not released within 24 hours (*Black's Law Dictionary* 1969, 837).

For Further Reading:

Knappman, Edward W., ed. 1994. *Great American Trials.* Detroit, MI: Visible Ink Press.

MURPHY, CORNELIUS F., JR. (1933–)

In a chapter of a book published a year after the bicentennial of the Constitution, *Philosophical Dimensions of the Constitution,* Duquesne law professor Cornelius Murphy recommended the convening of a constitutional convention. More concerned about the positive implications that such a convention would have for democratic theory than about advocating a specific agenda, Murphy sketched four areas for possible reform.

He suggested that a convention might seek to "delineate the boundaries between personal freedom and social order." He favored adding "economic, social and cultural entitlements," like those recognized in the Universal Declaration of Human Rights, to the Constitution. He wanted to combine states into more functional regional units. He also thought that problems created by the separation of the legislative and executive branches and the "fractionation of power" needed to be addressed. Murphy did not believe that the reforms he proposed could be adequately addressed "within the inherited constitutional structure" or by "piecemeal amendment" (C. Murphy 1988, 70).

See also Constitutional Convention.

For Further Reading:

Murphy, Cornelius F., Jr. 1988. "Constitutional Revision." In *Philosophical Dimensions of the Constitution,* ed. Diana T. Meyers and Kenneth Kipnis. Boulder, CO: Westview Press.

MURPHY, WALTER F. (1929–)

Walter F. Murphy is a retired Edward S. Corwin professor of politics at Princeton University. Known for his wide-ranging scholarship on matters related to the judicial process and constitutional interpretation, Murphy is one of the most articulate and persistent modern defenders of the view that there may be implicit and judicially enforceable limits on constitutional amendments within a true constitutional democracy. Murphy has defended his view in numerous essays over an extended time (W. Murphy 1978, 1980, 1987, 1990, 1992a, 1992b, 1995).

Drawing in part from judicial decisions in other constitutional governments, Murphy argues that the very notion of a constitutional democracy committed to principles of justice and the preservation of human dignity serves to limit the scope of change permitted within such a system. In a system that consists of a hierarchy of values, more important values must necessarily predominate over those with which they conflict. Moreover, the U.S. Constitution is informed by and based on the values of the Declaration of Independence, and the natural rights articulated there serve to limit what the Constitution can permit. The whole notion of amendments refers to those types of alterations that are consistent with the instrument being amended, not simply to changes that follow procedural guidelines.

Murphy has recently written a book involving creating a constitutional democracy for a mythical nation that he calls Nusquam. His detailed presentation of views to a caucus for a new political system for Nusquam incapsulates a life-time of work on "how to create a constitutional democracy, how to maintain it, and how to change it without destroying its integrity" (2007, ix).

See also Constitutional Amendments, Limits on.

For Further Reading:

Murphy, Walter F. 2007. *Constitutional Democracy: Creating and Maintaining a Just Political Order.* Baltimore: Johns Hopkins University Press.

Murphy, Walter F. 1995. "Merlin's Memory: The Past and Future Imperfect of the Once and Future Polity." In *Responding to Imperfection,* ed. Sanford Levinson. Princeton, NJ: Princeton University Press.

————. 1992a. "Consent and Constitutional Change." In *Human Rights and Constitutional Law: Essays in Honour of Brian Walsh,* ed. James O'Reilly. Dublin, Ireland: Found Hall Press.

————. 1992b. "Staggering Toward the New Jerusalem of Constitutional Theory: A Response to Ralph F. Graebler." *American Journal of Jurisprudence* 37: 337–357.

————. 1990. "The Right to Privacy and Legitimate Constitutional Change." In *Constitutional Bases of Political and Social Change in the United States,* ed. Shlomo Slonin. New York: Praeger.

————. 1987. "*Slaughterhouse, Civil Rights,* and Limits on Constitutional Change." *American Journal of Jurisprudence* 23: 1–22.

————. 1980. "An Ordering of Constitutional Values." *Southern California Law Review* 53: 703–760.

————. 1978. "The Art of Constitutional Interpretation: A Preliminary Showing." In *Essays on the Constitution of the United States,* ed. M. Harmon. Port Washington, NY: Kennikat Press.

————. 1962. *Congress and the Court.* Chicago: University of Chicago Press.

MYERS V. ANDERSON (1915)

In this case, a companion to *Guinn v. United States* (1915), the Supreme Court struck down provisions of a Maryland law regulating voting in Annapolis. This law, like the Oklahoma law at issue in *Guinn,* contained a grandfather clause that imposed a literacy test only on those—namely, African Americans—whose ancestors were not entitled to vote prior to January 1, 1868, that is, prior to ratification of the Fourteenth and Fifteenth Amendments.

Cheif Justice Edward White struck the law down as violation of the Fifth Amendment. In so doing, he implicitly rejected arguments for limits on the amending process that William Marbury and other attorneys for the state had offered. They had argued that "if construed to have reference to voting at state or municipal elections, the Fifteenth Amendment would be beyong the amending power conferred upon three fourths of the States by Art V. of the Constitution" (*Myers* 1915, 373)

See also Constitutionl Amendments, Limits on; Fifteenth Amendment; Marbury, William.

For Further Reading:

Myers v. Anderson, 238 U.S. 368 (1915).